FOR REFERENCE

Do Not Take From This Room

The Greenwood
Encyclopedia of Daily Life
in America

Recent Titles in
The Greenwood Press "Daily Life Through History" Series

The Civil War
Paul A. Cimbala

Civilians in Wartime Europe, 1618–1900
Linda S. Frey and Marsha L. Frey, editors

The Vietnam War
James E. Westheider

World War II
G. Kurt Piehler

Immigrant America, 1870–1920
June Granatir Alexander

Along the Mississippi
George S. Pabis

Immigrant America, 1820–1870
James M. Bergquist

Pre-Columbian Native America
Clarissa W. Confer

Post-Cold War
Stephen A. Bourque

The New Testament
James W. Ermatinger

The Hellenistic Age: From Alexander to Cleopatra
James Allan Evans

Imperial Russia
Greta Bucher

3 THE EMERGENCE OF
MODERN AMERICA,
WORLD WAR I, AND
THE GREAT DEPRESSION,
1900–1940

The Greenwood
Encyclopedia of Daily Life
in America

Francis J. Sicius
VOLUME EDITOR

Randall M. Miller
GENERAL EDITOR

The Greenwood Press "Daily Life Through History" Series

GREENWOOD PRESS
Westport, Connecticut • London

Library of Congress Cataloging-in-Publication Data

The Greenwood encyclopedia of daily life in America / Randall M. Miller, general editor.
        p. cm.—(The Greenwood Press daily life through history series, ISSN 1080–4749)
    Includes bibliographical references and index.
    ISBN 978–0–313–33699–7 (set)
    ISBN 978–0–313–33703–1 (v. 1)
    ISBN 978–0–313–33704–8 (v. 2)
    ISBN 978–0–313–33705–5 (v. 3)
    ISBN 978–0–313–33706–2 (v. 4)
    1. United States—Civilization—Encyclopedias.   2. United States—Social life and customs—
Encyclopedias.   3. United States—Social conditions—Encyclopedias.   I. Miller, Randall M.
E169.1.G7553   2009
973.03—dc22   2007042828

British Library Cataloguing in Publication Data is available.

Library of Congress Catalog Card Number: 2007042828
ISBN: 978–0–313–33699–7 (set)
        978–0–313–33703–1 (vol. 1)
        978–0–313–33704–8 (vol. 2)
        978–0–313–33705–5 (vol. 3)
        978–0–313–33706–2 (vol. 4)
ISSN: 1080–4749

First published in 2009

Greenwood Press, 88 Post Road West, Westport, CT 06881
An imprint of Greenwood Publishing Group, Inc.
www.greenwood.com

Printed in the United States of America

The paper used in this book complies with the
Permanent Paper Standard issued by the National
Information Standards Organization (Z39.48–1984).

10 9 8 7 6 5 4 3 2 1

Every reasonable effort has been made to trace the owners of copyright materials in this book, but
in some instances this has proven impossible. The editors and publisher will be glad to receive
information leading to more complete acknowledgments in subsequent printings of the book and in
the meantime extend their apologies for any omissions.

The publisher has done its best to make sure the instructions and/or recipes in this book are correct.
However, users should apply judgment and experience when preparing recipes, especially parents and
teachers working with young people. The publisher accepts no responsibility for the outcome of any
recipe included in this volume.

COPYRIGHT ACKNOWLEDGMENTS

The editor and publisher gratefully acknowledge permission for use of the following material:

Excerpts from *American Catholic* by Charles R. Morris, copyright © 1997 by Charles R. Morris. Used by permission of Times Books, a division of Random House, Inc. Electronic rights reprinted by permission of Russell & Volkening as agents for the author, Copyright © 1997 by Charles M. Morris.

Excerpts from Nash, Roderick, "The American Cult of the Primitive," *American Quarterly* 18:3 (1966), 517–537. © The American Studies Association. Reprinted with permission of The Johns Hopkins University Press.

Excerpts from Allan H. Spear, *Black Chicago*. Excerpts from pp. 147–149, 136, 20–30. University of Chicago Press.

Excerpts from Mayer, *Chicago: Growth Metropolis*. Excerpts from pp. 218–226, 252–262, 206–208, 224. University of Chicago Press.

Excerpts from *City Games: The Evolution of American Urban Society and the Rise of Sports*. Copyright, 1989 by Board of Trustees of the University of Illinois.

Excerpts from *Daily Life in the United States, 1920–1940,* copyright c 2002, 2004 by David E. Kyvig, by permission of Ivan R. Dee, Publisher.

Steven Reich, excerpts from *Encyclopedia of the Great Black Migration*, pp. 60, 288–289, 544, 664–665, 674, 880, 881–883. (Greenwood Press 5/30/2006).

Excerpts from Nancy Smith Midgette, "In Search of Professional Identity: Southern Scientists, 1883–1940," *Journal of Southern History,* LIV, No.4 (November, 1988), 597–622.

Excerpts from *It's Your Misfortune and None of My Own: A New History of the American West.* (Copyright 1993 by Richard White.) Used with permission of University of Oklahoma Press.

Excerpts from *Jack Dempsey: The Manassa Mauler.* Copyright Randy Roberts, 1979. (Baton Rouge: Louisiana State University Press).

Excerpts from *Pets in America: A History* by Katherine C. Grier. Copyright © 2006 by Katherine C. Grier. Published by the University of North Carolina Press. Used by permission of the publisher. www.uncpress.unc.edu.

Excerpts from *Philadelphia: A Three Hundred Year History.* (Copyright 1982 by Russel F. Weigley, et al.) Used with permission of the Barra Foundation, Incorporated.

Excerpts from William A. Link, "Privies, Progressivism, and Public Schools: Health Reform and Education in the Rural South, 1909–1920." *Journal of Southern History,* LIV, No. 4 (November 1988), 623–42.

Excerpts from Kingsdale, Jon M. "The 'Poor Man's Club': Social Functions of the Urban Working-Class Saloon," *American Quarterly* 25:4 (1973), 472–489. © The American Studies Association. Reprinted with permission of The Johns Hopkins University Press.

Excerpts from "Southern White Protestants at the Turn of the Century," (Copyright Kenneth Bailey, *American Historical Review*, vol. 68, no. 3 (April, 1963): 618–635. Used with Permission of the American Historical Association.

Excerpts from *The Transplanted* (Copyright 1987 by John Bodnar) Indiana University Press.

Excerpts from Harvey Green, excerpts from *The Uncertainty of Everyday Life, 1915–1945.* Copyright © 1992 by Harvey Green. Reprinted with the permission of the University of Arkansas Press, www.uapress.com.

Excerpts from *Veracruz is Dying.* (Copyright 1978 by Zevon Music.) Used with permission of Jordan Zevon.

Excerpts from "Women at Work' from *At Odds: Women and the Family in America from the Revolution to the Present* (1980) by Degler C. By permission of Oxford University Press, Inc.

The publisher has done its best to make sure the instructions and/or recipes in this book are correct. However, users should apply judgment and experience when preparing recipes, especially parents and teachers working with young people. The publisher accepts no responsibility for the outcome of any recipe included in this volume.

Dedicated to Mary T. Griesser

CONTENTS

Contents

Contents

TOUR GUIDE: A PREFACE FOR USERS

During the time of the American Revolution, the writer Hector St. Jean de Crevecouer asked the fundamental question that has dogged Americans thereafter: "What then is this new man, this American." Countless students of American history have searched every aspect of political, economic, social, and cultural history to discover "this American." In doing so, they have often focused on the great ideas that inspired a "free people" and defined public interest since the inception of the United States; the great events that marked American history; and the great changes wrought by democratic, industrial, communications, and other revolutions shaping American life, work, and identities. And they have been right to do so. But more recently other students of history have insisted that finding the *real* American requires looking at the details of everyday life. Therein, they argue, Americans practiced what mattered most to them and gave meaning to larger concepts of *freedom* and to the great events swirling about them. The ways Americans at home and at work ordered their daily life have become the subject of numerous community studies and biographies of the so-called common man or woman that were created by combing through all manner of personal accounts in diaries, letters, memoirs, business papers, birth and death records, census data, material culture, popular song, verse, artistic expression, and, indeed, virtually any source about or by common folk.

But making sense of so much individual study and providing a clear path through the history of Americans in their daily life has waited on a work that brings together the many and diverse ways Americans ordered their individual worlds at home and at work. *The Greenwood Encyclopedia of Daily Life in America* promises such a synthesis; it also promises to find "this American" in what Americans ate, who they courted and married, how they raised their children, what they did at work, where they traveled, how they played, and virtually every aspect of social life that Americans made for themselves. As such, it brings to life "this American" on his or her own terms. It also suggests that by discovering the ordinary it becomes possible to understand that extraordinary phenomenon of the American.

Features and Uses

The Greenwood Encyclopedia of Daily Life in America is a reference work and guide that provides up-to-date, authoritative, and readable entries on the many experiences and varieties of daily life of Americans from the dawn of the republic through the first years of the twenty-first century. In spanning the roughly 250 years from the mid-eighteenth century to the new millennium, the four volumes of *The Greenwood Encyclopedia of Daily Life in America* employ both a chronological and a topical, or thematic, approach. Doing so invites many uses for the volumes as reference guides; as touchstones for inquiries to a host of questions about the social, cultural, economic, and political history of Americans and the nation; and, taken together, as a broad view of daily life in the United States.

Users can read the articles separately or as a running narrative, depending on interest and need. The organization of the work collectively according to time period and within each volume according to time period, geography, daily activity, and group allows readers to explore a topic in depth, in comparative perspective, and over time. Also, because each section of each volume opens with a synthetic overview for purposes of historical context, the material in each section becomes more readily linked to larger patterns of American social, cultural, economic, and political developments. By structuring the volumes in this manner, it becomes possible to integrate and apply the encyclopedia within modern and flexible pedagogical frameworks in the classroom, in the library, and in home-schooling settings.

Cross-referencing within the articles and the cumulative subject index to the encyclopedia found at the back of each volume together expand the reach of individual topics across time and in different places. Thus, for example, the discussion of marital patterns and habits in the antebellum period of the nineteenth century, which includes mentions of courtship patterns, marriage rites, family formation, parenting, and even divorce, easily bridges to treatments of the same topics in other periods. Likewise, a reader wanting to compare foodways as they developed over time might move easily from representations of the early American "down-home" cooking of a largely agricultural society, through the increased portability and packaging of foods demanded by an urbanizing society during the nineteenth century, to the recent preference for such paradoxes in food choices as fresh foods, exotic foods, and fast food in the post-industrial United States.

Readers might go backward as well as forward, or even sideways, in following their interests, looking for the roots and then growth and development of habits and practices that defined and ordered the daily lives of Americans. In doing so, they might discover that each successive modern society has had its own search for the simpler life by trying to recover and reproduce parts of a supposedly more settled and serene past. They also will discover not only the changes wrought by ever more modern means of production, transportation, communication, and social and economic organization but also some striking continuities. Old ways often continue in new days. Americans have been a people on the go from the beginning of the nation and have become more so over time. As such, staying in touch with family and friends has ever been central to Americans' sense of place and purpose in organizing their lives. Whether carrying a daguerreotype image while heading west or to war in the nineteenth century, shooting photos with a Kodak camera from the late nineteenth century well into the twentieth century, or taking pictures with a video camera, a digital camera, or even with a cell-phone in the twenty-first century, Americans sought ways to keep visual images of the people, animals, possessions, and places that mattered to them. Letter writing also has become no less important a means of communication when the words move electronically via e-mail than when they were scratched out with a quill pen on paper. The encyclopedia provides a ready way to measure and map such social and cultural patterns and developments.

In its organization and with its reference supports, the encyclopedia encourages such topical excursions across time. Thus, the encyclopedia promises ways to an integrated analysis of daily life and of the core values, interests, and identities of Americans at any one time and over time.

Sidebars (found in volumes 3 and 4, and called Snapshots), chronologies, illustrations, and excerpts from documents further enrich each volume with specific examples of daily life from primary sources. They add not only "color" but also significant content by capturing the sense of a particular people or place in song, verse, speech, letters, and image and by giving voice to the people themselves. Readers thus engage Americans in their daily life directly.

The life and use of the encyclopedia extends beyond the physical volumes themselves. Because the encyclopedia derives much of its material from the vast resources of the Greenwood Publishing Group archive of works in ongoing series, such as the *Greenwood Press Daily Life Through History* Series and the *Daily Life in the United States* Series, to name the two most prominent, and on the many encyclopedias, reference works, and scholarly monographs making up its list, and on the many document-based works in its collection, the encyclopedia includes up-to-date and reliably vetted material. It also plugs into the *Greenwood Daily Life Online* database, which ensures a continuous expansion, enhancement, and refinement of content and easy searching capabilities. In that sense, *The Greenwood Encyclopedia of Daily Life in America*, like the American people, literally exists in a constant state of renewal to live beyond its original creation.

Organization and Coverage

The Greenwood Encyclopedia of Daily Life in America has a wide sweep in terms of time, topics, and themes related to the ordering of the daily lives of Americans. It also includes the many and diverse Americans, understanding that no one experience or people spoke or speaks for the variety of daily lives in the United States or explains even the unity of common experiences many different Americans have had and sought. That said, the encyclopedia is not a simple fact-by-fact description of every group or daily activity conducted in the United States. The encyclopedia is consciously selective in topics and coverage, with an eye always to relating the most significant and representative examples of the daily lives of different Americans.

The coverage of particular people and topics varies due to the availability of sources by and about them. Thus, for example, such peoples as the Iroquois, Cherokee, and Lakota Sioux get more explicit notice than, say, the Shoshone, simply because they left a fuller record of their lives and were observed and written about, or painted or photographed, in their daily lives more fully than were some other Native peoples. Then, too, the daily life of immigrant peoples receives extensive coverage throughout the volumes, but the extent and depth of coverage varies due to the size of the group and, more important, due to the available source material about any particular group. Thus, for example, when combined, the several major governmental and foundation studies of eastern and southern European immigrant groups in industrial America in the late nineteenth and early twentieth centuries, the rich tradition of publishing ethnic newspapers, the relating of personal lives in memoirs and oral histories, and a conscious effort to recover an immigrant past by the children and grandchildren of the first generation all explain the wider focus on such groups as representative types for their day. We simply know much about such people at work and at home. Such coverage of some people more fully than others does not mean any one experience counts more than others. It is, rather, mainly a matter of the critical mass of information at hand.

The encyclopedia includes all age groups in its coverage, but, again, the documentary record is richer for people coming of age through their adult lives into retirement than it is for the very young or the very old. Then, too, more is known about the daily lives of the upper classes than the lower classes, the privileged than the underprivileged, and the free than the unfree. The encyclopedia boasts significant inclusion of the many diverse American people, irrespective of wealth, circumstance, race or ethnicity, religion, or any other marker, and, indeed, it makes special effort to embrace the fullest range and diversity of experiences of daily life from birth to death.

The four volumes, each of which was edited by a prominent specialist or specialists in the field, are arranged by time periods as follows.

- Volume 1: The War of Independence and Antebellum Expansion and Reform, 1763–1861; edited by Theodore J. Zeman
- Volume 2: *The Civil War, Reconstruction, and Industrialization of America, 1861–1900*; edited by James M. Volo and Dorothy Denneen Volo
- Volume 3: *The Emergence of Modern America, World War I, and the Great Depression, 1900–1940*; edited by Francis J. Sicius
- Volume 4: *Wartime, Postwar, and Contemporary America, 1940–Present*; edited by Jolyon P. Girard

Each volume follows a similar format in that it organizes the material into seven principal topics, which are then generally divided into the following subtopics.

Those subtopics are sometimes arranged in a different order within the volumes due to emphasis, but they remain continuous throughout the encyclopedia.

1. *Domestic Life:* Covering such subtopics as Men, Women, Children, Pets, Marriage, and so on.
2. *Economic Life:* Covering such subtopics as Work, Trade, Class and Caste, Urban and Rural Experience, and so on.
3. *Intellectual Life:* Covering such subtopics as Science, Education, Literature, Communication, Health and Medicine, and so on.
4. *Material Life:* Covering such subtopics as Food, Drink, Housing, Clothing, Transportation, Technology, and so on.
5. *Political Life:* Covering such subtopics as Government, Law, Reform, War, and so on.
6. *Recreational Life:* Covering such subtopics as Sports, Music, Games, Entertainment, Holidays and Celebrations, and so on.
7. *Religious Life:* Covering such subtopics as Religion, Spirituality, Ritual, Rites of Passage, and so on.

Users are guided through this enormous amount of material not just by running heads on every page but also by *concept compasses* that appear in the margins at the start of main topical sections. These compasses are adapted from *concept mapping,* a technique borrowed from online research methods and used in *The Greenwood Encyclopedia of Daily Life.* The concept compasses will help orient readers in the particular volume they are using and allow them to draw connections among related topics across time periods. Following is an example of a concept compass:

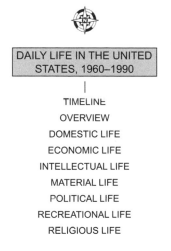

The individual volumes also have several variations in their internal arrangements and coverage of topics that speak to the particular chronological period under review. Volume 1, for example, does not begin at a fixed date, as do the other volumes, and it covers a longer time period than any of the other volumes. Its primary focus is on the period from the American Revolution through the Civil War, but it also looks back in time in its descriptions of many elements of daily life that continued from the preindustrial colonial period through the first rumblings of the so-called market revolution of the early nineteenth century. It does so to provide not only an understanding of the continuities in many aspects of life—from the ways people raised crops and livestock, manufactured and sold goods, organized family life, worshipped, and practiced the rituals of birth, marriage, and death, to name several—but also to mark the changes wrought by the age of revolutions that came with new understandings of political, economic, social, cultural, and even parental authority following the American Revolution. In the subsequent volumes, there is some overlap in terms of beginnings and endings for the chronological periods because social history does not have neat markers as does American political history with its election cycles. Each of the final three volumes covers roughly a half-century of time, reflecting the growing complexity of life in the modern era.

The encyclopedia covers the whole of the United States. The geography of the United States has expanded mightily over time, but the importance of geographical identity within the United States has varied at different times and more recently has declined. The first three volumes recognize the salience of regional variations in defining daily life and break the material, in varying degrees, into regions within the United States (e.g., Northeast, South, Midwest, Pacific West). But the fourth volume, covering the last half of the twentieth century—by which time a national market, telecommunications, and popular culture had done much to break down regional identities and create a national culture—discounts the importance of region in many areas of daily life. To be sure, as Volume 4 reveals, regional identities still persisted, even pridefully so, in "the South" and "the West" especially, but throughout the United States the rhythms of life moved in strikingly similar ways in a nation increasingly knit together by interstate highways, television, and, more recently, by the Internet and by a mass consumption economy and culture. Class, race, and occupation, more than regional cultures, now count more in defining daily life and social ties. Religion, too, matters much in ordering individual lives and distinguishing groups from one another in the United States, easily the most "churched" nation in the industrial world. In some cases, particular subtopics disappear from successive volumes because Americans at different times gave up particular ways of working and living or because the representative ways of working and living changed, from those of an agricultural world to those of an industrial and urban one and then to a postindustrial suburban one, for example.

Throughout the encyclopedia the most basic ways people arranged their daily life make up the principal content of the volumes. But the coverage of any topic is not constant. Take time, for example. It is useful to note that historically over time, *time* literally has been speeding up for Americans. Americans who lived by Nature's times of season and sunrise and sunset occupied a different world than people who have made time a commodity to be metered out in nanoseconds for purposes of productivity and even pleasure. The multiplicity of clocks and watches made possible by the industrial revolution, the imposition of factory time in the workplace, the dividing of the nation into time zones demanded by the railroads, the breakdown of time ordered by the moving assembly line, the collapse of time realized by telecommunications and then the radio, and the more current compression of time by microchips in all manner of computers, cell phones, and gadgetry that seemingly now run daily life and work—all this change in understanding and managing time transformed not only the pace but also the direction of life. Each volume marks the changing of time, the ways people used their time, and the times. Thereby, the attention to matters of time becomes a topic of growing importance with each successive volume of the encyclopedia.

Finally, in terms of coverage and content, the encyclopedia combines a *macro* with the *micro* view of daily life. External factors such as wars, natural disasters (e.g., fires, floods, hurricanes and tornados, ice storms, and droughts), epidemic diseases, environmental transformation, economic and political change, and population movements profoundly affected how, where, and why people lived as they did and, indeed, even which people lived at all. The Revolutionary War and the Civil War, for example, uprooted countless people from their homes as armies tramped about, armies that also liberated enslaved people who then used the upheavals to run to freedom or to fight for it. Daily life for refugees, for the "freedpeople," for the losers of political power and economic advantage was altered to its core by war. Dealing with the loss of loved ones in the Civil War changed the ways many Americans approached the meaning and management of death—in embalming, in funerary practices, in memorializing the dead, in shifting family responsibilities in the wake of a parent's death. The total mobilization of World War II touched every American household, and the G.I. Bill that came with it opened up opportunities for education, home ownership, and medical benefits that helped make possible a middle-class life for many Americans. So, too, massive floods, such as the 1927 flooding of the Mississippi River basin, swept away people, possessions, and patterns of living across a wide swath. Government actions also influenced, even determined, people's daily life. The many New Deal programs that insured bank accounts; underwrote home mortgage loans; brought electricity to rural America; built dams for hydroelectric power and economic development; constructed roads, bridges, airports, and public buildings; encouraged the arts, music, and literature, and so much more left a physical, social, and cultural imprint that still matters in Americans' daily living. Thus, relating the *macrohistory* of larger historical events and developments to the ways such factors informed and influenced the *microhistory* of individual daily life is essential to understanding the dynamics and consequence of changes and continuities in the daily life of Americans. The panoramic perspective plots the landscape of social history, while the microscopic examination observes its many forms. All that said, the primary focus of this encyclopedia remains on what students of social and cultural history term "the infinite details" of Americans' social and material arrangements in their daily life. The title tells the tale.

The Greenwood Encyclopedia of Daily Life in America, in the end, still makes no claim to comprehensiveness in trying to bring in all Americans and all manner of life. No reference work dare do so. Recognizing such a limitation rather than retreating from it, this encyclopedia serves not only as an introduction to the varied and complex American peoples in their daily lives but also as an invitation to bring other peoples into view, which responsibility, one hopes, the students and teachers using this encyclopedia will assume.

A Note on the Conception and Creation of the Encyclopedia

The encyclopedia is the product of many hands. It is both a collective work and, in its separate volumes, also very much an individual one. The encyclopedia was developed collectively by editors at Greenwood Press, who originally sought to provide a companion encyclopedia to the very successful six-volume *Greenwood Encyclopedia of Daily Life,* which covered the world from prehistory to the end of the twentieth century. The editors at Greenwood also sought to capitalize on the many reference works and individual volumes Greenwood Press has published on various aspects of daily life in the United States. At Greenwood, Michael Herman conceived of the idea for such an encyclopedia and drafted the broad design for it. John Wagner then stepped in and in many essential ways translated idea into product. He helped recruit volume editors, managed relations with the editors by means of correspondence and providing sample materials and other forms of guidance, read the individual volumes for content and fit regarding the collective set, and managed the details of moving manuscripts to production.

Each author/editor assumed the primary, almost complete, responsibility for his or her individual volume. Early in the planning process, several author/editors gathered by correspondence and even in person to discuss the scope of the work, to mark off the time boundaries of the individual volumes, to agree on essential topics, and more. The general editor coordinated such discussions; guided the works in progress; read the individual volumes for content, coverage, and fit with the other volumes and overall purpose and design of the encyclopedia; and in other ways moved production along. It is important to note that each author/editor has assumed principal responsibility for the content of his or her volume, from selecting, arranging, and editing the articles, to getting permission to use materials, to providing the context for the articles, to fact-checking and proofreading the volume, to ensuring the highest quality in content and presentation. The general editor thus disclaims any responsibility for the specific content of or in any volume. The individual author/editor's name on the title page of each volume places the responsibility where it deservedly should rest, with the true creators. It also is important to note that in creating each volume, the author/editor did much more than compile, collate, and arrange materials derived from other sources. Each author/editor wrote the introductions to the respective volumes, the introductions to the subsections of each volume, the transitions within each article excerpting materials from other sources, the headnotes in each volume, and some of the text in each volume. Because of the uneven, or even nonexistent, source material on daily life for the two volumes treating the twentieth century, both Francis Sicius and Jolyon Girard wrote much original material. This was so much so in Girard's case that he became more author than editor of Volume 4.

In sum, then, the creation of this encyclopedia mirrors the American experience. It was, and is, an example of the nation's guiding principle of continuous creation as a people—e pluribus unum. It also is a recognition that people make history. We hope that by discovering the American people in their day-to-day lives and the life they have sought to create and live, readers will find that elusive "new man, this American" and themselves.

—Randall M. Miller

VOLUME EDITOR'S PREFACE

This volume covers a period when the velocity of American life moved from the speed of a horse-and-buggy to that of an airplane. The final frontier was closed, and Americans looked to the future of a country that would become increasingly urbanized. Technology entered people's lives as never before. Houses became electrified; automobiles became a necessity; and radios brought music, drama, comedy, news, and even the president into Americans' living rooms. One-room schoolhouses became consolidated learning centers, sports nationalized, and government entered daily life in ways never dreamed of a generation earlier. In the midst of this whirl of change Americans attempted to anchor themselves in time-honored traditions. As this volume will demonstrate, while change became the norm in the first decades of the twentieth century, Americans in many ways clung to their regional traditions in order to navigate through this sea of transformation.

Documenting this American drama has been an adventure. I made new discoveries as well as remembered old stories told by my family around the dinner table years ago. I would like to thank Randall Miller for giving me the opportunity to make this journey, and for his careful editing and theme-enhancing suggestions. His voice was wise, encouraging, and constant throughout the process and without his help the final product would have been much less than it is. Finally my deepest gratitude goes to my wife Isabel Valenzuela, whose good humor, intelligent comments, and loving support brought me to the end of this journey intact. Despite all this help some blunders may remain, and those of course are mine alone.

Francis J. Sicius
St. Thomas University
March, 2008

CHRONOLOGY:
1900–1945

1900

January 29	The American League, consisting of eight baseball teams, is organized in Philadelphia with teams from Buffalo, Chicago, Cleveland, Detroit, Indianapolis, Kansas City, Milwaukee, and Minneapolis.
February 1	The first of the famous Brownie cameras is introduced. It sells for $1 and uses film that sells for 15 cents a roll. For the first time, the hobby of photography is within the financial reach of virtually everyone.
April 30	Hawaii is organized as a U.S. territory.
August 23	Booker T. Washington forms the National Negro Business League in Boston, Massachusetts.
November 3	The first automobile show in the United States opens at Madison Square Garden in New York City under the auspices of the Automobile Club of America.
November 6	Republican President William McKinley is reelected, defeating Democrat William Jennings Bryan, who had also been his opponent in 1896.

1901

March 1	The Pan American Exposition opens in Buffalo, New York.
March 4	William McKinley is inaugurated president for the second time.
April 25	New York becomes the first state to require automobile license plates; the fee is $1.
September 6	Anarchist Leon Czolgosz shoots President McKinley while the president is attending the Pan American Exposition in Buffalo, New York.
September 14	President McKinley dies and is succeeded by Vice President Theodore Roosevelt, who becomes the 26th president of the United States.
October 16	President Theodore Roosevelt invites black leader Booker T. Washington to the White House.
November 16	A cartoon appears in the *Washington Star,* prompting the Teddy Bear Craze, which started when President Teddy Roosevelt refused to kill a captive bear tied up for him to shoot during a hunting trip to Mississippi.

1902

January 1	The first Rose Bowl football game is held in Pasadena, California, with the University of Michigan beating Stanford 49–0.
March 4	The American Automobile Association is founded in Chicago.
March 29	Thirty-eight-year-old Henry Ford leaves the Detroit Automobile Company and begins his search for backers for his new Ford Motor Company.
April 14	James Cash Penney (J. C. Penney) opens his first Golden Rule Store for clothes, shoes, and dry goods in Kemmerer, Wyoming.
May 12	Over 100,000 miners in northeastern Pennsylvania call a strike and keep the mines closed all summer.
June 9	The first Automat restaurant opens at 818 Chestnut Street in Philadelphia, Pennsylvania.
November 18	Brooklyn, New York, toymaker Morris Michton names the teddy bear after President Teddy Roosevelt.

1903

July 23	The Ford Motor Company sells its first automobile.
October 1	By a score of 7–3, the Pittsburgh Pirates defeat the home team Boston Pilgrims (later renamed the Red Sox) in the first modern World Series game. Boston, however, goes on to win the series, five games to three.
December 1	*The Great Train Robbery*, the first western film, is released.
December 17	The first airplane flight occurs at Kitty Hawk, North Carolina, when the Wright brothers' Flyer I flies for 12 seconds.

1904

February 23	The United States acquires control of the Panama Canal Zone for $10 million.
April 30	President Theodore Roosevelt officially opens the St. Louis World's Fair.
May 14	The first Olympic games to be held in the United States open in St. Louis, Missouri.
August 16	New York City begins building Grand Central Station.
October 4	New York City subway service begins.
November 8	Theodore Roosevelt defeats Democrat Alton B. Parker to win the presidency in his own right.

1905

February 7	Congress grants statehood to Oklahoma, which becomes the 46th state to enter the Union.
February 23	The Rotary Club is founded in Chicago.
March 3	The U.S. Forest Service is formed.

September 22	Race riots in Atlanta, Georgia, kill 10 blacks and 2 whites.
December 16	The U.S. entertainment trade publication *Variety* publishes its first weekly issue.

1906

April 18	At 5:12 A.M., San Francisco is devastated by an 8.2 earthquake.
June 29	President Theodore Roosevelt signs a bill creating Mesa Verde National Park in southwestern Colorado.
June 30	President Theodore Roosevelt signs into law the Pure Food and Drug Act and the Meat Inspection Act.
August 13	At Fort Brown, Texas, some 10–20 armed men attack an all-black army unit; the attack results in a shooting rampage that leaves one townsperson dead and one police officer wounded.
August 22	The first Victor Victrola is manufactured.
December 10	President Theodore Roosevelt becomes the first American to be awarded the Nobel Peace Prize.

1907

July 18	Florenz Ziegfeld's "Follies of 1907" premiers in New York City.
August 28	Two Seattle teenagers begin a telephone message service that grows to become the United Parcel Service (UPS).
September 29	The foundation stone is laid for the Washington National Cathedral.
October 27	Union Station is opened in Washington, D.C.
December 6	The worst mining disaster in U.S. history occurs as 362 men and boys die in a coal-mine explosion in Monongah, West Virginia.
December 7	The first Christmas Seals are sold in Wilmington, Delaware, to help the fight against tuberculosis.
December 31	For the first time, a ball is dropped in New York City's Times Square to signal the arrival of the new year.

1908

February 18	The first U.S. postage stamps in rolls are issued.
March 4	The New York State Board of Education bans the act of whipping students in its schools.
October 1	The Ford Model T, the first car for millions of Americans, hits the market at a cost of $825.
November 3	Republican William Howard Taft is elected the 27th president of the United States, defeating three-time Democratic nominee William Jennings Bryan.
December 25	Jack Johnson of Texas knocks out Tommy Burns to become the first black world heavyweight boxing champion.

1909

February 12	The National Association for the Advancement of Colored People (NAACP) is founded.
February 16	The first subway car with side doors goes into service in New York City.
March 4	President William Howard Taft is inaugurated during a snowstorm that drops 10 inches of snow on Washington, D.C.
May 31	The NAACP holds its first conference at the United Charities Building in New York City.
August 2	The first Lincoln-head pennies are minted.

1910

February 8	The Boy Scouts of America is incorporated in Washington, D.C., by William D. Boyce, a wealthy Chicago publisher who learned of the "scouts" on a trip to England the previous year.
March 17	The Camp Fire Girls organization is formed in Lake Sebago, Maine.
March 23	The first auto race occurs at the Los Angeles Motordrome, the first U.S. auto speedway.
April 3	Alaska's Mt. McKinley, the highest mountain in North America, is climbed.
April 21	Author Mark Twain, who was born as Samuel Langhorne Clemens, dies at the age of 74 in Redding, Connecticut.
May 18	Earth passes through the tail of Halley's comet, which has been visible in the night sky for some weeks. Entrepreneurs peddle "comet gas masks" for people worried about Earth's passage through poisonous cyanogen gas in the comet's tail.
June 16	The first Father's Day is celebrated in Spokane, Washington, by Mrs. John Bruce Dodd. In 1924, President Calvin Coolidge recommends that it be celebrated as a national holiday.
June 25	Congress establishes a postal savings system in U.S. post offices, effective January 1, 1911; the system pays 2 percent interest on deposits not to exceed $2,500.
July 4	African American boxer Jack Johnson knocks out white champion James J. Jeffries in a heavyweight boxing match; the media had dubbed Jeffries "the Great White Hope" to keep an African American from winning the heavyweight crown.
July 24	James MacGillivray publishes the first account of the mythical lumberjack Paul Bunyan in the *Detroit News*.
August 9	Alva Fisher patents the first complete, self-contained electric washing machine.
August 20–21	The Great Idaho Fire kills 86 people and destroys some three million acres of timber in Idaho and Montana.
October 1	A bomb explodes at the *Los Angeles Times* building, leaving 21 dead and several injured.

November 12	In the first movie stunt, a man jumps into the Hudson River from a burning balloon.

1911

March 11	Charles Kettering creates the first successful electric self-starter for Cadillac.
March 18	Former President Theodore Roosevelt opens Roosevelt Dam in Phoenix, Arizona, the largest dam in the United States to date.
March 25	In New York City, the Triangle Shirtwaist Factory fire kills over 140 immigrant workers. Thirteen girls survive the fire that breaks out on the top three floors of the 10-story Asch Building as the workday is ending.
May 15	The U.S. Supreme Court orders the dissolution of Standard Oil Company, ruling it is in violation of the Sherman Antitrust Act.
August 15	Procter and Gamble unveils its Crisco shortening.

1912

January 6	New Mexico enters the Union as the 47th state.
January 10	The world's first flying-boat airplane, designed by Glenn Curtiss, makes its maiden flight at Hammondsport, New York. Curtiss is the first licensed pilot and Orville Wright is the second.
January 12	In Lawrence, Massachusetts, over 20,000 textile factory workers go on strike to protest wage cuts.
February 3	New U.S. football rules are set: the field is shortened to 100 yards; touchdowns become six points instead of five; four downs are allowed instead of three; and the kickoff is moved from midfield to the 40-yard line.
February 14	Arizona becomes the 48th state to enter the Union.
March 27	The first cherry blossom trees, a gift from Japan, are planted in Washington, D.C.
April 14	The luxury liner *Titanic* strikes an iceberg in the North Atlantic and sinks with the loss of over 1,500 lives.
August 7	The Progressive Party nominates Theodore Roosevelt for president.
October 14	Theodore Roosevelt, former president and Bull Moose Party candidate, is shot at close range by an anarchist in Milwaukee, Wisconsin. Although wounded, Roosevelt continues with his speech.
November 5	Woodrow Wilson becomes the first Democrat to be elected president since 1892, when he defeats incumbent Republican William Howard Taft and former President Theodore Roosevelt, who runs an independent campaign.

1913

January 15	The first telephone line between Berlin and New York is inaugurated.

February 3	The 16th Amendment to the U.S. Constitution, providing for a federal income tax, is ratified.
March 15	President Woodrow Wilson holds the first open presidential news conference.
April 8	The 17th Amendment to the U.S. Constitution, requiring direct election of senators, is ratified.
April 26	Thirteen-year-old Mary Phagan is killed at an Atlanta pencil factory. She had stopped to pick up her check on her way to Peachtree Street to see a Confederate Memorial Day Parade. Leo Frank, a Jewish factory manager, is falsely accused of raping and murdering the young working-class girl.
September 10	The Lincoln Highway (U.S. 30) opens as the first paved coast-to-coast highway.
October 7	Henry Ford adapts the assembly line method to automobile manufacturing, which reduces production time for a single car from 12 hours to 93 minutes. Output more than doubles and the price of the Model T is reduced from $600 to $550.
October 10	The Panama Canal is completed when President Woodrow Wilson, by pressing an electric button at the White House in Washington, D.C., triggers a blast that explodes the Gamboa Dike.
December 23	The Federal Reserve Act is signed by President Woodrow Wilson. The Owen-Glass Act establishes the decentralized, government-controlled banking system in the United States known as the Federal Reserve.
December 29	The first movie serial, the *Adventures of Kathlyn*, premiers in Chicago.

1914

January 5	Henry Ford announces that he will pay a minimum wage of $5 a day and share with employees $10 million of the previous year's profits.
April 4	*The Perils of Pauline* is shown for the first time in Los Angeles.
April 20	The "Ludlow Massacre" occurs as soldiers kill 45 during a mine strike in Ludlow, Colorado. Colorado militiamen called in by John D. Rockefeller Jr. to settle the strike torch a tent camp of 1,200 striking miners.
May 1	President Woodrow Wilson issues a proclamation designating the second Sunday in May as the first national Mother's Day.
July 11	Babe Ruth signs with the Boston Red Sox; he earns $2,900 in his rookie season.
July 15	Vaudevillian Henry Fox introduces the fox-trot in the Ziegfeld Follies.
July 28	Austria-Hungary declares war on Serbia, thereby initiating World War I in Europe.
August 5	Cleveland, Ohio, installs the first electric traffic lights.
August 13	Carl Wickman founds Greyhound, the first U.S. bus line, in Minnesota.
December 8	*Watch Your Step*, the first musical revue to feature a score composed entirely by Irving Berlin, opens in New York.
December 21	The first feature-length silent film comedy, *Tillie's Punctured Romance*, is released.

1915

January 12	The U.S. Congress establishes Rocky Mountain National Park in Colorado.
January 21	The first Kiwanis Club is formally founded, in Detroit, Michigan.
February 8	D. W. Griffith's silent movie epic about the Civil War, *The Birth of a Nation*, premiers at Clune's Auditorium in Los Angeles.
February 20	President Woodrow Wilson opens the Panama-Pacific Expo in San Francisco to celebrate the opening of the Panama Canal.
April 5	African American boxer Jack Johnson (1878–1946), the heavyweight champion since 1908, loses the heavyweight championship in Cuba to Jess Willard in the 26th round.
May 1	The luxury liner *Lusitania* leaves New York Harbor for a voyage to Europe. Warnings are issued by the German government in New York City newspapers that it regards the refurbished liner a battle target.
May 6	Babe Ruth makes his pitching debut with the Boston Red Sox and hits his first home run, but Boston loses to the New York Yankees 4–3 in 15 innings.
May 7	Almost 1,200 passengers die when the British liner *Lusitania* is torpedoed and sunk by a German submarine. The incident causes an upsurge of anti-German feeling in the United States.
May 17	The National Baptist Convention is chartered.
May 28	John B. Gruelle patents the Raggedy Ann doll.
July 28	10,000 blacks march down 5th Avenue in New York City to protest lynching.
August 17	Leo Frank, a Jewish factory manager, is lynched by a mob of anti-Semites in Cobb County, Georgia. Frank had been convicted in the killing of Mary Phagan, a 13-year-old girl who worked at his pencil factory. Georgia Governor John M. Slaton, believing Frank innocent, had commuted his death sentence to life imprisonment in June.
September 22	Southern Methodist University in Dallas, Texas, holds its first class, and Xavier University, the first African American Catholic college, opens in New Orleans, Louisiana.
October 4	Dinosaur National Monument in Colorado and Utah is established.
October 9	President Woodrow Wilson becomes the first president to attend a World Series game.
October 12	Ford Motor Company manufactures its one millionth Model T automobile.
October 23	25,000 women march in New York City demanding the right to vote.
November 19	Joe Hill, a labor leader and songwriter, is executed for murder.
December 4	The Ku Klux Klan receives a charter from Fulton County, Georgia.

1916

January	The five-member white Dixie Jazz Band from New Orleans led by Nick LaRocca cuts its first jazz records—"Darktown Strutters' Ball" and "Indiana"—for Columbia Records in New York City.

January 28	Louis D. Brandeis, a private practice attorney and leader in the U.S. Zionist movement, is appointed by President Woodrow Wilson to the U.S. Supreme Court, thus becoming the first Jewish justice.
February 5	Enrico Caruso records "O Solo Mio" for the Victor Talking Machine Company.
March 9	The forces of Mexican revolutionary General Francisco "Pancho" Villa raid Columbus, New Mexico.
April 20	Wrigley Field in Chicago opens.
June 1	The National Defense Act increases the strength of the U.S. National Guard by 450,000 men.
June 15	President Woodrow Wilson signs a bill incorporating the Boy Scouts of America.
June 17	American troops under the command of General Jack Pershing march into Mexico as General Pershing leads an unsuccessful punitive expedition against Francisco "Pancho" Villa.
July 4	Nathan's Famous Hot Dogs opens a stand at Brooklyn's Coney Island and holds a hot dog eating contest as a publicity stunt that becomes an annual event.
September 11	The "Star Spangled Banner" is sung at the beginning of a baseball game for the first time in Cooperstown, New York.
October 27	The first published reference to "jazz" appears in *Variety*.
November 7	President Woodrow Wilson is reelected over Republican challenger Charles Evans Hughes, but the race is so close that the final outcome is not known until November 11; Montana Republican Jeannette Rankin, a lifelong feminist and pacifist, becomes the first woman elected to Congress.

1917

January	The film *The Spirit of '76*, produced by Robert Goldstein, opens in Los Angeles. Goldstein is later arrested and convicted under the Espionage Act for producing an anti-British film.
January 19	The Zimmermann Note, a coded message sent to Germany's minister in Mexico, proposes an alliance between Germany and Mexico in the event war should break out between the United States and Germany. Intercepted and made public by the British, the telegram hastens U.S. involvement in World War I.
April 2	President Woodrow Wilson delivers his war message before a joint session of Congress and recommends that a state of war be declared between the United States and the Imperial German government.
June 15	At the urging of President Woodrow Wilson, Congress passes the Espionage Act, which makes it a crime for a person to interfere with the operation or success of the U.S. military or to promote the success of the enemies of the United States.
July 20	The U.S. draft lottery for World War I goes into operation.
October 23	American troops fire their first shot in battle in Europe.

October 24	The Bolshevik Revolution begins in Russia.
December 26	As a wartime measure, President Wilson places railroads under government control, with Secretary of War William McAdoo as director general.
December 28	The *New York Evening Mail* publishes a facetious and fictitious essay by H. L. Mencken on the history of the bathtub in America. Mencken claims, for example, that Millard Fillmore was the first president to have a bathtub installed in the White House.

1918

January 8	President Woodrow Wilson delivers his "Fourteen Points" address proposing the idea of a League of Nations. Mississippi becomes the first state to ratify the proposed 18th Amendment to the U.S. Constitution prohibiting the sale, manufacture, or transportation of liquor.
January 27	*Tarzan of the Apes*, the first Tarzan film, premiers at the Broadway Theater in New York City.
March	A flu epidemic begins at Fort Riley, Kansas, where 48 men die.
May 14	Sunday baseball becomes legal in Washington, D.C.
May 15	The U.S. Post Office and the U.S. Army begin regularly scheduled airmail service between Washington and New York through Philadelphia.
June 28	The U.S. Marines take the Bois de Bellcau in fighting on the Western Front in Europe.
September 11	The Boston Red Sox beat the Chicago Cubs in six games to win the World Series.
October	In a deadly month for Americans, some 195,000 Americans die of the worst global epidemic of the century; the cities of Baltimore and Washington run out of coffins.
October 8	Sgt. Alvin C. York single-handedly eliminates 35 machine guns, kills more than 20 Germans, and takes 132 members of a Prussian Guards regiment prisoner. A modest man, York shrugs off his heroic actions, saying, "It's over, let's forget it."
November 11	A truce is signed ending World War I, the so-called "war to end all war."
December 1	President Woodrow Wilson orders all U.S. breweries to shut down to save grain for the war effort.

1919

January 16	Nebraska, Wyoming, and Missouri become the 36th, 37th, and 38th states to ratify the 18th Amendment, the Prohibition Amendment.
January 18	The Versailles Peace Conference opens in France with President Woodrow Wilson in attendance.
March 15–17	The American Legion is founded in Paris by members of the American Expeditionary Force.
May 2	The first U.S. air passenger service starts.

June 14	The U.S. Congress passes the 19th Amendment granting suffrage to American women.
July 24	A race riot in Washington, D.C., leaves 6 dead and 100 wounded.
July 27	A race riot erupts in Chicago, killing 15 whites and 23 blacks and injuring 500.
August 23	The "Gasoline Alley" cartoon strip premiers in the *Chicago Tribune*.
October 1	In baseball's World Series, the Chicago White Sox face the Cincinnati Reds in a best-of-nine games series. The White Sox intentionally throw the series to satisfy gamblers in what becomes known as the Black Sox Scandal.
October 2	President Woodrow Wilson suffers a stroke that leaves him partially paralyzed.
October 8	The U.S. Senate and House of Representatives pass the Volstead Prohibition Enforcement Bill, which enforces the ban on the sale or consumption of alcoholic beverages.
October 17	The Radio Corporation of America (RCA) is created.
November 10	The American Legion holds its first national convention in Minneapolis, Minnesota.

1920

January 2	Some 2,700 arrests are made in raids in 33 American cities as part of a campaign against political radicals and labor agitators, spearheaded by the Department of Justice under Attorney General A. Mitchell Palmer.
January 3	The Red Sox sell Babe Ruth to the New York Yankees for $100,000, twice the amount of any previous player transaction.
January 4	The Negro National League, the first black baseball league, is organized by Rube Foster.
February 14	The League of Women Voters is founded in Chicago to encourage women's participation in government.
June 12	Republicans in Chicago nominate Warren G. Harding for president and Calvin Coolidge for vice president.
June 13	The U.S. Post Office Department rules that children may not be sent by parcel post.
July 6	The Democrats end their convention in San Francisco with the selection of James Cox of Ohio and running mate Franklin Delano Roosevelt.
August 2	Marcus Garvey presents his "Back to Africa" program in New York City.
August 18	Tennessee becomes the 36th state to ratify the 19th Amendment to the Constitution, which guarantees the right of all American women to vote.
November 2	Republican Warren G. Harding is elected the 29th president of the United States, decisively defeating Democrat James Cox, governor of Ohio. The first radio broadcast in the United States is made from Pittsburgh, where Westinghouse has built a radio station on its factory roof. KDKA in Pittsburgh broadcasts returns from the Harding-Cox presidential election.

November 20	The Nobel Peace Prize is awarded to U.S. President Woodrow Wilson.
November 25	Radio station WTAW of College Station, Texas, broadcasts the first play-by-play description of a football game between the University of Texas and Texas A&M; the first Thanksgiving Parade is held in Philadelphia.
November 28	The film *The Mark of Zorro*, with Douglas Fairbanks, opens in New York City at the Capitol Theater.
December 24	Enrico Caruso gives his last public performance, singing in Jacques Halevy's *La Juive* at the Metropolitan Opera in New York.

1921

March 4	Warren G. Harding is sworn in as the 29th president of the United States.
March 6	The National Association of the Moving Picture Industry announces its intention to censor U.S. movies.
April 2	Albert Einstein makes his first visit to the United States.
July 2	Heavyweight Jack Dempsey defeats Georges Carpentier of France in New Jersey in the first million-dollar gate boxing match.
August 25	The United States, which never ratified the Versailles Treaty ending World War I, finally signs a peace treaty with Germany.
September 8	Margaret Gorman of Washington, D.C., is crowned the first Miss America in Atlantic City, New Jersey.
October 5	The World Series is broadcast on radio for the first time. The New York Giants beat the New York Yankees five games to three in the best-of-nine contest.
October 23	The Green Bay Packers play their first NFL game and beat Minneapolis 7–6.

1922

February 5	The *Reader's Digest* begins publication in Pleasantville, New York.
April 12	A San Francisco jury acquits actor Roscoe "Fatty" Arbuckle in his third murder trial following two hung juries.
April 15	Wyoming Democratic Senator John Kendrick introduces a resolution that begins the Teapot Dome investigation, one of the most significant investigations of a public scandal in Senate history.
April 18	The office of Will Hays, head of the Motion Picture Producers and Distributors of America (MPPDA), announces that Roscoe Arbuckle is banned from working in motion pictures, effective immediately.
May 30	The Lincoln Memorial is dedicated in Washington, D.C., by Chief Justice and former president William Howard Taft.
June 14	Warren G. Harding becomes the first president heard on radio, as Baltimore station WEAR broadcasts his speech dedicating the Francis Scott Key memorial at Fort McHenry.
November 4	The U.S. Postmaster General orders all homes to get mailboxes or relinquish delivery of mail.

1923

January 2	A Ku Klux Klan attack on a black residential area of Rosewood, Florida, kills eight people. This all-black town, a north Florida community of 120 people, is burned to the ground.
February 22	U.S. transcontinental airmail service begins.
March 2	The first issue of the weekly periodical, *Time*, appears on newsstands.
April 18	The first game is played in Yankee Stadium, with the Yankees defeating the Boston Red Sox 4–1.
July 4	Jack Dempsey beats Tommy Gibbon in 15 rounds for the heavyweight boxing title.
August 2	Following a return trip from Alaska, and a bout with food poisoning, 57-year-old President Warren G. Harding dies in San Francisco at the Palace Hotel of a "stroke of apoplexy."
August 3	Vice President Calvin Coolidge is sworn in as the 30th president of the United States.
August 13	U.S. Steel Corporation initiates an eight-hour workday.
October 25	The Teapot Dome scandal comes to public attention as Senator Thomas J. Walsh of Montana, subcommittee chairman, reveals the findings of the past 18 months of investigation. His case will result in the conviction of Harry F. Sinclair of Mammoth Oil, and later of Secretary of the Interior Albert B. Fall, the first cabinet member in American history to go to jail.

1924

January 9	Ford Motor Company stock is valued at nearly $1 billion.
February 12	George Gershwin's symphonic jazz composition, "Rhapsody in Blue," premiers at Carnegie Hall in New York City.
February 22	President Calvin Coolidge delivers the first presidential radio broadcast from the White House.
May 10	J. Edgar Hoover is appointed head of the Federal Bureau of Investigation (FBI) at the age of 29.
May 21	Fourteen-year-old Bobby Franks is murdered in a "thrill killing" committed by Nathan Leopold Jr. and Richard Loeb.
June 2	Congress passes the Snyder Act, which grants full U.S. citizenship to all American Indians born in the United States.
June 9	"Jelly-Roll Blues" is recorded by blues great Jelly Roll Morton.
July 11	After 103 roll calls, the Democrats bypass New York Governor Alfred E. Smith and William G. McAdoo of California and nominate John W. Davis of West Virginia and Charles Bryan, brother of William Jennings Bryan, to run against Calvin Coolidge.
August 5	The comic strip "Little Orphan Annie" by Harold Gray debuts in the *New York Daily News*.
November 4	President Calvin Coolidge is elected to a full term in his own right.

1925

February 21	The first issue of the *New Yorker* magazine, founded by Harold Ross, hits the newsstands.
March 2	State and federal highway officials develop a nationwide route numbering system and adopt the familiar U.S. shield-shaped number marker.
April 10	The novel *The Great Gatsby,* by F. Scott Fitzgerald, is first published by Scribner's of New York.
July 10	The "Scopes Monkey Trial" begins in Tennessee.
July 26	William Jennings Bryan dies five days after assisting the prosecution in the Scopes Monkey Trial.
August 8	The first national congress of the Ku Klux Klan opens, with some 200,000 members marching in Washington, D.C.
October 16	The Texas School Board prohibits the teaching of evolution.
November 28	The WSM *Barn Dance*, later known as the *Grand Ole Opry*, the Nashville, Tennessee, home of country music, makes its radio debut.

1926

April 16	The new Book of the Month Club sends out its first selection: *Lolly Willows or The Loving Huntsman* by Sylvia Townsend Warner.
May 18	Evangelist Aimee Semple McPherson vanishes while visiting a beach in Venice, California; she reappears a month later, claiming to have been kidnapped.
August 23	The death of silent film actor Rudolph Valentino causes worldwide hysteria, with several women reportedly committing suicide, and riots breaking out in New York as thousands of fans try to view the body.
September 9	The National Broadcasting Company (NBC) is created by the Radio Corporation of America.
September 17	A hurricane hits Miami and Palm Beach, Florida, killing almost 500 people and marking the beginning of the end of the Florida land boom.
September 23	Gene Tunney defeats Jack Dempsey for the World Heavyweight Boxing championship in Philadelphia.
October 31	Magician Harry Houdini dies in Detroit as a result of a ruptured appendix.

1927

February 23	President Calvin Coolidge signs the Radio Act, a bill creating the Federal Radio Commission, forerunner of the Federal Communications Commission (FCC).
March 2	Babe Ruth signs a three-year contract with the New York Yankees for a guarantee of $70,000 a year, thus becoming baseball's highest-paid player.
May 21	Charles Lindbergh lands at Le Bourget Field in Paris after a 33.5-hour nonstop flight, the first solo transatlantic flight from Roosevelt Field on New York's Long Island.
May 25	Henry Ford stops production of the Model T and begins producing the Model A.

June 30	Clarence Birdseye, after years of experimentation, receives a patent for packing fish, meat, or vegetables into waxed cardboard containers, then flash-freezing them under pressure, reducing freezing time from 18 hours to 90 minutes.
September 30	Babe Ruth hits his 60th home run of the season off Tom Zachary in Yankee Stadium, breaking his own Major League record for most home runs in a season.
October 6	The era of talking pictures arrives with the opening of *The Jazz Singer*, starring Al Jolson singing and dancing in blackface.
October 28	Pan Am Airways launches the first scheduled international flight.
December 4	Duke Ellington opens at the Cotton Club in Harlem.

1928

January 31	Scotch tape is first marketed by the 3-M Company.
February 28	Smokey the Bear is created.
March 19	*Amos 'n' Andy* debuts on radio with the NBC Blue Network.
June 14	The Republican National Convention in Kansas City nominates Herbert Hoover for president on the first ballot.
June 28	New York Governor Alfred E. Smith is nominated for president at the Democratic National Convention in Houston.
November 6	For the first time, presidential election results are flashed on an electronic sign outside the *New York Times* building; Republican Herbert Hoover decisively beats Democrat Alfred E. Smith.
November 18	The first successful sound-synchronized animated cartoon, Walt Disney's "Steamboat Willie," starring Mickey Mouse, premiers at the Colony Theater in New York City.

1929

February 14	In Chicago, the "St. Valentine's Day Massacre" occurs in a garage of the Moran gang, as seven rivals of Al Capone's gang are gunned down.
March 4	Herbert Hoover is inaugurated as the 31st president of the United States.
May 16	Hollywood stages an awards event at the Hollywood Roosevelt Hotel that will become the Academy Awards extravaganza. The movie *Wings* wins the best production award, while Emil Jennings and Janet Gaynor are named best actor and best actress.
October 24	"Black Thursday," the first day of the stock market crash, sees the Dow Jones average drop 12.8 percent as 13 million shares changed hands.
October 29	"Black Tuesday" sees panicked survivors dump 16 million shares on the stock market, wiping out $30 billion in paper value in one day; the Great Depression begins.
December 31	Guy Lombardo and his Royal Canadians play "Auld Lang Syne" as a New Year's Eve song for the first time.

1930

February	President Herbert Hoover says that the worst effects of the Depression will be over within 90 days and that "prosperity is just around the corner."
February 24	President Herbert Hoover tells Congress to cut spending or face a 40 percent tax increase.
May 24	A poll shows that the majority of Americans favor the repeal of Prohibition.
July 31	The radio show *The Shadow* is broadcast for the first time.
August 11	A severe drought cuts U.S. corn output by nearly 700 million bushels.
October 8	The Philadelphia Athletes defeat the St. Louis Cardinals 7–1 to win the World Series.
November 5	Sinclair Lewis (1885–1951) becomes the first American to win a Nobel Prize in literature.

1931

February 21	Alka Seltzer is introduced.
March 25	In Alabama, nine young black men, arrested for riding a freight train, are taken to Scottsboro. Victoria Price (age 21) and Ruby Bates (age 17), who had worked as prostitutes in Huntsville, are also found on the train dressed as boys. The nine black men are soon charged with raping the two white women while riding on the freight train.
May 1	The 102-story Empire State Building opens in New York City.
October 4	The comic strip "Dick Tracy," created by Chester Gould, debuts.
October 24	Al (Alphonse) Capone, a Prohibition-era Chicago gangster, is sentenced to 11 years in prison for tax evasion.
October 26	Eugene O'Neill's *Mourning Becomes Electra* premiers in New York City.

1932

March 1	Charles Lindbergh Jr., the infant son of Charles and Anne Lindbergh, is kidnapped from his nursery at the family home near Princeton, New Jersey.
May 12	The character of Goofy first appears in "Mickey's Revue" by Walt Disney.
May 21	Amelia Earhart makes her first transatlantic solo flight from Newfoundland to Ireland.
May 29	World War I veterans begin arriving in Washington, D.C., to demand cash bonuses that they are not scheduled to receive for another 13 years.
June 16	President Herbert Hoover and Vice President Charles Curtis are renominated at the Republican National Convention in Chicago.
June 17	The U.S. Senate defeats a cash-now bonus bill as some 10,000 veterans mass around the Capitol.
July 1	New York Governor Franklin D. Roosevelt is nominated for president at the Democratic National Convention in Chicago. Roosevelt breaks precedent by flying to Chicago to accept the nomination in person.

July 28	Under orders from President Herbert Hoover, shacks built at Anacostia Flats in the shadow of the nation's Capitol by World War I veteran demonstrators are burned.
July 30	The Summer Olympic Games open in Los Angeles.
October 2	The New York Yankees win the World Series against the Chicago Cubs in four games.
November 8	New York Governor Franklin D. Roosevelt, a Democrat, defeats incumbent Republican President Herbert Hoover.
November 28	Groucho Marx performs on radio for the first time.
December 2	*The Adventures of Charlie Chan* is first heard on the NBC Blue radio network.
December 21	Fred Astaire and Ginger Rogers make their first movie together, *Flying Down to Rio*.
December 27	Radio City Music Hall opens in New York City.

1933

February 6	The 20th Amendment to the U.S. Constitution is declared in effect. The Lame-Duck Amendment changes the inauguration date of congressmen from March 4 to January 3.
February 10	The first singing telegram is introduced by the Postal Telegram Company in New York.
February 15	President-elect Franklin Roosevelt escapes an assassination attempt in Miami. Giuseppe Zangara, an unemployed New Jersey bricklayer from Italy, fires five pistol shots at the back of Roosevelt's head from only 25 feet away. While all five rounds miss Roosevelt, one hits Mayor Anton Cermak of Chicago, who dies from the wound.
February 17	*Newsweek* magazine is first published by Thomas J. C. Marchtyn under the title *News-Week*.
February 20	Congress passes the 21st Amendment repealing Prohibition.
February 28	Francis Perkins is appointed Secretary of Labor by president-elect Roosevelt; Perkins becomes the first woman to serve in the cabinet.
March 4	Franklin D. Roosevelt is inaugurated to his first term as president in Washington, D.C.
March 5	President Franklin D. Roosevelt orders a four-day bank holiday to stop large amounts of money from being withdrawn from the banks.
March 12	President Franklin Roosevelt delivers the first of his radio "fireside chats," telling Americans what is being done to deal with the nation's economic crisis.
March 20	Giuseppe [Joe] Zangara is electrocuted for the murder of Anton Cermak, the mayor of Chicago, whom Zangara killed while trying to assassinate president-elect Franklin Roosevelt in Miami.
March 22	President Franklin Roosevelt signs a measure to make wine and beer containing up to 3.2 percent alcohol legal.

March 31	Congress authorizes the Civilian Conservation Corps (CCC) to relieve rampant unemployment.
April 7	Prohibition ends when Utah becomes the 38th state to ratify the 21st Amendment to the U.S. Constitution.
May 18	The Tennessee Valley Authority Act is signed by President Franklin Roosevelt.
May 27	Walt Disney's Academy Award–winning animated short *The Three Little Pigs* is released.
June 6	Richard M. Hollingshead Jr., an auto products salesman, opens the first drive-in movie theater, in Camden, New Jersey.
June 16	Congress passes the National Recovery Act (NRA); the U.S. Federal Deposit Insurance Corporation (FDIC) becomes effective.
November 9	President Franklin Roosevelt sets up the Civil Works Administration as an emergency Depression agency to provide jobs for the unemployed.
December 17	In the first world championship football game, the Chicago Bears defeat the New York Giants, 23–21.

1934

February 15	The U.S. Congress passes the Civil Works Emergency Relief Act, allotting new funds for the Federal Emergency Relief Administration.
February 22	The romantic comedy *It Happened One Night,* starring Clark Gable and Claudette Colbert, opens at New York's Radio City Music Hall.
April 19	Shirley Temple appears in her first movie.
April 28	President Franklin Roosevelt signs the Home Owners Loan Act, saving thousands from foreclosure.
May 9	The San Francisco waterfront strike begins. The International Longshoremen's Association (ILA), headed by Australian immigrant Harry Bridges, shuts down seaports in Washington, Oregon, and California for three months.
May 23	Bonnie Parker and Clyde Barrow are shot some four dozen times in an early morning police ambush by Texas Rangers as the couple drives a stolen Ford Deluxe along a road in Bienville Parish, near Sailes, Louisiana. This ambush ends the most spectacular manhunt seen in America up to that time.
May 28	The Dionne quintuplets—Annette, Cecile, Emilie, Marchie, and Yvonne—are born to Elzire Dionne at the family farm in Ontario, Canada.
June 9	Donald Duck makes his first screen appearance.
July 22	John Dillinger is shot to death by federal agents outside Chicago's Biograph Theater.
November 22	"Santa Claus Is Comin' to Town" is first heard on Eddie Cantor's show.
December	Parker Brothers purchases the game of Monopoly from George Darrow and rewrites the rules.

1935

April 8	The Works Progress Administration (WPA) is approved by Congress. The WPA creates low-paying federal jobs to provide immediate relief. The WPA puts 8.5 million jobless to work on projects as diverse as constructing highways, bridges, and public buildings, and arts programs like the Federal Writers' Project.
May 24	The first Major League Baseball game played at night takes place at Cincinnati's Crosley Field as the Reds beat the Philadelphia Phillies 2–1.
May 27	The U.S. Supreme Court, in *Schechter Poultry Corp. v. United States*, declares President Franklin Roosevelt's National Industrial Recovery Act unconstitutional.
August 14	The Social Security Act becomes law.
September 2	A hurricane slams into the Florida Keys, claiming more than 400 lives.
September 8	Senator Huey P. Long, "the Kingfish" of Louisiana politics, is shot and mortally wounded in Baton Rouge.
October 10	*Porgy and Bess* debuts at the Alvin Theater on Broadway in New York City.
November 9	United Mine Workers president John L. Lewis and other labor leaders form the Committee for Industrial Organization to represent unskilled industrial workers.

1936

January 4	*Billboard* magazine publishes its first music hit parade.
January 15	The nonprofit Ford Foundation is incorporated.
January 29	The first members of baseball's Hall of Fame—Ty Cobb, Babe Ruth, Honus Wagner, Christy Mathewson, and Walter Johnson—are named in Cooperstown, New York.
April 3	Bruno Hauptmann, the man convicted of kidnapping and killing the Lindbergh baby, is executed.
June 30	Margaret Mitchell's novel, *Gone With the Wind*, is published in New York City.
August 9	American sprinter Jesse Owens wins his fourth gold medal at the Olympic Games in Berlin, Germany.
August 24	President Franklin Roosevelt gives the Federal Bureau of Investigation (FBI) authority to investigate fascists and communists.
October 16	American Eugene O'Neill wins the Nobel Prize for literature.
November 3	President Franklin Roosevelt is reelected for a second term in a landslide over Republican challenger Alfred M. "Alf" Landon.
November 17	Edgar Bergen and Charlie McCarthy are an overnight success on radio.
November 23	*Life* magazine hits the newsstands for the first time.
November 28	"Pennies From Heaven" by Bing Crosby hits #1 on the pop singles chart.
December 30	The United Auto Workers Union stages its first sit-down strike at the Fisher Body Plant No. 1 in Flint, Michigan.

1937

May 6	At 7:25 P.M., the giant German airship (dirigible or zeppelin) *Hindenburg* bursts into flames and crashes to the ground as it attempts to dock with a mooring mast at Lakehurst Naval Air Station in New Jersey.
May 27	The newly completed Golden Gate Bridge connecting San Francisco and Marin County, California, is opened.
May 30	The Memorial Day Massacre occurs; 10 union demonstrators are killed and 84 wounded when police open fire in front of the South Chicago Republic Steel plant.
June 1	Amelia Earhart and navigator Fred Noonan depart from Miami Municipal Airport in a Lockheed 10E Electra airplane; she is last heard from one month later trying to find tiny Howland Island in the middle of the Pacific Ocean.
June 22	Joe Louis becomes heavyweight champ by knocking out Jim Braddock.
August 14	The Appalachian Trail is dedicated.

1938

January 3	The March of Dimes is established by President Franklin Delano Roosevelt to fight polio.
February 4	The Thornton Wilder play *Our Town* opens on Broadway.
June 1	Superman makes his first appearance in D.C. Comics' Action Comics Series issue #1.
June 22	Heavyweight boxing champion Joe Louis knocks out Max Schmeling in the first round of their heavyweight rematch at New York City's Yankee Stadium.
October 30	On a Sunday night, Orson Welles and his troupe of actors in the Mercury Theater touch off mass panic with a CBS dramatic radio adaptation of H. G. Wells's 1898 novel of Martian conquest, *The War of the Worlds*.

1939

March 21	Singer Kate Smith records "God Bless America" for Victor Records; she had introduced the song on her radio program in 1938.
March 28	Philip Barry's *Philadelphia Story* premiers in New York City.
April 9	On Easter Sunday Marion Anderson sings a triumphant outdoor concert at the Lincoln Memorial in Washington, D.C., before a crowd of 75,000 and a radio audience of millions.
April 30	The New York World's Fair, billed as a look at "the world of tomorrow," officially opens.
May 1	D.C. Comics introduces Batman.
June 30	Frank Sinatra makes his first appearance with the Harry James band.
August 15	The MGM musical *The Wizard of Oz* premiers at Grauman's Chinese Theater in Hollywood, California.

September 1	World War II begins, as the Germans attack Poland with their strategy of *Blitzkrieg*, or lightning war.
September 5	President Franklin Roosevelt declares the neutrality of the United States in World War II.
October 24	Nylon stockings are sold publicly for the first time in Wilmington, Delaware.

1940

February 7	Walt Disney's second feature-length movie, *Pinocchio*, premiers in New York City.
February 10	Glenn Miller's "In The Mood" is the nation's #1 hit; the "Tom and Jerry" cartoon, created by Hanna and Barbera, is debuted by MGM.
February 12	The radio play *The Adventures of Superman* debuts on the Mutual Network.
February 29	*Gone With the Wind* wins eight Academy Awards, including best picture of 1939.
March 31	New York's La Guardia Airport is officially opened to the public.
June 28	The Republican Convention, held in Philadelphia, nominates Wendell L. Willkie for president.
July 18	The Democratic National Convention in Chicago nominates President Franklin Roosevelt for an unprecedented third term in office.
July 27	Bugs Bunny makes his official debut in the Warner Brothers animated cartoon *A Wild Hare*.
September 16	President Franklin Roosevelt signs into law the Selective Training and Service Act, which sets up the first peacetime military draft in U.S. history.
October 15	Charles Chaplin's first all-talking comedy, *The Great Dictator*, a lampoon of Adolf Hitler, opens at two theaters in New York City with Chaplin and his wife, costar Paulette Goddard, making appearances in both locations.
November 5	President Franklin Roosevelt wins an unprecedented third term in office, beating Republican challenger Wendell L. Willkie.
November 13	The Walt Disney animated movie *Fantasia* has its world premiere in New York City.
November 25	The cartoon character Woody Woodpecker debuts with the release of Walter Lantz's *Knock Knock*.

1941

January 6	President Franklin D. Roosevelt asks Congress to support the Lend-Lease plan to help supply the Allies.
January 20	Franklin D. Roosevelt is inaugurated for a third term as president.
May 1	The motion picture *Citizen Kane*, directed by and starring Orson Welles, premiers in New York City.

May 7	Glenn Miller and his orchestra record "Chattanooga Choo Choo" for RCA Victor; it becomes the first gold record in history.
July 17	The longest hitting streak in baseball history ends when New York Yankee Joe DiMaggio goes hitless for the first time in 57 games.
October 3	The film *The Maltese Falcon*, starring Humphrey Bogart as detective Sam Spade, opens.
December 7	Japan launches a surprise aerial attack on the U.S. naval base at Pearl Harbor, Hawaii.
December 8	The United States declares war on Japan.
December 19	The U.S. Office of Censorship is created to control information about World War II.
December 22	British Prime Minister Winston Churchill arrives in Washington for a wartime conference with President Franklin Roosevelt.

1942

January 2	The Philippine capital of Manila is taken by Japanese forces.
February 2	A *Los Angeles Times* column urges security measures against Japanese Americans.
February 9	President Franklin D. Roosevelt reemploys Daylight Saving Time (DST) in the United States; it remains in effect until September 30, 1945.
February 19	President Franklin Roosevelt signs executive order 9066, which gives the military the authority to relocate and intern Japanese Americans.
June 13	President Franklin Roosevelt creates the Office of War Information.
July 22	Gasoline rationing begins.
August 13	Walt Disney's animated feature *Bambi* premiers at Radio City Music Hall in New York City.
September 1	A federal judge upholds the wartime detention of Japanese Americans as well as Japanese nationals.
September 25	The War Labor Board orders equal pay for women in the United States.
October 3	President Franklin Roosevelt establishes the Office of Economic Stabilization and authorizes controls on farm prices, rents, wages, and salaries.
October 29	The Alaska Highway is completed.
November 13	The minimum draft age is lowered from 21 to 18.
November 23	The film *Casablanca* premiers in New York City.
December 2	A self-sustaining nuclear chain reaction is demonstrated for the first time at the University of Chicago.

1943

February 9	President Franklin Roosevelt orders a minimal 48-hour workweek in war industries.
March 29	Meat, butter, and cheese rationing begins.

June 9	The withholding of U.S. income tax deductions from salaries is authorized.
June 14	The U.S. Supreme Court rules schoolchildren cannot be compelled to salute the flag of the United States if doing so would conflict with their religious beliefs.
June 20	A race riot erupts in Detroit; federal troops are sent in to quell the violence that results in 34 dead and 600 wounded.
September 27	Bing Crosby, the Andrews Sisters, and the Vic Schoen Orchestra record "Jingle Bells" for Decca Records.
October 14	The Radio Corporation of America sells the NBC Blue radio network to businessman Edward J. Noble, who renames the network the American Broadcasting Company.

1944

April 3	The U.S. Supreme Court rules that black citizens are eligible to vote in all elections, including primaries. The *Smith v. Allwright* decision declares "white primaries" unconstitutional.
June 6	D-Day—a million Allied troops, under the overall command of General Dwight D. Eisenhower, move onto five Normandy beachheads over three weeks.
June 28	The Republican National Convention, meeting in Chicago, nominates New York Governor Thomas E. Dewey for president and Ohio Governor John W. Bricker for vice president.
July 1	Delegates from 44 countries begin meeting at Bretton Woods, New Hampshire, where they agreed to establish the International Monetary Fund and the World Bank.
July 20	President Roosevelt is nominated to run for a fourth term by the Democratic Party.
August 14	The government allows the manufacture of certain domestic appliances, such as electric ranges and vacuum cleaners, to resume on a limited basis.
November 7	Democratic President Franklin Roosevelt wins an unprecedented fourth term in office, defeating Republican challenger Thomas E. Dewey.
November 11	Private Eddie Slovik is convicted of desertion and sentenced to death for refusing to join his unit in the European Theater of Operations.
December 15	Bandleader Glenn Miller, a U.S. army major, is lost in a single-engine plane flight over the English Channel en route to Paris.
December 18	The U.S. Supreme Court upholds the wartime relocation of Japanese Americans.
December 23	General Dwight D. Eisenhower confirms the death sentence of Private Eddie Slovik, the only American shot for desertion since the Civil War.

1945

February 11	President Franklin Roosevelt, British Prime Minister Winston Churchill, and Soviet leader Josef Stalin sign the Yalta Agreement, which effectively divides Europe into two camps.

March 15	Bing Cosby and Ingrid Bergman are winners at the 17th Academy Awards along with the film *Going My Way*.
April 12	President Franklin Delano Roosevelt, the 32nd president of the United States, dies of a cerebral hemorrhage in Warm Springs, Georgia, at age 63. Vice President Harry Truman becomes the 33rd president of the United States.
May 8	VE Day—Germany surrenders, assuring victory in Europe for the Allies.
May 26	The United States begins dropping firebombs on Tokyo.
August 6	Hiroshima, Japan, is struck with the uranium bomb, Little Boy, from the B-29 airplane, *Enola Gay*, piloted by Col. Paul Tibbets of the U.S. Air Force along with 11 other men.
August 8	President Truman signs the United Nations Charter.
August 9	The 10,000-pound plutonium bomb, Fat Man, is dropped over Nagasaki, Japan. It kills an estimated 74,000 people.
August 14	Japan agrees to surrender.
August 15	This date is declared VJ Day, and gasoline and fuel oil rationing end in the United States.
September 2	The Japanese government signs the Instrument of Surrender aboard the U.S.S. *Missouri*, officially ending World War II.
September 5	Iva Toguri D'Aquino (1916–2006), a Japanese American suspected of being wartime radio propagandist "Tokyo Rose," is arrested in Yokohama, Japan. In 1949, she is tried in San Francisco and convicted for having spoken "into a microphone concerning the loss of ships." Although sentenced to 10 years in prison, she serves only six months.
October 29	The first ballpoint pen is sold by Gimbel's Department Store in New York for a price of $12.
November 23	Most U.S. wartime rationing of foods, including meat and butter, ends.

1

HISTORICAL OVERVIEW: THE UNITED STATES, 1900–1940

The Progressive Age and Theodore Roosevelt

Never had events marked the beginning of a century so clearly. On September 14, 1901, William McKinley, the last president of the nineteenth century and the first one elected in the new century, died from gunshot wounds suffered eight days prior at the Buffalo World's Fair, and 42-year-old Theodore Roosevelt (TR) succeeded him to become the youngest man to hold the office of president. Although the assassination of McKinley was tragic, many, including TR himself, recovered quickly, and a collective cheer rose from those who had championed progressive reform in government, business, family life, labor, conditions of women, and the environment. Mark Hanna and the stalwarts in the Republican Party may have complained about the "damn cowboy" in the White House, but the Progressive reformers rejoiced knowing that they had one of their own in the presidency, and now, they believed, the new century could truly begin. Under Teddy Roosevelt's aegis, Progressivism, which had been a loosely organized coalition of reformers who worked locally or regionally, soon became part of the national agenda.

Who were these Progressives? Historians have been debating that since the word was first used in the mid-1890s to describe reformers whose agendas crossed geographic, political, educational, and racial lines. Women joined the movement, often, as equals in expertise and interests, and, although Progressivism has been described as largely a middle-class movement, captains of industry as well as laborers joined its ranks.

Despite their eclecticism, Progressives had much that drew them together. First of all, they shared an idea, which philosopher William James defined as pragmatism.

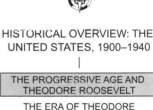

James and the pragmatists saw ideas as organic and therefore subject to Darwinian principles of natural selection and survival. Those theoretical designs that proved functional survived; those that did not died. Pragmatism determined that the central question of an idea was not, "is it true?" but rather, "does it work?" Secondly, the Progressives all accepted a psychological theory called behaviorism. The theory took its name from the belief that environment shaped (or as some even argued, determined) behavior, which meant that social, economic, cultural, and political influences and institutions could form and condition behavior. The conviction of these behaviorists was best expressed in the famous quote by the psychologist John Watson, who wrote that if given "a dozen healthy infants, and my own specified world to bring them up in," he could train any of them to be whatever he wanted, whether a "doctor, lawyer, even beggar man, and thief regardless of his talents, penchants, tendencies, abilities, vocations, and race of his ancestors." Although Watson admitted that his claim was "going beyond my facts," it illustrated the early twentieth-century confidence of behaviorists in the validity of their ideas (Watson 1930, 104).

Progressives believed that modern social science and social philosophy, correctly applied, could tame the tumultuous economic and social upheavals of the late nineteenth century. Caught amidst the convolutions created by massive immigration, the abuses of the factory system and workers' reaction to it, city bosses who undermined the democratic system, and corporate magnates who scoffed at the law, Progressives longed for a more orderly world that in their memory had existed in their childhood. In that remembered, if also idealistic, world, cities were well-managed living spaces, political leaders were true public servants, and employers and workers shared republican values. Local factories produced for local consumption, and fair competition and the eternal laws of supply and demand controlled their prices. In their world everyone spoke English, and those new immigrants that arrived accepted American values and quickly assimilated because they came from the same Anglo-Germanic soil as had the founding fathers.

From the Progressive point of view, events of the post–Civil War era had overturned their imagined world. Cities teemed with tenements, new immigrants without democratic traditions readily traded their vote to corrupt city bosses for personal favors, and small independent factories had merged into large conglomerates that choked competition and exploited their employees. Masses of workers had organized and threatened class war against these corporations and their oppressive labor policies. Progressives saw disruption of natural order everywhere, and they set out to bring order back to a world in terrible disarray. This sentiment, although primarily a middle-class phenomenon, had adherents that transcended geography, race, and class and became a powerful national political movement in the United States.

Some of the first Progressives were social workers who fought on the front line in the battle against the great inequities suffered by those living in cities without a social infrastructure to support them. Thanks to these workers and to the camera skills of Jacob Riis, middle-class Americans learned that they had a social problem in the cities. Awakened to the horrible conditions in the slums and tenement houses of America's cities, women took the lead in the early Progressive movement. Led by the example of people like Chicagoan Jane Addams, women began to demand a greater voice in social affairs. Some, like Addams, left their comfortable middle-class homes to live among the poor immigrants in settlement houses where they taught English, cared for children, provided food and shelter, and did whatever they could to alleviate the daily crises that occur in the lives of the destitute. They lived like "the early Christians," said one settlement worker, sacrificing their lives in service to the poor. Addams's Hull House was the most famous of the settlement houses, but at the turn of the century there were over a hundred such places across the nation, and they formed a powerful political base of activists who played an instrumental role in the development of the social legislation of the Progressive movement.

Women's clubs across the nation organized and lobbied for reforms as varied as temperance, child labor laws, "good government," women's voting rights, even birth control. The men followed, and soon the political structures within every state began to feel the pressure of this eclectic and widespread grassroots movement that everyone agreed to call Progressivism. Reform governments were elected across the country. Progressives such as Gifford Pinchot in Pennsylvania, Hiram Johnson in California, and Robert M. La Follette in Wisconsin won governorships, and state legislatures with Progressive majorities passed laws designed to improve social conditions. Many of these states pressed for common goals: control of monopolies, which distorted the eternal laws of supply and demand; education for all children, especially the immigrants so that they might learn to be good Americans; reform of local government; anti-vice laws, workman's compensation, and labor protection, especially for women and children. Good behaviorists that they were, they also concerned themselves with purifying the physical environment. They battled for new sewage and trash systems in the urban centers of the country. They also fought for pasteurized milk for children, for mass inoculation campaigns, and extermination of the hookworm in the South. They fought for more open space in the cities and expansion of the national park system in the countryside.

Sometimes this struggle went too far. In some cities, for example, in the name of cleaning up local government, Progressives drove city bosses from power, which effectively removed a powerful political voice for the poor urban immigrant. And in the South, good government and honest elections became an argument for disenfranchisement of blacks. On the other hand, blacks in the South did not have to depend on white middle-class Progressives to lead their struggle for social justice. They had their own advocates, such as Ida B. Wells, who used journalism and speaking to launch an antilynching campaign, which raised the national consciousness of the terrible wave of terrorism waged by whites against blacks at the turn of the century. Although she never realized her goal of a national antilynching bill, in 1896 she did establish the National Association of Colored Women (NACW), which advocated reforms in education, housing, and health care for blacks while they continued their campaign against lynching.

Black Americans also had a powerful advocate in Booker T. Washington, whose nonthreatening advocacy of technical education for blacks attracted a great deal of white philanthropy for his Tuskegee Institute, which, in addition to being a center for black education, became a focal point in the struggle for civil rights in the first decades of the twentieth century. Less accommodating than Washington, but articulate and passionate in his struggle for human dignity for African Americans, was W.E.B. Du Bois, who refused to accept Washington's premise that the road to equality lay in creating an economic and technical army of blacks on which the white power structure would become dependent. He refused to accept second-class citizenship for blacks, even as a temporary strategy, and demanded equal opportunities for all, which would allow the "Talented Tenth" of blacks to gain the power necessary to lift up the masses. He aligned himself with Progressive middle-class whites and blacks, and together in 1909 they formed the National Association for the Advancement of Colored People, an organization that took the fight for civil rights into the courtrooms. Their work would culminate in the landmark *Brown v. Board of Education* decision of 1954, which ended 60 years of state-mandated segregation in public school systems in the South.

Many Progressives were also influenced by the myriad socialist and utopian writers of the nineteenth century, who emboldened them to explore more radical solutions to contemporary social problems. Though not everyone followed the example of some states that elected socialist mayors, legislators, and governors (e.g., John Altgeld, the governor of Illinois, whom *Harper's Weekly* described as an "ambitious and unscrupulous . . . communist"), many did follow the socialist example of establishing ownership over such public essentials as water, sewage, public transportation, and electricity.

Religion also played a role in the emerging social consciousness that contributed to the Progressive movement. Persuaded by Baltimore's Archbishop James Cardinal Gibbons, Pope Leo XIII reversed the traditional papal stand against labor unions and also issued an encyclical entitled *Rerum Novarum*, which defended the workers' rights to a living wage. And many Christian ministers began to turn their flocks away from the idea that poverty was the result of personal depravity and toward the concept that to follow Christ's example meant they should work to bring the kingdom of God to Earth, which meant bringing social justice to everyone. This movement soon became known as the Social Gospel and was preached by important Protestant scholars like Walter Rauschenbusch, who from his ministry in the Hell's Kitchen section of New York convinced many fellow Christians that the gospels called them to service to the poor.

The Era of Theodore Roosevelt

After more than a decade of struggles fought at the local and state levels, the Progressives in 1901 finally had a champion in the White House. Teddy Roosevelt shared the Progressive belief that once cleansed of its corruption and entrusted to skilled professionals, a government of the best men using the best systems could bring order out of the disorderly nineteenth century and restore responsibility, efficiency, and integrity to the country. Like most Progressives, TR wanted a proactive government to replace the time-worn concepts of laissez-faire. In his energy and optimism over the capacity of Americans to realize progress through a systematic and educated attack on all social, political, and economic problems, he came to embody the Progressive ideal. Like many Progressives, he envisioned an empowered federal government that would be entrusted to act in the public interest, favoring no special interest or business. Those embracing this idea believed that government would speak for them in the unruly world of machine politics, big business, and big labor. An empowered federal government would be trusted to act for the little person, who had no alliance with large corporations or labor unions. Government representatives would be honest brokers, because an informed and honest public would elect them. In their view of things, cleaning up the ballot to ensure that the voting process was uncorrupted and that it attracted the right kind of men in office was critical. In many ways these Progressives were hardly that; for in reality they wanted to take the country back to a more ordered, bygone era, ideally when educated men made decisions for the common good, when favoritism and power held minor sway, and where fair play prevailed. Their collective memory of the past helped Progressives form their image of the future.

Roosevelt led the way by mobilizing the latent power of the presidency to promise a "Square Deal" to the American people. Republican boss Mark Hanna had told the sometimes impetuous TR to go slowly. But this man, who now added the presidency to his list of conquests that included the apprehension of cattle rustlers out West, confrontations with young toughs on the streets of New York, and the capture of Spaniards on San Juan Hill, could hardly restrain himself.

But without a Progressive mandate, and with a balky conservative Congress, Roosevelt had to choose his crusades carefully. He had no fight with big business per se and indeed thought that the well-managed corporation was the natural product of capitalism's development. But as a moralist, the politician Roosevelt also believed that both big business or corporations and big labor in the form of unions should act responsibly. Failing to do so threatened the public, whose only recourse was the government. Following the pragmatic model of the age, Roosevelt's ideas evolved in response to conditions.

The first opportunity for TR to test his philosophy of federal government came in 1902 when, as winter approached, he intervened in a coal strike for the public good. Suggesting that he might call in the army to run the mines if the unions and mine owners could not reach a bargain, he convinced both sides to accept a 10 percent wage hike, and Americans had coal to warm them that winter. In that same year he also launched an antitrust lawsuit against the giant Northern Securities Company, which held a monopoly over one of the nation's largest railroad systems and connected the northeastern states to the Pacific Northwest. Northern Securities, owned by J. P. Morgan Company and other powerful interests, had, through its excesses in controlling prices, become a political metaphor for the evil of trusts. Roosevelt took them on. Upon hearing of the investigation, Morgan suggested to Roosevelt that they each send their lawyers to meet and straighten things out. The president demurred, and two years later the Supreme Court ordered the company dissolved. TR gained a reputation as a "trust-buster" for his use of the 1890 Sherman Anti-Trust Act and his willingness to take on businesses abusing their power. He preferred negotiation and regulation to legal action. Nevertheless, Roosevelt and his successor William Howard Taft went on to bring suit against 44 giant companies, including Standard Oil and the American Tobacco Company, and established the precedent of using federal authority to regulate business competition. Roosevelt also joined the Progressive attack against the food industry, which was endangering American health with poorly processed foods, and launched the National Park System to preserve at least some of the nation's natural heritage and protect it from the exploitative hands of big business.

In 1912, the Progressive mantle passed to Woodrow Wilson, the reform governor of New Jersey and former president of Princeton University. Wilson represented a change in the guard of the old Democratic Party, which had nominated the Nebraskan populist William Jennings Bryan for three of the previous four presidential campaigns. Although incumbent president William Howard Taft was the Republican nominee, Wilson's real opponent was Roosevelt. Roosevelt, who had left national politics in 1909, returned to the political scene in 1912. Disillusioned with his hand-picked successor William Howard Taft, whom he believed had let the Republican Party drift away from its Progressive agenda, Roosevelt tried to wrest control of the Republican Party from him, but he failed. Rejected by anti-Progressive forces that controlled the political machinery of his own party, Roosevelt accepted the nomination of a third party, the Progressive Party, which, with a big game hunter and outdoorsman at the top of their ticket, became known as the Bull Moose Party after Roosevelt said he was as fit as a "bull moose" to take on the 300-pound Taft. Taft, the Republican candidate, almost became a nonissue in the campaign.

The real contest was between Wilson and Roosevelt, and the argument was not pro- or anti-Progressivism, but rather whose view of Progressivism should prevail. Wilson espoused the "New Freedom," which emphasized the need for government to restore fair competition, while Roosevelt called for the "New Nationalism," which accepted large corporations as an invariable fact, which necessitated regulation that only big government could provide. By 1912, TR also had moved toward accepting more radical Progressive ideas such as laws restricting child labor, establishing a minimum wage and maximum hours for workers, and protecting workers' health and safety on the job. Wilson defeated Roosevelt, but together these two candidates garnered over 10.4 million votes to Taft's 3 million. Adding the Socialist Party vote of roughly one million to the Progressive vote provided a strong mandate for an activist, reform-minded government. Clearly the American people had accepted the view that the complexities of the modern world demanded a proactive government that was socially and economically relevant to their lives.

Woodrow Wilson's Domestic Policy

Upon election as president, Woodrow Wilson rolled up his Progressive sleeves and went to work to establish what he had called in his campaign a "New Freedom" for the American people. An admirer of the British parliamentary system, Wilson was a policy-driven president who likened his role to that of the British prime minister, who initiated and proposed programs and legislation. He cajoled and persuaded Congress to lower the tariff, which he thought aided large corporations and hurt the average person. Tariffs had climbed steadily upward for half a century and continued upward during the Taft administration, despite Taft's efforts to lower them. Finally, in 1913, the trend was reversed when the Congress, now with a Progressive majority, passed the Underwood Tariff, which represented the largest reduction since the Civil War. Wilson also asked for and received a graduated income tax limited to the corporations and the wealthiest Americans. In fairness to Taft, it should be noted that he shepherded the 16th Amendment into being, which made the new tax law constitutional. Some historians have called this amendment and the tax law that followed the most significant piece of legislation of the twentieth century. Whether or not that is true, this legislation did change the financial basis of the country. For more than a century since its inception, land sales and tariffs had provided the federal government's primary source of income. From 1913 onward, however, the cost of running the U.S. government increasingly would become a direct expense of its citizens and corporations.

Wilson followed this momentous change with another. He established a Federal Reserve Board, which would take control of the money supply out of the hands of private bankers and put it into the hands of the government. Other progressive reforms instituted by Wilson included a new antitrust act to break price fixing by large corporations and to end the practice of having individuals sitting on the board of more than one corporation. He also took leadership on a Child Labor Act, an eight-hour-day law for railroad workers, and low-cost loans to farmers. In addition, he used his presidential influence to help establish the Federal Trade Commission (FTC), which created a bipartisan executive agency to oversee big business. When all was said and done, it appeared that Wilson had come closer to Teddy Roosevelt's ideas of an empowered federal government, with enhanced regulatory powers to control large corporations, than his own ideas of limiting corporate size to create a more decentralized competitive economy. As far-reaching and energetic as his program was, he never could fully implement his domestic plan, because soon after entering office, foreign affairs drew him into the international arena.

Overseas Expansion and the Mexican Revolution

In 1898, when the U.S. Navy destroyed the Spanish fleet, and the army mopped up a war that had been going on in Cuba intermittently for 30 years, the country announced to the world its presence as an emerging international power. In 1903

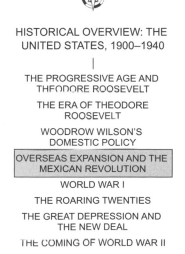

President Teddy Roosevelt confirmed U.S. intentions by taking control of the Panama Canal Zone and then spearheading the building of a canal that would connect the two great oceans of the world under the watchful eye of the American navy. "I took the Canal Zone!" Roosevelt boasted. "While congress debated I took the Canal Zone and as they continue to debate the canal is being built." Like its domestic policy, racism was woven into the fabric of Progressive diplomacy. Progressives developed a unique Social Darwinist rationalization for their imperialism by concluding that the Anglo-Saxon "race" had produced a superior society, and the movement of all the world should be toward that ideal. According to the Progressive worldview, other "races," especially non–Western European ones, were inferior and more prone to corruption, mismanagement, poor health systems, and inferior educational systems. Even the predominant interpretation of history taught at most American universities usually carried a title such as the "Progress of Western Civilization," which argued the premise that society had steadily progressed westward from the Greeks, to the Romans, to the French, to the English, and finally to the Americans. The conclusion of this thesis was that there was no being on earth intellectually or socially superior to the white male living on the East Coast of the United States. This privilege carried responsibility to bring the benefits of capitalist Christian civilization to the rest of the inferior world.

In 1899, *McClure's* magazine published a poem written by Englishman Rudyard Kipling that captured the sentiment and spirit that drove American expansionist ambition. Titled "The White Man's Burden," Kipling's poem called upon Americans to assume their proper role as white Europeans in the great race for empire and in the holy commission to save the world.

It was in this intellectual context that the United States entered the international stage, where it expected to be received as an equal partner at the turn of the century. In one sense this idea, with its subtle racism and its sense of social obligation, can be described as typically Progressive, but in another sense it demonstrated the persistence of an idea as old as the Puritan founding fathers, who strove to build, in John Winthrop's words, "A City on a Hill," an example to the world. However, in Wilson's brand of missionary diplomacy, rather than wait for conversion by example, his activist design exported and implanted American interests and institutions across the globe.

Wilson not only held both Puritan and Progressive beliefs, he had taught them to undergraduates at Princeton; now, as president, he would teach those values to the world. "We are chosen, " he declared, "and prominently chosen to show the way to nations of the world how they should walk in the paths of liberty." His first opportunity came in Mexico,

Snapshot

The White Man's Burden

Take up the White Man's burden—
Send forth the best ye breed—
Go, bind your sons to exile
To serve your captives' need;
To wait, in heavy harness,
On fluttered folk and wild—
Your new-caught sullen peoples,
Half devil and half child.
Take up the White Man's burden—
In patience to abide,
To veil the threat of terror
And check the show of pride;
By open speech and simple,
An hundred times made plain,
To seek another's profit
And work another's gain.
Take up the White Man's burden—
The savage wars of peace—
Fill full the mouth of Famine,
And bid the sickness cease;
And when your goal is nearest
(The end for others sought)
Watch sloth and heathen folly
Bring all your hope to nought.
Take up the White Man's burden—
No iron rule of kings,
But toil of serf and sweeper—
The tale of common things.
The ports ye shall not enter,

where in 1910 a revolution designed to overthrow the aged dictator Porfirio Diaz pushed the country to the brink of chaos and civil war. Out of the turmoil emerged Victor Huerta, the hero of the landed class, who had murdered the popular revolutionary leader Francisco Madero and taken control of Mexico at about the same time Wilson became president. Populists rebelled against Huerta's dictatorship and, in the name of their slain leader, launched a civil war against him and his followers. Although most European nations supported Huerta as the legitimate leader of Mexico, Wilson's politics of morality would not allow him to support a "government of butchers." After prohibiting the sale of arms to Huerta's government, Wilson threw his support to the rebel leader Venustiano Carranza, who immediately, in a burst of patriotic fervor and political sagacity, declined the offer of support. Wilson, for all his knowledge as a political scientist and historian, could not measure the strength of Mexican nationalism and the harm that his offer would do to Carranza.

Rejected by Carranza, Wilson pursued Huerta's downfall on his own. Landing troops first in Tampico and afterwards in Veracruz, the U.S. invasion disrupted the Huerta government sufficiently to allow Carranza to take control of the country. Bruised by Carranza's rejection, Wilson for a while supported the bandit revolutionaries Pancho Villa and Emilio Zapata, but soon he rejected this flight from reality and recognized Carranza. Angry at the U.S. rejection, Villa launched raids against the United States, and for two years American forces under General "Black Jack" Pershing pursued Villa unsuccessfully along and sometimes across the Mexican border. When the smoke finally settled, it was obvious that Mexican–American relations had sunk to their lowest level in 70 years.

> ### 📷 *Snapshot (continued)*
>
> The roads ye shall not tread,
> Go, make them with your living
> And mark them with your dead.
> Take up the White Man's burden,
> And reap his old reward—
> The blame of those ye better
> The hate of those ye guard—
> The cry of hosts ye humour
> (Ah, slowly!) toward the light:—
> "Why brought ye us from bondage,
> Our loved Egyptian night?"
> Take up the White Man's burden—
> Ye dare not stoop to less—
> Nor call too loud on Freedom
> To cloak your weariness.
> By all ye will or whisper,
> By all ye leave or do,
> The silent sullen peoples
> Shall weigh your God and you.
> Take up the White Man's burden!
> Have done with childish days—
> The lightly-proffered laurel,
> The easy ungrudged praise:
> Comes now, to search your manhood
> Through all the thankless years,
> Cold, edged with dear-bought wisdom,
> The judgment of your peers.
>
> *From McClure's Magazine, February 12, 1899.*

World War I

For a time, events in Mexico distracted Wilson from the drama that was occurring across the Atlantic. For a century, aside from two small skirmishes, Europe had been at peace, but for the last quarter of that century many had been spoiling for war. Swelling populations, expanding international trade, neocolonialism, and emerging nationalism were all combining to strain the European nations' tolerance for one another. The Industrial Revolution made arms manufacturers more efficient and abundant, and technology improved the range and firepower of weapons and ships. Soon every major industrial power of Europe was boasting of its new weapons, which included long-range Howitzer cannons, machine guns, and steel-plated warships. As the new century opened, even the new invention, the airplane, was being redesigned

Snapshot

Veracruz

More than 60 years after Wilson ordered the invasion of Mexico, while Mexico was threatened with financial collapse, poet-songwriters Warren Zevon and Jorge Calderón reminded Americans of their unsettling history with their neighbors to the south.

> I heard Woodrow Wilson's guns
> I heard Maria crying
> Late last night I heard the news
> That Veracruz was dying
> Someone called Maria's name
> I swear it was my father's voice
> Saying, "If you stay you'll all be slain
> You must leave now you have no choice
> Take the servants and ride west
> Keep the child close to your chest
> When the American troops withdraw
> Let Zapata take the rest."
>
> I heard Woodrow Wilson's guns
> I heard Maria calling
> Saying "Veracruz is dying
> And Cuernavaca's falling
>
> Aquel día yo juré
> *On that day I swore*
> Hacia el Puerto volveré
> *To the port I will return*
> Aunque el destino cambió mi vida
> *Although destiny changed my life*
> En Veracruz moriré
> *In Veracruz I shall die*
> Aquel día yo juré
>
> I heard Woodrow Wilson's guns
> I heard them in the harbor
> Saying "Veracruz is dying."

From *Veracruz is Dying*. (Copyright 1978 by Zevon Music.) Used with permission of Jordan Zevon.

as a war machine. As added insurance, the major powers of Europe entered into secret alliances, to ensure their advantage if war should break out.

These new inventions soon banged into gear in July 1914 when the Archduke Francis Ferdinand of Austria, heir to the throne of the sprawling Austro-Hungarian empires, while visiting Serbia, was shot by a Serbian nationalist. Austria demanded concessions that would have smothered an emerging Serbian nationalism. Serbia, although much weaker than Austria, bravely rejected the ultimatum, knowing that a strong Russia stood by in their support. Austria was aware of Russian support of Serbia but did not back down because it knew it enjoyed German support. The Russians were not afraid of the Germans because they secretly had an alliance with the English and the French. The Germans were not afraid of this alliance because they had a war plan that promised to put them in Paris six weeks before the Russians could even mobilize the Eastern Front. So, all the parties, convinced of their advantages, went to peace discussions in August with scant intention of working for peace. Soon all of Europe was at war. It would become a world war, because European nations had spent most of the nineteenth century extending their influence around the globe.

Wilson looked from afar with a feeling of hope and superiority—hope that the war would bring old regimes crashing down, and the superiority of knowing that American ideas of democracy would prevail in a new order. To become the leader of this new order at the end of the conflagration, Wilson believed that America must remain above the war. He reminded his fellow citizens, many of whom had recently migrated from the countries now at war with each other, that Americans must remain neutral in thought and deed.

Resisting early pressure precipitated by effective British propaganda, indiscriminant German submarine attacks, strong economic and cultural links to England, and his own Anglophile tendencies, Wilson refused to enter the war on the side of the French and British allies. He entered the 1916 election with the slogan, "He has kept us out of war," and he promised American mothers (although most could not yet vote) that he would not send their sons to die on a foreign battlefield. Accelerated events and amplified pressures soon made that promise an empty one. Slowly Wilson was pushed to the view that the moral thing to do was not to stay above the fracas but to join the war against the reactionary forces of Germany. The greatest persuasion for Wilson was the German use of submarines.

Invoking the principles of neutrality that harkened back to the early republic, Wilson issued a proclamation of neutrality in which he insisted on the protection and inviolability of Americans, their goods, and their properties from warring parties. He also asserted that Americans had the right to travel unmolested even in war zones, and as a neutral nation, America declared its right to trade with all belligerents. Geographic reality complicated this outward claim of commercial equanimity. England was physically closer to the United States than Germany, and there was no belligerent nation situated between England and the North American continent. Consequently, American products flowed freely to English ports. On the other hand, getting to Germany's single port of Bremen became a tricky maneuver. After crossing the Atlantic, American ships had to navigate the North Sea, which the British had been successfully blockading. During the first year of the war, trade with England increased as trade with Germany fell dramatically. When England had spent all it could, it began to borrow from American banks and the American economy boomed. By 1916, while trade with England and France expanded dramatically (from $800 million in 1914 to $3 billion in 1916), trade with Germany diminished to a trickle (Davidson, et al. 2001, 749). To counteract the British naval and commercial advantage, the Germans developed the submarine, with which they patrolled off the coast of England.

On May 7, 1915, the Germans sank the British luxury liner *Lusitania*. Among the passengers who died that day there were 128 Americans. Disregarding the facts that the *Lusitania* flew the British flag; that, as the Germans had warned, the ship most likely carried war munitions, thus making it a legitimate target; and that the Germans had warned Americans in newspaper notices to stay off British ships, Americans were outraged. Former president Theodore Roosevelt called the attack an act of piracy, which had to be avenged. The rage was fueled by an attack on two other ships that resulted in the loss of American lives. In March 1916, when the *Sussex*, a French ferryboat carrying passengers, was sunk, an enraged Wilson issued an ultimatum threatening war with Germany if it continued to sink unarmed ships without warning. The doves in Germany still had the upper hand, and Germany promised not to sink any more ships without warning. However, just as tensions seemed to be easing, Wilson and the United States discovered the so-called Zimmerman Note, a telegram revealing that the Germans had offered the Mexicans an alliance, which promised that in the event of war with America, if Mexico would attack the United States, Germany would provide guns, troops, and money to recover the Mexicans' lost territory in Texas, New Mexico, and Arizona. Americans were shocked to learn that the Germans would try to persuade the Mexicans to attack and that they would ever consider such an offer.

Finally in early 1917, the German hawks prevailed, reasoning that America was, by virtue of trade with Britain, already de facto in the war, and believing that their U-boats and military advances could knock the British and French out of the war before the United States could be sufficiently mobilized to be a factor in the conflict.

Germany decided to rescind the *Sussex* pledge and launch all-out submarine warfare. This new phase of the war included sinking all ships, including American ships perceived to be heading to an enemy port. The Germans announced to the world that they would institute this policy effective January 31, 1917. It did not take long for an incident and a cause for war to emerge, and on April 2, 1917, America entered the conflict.

Some say that the Great War, as it was called, ended Progressivism. Others call it the "Flowering of Progressivism." If by Progressive government one means the use of government bureaucracy to order, organize, and regulate every aspect of economic and public life, then the latter is true. Leaders of industry promised to create efficiently and rapidly a great American war machine; however, initial efforts to mobilize large corporations in the war effort failed due to mismanagement and competing interests. For example, the United States never built the "Great Fleet" it promised, and "liberty engines" designed to replace worn airplane motors were sitting on New York shipping docks when the war ended. It soon became evident that national mobilization required coordination and direction that only the federal government could provide. During the war years Wilson even more completely adopted the New Nationalism of Roosevelt by creating executive-appointed agencies to regulate and even manage the economy in the public interest.

Overnight, myriad bureaucracies were created to coordinate the war effort. Bernard Baruch, a Wall Street wizard, headed up the War Industries Board, which coordinated production, allocated scarce materials, set up work rules, and organized purchasing and distribution systems across the country. Herbert Hoover headed the Food Administration Board, which mobilized both consumers and producers of food. Convinced of the benefits of volunteerism over enforced regulation, Hoover launched a huge publicity campaign to encourage families to buy Liberty Bonds, eat and drink less, and plant "victory gardens." There were "wheatless Mondays," "meatless Tuesdays," and "porkless Saturdays." But probably the greatest sacrifice for many came on September 9, 1917, when under order of the president, empowered by the Lever Act, the liquor distilleries in the nation shut down. Beer and wine could still be purchased and consumed, but the war had given the latent forces of Prohibition the pretext and the power to realize a goal they had been seeking for decades, a country free of the horrors of demon rum.

The Fuel Administration was created to develop and implement energy conservation, and a Committee on Public Information was formed to explain to people how to think about the war. Knowing that Americans were not eager to enter this conflict, and fearing immigrant and ethnic division once the United States took sides, Wilson commissioned California publicist George M. Creel to launch a major propaganda battle for

Sow the seeds *of* Victory!

plant *&*
raise
your own
vegetables

WRITE TO THE
NATIONAL
WAR GARDEN
COMMISSION—
WASHINGTON, D.C.
for free books on
gardening, canning
& drying.

JAMES MONTGOMERY FLAGG

"Every Garden a Munition Plant"
Charles Lathrop Pack, President

A U.S. government poster from the Office of Public Information urging people to raise their own food during World War I. President Woodrow Wilson contributed to the effort by grazing sheep on the White House lawn. Library of Congress.

"the minds of men." Unlike other wartime organizations that contained an advisory board, supervisory board, and board of Cabinet members, the Committee on Public Information was a one-man show directed by Creel, who single-handedly ran the propaganda agency that employed over 150,000 persons. Creel mobilized every form of communication possible under the 1917 sun. He issued orders to newspapers listing what types of stories could and could not be printed, and he supplied them with stories. Some of these releases were pure propaganda, such as one that reported that excessive beer drinking by the Germans was responsible for their tendencies to commit atrocities; and others were upbeat, accompanied by still photos of people cheerfully participating in the war effort. He organized the motion picture industry, which produced short buoyant films with titles such as *Pershing's Crusaders*, *America's Answer*, and *Under Four Flags*. Creel also enlisted artists and cartoonists, resulting in the creation of an American art form, which became emblematic of the era. Among the most famous of these works was James Montgomery Flagg's Uncle Sam poster declaring "I Want You For the U.S. Army," which has become an American icon.

Creel also enlisted an army of speakers dubbed "four minute men," who gave short, upbeat speeches about the war effort in theaters, public meetings, and churches throughout the country. In some cases the propaganda effort of the government far exceeded expectation and created a wave of

James Montgomery Flagg's famous "I Want You" army recruitment poster from 1917. Library of Congress.

intolerance and sometimes violence against anyone (especially Germans) suspected of not supporting the war effort. Sauerkraut became liberty cabbage, frankfurters became hot dogs, and patriotic little boys tortured German breeds of dogs. The Poetry Society of America showed their superiority to the Hun by expelling the German American poet George Sylvester Viereck, and works by Richard Wagner and Ludwig von Beethoven were removed from orchestral performances. Dr. Karl Muck, conductor of the Boston Symphony, was forced to resign, but not until after he directed the orchestra in the "Star Spangled Banner." In Washington, D.C., the police superintendent warned Dr. Muck that if he attempted to fulfill a contract by playing in the district he would be subject to arrest. In the hysteria, any voice against war was scorned. Senator Henry Cabot Lodge was hailed for punching a pacifist lobbyist and knocking him to the floor, and Senator Robert La Follette was burned in effigy for voting against the war.

The government showed little more tolerance than its enraged citizens. Congress passed the Espionage and Sedition Acts, which made it a federal offense to speak against the war, denounce the draft, complain about wartime taxes, or say anything derogatory about the war effort. Under the law 1,532 persons were arrested for disloyal comments. Ninety-eight members of the International Workers of the World were sentenced to prison for speaking out against the war, as well as a number of leading socialists including Eugene V. Debs and Rose Pastor Stokes. Socialist Victor

Eugene V. Debs Responds to His Conviction under the Espionage Act

Upon being convicted for espionage, Eugene Debs, when asked if he had any final words for the court, said the following.

> Your Honor, years ago I recognized my kinship with all living beings, and I made up my mind that I was not one bit better than the meanest on earth. I said then, and I say now, that while there is a lower class, I am in it, and while there is a criminal element I am of it, and while there is a soul in prison, I am not free. (Zinn 2001, 368)

Berger, elected to Congress in 1918, was also indicted under the Espionage Act.

To shore up an unprepared army, Congress passed the Selective Service Act, which initiated the first draft since the Civil War. Over 24 million men registered for the draft, of which 3 million would eventually serve. Upon arriving in Europe, American soldiers soon discovered the horrors of trench warfare. For four years men had been living, fighting, and dying in ditches six to eight feet high that ran from the northeastern corner of France almost to the border of Switzerland. Germans, Frenchmen, and Englishmen had been slaughtering each other at close range in battles that demanded that young men armed with bayoneted rifles charge against a barbed wire-protected trench full of other young men armed with bayoneted rifles and machine guns. The men continued their attack until they died or machine gun barrels melted or warped. They then jumped over barbed wire into the trench where they engaged in hand-to-hand combat with their enemy. "Victory" meant moving the trench line back into enemy territory a few yards. Over the course of the war over 15,000 miles of trenches were dug and over four million young men died, of whom 116,500 were Americans. One battle at the Somme River emphasized the horror of it all. In just over a month of fighting, a million men died there. When the battle finally ended, the British generals could boast that they had gained seven miles of territory.

The American army that went to Europe reflected the change that had come to the collective face of the United States in the five decades that had passed since their last total war. Blacks, new immigrants, and women filled the ranks of the American Expeditionary Force that went to France under General Pershing. Although they represented 10 percent of the population, black soldiers represented 13 percent of the wartime army. Much to their disappointment, relatively few of these men saw combat duty. Although many might welcome this less dangerous status, it was received with disappointment among many blacks, who were aware that they were relegated to noncombatant status because of a policy that addressed white southerners' fears of black men receiving training in arms. Under American leadership, African American combatants served with mixed results for various reasons; however, under French command, the all-black 369th infantry regiment boasted an illustrious war record: it served 191 days at the front, the longest of any American regiment, and all members received the *croix de guerre* (war cross) from the French in recognition of their bravery under fire.

Newly arrived immigrants also contributed to the American war effort, as foreign-born men made up almost one-fifth of the American wartime army. Army officials worried that, despite their willingness to serve, foreign-born troops remained too far outside the mainstream culture to understand why they had to fight against the Germans. To ensure that the message reached the troops, camp commanders organized patriotic celebrations intended to bridge the cultural gap. Although there were language problems to be overcome and there were sporadic displays of nativist prejudice, the experience for the immigrant in the army was generally a positive one for all concerned (Keene 2006, 100–104).

Women also served overseas, not only as nurses on the

📷 Snapshot

An Immigrant Soldier's Experience

In their post-war recollections many foreign born soldiers felt satisfied with the service they rendered to their adopted country in the time of war. Louis Van Iersal from the Netherlands summed up the significance of serving in such a polyglot force by noting that he learned to get along and respect all people. When Van Iersal entered the military, he did not speak English. His fluent German and French, however, proved quite valuable for the American army in France. Van Iersal received the *croix de guerre* for infiltrating German lines and convincing a German officer to surrender his force of 60 men. He was also awarded the medal of honor for going behind enemy lines to gather information and then successfully warning his battalion that the Germans planned a heavy bombardment on their position. The thousands of lives that Van Iersal saved due to both his bravery and his distinct linguistic skills offer just one example of how the American army benefited from the unique abilities and dedication of foreign-speaking soldiers (Keene 2006, 113).

front line (over 200 were decorated for duty under fire, and 35 died), but also in skilled jobs as translators, telephone operators, and clerks. "For days I was on duty from eight in the morning until ten at night," recalled telephone operator Grace Banker, handling calls that transmitted status reports from the front and commands from headquarters. "But it seemed worth while when we gazed at the prison pen filling up with German prisoners." Despite women's wartime contributions, the press wrote more often about women's graceful and delicate female image of "hello girls" than their mastery of machines or contributions to the army's advance in battle. As in other situations where women find themselves in the company of men in the workplace, they suffered discrimination and sexual harassment; but they weathered the storm, and when they returned home they found their wartime skills, especially nursing and telephone operation, to be in great demand in a booming economy (Keene 2006, 114–20).

By the time the Americans arrived in Europe, both sides had been bled white. The fresh young troops from the United States, though inexperienced and undisciplined, made the difference. In the spring of 1918, the Germans were 50 miles from Paris; by September, although the French and English still carried the bulk of the load, the weight of the new American troops proved overwhelming and the tired and battered German army fell into retreat. The American navy also contributed to the cause by participating in a convoy system, which rendered the submarines ineffectual. But by far the greatest contribution of the Americans was the propaganda value of Wilson's "Fourteen Points." From the moment the United States entered the war Wilson began to envision the peaceful, prosperous world that would follow. His Fourteen Points called for: no recrimination, free trade among nations, freedom of the seas, open treaties openly arrived at, self-determination for the Balkan states, and an association of nations that would guarantee the political independence and territorial integrity of all nations great and small.

With their army in retreat, a seemingly endless flow of fresh young troops arriving on the other side, the vast production power of the United States now enlisted on the Allied side, and food supplies and civilian morale growing low, the Germans decided to sue for a peace based on Wilson's Fourteen Points. Much to Wilson's surprise, and the Germans' dismay when they met at Versailles, they discovered that the Allied forces of Europe had no intention of using Wilson's plan as an outline for peace. Disappointed but determined, Wilson held tenaciously to each of his principles until the vindictive victors chipped them away one by one. Finally, only the proposal for a League of Nations remained, and this Wilson refused to relinquish. Meanwhile, the victorious nations ignored a century of growing animosity and tension in all of Europe and declared Germany the sole perpetrator of the Great War. Therefore, reparations for the war fell on Germany. No one was sure what the war cost, but an immediate payment of $33 billion seemed adequate for the moment. When the draft of the peace treaty was handed to the German delegates in Versailles, they were horrified and then indignant, and when they returned to Germany, the treaty was met by violent opposition. It finally passed the Reichstag by the smallest of majorities when enough moderates became convinced that Germany could not continue the war.

Back in the United States, Americans were fighting another enemy, a great flu pandemic. Apparently the virus (an unknown factor at the time) had returned with the army from Europe. The first person with symptoms was a soldier in Kansas, but the disease, which many were calling "the Spanish Disease," soon spread from coast to coast, reaching its high point in the Northeast in October 1918. Unsure how the disease was spread, health workers tried many solutions to quell it. In New York City they experimented with a vaccine, while in other places like Schenectady, New York, the mayor ordered that "all schools, theaters, moving picture houses, churches, lodges, and places of public meeting and entertainment be closed until further notice" (Wells 2000, 187–89). By the time the scourge had worn itself out, over 675,000 Americans had died, but that number paled when compared to the worldwide number, estimated at 25 million (Davidson, et al. 2001, 760–62).

Wilson had his own bout with the epidemic while in Europe, but survived and returned to his country to discover that his fellow Americans were eager to forget the war and get on with the business of peace. The treaty that Wilson brought home with his beloved League of Nations still intact was rejected by the Senate, which believed that the League threatened American sovereignty. In response, Wilson wore himself out traveling back and forth across the country trying to rally support for his League.

Meanwhile, American soldiers began returning home to a country that had changed radically in a short two years. Industries, which prospered during the war years, had altered the demography of the country. Women had entered factories doing men's jobs, sometimes for the first time. Mexicans crossed the borders in droves to fill the demand for semiskilled workers. Blacks left the farms and towns of the South in great numbers seeking higher-paying jobs in the North. They brought their culture with them. Jazz and blues made their way up the Mississippi River to Chicago and other midwestern cities, and then east on the rails to New York City.

Many women went back to their homes after the war, but blacks did not return south, and their "Great Migration" of 1917 and 1918 continued into the new decade.

This exodus transformed the social and cultural complexion of America's larger cities and set the stage for a greater migration that continued through the first half of the century. Many whites reacted violently to the presence of newly arrived African Americans. Anti-black riots in Chicago, Detroit, East St. Louis, and elsewhere portended troubled race relations in northern cities in the subsequent decades.

For Americans the Great War ended quickly, and there were many manifestations at home that the government-fueled war fever had not had enough time to dissipate. Indeed, 1919 became one of the most violent domestic years on record, as a wave of brutality broke out with race riots, labor unrest, bombings, political terrorism, and lynchings across the country. In Florida, whites burned the entire black town of Rosewood, and those that were not killed scattered, never to return again.

Much of the violence in the 1920s, especially in the lower Midwest and South, could be attributed to the resurrection of the Ku Klux Klan, a Reconstruction-era terrorist group that found new life in the 1920s. The era of the new Klan began on Thanksgiving Day in 1915 on Stone Mountain, Georgia, just outside of Atlanta, where a group of 15 men burned a large wooden cross and declared their allegiance to the Invisible Empire of the Knights of the Ku Klux Klan. Unlike the old Klan, which terrorized Northern carpetbaggers and newly emancipated blacks in the name of protecting the women and property of the defeated South, the new Klan fed on fears generated by liberated women, uppity blacks, immigrants, Catholics, and Jews, who the Klan and its supporters believed were threatening the very fabric of American life. The new Klan drew on the culture of a small-town America that could not fathom, let alone absorb, the myriad changes occurring in their country because of the ascendance of so many groups that seemed to threaten their idea of what America ought to be.

Klansmen paid entrance fees and dues, which entitled them to a secret initiation, a white pointy-headed robe, participation in secret meetings, and a secret handshake. On Saturdays the Klan organized family barbeques, which ended in song and the burning of a large wooden cross. They organized their women into groups called the Women of the Ku Klux Klan. They saw themselves as the protectors of traditional American culture. Members had to be white native-born Protestant males. Members were mostly from the middle and working classes and many lived on the edge of poverty. Their mission was to keep their communities free of foreign and corrupting influences. When boycotts and rumor-spreading failed to cleanse their community of offensive foreign elements, especially Jews, or to pacify uppity blacks, or chasten daring women, the Klan resorted to flogging, kidnapping, mutilation, and lynching. Although they claimed to hearken back to a more orderly old-fashioned world, the Klan spread through the United States using the kind of modern promotional techniques used by many pyramid-based sales organizations.

Although scorned by the sophisticated, the Klan successfully seized political control of legislatures in four states and elected governors in six states. A future U.S. Supreme Court judge was even included in their ranks. Since their spectrum of hate went beyond blacks to include immigrants, loose women, and radicals, their appeal spread throughout much of the nation. Wherever there was a group of people suspicious of individuals not like themselves, the Klan had successful membership

Members of the Ku Klux Klan parade on the streets of Washington, D.C., in 1926, with the dome of the U.S. Capitol in the background. Library of Congress.

drives. The Klan's rapid rise abated somewhat in the mid-1920s when, in November 1925, the grand dragon of Indiana, David Stephenson, was sentenced to life imprisonment for rape and second-degree murder. However, the Klan survived and continued to have a dominant influence in many communities well past mid-century and remained a vital force in the southerners' resistance to the post–World War II civil rights movement (Davidson, et al. 2001, 796).

Despite the home-grown nativist nature of much of the violence, the government responded by blaming the social upheaval on the "Reds" (the shorthand term for communists, anarchists, and socialists). Preoccupation with Reds had been precipitated by the Bolshevik Revolution in Russia, which, beginning in 1917, had spread westward into Europe. Communists had even seized the Berlin government for a short time after the war. These events worried Americans, who feared that the breakup of old Europe would lead to social chaos and revolution throughout the continent. Americans also feared that their own soldiers returning from Europe had been corrupted by a degenerate Europe. Rumors of sexual liberty, social intermingling of the "races," gun-toting blacks being welcomed as heroes and treated as equals in Paris, and other social calamities, convinced many that they were witnessing the collapse of social order. The great pandemic, which soldiers had apparently brought to the North American shore, seemed to affirm this belief, and to some it provided a providential warning of the great dangers the country would face if Americans did not isolate themselves from the corrupt "Old World." The old American talisman of divine mission beamed once again, as politicians and preachers urged vigilance against the evils of decadence emerging from within and without.

In that context, A. Mitchell Palmer, the attorney general, began a campaign against political radicals. He launched raids across the country that led to the arrest or deportation of thousands of people suspected of anarchism, socialism, communism, or simple disloyalty. Over the course of a few months in late 1919 and early 1920, raids against radicals occurred in over 30 cities. Over 4,000 people were taken into custody, and hundreds of immigrants with radical ties as moderate as belonging to the Socialist Party were deported. In New York State five such socialists who had been elected to the state legislature were expelled.

The obvious abuse of power soon became repulsive to many, and, sensing the change in the electoral wind, politicians across the country railed against the government's repressive tactics. It became one of the issues leading to Democratic defeats in the November elections, as the man who would lead the Republicans in 1920, Senator Warren Harding of Ohio, denounced the actions of Attorney General Palmer, whose May Day, 1920 raids stirred up much havoc, but little evidence of revolution.

Meanwhile, Wilson continued traveling across the country campaigning for his League of Nations. In the midst of this crusade he suffered a debilitating stroke, and, like his battered body, the Progressive movement also for the moment became paralyzed. For over two decades, the Progressive movement had done much to improve government and make it responsive to the challenges of the new century. But as the second decade of the century came to an end, the movement seemed to have lost its vitality, and new forces were emerging in both parties.

One indication of this change was the successful passage of the 18th Amendment, which outlawed the sale and distribution of alcohol. An ironic legacy of Prohibition is that although it is generally viewed as reactionary, it captured many aspects of the Progressive mentality. Its proponents saw government as an instrument for social change, they believed in legislation to make people behave better, and they were sometimes racist and nativist. Examples of the latter two characteristics were the prohibitionists' assurances that the new law would improve the lot of the underclass, because the waves of immigrants in the North and the poor black farmers in the South comprised the largest group that abused alcohol and in turn abused their wives and families. Proponents of Prohibition (better known as the "Drys") also wrapped themselves in the mantle of patriotism, arguing that the new law was simply an extension of the restriction of alcohol production enforced during the successful war effort. The passage of this wartime measure had actually been the first national victory for the Drys in a decades-old campaign waged at the state level to rid the country of alcohol. The momentum of this victory carried them to a triumph, which would vanquish the "Wets" for more than a decade.

In 1920, Americans, weary of campaigns at home and abroad, elected a man who promised to let them rest and be normal for a while. And the United States entered a new era of prosperity and frivolity freed from the clutches of Puritans who hoped to redeem them.

The Roaring Twenties

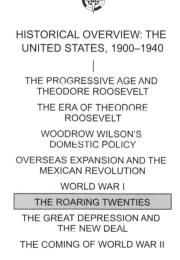

In the 1920s, foreign affairs took a distant back seat to the excitement of life at home. Electricity, the gasoline engine, Hollywood, sports, airplanes, bootleg whiskey, and the radio provided more stimulating distraction than one could absorb. Reflecting in 1930 on the recently ended decade, Frederick Lewis Allen surmised that one could hardly believe that it was "Only Yesterday" that the technological wonders of the 1920s barely existed or were nonexistent. Everything created in the 1920s seemed better, and faster. Speed was a virtue, and time was the new grace that one saved to realize the better life ahead.

Boasting of their new time-saving electric devices, General Electric assured readers that "to save time is to lengthen life." And Westinghouse boasted that the conveniences and comforts provided by electricity were unknown to the previous generation. Leading all the new time-saving and life-extending distractions was the gasoline engine automobile. Although invented in Europe, it quickly became absorbed into the American culture. The principal man responsible for this revolution, Henry Ford, determined to build a car everyone could afford. Applying the new principles of "scientific management," which included an assembly-line factory and ruthless time management, Ford and his engineers by 1925 had brought the price of his Model T down to $290, a price the average middle-class family could afford. At the same time, Will Durant's General Motors Corporation, comprising a collection of fancier, less successful producers, using windfall profits garnered during the war, offered credit for those who wished to buy something more attractive than Henry Ford's, "any color as long as it's black" product. Durant offered luxury automobiles for a little down and a little a month. With Ford's economical model available to the prudent, and Durant's credit-driven luxury styles for the wealthy and/or frivolous, automobiles drove straight into the national culture and radically transformed the nation's social geography. Paved roads connected town to city and city to city. Highway motels, gasoline stations, and restaurants sprang up along once-deserted roads. Auto clubs were formed for the sole purpose of keeping the roads operable and lobbying for more roads. Dating patterns among the young changed. For many middle-class youth, Saturday evening was no longer spent on the front porch under the watchful eyes of parents, but huddled in a car reveling in unchaperoned intimacies.

Propelled by the new automobile industry, the radio, and a host of other labor-saving electrical devices, the 1920s boomed. "The business of America," declared Republican President Calvin Coolidge, "is business." Large companies took over smaller ones, national markets expanded dramatically, and large corporations replaced the small-town business model. Large universities opened schools of business, which taught the new techniques of management, production, and distribution. The new American icon was the businessman. Even Christianity turned to the business model. Bruce Barton's bestseller, *The Man Nobody Knows*, presented Jesus Christ as the successful entrepreneur who took 12 ordinary men and founded the "greatest organization on earth." Aimee Semple McPherson adapted the new technology to the old-fashioned American revival and brought this distinctive form of American spiritual theater into the twentieth century of glitter and mechanized magic. Her Angelus Temple in California boasted a 75-foot rotating cross, a radio station, a miracle room for discarded crutches, a cradle room for babies, Holy Land slide shows, circuses, and healing sessions. Her performances revolutionized evangelization. One reporter wrote, "Sister Amy [sic] offered sinners flowers, music, golden trumpets, red robes, angels, incense, nonsense, and sex appeal." Charles Parham's Azuza Street revivals in California, which began with the new century when the Holy Spirit descended on his followers, enabling them to speak in tongues, also continued to attract and affect thousands in the 1920s as many Americans sought the solace of spiritual comfort in a world that seemed to be spinning out of their control.

The fact that the new religious revivalism depended on clever marketing reflected a greater reality of the 1920s. For many, consumerism had become the new obsession, and the clever salesman the chief priest of this New Jerusalem. Utilizing behavioral psychologists, the advertising industry began developing sophisticated techniques of commercial promotion that were provocative, powerful, and positive. They promised everything a consumer would want: good looks, healthier bodies (even from smoking), popularity, and sex. Packard Automobile Company, for example, featured an ad that declared that "A man is known by the car he keeps" and depicted a successful-looking handsome man behind the wheel of his luxury car with a beautiful woman standing by the door yearning for an invitation to join him. The advertisers for Lucky Strike cigarettes promised that cigarettes would make you slimmer and more courageous. Doctors recommended Camel cigarettes for calming the nerves. Camels also promised natural charm and assured the user that "pleasure would always be at your side."

To fuel the consumer age that advertisers had created, easy credit became more widespread. General Motors had spearheaded this trend, but buying on credit soon spread from cars to toasters, vacuum cleaners, refrigerators, watches, diamonds, and furs. Soon, with a little down and a little a month, Americans were luxuriating in items they never it was dreamed possible to own, and by 1929 national consumer debt jumped to twice the amount of the federal budget.

In the 1920s, sex became a household word, and the sophisticated set read or at least knew about Sigmund Freud. *Ego, id,* and *libido* became parlor words, and even women spoke openly about sex, birth control, and extramarital affairs. As the new decade opened, women finally became full-fledged citizens with the right to vote. But this movement fell short of the desired end of many women's rights reformers, who also wanted an equal rights amendment.

Despite their "liberation," women were still expected to remain in the home. The new domestic electric appliances promised freedom to do more than dust or mop, but advertisers still assumed that a woman's place was in the home. One of the ironies of the increased domestic technology was the expectation for a cleaner, better-managed home. With the new "time-saving" and "labor-saving" technology, middle-class homemakers began to let their maids go, but they ended up spending more time running the new machines of their modern houses than they had managing their helpers.

And the arrival of the Miss America pageant in 1921 reminded women that their chief asset remained their beauty. While men competed in sports and business, women competed in bathing suits. Samuel Gompers, president of the American Federation of Labor, praised the winner of the first Miss America contest as the type of woman America needs—strong, red-blooded, able to shoulder the responsibilities of homemaking and motherhood (Davidson, et al. 2001, 786–87). Such thinking not only affected concepts of proper roles, but also contributed to disparities in pay and responsibilities in the workplace. Certain jobs such as sales clerks, stenographers, telephone operators, and elementary school teachers became identified as women's work. These jobs remained at lower pay scales then those identified as men's work, because they were deemed less strenuous and because of the assumption that men were permanently established in the workforce, whereas women only worked to supplement the family income until they got married or had children, when they would assume their true vocation as wife and mother.

Among the new businesses booming in the 1920s was the movie industry. The multi-reel feature-length film, which had been invented in the early part of the century, came to maturity in the 1920s and became America's favorite form of entertainment. Lavishly appointed, palatial theaters dotted the major cities, and Americans stood in line for their chance to enter these cathedrals of escape. By the end of the decade over 100 million people a week were going to the movies.

Mass consumption helped produce a mass culture. Probably the greatest contributor to this phenomenon was the film industry, which created national models of speech, fashion, and custom. In the 1920s, Hollywood became the focal point of a national conversation. Adding to the newly emerging mass national culture was the radio. For the first time Americans could share a contemporaneous collective experience. In 1922, Americans could listen to the results of the World Series together, and in 1924 they could listen in on events at the Republican and Democratic National conventions. Popular magazines in the 1920s also contributed to the development of mass culture. Among the earliest were *Reader's Digest,* which began its run in 1922, and *Time* magazine, which appeared in 1923. They were soon followed by dozens more such as *Newsweek, Life,* and the updated *Saturday Evening Post,* which brought the newest information on national and international events, society, and fashions into homes across the country.

Electrifying became an overused metaphor in the 1920s, and rightfully so. For it was electricity that propelled this newly emerging urban middle-class culture. However, in the 1920s much of America lay outside the realm of this new miracle. As late as 1935, only 10 percent of America's rural areas had electricity. Despite the fact that the 1910 census suggested that America was a predominantly urban country, until the 1920s, most cities remained culturally and economically close to their rural roots. Electricity changed that. Never before in American history had the distinctions between urban and rural been so clearly defined. The many American subcultures based on region, ethnicity, and religion that continued to exist could all be divided into two major cultures in 1920s America: rural and urban.

While New York's Broadway glistened with artificial electric light, farmers' children still read with kerosene lamps. While women in urban areas mastered the new household appliances, women in rural areas continued to rake their clothes across a scrubbing board. While the sophisticated urbanite sought comfort in the most recent psychological insights, rural America sought solace in a revitalized fundamentalism that rejected evolution and any science that questioned the fundamental truths of the Bible. They embraced a literal interpretation of the Bible, which helped them maintain a well-ordered though rigidly defined universe that continued under God's protective and watchful eye. The urban bourgeoisie may have created a heaven on earth, but the rural fundamentalist took comfort knowing that this was a passing world, the Devil's distraction, and that true rewards lay in the hereafter. Despite their isolation, those living in the rural areas of the country were well aware of the newly emerging urban culture. Rural Free Delivery, parcel post, the *Sears Roebuck Catalogue,* battery-operated radios, and Saturday trips to town (and the local theater) kept rural America within the web of the new culture, if only on the margins of it.

The airline industry marked its birth also in this decade. Propelled by government mail contracts, the entrepreneurs began to link the large cities in two- and three-passenger planes. The most dramatic event of the decade belonged to the new airline industry, when in 1927 Charles Lindbergh crossed the Atlantic in a solo flight and captured the world's imagination with a single-engine Ryan NYP, dubbed the *Spirit of St. Louis*. His film-star good looks and his modesty projected a quiet, unassuming can-do attitude, which Americans liked to imagine was their own. His flight also gave solace to those who feared that machines were taking control of their lives, for in this case man was truly in control of the machine, but with the machine he could realize previously unfathomable dreams.

Sporting events also caught the national attention. In addition to the 16 big-league baseball teams, minor leagues, semiprofessionals, and amateur baseball thrived in towns across the country. Baseball became the national pastime, as newspapers regularly reported box scores and accounts of games and personal anecdotes of players in the sports pages, and radio announcers brought live games into homes. In the 1920s Americans also became avid fans of college football, and it soon surpassed Major League Baseball in attendance. Major universities built stadiums that seated from 60 to 70 thousand people, and every Saturday in the fall these stadiums filled with fans eager to cheer their team on to a mythical national title. Radio played a large part in this phenomenon, as announcers made living legends of Red Grange, dubbed the "Galloping Ghost," and Notre Dame's "Four Horsemen." The national media also helped create legends in boxing, tennis, golf, and swimming, making this decade the "Golden Age of Sports."

Not everyone was caught up in what has been described as an age of wonderful nonsense. As mentioned earlier, rural America remained outside the din, as did the large immigrant populations of the cities, who clung to traditions of their villages and shunned the morality and manners of their new country. Ironically, one of the new inventions of the age helped keep immigrants out of the vortex of change. Radio stations in most major cities usually dedicated at least a few hours a week to ethnic programs that gave many immigrants at least a virtual connection to their roots.

Many intellectuals also recoiled from the materialism and perceived "progress" of the 1920s. They sought refuge in Greenwich Village and low-rent districts of other American cities to read, write, and create their own bohemian culture. Preeminent among this group were the young writers who went to Paris and settled in on the Left Bank, gathered at Gertrude Stein's salons, and lamented the conformity and emptiness of modern mechanized and regimented civilization. Among this group were Ernest Hemingway, F. Scott Fitzgerald, Malcolm Cowley, and John Dos Passos. They had grown up, as Fitzgerald wrote, to "find all Gods dead, all wars fought, [and] all faiths in men shaken." Expatriate artists and writers discovered modernism in France, experimented with new forms of expression such as Dada, and created a new language in art.

The bitterest of all these disillusioned writers might have been Sinclair Lewis (the first American to win the Nobel Prize), who stayed in America. In his 1922 novel *Babbit*, Lewis satirized the absurd and blatantly dull life of Middle America. H. L. Mencken also railed against the ignorant middle class, whom he called the "Booboisie." His *American Mercury* magazine, which became a literary staple on college campuses, and his *The American Language*, a multivolume work on how English was spoken in the United States, helped remake American literature in the early to mid-twentieth century. The Algonquin (New York) Circle of writers and writers for the *New Yorker* magazine also contributed to the pages of satire directed against the gullibility and crassness of the American middle class. Not all of the great writers of the decade reveled in their angst. Disillusioned with the disillusioned, William Faulkner returned to his southern roots, where he explored the universal truths learned in a fictionalized postage stamp–sized Mississippi county that became the setting for a list of characters who told about the South and for whom the "past is never past." Faulkner received international recognition when readers noticed that these very localized and personalized stories held truths with universal human significance.

Disillusionment spread to the academic world also, where historians under the influence of Charles and Mary Beard began to see economic self-interest as the thread that tied together all American history. They insisted that even the most recent war, supposedly a noble cause that had seen the loss of so many lives, was fought for economic gain. According to the new revisionist history, the United States did not enter the war for democracy, but rather to ensure that a victorious England would pay back the millions owed to the house of Morgan.

The group, however, that had greatest reason to be disillusioned with the new America were the blacks. Despite some economic gains made in the Great Migration north during and after the war, African Americans remained the most underfed, underpaid, underemployed, and underhoused segment of the American population. They had also witnessed the rebirth of the Ku Klux Klan and a decade that opened with a rash of riots and lynchings the level of which had not been seen since the bloody post–Civil War era. Out of the mire of this dreadful condition rose the voice of a young Jamaican, Marcus Garvey, who told his fellow Africans they were a mighty race. His voice was heard, and at the first national meeting of his United Negro Improvement Association over 25,000 supporters jammed Madison Square Garden in New York City to hear his words of defiance against white racism and his quest for a new African nation based on self-help and patronage of black-owned businesses.

Other black voices rose in this decade also to decry the myth of racial inferiority, and the white practice of segregation and social and economic degradation of blacks. W.E.B. Du Bois, editor of *Crisis* magazine, advocated equal opportunities for blacks and set the agenda for the NAACP, which he cofounded. He also published young black writers like Langston Hughes and Jean Toomer, who were part of a group of extremely talented men and women who gathered in local coffee-houses, parlors, and theaters in Harlem, New York, to discuss their writing, their art, and their music. The energy that emerged from this group gave rise to a movement that became known as the Harlem Renaissance. In addition to Hughes and Toomer, scores of brilliant black people descended on the uptown New York neighborhood to practice their art. Among the more famous were the writers Richard Wright, James Weldon Johnson, Claude McKay, Zora Neale Hurston, and Countee Cullen, and the artists Augusta Savage and Archibald Motley. The Harlem Renaissance was an African American movement, created, supported, and sponsored by African Americans. But within a short time word spread of the genius residing in that part of town and soon whites were taking the "A train" to Harlem to share in this cultural explosion. A few white patrons contributed and supported a few black writers, and many more went to listen to black performances at venues such as the Cotton Club. Among the "smart set," African American culture became a fad in the 1920s. Probably the most obvious manifestation of this new white fixation was the production and success of George Gershwin's opera based on the life of poor blacks in the rural South, *Porgy and Bess*.

The fuel that energized the urbane 1920s was alcohol. Despite the fact that the 1920s Volstead Act forbade the production or transportation of alcohol, it flowed freely in the cities and in the back lands of rural America. Secret taverns called speakeasies flourished in the cities, and backwater stills in rural America pumped out gallons of sight-blurring liquid refreshment. Hip flasks tucked into garter belts or hidden in coat pockets accompanied couples to sporting events and dances. During this decade of Prohibition, a social revolution quietly occurred, as the male-dominated saloon of earlier decades gave way to the speakeasy where men and women drank together.

Sometimes seen as the last gasp of the faltering Progressives, Prohibition laid clear the class divisions that ran rampant in the United States. The middle class never had difficulty obtaining quality gin, rum, or whiskey from obliging neighbors in Canada or in the Caribbean. The poor, however, had to risk blindness and sometimes death to escape into an alcohol-induced refuge with moonshine locally made. Prohibition also increased the wealth and power of organized crime, as local gangs, following the corporate model, began to consolidate for the purposes of facilitating production and distribution of their product. The sale of illegal intoxicants became an important means of social mobility for some immigrant groups. Al Capone succinctly defined the class issue, which the Prohibition era magnified: "When I sell my product I'm bootlegging, when my clients serve it on Lake Shore Drive that's hospitality."

The decade of the 1920s also had its court cases "of the century." Each captured the imagination and attention of all Americans because each one could be seen as a metaphor for an aspect of American life in the 1920s. The first case to capture the national psyche was the Loeb and Leopold case, which took Americans into the

Snapshot

"If We Must Die"

In 1919, as violence against blacks in the form of lynchings and riots spread across the United States, Claude McKay wrote a poem titled "If We Must Die," which is often considered one of the works that initiated the post–World War I African American literary flowering known as the Harlem Renaissance.

> If we must die, let it not be like hogs
> Hunted and penned in an inglorious spot,
> While round us bark the mad and hungry dogs,
> Making their mock at our accursed lot.
> If we must die, O let us nobly die,
> So that our precious blood may not be shed
> In vain; then even the monsters we defy
> Shall be constrained to honor us though dead!
> O kinsmen we must meet the common foe!
> Though far outnumbered let us show us brave,
> And for their thousand blows deal one deathblow!
> What though before us lies the open grave?
> Like men we'll face the murderous, cowardly pack,
> Pressed to the wall, dying, but fighting back!

From the July 1919 issue of Liberator.

inner workings of that new branch of study known as psychology. The case involved the murder of a young boy by two disturbed boys who may or may not have been sexually involved. Using psychological argument, defense lawyer Clarence Darrow saved these two young men from the certainty of a death sentence for their crime. The second case, the Sacco and Vanzetti murder trial, revealed the racial and ethnic tensions of urban America as well as the anti-immigrant emotion that swept the country during that decade, and, finally, the Scopes Monkey Trial put the struggle between modernism and fundamentalism, which was a variant of the rural versus urban argument, on the front pages of newspapers across America.

Encouraged by the recently formed American Civil Liberties Union (ACLU), John T. Scopes, an unassuming high school biology teacher, challenged Tennessee's law that prohibited the teaching of evolution. Scopes was arrested, and the trial that ensued became a national spectacle. WGN radio in Chicago paid for a dedicated telephone line between the Dayton, Tennessee, courthouse and their station, and newspaper reporters from all over the country descended on the small town to see if the state of Tennessee would really enforce a law that prohibited the teaching of evolution in the classroom. William Jennings Bryan came up from Florida to help prosecute the case, and nationally known attorney Clarence Darrow defended Scopes. The climax of the trial came when Darrow put Bryan on the stand and made a mockery of fundamentalist belief. When the trial ended, Scopes was found guilty. Bryan died within the week, and urban America was convinced more than ever of the irredeemable backwardness of the rural South. H. L. Mencken, who was at the trial, described the South as an intellectual backwater, and blamed the southern preacher

who unable to move ahead with the more intelligent people of the South flings himself against every evidence of genuine advancement. He is against teaching the sciences, in schools; he is against the fine arts; he is against every infiltration of culture from without. He wants to keep his power and he knows intuitively that he can keep it only by holding the populace at his own level. (Mencken 1960, 198–99)

Politically, the 1920s decade of prosperity was a Republican decade, as the stock market, personal income, and American economic prestige rose, and Democrats seemed irreparably split between Wets and Drys, urban and rural, and Southern Baptists and urban Roman Catholics. One wondered if a Democrat would ever see the inside of the White House again. As humorist Will Rogers commented, "I don't belong to any organized political party, I'm a Democrat."

With the leadership of businessmen like Andrew Mellon, who served as Secretary of the Treasury for three presidents in the 1920s, and a tax policy that helped provide the foundation for prosperity, the Republican Party seemed invincible. They made policy decisions that propelled America's economy, while Democrats squabbled among themselves. Businessmen were the icons of the era, and Republicans spoke their language, particularly Herbert Hoover, who as Secretary of Commerce created the "associational" model of business-government cooperation, which brought business leaders together to agree on broad policies of prices and wages to avoid the painful disruptions of labor unrest.

The affirmation of Republican dominance came in the 1928 election, when Herbert Hoover defeated Al Smith by taking 58 percent of the popular vote and 444 of the available 513 electoral votes. Hoover even did something no Republican predecessor since Reconstruction could ever do; he cracked the solidly Democratic South in his landslide victory. Pundits wondered if the Democratic Party had not reached its demise.

No one could guess that the jubilation among Republicans would not continue well into the future. For in 1928 and most of 1929 no one could have predicted that the great upheaval known as the Great Depression was on the horizon. Very few understood or

> ## 📷 Snapshot
>
> ### A Florida Pioneer Remembers the Boom
>
> Thelma Peters, who was 20 years old and living in South Florida during the Florida boom years, later recalled those heady days.
>
> > Business areas, golf courses, a country club, marinas, apartment houses were on the blueprints. A 350 room ten story luxury hotel was to be built by a Detroit company at a cost of $2,000,000 on the Bay at the mouth of Arch Creek where there was a spectacular view of the Bay, and where it was stated the Atlantic Ocean would be visible from the balconies. First to go on the market was the Bay View Section, 3,500 lots for there the improvements were more advanced. The land had been cleared, the streets laid out though few were surfaced, street planting went along, and some sidewalks built. At the bay front a sea wall had been built a hundred yards from the shore awaiting fill, so some of the more expensive lots were still under water. The sale was set for December 4, 1925. It was flamboyantly advertised. The Shoreland Company had ten new Cadillac sedans purchased for the occasion lined up along Flagler street near the office. Within an hour after the sale opened all the lots facing the West Dixie Highway had been sold and before night some had been resold by their original purchasers at a good profit. In that one day, the sales amounted to $2,500,000.
> >
> > Within a few months that was small potatoes. The boom grew wilder and the purchasers more frantic. The next day was the sale of the Arch Creek property 1500 lots, again some under water, for the causeway, canals and boulevards were still largely a paper dream. Yet this sale over sold to two or more purchasers causing a nightmare of paperwork to unravel millions of dollars to be refunded. The sale was complete in one day bringing in the full value of the property $22,414,700. (Peters 1981, 292–93)

even suggested that there were fundamental imbalances in the American economy that spelled disaster. For one, in a world moving away from international trade, American production depended more and more on American buying power, which could not keep pace with production. Secondly, some important parts of the economy—agriculture, for example—had never prospered in the 1920s. Also, there was some unwise speculation on the part of those who were enjoying the wealth. The Florida land boom was but one example of a speculative investment gone awry. Mark Sullivan wrote in *Our Times* that "All of America's gold rushes, all her oil booms, and all her free land stampedes dwindled by comparison with the torrent of migration pouring into Florida during the early Fall of 1925." By spring 1926 the bubble had burst and with it millions of speculated dollars, much of which was underwritten by New York bankers, were lost.

Despite these basic flaws in various sectors of the economy, in the popular mind causes of the economic disaster focused on Wall Street, which had in the 1920s become the barometer of American economic strength. During the boom years, everyone wanted to cash in on the new prosperity, and Wall Street offered the public the opportunity to become part of the great corporate machine that was driving American prosperity. Stocks were sold on margin, meaning that a person could buy 100 dollars worth of stock for 50 dollars. With the price going up every day, few brokers worried about giving credit based on speculation. Creditor and debtor alike had no doubt that margins would quickly be covered in the ever-rising stock market. But it didn't stop there—once the margin was covered, the stock bought on borrowed money was used as collateral to buy more stock. The formula seemed perfect. The country was filling up with millionaires and those who thought they were on their way, at least on paper.

Then in October 1929 it all came tumbling down in a collapse that remained almost as unexplainable as the ascent. In the spring of 1929, the Federal Reserve raised rates in an attempt to tighten money and reduce the amount of loans. As this occurred, people had to sell stocks to cover outstanding loans. As more stock was sold, stock prices declined and therefore their collateral value declined. This meant more loans had to be covered, which caused the selling of more stock. This was occurring quietly throughout the summer, and as long as it was private fortunes being lost there was no panic. In October, the loan crisis and the sale of stock it precipitated hit the major players and it all came to a head on October 24, 1929, thereafter known as Black Thursday. Stocks plummeted as 13 million shares were traded that day and three billon dollars were lost. To stop the flow, a group of bankers headed by J. P. Morgan got into the market at the beginning of the next week to bolster prices, but even the great house of Morgan proved to be but a finger in the dike. On Tuesday the bubble burst, and when the dust settled, stocks that had a collective value of $87 billion at the beginning of the year were now worth about $18 billion. Optimism was gone, capital was dried up, and confidence in the unending prosperity promised by Hoover and others was gone. The Depression had not yet arrived, but its harbingers certainly had settled in.

The Great Depression and the New Deal

During the 1928 presidential campaign, Hoover said, "We are nearer today to the ideal of the abolition of poverty and fear from the lives of men and women than ever before in any land." If ever a man seemed qualified to handle the country in the throes of economic depression, a word he coined, it was Herbert Hoover. In 1914, he directed food relief that fed over nine million Belgians, and at the end of the Great War he directed the American Relief Administration, which fed millions of starving Europeans. In Finland the word *to Hoover* meant to help. When he was nominated for the presidency in 1928, conservatives in the party were opposed because of his perceived hostility to laissez-faire government.

Hoover alone did not deserve to be blamed for the economic catastrophe of the Depression. Nevertheless, during the Depression Hoover's name entered the American lexicon as a synonym for failure, indifference, misfortune, and despair. Cardboard shanties on empty lots where thousands of homeless were forced to sleep were called "Hoovervilles." When a homeless mother bundled her child in newspapers to keep her warm she was covering her with a "Hoover blanket," and when thousands gathered in the great underground loading docks of Lower Wacker Drive in Chicago, they said they were staying in the "Hoover hotel." The president took the blame because he headed a government that was politically and bureaucratically unprepared for the crisis it faced. By the time the Depression had ended, an active interventionist socially concerned federal bureaucracy would replace laissez-faire government.

Although the Republicans had begun the drift away from laissez-faire at the beginning of the century, they were unable and unwilling to make the radical departure necessitated by the crisis at hand. Political leadership seemed to drift aimlessly while the country's economy sank deeper into the abyss. For the first three years of the Depression unemployment rose to 13 million, or 25 percent of the workforce, and 60 percent of American families lived below the minimum income necessary for the barest necessities, but Hoover and his party failed to take the leap of faith into deficit spending and government investment that many economists were advocating. Therefore, then and for decades thereafter, Americans held them responsible for the collapsing economy that continued to spiral downward under their watch. With the Depression deepening in 1930, Hoover did not remain indifferent. Understanding that public confidence was essential to a recovering economy, he promised, "prosperity is just around the corner." He rallied business leaders and urged them to pledge to maintain employment and wages. He authorized one billion dollars in public works, and in 1932, with banks failing at the rate of 70 a week, Congress passed and Hoover approved the creation of the Reconstruction Finance Corporation, which could lend money to banks and their corporate debtors. Through the Glass-Steagall Banking Act passed the same year, the government added $2 billion to the money supply, making it easier for banks to loan money. Hoover even pushed a tax cut through Congress in 1932, but when that action threatened to create an unbalanced budget, he retreated and agreed to tax increases when just the opposite was needed. Also, in an attempt to protect American jobs he endorsed a higher tariff, which by reducing foreign trade proved equally disastrous.

Given their understanding of the economic universe, Hoover and his Republican colleagues did all they could to set the economy straight. Ultimately, they believed that the eternal forces of supply and demand would eventually equilibrate the economy and there was little more they could do. All their efforts betrayed a lack of understanding of the scale and complexity of the crisis. Hoover and his aides were products of almost two centuries of economic liberalism that believed the best government was that which governed least. They firmly believed that the current crisis represented a normal (albeit harsh) and necessary economic adjustment, and that prosperity would soon return. Whether they were correct or not, they created an image of a government indifferent to the pain of the average citizen, and this devastated the Republican Party. After Hoover's term ended, 20 years would pass before Americans would trust the Republicans in the White House again. But until they could make an electoral change, the American people could not look to the federal government for much help.

Some reacted with deep emotional depression, and some left their families and took to the roads. Men were especially distressed as they lost their jobs and sense of purpose. Women took on new responsibilities for keeping the household together by practicing economies in cooking and consumption, taking in work, postponing childbearing, and giving up entertainment outside the house. Most families stuck together, planted small gardens, bartered with neighbors, sewed up the holes in old clothes, put cardboard in their shoes and old blankets in their overcoats, and got by. Some got angry.

One such group was the "bonus" army, a collection of World War I veterans who in 1932 marched on Washington simply to ask the government to pay them money they had been promised as a bonus for enlisting in the war. Some 20,000 veterans came to Washington to petition Congress. When the House of Representatives voted against their request, most went home. But about 2,000 of them camped in Anacosta Flats with their families. When they refused to leave, Hoover ordered the U.S. army to drive them out, which they did with a vengeance, destroying and burning the camp and terrorizing the men and their families. This event was the last straw for many, and that fall the American people turned Herbert Hoover out of the White House.

Franklin D. Roosevelt (FDR), the man who would replace Hoover as president, made a lot of people nervous. Walter Lippmann wrote:

His mind is not very clear, his purpose is not simple. and his methods are not direct. . . . Mr. Roosevelt does not ring true. . . . He is no enemy of entrenched privilege. He is a pleasant man who, without any important qualification for the office, would very much like to be President. (Harrell, et al. 2005, 893)

Roosevelt may have had many detractors, but the truth remained that almost any Democrat could have been elected in 1932. When he entered office in March 1933, the country could have been no worse. First Lady Eleanor Roosevelt remembered wondering if there was anything that could save the country. Twenty-five percent of the nation was unemployed, 30 million families had no means of support, and banks were closing daily. Children who lived near train tracks would walk along the rails gathering coal that fell from the coal car; men made gin in their bathtubs and sold it for 25 cents a half pint. People were getting by as best they could. Roosevelt had no real plan, but he did have what America needed; he exuded confidence. He also had the magical Roosevelt name (he was a cousin of Teddy Roosevelt), a sunny disposition, and a can-do attitude. And although from the upper class of American society, his own bout with polio provided him with a sense of solidarity with the millions at the time who felt they too had overwhelming obstacles to overcome. When Roosevelt took office the Depression was three years old, and in that span over 107,000 commercial and industrial businesses had collapsed, the Dow Jones Average had sunk from $125.43 to $26.82, banks were failing daily, and there were over 12 million people out of work. Americans looked to the optimist from New York to do something.

At his inauguration, speaking to a crowd of 100,000 and millions more listening on the radio, Roosevelt told Americans that they had "nothing to fear but fear itself." Whatever that meant, it made people feel that finally they had a government that would do something about the crisis. The first hundred days of Roosevelt's term were the most frenetic in the history of the presidency and Congress. To stop the run on banks, he declared a bank holiday and then pushed through legislation that would protect sound banks and insure depositors' money. To protect the fragile dollar, Congress also took the country off the gold standard.

To explain to the American people what he was doing, he got on the radio. By 1934, 60 percent of American households had a radio, which was often the centerpiece of the living rooms in most urban households. In rural areas, people got by with a two-dollar "crystal set" that could be purchased at the local hardware or general store. Every night families would gather around their radios to listen to variety shows, classical music, sporting events, news, or to discover what trick Molly had played on Fibber or what trouble Amos and Andy were getting into. In the South the *Grand Old Opry*, which had begun broadcasting out of Nashville in 1927, was a favorite. The next day at the office or over the back fence people would talk about radio characters as if they actually shared time with them the night before. Roosevelt understood the power of this new invention, and he knew how to use it. After pushing through the banking reforms and taking the country off the gold standard, on March 12, 1933, he began a practice he would use throughout his presidency. He entered the living rooms of the American people via the radio and talked to them directly. He called his talks "fireside chats." To the still unsophisticated listening audience it was as if the president had just come over to their house and sat down to explain the intricacies of bank solvency, deposit insurance, and the international gold standard. His strategy worked. When the banks opened the next day, deposits exceeded withdrawals even though Roosevelt's banking legislation had not yet passed Congress. In marked contrast to how the emerging totalitarian leaders of Europe used the new invention, placing loudspeakers on every corner to control what was heard and making broadcasts a collective experience, FDR's approach personalized the experience and made the intricacies of government seem more comprehensible to the average person.

Roosevelt's first hundred days would become a political benchmark by which future administrations would be measured, but such comparisons are meaningless if not unfair. Never had the country faced such a crisis at the beginning of a presidential term, and never again would there be such a flurry of legislative activity in such a short period of time. In an attempt to return depressed farm prices back to the parity of 1909–1914, the last time industrial and agricultural buying power were more or less equal, Congress passed the Agricultural Adjustment Act (AAA), which would pay benefits to farmers for not producing at capacity. To have an immediate impact, with crops already in the ground and sows ready to farrow, farmers were paid to plow their crops back into the soil (over 10 million acres of corn) and slaughter their pigs (over 7 million). To help those in danger of losing their homes and on the brink of starvation, Congress passed the Federal Emergency Relief Act (FERA). Directed by a former social worker, Harry Hopkins, this agency utilized state, local, and private charities to distribute over a billion dollars to families in immediate danger of starvation or eviction from their homes.

Charity alone would not lift the country out of its economic malaise. The dignity of the workers of America had to be restored, as Hopkins argued, by paying them to do useful work. In response, the government began a series of various work programs, which would last right up to the beginning of World War II. Many criticized the programs for being inefficient, wasteful, and even exploitive of desperate people. But however one felt about the programs, the fact is they did restore a sense of self-worth to many and often provided a protective barrier, albeit a fragile one, from starvation and eviction for thousands of families. Starting with the Civil Works Administration (CWA), the Progress Works Administration (PWA), and continuing with the National Youth Administration (NYA), which put young people to work, and the Works Progress Administration (WPA), whose employees included writers, artists, and scholars, and the Civilian Conservation Corps (CCC), which gave young men from cities the chance to get out in the fresh air planting trees and building parks and trails while earning money for their families, the government throughout the 1930s became the employer of last resort for hundreds of thousands of Americans. Although planned to be temporary, the agencies created to administer these temporary jobs became amalgamated into the ever-expanding federal bureaucracy and provided thousands with permanent employment.

FERA grants kept foreclosure away a month at a time; however, to put the American family and the housing industry on a more secure footing, a more permanent system had to be applied, and in 1934 Congress passed the Home Owners Loan Act, which made federally guaranteed home loans available. This agency would eventually become the Federal Housing Authority (FHA), which created amortized loans that made home ownership feasible for millions of Americans who had never dreamed of such a possibility.

The New Deal, as Roosevelt's policies were described, also revolutionized thought concerning regional development by creating the Tennessee Valley Authority (TVA), which tamed the Tennessee River and used its energy to bring electricity, parks, jobs, and income to a large portion of the rural South. In the West, the government expanded a dam project begun by the Hoover administration and brought electricity, irrigation, and flood control to thousands in the Southwest while freeing them from the ravages of the wild Colorado River.

In 1935, Congress also established the Rural Electrification Agency (REA), which brought electricity to millions of rural Americans. No single act revolutionized the lives of so many as the REA. The cost of stringing electric wire to far-flung villages made it unprofitable for private industry; therefore, rural America remained in the dark without benefit of light bulbs, electric radios, and other new electric appliances; rural folk read by kerosene light, cooked with wood, and refrigerated with ice. In 1935, only 10 percent of rural America had electricity. Thanks to the REA, by 1939 that number had increased to 40 percent and by 1950, 90 percent of rural America had electricity and became connected to the technological rhythms of the country.

In the first months of the New Deal, the immediate focus had centered on the immediate relief of the effects of three years of poverty and unemployment. Families, as Harry Hopkins had pointed out, needed to eat every day, not in the long term, but Roosevelt's advisors and others in Congress understood that in the long run government must do what it could to resuscitate and reinvent the American capitalist system. To that end the administration embarked on what they thought would be more permanent economic reforms, and in 1934 Congress passed a plan known as the National Industry Recovery Act (NIRA), which called for voluntary state corporatism that would control prices, wages, supply, and demand. This plan would eventually be declared un-

📷 *Snapshot*

Ain't No Law That You Got to Go Hungry

Conservatives railed against the New Deal's experiment with socialism, and Nobel Prize–winning author Ernest Hemingway added his voice to the protest. He expressed these feelings in his novel *To Have and Have Not.* His comments may have surprised readers, since at the time of writing this work he had been recently published in the leftist *New Masses.* He also had been a vociferous and active supporter of the Spanish Republic, one of the great liberal causes of the 1930s. Hemingway's book is peppered with anti–New Deal comments; some even get personal, as, for example, the following: "Anyone would have to be a writer or a FERA [Federal Emergency Relief Act] man to have a wife look like that. God isn't she awful?" At one point in the novel Captain Harry Morgan tries to convince a friend who is working for the WPA to join him in a smuggling scheme, by telling him the following:

> You're making seven dollars and a half a week. You got three kids in school that are hungry at noon. You got a family that their bellies are hurt and I give you a chance to make a little money. . . . Let me tell you, my kids ain't going to have their bellies hurt and I ain't going to dig sewers for the government for less money than will feed them. . . . I don't know who made the laws but I know there ain't no law that you got to go hungry. (Hemingway 1936, 97)

constitutional, but many of its provisions were later adopted as law and, contrary to fears at the time, its overall concept of the feasibility of increased wages, stable prices, and improved profits through full employment strengthened the American capitalist system and became part of future fiscal policy.

Not all the New Deal's plans were successful, but at least it gave the American people the idea that the government was doing something. In the short span of a year, FDR's New Deal and his "alphabet soup" of agencies (as some described them) had revolutionized the American economy. Laissez-faire was dead, and the federal government had become an active senior partner in the business of running the American economy.

Indeed, from the beginning the genius of the New Deal was its experimental nature. Although not an ideologue, FDR embraced the philosophy of pragmatism—if an idea worked, it survived. New Deal programs at once called for seemingly contradictory actions such as belt tightening and deficit spending, for aid to workers and help to business, for regulation of business and promotion of free competition, for destroying farm products when people were hungry. FDR also drew on a wide range of people with varied interests for advice, and in the pressure cooker of the first hundred days almost any idea got a hearing and often support. Those who had ideas that survived remained as Roosevelt's advisors. They remained outside the regular cabinet and therefore politically and intellectually free to state their opinions. They came to be known as Roosevelt's "Brain Trust." The result of this open and free flow of ideas was often confusing and contradictory but also exhilarating and hopeful, and for this FDR was able to garner the support of the people. After voters enthusiastically affirmed the New Deal in the congressional elections of 1934, Will Rogers observed that the people were with him (Roosevelt) so much that even if he had burned down the capital they would say, "at least he got a fire started."

After a year of Roosevelt's Brain Trust fine-tuning the economy, the Depression had reached its fifth year, and although things began to look a little better Americans were growing impatient. Industrial production had declined in the second half of 1933, sputtered upward in early 1934, then slid back down in the second half of that year. The number of people on payroll had risen steadily in 1933 from 40 to 75 million but in mid-1935 slid backward to 65 million (Mitchell 1947, 447). Many were beginning to grow impatient with the process of recovery. Radicals on both the right and the left were gathering strong followings. Most accepted as fact the demise of the capitalist system but argued over which model the country ought to follow, that of Italy and Germany, or that of the new Soviet Union.

In California, the socialist Upton Sinclair was nominated for governor. In Louisiana, Huey Long was creating a new populist form of democratic politics, demanding that the government limit the size of fortunes and distribute the surplus to the people. Dr. Francis Townshend advocated a monthly payment of $200 to elderly Americans who would quit their jobs and promise to spend the money in 30 days. From his Little Flower church and broadcast station in suburban Detroit, Father Charles Coughlin, the "Radio Priest," who in 1933 had supported Roosevelt's policies as an embodiment of the papal encyclical on social justice, *Rerum Novarum*, began to attack Roosevelt. He claimed that the president was protecting "international bankers" (many believed that to mean Jews) who manipulated currency, causing havoc in the economy. He called on Roosevelt to nationalize the banks and expand the money supply, which would help the working class. Thanks to the radio, newsreels, and their own publications, all these critics had a national voice and following. For all their differences, these radical reformers struck a similar chord that rang true to many average Americans: the money supply was inadequate, the elderly needed a plan of financial aid, the unemployed needed assistance to keep their lives together until they could find work, and the terribly unequal distribution of wealth in the country needed to be adjusted.

The political instincts of Roosevelt were not deaf to the voices of protest. In 1935 he expanded public works projects, but more importantly he pushed for the passage of the Social Security Act, which would provide the unemployed with a partial income until they found a job and would provide retirees a monthly allowance that would allow them to live out their lives with dignity. And at the urging of New York Senator Robert Wagner, Roosevelt took a giant step in the direction of government support for the average worker when he pushed for the creation of the National Labor Relations Board. Congress passed the National Labor Relations Act of 1935, by which the federal government guaranteed the rights of workers to organize and if necessary to strike. Armed with this new prolabor legislation, the Congress of Industrial Organizations (CIO) split from the older American Federation of Labor (AFL) and organized the industrial mass production workers, those considered unskilled by the craft union dominated by carpenters, electricians, and plumbers. CIO leaders first took on the steel industry, and then in their most famous action of the 1930s they took on General Motors. In this strike, to avoid being locked out and to prevent replacement workers from taking their positions, and taking a page from the successful civil disobedience tactics of Gandhi in India, the men sat down in the factories. The union won these strikes, and by 1941 every major automaker and U.S. Steel had been organized.

By 1936, the New Deal seemed to be working. Production was rising, unemployment was falling, and America was slowly recovering. In this process a quiet political revolution was unfolding, as the government assumed an active role in creating economic policy that regulated the workplace, business, wages, banking policies, and more. Some question the reforms of the New Deal and claim they did not change the system but rather saved it. Nevertheless, Roosevelt's New Deal had changed the federal government's relation to the economy in ways that his Progressive predecessors could only dream of.

Those who saw these changes as creeping socialism did not take this movement sitting down, and they rallied around the last bastion of laissez-faire in Washington, the U.S. Supreme Court. In his first term in office, Roosevelt did not have the opportunity to name a Supreme Court justice. He was the first president since James Monroe not to have had this opportunity, and in 1937 a politically conservative Court threatened to undo much of his legislation and thereby overturn every advance the New Deal had achieved. Conservatives chose the Court as the place where the final battle between laissez-faire and welfare capitalism would be fought. The Court had already declared the NIRA and the AAA unconstitutional, and by going after a minimum wage law in New York, Roosevelt had every reason to believe that now they were setting their sights on Social Security. With his second mandate in hand, Roosevelt decided something ought to be done about what he described as an "aging" and conservative Court. He proposed that every judge over 70 years old who had served on the bench for 10 years should retire and if he refused, the president could then appoint another judge to help with the workload. Such a policy might be repeated up to six times, which meant it might lead to adding up to six new judges to the Supreme Court.

Reaction to his plan was not what FDR expected. There was a huge public outcry against his attempt to "pack" the Supreme Court. As the debate raged, however, other events defused the issue. The Supreme Court got the message, and in 1937 it upheld Social Security and the Wagner Act, which had created the National Labor Relations Board. Also, one of the most conservative opponents of the New Deal, Justice Willis Van Devanter, resigned, and Roosevelt was finally able to appoint someone more sympathetic to his political philosophy. Pundits referred to the events as the "switch in time that saved nine." Other resignations followed so that before he died in 1945, after being elected president four times, Roosevelt was able to remake the Supreme Court into what became known as the New Deal Court through most of the next generation. But FDR paid a political price for his attempt at "court-packing." Conservatives who otherwise had ceased opposing him now cloaked themselves as protectors of the constitutional balance of powers and criticized FDR and his New Deal for coalescing so much power into the hands of the executive branch.

By the end of 1936, with the economy seemingly well on the way to recovery, Henry Morganthau, the Secretary of the Treasury, suggested that it was time to "strip off the bandages, throw away the crutches, and let the economy stand on its own feet." Roosevelt, eager to get the budget back into balance, ordered federal spending cuts and slashed welfare rolls. The economy responded by collapsing, and within six months of these cuts it appeared that the country was headed for a return to the quagmire of 1932. Roosevelt's actions in 1937 demonstrated that he never really accepted or understood the concept of deficit spending completely and never totally bought into the philosophy of John Maynard Keynes, whose theory was that governments should tax heavily in times of prosperity and spend that money in times of economic decline. Eventually the government would spend the country out of the economic downturn, not because of their conversion to Keynesian economics, but rather because of events on the other side of the Atlantic.

The Coming of World War II

Across the Atlantic a few countries were following Keynesian economics, but the spending was not on public works, but rather on armaments, and as the United States, England, and France floundered in the 1930s, Germany, with mass expenditures on armaments, created a strong, vibrant economy. England, France, and the United States wanted to leave the Great War behind. Conversely, Germany's new leader, Adolf Hitler, reminded his people of the war every day, and in the collective war memory that he and his Nazi party fabricated, Germans were victims, not the aggressors. In the Nazi interpretation of recent history, communists, international bankers, Jews, and the Weimar government that in 1919 had voted in favor of the Versailles Treaty had betrayed Germany.

The betrayal was a significant element of the new philosophy Hitler had borrowed from Benito Mussolini. Mussolini called his new political economic system fascism. The communists had gotten it all wrong, preached Mussolini. Conflict between worker and capitalist was not inevitable. Both had greater common interests, which were represented by the nation. Together worker and capitalist should struggle to create a greater Italy in the tradition of ancient glories of Rome. For this system to work, Mussolini declared, the people must have a trusted leader who embodied the nation and its values. This leader would have no ulterior motives; his only desire would be the emergence of the nation into greatness. Worker and capitalist would both have

Snapshot

New York World's Fair of 1939

For those that could afford to go to New York in 1939, another World's Fair opened its doors. It had been planned as a celebration of the future and the exciting prospects of a world of science. But for most Americans the world of science was coming under question. It had brought many gifts but also many more new burdens. Scientific management had promised greater and more efficient production and distribution of goods, but it had not saved them from a catastrophic economic depression. Science had brought technological advance, but now those advances were being used to decimate Europe for a second time in a generation. The automobile and radio were certainly blessings, but what about the fragmentation that accompanied these inventions? What had happened to community and to family in the new age of technology? The New York World's Fair of 1939 did not attract the large numbers expected. Whether it was because Depression-burdened Americans still couldn't afford it or because its message did not resonate, historians still debate.

faith in the leader and his ministers. Conflicts between workers and owners over such things as working conditions or pay would be resolved by the leader and his ministers, who would advise him on what is best, not simply for workers or capitalists, but for the nation.

In this line of thinking, those who did not go along with the leader's decisions were no longer disgruntled workers or reactionary managers, but rather they were enemies of the state. In Italy, Benito Mussolini emerged as this trusted leader or *Il Duce*; in Germany, it was Hitler, known as *Der Fuehrer*. Hitler, following Mussolini's model, turned Germany into a well-oiled fascist machine. Production soared, prosperity returned to Germany, and most Germans saw Hitler as their savior. For fascism to work, it must have a viable national myth, which serves as a glue to bond the disparate members of the nation together. For Italy it was a return to the glories of ancient Rome; for Germany it became the myth of Aryan supremacy and their betrayal by non-Aryans. According to the Nazis, there were many non-Aryan betrayers in Germany: communists, gypsies, and Catholics to name a few, but the people that became the focal point of their anger were the Jews. In the 1930s in Germany, to be a patriot meant also to be anti-Semitic, and the country that up to that time had been the most hospitable to the children of Moses now became their greatest enemy.

Poster showing the Trylon and Perisphere buildings for the 1939 New York World's Fair. Library of Congress.

Americans watched events in Europe with suspicion, yet they were not eager to get involved in another war. Even when Germany helped the Spanish military overthrow the legitimate government of Spain in a bloody civil war, the Americans declared themselves neutral. The successful end of the Spanish Civil War in their favor in the spring of 1939 convinced the fascists of Germany that the time was right to implement their plans of expansion. And a few months later in September 1939, Hitler invaded Poland. After a winter of false negotiations and military maneuvering, the war broke out again in April and within six weeks the German army handed all of Western Europe over to the Nazis. England now stood alone against the combined fascist powers of Europe. Still Americans remained neutral. Although an internationalist who understood the threat Germany represented, Roosevelt could not lead where the people would not follow. Isolationism dominated the collective American mind. With popular spokesmen such as Charles Lindbergh arguing for an "America First" policy, there was little Roosevelt could do.

Without the necessary political support for more decisive action, he did everything in his power to put the economic and military strength of the United States at the disposal of the British, and in 1940 he signed the Lend-Lease Act, which would lend, lease, or otherwise dispense arms to countries whose defense was vital to the United States. In explaining this new policy in a fireside chat, Roosevelt likened his actions to a man lending a neighbor a hose when his house is on fire. But more than a garden hose would be needed to quell the conflagration in Europe. While Roosevelt searched for means to get American aid to Europe and for an opportunity to engage the Nazis and come to the aid of England, events in Asia were drawing the country closer to war, and more rapidly than they expected.

Since 1932, when the Japanese had invaded Manchuria and set up a puppet government there, the United States had been quietly using diplomatic and economic pressure on Japan to convince them to abandon their imperialist designs on China. The Japanese ignored diplomatic pressure, even withdrawing from the League of Nations in 1933, and continued their policy of expansion, insisting that just as the United States in the Monroe Doctrine had claimed a right to determine the political destiny of the Western Hemisphere, they had a right to maintain a political and economic sphere of influence in Asia. Finally, in 1941, when the Japanese, taking advantage of a neutralized French government controlled by their German allies, marched into French Indochina, Roosevelt took action. He froze Japanese assets in the United States and announced an embargo on petroleum and metal scrap products being shipped to Japan. This action put those in favor of war with the United States in control of the Japanese government, and on December 7, 1941, Japan attacked American bases in the Pacific. The following day Roosevelt asked for a declaration of war against Japan, and within a week Japan's ally Germany declared war on the United States. For the second time in a generation the United States found itself embroiled in a world war.

The second time Americans went to war in Europe, there were no songs, no fanfare, simply a grim determination to finish what their fathers had started. In the winter of 1942, the world looked rather grim. Nazi Germany controlled all of Europe, and they were meeting little resistance as they rolled into the Soviet Union, which stood alone against the seemingly unstoppable force of the Third Reich. In the Pacific, the Japanese surprise attack had given them temporary dominance in the region and they were threatening an attack on and occupation of Australia.

Although news on the battlefront was bleak, at home determined Americans went to work to build the most formidable arsenal the world had ever seen. By 1943, the American industrial output exceeded that of the Axis powers, and Americans were producing planes, tanks, and guns much faster than enemies could destroy them. The massive war production created unprecedented economic and demographic changes in the United States. During the war the average weekly income increased by 70 percent—while inflation rose 47 percent—and for the first and only time in American history there was a downward redistribution of income. The share of the nation's wealth taken by the top 5 percent of the population declined from 22 to 17 percent, with most of the difference going to the bottom 40 percent. Also during the war years, people migrated around the country as never before. Some nine million Americans moved to the cities that offered jobs in the newly burgeoning defense industry. In addition to the traditional urban destinations of the North and Midwest, Americans also moved to the Pacific and Gulf Coast, and in the process they created an entirely new demographic region that became known as the Sunbelt.

The new prosperity of the war years also set off a consumer boom. With higher incomes and rationing restrictions, Americans had money to spend. Although the restrictions of war limited access to high-ticket items such as cars and houses, Americans did spend their money on entertainment, and theater revenues soared. Americans also used their extra income to hoard rationed items such as sugar, coffee, spices, rubber goods, golf balls, clothing, and shoes. The shortage of male labor brought countless women into jobs where they had not been seen before, which forced Americans to change their attitudes toward gender roles in the workplace. Women took positions as metal workers, millers, welders, lumberjacks, and machinists. One of the lasting icons to emerge from the war is the Norman Rockwell poster of "Rosie the Riveter," an attractive girl pictured baring her muscular bicep while telling American women, "We can do it!"

Black Americans used World War II to attack discrimination more directly than they had ever done before. In 1941, as the government was preparing for war, A. Phillip Randolph, head of the Brotherhood of Sleeping Car Porters, threatened a massive march on Washington unless Roosevelt issued an executive order banning discrimination in the defense industry and armed forces. Roosevelt acceded to the demand, and as a result, by war's end, two million African Americans were employed in war-related jobs. These job opportunities outside the cotton South added another chapter in the history of black migration, as over 800,000 southern blacks moved to the urban North, Midwest, and West in the 1940s.

By the time World War II began, German Americans had been well assimilated into the American culture, and they did not suffer the same prejudices experienced in World War I. This time American nativists directed their venom against the Japanese, especially in the Pacific West, where the war fanned smoldering anti-Asian feelings. Bowing to this prejudice, President Roosevelt ordered the relocation of 120,000 Japanese Americans to 10 hastily built camps that were nothing more than shacks surrounded by barbed wire. These detention camps remained in operation until March 1946, and not until 1983 did the government officially admit its mistake and pay compensation to survivors (Harrell, et al. 2005, 976–78). When the war ended, Americans knew that they had entered a new, much more complicated world. Women had entered the workforce in unprecedented numbers and in positions they had never held before. African Americans had left the South for northern and western cities as they had never done in previous eras, and they were demanding with a more militant voice rights that had been denied for far too long. Seemingly benevolent science, which in previous decades had entertained, fascinated, and promised an ever-improving life, had, in one moment over Hiroshima, become demonic. And Americans had defeated one totalitarian menace only to be confronted with a new challenge from international communism. On the other hand, wages were rising, birthrates were at an all-time high, and Americans who had learned to accept change seemed willing to face the challenges of a not-too-certain future.

FOR MORE INFORMATION

Davidson, James West, William E. Gienapp, Christine Leigh Heyrman, Mark H. Lytle, and Michael B. Stoff, *Nation of Nations: A Narrative History of the United States*. Boston: McGraw Hill, 2001.

Harrell, David Edwin, Edwin S. Gaustad, John B. Boles, Sally Foreman Griffith, and Randall Miller. *Unto a Good Land: A History of the American People.* Grand Rapids, MI: Eerdmans Publishing Co., 2005.

Hemingway, Ernest. *To Have and Have Not.* New York: Charles Scribners and Sons, 1937.

Keene, Jennifer. *American Soldiers Lives: World War I.* Westport, CT: Greenwood Press, 2006.

Mencken, H. L. *On Politics: A Carnival of Buncombe.* New York: Vintage Books, 1960.

Mitchell, Broadus. *Depression Decade: From New Era through New Deal 1929–1941.* New York: Harper Torch Books, 1947.

Peters, Thelma. *Biscayne Country, 1870–1926.* Miami, FL: Banyan Books, 1981.

Watson, John B. *Behaviorism.* New York: W. W. Norton and Company, 1930.

Wells, Robert. *Facing the King of Terrors: Death and Society in an American Community 1750–1990.* Cambridge: Cambridge University Press, 2000.

Zinn, Howard. *A People's History of the United States.* New York: Harper Perennial, 2001.

2

THE NORTHEAST

Overview

In the early decades of the twentieth century, the northeast quadrant of the United States comprising New York and New England remained the most densely populated and wealthiest sector of the country. Over half of the nation's 106 million people lived in the Northeast and the per capita income was higher than in any other part of the country.

In the first four decades of the twentieth century, five major events defined the history of the Northeast: immigration, urbanization, war, technological innovation, and the Great Depression. Populations of the urban Northeast swelled as immigrants, especially southern and eastern Europeans, filled the major cities of the Northeast. Most of these new immigrants came through the new federal immigration processing center at Ellis Island, New York.

During World War I and continuing for over the next half century, great numbers of blacks migrated northward, leaving the dismal life of tenant farming, Jim Crow laws, and urban poverty in the South for the promise of a better life in the urban Northeast. Previously small black sections within the cities of the Northeast would be transformed into large lively African American communities. One major result of this migration in New York was the blossoming of Harlem and the Harlem Renaissance of the 1920s.

In addition to immigration, three major technological changes took place in the early twentieth century that revolutionized American culture: electricity in the home, the automobile, and the radio. The introduction of electricity into the home changed house designs, revolutionized housework, and put lights into children's rooms, allowing them to read into the night. For better or worse, by 1914 the automobile, thanks to Henry Ford and his efficient assembly-line production and effective marketing, was no longer a plaything for the rich but a part of many middle-class families. The family car brought people and places closer together, enabling weekly trips to places that were once prohibitively far for a weekend jaunt. On the other

Ellis Island, in New York Harbor, where thousands of immigrants to the United States were processed in the late nineteenth and early twentieth centuries. Library of Congress.

hand, it separated the nuclear family as the automobile became for the middle class, as it had become for the privileged rich, an expression of independence and freedom. It did not take long for young people to begin using the family car as a dating place where they could have some time alone and away from adult supervision. In the 1920s the radio changed the way people saw the world by bringing that world literally into their living rooms. Events that only a few years prior were read about a day after they occurred (such as presidential elections and baseball games) were now being heard as they happened.

In 1917, the United States entered a "war to end all war" to "make the world safe for democracy," as President Wilson declared. Many Americans took up the cause, growing victory gardens, rationing gas, abstaining from strong spirits, and hating the Germans. For many, the war evoked a new sense of national community; however, it also divided some Americans across immigrant and ethnic lines.

In 1920, decades of women's organizing, petitioning, and demonstrating culminated in the passage of the 19th Amendment, which gave women the right to vote. Both those who had predicted disaster and those who had predicted the dawning of a new age of political reform and morality with women's enfranchisement were disappointed and surprised to learn that women ended up splitting into factions and voting in patterns similar to their male counterparts.

In the same year women won the right to vote, they, along with the men, lost their right to buy or drink alcohol in public places. In a flurry of postwar enthusiasm and conservative Protestant exhortation, Americans attempted the "noble experiment" of closing the saloons and drying up America. A new dawn was predicted: sober men would become more industrious and, in turn, the country would become more productive and prosperous. Men would stay home at night, making the family stronger and, in turn, the country stronger. Noble or not, the experiment failed, especially in the urban Northeast where immigrant and ethnic cultures and urban "moderns" rejected the imposition of largely small-town, rural "middle America's" values on their habits. Although, statistically, national consumption of alcohol decreased, the long-term success of the experiment hinged on local support and law enforcement, which in many areas of the Northeast remained less than enthusiastic. In the urban Northeast, speakeasies, clubs, and a host of distributors provided illegal alcohol to thirsty clients. Organized crime capitalized on the demand for beer and wine especially to muscle in and control large distribution systems in the cities.

The industrialized Northeast, except for New England, which saw their textile mills move to the South closer to the raw material of their industry and to cheaper unorganized labor, experienced economic prosperity in the 1920s. Propelled by the new technology of the automobile, radio, and electricity, the Northeast went through a period of exceptional economic growth in this decade. Out of this economic explosion came AT&T, RCA, General Electric, Westinghouse, and other corporations based in the Northeast that would dominant the American economy for the next 50 years.

At the end of the 1920s the boom that helped define the decade ended in a terrible economic crash, the worst the nation had ever experienced. The urban industrial areas of the country felt the crash worse than other areas and the Northeast worst than most. Soup kitchens and breadlines and shelters for the homeless tried to soften the blow in an era when the federal government's policy remained hands-off during times of economic crisis. Economically, the decade of the 1930s became one of the most terrible the Northeast had ever experienced. However, by the end of the decade, through new federal economic policies established by the New Deal and the economic stimulation provided by government spending for a new war on the horizon, the industries of the Northeast once again by 1940 were supporting a growing and prosperous economy. Workers were taking home regular paychecks, the flood of foreclosures abated, and Americans were once again on the road to the promised land of economic security. They had survived the Great Depression, but a greater threat to democracy and the American way of life lay just over the horizon in Europe, where democratic government had been crushed under the iron boot of totalitarianism. By 1940, Great Britain stood alone against this threat, and the English looked to their long-time ally, the United States, for assistance. For the second time in a generation, Americans would find themselves embroiled in world war. This section will explore the changes to daily life of the people of the Northeast as technology, mass migration, war, and economic depression propelled them through one of the greatest periods of change in the nation's history.

Domestic Life

FAMILY LIFE

No aspect of American life changed more radically in the first decades of the twentieth century than the family. Many factors precipitated this change, including the move from rural settings to urban ones, the new technology entering the home, and the changing perceptions of the role of women in modern life. In the urban Northeast, large families were no longer an asset and, as families moved to cities, the number of children decreased. This decline was especially true among the middle class. Homes of immigrants still remained full of children, as did the houses of the urban poor regardless of their origins. In some cases the power of tradition overwhelmed the new trend toward smaller families, and in other cases children remained an economic necessity, for as soon as they were able, the children of the poor were often sent out to find work to help support the family.

As the population of the Northeast became more urbanized, attitudes toward marriage also changed. In many urban middle-class families, the motivation for marriage itself changed also as women began to demand more than simple economic security from the relationship. Indeed, new sociological and psychological studies suggested that the well-adjusted family was one that women found to be emotionally and socially fulfilling. As expectations for a happy marriage increased, so did the desire to leave unfulfilling marriages. Divorce rates increased rapidly in every decade of the twentieth century except the Depression decade of the 1930s.

In the urban Northeast, as young people were exposed to a greater number and variety of potential partners, the decision to marry was cast in a new light. Marriage had traditionally been regarded as a partnership established for economic, educational, and welfare purposes as much as a social relationship, but during the late nineteenth and early twentieth century, additional forces, including birth control, new attitudes toward child rearing, and an emphasis on individual personal development and fulfillment, influenced the expectations and function of the family in middle-class urban America. One by-product of these changing values in marriage was the reduction in the number of children born to a typical urban middle-class family. Increasingly women's magazines and journals emphasized not only the female role of the loving mother, but also that of caring and careful home manager.

By the 1920s, the urban middle-class wife was a "homemaker," in charge of the family budget and running an efficient, clean household aided by the new appliances and improved time management. In urban areas and even some rural areas, institutions assumed educational and welfare responsibilities traditionally relegated to the preindustrial or rural family, and more people were involved in work settings where cash wages allowed individuals to purchase daily necessities that in an earlier era had been provided at home. As a result, different expectations of marriage began to develop. After 1890, native-born men and women married earlier. Contraception provides the key to the increase in early marriage among the middle class at the turn of the century. In the late nineteenth century marriage had been postponed for economic reasons as men and women, especially in the newly emerging urban population, delayed marriage in order to permit men to work for a time without the burden of providing for a growing family. Delayed marriage also served as a form of birth control by limiting the amount of fertile years that a couple lived together. By the twentieth century, growing knowledge and availability of contraception alternatives permitted family planning after marriage rather than before. Birth control allowed husband and wife to delay first birth and, just as important, to space subsequent births according to family goals and resources. By 1920, a low urban birthrate was positively and strongly correlated with a high marriage rate among the young.

Indeed, birthrates declined among middle-class white women in the first decade of the century from 3.5 to 2.3 children per family.

Like the sharp decrease in family size, the increase in early marriage showed the new potential for planning and cooperation within marriage. As husband and wife gained control over family life, the companionship possibilities in marriage were freed from earlier restraints. Marriage could become first a relationship between two people rather than a necessary and determinant step toward family formation. Contraception thus broke down rigid traditional roles and definitions in the family.

The idea of the "modern" family emerged, popularized by psychologists, social service professionals, and educators. These experts determined that a successful marriage was based primarily on affection and companionship. As a result of these changing attitudes, divorce began to be seen as an alternative to a marriage that was not emotionally fulfilling. Some but not all states eased divorce requirements, and in the Northeast divorce increased from 1 in 18 marriages in 1880 to one in six in the 1920s. But this trend did not signify a decline in a desire to be married. Remarriage became much more common than in previous eras when divorce was a rarity. The 1930 census reported that only 1 percent of adults listed their current status as divorced. People were not turning against marriage; rather they were expressing a desire to have a happy and fulfilling family life, and if disappointed in one attempt they were willing to try again. As the new century unfolded, emotional and sexual satisfaction was replacing economic security as the standard of marital choice and contentment (Kyvig 2002, 134–36; Fass 1977, 68–69).

The rising frequency of divorce among the urban middle class caught the attention of the Progressives of the new century. In Boston the New England Divorce Reform League, founded in 1881, lobbied for more legislative curbs on divorce and sponsored studies to investigate the "family problem." In 1906, Governor Samuel W. Pennypacker of Pennsylvania hosted a National Divorce Congress attended by delegates from 42 states. Although they drafted a set of rigid divorce laws designed to become national law, the proposals were rejected in Congress. Despite the determination of Progressives and Christian leaders to create uniform national legislation that would check the soaring divorce rate, the legal status of divorce remained a state issue. Church groups played an important role in the process of defining marriage laws. In New York, for example, an alliance between a strong Catholic Archdiocese of New York and an equally powerful Episcopalian bishop persuaded the New York legislature to maintain highly restrictive divorce laws. Similar coalitions produced the same results throughout the Northeast.

Modern ideas of marriage were not limited to the urban middle class; the phenomenon was also occurring in the rural areas of the Northeast. However, in the rural Northeast the reasons for one modernizing trend, birth control, were most often connected to economics. In some cases the diminishing availability of arable land in the Northeast reduced the possibility for men to make a living off the land and resulted in postponement of marriage until later in life. Even when young people took the economic risk and did marry, they often decided to practice birth control in order to maintain a smaller, more manageable family. Poor nutrition in rural areas also may have contributed to a reduction of female fertility in the first decades of the twentieth century. Whatever the reasons—social and intellectual in urban areas or economic in rural areas—throughout the Northeast, female fertility continued a decline that had begun in the nineteenth century and would continue until World War II.

When African American families migrated from the South to the urban Northeast, their numbers declined also. The average African American family in the South contained five people, while those in the North had four members. In addition to declining size, the black family in the North faced numerous challenges that threatened its ability to function as a viable unit. Contributing to family instability was a variety of problems including high delinquency, unemployment, and substandard living conditions. Documenting the combined impact of forced relocation, economic exploitation, and institutional racism, which caused havoc and disorganization in black urban areas, black sociologist E. Franklin Frazier explained that problems of black urban families were socially constructed rather than culturally inherited (Reich 2006, 544).

Urban immigrants from Europe resisted modernizing trends in the family. Many who came to the cities had come from rural areas of their own countries where, like those living in the countryside in the United States, they resisted the intellectual and social fashions of the cities. When they arrived in the United States, they held to traditions centuries old that served to insulate the immigrant families somewhat from the social experiments going on around them, and to bind them together in what they viewed as an ever more fragmenting world. For the most part they continued to have large families and, well into the twentieth century, they continued to celebrate religious festivals that reconnected the generations and brought family members back to long-abandoned neighborhoods at least for a day. Catholics especially, under the rigid marriage guidelines of the Church, were less likely to witness the breakup of the family. And Italians, although by tradition not as cowed by the Church as other immigrants, did have a litany of saints that helped and supported the family in time of crisis. Among these spiritual helpers were saints who found lost articles, others who helped sell a house, and various others who alleviated family sickness. Young girls even had a saint who protected their virginity.

The explanation for differences in fertility between classes or between ethnic women and native-born American women is complex. In part it may have to do with religious tradition or class concerns about the costs or advantages of having children. But certainly a part of the explanation was simply lack of sufficient information. Oral interviews with working women around the turn of the century suggest that few women of that class knew of mechanical methods of birth control like the diaphragm. For family limitation they relied on abortion or abstinence. In fact, some of the women recalled that abortion was much more commonly talked about among them than contraception as a means of birth control (Degler 1980, 221–22).

As people began to live longer, poverty among the elderly became a serious problem and another burden on families of every class, as children were expected to care for poverty-stricken aged adults. The Social Security Act of 1935 eventually addressed the problem of old age and survivor needs, though it hardly provided the resources to meet the growing needs and expectations of America's aging population. It was not until the 1940s that the first payments to the elderly were made, and few people were covered in any case. Helping the elderly remained a personal obligation, with states and local government providing assistance in varying degrees.

American family life was severely challenged by the Great Depression. Many families, in the Northeast as elsewhere, planted gardens and did home canning, pickling, and baking. They ate less meat and more beans and pancakes. Women returned to making their own clothes, and men did their own home repairs. Families bought day-old bread from the bakery, repaired their shoes with cardboard, and relined coats with old blankets. Confronted with the loss of jobs and income, families struggled to pay mortgages, rents, and bills. Many suffered deprivation, hardship, and humiliation. Men especially suffered terrible blows to their pride when they could no longer see themselves as the "breadwinners" of the family.

Despite these trials, most families remained intact. The divorce rate actually declined in the 1930s. Some historians suggest a more scrutinized view of this statistic would reveal that divorces declined because of the costs involved, and they point out that frequently men just left their families without formal legalities. Desertion and abandonment became "the poor man's divorce," and the number of such incidents soared during the Depression era. The Depression also affected the number of marriages during the decade. Many couples decided not to start families and, as a result, marriage rates plunged, and birthrates fell to their lowest in the nation's history. Whereas the population had grown by 16 percent in the 1920s, the growth plummeted to 7 percent in the 1930s. The generation born in the 1930s would be the smallest of the century.

MEN

As in earlier periods, patriarchy remained the central concept for understanding men's lives. Throughout the century, in the United States, men reaped the benefits of a social system that provided them with a dominant position in the family, in politics, and in the economy. This position did not go unchallenged. Throughout the century American women gained social, economic, and political power. But such things as the 19th Amendment to the U.S. Constitution, the increase in the numbers of women workers in factories, shops, stores, and offices, and new laws giving women the power to divorce and claim full custody of children did not eliminate men's overriding power. Thus, although feminist groups made inroads against the system, the basic assumptions of patriarchy remained largely intact. One can see this in terms of wages. Regardless of education, qualifications, and experience, men made more money than women for the same work.

In the first decades of the twentieth century, before Prohibition caused its immediate if only temporary demise, the saloon was a bastion of masculinity. From the sawdust floors, to the boxing posters on the wall, to the all-male presence (except for prostitutes relegated to the back room), the saloon was a man's world. It represented a male culture that still dominated society but was slowly losing ground to female emancipation and equality. In the male world of the first two decades of the twentieth century the local saloon provided a retreat from the world of women and children. The saloon supported the stereotypical masculine image, separate and unfettered by the chains of domesticity. Saloons provided many services for men. First of all they were centers of political organization. In New York, for example, at the turn of the century 11 of 24 aldermen were saloonkeepers. They also formed the basis of community in many working-class neighborhoods as a place where people of similar ethnic background, class, and occupation could gather. The neighborhood saloon also served as a private club rather than a public place. At the saloon many men received mail and messages, made deposits, and sometimes got loans, ate, and even slept. Men played cards, sang, played musical instruments, got live sports information from a ticker tape, and engaged in boisterous, raucous, and often coarse conversation. Since working men of similar occupations gathered together at many saloons, they also served as employment agencies, putting prospective employers in contact with potential employees.

Although in the late nineteenth century the Knights of Labor prohibited saloonkeepers from joining their union, by the new century many unions used bars as their meeting places. In Buffalo, New York, for example, in the first decades of the twentieth century 63 of 69 unions met in bars. In New York in the pre-longshoreman union era, saloonkeepers hired dockworkers. Saloons often provided the working man with his best and sometimes only meal of the day for free. Most saloons offered a free lunch, and in Boston, saloons were required by law to offer free food to their patrons. So for five cents, the price of a beer, a man could have a lunch far better than what most eating establishments were offering for five times that price, and without the beer. Some bartenders would serve heavily salted food, which caused men to buy more than one beer to wash down the free food. Finally, saloons in the early decades of the century served as models of manhood for young boys, who would gather at the doorways of bars to watch with fascination what the men were doing inside (Kingsdale 1973, 472–89).

The writer Jack London recalled this boyish fascination as he passed a number of saloons daily while he was delivering newspapers.

In saloons life was different. Men talked with great voices, laughed great laughs, and there was an atmosphere of greatness. Here was something more than everyday where nothing happened. Here life was always very live and sometimes even lurid. . . . Great moments these, for me, my head filled with all the wild valiant fighting of the gallant adventurers of sea and land. There were no big moments when I trudged along the street throwing my papers in at doors, but at the saloons even the sots, stupefied sprawling across tables or in the sawdust were objects of mystery and wonder. (London, 1989, 24)

In the African American community, traditional concepts of masculinity and manhood became one of the motivating factors that precipitated the great black migration to the North. Disenfranchisement, segregation, and economic marginalization militated against the African American male's claim to manhood. In the South, most black men could not vote, which continued as a gender-specific privilege during the first two decades of the twentieth century; the tenant farmer's economic dependence on white landowners took the male privilege of breadwinner away from many blacks in the South; then, too, the humiliating Jim Crow laws also militated against the black man's sense of self-worth and pride. Given this reality, the advertised egalitarianism and economic opportunities of the urban North attracted black males to the region. Letters to black newspapers frequently repeated the themes stated in the following letter: "I will gladly take a position in a northern city or county where a man is a man." Although the black migration experience encompassed black men and women of all ages, classes, and skill levels, black males were the first and the largest group to migrate in the years around World War I, when the great black migration north began (Reich 2006, 544).

WOMEN

In the urban areas of the Northeast, the twentieth century ushered in a new age of individuality for young women. This great leap forward in women's involvement in the work economy occurred primarily between 1900 and 1910, as there would be little percentage increase of women working between 1910 and 1930. The movement into the workplace freed young women from the social customs reinforced by family, church, and community. In the city the young urban woman could individualize her own moral norms. The phenomenon of the liberated working girl dominated the themes addressed by those concerned with domestic tranquility. As early as 1904, the family in peril became the theme of many magazine articles. Dorothy Dix observed in 1913, "there have been so many changes in the conditions of life over the last twenty years that the parent of today is absolutely unfitted to decide the problems of life for a young woman today." In fact, she pointed out, the "whole social and economic position of women has been revolutionized since mother was a girl." Magazine articles lamented the passing of the home daughter, as the modern women preferred the blessed anonymity of the city to dying of what felt like asphyxiation at home. Women's individualization was occurring because, whether married or single, employed or not, women were spending more time outside the home.

And a sexual revolution was well underway. In 1900, Wellesley College, in Massachusetts, reflecting the morals of the time, forbade a junior prom, because it did not want the women mixing with "promiscuous" young men. A mere 16 years later, *Puck* magazine featured a young girl with puckered lips urging the reader to "Take it from me." A popular song of 1916 entitled "Dangerous Girl" proclaimed, "You dare me, you scare me, and I like you more each day." In 1915, Dorothy Dix noted that it was literally true that the average father did not know who was taking his daughter out, and she lamented the terrible things that were going on in the back seats of cars, which she called the "devil's wagon." The change in morals that decidedly occurred in the decade from 1910 to 1920 became embodied in the flapper. The flapper was young, whether in fact or fancy, self-assertive, and independent. She joined men as a comrade, and the differences in behavior of the sexes narrowed. She cropped her hair, wearing it in a short bobbed style, and wore dresses that emphasized a boyish figure. She conscientiously became desexualized. This style, often attributed to the postwar era, actually had its beginning a decade earlier. In the Northeast, the Boston *American* defined the "1914 girl as a slim boy-like creature with narrow hips." This new style deemphasized hips and bust. By 1914, even Newport ladies, models of decorum in fashion, were wearing short hair. Although the flapper's speech, her interest in thrills and excitement, her dress, and her aggressive sexuality made her less feminine in the traditional sense, she paradoxically became more attractive to the opposite sex.

A major contributing factor to the changing status of women was changing attitudes toward women's sexuality. Sexuality became part of a woman's physical attributes and an aspect of her emotional expression. And the emphasis on sex highlighted the new marriage ideals, which equalized some rights, responsibilities, and roles between men and women in marriage. The legitimization of female sexuality and the pointed sexualization of marriage were perhaps the most significant departures of the marriage literature of the 1920s, for they reflected specific changes that had already taken place and in turn implicated all facets of marital interaction. Behind this change was the increase in availability and knowledge of contraception. With contraception, female sexuality could be freed from its necessary connection with motherhood. As long as childbirth was implicit in sexual relations, sexual intercourse defined woman's role as submission, obedience, and childbearing. Women fulfilled "marital duties" by submitting to their husbands in the effort to conceive. Contraceptives, however, permitted women to be sexual partners first and mothers second, if and when husband and wife chose that role for her. Contraception released men and women from imposed roles and permitted new choices in roles and relationships (Fass 1977, 69–72).

The emergence of the film industry in the 1920s also had a great influence on the perception and portrayal of the "modern" woman. Films with contemporary urban settings were especially likely to feature restless young women, single or married, eager to escape the home and obtain status equal to men. Nevertheless, with threats of censorship in many communities, the triumph of conventional virtue, after some audience-attracting misconduct, proved to be a constant theme. Even a free-spirited and apparently sexually liberated female star such as Clara Bow in *The Plastic Age* (1925) or *It* (1927) demonstrated in the end that chaste goodness under the surface of her outwardly naughty behavior would win her man. Films also provided a source of sexual information for young adults when none other was available. One young woman reported that she learned to close her eyes while being kissed from observing actresses on the screen doing it. A young man confessed that he learned to kiss a girl on the ears, neck, and cheeks as well as the mouth from the movies. And a 16-year-old sophomore revealed, "I know love pictures have made me more receptive to love making, I always thought it rather silly until these pictures where there is always so much love and everything turns out all right in the end, and I kiss and pet much more than I would otherwise" (Kyvig 2002, 95–96).

Another contributing factor to the liberation of women were the so-called kitchen and housework revolutions, which were well underway by 1909. Electricity radically altered the lives of urban women after the turn of the century. After lights, electric irons became one of the first acquisitions for newly wired homes. Then came the vacuum cleaner. These new inventions, along with canned goods and prepared foods, transformed women's work habits in the house. Images of women in magazines from 1900 to 1920 document changes in womanhood. In 1900, the middle-class women in magazine advertisements appear well-rounded with soft billowy hair, delicate hands, and motherly expressions. By 1910, the idealized woman in advertisements changed. She was depicted with a more active figure and in more activity outside the home. One ad presented a woman on the telephone saying, "Yes drive over right away, I'll be ready. My housework? That's all done! How do I do it? I just let electricity do my work these days."

Women were expressing their desire for freedom in other ways. Smoking in public and drinking with men in bars (and speakeasies in the Prohibition 1920s) were becoming fashionable, at least for middle- and upper middle-class women. New dance styles motivated by the syncopated rhythms of black music also became the rage in the urban Northeast.

Women's newfound sexuality and liberation did not occur without a backlash. In 1913, a New York grand jury outlawed the turkey trot and kindred dances that were deemed too sexually inviting. In Boston, the mayor ordered the removal of a showgirl from a store window where she was posing cross-legged on a sofa. And in both Boston and New York, advocates of contraception, Van Allyson and Margaret Sanger, were arrested for distributing birth control information to women. A number of states in the Northeast created film commissions to pass judgment on the decency of films. The Pennsylvania commission, for example, forbade films that included nudity, prolonged passion, women drinking, or infidelity.

An important milestone in the movement toward women's sexual, domestic, and social liberation arrived with the passing of the 19th Amendment in 1920. In the Northeast, the amendment met strong resistance from rural, immigrant, and Catholic populations who often feared it as an assault on traditional family values and a threat to social cohesion. Only in New York did both legislative assemblies vote unanimously in favor of the amendment. In Delaware, Vermont, and Connecticut, the governors refused to call special sessions to vote for the amendment. Despite the myriad debates over how the women's vote would change society, the results were disappointing. Women tended to vote and divide over issues the same way that men did. Still, the amendment had symbolic weight, if only as an assertion of women's status as fully empowered citizens.

The American woman had been the social stabilizer of the nineteenth century, and changes in her behavior underlined the overall changes taking place in society in the new century. The new woman of the twentieth century redefined equality. The new woman demanded not only political and economic rights, but a much more threatening and subtle freedom, the right to self-expression, self-determination, and personal satisfaction. To traditionalists this smacked of immorality, self-indulgence, and irresponsibility. Asking for more than merely to have a man choose her for a wife and the mother of his children, the new woman expected to be satisfied as a lover and companion, and she insisted on more freedom and honesty within the marriage. To conservatives, rural and small-town Americans, and various immigrant and religious groups of the Northeast, all this appeared to portend the collapse of noble womanhood, as it had been understood. Such groups worried that once released from previous controls and well-defined roles, women risked the danger of succumbing to a path from which there was no return, of teetering on the edge of sexual promiscuity. The change in female behavior was especially apparent in the cities. Indeed, the *Literary Digest* warned country girls of the dangers of migrating to the city for work. Theodore Dreiser's *Sister Carrie* (1900) had signaled the danger of a woman giving herself over to the pleasure and the allures of city living. The "new woman" of the 1920s only intensified such worries in fact (Fass 1977, 23–24).

To be sure, women of color also joined in the new freedoms of their gender, but the majority of black women migrating from the South to the Northeast often left children and husbands behind out of economic necessity, not in search of gender equality. The most common life for a black urban woman was working in the home of a white middle-class family. This created a working situation that deprived black women of their privacy and continued their isolation from their own families. In the 1920s African American women in the urban Northeast struggled, not to leave household service for better jobs, but to leave "live-in" circumstances in order to have time off and an opportunity to reunite with their families. Once they did reunite, they often encountered problems of segregation in housing and prejudice in the workplace, problems they felt they had left behind in the South, continuing to plague their families (Reich 2006, 288–89).

CHILDREN

The movement to the cities and the new technology of the late nineteenth and early twentieth century also affected children. For one thing, there were fewer children per capita in middle-class families. As people began moving to the cities, they discovered that children were a liability, not an asset as they had been in rural and farm communities. And with the increasing availability of birth control information and women's new sexual assertiveness, urban families were becoming smaller. Those children who were born in this era benefited from the emphasis on love-centered child rearing, social science guidance emphasizing rewards over punishments, and new technology that made homes healthier and more comfortable living spaces. Electric lights on Christmas trees began to appear as early as 1882, and by the 1890s children's toys such as electric-powered model trains for boys and lighted doll houses for girls began to appear. The appearance of electric lights in the house stimulated reading at home. Children could not be left alone with dangerous gaslights or candles, but they could easily and safely read by electric light without supervision.

In rural areas, life revolved around the family, but as families moved to urban settings, children discovered expanding opportunities for extrafamilial activities that gave them more opportunity to meet and interact with peers. Some of these groups such as the YMCA, YWCA, the Boy Scouts, and the Girl Scouts were designed to keep maturing young males and females away from each other, occupying them in outdoor activities and crafts for hours each week. Schools also sponsored social activities such as dances and proms.

For the urban poor there were other outlets. City boys tried as best they could to maintain control of their traditional playing areas. At the turn of the century, for example, boys continued to swim off public or private docks despite the danger of polluted water, drowning, or arrest. Most swimming was without suits; one old New York swimmer remembered that swimming was legal in the East River "provided one wore one's underwear." Young athletes mainly relied on the streets in front of their homes for their entertainment. As George Burns reminisced,

Our playground was in the middle of Rivington Street. We only played games that needed very little equipment, games like kick the can, hopscotch, hide and go seek, follow the leader. When we played baseball we used a broom handle and a rubber ball. A manhole cover was home plate, a fire hydrant was first base, second base was a lamppost and Mr Gitletz, who used to bring a kitchen chair down to sit and watch us play, was third base. One time I slid into Mr Gitletz, he caught the ball and tagged me out. (Riess 1991, 127)

The most popular game for young boys was baseball. It was America's pastime and second-generation immigrant youth loved the game, which was not only fun, but proved that they were not greenhorns but true Americans. On the fringes of the city in the new suburban areas, makeshift ball fields sprang up on empty lots everywhere, but in the inner city, the lack of playing space limited the possibilities for a normal game. Consequently, few immigrants made it to the big leagues in the first decades of the century. Ball playing there was constricted to cognate games like stickball, and they had to develop special rules to conform to the idiosyncrasies of their playing area (for example, anything hit to left field is an out). Other factors also limited the playing time of the urban poor and immigrant, such as working a regular job, Hebrew school, parental opposition, and limited community support.

Settlement houses and community centers in the inner city often provided space for young boys to play indoors. Consequently, sports that could be played in limited space like boxing and basketball became very popular among the poor and immigrants in the urban Northeast. Whereas baseball produced few ethnic stars in the period 1900–1920, boxing was dominated by the Irish, and then the Italians, and later urban blacks. Basketball followed a similar development determined by class or race.

Among young urban blacks in the Northeast, access to semi-public or public sports facilities was limited by expense, free time, accessibility, and discrimination. In the Northeast black YMCAs were established in Brooklyn, Boston, and New York. The most popular sports among young black males were prize-fighting and baseball.

Among the middle class, sport and games were only some of many diversions for young people. From the 1900s through the 1930s middle-class youth engaged in a school culture more than any generations before them. One positive result of this was a radical increase by 1940 in the number of 18-year-olds who were staying in school long enough to obtain a high school diploma. With more people finishing high school, more went to college. From 1910 to 1930 the number of 18–20-year-olds enrolled as students increased from 114,228 to 228,342 nationwide.

Collegiate social life flourished in the 1920s. Since college students had substantial hours of free time to spend with one another, free from the company of their elders, they devoted themselves to their own entertainment. Attendance at school events grew popular, and going to movies and dances more so. For young adults, the thrill of doing things that their parents might not approve of sent them to speakeasies. Dating and sexual exploration remained at the top of most students' lists of favorite diversions. Student social life set the collegiate culture apart, drew attention to innovations in fashion and conduct, and provided a model for behavior of high school students and young people already at work.

In the 1930s, college life took on a more serious tone. More puzzled and concerned over contemporary conditions than their immediate predecessors, many students became involved in political and economic discussions. Some were drawn by their professors or their own analysis to advocate reformist or even radical political solutions to the nation's economic woes. More students had to find part-time jobs to keep themselves in school, leaving less time for the leisure activities that had been a hallmark of college life in the 1920s. Still despite the Depression or perhaps because of it, more people enrolled in college than ever before. At the end of the Depression decade there were 400,000 more students enrolled in colleges and universities than there had been when the decade began (Kyvig 2002, 148–49).

PETS

In the Northeast, as Americans moved from rural to urban environments, their relations to their animals changed also. People remained close to their animals but in different ways. Farm chores in the rural environment, which included helping a cow deliver a calf, shoveling mountains of manure out of a barn, and sticking a hand under a hen to check her eggs, necessitated familiarity with each animal's needs and habits. As people and their animals moved into an urban environment, intimacy remained, but animals were no longer producers of commodities or commodities themselves. The urban animal or pet represented a source of amusement and companionship, not economic necessity. Pets often shared living space with their owners, and many pets enjoyed petting, holding, and cuddling, contacts that society otherwise only permitted between adults and young children, close relatives, or lovers. Despite this domestic familiarity, family dogs and cats (then as now the most popular of pets) in the early twentieth century lived more of their lives outdoors than indoors.

Well into the twentieth century, many city and suburban houses had outbuildings that were the pet's primary shelter. This was especially true if the animals were large or still worked for their owners. For example, owners needed cats to prowl attics and sheds and hunt rodents that lived off goods in the pantry, spilled livestock feed, and family trash. Rabbits, bantam chickens, and fancy pigeons usually lived in outbuildings or outdoor hutches because of their numbers and the mess they made. Doghouses ranging from elaborate miniature versions of human dwellings to a large wooden barrel laid on its side with a hole cut in one end as a door were common features of house yards. To keep them from wandering, dogs were often chained to their houses at least part of the time. During the warm months in the Northeast, dogs and cats were more likely to live outside because of the fleas they harbored (Grier 2006, 61–63).

By the early twentieth century, public health officials in the largest urban centers had turned their attention to remaking cities into orderly, healthier environments with safe water, clean streets, and regular trash pick-up. In this context the urban tramp cat was no longer a joke or even an unpleasant yet acceptable fact of life. Cities had needed them, but now the misery of half-starved feral cats and increasing if sometimes misguided public concern about cats as carriers of disease, including poliomyelitis, led to new efforts to control their numbers. Whether or not populations of stray cats had increased drastically in those years as advocates of control claimed, it is true that hundreds of thousands of cats were captured and killed between 1890 and 1910.

By 1911, the New York Society for the Prevention of Cruelty to Animals (SPCA), founded in 1866, killed upwards of 300,000 cats annually, most of which were kittens. Philadelphia disposed of 50,000 and Boston destroyed another 25,000 that same year. The author of a *McClure's* magazine article that startled readers with those figures excoriated pet owners who abandoned their cats for the summer or refused to euthanize unwanted kittens. "It does not fit in with the decencies of civilization," he criticized, "that so much living and dying should go on casually in lofts and cellars and coal pockets and vacant houses." By the turn of the century, many cities of the Northeast had created agencies that attempted to save stray dogs and cats rather than simply destroy them. The Animal Rescue League of Boston, and the Ride a WEE Home in New York, among other animal protection agencies, were committed to saving as many abandoned pets as possible through adoption (Grier 2006, 216).

As in other aspects of life in the twentieth century, pet care became commercialized. The Spratts Company of England was the first to manufacture dog food, which it began marketing in the United States in the last decades of the nineteenth century. By the early twentieth century American companies in the Northeast got into the competition. Potter and Washington, a Massachusetts company that specialized in hygienic health foods for family use, introduced Old Grist Mill Dog and Puppy Bread around 1905. The makers mixed their special whole grain flour with beef bone meal, rice, and vegetables and baked them into cakes. They also offered a special Boston terrier biscuit. The A. C. Daniels Company of Boston began to offer medicated dog bread as an aid for convalescent or chronically ill pets. Canned dog food, which first appeared in the 1910s, also developed as a regional business.

Factory locations were determined by proximity to sources of meat and meat byproducts. There was an abundance of meat by-products for dogs, especially after the passage of the Pure Food and Drug Act that determined that certain meats and their by-products were not fit for human consumption. The packers of wet dog food always depended on multiple animal sources for their meat. Horse meat became available in large quantities in the first decades of the twentieth century as the American cities turned from horse-drawn vehicles to electric trolleys and gas-powered trucks and automobiles. The Hugo Strauss Packing Company of Brooklyn offered Purity dog food, composed of solid horse meat, and Laddie Boy Kennel Ration offered a mixture of horse meat, cereals, and cod liver oil. In addition to food products, the market in the 1920s and 1930s was deluged with pet care products. By the 1930s owners could buy dog scrubbers that attached to a bathroom faucet and dispensed flea soap. Another breakthrough was the discovery of pyerthum, or flea powder.

Connected to marketing of dog products was their training. As early as 1878 books on dog training for pet owners began to appear. By the 1920s, the companion dog was an increasingly regulated creature, and a wider range of typical behaviors—chasing cars, approaching other dogs, pulling on the leash, and urinating on neighbors' shrubbery—were now defined as unacceptable. Ralston Purina Company began publishing books with titles like *Dog Etiquette*. In 1936, the American Kennel Club instituted standards for highly codified obedience competitions. While only a handful of family dogs ever competed, this development suggests even more self-conscious improvement in dogs' behavior as an outlet for leisure time, and for orderly urban and suburban living. At least a few dog owners now felt they needed the advice of multiple experts when once they had simply known what to do with their pets.

Memorializing animals also became a part of American culture in the twentieth century. On the farm and in the open suburbs departed pets were often buried on the grounds somewhere without much ado. In congested cities of the Northeast most deceased pets simply went out with the household trash. This undoubtedly caused much distress, but there was no alternative. By the end of the 1890s, however, well-to-do pet lovers in greater New York had an option. In 1896, a small animal veterinarian practicing in Manhattan, Dr. Samuel Johnson, allowed a grieving client to bury her dog in a corner of his apple orchard in rural Hartsdale, New York. After a reporter friend publicized the burial, Dr. Johnson began to receive many more requests. The graveyard soon began to look like many picturesque cemeteries for people of the era, a place of repose for grieving survivors. Hartsdale Cemetery became a corporation to guarantee its existence into perpetuity, and it was soon imitated in other areas of the urban Northeast.

Singing canaries continued to be a popular pet in the twentieth century. Their breeding was an important cottage industry in Europe that no longer affected the Canary Island bird population. Breeders in the Harz Mountains in Germany provided the largest number of birds. They shipped out over 4,000 birds weekly. George Holden, owner of a grand pet store in New York City, informed his customers that the strongest canaries were held for the long trip to America. "Few ladies," he noted, "while caressing their pets and bestowing on them daily delicacies, imagine for a moment what dangers the feathered immigrants have passed in their younger days." In 1914, Philadelphia's Cugley and Mullen offered its best birds, golden opera singers, for $5.00, while an ordinary male canary cost $2.50. Among other favorite small pets were goldfish. Following a tradition that had begun in the mid-nineteenth century, households of the twentieth century often had a small glass globe with a short-lived goldfish that served as an "animated ornament." Commercial goldfish farming seems to have been the first successful aquaculture business in America. By the 1870s, fish farms had been established on Long Island, and goldfish were shipped throughout the United States from this northeastern breeding farm (Grier 2006, 245–47, 251–52).

Economic Life

WORK AND WORKPLACE

In the first four decades of the twentieth century, the number of people engaged in manufacturing remained steady. In 1900, 1.8 million people or 15 percent of the population of the Northeast were employed in manufacturing. By 1920, that figure rose to two and a half million people, which represented 14 percent of the population. In 1930, the first full year of the Great Depression, 2 million or 10 percent were employed in manufacturing, and in 1940, 1.9 million people or 9 percent of the population of the Northeast were engaged in manufacturing. By the mid-1920s, one of eight American workers was somehow engaged in the production, sales, service, or fueling of American automobiles, making that business the biggest American industry. At the end of the economic boom of the 1920s, the northeastern area of the United States (anchored by New York and Boston) had the highest annual per capita income in the country, about $1,000. Farmers in the Northeast made about $366 annually (U.S. Census 1920, 1930).

The nature of work, particularly in the industrial sector, was dramatically changed by the increased use of electricity. In 1905, less than 10 percent of all automated power nationally was electrical, but thereafter usage grew so rapidly that by 1930 the figure reached 80 percent. Electricity could drive small motors, reducing the need for elaborate systems of drive shafts, gears, and belts linking every factory mechanism to a central power source. Electricity could coordinate a series of machines with automatic feeding devices and moving belts, and it could also regulate other systems of production with temperature gauges, flow meters, shut-off devices, and other control mechanisms. The growing application of time-motion studies, based on Frederick W. Taylor's "scientific management," fit neatly with the shift to electricity to coordinate or run more complicated processes and order systems. Likewise, electric mixers and cranes sharply reduced the need for unskilled heavy labor. Although electrification displaced many workers, it did not reduce employment. Instead, it fostered new enterprises and created demand for different kinds of labor, for the most part semi-skilled, clerical, or service work. Electrification of the workplace helped account for the great surge in productivity per American worker in the 1920s and 1930s (Kyvig 2002, 55–56).

TRADE AND MARKETS

In 1919, enjoying an immense cash surplus from World War I profits, General Motors founder Will Durant established the General Motors Acceptance Corporation (GMAC) as a means of financing his automobiles. Credit buying soon spread to other areas of the American economy and revolutionized buying and marketing in the 1920s. Credit had always been available at the local general store in rural areas, and since the late nineteenth century it was available in city department stores, but GMAC made consumer credit possible for myriad larger durable goods.

Soon everything from cars to washing machines and vacuum cleaners could be bought for a little down and small monthly payments. Where previously Americans had been weaned on nostrums concerning the avoidance of debt, now ad men, salesmen, and marketers urged Americans to "increase your credit." Among America's middle class the measure of one's worth was not what one did or made, but what the family consumed (Kyvig 2002, 29–31).

Adding to the marketing boom of the 1920s was the radio. Radio advertising at first consisted of sponsoring entire programs. Advertisers counted on boosting sales by virtue of the good will generated by having their brand name associated with a popular program. Initially, broadcasters and advertisers alike were reluctant to intrude upon an audience by describing a specific product, much less proclaiming its virtues or indicating a price, but the potential power of radio as a marketing instrument overcame the early hesitation. Taking advantage of the preoccupation with hygiene, commercial advertising gave new emphasis to cleanliness and introduced new "social diseases" of body odor and bad breath, which could be cured with their products. Lifebuoy soap featured a man with "b.o." who luckily discovered what they were saying behind his back and saved himself future embarrassment and social ostracism by lathering up with Lifebuoy soap. Similar strategies were used for toothpaste and mouthwash. Listerine reached into an obscure medical journal to discover the word "halitosis" and produced a mouthwash that could rescue victims from this terrible affliction. Colgate initially dominated the toothpaste market, but Pepsodent sales skyrocketed after the company began sponsoring the popular radio show, *Amos 'n' Andy*.

Cigarette manufacturers devised new ad campaigns to keep their brands in the public's mind and to sustain the surge in cigarette use spurred by World War I military service and the disappearance of alcohol. "I'd walk a mile for a Camel" ads began appearing in 1921. Women smoking, formerly a sign of dubious character, was now encouraged as a symbol of newly achieved equality and youthful vigor. Ads depicted smokers as invariably attractive, fashionable, and healthy. And more specific reassurances such as "Not a cough in a carload" helped per capita cigarette consumption double during the 1920s.

The first decades of the century saw other marketing innovations, most of which were directed toward women and the home. Processed foods such as Van Camp's beans and Campbell's soup promised to reduce time spent in the kitchen; and vacuum cleaners, electric irons, and washing machines promised to reduce the time spent keeping the house tidy (Kyvig 2002, 128–30, 190–94).

CASTE AND CLASS EXPERIENCE

During the First World War over 500,000 African Americans migrated to northern cities looking for jobs that had been promised to them in wartime industry, and many of these migrants ended up in the Northeast urban corridor. This massive influx into cities caused tension with working-class whites competing for the same jobs, and sometimes space to work and play. Tensions ran high between the newly arrived African Americans and the native white population and also other newly arrived immigrants, particularly those from southern Italy.

As southern Italians moved into the Northeast, especially Boston, New York, and Philadelphia, at the turn of the century they experienced a level of racial prejudice not experienced by other European groups that had preceded them. These olive-skinned, kinky-haired, southern Italians represented a genetic ambiguity that upset previous American notions of black and white. Most Americans would have agreed with Senator Henry Cabot Lodge, who found the "Teutonic Italians" of northern Italy acceptable but who could not welcome the dark-skinned southerners whom nativists would have described as lazy, criminal, sexually irresponsible, and emotionally volatile.

Jack London's mother advised her son to avoid the Italians. "My mother had her theories," he recalled:

First, she steadfastly maintained that brunettes and all the tribe of dark eyed humans were deceitful. Needless to say, my mother was a blond. Next she was convinced that the dark eyed Latin races were profoundly sensitive, profoundly treacherous, and profoundly murderous. Again and again I heard her state, that if one offended an Italian, no matter how slightly and unintentionally, he was certain to retaliate by stabbing one in the back. That was her particular phrase, "stab you in the back." (London 1989, 14)

Among the derogatory names for Italians arriving at the turn of the century was "Guinea," implying their connection to the African slaves who had come from Guinea in western Africa. The Dillingham Commission's report on immigration to the 61st Congress in 1910 did not even include Italians in the white race. Described as *mezzogiorno* ("mid-day" people because of their dark tanned skin) by their northern compatriots, southern Italians struggled with blacks for jobs at the bottom of the social scale. In cities such as Philadelphia, Boston, and New York, southern Italians began taking over professions such as barber, bricklayer, garbage remover, and restaurateur, formerly the domains of blacks. This set the background for the most intense immigrant rivalry of the period from 1900–1940, especially in cities of the Northeast. Historian Arnold Shankman divides the black–Italian relationship into three periods prior to World War II: the first period from 1880 to 1900 of intense rivalry over housing and jobs, a second period of relative peace and accommodation from 1900 to 1930, then the third period from 1930 to 1936 of renewed competition spurred on by the Great Depression. The third period of animosity was also aggravated by Mussolini's attack on Ethiopia (Orsi 1992, 313–47).

URBAN AND RURAL EXPERIENCE

One of the most important defining events of the first decades of the twentieth century, along with war and immigration, was the population shift from rural to urban areas of the country. In the Northeast, urbanization was a trend that had begun before the Civil War era. Census information documents the remarkable growth in the major cities of the Northeast in the last decades of the nineteenth century. From 1870 to 1890, for example, the city of New York grew from 1.4 million to 2.8 million, which represented a growth of over 100 percent, while the state in general grew from 4.8 to 6 million, a growth of 36 percent. A look at Boston, another major city in the region, reveals similar numbers. Boston grew from 270,00 to 611,000, or 122 percent, in the two post–Civil War decades, while the state of Massachusetts grew from 1.5 million to 2.2 million or 46 percent. This trend continued into the twentieth century and accelerated as major urban areas of the Northeast became home to a new wave of immigrants arriving around the turn of the century.

Differences between urban and rural life are as old as the republic. In the new century, however, because of revolutions in technology, corporate management, and transportation, cities were changing and adapting rapidly to a new life, while rural areas seemed to remain the same. Cities, where young innocent girls worked next to men, many of whom were immigrants, where saloons could be found on every corner, and where dance halls and nickelodeons thrived, seemed to those of rural America to be threatening the very moral fabric of the country. On the other hand, the city dweller who could read the latest news from his daily paper, and a decade later could listen to the radio, and could go downtown to see the latest films, and discover the latest fashions, and read the latest magazines, began to see the rural dweller as someone hopelessly mired in a passé irrelevant world.

The self-proclaimed spokesman in the 1920s of the superiority of the city over rural life was H. L. Mencken, a Baltimore writer and publisher of magazines such as *The Smart Set,* who waged his personal war against prejudice, bigotry, and ignorance, which he believed was cultivated in the decaying soil of rural America. Often referring to the inhabitants of rural America as "yokels," Mencken believed that rural Americans, with their best blood all drained to the cities, were probably hopelessly uneducable. Sound ideas make no more sense to them, he chortled, than decent drinks. But "educate them we must," he insisted, and although "the job of enlightening [the yokel] may be difficult, it should be worth trying. . . . For in the long run," he asserted, "the cities of the United States will have to throw off the hegemony of these morons. They have run the country long enough," he protested, "and made it sufficiently ridiculous. Once we get rid of camp meeting rule," he concluded, "we'll get rid simultaneously of the Klan, the anti saloon league and the Methodist board of temperance, prohibition, and public morals, and we'll get rid of [those politicians who] flatter and fawn over the hookworm carriers to further their own fortunes" (Mencken 1960, 213).

One aspect of life that dramatically drew differences between urban and rural life was the family. A White House Conference in 1932 discovered in the middle-class urban family a pattern emphasizing emotional ties and unity that differed from an existing rural pattern stressing discipline, authority, and hierarchical responsibilities. Urban children, for example, confided in parents much more frequently than rural children and were decidedly less hostile to parents. Children in urban families were punished less frequently, and open demonstrations of affection like kissing were more common. So, too, children in urban families were less often incorporated into a household work routine with specific allocation of chores and responsibilities than were children on the farm. Urban families required a minimal number of tasks, usually related to the care of one's own things, rather than active participation in a family work regime. Urban families shied away from elaborate household routines of all kinds and engaged in fewer activities as a unit. Church going, for example, was a less common family activity in the city than in the country. There was altogether less physical interaction and a larger measure of personal independence granted to urban children, who were given time and occasion to engage in extensive extrafamilial activities, especially with peers.

The average urban adolescent was away from home between four and six evenings every week. Rural adolescents, in contrast, were home much more frequently. Urban adolescents were granted a large measure of independence. In describing different patterns of family organization, the White House report concluded, "At one extreme is the family with harsh and stern methods of control . . . [with] little effort on the part of the parent to understand the child or gain his confidence. At the other extreme is the family with guidance rather than punishment as the means of control and a sympathetic understanding of children." By the 1920s and 1930s, middle-class urban families were clearly moving in the direction of the latter norm.

Democratically integrated, and emotionally bound together, middle-class urban families had become small, informal, emotionally intense, and private units. A very specific kind of family style had developed among the native urban middle class. Families were small, planned, and actively concerned with the welfare of the children. Women expected that marriage and family would provide them with a variety of personal satisfactions and a scope for personal expression. Children were less tied into a household routine of work and play and were permitted to partake freely in peer-centered activities. The decline in family size in urban areas resulted from this new sense of family. To the urban family that was to a larger degree a unit of consumption than production, children were not an economic asset, whereas rural children were usually incorporated into a work routine in which they could contribute their part to a productive enterprise. In this rural context, the father was production director, manager, and instructor as well as parent.

This description of the native middle-class family does not hold for the masses of lower-class immigrants living in cities. No doubt the children of immigrant families were sent to work at an early age and they were expected to contribute their meager salaries to the family income. Nevertheless, from childhood to adulthood, a gulf in manners of life, education, family, labor, and entertainment between rural and urban societies grew much deeper in the first half of the twentieth century (Fass 1977, 88).

ANIMAL HUSBANDRY AND HUNTING AND FISHING

From the mid-nineteenth century through the first decades of the twentieth century, economic forces had been drawing dairy farmers into the commercial farming industry. Many farmers in the Northeast sought a cash crop that would be suitable for intensive mixed farming on relatively poor but high-priced land and that would also shelter them in some way from competition with products grown on the better, cheaper land further west. Production of fluid milk for consumption in the large cities of the Northeast filled this need. Drawing on a long tradition of providing milk, cheese, and other dairy products, farmers in the Northeast expanded such activities as market demand, improved transportation, especially trucks and refrigerated railroad cars, and changing production techniques such as better feed, pasteurization, and mechanized milking made dairy farming profitable. Distribution was limited until refrigerated cars expanded the market reach from a mere 10- to 30-mile range in the nineteenth century to as far as 275 miles away by 1910 (Bateman 1968, 255–73).

On the morning of August 10, 1913, the Boston *Post* headlined its lead story "Naked He Plunged into Main Woods to Live Alone Two Months." The article that followed told how six days previously Joseph Knowles, a husky part-time illustrator in his mid-forties, had disrobed in a cold drizzle at the edge of a lake in northeastern Maine, smoked a final cigarette, shaken hands around a group of sportsmen and reporters, and trudged off into the wilderness. The *Post* explained that Knowles had gone into the woods to be a primitive man for 60 days. He took no equipment of any kind and promised to remain completely isolated, living off the land "as Adam lived."

For the next two months Joe Knowles was the talk of Boston. He provided information about his experiment with periodic dispatches written with charcoal or birch bark. These reports printed in the *Post* revealed to an astonished and delighted public that Knowles was succeeding in the planned reversion to the primitive. Using heat from the friction of two sticks, he obtained fire. Clothing came from woven strips of bark. Knowles's first few meals consisted of berries, but soon he varied his diet with trout, partridge, even venison. On August 24, a front-page banner in the

Post announced that Knowles had lured a bear into a pit, killed it with a club, and fashioned a coat from its skin.

When on October 4, 1913, a disheveled but healthy Knowles finally emerged from the Maine woods extolling the virtues of the primitive way of life, he was swept up in a wave of enthusiasm. His triumphant return to Boston included stops at Augusta, Lewiston, and Portland with speeches before throngs of 8 to 10 thousand people. The cheers persisted in spite of a fine of $205, which the unyielding Maine Fish and Game Commission imposed on Knowles for killing a bear out of season. But Maine's welcome paled next to Boston's. The city had not had a hero like the "modern primitive man" in a generation. Thousands lined the streets through which his motorcade passed. Still clad in bearskin, Knowles went to Boston Common, where an estimated 20,000 persons waited. Even when the *Post*'s rival newspaper the Boston *American* presented evidence that Knowles was a fraud whose wilderness saga had actually occurred in a secret snug cabin, a vociferous denial arose in reply. Quite a few Americans wanted to believe in the authenticity of the "Nature Man."

The most significant fact about the Joe Knowles craze was that it occurred at all. One hundred fifty years earlier, or even 50 years earlier, anyone undertaking such an intentional and complete reversion to the primitive would have been thought demented. Aside from a few artists and writers, Americans before Knowles's generation regarded the wild as something alien and hostile. Their energies were largely directed to conquering wilderness and destroying savages in the name of progress, religion, and indeed survival.

But, by 1890, the census takers had told Americans that the frontier was closed. The last dangerous Indians had been subdued at Wounded Knee, and the wilderness had been transposed into gardens and farms. With the passing of the frontier there was a collective nostalgia for the untamed wilderness and a sense of something being lost in the American tradition. Clear cutting had mowed down woodlands, and unplanned growth and the use of chemicals in manufacturing and even agriculture polluted many water sources in the Northeast. The disappearance of various birds associated with America's noble past added to a sense of urgency. In three widely read articles published in the *Atlantic Monthly* between 1896 and 1906, historian Frederick Jackson Turner suggested that the nation had reason to be alarmed at the distance it had come from its primitive past. Turner's articles verbalized a concern that went beyond the readership of the *Atlantic Monthly*, prompting at the turn of the century an interest in developing a national park system to save the last of the American wilderness. The state constitution of New York in 1894 declared that the purpose of the Adirondack State Park would be to preserve the American wilderness. And in 1895 the New York legislature created the Fisheries, Game and Forest Commission to take on functions related to fish and game regulations, hunting seasons, and poaching. Similar actions were taken in other states of the Northeast as well as the rest of the nation, as legislators responded to the concerns of many Americans that in losing the wilderness the country was losing at least a part of its soul. These events, along with the founding of the Boy Scouts in 1910 to give boys representing the next generation a chance to return to the wilderness, document a dramatic change in the thinking of many Americans, who were now more concerned with preserving the wilderness than with taming it (Nash 1966, 517–37).

Intellectual Life

SCIENCE

Perhaps the most curious folk hero of the early twentieth century was a scientist, Albert Einstein. From the moment he first visited the United States in 1921, the mild-mannered and eccentric physicist captivated the American public. The disheveled, odd-looking Einstein became synonymous with the word *genius*. Few scientists, much less the general public, understood Einstein's theories of relativity, made public in 1905 and 1916 and formulated in the deceptively simple equation $E = mc^2$. When the scientist visited President Warren G. Harding in 1923, the *New York Times* reported in a comically understated headline: "Einstein Idea Puzzles Harding." Einstein's theory of relativity illustrated that time, space, and motion are not absolute but rather are relative to the observer and the observer's motion. Relativity posited a radically different universe from the orderly machine described by Isaac Newton more than two hundred years earlier. The Einsteinian universe seemed shockingly relativistic compared to the orderly Newtonian universe it replaced (Harrell, et al. 2005, 864).

During much of the twentieth century, scientific invention and technological advancement in the United States were integrally tied to the nation's intense entrepreneurial spirit. Perhaps like all great scientists and experimenters in the past, Americans like Thomas Alva Edison sought to move science and technology forward to (among other things) make money. Edison's invention of the incandescent light bulb in 1879 marked the beginning of its practical use. Edison and his laboratory assistants quickly thereafter developed lamp sockets, household wiring, and generators to make electric lighting systems functional. In 1882, Edison began offering home electric generators. In the same year he also opened in New York City the first central generating station to provide power over utility lines. Within two years 500 homes and several thousand businesses were using electric lights. Also by the beginning of the twentieth century, direct current arc lamp streetlights had replaced older gas-powered lighting systems in cities in the Northeast and elsewhere. Electrically driven streetcars, industrial machinery, and elevators for new high-rise buildings appeared as well (Kyvig 2002, 55–56). In the end, the Westinghouse alternating current proved safer and more economical than direct current in supplying electricity for homes and businesses. But whatever the method, electricity remade daily lives in urban America.

EDUCATION

By 1900, compulsory attendance at a public or private school was universal in the Northeast. According to the 1920 census, 85.7 percent of children aged 5 to

17 years old in the Northeast were in private or public schools. This percentage would rise to 95.5 percent by 1940. The average school year was 35 weeks in length. While segregation was not the law outside of the South, most communities in the Northeast experienced de facto segregation, because in urban areas the tradition of neighborhood-based schools continued. In the poorer sections of cities, however, schools were as diverse as their neighborhoods. John Loftus, principal of an elementary school in Brooklyn, described his school in 1920 as typical of the area, being large and overcrowded, with a significant foreign-born, shifting population.

When the century began, students in the Northeast were learning much the way their grandparents did, that is, by rote memory and recitation. Recalling his classroom days around the turn of the century, one person recalled, "the drill was very thorough in what was then called mental arithmetic." In this drill a student had to stand on his feet and think quickly and accurately before the gaze of the whole class and his teacher, who fired questions such as, "How many square inches in a piece of paper six inches long and four inches wide," or "reduce to lowest terms: 12/16; 24/36; 28/49." These tests in addition, multiplication, and division were designed and thought to be a good form of mental gymnastics. After the math session the students' attention turned to spelling. One Buffalo student recalled spelling as the *pièce de resistance* and test of scholarship in all district schools. Teachers often raised the art of spelling to a competition called spelling bees, where students stood along a classroom wall facing another group of students. They stood until they misspelled a word. The last person standing was declared the champion speller. "Bees" were held between classmates, between different classes, even between different schools. Disputes were adjudicated by the *Webster's Blue Back Speller,* which entered the American classroom in the late eighteenth century and was still around to greet students in the early twentieth. Published in the United States by the D. Appleton Company, by 1890 it was the company's best-selling book, reaching the 90 million mark that year. Not restricting itself to spelling, the book also included moral lessons for its young readers. A typical sentence in the book advised, "If good words and gentle means will not reclaim the wicked, they must be dealt with in a more severe manner."

Ranking with spelling and arithmetic as studies good for mental discipline stood the study of grammar. For hours students would drill and memorize parts of speech and their use. "Grammar," declared Clarence Darrow, "was a hideous nightmare. I tried and tried but even now can hardly tell an adjective from an adverb, and I do not know that I care." Equally important to grammar, spelling, and mathematics was the art of writing. By the 1890s, good handwriting became considered a sign of social class, and a key to upward mobility. This belief continued well into the twentieth century, as farmers, laborers, mechanics, and others who worked with their hands and who wanted their children to have white-collar jobs urged them to practice their handwriting. Neat penmanship was a requirement to be a bookkeeper or a clerk in a government office and thus promised a working-class child a more refined occupation and a foothold into the middle class. Every day, students took out paper and pen and practiced their cursive writing. The Palmer teaching method promoted by Austin Palmer in the early 1900s soon became the most popular handwriting system in the United States. Under it, students were taught to copy a uniform style of cursive writing with rhythmic motions. Left-handers were usually made to use their right hands. Whether in rural or urban areas, in the first decades of the century, the school day maintained the same monotonous demands of repetition, memorization, and recitation (Sullivan, 1927, vol. 2, 120–37).

In the 1920s, with the advent of the school bus, consolidation became possible, and improvement in education came rapidly as it became possible to bring students from a wide area to one central location. Consolidated schools allowed teachers to concentrate in specific subjects or age groups, and they permitted students to attend classes with people of equal age and abilities. By the end of the 1920s the number of one-teacher schools had dropped by 25 percent, and by the end of the 1930s it had dropped by half. Those one-room schools that remained were for the most part in rural areas, not in the predominantly urban Northeast.

Teaching methods also changed radically in the 1920s as a curriculum based on indoctrination, repetition, drills, and conformity gave way to a project- or activity-based curriculum. Typical of the new style were the following classroom activities outlined by the principal of a Brooklyn elementary school:

1. *Conference and Discussion*. Holding frequent class or small conferences providing real discussion by children with other children.
2. *Trips and other exploratory activities*. Providing experiences outside the class or school.
3. *Research activities*. Raising problems and placing responsibility on children to seek solutions in their textbooks or wherever else they can be found.
4. *Dramatic experiences*. Making believe, playing store or travel bureau, writing and acting plays and performances, reproducing plays in books, giving puppet shows.
5. *Construction activities*. Reproducing in miniature the signal features of whatever is being studied.
6. *Pictorial and graphic representations and interpretation*. Illustrating with maps, charts, scrapbooks, logs, or other written, visual, or graphic records.
7. *Culminating Activities*. Organizing exhibits or assembly programs or demonstrations for other classes or parents.
8. *Evaluation Activities*. Preparing summaries, outlines, reviews, reports, tests, and listing most important things to remember.

"These activities are not to be isolated," the principal advised, "trips for example are one form of research." He also suggested that, "In all of the procedures the children should have as large a responsibility as possible." The Brooklyn principal's directives show that in a very short time education in grammar schools, at least in some sections of the urban Northeast, had come a very long way (Loftue 1943, 71–72).

Increasing the quality of schools meant raising requirements for qualified teachers. By World War I, at least a two-year associate's degree was required to teach in grammar schools, and a four-year degree was required for high school teachers. In larger urban areas of the Northeast, school curriculum expanded beyond science, reading, history, and mathematics, and some high schools began to offer vocational education in agriculture, home economics, and mechanical arts such as wood and metalwork. Attention also began to be paid to music and physical education. One area that declined in these decades was foreign language, as the rising tide of postwar isolationism found its way into the classroom.

The increase in high school graduates, together with the growing demand for better-educated teachers, helped stimulate a rise in college attendance in the 1920s and 1930s. The number of 18–21-year-olds attending college doubled between 1919 and 1940 from 8 percent to 16 percent and overall enrollment grew from 600,000 to 1.5 million. The private and elite colleges and universities more prominent in the northeastern states, generally smaller to begin with and often restricted to a single sex, grew more slowly than the public ones. These elite schools regularly excluded or severely limited the admission of immigrants, Jews, and African Americans. All but the latter found public institutions, especially urban schools such as City College of New York, more hospitable.

Like secondary schools, colleges and universities underwent curriculum reform and expansion in the years between the wars. As the number of faculty tripled, the variety of courses increased proportionately. Courses and programs such as business, engineering, fine arts, and education, and new approaches to the study of human society such as anthropology, political science, and social science were added to the traditional liberal arts courses.

In this era, W.E.B. Du Bois, born on February 23, 1868, in Great Barrington, Massachusetts, began a revolution in African American scholarship. After receiving a bachelor's degree from Harvard in 1890, Du Bois immediately began working toward his master's and doctoral degrees. His doctoral thesis, *The Suppression of the African Slave Trade in America*, remains an authoritative work on that subject and is the first volume in Harvard's Historical Series.

In 1896, with his doctorate degree behind him, Du Bois accepted a special fellowship at the University of Pennsylvania to conduct a research project in Philadelphia's seventh ward slums. The outcome of this work was published as *The Philadelphia Negro*. This was the first time such a scientific approach to studying social phenomena was undertaken, and as a consequence Du Bois became acknowledged as a father of social science.

After the completion of the study, Du Bois accepted a position at Atlanta University and for the next 13 years there he wrote and studied Negro morality, urbanization, Negroes in business, college-bred Negroes, the Negro church, and Negro crime. He also repudiated the widely held view of Africa as a vast cultural cipher by presenting a historical version of complex, cultural development throughout Africa. His work became the cornerstone of all the work done on black studies in the ensuing decades, and every black studies academic program that currently exists owes a great intellectual debt to Du Bois (http//:www.duboislc.org/man.html).

LITERATURE

In literature the century opened with a new movement called naturalism. One of the leading figures of this movement was Theodore Dreiser, who used the Northeast as the setting for some of his work, which searched for some pattern of order other than theological, romantic, or idealistic in what he perceived to be the prevailing chaos. In his most famous work, *Sister Carrie*, which is set in Chicago (although it could have been New York or any other large city of the Northeast), he presents individuals as powerless figures caught between their own animal natures and the pressures of their social environment. In addition to Dreiser, other popular writers of the prewar era included naturalist Jack London and Stephen Crane, who despite dying at age 29 in 1900 remained popular in the first decades of the new century.

Books that raised social consciousness were also popular in America in the first decade of the twentieth century. Among them were Upton Sinclair's *The Jungle* (1906), which exposed abuses in the meatpacking industry; Frank Norris's *The Octopus* (1901), which revealed the unethical practices of the Southern Pacific Railway; Ida Tarbell's *The History of Standard Oil* (1904), which warned of the power and abuses of monopolies; and Jacob Riis's *How the Other Half Lives* (1890), which raised middle America's consciousness of the slum conditions suffered by America's urban poor.

Finley Peter Dunne's fictional Mr. Dooley, the barkeeper, and his friend Mr. Hennissy shared humorous folk philosophy with the readers of the daily newspapers of the first decades of the twentieth century. Mark Sullivan, author of *Our Times*, noted that "Mr. Dooley was not only popular but a useful institution to a whole generation of American Life." He supplied Americans with folk philosophy, wisdom, and compact common sense, and to public figures he provided a good dose of satire. After Theodore Roosevelt wrote an account of his exploits in the Spanish American war, Mr. Dooley proclaimed, "If I was him I'd call the book 'Alone in Cubia' [sic]." And as far as building monuments to heroes was concerned, Mr. Dooley believed that when a grateful republic builds an arch to a conquering hero they ought to build it of brick so that we can have something convenient to hurl after him when he has passed by (Sullivan 1927, vol. 1, 290, 340).

In the postwar era, American reading tastes changed; naturalist influences of Dreiser and London continued, especially in the writing of Ernest Hemingway, but other young writers of the 1920s and 1930s, like F. Scott Fitzgerald and John Dos Passos wrote popular novels such as *The Great Gatsby* (1925) and *Manhattan Transfer* (1925), which caused Americans to look inward and critically take measure of their own changing values. In the 1930s, as economic hardship gripped most Americans, novels with a social message such as Hemingway's *To Have and Have Not* (1937) and John Steinbeck's *Grapes of Wrath* (1939) became popular once again, and even Margaret Mitchell's dreamy and romantic journey into the antebellum South, *Gone with the Wind* (1936), had a message for the Depression-wracked country: like those southerners who saw their lives destroyed by the Civil War, those who were broken by the Depression could rise up again. As the heroine Scarlett O'Hara proclaimed "Tomorrow is another day!"

In the 1920s, the black neighborhoods of Harlem in New York City witnessed a flourishing of various arts, particularly literary. Dozens of writers, led by Langston Hughes and Countee Cullen and novelists Claude McKay and Zora Neale Hurston, created an impressive body of new literature dealing with the African American perspective and experience. The philosopher Alain Locke gathered some of the best black writing into a 1928 book titled *The New Negro*. Two years later in *Black Manhattan*, James Weldon Johnson underscored the progress African American intellectuals were making. The visual art of the Harlem Renaissance was an attempt at developing a new African American aesthetic in the fine arts. African American painters, sculptors, and graphic artists set out to establish their artistic community mainly through improvisation and style. Believing that their life experiences were valuable sources of material for their art, these artists created an iconography representative of the Harlem Renaissance era. Thematic content included Africa as a source of inspiration; African American history, folk idioms, music, and religion all figured into the art, as did a keen sense of social injustice. The main factors contributing to the development of the Harlem Renaissance were African American urban migration, trends toward experimentation throughout the country, and the rise of radical African American intellectuals.

The Harlem Renaissance transformed African American identity and history, but it also transformed American culture in general. Never before had so many Americans read the thoughts of African Americans and embraced the African American community's productions, expressions, and style. Their collective efforts not only established this new African American identity, but also contributed significantly to the development of modern American culture.

COMMUNICATION

Newspaper and magazine reading was a widespread activity in an era when it remained the best means to obtain low-cost, detailed, up-to-date information about what was happening in the world beyond a person's immediate reach. Cheap mass-distribution newspapers appeared in the late nineteenth century, and by the end of the century great rivalries such as those between the Boston *American* and the Boston *Post,* and the New York *Herald* and the New York *Journal* developed among the major publishers in the big cities. Such competition often led to the publication of outlandish stories that critics decried as "yellow journalism." By the 1920s, the ratio of the number of copies of newspapers sold to the total population stood at one to three. The advent of the newspaper syndicates and the expansion of wire services meant that other than local matters, the same stories, written by Associated Press, Hearst, or Scripps-Howard, would routinely appear in newspapers across the country. While across the country more than two thousand daily and six thousand weekly newspapers, each with their own editorial position, were being published, throughout the period the bulk of the news came from relatively few sources.

Magazines were just as available as newspapers to a widely read public. Nearly 4,500 periodicals were published each year by 1925, with a combined circulation of 180 million copies per issue. Thanks to Rural Free Delivery, which was established in 1896, rural families also shared the benefits of the rapid rise of newspaper and magazine publication. In the first decade of the twentieth century, the urban middle class enjoyed magazines such as *McClure's,* a New York magazine that exposed wrongdoers in the public arena. In 1902, *McClure's* hired Lincoln Steffens to do an exposé on corruption in politics in the major cities of America; the magazine also hired Ida

Tarbell to investigate the excesses of the Standard Oil monopoly, and Ray Stannard Baker to expose the transgressions of the U.S. Steel Trust. In response to what he considered the heavy-handedness of these exposés, President Theodore Roosevelt called them "muckrakers," a name that stuck throughout the century. In the rural Northeast, the preferred magazines were those that provided farm and livestock information; the most popular of these publications included *Grit*, *Farm Journal*, and *Rural New Yorker*.

During the golden age of magazines, from 1890 until 1915, a number of developments converged to enable Northeast publishers, such as *McClure's*, and its chief competitors, *Munsey's* and *Cosmopolitan*, to spread their message across the nation. Postal rates decreased, while Rural Free Delivery rapidly expanded. High-speed presses were becoming commonplace, and Frederic Ives's perfection of halftone photoengraving enabled magazines to print high-quality illustrations at a fraction of their original cost. The middle-class market for inexpensive periodical literature expanded, causing advertising revenues to soar as manufacturers scrambled for a share of the profits. By 1903, the yearly flow of customer goods exceeded 25 billion dollars, and magazines and newspapers soon accommodated this tremendous growth by becoming the central medium for commercial advertisement. Economic and technological factors enabled the magazine business to thrive. Inexpensive periodicals flooded newsstands, and had an "unprecedented . . . influence on the social scene." During the 1920s and 1930s, new advertising-laden magazines catering to middle-class urban and suburban readers continued to appear, among them *Time* (1923), *Better Homes and Gardens* (1924), *The New Yorker* (1925), *Life* (1936), and *Look* (1937). *Look* and *Life* were new magazines that appeared rather late and that developed in response to the new communication rival, radio. *Look* and *Life* magazines relied on striking photographs more than text to provide the public with something radio could not: visual images of newsworthy events and people. But radio would revolutionize communication by bringing live events into the family home, an accomplishment that no magazine could rival (Kyvig 2002, 190–92).

Much of the pioneer experimentation in radio occurred in the Northeast. The first known radio program in the United States was broadcast by Reginald Aubrey Fessenden from his experimental station at Brant Rock, Massachusetts, on Christmas Eve of 1906. Two musical selections, the reading of a poem, and a short talk apparently constituted the program, which was heard by ship wireless operators within a radius of several hundred miles. In 1915, Lee Fe Forest, using the vacuum tube equipment he had developed during the previous decade, began broadcasting phonograph music and lectures in New York. In 1916, he broadcasted the Harvard–Yale football game and the presidential results, including an incorrect report that Woodrow Wilson had been defeated. Also in 1916 in New York, David Sarnoff proposed as entirely feasible the broadcasting of music, lectures, news, and sports over several channels to radio music boxes that combined receivers and loudspeakers. In Pittsburgh at 8:00 P.M. on November 2, 1920, Westinghouse station KDKA went on the air, broadcasting from the roof of the company's factory. KDKA was the first station to obtain a government license to operate a general broadcasting company. Soon Westinghouse established stations throughout the Northeast, providing regular programming in music, news, and sports to listeners. In the fall of 1919, the Radio Corporation of America was formed with government encouragement and the support of the General Electric Corporation (G.E.).

One of radio's early and important influences was the development of an appreciation for classical music. Once introduced to classical music, the general public took a liking to it, and between 1928 and 1939 the number of professional symphony orchestras in the country increased from 10 to 17. Including the number of part-time or less professional ones in smaller cities, the number came to 286. And whereas music instruction in public schools was almost unheard of before 1920, by 1940 there were 30,000 school orchestras and 20,000 bands. Some radio stations even had their own orchestras, such as the NBC Symphony Orchestra led by the internationally renowned conductor Arturo Toscanini. In 1932, Texaco Oil Company began sponsoring weekly performances from the Metropolitan Opera House in New York. It was also through the radio that Americans became familiar with regional music, which until the radio could only be heard where it had originated. In addition to music, drama and comedy became regular fare on the radio. The first shows were largely directed at middle-class women and were broadcast in the daytime hours when it was assumed that the stay-at-home audience would be primarily female. Thus advertisers of domestic products dominated the airwaves. These shows thus received the pejorative name of "soap operas."

HEALTH AND MEDICINE

Ever since the Civil War, a belief in the importance of keeping clean had been spreading in the United States as a result of new theories, which related germs and disease to dirt and spoiled food and sewage. The increased availability of piped water and indoor plumbing in the post–Civil War era gave way in the early twentieth century, at least among middle-class families, to the dedication of an entire room in the house as a separate toilet and bathroom. World War I stirred further concern about personal hygiene. The shocking rejection as physically unfit of nearly one-third of World War I draftees called notice to the deficiencies in American hygiene.

Further anxiety was aroused by the influenza epidemic of 1918–1919. This worldwide scourge was one of the most fatal in history. Estimates put the number of dead at 20 million worldwide and perhaps as many as 500 thousand in the United States. Appearing first on the Eastern Seaboard in military bases, it spread quickly across the country as World War I came to an end. On September 19, 1918, the *New York Times* raised suspicions that the epidemic was part of a germ warfare plan launched by the Germans. At another point it was suspected that it was a variant of the pneumonic plague that had been present in China since 1910 and had been brought to the United States in 1918 by 200,000 "coolies" who entered the United States in 1918 in transit to France. All these rumors fueled the rising anti-immigration feelings that would lead to strong anti-immigration laws in the 1920s. Finally health officials decided the flu originated in Spain and it became known by that name. On September 25, the Schenectady *Union Star* ran a report, "Spanish Disease Hits Schenectady," and in the month of October the town lost 325 people to the disease. While the disease reached its peak that month, the local governments in the Northeast ordered all schools, movie theaters, churches, lodges, and places of entertainment closed. Newspapers began to print rules of hygiene along with reports on the death toll. Of every 1,000 affected with the disease, 19 died. In Philadelphia the normal death rate went up 700 percent and there was a shortage of coffins until J. G. Brill, the streetcar makers, began making them in their woodworking shop. Workers stayed home or worked in staggered shifts to avoid public congestion. Shipyards and munitions factories in the Northeast shut down. People also avoided streetcars and stopped using the telephone.

The city bacteriologist of New York City announced on October 2 that he had discovered an antiflu serum, and a similar announcement came from Dr. Warren Stoen, the city bacteriologist of Schenectady, New York. The local paper reported that the vaccine "is proving highly effective." Responding to the news, 12,362 people in Schenectady were vaccinated. By the end of the month the worst had passed. By November 4, churches, schools, and theaters throughout the Northeast reopened, and what local papers described as the worst epidemic in history had passed. By early 1919 the pandemic vanished as spontaneously as it had erupted, but for years thereafter it would haunt Americans. Everyone knew someone who had died from the pandemic, and for years thereafter it left a train of Bright's disease, cardiac illness, and pulmonary tuberculosis (Wells 2000, 187; Sullivan 1927, vol. 5, 652–53).

The epidemic accelerated a concern for hygiene that had been developing since the early years of the century. In the early 1900s, elementary schools' curricula began to include health classes, which instructed children to wash their hands before each meal, brush their teeth twice a day, and practice other habits of cleanliness. Commercial advertising of deodorants, bath soaps, and toothpaste also raised personal hygiene consciousness, and the new electric household appliances like the vacuum cleaner and washing machine in electrified urban areas helped women wage war against dirt in the home. Practices of women's personal hygiene also changed with the mass production of sanitary napkins, which by the turn of the century could be purchased from the *Sears Roebuck Catalogue*. In the 1920s, Kimberly Clark Company began advertising a mass-produced disposable sanitary napkin it called Kotex. Originally a middle-class measure of refinement, the product transcended class by the 1930s and was used by working-class and immigrant women as well (Kyvig 2002, 128–30).

Revolutions in medical technology, and the major social changes occurring in the first third of the twentieth century, radically altered the mission of hospitals, especially in the urban areas. In response to the growing need for health services, particularly in the cities, in 1904 Dr. John Brannan promised that the greatest hospital in the world would be erected in New York City. With those words he unveiled plans for the rebuilding of Bellevue Hospital. The project would take 10 years and $11 million to accomplish and when completed would cover three city blocks and house

3,000 patients. The hospital was a reflection of what the residents of large American cities had come to expect. Like public libraries, parks, waterworks, subways, and great bridges, the new hospital was an expression of urban vitality and resourcefulness. Around the same time, the great and ancient private New York City Hospital also made a historic decision. Resisting pressures by some members of the board to relocate to White Plains, the city decided to seek a new location in Manhattan, where they could continue their mission to serve the people of New York City.

Both of these hospitals were responding to challenges the new century brought them. Up until the twentieth century, a hospital could provide little more remedial care for a person than could be received at home. But with the advance of scientific medicine at the end of the nineteenth and early twentieth century, including the use of antiseptics and anesthetics during surgery, introduced at the end of the nineteenth century, and the introduction of the x-ray in the first decade of the twentieth century, blood transfusions in the 1920s, and antibiotics in the 1930s, new technology rapidly transformed the field of medicine, and hospitals from the first decade of the twentieth century onward began to provide a scientific health care that homes could not provide. Prior to the twentieth century, a hospital was basically a place to rest, and middle- and upper-class patients preferred to remain at home to recover or die, rather than expose themselves to the germs, diseases, and odors of the hospital wards dominated by the working class. But as science expanded, so too did the possibilities for surviving illness, and the hospital alternative began to appear more favorable.

This explosion of medical technology transformed the mission of hospitals. Until the twentieth century, public and private hospitals shared a common mission. Regardless of the source of funding—philanthropy in the case of private hospitals, and taxes in the case of public hospitals—the purpose of each was to provide a place of rest and recovery for the poor. An occasional wealthy patient might check into a private hospital from time to time, but this was not the normal patient. As technology made hospital care more complex, and care became more specialized and more expensive, private and public hospitals began to move into separate spheres in search of funding. The private hospitals such as New York City Hospital, depending on private funding, saw patient revenue as a new source of income and would create such innovations as the semi-private room and health insurance in order to court middle- and upper-class patients. The public hospitals such as Bellevue also built alliances with universities, providing patients and space in return for qualified doctors and new technology. And to increase public funding, they began to offer high-quality health care to the poor for little or no cost. Being publicly funded, public hospitals would also be less resistant to the social changes of the first decades of the twentieth century. They would admit female physicians, they would integrate, and they would accept unionization long before private hospitals did so (Opdycke 1999, 17–39).

In the Northeast, cities large and small began to see health care as a public responsibility. In 1905, for example, Schenectady issued a series of health codes regulating a variety of health matters. Perhaps the most important of these was the effort to provide a cleaner, healthier food supply. In 1909, the Schenectady Bureau of Health claimed that its efforts since 1905 to inspect milk producers and dealers deserved credit for reduced infant mortality. By 1917 northeastern towns and cities required milk to be sold in sealed containers and to be pasteurized. Education joined science in the fight to improve life expectancy. A campaign to control tuberculosis in 1908 combined direct action such as fumigation with a broad effort made to inform the public of the causes of tuberculosis. Diphtheria, one of the few diseases that could be cured by an antitoxin developed in 1894, was also aggressively attacked through education and injection. The campaign began in 1909 but was not considered a success until 1926, because many parents, especially immigrants, refused to call a doctor in time to avail their children of the free antitoxin. Schenectady's public health measures seem to have been remarkably successful, and in 1920 it was considered a model city regarding public health (Wells 2000, 181–82).

Material Life

FOOD

In upper middle- and middle-class homes in the Northeast, eating patterns began to change in the new century. Well-to-do Americans in urban areas, particularly in the Northeast, made French cuisine fashionable. The diet included various entrées with sophisticated sauces, soups, salads, and desserts. French diets demanded servants for preparation and serving, so the French menu became a symbol of status in the late nineteenth and early twentieth century. The urban middle class attempted to copy this style as much as they were able. With less domestic help the middle class made use of the rapidly developing convenience of processed foods. Fine cuts of meat previously only available on a daily basis from the local butcher were becoming available in packaged and processed form from the great meatpacking companies led by Armour and Swift. Professional bakers, canners of fruits and vegetables, processors of dairy products led by Sealtest and Borden, all contributed to the ever more sophisticated and varied processed food industry, which made practically everything edible available in some packaged form or another at reasonable prices. By the end of the 1930s, even frozen foods were available to the consumer fortunate enough to have a freezer in which to store them. Sugar refiners completed this processed meal diet. After World War I, with the decline of immigration and thus the decline of servants in middle-class households, more families came to depend on the convenience of processed food as food preparation became part of the housewife's responsibility. Immigrant families resisted the trend in modernization and continued to eat foods familiar to them. Italians and Chinese especially would remain steadfast in their eating habits, and eventually many of their foods would be assimilated into the American cuisine.

As the urban workforce expanded, eating the midday meal outside the home became common practice. In the first decades of the century before Prohibition, the neighborhood saloon often provided the working man with his best meal of the day. For the price of a beer, usually five cents, saloons in Boston, Philadelphia, and New York offered bread or crackers, bologna or weinerwurst, stewed tomatoes, salad, pickles, onions, radishes, soup, and meat stew. In Boston, saloons were compelled by law to offer something to eat free of charge.

> 📷 *Snapshot*
>
> **Horn & Hardart's Automats**
>
> A coin-operated glass-and-chrome wonder, Horn & Hardart's Automats revolutionized the way Americans ate when they opened up in Philadelphia and New York in the early twentieth century. In a country where the Industrial Revolution had just taken hold, eating at a restaurant with self-serve vending machines rather than waitresses, and art deco architecture instead of stuffy dining rooms was an unforgettable experience. The Automat served freshly made food for the price of a few coins, and no one made a better cup of coffee. By the peak of its popularity—from the Great Depression to the postwar years—the Automat was more than an inexpensive place to buy a good meal; it was a culinary treasure, a technical marvel, and an emblem of the times.

With the passage of the 18th Amendment and the Volstead Act that quickly followed, the saloons of America closed and with them the free lunch for the working class. Prohibition also affected the culinary habits of the middle and upper classes as French restaurants and cooking, both of which depend heavily on wine, could not survive without this essential product.

In the 1920s, when Prohibition not only took away alcohol but also the free lunch, a new phenomenon, the fast-service restaurant, emerged. The number of restaurants that opened in the 1920s tripled the number that had existed before that decade. In the Northeast, the leaders of this industry were Howard Johnson's New England Seafood Restaurants, and in New York and Philadelphia Horn and Hardart's, which introduced the coin-operated cafeteria restaurant called the Automat.

After 1910, in major cities of the Northeast, pasteurized milk was rapidly entering the diet, improving the health of children and lowering infant mortality rates. Other aspects of children's food in the urban Northeast also changed dramatically as baby foods, or well-pureed fruits, vegetables, and even meats were being processed and sold in small bottles for the exclusive use of babies six months and older.

With the end of Prohibition in 1933, the saloons reopened to an enthusiastic clientele in the urban Northeast. Although the free lunch was not as common as it had been, the beer flowed freely and for this, thirsty northeasterners were grateful.

Whether rich or poor, young or old, everyone in New York City ate at Horn & Hardart's Automats; this photo is from 1936. AP Photo/HO/Courtesy of The Museum of the City of New York/Berenice Abbot.

DRINK

By the turn of the century beer had become the beverage of choice for most men. Consumption of beer per capita had increased from 2.7 gallons in 1850 to 29.53 gallons in 1899. The usual place of consumption for this beer was the local saloon. In 1915 New York had over 10,000 licensed saloons, or one for every 515 persons. Boston, with a population of less than half a million at the turn of the century, counted 277,000 people (over half the population) entering saloons on any given day. Other cities of the Northeast could boast similar numbers. The doors of these saloons closed with the passage of the 18th Amendment, which attempted to change the drinking habits of millions of Americans.

By some estimates, alcohol consumption was cut in half by Prohibition. From the outset, however, enforcement was unenthusiastic, understaffed, and underfunded. In large cities of the Northeast, as elsewhere, speakeasies or underground taverns opened and prospered. The new speakeasies, unlike the saloons that preceded them, welcomed women. Prohibition also changed drinking habits by reversing a 50-year-old trend toward beer. Liquor, which was more easily transportable, easier to conceal, and brought greater profits to suppliers, became much more available than beer and became the beverage of choice. The era of Prohibition contributed new words to the American vocabulary, such as *speakeasy*, *hip flask*, and *bathtub gin*. Probably the most profound effect that Prohibition had in the long run was that it provided opportunities for the growth of organized crime, which traces its economic take-off to this era (Davidson, et al. 2001, 795).

Steve Brodie's bar in New York City, c. 1895. The Granger Collection, New York.

The new film industry did not leave the Prohibition campaign without commentary. In so doing it left a permanent collective memory of this era, which is reinforced by moving image documents. "No picture [about the 1920s] would be considered properly finished," observed one New York film reviewer, "without a number of scenes depicting the shaking up and drinking down of cocktails and their resulting effect on those who partake of them." In a representative sample of 115 films from 1930, liquor was referred to in 78 percent of them and drinking depicted in 66 percent. Further analysis of 40 of those films reveals that while only 13 percent of male villains and 8 percent of female villains could be seen consuming alcohol, no less than 43 percent of heroes and 23 percent of heroines were shown doing so. Moviegoers could hardly avoid the impression that drinking was widespread and that Prohibition violation was socially acceptable (Kyvig 2002, 97).

HOUSING

Electric wiring at the turn of the century, along with indoor plumbing, added substantially to the cost of house construction. To keep house prices stable while adding these new technologies, builders cut costs by reducing the size and number of rooms in the average house. Early twentieth-century house plans began to eliminate formal front parlors, merging them with the family sitting room to create a single living room, often opening directly to the dining room. Large entrance halls were eliminated or reduced in size. In a moderately priced two-story house there were usually only three downstairs rooms: living room, dining room, and kitchen. In the Northeast a familiar form of architecture, the row house, remained the dominant form of moderate-priced housing and fit the new demand for reduction in space. The row house had first appeared in the United States in the 1700s in Philadelphia and continued to be the dominant family architectural form in that city well into the twentieth century. This style was also adapted in the northeastern cities of Boston and New York.

An important influence on housing, which began in the early twentieth century in the Northeast, was the emergence of the black ghetto, which began when real estate and financial institutions along with property owners, managers, and neighborhood property owners' associations actively pursued policies, legal and illegal, that restricted African Americans to ghetto housing. While real estate agents refused to show or rent properties outside of the ghetto, white financial organizations refused loans for black home building or purchase. White neighborhood improvement or protective associations, real estate interests, and homeowners placed racially restrictive covenants on neighborhood properties prohibiting blacks and others from buying or renting in those areas. State and local governments failed to enforce antidiscrimination laws, and police often ignored physical attacks against blacks who attempted to move outside of restricted areas. In the Northeast, ghettoes first appeared in New York and then Philadelphia around 1915. Population growth stimulated by the great black migration and restrictive living areas caused housing prices to skyrocket in some ghettoized areas of the urban Northeast. As a result, blacks paid almost twice as much in rent as their white counterparts living in similar housing outside the ghetto. Nonetheless, institutional development within the ghetto exploded: newspapers, businesses, and professionals increased to serve the expanding population. In Harlem and elsewhere a cultural renaissance stimulated by artists, writers, and musicians demonstrated a cultural vitality that contrasted with worsening housing conditions. Ghetto residents revealed other positive adaptations to difficult conditions by taking in boarders, and holding parties to obtain rent money for someone in need (Reich 2006, 340–41).

CLOTHING

Machine-made mass-produced clothing had become common in the late nineteenth century, but at first it was largely confined to exterior garments for adult males. Much women's and children's clothing continued to be made at home. Making their own and their children's garments had been considered one of the major responsibilities of a woman. After World War I, this practice changed rapidly, especially among middle-class women, who in the first decades of the century had remained reluctant to adopt manufactured ready-to-wear clothes.

Women's fashions changed radically after 1908 but then remained basically the same through the 1920s. The optimum style with little variation was a modified sheath straight up and down and clinging. In 1912, the president of the New York Cotton Exchange commented that the virtual elimination of undergarments for women and the clinging fashions had reduced the amount of fabric used by at least 12 yards for each female. By the 1920s plunging bodices and backs were also in vogue. In the early 1930s full-figured women came back into fashion and with it styles that emphasized bosoms and hips.

The last type of clothing to make the transition from predominantly homemade to manufactured proved to be undergarments. Both men and women had dressed in winter flannel and summer cotton "union suits" with knee-length or longer underdrawers and shirts that were long-sleeved in winter and short-sleeved in summer.

By the early twentieth century, the fashion of girls and women was shifting away from the stiff corsets of fabric bone and steel designed to severely pinch the midsection and heighten the appearance of ample hips and chest. The corset was at least loosened, if not replaced by a less restrictive one-piece fabric waist or camisole, still intended to accentuate a small waist and large bust (Kyvig 2002, 120–21).

An important technological invention that contributed to the demise of the corset was the bicycle. Although versions of the bicycle had been around for decades, only in the 1890s did the introduction of the safety bicycle generate mass appeal and consequently mass production. Women responded enthusiastically to this new craze. For proper breathing during bicycle excursions, many women abandoned their corsets for the first time. For those reluctant to go that far, corset manufacturers provided alternative designs that were shortened to the waist and constructed with less-constricting fit. By the middle of the 1890s some daring women even rode their bicycles in divided skirts or breeches called knickerbockers (Hill 2004, 22–23).

A new undergarment given the French name *brassiere* came into use shortly before the Great War. The first brassieres were designed to flatten the breast for the chemise or flapper dress just beginning to be popular, especially among women who wanted to deemphasize their reproductive role and assert their independence. Gradually, as fashion evolved in the 1930s, and designs once again emphasized motherhood, bras to shape and emphasize the roundness of breasts were developed, and in the 1930s bra cups in standard A, B, C, and D sizes appeared (Kyvig 2002, 120).

World War I dietary habits also changed fashion. In the late nineteenth century right through the first decade of the twentieth century, when getting enough to eat was often still a challenge and the understanding of good nutrition was limited, being stout was a sign of health, success, and beauty. Late nineteenth-century clothing had tended to emphasize or even create a plump figure. Both men's and women's clothing had featured layers of heavy fabrics, padded shoulders, and a loose fit. Women's dresses, normally with flared and pleated ankle-length skirts, were made fuller by being worn over petticoats. Around the turn of the

> ### 📷 *Snapshot*
>
> **A Philosophy of Clothes**
>
> The following excerpt from Theodore Dreiser's novel *Sister Carrie* (1900), about a wayward country girl, offers a philosophy of women's clothes.
>
> > A woman should some day write the complete philosophy of clothes. No matter how young, it is one of the things she wholly comprehends. There is an indescribably faint line in the matter of man's apparel which somehow divides for her those who are worth glancing at and those who are not. Once an individual has passed this faint line on the way downward he will get no glance from her. There is another line at which the dress of a man will cause her to study her own.

century, as more women began to work outside the home, simpler styles such as tailored suits or long dark skirts without petticoats and white blouses (or shirtwaists) became common. Just before World War I, fitness rather than girth emerged as the standard for male attractiveness, and therefore male fashions began moving toward defining a more slender body. The war accelerated this tendency. Wartime shortages of food and fabric stirred government conservation efforts, and the Wilson administration sought to educate people on the advantages of eating less and consequently weighing and wearing less. Good nutrition was reflected in erect posture, healthy-looking skin, shiny hair, and a slender figure. These characteristics replaced plumpness as signs of beauty.

Women's clothing styles in the postwar era—at least those favored by younger women—were the most notable symbol of the new fashion. Flapper-style dresses used light fabrics that hung straight from the shoulders and gathered low on the hips rather than at the waist. This style deemphasized both the bust and the hips in order to create a slim profile. Corsets disappeared almost altogether, and multilaced petticoats gave way to single-layer slips or just knickers under skirts. Hemlines, which had only just risen from ankle to mid-calf, rose to the knee and beyond in the 1920s. Exposed lower legs acquired further emphasis with sheer silk stockings.

Cosmetics in small amounts became acceptable fashion in the 1920s, and women, especially younger ones, abandoned long-standing views that cosmetics were used only by "painted ladies" of loose morals. Among the most common cosmetics that women used were face powder, rouge for color in cheeks, lipstick, eyebrow pencil, and eyelash curlers. Among urban black women of the Northeast, skin lighteners and hair products developed by Madam C. J. Walker created a culture of African American female beauty. Madam Walker's grooming products made her the wealthiest African American woman in the country. She built a mansion on the Hudson River 20 miles from New York, and her philanthropy helped support the budding cultural world of Harlem (Reich 2006, 868).

Bobbed hair became another central element of the flapper style in the 1920s. Short hair not only emphasized the desired slender look, but for many it was also an act of defiance against the long-standing tradition of long hair being the crowning glory of a woman. Until the second decade of the twentieth century, hair was worn well-coifed and elaborately arranged, and a woman only "let her hair down" (an invitation to intimacy) in the presence of her mate. By the 1920s, short hair announced the "liberation" of the American urban woman.

Men also began to wear their hair much shorter in the post–World War I era. Short slicked-back hair in imitation of such movie stars as Rudolph Valentino became the favored fashion. Beards disappeared, and soon mustaches and sideburns followed. The clean-shaven look became fashionable. Inexpensive mass-produced safety razors made the new look possible, and advertisers played up the sexual appeal of the smoothly shaven face.

The economic downturn of the 1930s did little to affect clothing and style, since people in an economic pinch tended to make clothes last longer. Still, some notable changes in fashion occurred. Designs for women once again began to emphasize hips and bust, hemlines fell to the ankles, and fitted waistlines reappeared. Men's suits once again acquired padded shoulders, and fuller cuts reemerged as standard for men as well as women. The trend toward mass-produced clothing continued, and with it the ability to disguise one's individual economic circumstance by conforming to standard patterns of dress.

The film industry also had an effect on clothing. When Clark Gable took off his shirt to reveal he did not wear an undershirt in the movie *It Happened One Night*, supposedly the men's undershirt market collapsed. Movie magazines set the tone, and the fashion with more femininely fitted dresses and curlier locks suggesting what the smart American woman should wear. During the 1930s, Shirley Temple, a plump preteenage girl with curly hair and deep dimples, captured the hearts of middle America. Mothers rushed to stores to buy their girls Shirley Temple dresses and coifed them with Shirley Temple curls. In the 1930s, Sears Roebuck catalogues filled pages with Shirley Temple fashions. Films also encouraged the unveiling of the female human body, baring arms and legs and putting the body on display as never before (Kyvig 2002, 120–26).

MANUFACTURING

In the Northeast from 1900 to 1930, the number of wage earners engaged in the manufacturing industry increased from 1.8 million to 2.1 million. In the Depression decade of the 1930s this number dropped off slightly to 1.9 million.

Industrial workers in the Northeast were unorganized, and they usually worked under harsh conditions. No matter what the product, most industrial workers shared the common characteristics of industrial work—the use of machines for mass production; the division of labor into intricately organized, menial tasks; and the dictatorship of the clock. At the turn of the century, two-thirds of all industrial work came from large-scale mills. Factory workers held jobs that required more machines and fewer skills. Repetition of small chores replaced fine craftwork. Workers could expect no payment from employers or government for injury or death on the job. Accidents were considered to be their own fault. By 1900, most of those earning wages in industry worked 6 days a week, 10 hours a day. These conditions would continue through the 1930s, until the Wagner Act, which protected the workers' right to organize, was passed, and then the Congress of Industrial Organization set out to organize unskilled workers.

Not only adults worked in industry. By 1900, the industrial labor force included some 1.7 million children. Parents had no choice. As one union leader observed, "Absolute necessity compels the father to take the child into the mine to assist him in winning bread for the family." On average, children of the working class worked 60 hours a week and carried home paychecks a third of the size of those of adult males.

In the new century, new methods of management and marketing opened white-collar positions for women as typists, telephone operators, bookkeepers, and secretaries. On rare occasions women entered the professional ranks through law and medical schools, but they were for the most part unwelcome.

Even more than women, African American men faced discrimination in the workplace. They were paid less than whites and given menial jobs. Their greatest opportunities in industry often came as strike-breakers to replace white workers. Once a strike ended, however, black workers were replaced and hated by the white regulars whom they had replaced. The service trades furnished the greatest source of jobs for African Americans. Craft workers and a sprinkling of black professionals could usually be found in the cities, and after the turn of the century, black-owned businesses thrived in growing black neighborhoods of the Northeast (Davidson, et al. 2001, 629–73).

TECHNOLOGY

At the turn of the century electricity's primary use was for large-scale power needs for streetlights, public transit, elevators, and factory machinery. But electricity as a power source in the home had begun in the previous century when Thomas Edison in 1882 began producing home generators, lamp sockets, and home wiring. That same year he developed the first central generator that could deliver power over utility lines. Nevertheless, home use of electricity in the nineteenth century remained scarce. By 1884, only 500 homes were electrified, while several thousand businesses were using electric lights, and electricity was driving streetcars, powering industrial machinery, and lighting street lamps.

At first, home use of electricity in the Northeast was limited to lighting and remained somewhat of a novelty.

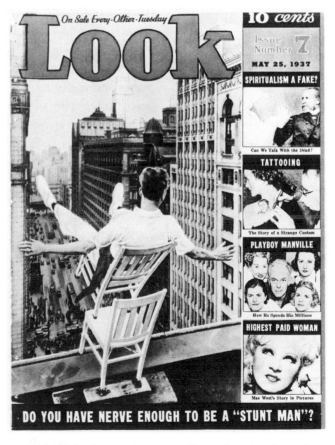

A May 1937 *Look* magazine cover illustration showing a daredevil balanced on chairs on the edge of a building. Library of Congress.

In New York City, for example, Mrs. Cornelius Vanderbilt would greet visitors to her home in a dress covered with tiny electric bulbs. Electric lights on Christmas trees became popular by the end of the century, and electric children's toys, particularly model trains for boys and electrified doll houses for girls, became popular by the turn of the century. By 1900, electricity gradually began to replace gas as the primary source of illumination in the house in the urban Northeast. After 1910, the standardized transmission of electricity at 120 volts of alternating current increased availability of electricity in the home. The percentage of gas used for illumination fell from 75 percent at the turn of the century to 21 percent by 1919.

In the postwar era, especially in urban areas of the Northeast, electricity began to influence American lives as it never had before. After World War I, electricity began to be generated and controlled for personal human use. This not only changed the personal lives of millions of Americans, but it also introduced mass marketing and production on a scale never before seen. In the 1920s electricity accentuated the differences between the electrified urban Northeast and the less developed rural parts of the region. When electricity began to enter the house, it was initially directed at easing the burdens of housekeeping. General Electric created several small appliance companies including Hotpoint, which dedicated considerable technological skill to developing the home appliance market. After lights, electric irons were usually the first acquisitions in newly wired homes. Soon to follow were sewing and washing machines and vacuum cleaners. From 1909 to 1929, the amount spent on household appliances increased from 235 million dollars to over one and a half billion dollars.

Rapidly, home appliances went from being expensive unreliable toys to dependable and useful tools for the mass of middle-class urban Americans. All of these inventions promised to free women from excessive housework, but some studies show that was not always the case. These studies done in the 1920s showed that women spent from 51 to 60 hours a week on housework. The increase in electrical power caused expectations to increase, and demands increased for greater variety in meals, cleaner homes, and more frequently laundered clothes. In addition, as the acquisition of appliances became more and more a defining feature of middle-class life, women found it necessary to work for wages outside the home so the family could have the financial resources to maintain middle-class status. Whether appliances added or reduced women's work can be debated, but what is certain is the appliance revolution gave women an influence in the market and workplace they had previously not enjoyed (Kyvig 2002, 53–71).

NAVIGATION

The classic liberal model in practice before World War I, with relatively free and massive migration, the gold standard, large capital flows, and rapid industrialization and expansion of the American economy, created one of the greatest eras of international trade in the history of the world. New York, as the principal port of the United States, benefited greatly from this explosion in international trade. It was a period during which both continental and intercontinental transport costs continued to fall as steam power became the norm for ocean transport and as railroad expansion progressed in the United States, Europe, and elsewhere.

In navigation, the most significant event for the shipbuilders of the Northeast was the passage of the Shipping Act of 1916. The law created a government merchant marine that in less than five years became the world's largest shipping company. From 1917 to 1922 the government constructed more than 2,300 ships at a cost of more than $3 billion (current), an unprecedented sum. The greatest beneficiaries of this were the great shipbuilders of the Northeast (Sicotte 1999, 103).

TRANSPORTATION

Urban transportation became transformed at the turn of the century as electric trains and cars dominated the cityscape of major urban areas, and the popularity of the "Tin Lizzie," as the Model T came to be called, helped account for the jump in the number of automobiles from fewer than half a million in 1910 to 2.5 million in 1915 and 9 million by 1920. At the same time that Henry Ford was promoting the Model T, another Detroit businessman, William C. Durant, was creating the General Motors Company. He bought up numerous auto-manufacturing companies including Buick, Oldsmobile, Cadillac, and Chevrolet, as well as parts makers Fisher Body and Charles Kettering's electric starter and battery company. In 1919, awash in war profits, Durant established the General Motors Acceptance Corporation as a means of financing his automobiles. Within two years half of all automobile buyers were entering into credit purchase agreements. By 1926 the figure reached three-fourths.

Credit buying dramatically enlarged the population that could afford to buy automobiles, and it altered the buying habits of those who already owned cars. More drivers began to eschew the economical, reliable, but unchanging Model T Ford for the more expensive but colorful and ever-changing styles and optional luxuries of General Motors cars. There were few paved roads between major cities until the limited number built in the 1920s were finished. The traveler who left the city on a long trip had to be intrepid. Maps of rural America were virtually nonexistent, road signs were scarce, and it was easy to get lost and completely turned around. Mechanics and filling stations were widely scattered and difficult to locate before the advent of roadside advertising signs in the late 1920s. Bridges could be rickety, with no standards of construction or inspection at least to give the impression of safety. Many were built in the distant past and were meant for the slower and perhaps lighter weight of the horse and carriage. Even in mountainous areas, guardrails were the exception rather than the rule.

More than one-half of all American roads that were categorized by local, state, and federal officials were classified as "unimproved." There was no great comfort if one traced an itinerary on a map that stayed on "improved" roads, since that designation was applied to graded dirt and gravel, which could be washed out or have become a quagmire, depending on the age of the map or recent weather conditions.

The federal government had high-minded intentions to connect all cities of greater than 50,000 population with paved roads, or so the Federal Road Acts of 1916 and 1921 intended. World War I hamstrung the first act; lack of funding and the high local funding requirements of the second limited its effects. Only after the New Deal put people to work on the federal payroll did road building take off (Green 2000, 217–18).

In 1903, the Wright brothers' first successful flight in Kitty Hawk, North Carolina, marked the beginning of the aviation age. In the early years, the public did not embrace airplane travel as an option, thinking that it was too dangerous. Although during World War I the government did fund flight research, it abandoned support when the war ended. Still, in the 1920s the government continued to subsidize the nascent industry with airmail contracts. The original "Big Four" (Pan Am, TWA, Eastern, and United) airline companies, which would come to dominate the industry in its first 50 years, all survived this early era of public indifference by carrying mail across the country for the U.S. government.

Public apathy for flying continued until 1927 when Charles Lindbergh successfully completed a solo flight across the Atlantic Ocean. Lindbergh captured the public imagination and, while becoming the hero of the century, he also stimulated an interest in airline passenger flight. As a result of this new interest in flight, a variety of air transport holding companies began, including one called Aviation Corporation. The air transport division of the company was called American Airways and later grew to become American Airlines, one of the largest commercial carriers in the United States. In 1933 American Airlines ordered its first Curtiss Condors, which were twin-engine biplanes with an 800-mile range and fitted with sleeping berths. On June 25, 1936, American Airlines flew the world's first commercial DC-3 trip from Chicago to New York.

Eastern Airlines traced its roots to Clement Keys, a former financial editor of the *Wall Street Journal* who was an untiring promoter of multimillion-dollar aviation corporations in the 1920s and 1930s. In early 1929, Keys decided to purchase a small Philadelphia-based airline known as Pitcairn Aviation, Inc. Keys sold Pitcairn to North American Aviation, then a holding company for a number of airline and aircraft companies in which he was one of the key shareholders. On January 17, 1930, Pitcairn's name was changed to Eastern Air Transport, Inc., and soon after, the airline expanded its routes to include Atlanta, Miami, Boston, and Richmond, Virginia. Its fleet

A 4-cylinder Model T Ford from 1908. Library of Congress.

4 CYL. MODEL T
FORD, 1908

at the time consisted of three Ford Trimotors and two Fokker F-X aircraft. These were joined soon by Curtiss Condors and Kingbirds. Pitcairn hired World War I ace Eddie Rickenbacker to serve as general manager of Eastern. While most of the major airlines were focusing on transcontinental flights, Eastern's specialty was the East Coast, where it established a near monopoly. Through 1933, the airline acquired contracts for a number of routes that spanned from New York to Miami. Eastern catered to the high demand for quick passenger travel between the northeastern states and the vacation areas of Florida.

In 1928, Boeing and its air transport division, United Aircraft, created United Aircraft and Transportation Corporation. In 1931 the four air transport divisions of United Aircraft became United Airlines. With the advent of larger aircraft, such as the Boeing and Ford Trimotors, came stewardess service. Boeing Air Transport traffic manager Steve Stimpson took the suggestion of nurse Ellen Church and proposed that nurses serve coffee and sandwiches and minister to the comfort of apprehensive flyers. On May 15, 1930, Boeing Air Transport—one of United's predecessor subsidiaries—introduced the world's first stewardess service. The idea was such a success that stewardesses quickly became a fixture of commercial air travel. Church was the world's first stewardess.

With a plan to establish routes to South America and then over the closest southern route to Europe from Rio to Lisbon, Juan Tripp created the Pan American Airways system. To avoid needless delays in the construction of airports in South America, to say nothing of the ambiguities of aviation legislation in South American countries, Tripp commissioned Sikorsky Company of Philadelphia to build a fleet of planes that could land on water. Once on the water the airships followed already established navigation rules and taxied up to their own floating docks to discharge and receive passengers.

In 1938, the Civil Aeronautics Authority, an independent regulatory bureau, was developed. That same year, many air transport companies were flying the new DC-3s. These planes, created to carry both mail and passengers, were wide enough to seat 21 people. The design of the DC-3 also allowed for 14 seats and three berths for sleeping on long flights. Famous child actress Shirley Temple was the first to purchase a sleeping berth ticket on an American Airlines DC-3. Thus, by the

Completed Model T Fords ready for delivery from this Detroit, Michigan factory, c. 1916. Library of Congress.

outbreak of World War II, the American aviation industry was on sound footing, and the companies that would carry the industry through its first half century were well established (http://scriptorium.lib.duke.edu/adaccess/airline-history.html); (http://www. united.com/page/middlepage/0,6823,2286,00.html).

Despite the great advances made in methods of travel in the first decades of the twentieth century, most Americans, especially in the urban areas, continued to depend on public transportation to move from one place to another. Every day, hundreds of thousands of commuters traveled back and forth from home to work on subways, and the newly created gasoline or diesel engine buses, which began to replace streetcars.

Political Life

GOVERNMENT

In the early decades of the twentieth century, powerful political machines ran the major cities of the Northeast. Using the newly arrived immigrants as a political base, street-savvy political organizers overthrew a privileged plutocracy that had been running the cities of the Northeast in most cases since the early years of the republic. For example, until the beginning of the twentieth century the local politics of Boston had been dominated by the prosperous and powerful descendents of the city's seventeenth-century English immigrant founders. This group had participated in the founding of the Republican Party, which dominated local politics. The new immigrants, beginning with the mid-nineteenth-century Irish, rallied to the Democratic Party as their only alternative, and as new immigrants arrived at the end of the century they too eventually found their way into the Democratic Party. By the mid-1920s, the immigrant coalition led by the more politically experienced Irish dominated Boston politics.

With a population much larger than Boston, New York became home to the most famous political machine in the country, Tammany Hall. Tammany had dominated New York politics since 1798 when Aaron Burr used it as the central organizing force for the Jeffersonian Democrats to defeat John Adams in 1800. When the Irish immigration began in the late 1840s, Tammany Hall provided housing, jobs, food, coal, and sometimes even a fiancé to the new arrivals and in return gained their political support. They divided the wards of the city into small principalities headed by a ward heeler, who made sure that the social needs of the citizens in his assigned area had the help of city hall for whatever problem they might have. In return, the ward healers and in turn the party had the complete loyalty of these voters and control of the city government and its coffers. Progressive historians of the first half of the twentieth century usually painted the city bosses in a bad light. However, in the later decades of the twentieth century some historians began to take a kinder look at machine politics, explaining that the machine provided social services to people who had no other recourse. George Washington Plunkitt, a boss in the Tammany machine at the turn of the century, explained its purpose to William Riordon, a young reporter for the New York *Evening Post*. As Plunkitt described it, he held a grip on his district by going

right down to the poor families and help them in different ways they need help. I've got a regular system for this. If there's a fire in Ninth Tenth or Eleventh Avenue, for example any hour of the day or night, I'm usually there with some of my election district captains as soon as the fire engines. If a family is burned out I don't ask whether they are Republicans or Democrats, and I don't refer them to the Charity Organization Society, which would investigate the case in a month or two and decide they are worthy of help about the time they are dead from starvation. I just get quarters for them, buy clothes for them if their clothes were burned up, and fix them up 'till they get things runnin again. It's philanthropy, but its politics too—mighty good politics. Who can tell how many votes one of these fires bring me? The poor are the most grateful people in the world, and, let me tell you, they have more friends in their neighborhoods than the rich have in theirs.

If there's a family in my district in want I know it before the charitable societies do, and me and my men are first on the ground. I have a special corps to look up such cases. The consequence is that the poor look up to George W. Plunkitt as a father, come to him in trouble—and don't forget on election day.

Another thing I can always get a job for a deservin' man. I make it a point to keep track of jobs, and it seldom happens that I don't have a few up my sleeve ready for use. I know every big employer in the district and in the whole city, for that matter, and they ain't in the habit of saying no to me when I ask for a job. And the children—the little roses of the district! Do I forget them? Oh no! They know me, every one of them, and they know that a sight of Uncle George and candy means the same thing. Some of them are the best kind of vote getters. I'll tell you a case. Last year a little Eleventh Avenue rosebud whose father is a Republican caught hold of his whiskers on election day and said she wouldn't let go till he'd promised to vote for me. And she didn't. (Riordon 1994, 64)

LAW, CRIME, AND PUNISHMENT

At the turn of the century in New York City, clergymen and reformers referred to a neighborhood stretching from 23rd to 57th Streets between Sixth and Tenth Avenues as Satan's Circus. Here one could find the most intense concentration of saloons, brothels, gambling parlors, dance halls, and clip joints in the city. It also offered police the richest grafting territory in the city, which gave the area the name by which most New Yorkers knew it. When police Captain Clubber Williams was transferred to the district, in the late 1870s, he said, "I've been eating chuck steak for a long time. Now I'm gonna get me a little of the tenderloin." The name stuck and New Yorkers contributed a new word to the American vocabulary, which defines similar areas in other cities.

In 1912, on a sweltering night in the Tenderloin, Herman Rosenthal, a gambling house owner, was gunned down, and when his murder became connected to a corrupt police lieutenant, Charley Becker, it soon became New York's first "trial of the century." Charles Whitman, the New York district attorney, prosecuted Becker. Knowing that securing the conviction and execution of a corrupt police officer would propel his career, he launched a spectacular trial that captured more newspaper space than the sinking of the *Titanic*. Coercing criminal witnesses with the promise of immunity, Whitman secured the conviction of Becker, who was executed at Sing Sing in 1915. With his electrocution Becker earned the notoriety of being the only policeman ever executed for murder in the United States (Patrick 2007, 51).

In the 1920s a number of "crimes of the century" captured the attention of numerous Americans, many of whom became convinced that they were living amidst a crime wave propelled by immigrant gangsters and rapacious blacks. One such crime occurred in April 1920 in South Braintree, Massachusetts, when two men shot a guard and the paymaster at Slater and Merrill Shoe Company, then fled in an automobile with the company's payroll. Police soon arrested two pistol-carrying Italian immigrants and charged them with robbery and murder. Nicolo Sacco and Bartolomeo Vanzetti were interrogated for two days, mainly about their political beliefs, without being told the charges against them or their legal rights. Witnesses to the crime were asked to identify them standing alone as opposed to in a lineup. At their trial Sacco and Vanzetti's anarchist political beliefs and their ethnic background appeared to carry more weight with the judge and jury than the weak case presented against them or the defense witnesses that placed Sacco miles away at the time of the robbery. The judge, Webster Thayer, repeatedly referred to the defendants as those "anarchist bastards." Even a confession by another death row inmate who bore a striking resemblance to Sacco failed to impress the judge, and the two men were condemned to death. They were executed in the Charleston Prison electric chair in August 1927. The case drew international attention as a blatant example of ethnic prejudice and political oppression in America and the harsh and socially uneven justice system that existed there.

One reason the Sacco-Vanzetti trial attracted such attention may have been the general decline in crime during the first half of the twentieth century. Despite a perceived crime wave in the first decades of the twentieth century the United States actually experienced a decline in crime, which sociologists agree continued through 1960. The 1920s, which experienced a slight increase in felonies and misdemeanors, provided an exception to the statistical decline of crime in the first half of the twentieth century; however, over 60 percent of the criminal offenses in that decade involved the violation of Prohibition, an act that would not have been a crime prior to 1920 or after 1934 (Kyvig 2002, 177–78).

REFORM

As the new century opened, a rejuvenated white middle class, appalled by the excesses of corporations, revolted at the conditions of the working class, horrified at the prospects of socialism, and guided by a Calvinist sense of being blessed and therefore obligated to improve society in God's image, began to organize politically with reform as their common goal. Reform came in most cases in the form of legislation. Conservation, antitrust suits, health reform, child labor laws, women's labor laws, housing laws directed at slum landlords, and local political reform topped the agenda of these reformers, who called themselves Progressives. This soon became a national movement, but it began locally and regionally.

Typical of these reformers in the Northeast were the New York Progressives who waged war against the Tammany political machine, which they claimed had manipulated ignorant immigrants in order to gain control of the city and in the process had created a dynasty of corruption that robbed honest taxpayers and in no way helped those whose interests they claimed to champion. In 1901 the Progressive anti-Tammany forces elected reformer Seth Low, a Republican, as mayor. After the election, Lincoln Steffens praised New York City as the leading exponent of the great "American anti-bad government movement for good government. New York by persistence has at last achieved a good administration." But Steffens wondered, "Will New Yorkers continue?" Although it took another 30 years of struggle, the reformers would finally win out. In 1932, the Tammany machine suffered a dual setback when Mayor James Walker was forced from office because of corruption and opponent Franklin D. Roosevelt was elected president of the United States. Roosevelt stripped Tammany of its federal patronage—much expanded because of the New Deal—and handed city patronage to Ed Flynn, "boss" of the Bronx. Roosevelt helped Republican Fiorello LaGuardia become mayor on a fusion ticket, thus removing even more patronage from Tammany's control. Tammany never recovered.

Reform was not only political. There were reform movements in public health, education, and housing, to name a few. Most reform movements were directed at the issues created by the massive migration to the cities and the problems this caused. Urban infrastructure, especially housing, simply was not prepared to deal with the massive influx of people begun after the Civil War and then augmented by mass immigration from Europe at the turn of the century. As a result of Progressive reforms of the first decades of the twentieth century, life for many Americans improved notably. Children stayed in school longer, workers received compensation when they were injured on the job, housing standards were improved, water became safer to drink, children had parks to play in, and family meal tables were protected from tainted meat and from harmful additives that often had been mixed into processed food.

WAR

One of the most important defining events of the first decades of the twentieth century was what people at the time called the Great War. President Woodrow Wilson had promised to keep America out of the European conflagration, but soon the country for various reasons was swept into the whirl. The United States did not enter the war until April 1917, but as early as the spring of 1915 Americans began to realize that they were not immune to events occurring across the ocean. On

The British luxury ocean liner *Lusitania* arrives in New York for the first time on September 13, 1907. Library of Congress.

April 28, 1915, the British-owned Cunard Line announced in the travel section of the *New York Times* that the *Lusitania*, "The fastest largest steamer now in Atlantic Service" would be departing New York on May 1. Then on the day the ship was to sail an ominous advertisement was placed in the *New York Times* travel section. It reminded travelers that a state of war existed between England and Germany and that all ships flying the British colors were subject to attack. The Imperial German Embassy had signed the message. Charles Sumner of Cunard Lines dismissed the threat. He told a reporter, "No passenger is permitted aboard unless he can identify himself, [and] every passenger must identify his baggage before it is placed on board." Furthermore, he assured that the British navy had responsibility for all British shipping, especially Cunard's, and as "for submarines," Sumner declared " I have no fear of them whatever."

Six days later, the *Lusitania* lay at the bottom of the Atlantic Ocean off the British coast, sunk by a German submarine. Among the 1,200 dead were 128 Americans. Many Americans at that time called for war with Germany, but Woodrow Wilson counseled restraint, arguing that "There is such a thing as being too proud to fight." But events over the next year and a half, including German espionage activity in the Northeast and more ships sunk, and German overtures to America's Mexican neighbors to join in a war against them, finally pushed America to the brink, and when Germany announced that it would continue unrestricted submarine warfare despite protests from the United States, America entered the war. Immediately Woodrow Wilson used his war powers to mobilize the American people. Some call the war the end of Progressivism; others say it was Progressivism's greatest triumph up to that moment. If one interprets Progressivism to mean government control over economic and social life, then the war could be called the flowering of Progressivism.

One of Wilson's first acts was the creation of the War Industries Board, which coordinated production through a network of industrial and trade associations. A food administration was established that encouraged farmers to grow more and citizens to eat less. Wilson placed Herbert Hoover in charge of the Food Board, and upon his appointment, he received a letter from the mayor of New York, John Mitchel, assuring him of every New Yorker's cooperation with the new bill. One aspect of the bill, which passed almost unanimously, did give many New Yorkers pause. The production of alcoholic beverages was prohibited and the president was given the authority to seize for defense purposes all of the 300 million gallons of whiskey that were currently in storage. The *New York Times* objected that the antisaloon crowd was using a food bill to establish prohibition. Rather than admit that the law would disrupt what was an essential part of life in New York and other urban areas of the Northeast, the *Times* pointed out that the prohibition of the sale of whiskey would deprive the government of many needed tax dollars. Samuel Gompers, head of the American Federation of Labor (AFL), protesting from his New York office, was more forthcoming. He declared that the American workmen should be allowed to have their beer, and that the war should not alter the traditions of life. The president finally relented and excluded beer and light wine from the ban on alcohol, but prohibitionists had finally won an important battle and they promised to return to successfully complete their war against alcohol.

A federal board was established to limit fuel consumption and to divert more of it to the military. The National War Labor Board arbitrated over 1,000 labor disputes and gave a great impetus to growth of the AFL, as union membership jumped from 2.7 million in 1914 to over 4 million by 1918. The U.S. Railroad Administration took over management of the railroads for the duration of the war, a condition that many Progressives would like to have seen made permanent. As young men went to war and war industries cranked up to full capacity, a shortage of labor developed, which gave opportunities to those who had been denied possibilities of higher-paying factory jobs. The war brought over a million women into the workforce, many at jobs that had been exclusively a male domain, such as train engineers and drill press operators. Southern blacks also benefited from the labor shortage in northern cities, and the war years witnessed the first of the great African American migrations north. In northeastern cities like New York, Buffalo, and Boston, blacks from the South created their own uniquely characteristic neighborhoods. As a result of the great influx of blacks into New York, Harlem, a formerly multiethnic area with defined boundaries negotiated by various immigrant groups, became recognized as a predominantly black domain.

In the Northeast as well as the rest of the country, George M. Creel's "four minute men," salesmen for the war, delivered patriotic speeches and sold war bonds wherever people gathered: in church, in theaters, and at vaudevilles. In response northeasterners, like the rest of the country, planted victory gardens, conserved fuel, and collected metal for the war effort. Like the rest of the country, many were stirred up against Germans. Mayor Victor Mravlag of Elizabeth, New Jersey, an Austrian by birth, refused to accept a flag from the Patriotic Tenth Ward Club when their presentation speech was filled with anti-German sentiment, which, he said, made people feel as if all Germans were disloyal. Even the *New York Times* was guilty of fanning the flames of prejudice when they suggested that the Spanish flu epidemic had been planted in New York by Germans.

Not everyone became caught up in the pro-war sentiment. On July 1, 1917, radicals organized a parade in Boston against the war with banners that read "If This Is a Popular War Why Conscription?" and "We Demand Peace." Although schools and universities discouraged opposition to the war, many did speak out, including the famous historian Charles Beard, who resigned from the Columbia University faculty and charged the trustees with being "reactionary and visionless in politics, narrow and medieval in religion" (Zinn 2003, 370–71).

The coastal areas of the Northeast came to feel direct effects of the war as German U-boats patrolled off the shoreline and took as easy prey fishing boats out of the Cape Cod area and coal boats moving along the coast. One such event took place in July 1918. Sixty miles off the Cape a German U-boat sank a Boston-bound schooner filled with halibut. This submarine was one of two that patrolled off the coast of New England during the war years. Closer to home in New York Harbor, German agents blew up a munitions storage area on Black Tom Island and in the process destroyed the entire island and created a blast that was heard in Baltimore and shattered windows as far away as midtown Manhattan (Green 2000, 204–5; Millman 2006, 90–96).

Recreational Life

SPORTS

At the turn of the century, sports remained for the most part a male-dominated phenomenon that tended to preserve class lines, yet at the same time sports served as a vehicle for assimilation for many new urban immigrants. Boxing, which had been popular in the Northeast in the nineteenth century, lost its appeal after the demise of the Bostonian John L. Sullivan, and the entire business moved to the West during the first decades of twentieth century, only to return to the Northeast with a flourish in 1921 with the Dempsey-Carpentier fight. Spectator sports, especially college football and professional baseball, attracted tens of thousands of fans in the 1920s, and this phenomenon would continue through the 1930s. The growth of cities and the invention of the radio in the 1920s contributed greatly to the increased interest in sports in the early decades of the twentieth century.

The urban social structure in the Northeast invited men to display their status, and sports became one showcase for them. The New York Athletic Club, for example, had a very exclusive membership throughout the late nineteenth century and into the twentieth. Here wealthy men not only exercised together or watched competitive events, they made business contacts and solidified their identification with each other. Sporting clubs and organizations tended to observe class lines; skilled blue-collar and low-level white-collar workers might play together in a neighborhood baseball league, but rarely if ever did the steel magnate and his puddler share a democratic game of squash. Ethnic groups too—especially the first American-born generation—found in sports a powerful source of identification with the nation, and at least the hope of social mobility. Yet sports did not propel ethnic peoples into the larger culture only to have them lose their Old World identities. On the contrary, games and clubs were organized along lines of nationality, race, and religion. A bowling alley in a working-class section of New York might bring Irish, Italians, and Jews to the same lanes, but it was more as rivals than as chums. Sports could simultaneously enhance people's new American identity and their ethnic consciousness (Riess 1991, 60–92).

Sports for both participants and spectators increased dramatically after World War I. The common war experience exposed many young men to baseball and boxing for the first time. And the American Legion after the war kept men interested in sports, both as participants and as coaches for younger men. By the 1920s a large enough proportion of the population had become familiar enough with sports to create a great explosion in spectator sports. Not only live audiences but also radio audiences propelled spectator sports forward as an important leisure activity. Baseball drew the largest crowd of spectators. The big leagues began in a quadrant north of St. Louis and east of the Mississippi where proximity of urban areas and access to transportation made the formation of two eight-team leagues, 16 in all in 10 cities, possible. Radio and newspapers carried accounts of the big league games to the rest of the nation. By the 1920s there was no area of the country where the game was not played from spring to early fall, making it truly a national pastime.

Since the 1890s, football had become extremely popular at high schools and colleges. As enrollments grew, football increased in popularity. Not only did students and alumni come to games, but so too did people whose only connection to the school was an enthusiasm for its teams. Recognizing the potential financial bonanza, colleges and universities in the Northeast, as elsewhere, built stadiums seating several times their student enrollment and began offering scholarships to talented players. Unprecedented crowds of 60,000–80,000 came to college campuses on Saturday afternoons to watch football. By the end of the 1920s college football brought in an estimated $21.5 million yearly, $4.5 million more than professional baseball. Professional football, employing ex-college stars, began playing in the same cities that supported Major League Baseball, but the attraction remained far less than that for the college game.

At the turn of the century boxing left the Northeast for the West where, except for the brief reign of Jack Johnson, it received little national attention, and outside of the black community that attention remained negative. When boxing did return to the Northeast, precisely Atlantic City in 1921, it did so in great fanfare. Jack Dempsey fought Georges Carpentier in a bout that drew attention from around the world. Newspapers from America, Europe, and even Japan detailed each day's events leading up to the fight. The news-hungry public greedily consumed every scrap of information about the bout, each prophecy and speculation. The majority of experts wisely picked Dempsey to win, which he did, but the greater question was why all of a sudden, after 20 years, was boxing so popular once more? Explanations of the phenomenon were as many and as complicated as the predictions of the outcome. But through the most reasoned explanations ran a common thread: the bout symbolized the triumph of man over systems and machines. In an age where man seemed to be guided by amoral forces beyond his control, the Dempsey-Carpentier fight represented man as a master of his fate. "In days when we think in terms of politics and theologies and economic systems," wrote psychologist P. W. Wilson, "Dempsey and Carpentier declare unto us that it is, ultimately, the man who counts. His food, his muscles, his habits, his frame of mind, his morale, matter infinitely to the whole world" (Roberts 1979, 118–19).

Except for baseball, boxing, horseracing, and football, sports that attracted crowds of spectators and quickly gained a radio audience as well, most sports remained predominantly "kids'" games. Large numbers of children and younger adults in the Northeast played baseball, bicycled, swam, ran, and, in winter, ice skated, sledded, and skied. But these sorts of activities tapered off rapidly as one approached adulthood.

The one exception to this rule was golf. By the end of the 1920s an estimated three million players played on some 4,000 courses nationwide. The Depression caused interest in golf to sag, but an alternative, miniature golf, took its place. Although it was not invented until 1920, by the 1930s there were over 40,000 miniature golf courses in operation across the United States (Kyvig 2002, 158–62).

MUSIC

The record business started in various regions at various times, and its origins reach back into the nineteenth century with gramophone recordings. But in the Depression years many of the regional companies, except those in the South, which benefited from the genius of the Carter family, began to go out of business. Commercialism had trumped artistry as businessmen in New York began to stimulate the development of a more homogenized popular music.

The roots of the New York–based popular music production industry began in England with the formation of the Decca Record Company in 1914. By 1919 Decca was the largest recording company in the world, and in 1934 a U.S. branch of Decca was launched, which quickly became a major player in the depressed American record market, thanks to its roster of popular artists, particularly Bing Crosby, and to the shrewd management of Jack Kapp. Artists signed to Decca in the 1930s and 1940s included Louis Armstrong, Count Basie, Billie Holiday, the Andrews Sisters, Ted Lewis, Judy Garland, the Mills Brothers, Billy Cotton, Bing Crosby, Jimmy Dorsey, and Jack Hy.

Kapp decided that a smaller inventory of highly promoted releases was more economically prudent than a large eclectic collection, and through improved management, and the reduction in variety of music produced, he was able to reduce the price of a record by half to 35 cents. These strategies helped produce music that reached a larger public audience. Kapp developed hit records by blending elements of various musical genres. He encouraged the orchestras of Guy Lombardo and Jimmy Dorsey to emphasize clear, simple melodies as well as light rhythms that would be good for dancing. He also promoted singers with soft, pleasant voices like Bing Crosby and the Mills Brothers. Decca's upbeat music appealed to the Depression-era audiences and helped shape a mass popular music market that would explode in the post–World War II years.

Kapp's chief rival, John Hammond of Columbia Records, used newly developed recording technologies to improve sound. Like Kapp, he produced records that softened the style of jazz and blues. He played an important role in creating new dance music that by the 1930s was beginning to be called swing. Hammond helped clarinetist Benny Goodman increase his band's already considerable appeal by adding flamboyant drummer Gene Kruppa and rhythmically steady piano player Jess Stacy. Hammond also brought band leader Count Basie and singer Billie Holiday national attention. Hammond remained far more aggressive than Kapp in bringing African American music and artists into the cultural mainstream (Kyvig 2002, 204–5).

In Tonawanda, New York, the first coin-operated automatic phonograph, the *Wurlitzer*, was developed. The music machines quickly began appearing in restaurants, nightclubs, soda fountains, and taverns, first in New York and then in the rest of the United States. Other companies joined the market and, in all between 1933 and 1937, produced over 150,000 jukeboxes. This word was probably borrowed from the juke joints of the South (see Chapter 4, the section on Entertainment). Each jukebox held about 50 records that were popular throughout the United States. Jukeboxes boosted the popularity of dancing throughout the United States in small communities as well as large. Until the turn of the century the waltz was the most popular dance, but major modifications to this stiff though once scandalous dance step rapidly transformed dancing in the early 1900s. By 1910, more informal and physically intimate social dancing was being transformed from a morally questionable activity restricted to lower-class urban dance halls and saloons into such a popular pastime that it was frequently referred to as the dance craze. By World War I new dances were constantly being introduced, including the fox-trot, the tango, and dozens of briefly popular dances (Kyvig 2002, 205–6).

Jazz music, which had little respectability given its southern and black roots, was dressed up by white orchestras and composers in the early 1920s and became acceptable to middle-class white audiences. By the mid-1920s, Paul Whitman's orchestra and his style of jazz became regular features of radio music that would continue over the next quarter century. Other bands, led by Guy Lombardo, Ozzie Nelson, Rudy Vallee, Duke Ellington, Glen Miller, and Tommy and Jimmy Dorscy helped make jazz an important part of radio broadcasting in the 1920s and 1930s.

Traditionalists looked at pastimes like dancing and jazz and saw dangerous, rude passion and sensuous movement. In the early 1920s the *Ladies' Home Journal* railed against "unspeakable jazz" and launched an anti-jazz crusade that it believed to be "of as great importance today to the moral well being of the United States as the prohibition crusade in the worst days of the saloon." Critics warned that jazz and modern dancing were the sign of American decadence heralding the collapse of civilized life. "Anyone who says that youths of both sexes can mingle in close embrace—with limbs intertwined and torso in contact—without suffering harm lies." The *Ladies' Home Journal* warned, "Add to this position the wriggling movement and sensuous stimulation of the abominable jazz orchestra with its voodoo born minors and its direct appeal to the sensory center, and if you believe that youth is the same after this experience then God help your child." Jazz dancing, it was believed, relaxed morality and undermined the institution of the family. New York, the corrupt Gotham, laying waste to the virtues of the republic, came in for the lion's share of denunciation, and there was the inevitable comparison to Rome in her final orgiastic plunge to destruction (Fass 1977, 22–23).

GAMES

As they had been for centuries, games continued to be part of the repertoire of entertainment possibilities. In addition to the old standbys of Parcheesi, chess, and checkers, card games like mah-jongg, canasta, rummy, casino, and bridge became favorite pastimes for many middle-class Americans. Poker remained a popular card game, particularly among working-class males. Among children the most popular games for boys were playing baseball, rollerskating, kites, marbles, hide and seek, tag, and card games like penny pinching, where cards were tossed and won or lost depending on the skill of the participant in "flipping" his cards. The cards came out of cigarette packs. Among girls the most popular games were tag, jump-rope, jacks, roller-skating, dolls, and ball playing. In the 1930s, Monopoly®, a new board game based on buying and selling property named for streets in Atlantic City, captured the imagination of families of all classes.

ENTERTAINMENT

For the working class the weekend, which often consisted of Saturday afternoon and Sunday or only Sunday, was a special time of some relaxation, at least for men. Women still had to keep up with the daily regimen of cooking, cleaning, and minding the children, and often had to work extra because of the expectation of a special meal on Saturday night or Sunday. On Saturdays immigrant neighborhoods would wait for the beer wagon, which would drop off quarter kegs at various houses. On Sunday working-class families in good weather would often gather in a neighbor's back yard and listen while someone played the guitar or mandolin, while the rest listened or played cards.

Seasonal festivals, usually associated with the church, provided outdoor street theater and social interaction for urban ethnic enclaves of the Northeast. These were the twentieth-century descendants of the urban fairs and festivals of medieval Europe and the urban counterparts of American county and state agricultural fairs and usually included music, food, and religious pageantry. The workplace analog of the street fair was the company picnic. Paid for by the firm, these food and drink extravaganzas often turned the activities of the job into contests. Loggers competed in sawing and chopping contests, and miners in drilling events. Pennsylvania coal miner John Parraccini remembered going to many company-sponsored affairs. "There were a lot of picnics. The mines used to hold picnics every year. There used to be all kinds of games on those picnics. Many times we used to have big rocks, and fellas would see who [could] drill the hole through first."

Modernization also greatly affected the development of recreation in the new century. By the 1920s, most cities of the Northeast boasted an amusement park nearby. These parks consisted of combinations of mechanical rides, cheap foods, and games of chance. Coney Island, near New York, was probably the most famous amusement park in America, but throughout the region hundreds of parks, such as Steeplechase

Island and Pleasure Beach in Connecticut; Electric Park in Albany; the Boardwalk on Long Island; and Merrimack Park, Riverside Park, and Nantucket Point in Massachusetts, provided families in the Northeast the possibility of a day at an amusement park that was only a short train ride away. Often urban trolley companies and amusement park builders formed partnerships, ensuring that a trolley line would be built to serve the park. When there was water around for swimming and bathing, the combination often proved irresistible for both sweltering urbanites and entrepreneurs. Nantucket Point, Coney Island, and Boardwalk Park had seawater; at Rochester, New York, Ontario Beach had Lake Ontario. All were served by public transportation, and all were jammed with people in the summer.

By the 1920s, Americans were also beginning to enjoy annual vacations. Salaried workers increasingly benefited from a two-week annual release from their duties. Rarely did hourly wage earners enjoy such a benefit, but employers would often let them take a week or two off without fear of losing their job. Farmers, of course, who were caring for livestock, had no time for vacation. For those in the Northeast fortunate enough to be able to take automobile vacations, the most popular destinations were Cape Cod, Niagara Falls, New York City, and the beaches of southern New Jersey, especially Atlantic City.

Before 1915 motoring was too expensive for any but the wealthy to enjoy for recreational purposes, but by the end of World War I the economic crunch on motoring began to ease. Filling stations and mechanics were more numerous in cities and suburbs, and prices for automobiles and parts were declining, especially for Henry Ford's basic black Model T. For the urban and suburban middle class, the Sunday drive in the country became a ritual in passable weather, as did the one- or two-week vacation, in spite of the challenges of long-distance trips.

Travelers who made it over the roads and bridges needed overnight accommodations that had ample parking space, a demand that hotels could not always meet. Traditionally, hotels were located in city and town centers, convenient to businesses and train terminals. They usually had little space for parking and could obtain none because central city real estate was expensive and crammed with buildings. Thus the motor hotel, or motel—at first a conglomeration of little cabins placed side by side on major roads outside of cities—was born. Rarely equipped with private bathrooms or toilets, they were inexpensive and offered more privacy than guesthouses, which were usually a family's home that had been turned into a seasonal moneymaker. By 1926 (the year the term *motel* was coined), there were an estimated 2,000 motels in the United States. In the mid-1920s some cities had opened municipal campgrounds for motoring travelers, equipping the sites with cold-water spigots and outdoor toilets. These became more popular as the car-drawn trailer caught the fancy of many travelers. Seven hundred companies manufactured trailers in the 1930s, and by 1940 more than 100,000 trailers were in use.

Many, especially in the middle class, found recreational outlets in various

An early twentieth-century panoramic view of Luna Park, an amusement park at Coney Island in Brooklyn, New York, that ran from 1903 to 1944. Library of Congress

voluntary organizations and clubs, both church sponsored and secular, which allowed men, women, and teenagers in communities of practically every size to explore shared interests and common concerns and backgrounds. Men had business clubs such as the Rotary clubs and Kiwanis, as well as fraternal organizations such as the Knights of Columbus, the Elks, the Moose, and Lions clubs. In large urban areas of the Northeast with large Catholic populations such as New York, Boston, Rochester, and Buffalo, the Catholic Youth Organization provided an alternative to the activities offered by the YMCA and YWCA. Young Men and Women's Hebrew Associations did the same for their coreligionists. Women belonged to various clubs and informal social educational and charitable groups as well.

Drinking, which never died out entirely during Prohibition, especially in the speakeasies of large cities, became a more affordable and commonplace form of recreation after repeal in 1933. The working class patronized taverns, while the middle class increasingly drank at home. Otherwise, dancing was perhaps the most widely shared recreational activity.

A 1936 sociological study of junior high school children on the Lower West Side of New York revealed that 75 percent of the leisure time of these children was spent indoors. Listening to the radio, going to movies, and reading were their favorite activities. Among the radio shows they listened to were adventure serials, family serials, comedies, and musical variety shows. Girls preferred family serials and the boys the adventure serials, while both enjoyed musical variety shows and comedies. Reading was the third most important indoor leisure time activity for young people with newspapers (because of the comics) preferred over other reading material, followed by books, then magazines. Girls preferred *Liberty, Saturday Evening Post,* and *Colliers* magazines while the boys preferred aviation and science magazines. In the 1930s, comic books, building on the popularity of newspaper comics, became popular leisure reading fare for young people. Among the first were *The Shadow* (1931), *Detective Comics* (1937), *Superman* (1938), and *Batman* (1939). Both boys and girls preferred novels of fantasy far removed from the reality of their everyday lives. Boys spent much more time in outdoor activities than girls. While outdoors, "hanging around" followed by baseball remained the most popular activities for boys, while young girls preferred tag and jump-rope, which they did to rhymes that had been part of the culture for centuries yet modified to meet the expressional needs of each new generation that recited them (Robinson 1936, 484–93; Green 2000, 204–8).

Live stage entertainment (and there was no other in the first decades of the century) remained close to its nineteenth-century minstrel and vaudeville roots, but in the Northeast, specifically New York City, a number of musical innovators led by George M. Cohan introduced a new form of entertainment, the musical, to the American public. This form of entertainment, which combined popular music with storylines about average everyday people, gained immediate popularity and became so identified with New York that soon the term *Broadway musical* had a universal connotation. The great American composers and lyricists of the first half of the century all became involved in this new musical form, including Irving Berlin, George M. Cohan, Jerome Kern, Leonard Bernstein, Oscar Hammerstein, Cole Porter, and the Gershwin brothers, George and Ira.

The pioneer in this new creation was George M. Cohan, who wrote both lyrics and music for his shows, which were extravagantly patriotic odes to America and show business. "You're a Grand Old Flag," "Give My Regards to Broadway," and "Over There" were easy to remember and they punched hard with their marching syncopated rhythms. His first hit show, *Little Johnny Jones* (1904), set the pattern for the future Cohan shows as fast-moving musicals. Jerome Kern brought to Broadway the idea of writing shows based on stories about believable people rather than romantic characters from a never-never land. Kern contributed songs to the Ziegfeld Follies of 1916. The follies, of which there were almost annual editions through 1936, represented another form of musical, the storyless revue. Everything about the follies was spectacular. There were opulent settings, music by Kern, Irving Berlin, and Victor Herbert, and of course the elegant Ziegfeld Follies girls, who did little more than make grand entrances in exquisite gowns, stroll around the stage, and pose in tableaux to the "national anthem" of the follies, Berlin's "A Pretty Girl Is Like a Melody."

The revue dominated the Broadway stage of the early 1920s. Most important of the revues were the Garrick Gaieties of 1925 and 1926, because they brought to light two great talents, Richard Rodgers and Lorenzo Hart. The revue was a fast-paced alternation of romantic or topical songs, bright and often satirical sketches, and dances that combined elements of tap, ballet, and ballroom dancing. The 1920s Broadway shows brought together the composers who would dominate the American musical stage for the next two decades: the Gershwins, Rodgers and Hart, Cole Porter, Vincent Youmans, Jerome Kern, and Oscar Hammerstein. It was the last two who brought musical comedy to its maturity in 1927 with their memorable *Show Boat*. It featured blacks not as caricatures but as real suffering people, and all its characters, white and black, were believable figures. Hits from the musical, such as "Ole Man River," became American standards. As Broadway and its composers matured in the early 1930s, it was ready for its closest approach to a true American opera—George Gershwin's *Porgy and Bess* (1935). This work, with its recitatives linking its arias and its orchestration carefully worked out by Gershwin, remains a landmark in American musical history. Broadway musicals had created a genre that would continue into the present, but the high point of this initial era was reached in the mid-1930s. After that, this brilliant group of composers was attracted to Hollywood, where gleaming sets and the introduction of sound provided them with a brand new medium to present their work. Although they left for Hollywood, they had left behind a legacy, which continues to today and has come to represent American popular music to the world (Lloyd 1968, 347–51).

As the new century unfolded, the movies introduced a new form of entertainment that captured the American imagination. American enthusiasm for motion pictures began taking shape in the 1890s with the introduction of Kinetoscopes, followed in 1896 by large-screen projection. Within a few years middle-sized and large cities throughout the Northeast all had nickelodeons offering 15- to 20-minute programs composed of a potpourri of unconnected black-and-white scenes that included brief presentations of dancing, travel scenes, speeding locomotives, and re-creations of historic events. In its early years, the nickelodeon was almost exclusively a popular

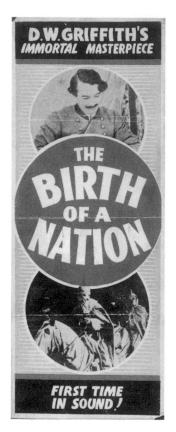

Motion picture poster for D. W. Griffith's 1915 film *The Birth of a Nation,* which was highly controversial due to its promotion of white supremacy and its glorification of the Ku Klux Klan. Library of Congress.

entertainment for the urban working class, but in 1915, D. W. Griffith revolutionized the medium with the first feature-length film, *Birth of a Nation*. The film presented a racist interpretation of Reconstruction and was even partly responsible for the resurrection of the Ku Klux Klan; nevertheless, its technological innovations, in length, staging, and photography, opened new vistas for the fledgling film industry, which in the 1920s and 1930s transcended class to become America's most popular form of entertainment. By the 1920s feature-length as well as shorter films, often accompanied by live vaudeville acts, had become a popular form of cheap entertainment in large and medium-sized cities. In January 1923, the United States had 15,000 silent movie theaters with an average capacity of 507 and a weekly attendance of 50 million.

Although the first generation of films was dubbed silent films, the theaters were anything but. An organ or piano player accompanied pictures, and audiences felt free to comment out loud if scenes called for it. In the 1920s, Hollywood also established the star system, and actors, bigger than their pictures, almost bigger than life, captured the imaginations of many who followed the on- and off-screen adventures of their favorite stars, such as male sex symbol Rudolph Valentino, the comics Charlie Chaplin and Buster Keaton, the "It" girl Clara Bow, and Mary Pickford, "America's Sweetheart," who married the dashing Douglass Fairbanks. By 1927, the movies began talking when in October of that year Al Jolson starred in *The Jazz Singer*. Sound influenced the direction the industry would take over the next 10 years. Western action films that could include compelling sounds such as horses, guns, and saloon sounds became popular, as well as horror movies with their screams and creaking doors. Contemporary crime dramas with gunfire, breaking glass, and screeching tires also provided a popular theme in the 1930s. By the end of the decade the movie industry had secured its position as America's most popular form of entertainment, with weekly attendance at films exceeding one million viewers.

The Depression at first caused a downturn in film attendance, but by 1933 the industry had recovered. Some of the most popular movies of the era were gangster films such as *Little Caesar* (1930), and *Public Enemy* (1931) starring Jimmy Cagney. Backstage "confidential pictures" such as *Footlight Parade* (1933) and *42nd Street* (1933), which supposedly took viewers behind the scenes of the entertainment industry, also enjoyed popularity. The audiences also flocked to comedies in the 1930s. Among the most popular were those in which either the Marx Brothers, W. C. Fields, or Mae West starred. While becoming America's favorite form of entertainment, the movies with their standardization of speech, fashion, and manners also contributed significantly to the creation of a national culture. Another popular form of entertainment that

A casino in Harlem, New York, 1927. The Granger Collection, New York.

contributed to the development of a national culture was the radio (see the section on Communication). With broadcasts that could be heard across the country, the radio allowed Americans for the first time to share a common live experience. National political events and World Series baseball games were the first of these collective radio experiences (Kyvig 2002, 50–52, 156–62).

HOLIDAYS, CELEBRATIONS, AND FESTIVALS

For many Americans, holidays represented the high points of their leisure time. Christmas was the most important holiday for the 90 percent who were Christian. Protestants had traditionally dedicated more time to Easter, but within the previous century American Christmas celebrations had come to combine Catholic and Orthodox religious festivals, along with German and Scandinavian traditions of decorating a tree, the domestically evolved traditions of greeting cards and the jolly old elf Santa Claus, and at the center of the celebration extensive gift giving. New Year's Day, Easter, Memorial Day, Fourth of July, and Thanksgiving were generally important holidays, while children enjoyed Halloween, and ethnic groups celebrated their own special occasions such as St. Patrick's Day and Yom Kippur (Kyvig 2002, 162).

SECULAR RITES OF PASSAGE

One of the most respected of the secular rituals, particularly in the Northeast, involved the process by which one chose one's lifetime companion. In the first decade of the century much courtship had taken place in the home according to well-defined customs. A young man would be encouraged to call on a young woman. In doing so he would meet her parents, talk to her in the family parlor, perhaps be offered refreshments, possibly be entertained by her piano playing or singing, and ultimately be encouraged to call again or discouraged from doing so. This social ritual, originating with the upper classes, common within the middle class, and copied insofar as possible by families of more modest means, gave eligible women and watchful parents some power over the courtship process. Men could, of course, decline to call, but if they did proceed, they ventured into the woman's environment. If the courtship progressed, the couple might move from the parlor to the still highly visible porch, or attend public functions together. But only well along in the process could a young lady properly consent to the privacy of going out alone with her suitor. Early in the twentieth century "dating" began to replace calling. Urbanization in the new century had led to the demise of the tradition of visiting a girl and being entertained in her home. In the urban Northeast, apartment living limited space for receiving and entertaining guests, and for poorer people living in tenements in cramped boarding houses, there was no private space at all.

At the same time cities offered greater possibilities for courting outside the home. Gradually, couples began to go out on dates, prearranged excursions to the soda and coffee shops, movie theaters, restaurants, and other places where even in the midst of a crowd they experienced less supervision and greater privacy than in the parlor. The automobile further extended the range of possibilities for dating couples, not only as transportation to entertainment, but also as a place for private intimacy. Because dates cost money and males were far more likely to earn cash for such purposes, dating tended to give men greater control over courtship. Since they were now the hosts, men gained control over the choice of activity and the dating process. Indeed, it was considered improper for a woman to propose a date.

The increased popularity of dating in the second decade of the twentieth century encouraged greater sexual exploration. Promiscuity is often connected to the 1920s, but a study of the literature demonstrates that this quiet revolution had been going on since at least the turn of the century as women began to demand looser corsets, greater equality with men, and more information on the control of their reproductive lives. Long before the rise of the dating system young people regularly experimented with kissing games. Engaged couples often enjoyed what was coming to be known as heavy petting, and enough people engaged in premarital intercourse that nearly 1 in 10 late nineteenth-century brides went to the altar pregnant. Dating, however, brought more open attitudes about sexuality and more freedom to explore them. Prolonged kissing and embraces became accepted aspects of romantic relationships. Necking and petting were customary if not universal practices. Evidence compiled later pointed to a sharp rise in premarital intercourse after World War I, with over 80 percent of males and nearly 50 percent of females acknowledging participation (Kyvig 2002, 132–34).

Religious Life

THE NORTHEAST

|

OVERVIEW

DOMESTIC LIFE

ECONOMIC LIFE

INTELLECTUAL LIFE

MATERIAL LIFE

POLITICAL LIFE

RECREATIONAL LIFE

RELIGIOUS LIFE

RELIGION AND SPIRITUALITY

Despite what some described as a growing laxity in morals during the first decades of the twentieth century, religion continued to play a role in most Americans' lives in the 1920s and 1930s. Most people belonged to a religion, almost always a Christian one. Two-thirds of the Christians, however, affiliated with one or another Protestant sect. In the Northeast, the predominant sects were Episcopalians, Presbyterians, Methodists, and (especially in the New England area) Congregationalists. New York had significant Jewish populations. Despite the number of denominations, they generally shared certain characteristics. Homes more often than not had religious icons such as pictures, crosses, crucifixes, or menorahs, and most families routinely prayed before meals. Otherwise, religious matters were centered in the church. Conducting prayer services at home was mostly a thing of the past.

Sunday was the day most given over to religious activities. Religious education programs had developed over the previous half century with graded curriculums that were patterned after secular education but centered on Bible study and conducted by church volunteers. Sunday schools had shifted the responsibility for religious training from the home to the Sunday schools. By 1920, more parents sent their children to Sunday school than went to services themselves (Kyvig 2002, 149–55).

With 12 million Catholics in the country, they were by far the single largest denomination of Christians in the United States. Half of those Catholics in the United States were concentrated in the Northeast. And their religion was not limited to the spiritual; their entire social, cultural, and material lives revolved around their Catholicism and their church. Catholics for the first decades of the twentieth century in the major dioceses of the Northeast created and maintained a separate social structure of Catholic schools, orphanages, welfare centers, hospitals, universities, even cemeteries. They also were guided by a rigid set of rules, which demanded weekly church attendance, catechism, and a Catholic education for their children either through Sunday school classes or preferably by attendance at a Catholic school. The big urban diocese set the tone for and defined the public image of the American Catholic Church.

Bishops of big dioceses such as Philadelphia, New York, and Boston were sole corporate heads of major business enterprises. A small number of men, all of whom became cardinals, had unusually long tenures as archbishops of the largest dioceses: William O. Connell in Boston (1907–1944), Dennis Dougherty in Philadelphia (1918–1951), John Farley in New York (1902–1918), and then in New York Patrick Hayes (1919–1938). Differences of style and personality notwithstanding, they were all like-minded centralizers, standardizers, and disciplinarians. They also were all Irish Americans. In the established dioceses of the Northeast the priesthood offered an inviting package of security and social rank to any young man with upper middle-class aspirations, particularly among the Irish. Compared with other high-status professions like medicine or the law, the priesthood was much more accessible to a young man without family connections or the means to finance an extended education. All of the post–World War I cardinals were sons of working-class families.

In the hierarchical structure of the church, nuns were at the bottom of the religious pecking order, but they were essential to the maintenance and administration of the complex and massive Catholic system of education, health care, and social services. A major motivation for joining the sisterhood in this era was the fact that at the turn of the century and well into the twentieth century there were few lay positions open to women that carried the responsibilities and prestige of a Catholic nun. As one nun recently recalled, the pre–World War II generation of nuns were "pretty independent ladies. They were engineers who fired up boilers in the morning. They fixed things. They managed investments; they approved building plans and managed construction. [In those days] we didn't know women could do all those things" (Morris 1997, 115–16).

The issue of alcohol divided Baptists, Methodists, and other firm Prohibitionists from Catholics, some Lutherans, and others who, largely because of their ethnic background, were not opposed to drinking. Race created other religious divisions throughout the first half of the twentieth century. Large Protestant denominations such as the Methodists and Baptists remained divided by color, as 99 percent of black Protestants worshiped only with other African Americans in self-segregated congregations. Most African Americans (seven and a half million) belonged to their own separate churches. The largest black Protestant congregation was Harlem's Abyssinian Baptist Church. Harlem was also home to the flamboyant mystic George Baker, who called himself Father Divine.

In urban areas especially, American religious expression in the 1920s consisted of a general approval of the way things were. Many American Protestants, who collectively represented the religious majority, shared a Calvinist view that explained success as a reward for virtue and difficulty as a test of character. The self-contented Protestant pro-business view was expressed in Bruce Barton's 1925 book *The Man Nobody Knows*, which depicted Jesus Christ as a dynamic business leader who picked up 12 men from the bottom ranks of society and forged them into the world's most successful organization. At the same time the Social Gospel movement, which contributed to a host of social reform movements, thrived among many urban congregations.

SACRED RITES OF PASSAGE

Sacred rites of passage in the Catholic Church included receiving a series of sacraments: baptism, at birth; first communion, around age 7; confirmation, at age thirteen or fourteen; followed by matrimony, which the Catholic Church also considers a sacrament. Among the Protestant faiths, the Episcopalians followed rites similar to the Catholics, but for other Protestant faiths the most sacred rite of passage remained baptism, which in some denominations could not be administered until the person had reached the age of reason, at which they could make the decision to accept Christ as their savior. Aside from circumcision of boys at birth, for the Jewish faithful there remained only one sacred rite of passage, the bar mitzvah, which declares a boy a man at 13 and a girl a woman at 12.

An important sacred rite of passage that all religions shared was the rite of burial. In the 1920s, especially in urban areas of the Northeast, mourning and burial of the dead began more and more to be taken over by professional funeral directors. It became common practice to embalm the body and display it in an open casket either in the home of the deceased or in a funeral parlor. Burial of the remains in a cemetery remained the norm, and cremations were rare. In northeastern cities and towns the advent of professionally conducted funerals had a profound impact on the next three stages of the rituals of death services: services before the burial, the procession, and services at the grave. One of the most powerful symbolic actions associated with the rituals of death had been the procession from the home to the grave, marking the separation of the living from the dead. As more and more people were taken to hospitals to die, and then buried from hired chapels, the effects of the pointed and poignant transition were greatly muted.

From 1900 to 1915, only 3.3 percent of funerals in the Northeast occurred at undertakers' establishments. No doubt more families used an undertaker's service, but they kept the body at home for the funeral. By 1930, the proportion of families who chose to have the funeral service at the undertaker's parlor rose to 13.8 percent, and it had jumped to 55.3 percent by 1945. Several reasons exist for this change. For many, having a body in the house for several days must have been a strain, no matter how close the relationship, and to remove it must have been a relief. Most must have welcomed funeral homes once they were available without charge, as they were in many cities of the Northeast after 1914.

The last two stages of the ritual of death include actions taken to remember the dead and the reintegration of the mourners into the community of the living The various forms used in remembrance and reintegration, such as memorial pamphlets, resolutions passed by organizations on the death of a member, letters and other written expressions of consolation, and obituaries were all present before the turn of the century, but all underwent significant transformation in substance and symbols in the new century. As the new century opened, memorial biographies began to replace sermons, and the death was used not as opprobrium to the living but rather as a celebration of the life of the deceased. Memorial cards also came into frequent use. Such cards were sometimes printed on black-bordered paper and represented an inexpensive option for distribution to family and friends. The messages were simple and brief, like an obituary, with some appropriate symbol or verse.

Written condolences continued to be important means for remembering the dead and reassuring the survivors that they were still part of the community. In the first half of the twentieth century these cards became less religious, and with the advent of the commercial greeting card, those who were sympathetic but could not easily express their concern personally had an opportunity to express their sympathy. Consideration of rituals of death associated with remembrance and consolation naturally leads to the evolution of cemeteries and grave markers. In many towns and cities of the Northeast, cemeteries ranged from large elaborate grounds open to the whole community to small churchyards. Size of markers has reduced significantly over the years; the oldest parts of cemeteries in towns and cities in the Northeast have a variety of types of monuments. Between 1870 and 1950 taste in grave markers continued to evolve. From 1840 to 1920 an eclectic style of large monuments reflecting both individualism and a defiance of death was common. Around 1900, a modern plain style emerged Part of this more modern style owed to attitudes that, if not denying death, attempted to maintain a degree of indifference to it. In addition, with longer life expectancy, most of those who died were older, so their deaths were neither unexpected nor tragic—hence the need to commemorate the individual and express grief were reduced. This trend would continue through the first half of the twentieth century (Wells 2000, 204–6).

RITUAL

Among immigrant communities of the urban Northeast ritual often involved the amalgamation of the sacred with the profane—or at least the practical. One example of this is a religious celebration in New York, which began in the 1880s and continues to the present. It is known as the festival of Our Lady of Mt. Carmel the Virgin of 115th Street. Although its roots were in the nineteenth century and the energy of collective memory resuscitates this celebration every year, the vibrant and crucial era of this religious celebration was the first half of the twentieth century. In the 1880s, the celebration began as a devotion imported from the Italian village of Polla. Soon the celebration was joined by Italians from other villages, and the devotion, mostly attended by men who had come without their families to this country, was an expression by the men of their loyalty to the women they left behind. In the early twentieth century, when bitter generational disputes arose, the festival of the Virgin to which all Italians were compelled to go reminded wayward youth of the family-centeredness of the Italian community and cajoled wayward youth who were obligated to go to the festival back to their family roots. In the 1930s and 1940s as other ethnic groups began to enter what Italians considered their Harlem, particularly the newly arrived Puerto Ricans and the expanding community of blacks, the celebration took on greater significance as a means of defining space. The streets through which the Virgin was paraded every July 15 marked the Italian streets of Harlem.

SACRED SPACE AND SACRED TIME

As the new century unfolded and as Americans searched for a language of restitution and wholeness, they demanded institutions larger than the separated churches for its embodiment. A new religion of Americanism emerged. Leaders grafted religious symbols onto their imperial mission. They used wars, a small one in 1898 and a much larger one in 1917, to serve as the major ecumenical and interfaith instrument, while the nation itself became a transcendent religious symbol.

In this spirit, sacred spaces of American history became places where the religious symbol of America was memorialized, and the Northeast was replete with such places. The pilgrim could start in Boston with Plymouth Rock and then go to Concord and Lexington, then travel to Gettysburg where none other than Abraham Lincoln called the ground "consecrated" by brave men. And finally, the traveler could visit Independence Hall, the Bethlehem where the nation was born. As the automobile made people more mobile, weeklong vacations became pilgrimages to the hallowed spots of the nation's heritage.

In the predominantly Christian Northeast, Sunday had always remained the day of worship and rest, but as the century progressed it began to be seen more as simply a day of rest in which secular entertainment and relaxation rivaled and in many areas surpassed the spiritual recreation of church. By the 1920s, golf courses were reporting more players on the links on Sunday morning than any other day of the week. Sunday also became the most popular day of the week for moviegoing, and finally, professional baseball teams chipped away at blue laws that prevented charging for tickets for Sunday games. Midwestern cities led the way before the turn of the century; they were joined by Washington and New York after World War I. Boston held out against Sunday baseball until 1929, and Pittsburgh and Philadelphia held steadfast until 1934, but with those two cities the last bastions against Sunday baseball fell.

WORLDVIEW

In the Northeast, where the population remained the most eclectic in the country, it would be difficult to define a single worldview. For the dominant middle-class Protestant population of the Northeast all space was sacred space. Jesus was depicted as a super salesman, John D. Rockefeller claimed that God gave him his money, and the middle-class Christian spirit told people that if they abided by the scriptures and led forthright lives they would be prosperous and if they weren't prosperous it was because of their own vice. Thus the politics of the new era were tinged with a great deal of morality and the Christian obligation of those who had followed the straight and narrow and had become successful to help those less fortunate find the way.

For immigrants another view prevailed. It could probably best be summarized by a Jewish immigrant's son who served in World War I. "When my turn to be drafted came," he said, "it didn't bother me at all. As a matter of fact, if I hadn't been drafted, I think I would have gone anyway. Both my parents had been Jewish immigrants from Europe and this country has been good to our family" (Keene 2006, 109). Like many other immigrants who left Europe in the late nineteenth and early twentieth century, they ignored the prejudice they experienced in their new country, which probably seemed fairly benign when compared to the oppression, starvation, and poverty they had left behind. They clung to their traditions and their faith but looked forward to a bright future that America promised them. The American dream was not always realized, but the myth was strong enough to maintain them.

For blacks in the new urban ghettos of northern cities their worldview was probably distinct from that of the immigrants from Europe, and they certainly did not share the chauvinistic worldviews of the white Protestant middle class. Some may have shared the optimism of the European immigrants, but they also had to face the dismal reality that while the Europeans had been able to escape the social constrictions of their European villages, racial prejudice, which had caused so many social and economic problems in the South, had followed them northward.

All groups in these early decades of the twentieth century, however, had shared in a world war and were witnessing the beginning of another, and experiencing a technological explosion that had taken them from horse and buggies to autos, and a Great Depression that had left many in financial ruin. Despite their differences of class, race, or religion, Americans shared the common dilemmas of living and working in a world where change had become the norm, war was ever present, and economic calamity was a constant possibility.

FOR MORE INFORMATION

Books

Davidson, John West, William E. Gienapp, Christine Leigh Heyrman, Mark H. Lytle, and Michael B. Stoff. *Nation of Nations: A Narrative History of the American Republic*. 4th ed. New York: McGraw Hill, 2001.

Degler, Carl N. *At Odds: Women and the Family in America from the Revolution to the Present.* New York: Oxford University Press, 1980.

Fass, Paula S. *The Damned and the Beautiful: American Youth in the 1920's.* New York: Oxford University Press, 1977.

Green, Harvey. *The Uncertainty of Everyday Life 1915–1945.* Fayetteville: University of Arkansas Press, 2000.

Grier, Katherine C. *Pets in America.* Chapel Hill: University of North Carolina Press, 2006.

Harrell, David Edwein, Edwin S. Gaustad, John B. Boles, Sally Foreman Griffith, and Randall Miller. *Unto a Good Land: A History of the American People.* Grand Rapids, MI: Eerdmans Publishing Company, 2005.

Hill, Daniel Delis. *As Seen in Vogue: A Century of Fashion in Advertising.* Lubbock: Texas Tech University Press, 2004.

Kyvig, David E. *Daily Life in the United States 1920–1940: How Americans Lived Through the Roaring Twenties and the Great Depression.* Chicago: Ivan R. Dee, 2002.

Lloyd, Norman. *The Golden Encyclopaedia of Music.* New York: Golden Press, 1968.

London, Jack. *John Barleycorn: Alcoholic Memoirs.* New York: Oxford University Press, 1989.

Mencken, H. L. *On Politics.* New York: Vintage Books, 1960.

Millman, Chad. *The Detonators: The Secret Plot to Destroy America and an Epic Hunt for Justice.* New York: Little Brown and Company, 2006.

Morris, Charles. *American Catholic: The Saints and Sinners Who Built America's Most Powerful Church.* New York: Random House, 1997.

Opdyke, Sandra. *No One Was Turned Away: The Role of Public Hospitals in New York City Since 1900.* New York: Oxford University Press, 1999.

Reich, Steven A. *Encyclopedia of the Great Black Migration.* Westport, CT: Greenwood Press, 2006.

Riess, Steven A. *City Games: The Evolution of American Urban Society and the Rise of Sports.* Chicago: University of Chicago Press, 1991.

Riordon, William L. *Plunkitt of Tammany Hall,* ed. Terrence McDonald. New York: Bedford Books/St. Martins Press, 1994.

Roberts, Randy. *Jack Dempsey: The Manassa Mauler.* Baton Rouge: Louisiana State University Press, 1979.

Sklar, Robert. *Movie-Made America: A Cultural History of American Movies.* New York: Vintage Books, 1994.

Sullivan, Mark. *Our Times: The United States 1900–1925.* 6 vols. New York: Charles Scribners, 1927.

Tygiel, Jules. *Past Time: Baseball As History.* New York: Oxford University Press, 2000.

Wells, Robert V. *Facing the King of Terrors: Death and Society in an American Community 1750–1990.* New York: Cambridge University Press, 2000.

Zinn, Howard. *A People's History of the United States 1492–Present.* New York: Harper Perennial, 2003.

Articles

Bateman, Fred. "Improvement in American Dairy Farming, 1850–1910: A Quantitative Analysis." *Journal of Economic History* 28, no. 2 (June 1968): 255–73.

Kingsdale, Jon M. "The 'Poor Man's Club': Social Functions of the Urban Working Class Saloon." *American Quarterly* 25, no. 4 (October 1973): 472–89.

Loftue, John J. "The Activity Program in New York Elementary Schools." *Journal of Educational Sociology* 17, no. 2 (October 1943): 71–72.

Nash, Roderick. "The American Cult of the Primitive." *American Quarterly* 18, no. 3 (Autumn 1966): 517–37.

Orsi, Robert. "The Religious Boundaries of an In-Between People: Street Fest and the Problem of the Dark-Skinned Other in Italian Harlem, 1920–1990." *American Quarterly* 44, no. 3 (September 1992): 313–47.

Patrick, Vincent. "Crime Story." *New York Times Review of Books*, September 9, 2007, 31.

Robinson, Reginald. "Leisure Time Activities of the Children of New York's Lower West Side." *Journal of Educational Sociology* 9, no. 8 (April 1936): 484–93.

Sicotte, Richard. "Economic Crisis and Political Response: The Political Economy of the Shipping Act of 1916." *Journal of Economic History* 59, no. 4 (December 1999): 103–10.

Web Sites

Diehl, Lorraine B., and Marianne Hardart. "The Automat: The History, Recipes, and Allure of Horn & Hardart's Masterpiece." http://www.theautomat.net/.

"Duke University Libraries—Airlines History." http://scriptorium.lib.duke.edu/adaccess/airline-history.html.

"United Airlines History." http: //www. united.com/page/middlepage/0, 6823,2286,00.html.

W.E.B. Du Bois Learning Center. http://www.duboislc.org/man.html.

3

THE MIDDLE ATLANTIC STATES

Overview

THE MIDDLE ATLANTIC
STATES
|
OVERVIEW
DOMESTIC LIFE
ECONOMIC LIFE
INTELLECTUAL LIFE
MATERIAL LIFE
POLITICAL LIFE
RECREATIONAL LIFE
RELIGIOUS LIFE

As in other areas of the country, in the Middle Atlantic region (which includes Pennsylvania, New Jersey, Delaware, Maryland, and the District of Columbia), immigration and migration, technology, and a great war followed by an economic boom and collapse brought great changes to daily life from 1900–1940. The major cities of the area, including Philadelphia, Pittsburgh, Baltimore, and Washington, absorbed part of the great immigration from Europe and the continued significant migration of blacks from the South. This demographic upheaval affected almost every area within the Middle Atlantic region. Migration changed people's neighborhoods, living conditions, eating habits, and even the way they viewed each other. Technology, particularly the wide application of electricity in factory production, businesses, and households, changed how people lived not only at home but in the workplace. The expansion of trolleys, elevated trains, and subway systems, and the advent of the automobile expanded and redefined space and accelerated the growth of suburbs. The convulsions of the "Great War," followed by the Great Depression, affected people's perspectives on the security of daily life as they had known it as children. This chapter will investigate how these changes shaped daily life in the Middle Atlantic region and the nation in an era that many historians have described as the decades of change and uncertainty.

Domestic Life

THE MIDDLE ATLANTIC
STATES
|
OVERVIEW
DOMESTIC LIFE
ECONOMIC LIFE
INTELLECTUAL LIFE
MATERIAL LIFE
POLITICAL LIFE
RECREATIONAL LIFE
RELIGIOUS LIFE

FAMILY LIFE

In the Middle Atlantic region, as elsewhere, the middle-class family household, whether as an apartment or detached dwelling in city, suburb, or small town, was supposed to be a place of refuge from the harsh world of the workplace. In the nineteenth

Typical Pennsylvania farm kitchen at the turn of the twentieth century. Library of Congress.

century this conception of the home was refined and codified in popular literature, architectural form, and home furnishings. In these "secular sanctuaries," as writers referred to them, beauty, religion, learning, and other high-culture pursuits were preserved, encountered, and appreciated, and here they exercised their alleged influence upon the character of men hardened by the highly competitive world of capitalism. In this protected environment, women supposedly assumed the roles of civilizer and softener, nurturer, and helpful companion. These roles gave them new moral authority within the household, supposedly with a concession to men to control the public sphere. This image of family, which had been carefully crafted in women's magazines, advice columns, and fiction during the mid- to late nineteenth century, would be radically altered in the new century.

The Great War, the middle-class expansion of the 1920s, the crises of the Depression, and technological innovations in consumer goods altered family relationships, challenged traditional gender roles, and offered new social and economic expectations for many Americans. Many World War I soldiers returned from Europe with knowledge and experience of a more open (or at least less straight-laced) attitude toward sex and marriage. In the 1920s, young people with access to automobiles took advantage of the mobility and the privacy that the car offered to escape parents and chaperones while courting, thereby undermining the Victorian codes of conduct their parents had experienced. The economic and social dislocation wrought by the Depression disrupted family roles when fathers could not find work, and many men, women, and children lost their homes and drifted.

Yet certain images, and to a greater extent roles, of the sexes remained powerful. Men were to be responsible breadwinners and physically strong and dominant. Women were supposed to be nurturing and emotional, physically weaker, but bedrocks of familial stability. In the Middle Atlantic region, as elsewhere, the archetypical family structure of popular culture, husband and wife and children in one household, was predominant enough to maintain the stereotype, but there were many variants.

With larger families than their middle-class and wealthy counterparts, as well as boarders, newcomers, and relatives looking for work, home life for the working class of the Middle Atlantic region was characterized by little space and few conveniences. In a 1913 article in the *Journal of Home Economics*, Mabel Kittridge identified a typical working-class family and described their living situation. Eight family members and one boarder occupied a four-room flat that cost $19 monthly. The father and two of the children worked in a local factory (the father earned $12 weekly), and the mother made artificial flowers at home. All slept in the same room and each child shared a bed with two or three siblings. Margaret Byington's 1910 study of workers near Pittsburgh revealed that only 15 of 90 (17 percent) working-class living units had indoor toilets.

Crowded living conditions were common among the working class because boarders were both a financial necessity and a neighborhood service. Newly arrived immigrants expected lodging with people from their home village until they could get on their feet; so too did relatives. But most households brought in boarders for the income they generated. Joe Rudiak, of Lyndora, Pennsylvania, "lived in company houses owned by the Standard Steel Company, and each . . . were all frame and painted red. . . . They had, lined up for let's say half a mile and about five hundred feet deep, rows of these shanties. . . . As high as five, six, seven boarders would come in. . . . There was nine of us and as high as four boarders. Mostly it was all relatives and folks from home." Rose Popovich's mother started a boardinghouse in Monessen, Pennsylvania, immediately after arriving in the United States in 1912. She had hoped to pack the beds with boarders each night, and she succeeded. Renters were "so in need of housing that they were willing to sleep even three on one bed." The real entrepreneurs took in people working different shifts to maximize the number of bodies that could sleep on a few beds. Five dollars each month got a boarder laundry and room; the weekly food bill was divided among the boarders, which meant that the proprietors' food costs were met by the boarders. Rose shined the boarders' shoes on Saturday nights for 25 cents for each pair. She remembered that some boarders bought her presents at Christmas and Easter.

Black family structure in the city and in the countryside was most often that of the two-parent household. In the alleys and residential streets to which they were confined by poverty and racism, extended kinship and community care were provided by the neighborhood. In the black community kinship networks remained strong over substantial distances. Throngs of relatives of three and four generations reconvened for births, annual "homecomings," and funerals. Among poor rural families in the Middle Atlantic region, there was a great deal of turnover, but, as George McDaniel has shown in his study of rural Maryland, those who moved in were often kin to those who had left.

In the 1920s, young people in the Middle Atlantic region, as in other highly urbanized sections of the country, encountered a new set of conventions regarding marriage and family life. Compatibility replaced economics as the major factor of a successful marriage. Academics, sociologists, and some health professionals studied courtship and issued studies, even manifestos that identified the secrets of a happy marriage and effective child rearing. Colleges and universities began to offer courses in "modern marriage." A product of the new sexuality, such courses also owed some intellectual debt to the continuing power of eugenics and high school hygiene courses that touched lightly and cautiously on matters of anatomy and sex. Ernest Groves, a prominent sociologist who had written a textbook on marriage in 1926, taught the first course and then reached a broader audience with his "lecture" in *Good Housekeeping*'s "College Courses on Marriage Relations" series, which began in September of 1937.

"Companionate marriage" was the fashionable term for the ideal marriage relationship of the 1920s. A "good sport" and shared interests, rather than the nineteenth-century concept of "separate spheres," were the keys to happiness. Promoters of the new kind of relationship encouraged couples to socialize together with other couples, instead of the traditional middle-class and wealthy social practices that separated the sexes. Reformers criticized men who were constantly slipping off to clubs, bars, or golf courses that excluded women, and they attacked women who for their social lives relied primarily on entertaining other women at home, or on meeting them in restaurants or department store salons, or at their own clubs. The companionate marriage concept explains the surge in middle-class women's interest in sports such as golf and tennis, which they could play with their husbands or boyfriends.

Marriage and family life among the urban and rural working class received far less attention from these reformers, and couples from lower economic levels experienced the companionate marriage ideal less than did those who were more affluent. Traditional gender roles also remained strongly entrenched among urban immigrant workers and African Americans, as they moved to major cities of the Middle Atlantic region and elsewhere. In part this was a result of the exigencies of trying to eke out a living. Leisure was a scarce commodity, and the free time that the middle class and the wealthy enjoyed simply did not exist for workers. Entertainment and social life often turned on activities run by church and ethnic organizations, and mutual aid or labor associations. In cities, access to amusement parks, movie houses, and other public entertainment provided relief to working-class family lives.

The increased availability of contraceptive devices and information also contributed to a transformation of gender relations in the first decades of the twentieth century and demanded new conventions for intimacy. As the new rules were negotiated, the limits were allegedly set by women, and the boundaries of behavior were based on the assumption that men would not force themselves on women after an inexact but generally acknowledged number of protestations. Physical and economic powers were male attributes and advantages, but the responsibility for chastity ("keeping one's worth") rested with the women. "A man is only as bad as the woman he is with," wrote the author of *How to Win and Hold a Husband* (1945) (Green 2000, 132). Emily Post, the famous arbiter of good behavior and taste, offered more blunt advice. She warned young women that "petting and cuddling have the same cheapening effect as that produced on merchandise which has through constant handling become faded and rumpled, smudged or frayed and thrown out on the bargain counter in a marked-down lot." The proliferation of warnings against sexual activity by the young is an indirect but credible indicator of the persistence of premarital sexual intercourse (Green 2000, 119–21, 131–32).

Although the archetypical family structure of popular culture—husband and wife and children in one household—was predominant enough to maintain the stereotype, there were many variants. Working-class Americans took in boarders to make ends meet, and their parents and other relatives sometimes moved in during difficult times or as their health declined. In the working-class world, children often went to work as early as they could to increase family income.

In many ways, Polish families in Pennsylvania typified the Middle Atlantic immigrant family experience in the first decades of the twentieth century. Polish families could be divided into three groups according to family composition—nuclear, extended, and augmented—and into four groups according to stage in life cycle—newlyweds, young families, midstage, and mature. A nuclear family consisted of one or both parents and their children; an extended family included other relatives living in the home; an augmented family included nonrelative lodgers and boarders whose presence was intended to supplement the family income. Newlywed families were defined as childless couples; young families were those in which there were no working children and the wife was under age 45. Midstage families had employed children and/or a wife over age 45; mature families had children living outside the home. Characteristically, kinship was also crucial for Poles moving to western Pennsylvania. For example, the mother of Joseph D. was brought from Gdansk (Prussia) to "Polish Hill" by an uncle who ran a grocery store. Valerian D. was brought to McKeesport, Pennsylvania, by his father in 1906. Peter L. avoided service in the Russian army by following a brother to Pittsburgh. The parents of Joseph B. were brought from Russian Poland by relatives. With two sisters and a brother already working in the city, the father of Stephanie L. left German Poland in 1899 with his wife and daughter. Joseph B. sent passage for two brothers and a sister to join him on the south side of Pittsburgh. Joseph Z. attracted two brothers to the Oliver Iron and Steel plant, also in Pittsburgh (Bodnar 1985, 562).

In the Mid-Atlantic region, as elsewhere, the Great Depression put great strains on families, and they did whatever they could to survive. In industrial regions of the Mid-Atlantic, the Depression crushed many of the working class, especially those who constantly lived on the edge of insolvency. Entire factories closed down, leaving thousands unemployed. The majority of those lucky enough to find work only did so sporadically. Joe Rudiak, who worked in Lyndora, Pennsylvania, building flatcars, remembered "making good money in 1929, more than $4 a day until about two, three weeks after [the crash when] the place closed down. Everybody lost their jobs," he recalled. "There was no work. I didn't get back to work up at the plant again up till about 1936—'35 maybe."

By 1931, out-of-work urban families, both adults and children, were scavenging in dumps. Orderly lines formed at some dumps as people waited their turn to hunt for food. Some enterprising men made and sold gin from their homes. Those who did manage to fend off the bankers and other lenders, and who found some sort of food, faced another trial finding fuel for warmth and for cooking. People foraged firewood from forests if they were nearby. Unemployed coal workers around Steelton, Pennsylvania, dug coal from abandoned mines, hauled it out, and distributed it first to widows and then to those who dug it. In Philadelphia, Mary Griesser recalled poor children walking along railroad tracks with empty fruit baskets collecting coal that had fallen from passing coal-driven trains. They would either sell their black treasure for a few pennies or take it home to provide a little fuel for the family stove or furnace.

Most families survived, but for many the effects of the Depression were devastating. In some families, domestic violence and child abuse increased as men found it difficult to cope with unemployment and families scrapped over money. Men and boys (and some women and girls) ran away from home in ever-increasing numbers. Labor organizer Larry Van Dusen admitted, "My father led a rough life. [In normal times] he drank. During the Depression, he drank more. There was more conflict in the home. A lot of fathers, mine among them, had a habit of taking off. . . . And there was always the Saturday night ordeal as to whether or not the old man would get home with his paycheck."

Many families came apart when father, children, or mother simply left. Hundreds of thousands of single men and women, young and old, married and single, rode the rails, trying to find work, swiping a meal, doing odd jobs here and there, sleeping where they could. Many children and young adults left home because they could not get food or work there. Joe Morrison, a coal miner and steelworker recalled that "In '30 and '31, you'd see freight trains, you'd see hundreds of kids, young kids, lots of 'em, just wandering all over the country" (Green 2000, 79–80).

As people began to live longer in the new century, the elderly began to have a greater presence in the family for longer periods of time. The lack of retirement plans or government social security, and an extension of relatively useless years after a life of productive work for many, often created a humiliating experience, especially when an elderly person had to accept an inferior role in the home of his or her child. Popular concepts of the elderly did not help. Advertising celebrated youth. When an elderly person made an infrequent appearance in an ad, he or she was depicted as an object of nostalgia or an anachronism and usually as a background subject.

There were few if any "safety nets" for older Americans until Social Security became functional in the mid-1940s, and even that was little help to those already old, infirm, and poor, and the vast number of Americans who were not yet included in the coverage. The working class, especially in the extractive industries, also often suffered from job-related injuries or chronic disabling conditions that aged them prematurely. Miners hacked from black lung or silicosis. Farmers often lost digits or limbs in machines, or contracted lung diseases from the dust raised while working dry ground or harvesting grain and hay, or became deaf as a result of driving tractors that normally had no mufflers. Few workers had company pensions, and those who did found them to be meager.

But aging was not simply a tale of woe and unmitigated disaster, even for the working class and the poor. When the last of the children left home, for those parents who could still work, it was the beginning of a time of freedom as well as the end of an era. And not all children disappeared from their parents' lives. Many settled near their siblings and their parents, especially because in many cases working-class children starting out on the job often did so in the same place where their parents or relatives already worked. There were also some organizations that provided social comforts, if not physical protection, for the older American. Synagogues, churches, and fraternal groups such as the Knights of Columbus, the Elks, the Moose, the Odd Fellows, the Grange, and the Masons provided camaraderie and understanding for their members. Older women had fewer structured opportunities for socializing but had more continuity in their social relationships, because many had for years centered their social lives in their homes and neighborhoods among friends their own age. Excluded from many clubs and lodges because of their gender, they built networks of women friends and neighbors as they grew old (Green 2000, 139–40).

WOMEN

By the early twentieth century, people of the Middle Atlantic region were being influenced by movies, magazines, and advertisements, which had been busy building a national consensus of opinion on the qualities of the "ideal woman." Women, supposedly more emotional, and invariably physically weaker than men, were to be the bedrocks of familial stability. Women were responsible for cushioning the uncertainties of war and economic dislocation and were the arbiters of the new rules of courtship and child rearing of the era. These were roles of complexity and contradiction, because the mass media often portrayed women as weak, even frivolous. The "Mom" who was the foundation of the family was the roundish figure of comfort and steadfastness. This image was reinforced by the women portrayed in the soap operas introduced after 1930 and brilliantly lined by Norman Rockwell in his rendition of "Freedom from Want" in 1943. But the matronly figured mother image had her competition: the elongated lithe figure of advertising's "smart" set. The latter offered little comfort in the Depression. In fact, "smart," stylish women were implicitly humiliating to those men who had lost their jobs after the crash.

Women were also the "homemakers." Household maintenance had been an important part of nineteenth-century prescriptive literature, but after World War I, housework became perhaps the most important measure of a woman's personality, her affection for her family, and her responsibility to the nation. Love for the husband and children could be proven in the degree of whiteness in clothes, and the strength and stamina of the family. So important were these responsibilities that women were cautioned not to leave them to servants. Thus emerged the idea of housework as "different" work, labor that did not require any financial reward because of the returns of emotional fulfillment it brought. The long hours, unending repetition, difficult and unpleasant tasks, and the loneliness of the job were subsumed under the rubric of responsible motherhood.

The tasks could be made easier, however. That was the marketing strategy and mantra of the appliance advertisers and dealers, especially those implying they could bring the house worker a "mechanical servant." This enabled the literati of household advice in magazines and books to evade the central ironies of the servantless household of the expanding middle class. During the 1920s especially, what had been the work of servants and the "lower orders" was endowed with a special importance, like that of a craft or a profession. Widely circulated publications such as *Good Housekeeping* magazine promoted this image.

The cult of the well-managed household increased women's workload. Ironically, the new electrically powered vacuum cleaners, washing machines, refrigerators, and, less commonly, dishwashers or garbage disposals expanded the work expectations for middle-class women. And often women went outside the house to find part-time jobs to pay for these labor-saving devices. More complex meals became fashionable status symbols, clothes were laundered more often, and increasing social pressure to wear whiter clothing transformed the laundry process nearly as much as the electrically powered washing machine.

As ever, for the working class and now most of the middle class, the unpaid labor of the household fell to women. Middle-class women were increasingly doing more of their own work, because the number of servants had declined and the cost of hiring them had increased, thereby taking many middle-class families out of the market for service. Even those women who worked full-time jobs outside of the home and those who did piecework in their homes still had nearly all the household chores left to them. Historian Ruth Cowan estimates that between 1920 and 1940 the average middle-class woman at home worked between approximately 48 and 60 hours weekly (Green 2000, 60–61, 120–21).

In the major cities of the Middle Atlantic region, some women eschewed the mother model for the professional world. Although women were not a minority, they did have minority status when seeking positions available to them in the workplace. With the ratification of the 19th Amendment on August 26, 1920, better times seemed in view. On September 26, 1920, Philadelphia women, for example, celebrated this, their first step into a fuller citizenship. Before year's end they had voted for a president of the United States and elected three women to the state legislature. Women's names were placed in the jury wheel; there were two women on the school board and a woman on the Art Jury. Violet E. Fahnestock, the city's first woman magistrate, was sworn in on January 2, 1925, and heard her first case a week later. Before the end of the decade amenities available for women were enlarged as the Women's City Club settled into its spacious new quarters at 1622 Locust Street, and also before decade's end, Warburton House, Philadelphia's hotel for women, opened.

Despite aspirations for the exciting new world of offices and business, the greatest numbers of working women in Philadelphia were employed in factories or domestic service. Others were clerks, saleswomen, bookkeepers, stenographers, or teachers. The city also counted a small but important group of professional women in the city, including lawyers and doctors, many of whom had been trained by the University of Pennsylvania and Women's Medical College of Philadelphia. Women held graduate degrees in the liberal arts and sciences, but if they wanted a Bachelor of Arts degree as an undergraduate, they could not expect the University of Pennsylvania to admit them to its program. For these undergraduate degrees they had to depend on Bryn Mawr and other area colleges that provided all-women or coeducational education. But Philadelphia's example did not reflect patterns elsewhere in the degree of women's involvement in public life and work outside the home. Philadelphia had a longer history of women's activism than other Middle Atlantic places, and its diverse economy provided a greater variety of employment opportunities for women and men than any other area in the region. In places where eastern and southern European cultures were powerful, women were restrained from political activity and outside work. Indeed, in Pennsylvania, ethnic and religious factors had retarded even women's support for women's suffrage (Weigley 1982, 591–92).

In their adolescent years immigrant women of the Middle Atlantic region, as in other regions, worked outside the home to supplement the family income, but once they left their parents' homes and married, immigrant women tended to remain at home, focusing attention on their role of wife, mother, and homemaker. Although married immigrant women usually raised the children and cared for boarders because they really had few opportunities outside the household for employment, in some immigrant families, cultural traditions were what kept the woman in the home. Irish immigrants, for example, strongly believed that married women should not work at all, because it was believed that a working married woman diminished the status of her husband. To the average southern Italian, who remained somewhat powerless in the larger society, the conquest and possession of a woman offered a sense of control and authority. And Greek families actually considered it a disgrace for a wife, and sometimes a sister, to work outside the home. For various reasons the celebration of female domesticity was as strong in immigrant communities as it was in middle-class native-born communities. There were exceptions to this general rule. Sometimes the skills possessed by immigrant women, such as Italian seamstresses, caused certain women to be in high demand in the marketplace. But even when relegated to the home, immigrant women wielded a great degree of power within the household. Usually they managed household financial resources, and because they had such intimate knowledge of family finances and needs, women usually made the decisions to initiate small immigrant family business concerns. Among Hungarian newcomers in New Brunswick, New Jersey, for example, the idea of buying a farm or opening a saloon originated with women, who had more energy and ideas than the men (Bodnar 1985, 78–80, 82).

CHILDREN

In the first decades of the twentieth century in the Middle Atlantic region the number of children born in hospitals (as opposed to home) increased. By 1938, more than 50 percent of all infants were delivered in hospitals. In part this change was due to an alteration in Americans' image of the hospital from that of a building full of sick, infectious, and dying people to that of a center of medical science with practices capable of curing diseased or damaged bodies. Other important factors in the increased number of hospital-born children included a growing trust of physicians and the successful marketing techniques of the baby food industry. All created strong pressures on parents to allow professionals to supervise the birth and direct the feeding of infants. In rural areas, home births with midwives or male physicians in attendance were more common than they were in cities, but there too they were declining in frequency. The automobile made it possible for physicians to get to a bedside faster and for patients to travel to hospitals with more ease than either could previously. Still, hospital childbirth in the first decades of the new century remained for the most part a middle-class white phenomenon. Infant mortality among urban black Americans was twice that of urban whites in this era. Medicine's bright promise was as white as the inside of a hospital.

Child care in the new century became a "science." Infant feeding practices and intestinal disorders in children were major concerns for physicians, government bureaucrats, and parents, as many infant deaths resulted from diarrhea and dehydration. The breast-versus-bottle debate that had heated up popular and professional medical discourse in the late nineteenth century continued through 1945, but with the critical difference that bottle-feeding became the more acceptable and, for many, the more desirable choice. The decline of breast-feeding among the middle class and the wealthy was in part a result of the increasing popular acceptance of medicine and nutrition as "scientific" in the late nineteenth and early twentieth centuries. For working-class women the shift to bottle-feeding was linked to this culture-wide faith in science, the increased availability of cheaper bottles and other feeding paraphernalia, and the necessity for many of these women to work outside the home. Some physicians buttressed their arguments in favor of bottle-feeding by erroneously warning that working-class women's breast milk was probably less healthy than scientifically developed "formula." They maintained that the diet of the adult working class was likely to be deficient in "vital" substances, especially the new miracle "vital amines," or vitamins, that were first isolated in the early twentieth century.

The everyday experience of child rearing, at least for the middle class and the wealthy, was also altered somewhat by the increasingly popular awareness of the work of child psychologists. As they had a century earlier, Americans of the era perceived a "wave" of crime threatening to overwhelm them, and they sought answers for the seeming increase in lawlessness in the childhood experiences of the outlaws. Countless sociological studies of adult prison inmates helped generate a multitude of articles in popular and professional journals, nearly all of which linked antisocial behavior to economic, social, and emotional deprivation in childhood. Sensationalist newspaper stories, the actions of the underworld, and movies also turned attention to the child as the source of future antisocial behavior. Movies such as *Angels with Dirty Faces* (1938) and *Dead End* (1937) portrayed children as basically good, but corrupted by their environment. The burden of blame rested upon the parents. Feed the little tykes the wrong stuff, avoid playing with them, take little interest in their studies, and a potential Al Capone, Bonnie Parker, or Clyde Barrow was liable to emerge. Advice was easy to find: columns in newspapers and in periodicals such as *Ladies' Home Journal* abounded. *Parents* magazine began publication in 1926 and purveyed countless articles with advice on "good parenting" (Green 2000, 121–24).

Among urban immigrant families of the Middle Atlantic states, children were more commonly seen through an economic rather than a sociological prism. In the early twentieth century, an immigrant family could not live on the income of a single wage earner. Children who reached working age at about 14 were expected to fill the economic gap. The percentage of family income generated by children in 1911 in eastern Pennsylvania was 46 percent among Poles and 65 percent among unskilled Irish workers (Bodnar 1985, 76–77).

Socialization in Polish families in western Pennsylvania functioned in a manner that ensured both the inevitability of child labor and the relinquishing of earnings for family use at least until marriage. Before 1930, young Poles learned their lessons well. Ray C. expressed his reason for remaining in Lawrenceville as a young man. "I felt down deep I had an obligation to take care of my mother." Joseph D. never had to be told to assist his family. "I always thought dad had hard luck so I would stick with them [parents] until the other kids got old enough to work," he explained. The tendency of young Poles to consider family obligations was stated clearly by Edward R.: "We looked forward to the time when we got to the legal age. When we got to that point we quit school and got a job because we knew the parents needed money. . . . That's just the way we were raised."

Carrying out the dictates of their upbringing, Polish youth nearly always gave their earnings to their mothers, the usual managers of Polish family finances. Stanley N. "hustled newspapers" at mill gates and gave his three-dollar per-week profit to his mother. Joseph B. and his brothers sold enough newspapers on Polish Hill to nearly equal his father's weekly salary of $12.50. Young Polish girls were also expected to assist parents until marriage. In fact, it was not uncommon for Polish children to live in the same house with their parents for several years after marriage. On Pittsburgh's south side, Polish girls packed and inspected nuts and bolts at Oliver Iron and Steel. Stephanie W. recalled that all her sisters worked at either H. J. Heinz or the South Side Hospital and contributed their wages to their mother. At age 16 Stephanie worked in a store that needed a "Polish girl" for its Polish clientele. Josephine B. left school after the eighth grade and did "day work" in Mount Lebanon, an upper middle-class suburb. She and her brother, who worked in a nearby coal mine, relinquished all their earnings to the family. The presence of children was crucial to the smooth functioning of the immigrant family economy. Besides offering economic benefit, in the long run children could care for immigrants in their old age (Bodnar 1985, 562).

Economic Life

As the new century opened, the people of the Middle Atlantic region experienced a great many changes in their economic life. White-collar workers became more numerous and in turn more regimented than they had ever been. As industry grew in the region, the working class struggled to survive the precariousness of work opportunities and the physical danger of the workplace. In response, industrial workers finally began to organize into unions with success.

Both the working class and the urban middle class saw a changing marketplace and advertising techniques that turned many products they didn't know existed a few years prior into necessities of life. The greatest economic changes of the era, however, were not caused by new marketing techniques but, rather, by the massive influx of new immigrants, especially to the cities of the Middle Atlantic region. Escaping from political and economic oppression in their home countries, these immigrants faced new and various problems primarily caused by discrimination. But for the most part they overcame these challenges to create a better life for themselves and their families.

New technology rapidly entered the daily lives of urban Americans in this era and created even greater contrasts between urban and rural life. Those in rural areas responded by joining the Grange or other cooperative movements and 4-H clubs in an attempt to enjoy collectively what they could not obtain individually. Through the various farm organizations and their religious institutions, people in rural areas began to enjoy some of the social, economic, cultural, and educational opportunities that people in the city were beginning to take for granted. This section will study the economic changes that occurred in the Mid-Atlantic region in the first decades of the twentieth century and the effect these changes had on the daily lives of the people that lived there.

WORK AND WORKPLACE

The turn of the century brought many changes to the workplace, and some working-class men did enter the white-collar world, if not its power structure. Errand boys, couriers, and clerks most often came from the white Anglo-Saxon or northern European working class, and they hoped, like Andrew Carnegie or the heroes of Horatio Alger novels, to get ahead with savvy, hard work, a stroke of luck, or a little of all. As the American economy became more bureaucratic and service- and sales-oriented, the managerial and sales segments of the workforce mushroomed. The great age of advertising began after World War I, and the duties of financial control, personnel management, and planning expanded as industries did. The irony in this growth was that as the numbers of workers not directly connected with the tangible production of goods increased, managers were bringing the office environment closer to the mechanistic world of the plant or factory.

Office workers of the Middle Atlantic region saw their work environment changed by the application of the principles of the "scientific management" of Pennsylvania-born Frederick Taylor, who was the high priest of this crusade, which had seen great success in the factory by regulating workers' movements on assembly lines. Taylor expanded his research to the office, proposing that efficiency would be enhanced if employees did one job only, such as opening mail, carrying papers from one desk to another, accounting, or sales.

Taylor's principles directly attacked the nineteenth-century office system of the somewhat independent clerk and his private office within the office, with his locking rolltop desk with its myriad pigeonholes and drawers big enough for filing papers. Scientific managers termed this behavior wasteful and potentially dangerous, because clerks could mislay or hoard papers vital to the smooth running of the firm. By 1915, the rolltop desk was disappearing from larger office buildings.

The newly designed flat-top seven-drawer desk for mid-level executives and the three-drawer flat-top for clerks and typists replaced the old compartmentalized workstation. Files were centralized for access by the entire office, and even the occupants of seven-drawer desks were urged not to keep files or important papers in them. Runners routinely collected and filed papers throughout the day, and speed and ease of handling paperwork became an important measure of success in the offices of corporate America. Pigeonholes and privacy were gone and discouraged, and some offices had rules commanding strict silence during the workday to avoid distracting workers. Desktop neatness and cleanliness and the ability to find paperwork at a moment's notice were openly equated with productive work habits. The hierarchy of writing instruments recommended by the scientific managers reinforced status differences. All clerks were to use the same nib on dipping pens (which tied them to their desks to write and discouraged individuality). Mid- and high-level executives were permitted more freedom, because they could use fountain pens, which allowed them to move about and write presumably important words.

The visual distinctions in desks also applied to desk chairs. Executives at the highest level earned upholstered chairs. Those a level downward got caned seats and chairs that swiveled and tilted back like the padded ones of their superiors. Clerks and typists were issued wood saddle-seat chairs with slat backs. These generally could be rotated, and some provided flexibility for the back by means of a spring steel connecting band. Eventually steel replaced wood as the material in many pieces of furniture, allegedly because it was lighter and more durable, but it may not have been popular, because it transformed the office into an environment that looked more like a factory. Office machines—typewriters, addressing machines, Dictaphones, and accounting machines—were all in widespread use by the 1920s and resembled tools of industry. It would take another generation to change the environment to a more modern and perhaps domestic scene, allegedly to attract more women into the office labor force.

One obvious message of this office revolution was that appearances mattered as much as—and perhaps more than—did performance, because measuring the latter was problematic in most offices. In the period in which workers were paid on a piece-work basis, measuring success was easy. In the factory in which workers were paid on an hourly basis, it was punctuality and the surveillance of foremen that was supposed to guarantee productivity. In the office, the amount of paper passed over a desk may be one measure of worth, and for typists the number of characters typed per hour (on typewriters equipped with counters) would work for supervisors obsessed with quantification. But so much of the work of the office was intangible that the superficial characteristics of dress, deference, collegiality (at the proper times, and only then), and the appearance of one's desk became important measures of worth. (Salesmen had the pressure of the easily quantified number and amount of sales, but most of them worked on a commission basis, unlike office and management workers.)

White-collar workers' socioeconomic aspirations and egos depended on their ability not only to maintain their material way of life but also to advance to higher-paying jobs. But the chance of moving up also carried with it the possibility of falling back. White-collar workers' anxiety levels were constantly in flux, whatever their situation. Subjective judgments by superiors determined success and failure in the business office, and conformity in nearly all aspects of work life became highly valued (Green 2000, 19–20).

For the working class employment was probably even more uncertain than it was for their white-collar colleagues, but for different reasons. In western Pennsylvania, going back to the nineteenth century, a number of medium-sized towns had developed around the steel industry. For example, Aliquippa, Pennsylvania, with its 27,000 residents, was dominated by the Jones and Laughlin Steel Corporation. These companies dominated local government, school boards, and the press. Given this control, steel mills were able to resist unionization effectively until well into the 1930s

---

Snapshot

Report of Factory Inspector in Pittsburgh, 1914

Among dust-producing occupations examined in Pittsburgh are stogy making, garment and mattress making, mirror polishing, broom, cork, and soap making. Most of these occupations are productive of vegetable dust. The high percentage of tuberculosis among tobacco workers, second only to that among stone cutters, has led to the supposition that there is something inherently dangerous in the trade itself. The amount of dust varies greatly, however, according as the tobacco is dried by air or by heat. . . . With reference to present conditions, Dr. Kober states that "Workers in tobacco suffer more or less from nasal, conjunctival and bronchial catarrh, and digestive and nervous derangements, and although the mucous membranes gradually become accustomed to the irritation of the dust and fumens, the occupation appears to be dangerous." (Vol. 1, 359)

Industrial work and environment must induce health and not disease if the future shall justify us in employing women in factories. Processes can be made harmless if we work at the problem long enough; workrooms can be made wholesome, speed cut short before the point of depletion. In such an industrial city as Pittsburgh, the medical profession or the department of factory inspectors might take the initial steps toward overcoming the tendency to trade disease by giving employers and legislators more facts about industrial hygiene, exact knowledge of what and how a trade contributes to ill health. (Vol. 1, 359)

I began my study of the [steel] industry with no preconceived ideas as to health. . . . I discovered that there is always a fine dust in the air of the steel mill. It was not very noticeable at first, but after being in a mill or around the furnaces for a time, I always found my coat covered with minute, shining grains. A visitor experiences no ill effect after a few hours in a mill, but the steel workers notice it and then declare that it gives rise to throat trouble. . . . Many a workman justifies his daily glass of whiskey on the ground that it "takes the dust out of my throat."

I began to notice after a time that the men with whom I talked were often a little hard of hearing. It was some time before I connected this fact with the noise of the mill. The rolling mills are all noisy, the blooming mills and the plate mills especially so, while the cold saw bites in the steel with a screech that is fairly maddening. When I finally began to make inquiries I found that among the men I met, partial or slight deafness was quite common, and that they all attributed it to the noise. (Black 2006, 43–44)

---

when the Wagner Act, which protected workers' rights to organize, was declared constitutional by the 1937 Supreme Court (Kyvig 2002, 285, 289).

Even in the boom times of the 1920s, roughly 10 percent of the workforce was out of a job at any given time; about one-half the men and two-thirds of the women were unemployed for more than 10 weeks of the year. With little or no formal insurance to fall back upon other than limited state and municipal relief funds (usually in cooperation with private agencies such as the Red Cross and religious organizations) until the passage of the Federal Unemployment Relief Act in 1933, unemployment meant very hard times. In the Depression, the conditions and the suffering were exacerbated beyond anything workers had encountered before.

Finding a job was a trying experience for many in the working class, especially immigrants, especially if they did not know someone already employed in a factory, mine, or other line of work. Workers interviewed by John Bodnar for his book *Workers' World* remembered how connections worked and how the rules were bent. For some, a parent eased the path. Ray La Marca of western Pennsylvania started work at the Fort Pitt Spring Company when he was 16, able to land a laborer's job because his father got it for him. Later, during the Depression, he paid an agency to get him a job at Union Switch and Signal. Stacia Treski, from Nanticoke, Pennsylvania, had a harder time. She remembered that every morning "you would make the rounds from one of the three silk mills, the cigar factory, and the sewing mill to another. You just stood there and maybe they would hire someone." Eventually she went to New York City to get a cleaning job after she married her husband, George. Dock worker Charles Oliver's experience was similar: "To get a job on the docks men would line up each day. The bosses would hand out numbers and give you slots."

Steve Kika's father got him his first job as a waterboy in the mills when he was 13 in 1914. He worked a 10-hour day and commuted between Reading and Philadelphia. Sometimes bribery greased the wheels of employment hunting. "There used to be lots of payoffs to foremen for jobs," according to John Sarnoski, a laborer in the coal mines in the 1920s. Louis Heim, son of a German-born Lutheran family, recalled that in the 1920s some men in the Bethlehem Steel plant "would give the boss money; some farmers would bring in potatoes, chickens, eggs [to get special treatment or a job] . . . until the union came in." Occasionally, a service organization helped. Ray Czachowski got his first job through the Boys Club in Pittsburgh.

Members of ethnic and racial groups usually stuck together in the workplace. Stanley Brozek, born in 1910 of Polish immigrant parents, recalled that "the Irish had, when I was a youngster in the open hearth [steel mills], the first helper, second helpers, and most of the slaggers. . . . The Irish also predominated in the machine shop, and the Scotch, Irish, and English were roll turners." Similarly, Louis Smolinski remembered that "at the Edgar, Thomson [steel] mill the maintenance department was mostly Irish people. . . . The Polish people dominated the foundry. And in the finishing department there was Polish, Slavish [sic], and colored, not too many colored."

Life in the workplace for the industrial blue-collar worker was dangerous. There was virtually no regulation, no insurance, and no company fear of a lawsuit when someone was injured or killed. Louis Heim remembered how he "got a job over [at the foundry]. They put me on chipping. But after two weeks the dust was so bad that my lungs were polluted. When I coughed, black dirt would come out." Blue Jenkins, an African American man working as a grinder, recalled that "you'd have goggles on, naturally, because of the sparks flying, but when you'd take off your goggles, you'd just see the part where your goggles were and the rest of your face would be black. And your lungs, you'd just spit up big clots of dirt."

Unsafe working conditions, poor pay, and layoffs with little or no warning were not limited to the Middle Atlantic region. In the early twentieth century such conditions were common to workers in all areas of the country, and there remained little that workers could do in response. Although strikes had been a prominent part of the American working scene since at least the last quarter of the nineteenth century, there was relative peace between capital and labor after World War I began. In large part this wartime domestic peace had been a result of the governmental controls imposed for the war effort. The White House had created the National War Labor Board, which heard more than 1,000 cases and issued decisions by which both labor and capital agreed to abide. President Woodrow Wilson had recognized the American Federation of Labor (AFL) as a legitimate negotiating body, and for its part the conservative union distanced itself from the more militant International Workers of the World (IWW), known as the "Wobblies." The "Wobblies" were powerful. They had tremendous influence in the famous Paterson, New Jersey, strike against the textile industries in 1913. The AFL grew too, from 2.7 million members in 1916 to 4 million in 1919 (Green 2000, 26–27, 31–32).

One of the truly revolutionary developments of the twentieth century was the advance of labor, in that it at last achieved organization as well as recognition of its concerns by government and the general public. The story of labor in Pennsylvania always had a significant bearing on the national labor pattern, because of the dominant industrial position of the state; this continued in the twentieth century. At the turn of the century labor was in travail, as the power of huge corporations literally broke the backs of such organized labor as had reared its head. Conditions were slow to improve, and as late as 1910 a 12-hour day was common for about one-third of all western Pennsylvania steelworkers, of whom nearly 60 percent remained first-generation European immigrants. A steel strike in 1919, according to investigators, was provoked by "excessive hours" and the "boss system" of supervision in the mills that denied workers any individual rights.

The United Mine Workers, organized in 1890 in the coalfields, gradually increased its strength under the leadership of John Mitchell and his stalwart associate, William B. Wilson; both were schooled in the old defunct Knights of Labor. Wilson became secretary-treasurer of the United Mine Workers in 1900. Thomas Kennedy, a native of Lansford, Pennsylvania, was another early mine union leader. Another Pennsylvanian leading in the growth of the miners' union was John Brophy, born in England, who came to Pennsylvania at the age of 12 and by 15 was a mine worker near Philipsburg, in central Pennsylvania. Mitchell in 1900 called a strike for higher wages and recognition of the union in the anthracite coalfields, though he then had only some 8,000 members in his union. Wages averaged perhaps $300 a year, and a 10-hour day in unsafe mines was common. The anthracite mines were owned for the most part by powerful railroad corporations, which in turn were allied with J. P. Morgan's banking empire. This was some challenge to be issued by a brash new union. Shrewd Mark Hanna, architect of the theory that what is good for President William McKinley is good for big business, saw the issue as politically explosive when some 100,000 miners responded to the strike call; he negotiated a quick settlement.

Two years later Mitchell forced the issue again with demands for union recognition, a nine-hour day, and a 20 percent wage increase. George F. Baer, president of the Reading Company, took the lead in refusing to arbitrate or mediate with the miners. Baer made the statement, "The rights and interests of the laboring man will be protected and cared for, not by labor agitators but by the Christian gentlemen to whom God in his infinite wisdom has given control of the property interests of the country, and upon whose successful management of which so much depends." This was literally "divine right" capitalism. The New York Times called the words close to "unconscious blasphemy." President Theodore Roosevelt in October called upon both sides to meet with him in Washington to consider the idea of an impartial arbitration commission. The miners accepted, but Baer and his associates refused. Roosevelt then threatened the use of federal troops to take over the mines unless the owners came into line. The settlement secured for the miners their nine-hour day and a 10 percent wage increase but left the question of union recognition unsolved.

Organized labor had won its first great battle, but it had not won the war. The National Association of Manufacturers, organized in 1895, began a program of active opposition to unions. In 1904, while saying that the association was not opposed to "organizations of labor as such," it did disapprove "absolutely of strikes and lockouts," along with the closed shop. The same leadership in 1900 had accused labor of "organized coercion" and attempting to force "socialistic or semi-socialistic" legislation that would deny "free competitive conditions in the labor market." Unions were further denounced as trusts and "a dangerous institution in a free country." They accused union leaders of preaching doctrines "not only of anarchy but also one based on woeful ignorance of economic laws of wages."

Labor organizations continued to grow in strength as the American Federation of Labor steadily increased its membership. The Pennsylvania Federation of Labor was organized in 1902. In 1919, new efforts to organize the steel industry were started. By this time there was a Department of Labor in Washington. Congress created it in the Wilson administration in 1913 to "foster, promote, and develop the welfare of the wage earners of the United States; to improve their working conditions, and to advance their opportunities for profitable employment." The first head of this new department was Pennsylvania miner and labor leader William B. Wilson, who had written the legislation that created it, along with many other labor laws, while serving in Congress. His successor in the Harding administration was James "Puddler Jim" Davis, a laborer who had started work as a puddler in the steel mills of Sharon, Pennsylvania. Davis served as Secretary of Labor until 1930. Many looked upon Davis as a labor politician more or less kept by big business, and by no means the equal of Wilson.

Organization of the steelworkers was a reality by 1918, but the industry leaders successfully broke their great strike of 1919. By 1936, efforts at a stronger union produced the United Steel Workers of America. Among its major leaders were Philip Murray and David McDonald. The United Mine Workers and the United Steel Workers formed the nucleus for the Congress of Industrial Organizations, the CIO, which was formally organized in Pittsburgh in 1938, continuing the Pennsylvania tradition as the birthplace of national labor unions (Stevens 1964, 316–18).

In the early decades of the twentieth century, the International Workers of the World (IWW), also made great inroads in union organization. With a philosophy greatly influenced by European socialism, this union evoked more fear among capital than any other union. Although they remained most powerful in the West, in the Middle Atlantic region they exerted a great influence in the textile industry of New Jersey.

Since the mid-nineteenth century, Paterson, New Jersey, had been the center of the silk textile industry in the United States and the factory owners, known as the "silk kings," controlled every aspect of life in the city and maintained oppressive working conditions, long hours, and low wages free from scrutiny. By the turn of the century eastern and southern European workers had replaced Irish and English laborers, and their oppression was no less severe than that of their predecessors. Frustrated by failed political strategies and attempts at organization, immigrant workers in Paterson often expressed their anger violently, and in the first decades of the twentieth century Paterson became a central battleground in the virtual war going on between labor and capital. Riots were a frequent feature of Paterson strikes. Machinery was wrecked and factories torched. Vandalism of public property was a constant problem. When one of the silk industry kings donated a park to the city, the workers smashed vases and urns, chipped noses and ears off statuary, and even cut branches from the trees until the place was a denuded, polluted wreck.

In February 1913, leaders of the IWW arrived in Paterson to organize the silk workers, and in that same month 8,000 workers and dyers walked off the job and began one of the most memorable struggles in American labor history. The workers demanded recognition of the IWW as their bargaining agent, an eight-hour day, and a minimum wage of $12 a week. The Wobblies took control of the strike and brought a who's who of American radicalism to Paterson. At the head was William D. "Big Bill" Haywood, a huge one-eyed man with "a face like a scarred battlefield." At his side was the fiery "rebel Girl," Elizabeth Gurley Flynn, the anarchist Carlo Tresca, novelist Upton Sinclair, and the journalist turned agitator John Reed. For five months Paterson was torn by insurrection. Gangs of workers and police roamed the streets attacking each other. The owners refused to negotiate with the IWW, calling them radicals and subversives who threatened American society. Haywood and other IWW leaders played into the owners' hands with statements declaring, "We will have a new flag, the red flag, the color of the workingman's blood." Another IWW leader warned that "We are going to win this strike or Paterson will be wiped off the map" (Fleming 1985, 164).

The owners remained intransigent, and the courts backed the bosses with harsh sentences for IWW leaders. Patrick Quinlan, for example, was arrested even before he spoke and was sentenced to a term of from two to seven years. By July some 1,300 picketers had been arrested and jailed. Finally, Summit Mills, located near Paterson, offered its workers an eight-hour day and a 25 to 35 percent wage increase if they withdrew their insistence on IWW recognition. The battered starving workers accepted the offer and the great strike collapsed. When it was finally over the workers had lost $5 million in wages and the mill owners $10 million in profits. The strike left Paterson a spiritual and economic wreck.

Labor outcomes were not always as bloody as the Paterson strike, but until the 1930s most labor struggles usually ended in the favor of owners. Not until the establishment of Franklin Roosevelt's New Deal in 1933, which ushered in legislation that leveled the playing field in labor negotiations, would the labor movement have a just place in the nation's politics and government (Fleming 1985, 160–66).

Black workers were able to obtain some of the benefits of the industrial expansion and economic growth of the new century, especially when the United States entered World War I. Many working-class white men joined in the campaign and this, along with a virtual halt to immigration, reduced the available pool of workers in many heavy industries, thereby opening job opportunities to blacks and women. Sometimes manufacturers worked deals with the railroads to provide free or discounted transportation northward. Throughout the South, black railroad porters left copies of black-owned newspapers, such as the Pittsburgh *Courier*, that advocated migration to the North where jobs beckoned and Jim Crow laws did not apply.

Black workers (primarily men) moving to the Middle Atlantic cities found work in the steel and manufacturing industries, as well as in domestic service, teaching, and racial and neighborhood service industries such as newspaper production and distribution, funeral homes, moving companies, barber and beauty shops, restaurants, and entertainment. Although the tasks they were assigned in the factories and mills were predictably the hardest and lowest paying, and the unions often refused them membership, blacks found that the pay opportunities were better in the North. Some union resentment of black workers was based on feelings in addition to or other than racial antagonism. African Americans were sometimes brought in as strikebreakers, although they were not always aware of what they were walking into when they arrived at the job on the first day.

In urban ethnic and racial enclaves, small businesses—green grocers, butchers, barbers, shoemakers, and small general stores—provided special ethnic supplies and credit to neighborhoods and spoke the language of the district. In the towns and villages scattered throughout the rural countryside the general store functioned as post office and supply depot for the necessities and niceties of life. They were small versions of the department stores that were taking command of urban shopping. These operations taxed the owners with long hours, bookkeeping chores, carrying unpaid bills and debts, and an assortment of physically demanding tasks, especially if they sold heavy goods such as furniture and agricultural supplies (Green 2000, 30–32).

TRADE AND MARKETS

In the Middle Atlantic region, the new advertising industry could not ignore the working class, who constituted by far the largest single segment of the public. Advertisers in addressing the working class assumed that they shared, or could be persuaded to accept, middle-class aspirations and anxieties regarding status, decorum, and consumption. But to succeed in convincing these potential consumers to buy newer and more goods and to define themselves by the goods they could own, advertising executives had to overcome centuries-old Protestant values of thrift, disciplined work, delayed gratification, and contentment with one's material lot. These beliefs had to be replaced with an acceptance for quickly acquired wealth, installment buying, immediate pleasure, and dissatisfaction with the goods one already owned. Guiltless discard of things that still worked or that could be fixed was necessary in this new calculus of consumption; otherwise, the economy could not continue to expand. Important, too, especially in the world of the office, was the implied power of new and expensive clothes and other accessories. To these ends, companies spent ever-increasing amounts on advertising throughout the 1920s, trying to convince consumers to spend and white-collar households in particular to adhere to standards of consumption that stressed the superficial. In 1914 American firms spent $682 million on advertising; in 1919 they spent $1.4 billion; and in 1929 nearly $3 billion was devoted to promotion of goods and services.

The most common advertising appeals centered on guilt, status, and celebrity. Even Henry Ford, who detested the idea of spending money on what he considered nonproductive elements, in 1924 finally approved an ad campaign that promoted the Model A because of its stylish colors and alleged associations with the wealthy. Ford cars were depicted in front of estates and mansions, and the idea was to give a "look" or a sign that the car meant success. Celebrities were used more and more to offer testimonials for products. The testimonial was an old technique, dating to at least the last quarter of the nineteenth century, but the extent to which the celebrity's importance replaced that of the product was the new component in the 1920s and 1930s (Green 2000, 23).

In 1924 a Philadelphia publication, the *Saturday Evening Post*, complained that "the firmly rooted aversion to debt in any form which prevailed a generation ago has almost completely evaporated." However, the 1920s campaign to convince Americans to accept manageable debt may not have been as revolutionary as the Philadelphia magazine and many others presumed. Recent studies of American spending have discovered that there never was a golden age of thrift in American history, and that debt has always played an important role in American lives—not only as a means of instant gratification but also as a strategy for survival and a tool for economic advance. American indebtedness, historians note, even precedes Mark Twain's lament of 1873 over the loss of the "antebellum horror of debt which had almost completely evaporated." In fact, the American tradition of indebtedness goes back at least as far as the Founding Fathers; men like Jefferson and Washington carried significant debt throughout their lives. One could say that those who found themselves in debt in the first half of the twentieth century were participating in one of America's great traditions (Lears 2006, 13).

In the first decades of the twentieth century, magazines and the airwaves of the Middle Atlantic region, as elsewhere, were inundated with hawkers for cosmetics, foods, clothing fashions, and hygienic products, who indicated that social ostracism and shame were the prices for failure to use the recommended product. Much of this advertising placed women in a situation full of responsibility. Advertisers charged women with the responsibility for their husbands' successes or failures. They were expected to understand clothing fashions and to make certain that their husbands were well-dressed. Failure to make a good impression at the office because of fashion anachronism or ignorance was identified as a potentially critical factor for failure to secure a promotion or a new job. Another element in the formula for success was the wife's knowledge and acquisition of the right soaps, sock garters, breakfast foods, laundry detergents, laxatives, and other products that were essential for her husband to be at his best in the competitive world of business in which many worked and to which many aspired. With the exception of the hunting, fishing, mechanics, and other male-oriented popular magazines, nearly all advertisements for these goods were directed to women.

The world the ads portrayed had no problems that the right products could not solve. A new pharmacopoeia of "diseases" appeared: halitosis (bad breath), body odor (b.o.), bromodosis (odiferous feet), homotosis (furniture in "bad taste"), acidosis (sour stomach), dandruff, constipation, and others. The victim never knew why he didn't get the girl or the job or the promotion, or why she never got asked to the best parties or her children were playing alone. Since even one's best friends often would not tell the offender of a problem, how could the aspirant know why good fortune seemed to be so elusive? There was no answer except to be safe.

In a menacing reference to Darwinian biological theory, advertisements stressed that in the struggle to survive and thrive in the capitalist system, the line between success and failure was thin and the competition keen and close. Failure to achieve the middle-class goals of material success was the individual's fault alone. But the relationship between appearance, effort, and material success could be altered at any given moment by forces that were unknown or out of control, adding constant uncertainty and anxiety to the equation. In the early twentieth century, a culture of personality that emphasized appearance and "fitting in" emerged among the growing American middle class. This replaced the emphasis on morality and work discipline that had constituted the proper character identified in nineteenth-century advice books. This became a formulaic strategy both for domestic advisors invented by advertisers, such as General Mills' Betty Crocker (1924), and counselors such as Emily Post, who continued churning out successful etiquette books (Green 2000, 24–25).

CASTE AND CLASS EXPERIENCE

Philadelphia

Like other major metropolitan areas of the country, the most significant changes in the Mid-Atlantic cities could be attributed to the demographic convulsions of the early decades of the twentieth century. Between 1901 and 1915 Middle Atlantic cities experienced their greatest numerical population increase, more than any similar period before or since. In Philadelphia for example, the number of inhabitants grew by almost a third—from 1,293,000 to 1,684,000.

The proclivity of Philadelphians for large families accounted for part of the increase, but much of it resulted from the flood of immigrants to America before World War I. Between 1905 and 1914 over nine million aliens were admitted to the United States. Although Philadelphia still did not attract the new immigrants from southern and eastern Europe in the same numbers or proportions as other cities (it ranked fourth as an entering port behind New York, Boston, and Baltimore), it did feel their impact. The percentage of foreign-born in the city's population rose from 23 percent in 1900 to 25 percent (421,000) in 1910. The percentage of Italians, Russians, and Poles in the total foreign-born population increased from 16 to 33 percent, a trend that continued until the European war drastically cut immigration in 1915.

Largely poor, these new Philadelphians usually settled in the shabbiest sections of the central and southern wards along the Delaware River. Joining those who had preceded them, they created ethnic ghettos that offered the security of familiar languages and customs and helped to perpetuate traditional social and religious institutions. All the new arrivals shared the problem of finding housing—any housing—in an area that was already overcrowded. Increasing competition for living space led to more division of dwellings for multifamily use, the construction of back-alley shacks, and a general deterioration of sanitary conditions, particularly in the river wards. Those who lived in them did not soon forget the vermin-infested matchboxes, boiling in summer, freezing in winter.

One of the largest ethnic communities in the city consisted of the Italians in South Philadelphia. Between 1870 and 1900, Philadelphia's Italian population increased 60-fold, from about 300 to 18,000. By 1910, it jumped dramatically to 77,000, creating an immigrant city within a city. The center of "Little Italy" was the market area in the vicinity of Ninth and Christian Streets, where dozens of shops offered enough cheese, fish, eels, artichokes, Ligurian mushrooms, and rich pastries to satisfy the most homesick Sicilian. Italian theaters and restaurants between Seventh and Eighth Streets recreated a Neapolitan atmosphere for local residents while providing a continental adventure for visitors. In the early years of the twentieth century, Italians from Sicily and southern Italy were drawn to Philadelphia, usually by reports that jobs could easily be found there and by the knowledge that "their people were there." Those already in the city often provided the stimulus for relatives and friends to leave the old country and sometimes contributed passage money as well. And the newcomers did find jobs, particularly as general laborers in unskilled occupations: construction work, road grading, street cleaning, railway maintenance, and trash collection. It was largely Italian labor that built City Hall, the Reading Terminal, and the Broad and Market Street subways. Skilled Italian workers could also be found among the city's bakers, shoemakers, masons, plasterers, stonecutters, waiters, and garment workers. Unlike some immigrants, many of the Italians, especially men who had come over without their families, wanted only to return home as the rich American uncle after a sojourn in America. From South Philadelphia Italians moved westward toward the closer suburbs—Overbrook, Manayunk, and Germantown.

The Philadelphia political machine tended to organize Italians, displacing the system of the *padroni*. As a result, instead of depending on the *padroni* for food and lodging, as they had in the old country, Italians, like other Philadelphians, rented or bought houses of their own. Many of them worked in their homes as tailors or finishers or on the streets in the familiar roles of bootblacks, organ grinders, and fruit vendors. For Philadelphia's 55,972 Italian adults, the 1920s were a time of change and adaptation. Although Italians had lived in South Philadelphia in sufficient numbers to make possible the establishing of their own churches—for example, St. Mary Magdalene de Pazzi, in 1851—it was not until the Pennsylvania Railroad began to invite Sicilian laborers to come to Pennsylvania to work on the railroad that Sicilians and southern Italians became a major presence in the city. The earlier nineteenth-century immigrants were northern Italians—generally skilled craftsmen, musicians, and others with specific contributions to make to Philadelphia's culture and diverse economy. The later comers were generally laborers, employed by the railroads, or in construction work on public buildings like City Hall, or in building subways. By the 1920s, marked differences in the Italian community, both cultural and economic, increasingly divided the middle-class minority from the working-class majority.

The separation between them was most evident in their attitudes toward education. For the laborer and his wife, both often illiterate, economic need determined that a son's attendance at school should end at 14 when he could obtain working papers. Italian boys aged 14 to 16, working as messenger boys, office boys, or in various capacities in the clothing industry, were the largest number of white youths employed in Philadelphia. Meanwhile, the sons of the middle-class families were able to finish high school and even go on to college. Middle-class parents—skilled artisans, specialty manufacturers, and merchants—saw education as a way to preserve their Old World status as well as a means of advancement in the New World. Given these aspirations, Philadelphia's public schools, with their emphasis on vocational training as the most appropriate kind of education for the children of immigrants, regardless of their inclination and ability, and the emphasis on a standardized variety of Americanization, irritated many Italians (Weigley 1982, 490–91).

Equally hard for the Philadelphia Italians to accept was the determination of the Irish hierarchy of Philadelphia's Catholic Church, under the leadership of Dennis Cardinal Dougherty, to bring the "individualistic" and often anticlerical Italians into the fold of an Americanized church and his own program of "obedience and orthodoxy." Ten Italian parishes had been created before 1920, and five more were added in the 1920s. The Italian priests assigned to serve these were "carefully screened," and great efforts were put forth to bring the religious practices of the Italians into harmony with the cardinal's ideas of sound doctrine. An able administrator, Dougherty had a limited "ability to convey a sense of warmth, charity and human sympathy to the immigrants." In time, and not without some open rebellion, the Italians "made an accommodation" with Dougherty's church, but they did so "in their own fashion and with traditional reservations" (Morris 1998, 128, 181).

Most Italians, unlike many of their Jewish neighbors, elected to remain in South Philadelphia in spite of improvement in their financial position. Many had invested in South Philadelphia real estate and found that ownership of property offered a useful way up the economic ladder. Their holdings were often small and not infrequently placed the owners in the category of slumlords, operators of licensed tenements. Charles C. A. Baldi, banker, undertaker, and politician, was one of the first and most successful of the Italian real estate tycoons, owning a hotel, a factory, a warehouse, an office building, and numerous houses. His activity and that of his lesser comrades in this business show that Philadelphia slum properties were often in the hands of a member of an ethnic minority who might himself have lived in a tenement that he owned.

Like the Italians, the Irish had first settled in South Philadelphia, in Southwark and Moyamensing. After the Civil War they began to scatter through the city into Port Richmond, along the South Street-Bainbridge Street corridor to the Schuylkill, Germantown, Chestnut Hill, and the northeastern sections of the city. Both Italians and Irish subscribed to the Roman Catholic theology, but if the Italians found the American church uncongenial, the Irish, whose fellow nationals formed Philadelphia's archdiocesan hierarchy, were on familiar ground. Their children went, as they were expected to do, to the parochial schools; families, not just the women, went to Mass; contributions were made to the parish for the building of churches, schools, and other useful projects, not for colorful festivals with the pagan undertones the parishioners of the Italian churches enjoyed. Again, unlike the Italians who gave total allegiance to the Republican Party (GOP), the Irish, perhaps more given to faction, supported both parties with little real power in either until the 1928 presidential election united them behind the twin issues of religion and ethnicity. Then the builder-developer or contractor-boss with the right political connections, a breed that first came to prominence in Philadelphia in the 1850s, found in the Democratic Party a suitable vehicle for political and financial advancement, a means used with increasing effectiveness ever since.

Most of the Russian immigrants to Philadelphia, as well as large numbers of Poles and other eastern Europeans, were Jews. Forced from their homelands by poverty and pogroms, they came to America as true immigrants. While others had thoughts of returning to Europe, and some did go back, the Jews tended to settle in Philadelphia and remain there. Between 1905 and 1918, their numbers grew from 100,000 to 200,000. Concentrated in South Philadelphia at the turn of the century, the Jewish population soon spread north of Market Street and came to dominate the small-business life of the north-central part of the city. The corner of Marshall and Poplar Streets, where the German Jews who had preceded them once lived, became the hub of a bustling business district that resembled a European shopping bazaar, complete with exotic shops and dozens of pushcart vendors. While many Jews were engaged in commerce as peddlers, shopkeepers, and merchants, even more could be found in the skilled occupations for which the city, given the nature of its industry, had exceptional demand. In particular they became preeminent in the "needle trades" (all forms of clothing manufacture) and contributed many shoemakers, carpenters, butchers, coppersmiths, and similar artisans to the city's labor force. Solid evidence of Jewish mercantile enterprise was three large department stores on Market Street East: Snellenburg's at Twelfth Street, Gimbels at Ninth, and Lits at Eighth.

For several decades prosperous Jewish families had been moving away from their old communities to apartments in the Rittenhouse Square area and to a band several streets wide on either side of Broad Street between Girard and Diamond. A movement farther north had already begun with some families seeking tree-shaded lawns and the advantages of suburban living in Oak Lane and Cheltenham Township, closer to their Philmont Country Club.

At the same time, numbers of eastern European Jews were climbing up the economic and political ladder, foremost among them Lithuanian-born Albert M. Greenfield. In South Philadelphia, the center of Jewish orthodoxy, Rabbi B. L. Levinthal held sway. As they prospered, these immigrants also moved away from their first place of residence to nicer homes in West Philadelphia and Strawberry Mansion, at the same time abandoning orthodoxy for the less stringent demands of Conservative Judaism. A spread of settlement from Parkside by the end of the 1920s included Wynnefield, where the Conservative synagogue Har Zion rapidly grew in size and influence. To be sure, a good many Jews of the prewar waves of immigration—the war and the restrictive Johnson Act of 1924 brought an end to the eastern European flow as it did to those from Italy and Greece—remained in the older areas of settlement, but the census figures for 1930 showed that South Philadelphia had 41 percent fewer Jews living there than in 1920. In 1919 the Federation of Jewish Charities, the community's central fundraising organization for health and welfare agencies, which had been dominated by members of the older German-Jewish families, expanded its scope by taking in under its aegis a host of agencies founded by and for the new immigrants. These included Mount Sinai Hospital, which became the Daroff branch of the Einstein Medical Center, and the Associated Talmud Torahs, traditional Hebrew schools. So began the slow melding of the Jewish community.

Poles, largely unskilled laborers, competed unsuccessfully with the more numerous and already established Irish and Italian workers for general labor jobs. Consequently, many Poles continued to move on to those Pennsylvania regions having more heavy industry than Philadelphia, and thus a greater need for unskilled labor, such as northeastern, central, and western Pennsylvania.

At the same time that they were competing among themselves for jobs and territory, the new immigrants faced the common problem of overcoming the nativism of the Philadelphia population. They were more "different" than earlier immigrant groups and found acceptance more difficult in the city that was still called "the most American of American cities." Native-born workers, fearful of the loss of jobs to the immigrants, bitterly resented them; industrial employers often paid lower wages to them than to other workers; Anglo-Saxon homeowners generally viewed them with suspicion if not with contempt. One did not have to look beyond the newspapers' classified ads for domestic help—which required that the candidate be Protestant as well as white—to realize that the roots of intolerance ran deep in the City of Brotherly Love.

Of all the city's incoming groups, the most consistent flow was the result not of foreign but internal migrations. Philadelphia's foreign-born population was small compared with other cities', but its black population was the largest of any northern urban center. Only the southward cities of Baltimore, Washington, and New Orleans had larger black populations. By 1890 this population was close to 40,000, 4 percent of the city's total and a 24 percent increase over 1880. By 1900, the number had risen 60 percent to more than 62,000 and made up 5 percent of the total.

In 1896, the University of Pennsylvania invited W.E.B. Du Bois to Philadelphia to study the city's black population. His book, *The Philadelphia Negro*, was a pioneer study using sociological and environmental research and is today a classic. Du Bois found that most blacks lived in center city and had for many years. The heaviest concentration was in the Seventh Ward (Spruce to South, Seventh to the Schuylkill), where they were about 40 percent of the population and lived near the white families for whom they were domestic servants. This ward provided both high and low aspects of black life. The more prosperous blacks, perhaps 3,000, lived on Lombard Street west of Eighth and on Rodman and Addison Streets. They comprised an aristocracy of wealth and education that was not recognized by or even known to the whites. They tended to be alienated from their own people, for whom they provided little or no leadership. They were largely Philadelphia-born, many of them descendants of freedmen of the past century.

The vast majority of black males were manual laborers, filling the ever-present need for cheap, unskilled labor—stevedores, street and sewer cleaners, trash collectors, livery men and bootblacks, porters, and waiters. Black women, who outnumbered the men, were virtually limited to domestic service and sewing; however, none of them found work in the sweatshops of the garment trade. Some blacks, however, were able to pull themselves out of this economic pit. By 1896, there were some 300 black-owned businesses in the city, mostly catering firms, restaurants, and barbershops. Christopher J. Perry founded the *Philadelphia Tribune*, a newspaper for blacks, in 1884. Walter P. Hall was one of the wealthiest blacks in 1892, making his money in the wholesale poultry business and using it lavishly through churches and welfare organizations.

Two of the four black undertakers in the city were women. Professionally, the black community had 15 "reputable" physicians, 3 dentists, and 10 lawyers in 1896. There were about 40 teachers and more than 60 ministers. About 1 percent of the blacks were clerical or semiprofessional workers. In 1896 there were 60 black policemen, working in or near black areas. Although blacks had no equal chance for a job at Strawbridge & Clothier or Wanamaker's department stores in 1888, a decade later the black postmaster and postal employees at Wanamaker's were highly successful in running the city's second-largest substation.

To ease their existence, Philadelphia blacks joined beneficial and mutual-aid societies and "secret" or fraternal organizations, paralleling similar groups in the white community. The Odd Fellows were perhaps the most influential of the fraternal societies. The Freemasons too were active, celebrating the centennial of black Masonry in 1884.

The principal organizing and stabilizing body among the blacks remained the church. The church was the center of social life and amusements and a communication center. Each congregation formed its own circle, some being neighborhood-bound, some class-conscious or work-oriented. In 1885, there were 25 black churches and missions in the city, but with the migration of Negroes from the South their number more than doubled to 55 in 1897. The Methodists had the greatest number of communicants, followed by the Baptists, Presbyterians, and Episcopalians, and "springing up and dying a host of little noisy missions which represent the older and more demonstrative worship." In the 1890s, the Catholic Church, because of its "comparative lack of discrimination," made many converts among the blacks, enough in fact that in January 1892 Philadelphia was host to the third black Catholic congress of the United States (Weigley 1982, 494).

As a group, blacks were generally still poorly paid and relegated to the least desirable jobs, but individual achievements indicated that chances for economic advancement were improving. The *Philadelphia Colored Directory* of 1910 revealed that blacks were engaged in almost any enterprise to be named, including all the professions. Among those listed were 169 clergymen, 143 musicians, 78 physicians, 16 dentists, and 13 lawyers. One member of the black community, tobacco dealer Richard A. Cooper, served on the city council. The first black member of the Pennsylvania state legislature, attorney Harry W. Bass, was elected from Philadelphia in 1910. John T. Gibson established a successful theater for black performers, the Standard, on South Street in the early 1900s. Publisher Christopher James Perry had built the *Philadel-*

phia Tribune into one of the most prosperous, respected, and influential black newspapers in the country. The first black to win a Rhodes Scholarship was Central High and Harvard graduate Alain LeRoy Locke. After studying abroad, Locke became a teacher at Howard University in 1912 and later earned a doctorate from Harvard in 1918. He was to have a long career not only as a philosophy professor at Howard but also as a prominent literary figure who published more than a dozen books on African American life and culture before his death in 1954.

The northward migration of blacks during the war had a significant impact on Philadelphia. By the early summer of 1917 more than 800 migrants were arriving in the city each week. The *Philadelphia Christian Recorder* (the official organ of the African Methodist Episcopal [AME] Church and the oldest black newspaper in America) published a special migration edition to instruct blacks on how to arrange their affairs in the South upon leaving, how they should comport themselves in the North, and how to find jobs at their destinations. By 1920, the city's black population had grown to 134,000, more than double that of 1900 (63,000).

If the foreign-born contributed but a relatively small part of the city's total numbers, the blacks, although only about 7.4 percent of the whole in 1920, added a preponderantly large part for a northern city. Many black families still lived along the corridor of Lombard Street in the neighborhood of Mother Bethel AME Church and on other streets in the Fourth, Seventh, and Thirtieth Wards. A strong if small black community had also developed in the Northern Liberties close by Zoar Church, around the Berean school and Presbyterian Church, opposite Girard College, on Diamond Street near Twenty-ninth, and in West Philadelphia. After World War I blacks began to take over houses left vacant by Jews "moving up the ladder," and North Philadelphia started to assume its present orientation (Weigley 1982, 526–28).

The southern migrant who arrived in Philadelphia during World War I through the 1920s found steady, if also rigidly routine, employment. Ready jobs and steady pay were available at both the Pennsylvania and the Erie railroad companies, which had contracts to supply war materiel. Black migrants to Philadelphia also found jobs in industrial and textile factories, shipyards, and sugar refineries. The Philadelphia Rapid Transit Company employed blacks for track-laying work, and the foundry of the Griffin Wheel Company employed many migrants (Reich 2006, 664). Although the opportunities were severely limited, by 1930 Philadelphia was home to nearly 220,000 African Americans.

Among the more secure older families, the professions, particularly law, medicine, teaching, and the church, offered both men and women the best chance for advancement. Two hospitals—Mercy, founded in 1907 by Dr. Henry M. Minton, a graduate of Thomas Jefferson University, and Douglass, then at Sixteenth and Lombard, founded in 1895 by Dr. Nathan F. Mossell, a graduate of the University of Pennsylvania Medical School—supplied the best healthcare services generally available to the community. A newspaper, the *Tribune,* a bank, the Citizens and Southern, beneficial societies, organizations like the Armstrong Association, and the many black churches tried to help the newcomers withstand the frustration and loneliness of life in an inhospitable city. The churches, however, were not always seen as the stabilizing force they had been in the nineteenth century. Writers like historian Carter Woodson accused the clergy and the educated blacks of shirking their responsibilities as the black community, like its white counterpart, divided along social and economic lines.

Political exploitation of the black community, most of whom were "Lincoln Republicans," was easy for the city's political machine. There was only one black ward leader in 1925, Edward W. Henry, and most of the jobs he had in his pocket were the traditional ones, plus a handful of appointments to the police force, or to positions as marshals' or sheriffs' deputies. When the organization failed to deliver its expected aid, the black voters could and on occasion did make their displeasure felt. For example, when Amos Scott, a black tavern keeper of 1140 Pine Street, failed to receive a promised magistrate's office, G. Edward Dickerson, a black attorney with offices at 628 South Sixteenth Street, made sure that the Thirtieth Ward blacks heard the story. The result at the next election was "evident." In the main, however, residents of the largely black Twelfth, Fourteenth, Twentieth, and Thirtieth Wards remained subject to the Republican organization's whims until the New Deal's humanitarian response to the misery caused by the Depression drastically altered their affiliation (Weigley 1982, 588–91).

As elsewhere, the rapid expansion of the black population in the urban areas of the Middle Atlantic region led inevitably to increased tension and conflict between the races. Although Philadelphia was able to escape a repetition of its nineteenth-century racial riots and the disastrous twentieth-century racial wars that occurred in East St. Louis, Chicago, and Washington, D.C., the competition for jobs and housing gave rise to bitterness on both sides. Housing, already overburdened because of the new immigrants, became a particularly acute problem for blacks. In one of many such instances, 10 black families lived in one three-story house in the Thirtieth Ward with only a single bath and toilet for all the residents. Whites, who expected blacks to remain in those parts of the city where they had traditionally lived, resented their movement into other areas. The resentment erupted into violence in July 1918 when a black woman moved into a house at 2936 Ellsworth Street, in a white neighborhood. Angry white mobs gathered in the street, stoned the house, and attacked blacks near the scene. Two days of sporadic rioting and fighting between the two races followed, resulting in the deaths of two whites and one black. Peace was gradually restored, but the tensions and resentments lingered on (Weigley 1982, 531–32).

In response to the riots of 1918, black Philadelphians organized the Colored Protective Association, which operated much like the National Urban League. Although the city's black newspaper, the *Philadelphia Tribune*, unlike its counterparts in other northern cities, did little to encourage black migration north, the paper did join the migrants' struggle against racial injustice. During the riot of 1918, for example, the editors urged black Philadelphians to defend themselves as American citizens. The *Tribune* also encouraged black churches to do more to support the migrants. In the first half of the twentieth century, black churches played a major role in easing the burden of migration and discrimination suffered by blacks in the urban Middle Atlantic region. Often functioning as settlement houses, the churches not only cared for the social, economic, and spiritual needs of early migrants, but defended them by pressuring city officials for improvement of unsanitary living conditions, inferior schools, inaccessibility to medical care, and other consequences of discrimination (Reich 2006, 664–65).

Baltimore

Migrants and immigrants from myriad cultures and places settled in Baltimore in the post–Civil War era. Among those seeking a new home in Baltimore were ex-Confederates from Virginia, farmers from rural interior counties, black farm workers from south Maryland, and immigrants mostly from eastern Europe who differed greatly in habit, custom, and language from the Germans and Irish who had preceded them in the first half of the nineteenth century. By 1900, Baltimore was home to 10,000 Russian Jews, and in lesser numbers Poles, Greeks, Bohemians, and Lithuanians.

In 1920, Germans continued to be the largest foreign-born group in Baltimore. They numbered 30,000 and maintained a variety of institutions that their predecessors had established in the early nineteenth century, including churches, turnverein athletic clubs, schools, and music clubs. Germans made important contributions to Baltimore's labor movement and many served the city in political offices (Chapelle 2000, 153–54).

The eastern European newcomers who arrived in Baltimore in the late nineteenth and early twentieth centuries faced many of the same problems that had greeted the Germans and Irish in the mid-nineteenth century. Most landed with little or no money and without the ability to read, write, or speak English. They also had trouble obtaining anything other than menial employment and had to live in the worst housing. Eastern Europeans also suffered prejudice and discrimination from both native English-speaking Americans and earlier immigrant groups.

Bohemians began arriving in Baltimore at the end of the Civil War. They had emigrated to escape exploitations of the Austro-Hungarian Empire and to avoid service in the Austrian army. Upon arriving in Baltimore, they built a community around a national church and school, where they maintained their native Czech language until 1910. In 1900, a group of Bohemians formed the Slavic Savings and Loan Association, the first of many similar institutions that made it possible for a high percentage of Bohemians to buy homes.

In the early 1920s, Poles began to arrive in Baltimore in large numbers to escape the hardships of the post–World War I era in their homeland. Many were peasants driven from their small farms by hunger and desperation. Although a number of Poles knew German, almost none of them could speak English. Nevertheless, their reputation as hard workers preceded them, and many were able to find employment working for the railroads, the shipyards, construction companies, clothing manufacturers, canneries, and steel mills.

Because the Polish immigrants were extremely poor, it often took them more than one generation to buy a house, and they frequently had to live in crowded unsanitary conditions. Families were large, and many women went to work, often in canneries, to make ends meet. Like the Germans and the Bohemians, Poles began to found building and loan societies—20 of them by 1914—and to buy homes. The Polish community also created numerous other institutions, which provided various social, educational, and recreational activities. In 1923 the Polish community began to establish a political voice when they elected their first city councilman, Edward Novak (Chappelle 2000, 158).

Little Italy, Baltimore's most enduring ethnic community, traced its roots to the nineteenth century and continued through the twentieth. Italians first arrived at the end of the nineteenth century, driven from their homeland by drought and privatization of common lands by the national government. They spoke little or no English, but they went to work on the railroads, first as common laborers and later as machinists. Some, such as stone masons and barbers, were able to utilize skills they brought with them from Italy, and others became independent merchants, starting by selling vegetables and fruits in carts from door to door, or on street corners. In the Italian community the women were not expected to enter the public workplace; their domain remained the home, where their obligations were rearing the children and maintaining the house. If women brought in any outside income at all it was usually by taking in boarders (Chapelle 2000, 162).

Italians gained political power relatively soon after their arrival compared to other immigrant groups. The community's first political leader, Vincent R. Palmisano, was elected to the Maryland House of Delegates in 1914, to the Baltimore City Council the following year, and to the United States Congress in 1926. Thomas D'Alesandro succeeded Palmisano and became Little Italy's best known Baltimorean. D'Alesandro, son of an immigrant, was elected to the Maryland House in 1926, then went to Congress in 1938 (Chapelle 2000, 160).

The Russian Jews who began arriving in Baltimore during the 1880s were by far the largest group of newcomers. By 1900, over 10,000 Russians lived in the city, and by 1910 almost 25,000 lived there. Most fled from persecution in Russia and nearby countries like Poland and Lithuania, which were subject to Russian domination. The vast majority of eastern European Jews became garment workers in the factories of East Baltimore, and they became active in the formation of one of the country's most important unions of the era, the International Ladies Garment Workers Union (ILGWU) (Chapelle 2000, 162).

European immigrants who came to Baltimore at the turn of the century followed patterns similar to those who had arrived in this country in an earlier era of immigration. They arrived with little knowledge of English or of American culture and therefore sought security by settling initially in areas where they could communicate in their own language. As soon as they could, they built churches or synagogues, which in addition to serving the spiritual needs of the new community also provided a place for social gatherings. Churches and synagogues also provided a safety net in a country where social services were minimal.

Gradually these immigrants, who usually started out in low-paying jobs, began to improve their economic situation. The more fortunate of the immigrants often established mutual-help societies—often church- or synagogue-based—and chartered banks, which helped their compatriots secure loans for houses or small businesses. Eventually, each of these groups, often within their own generation, but certainly within the generation of their children, began to climb the social and economic ladder of American life.

The same pattern was not true for the black migrants to Baltimore. Blacks spoke the same language and understood the American culture far better than most European immigrants. They were also willing to work in the lowest-paying jobs. But because of the persistence of racism in the country, most blacks were not able to make the same steady social and economic progress that most white European immigrants enjoyed. The majority of Europeans eventually were able to work their way out of the terrible living conditions they encountered upon arrival, but color kept blacks restricted to the poorest, most unsanitary neighborhoods with the worst public services, including inferior schools. For many, these neighborhoods became inescapable ghettoes. This pattern was familiar throughout the urban Middle Atlantic. Each city had its black ghetto, often with its own derogatory name. In Baltimore the black ghetto was known as "Pigtown," which was the dirtiest and least healthy place to live in all of Baltimore. Discrimination in the workplace and an unequal and segregated school system also prevented a majority of blacks in Baltimore from following the pattern established by European immigrants.

Despite these many impediments, a small black middle class did emerge in Baltimore. Their social mobility began with the ballot box. Unlike their counterparts in the South, blacks were able to maintain their franchise in Baltimore, and beginning in 1890, black Republicans won seats on the city council in almost every election until 1931. Although black councilmen never possessed a great deal of political power, they were able to push for improvement of the black schools and funnel some jobs into the black community. These efforts provided opportunity for at least some to rise above their grave circumstances.

By the outbreak of World War I, the newly emerging black middle class began to move out of the ghetto and into nearby neighborhoods that had formerly been occupied by European immigrants. Still, the vast majority of blacks lived in poor conditions, received poor wages, and had little or no opportunity to get a good education. While the immigrants became more thoroughly assimilated, most African Americans remained in a segregated world with limited opportunities through the first half of the twentieth century (Chapelle 2000, 166, 168).

Maryland, historically a slave-owning border state, had a spotted attitude toward race. Some facilities and institutions such as schools, restaurants, and many stores were segregated, while others such as streetcars were not. Several attempts from 1910 through 1913 to pass ordinances to establish segregated neighborhoods were defeated, when local black lawyers challenged their constitutionality in court. The single most difficult problem faced by blacks was unemployment. Blacks were often fired in favor of white workers, and almost always paid less, and because of this overt discrimination most black workers were unable to build the financial base that the immigrants gradually did (Chapelle 2000, 166, 168).

Washington

The late nineteenth-century migration helped make Washington, D.C., the city with the largest percentage of African Americans in the Middle Atlantic region. While several cities surpassed Washington's numbers of black migrants, as the great migration progressed, proportionally Washington's black population remained one of the largest in the region.

Migrants came for reasons that varied by individual and epoch; they were pushed by intolerable conditions and attracted by the city's possibilities. The size of Washington's black population and its extensive organizational infrastructure, including churches and educational, cultural, civic, and recreational facilities, made it a mecca for rural and urban migrants alike.

Washington's proximity to Virginia and Maryland meant that poor migrants did not have far to go. Some came by walking, others by wagons or boats. But most frequently they arrived by railroad. On the Atlantic Coast Line, which passed through the heart of the South and into Washington, black migrants sat in segregated Jim Crow railroad cars and provided their own food. In later years they also came by bus and car. Migrants carried their belongings in small suitcases called "freedom bags," symbolic of their hopes and laden with southern black traditions.

Their decision to migrate resulted from a variety of factors, personal, familial, and more general; the process involved considerable planning. The immediate decision to leave often resulted from personal events such as a parent's death; general forces included worsening agricultural conditions or the promise of better opportunities in Washington. Families regulated the migration process for individuals and family groups; potential migrants wrote to relatives and friends in the city to locate employment, housing, and city information. The first migrants often sent money home, encouraged a chain migration of family and friends, then housed the new arrivals and helped them find housing. Migrants maintained ties by visiting home and joining hometown clubs in Washington.

Washington was a southern border city, and its residential patterns reflected those of the deep South. Although African Americans resided throughout the city, they often lived in small clusters near whites. By 1920, three large black residential concentrations emerged in the southwest, in the northwest along North Capitol and Florida avenues, and near Foggy Bottom in the northwest. Many prominent blacks continued to reside in predominantly white neighborhoods, but it became increasingly difficult to move into these neighborhoods.

Unlike other border cities in the early 1900s, Washington did not have a segregation ordinance; nevertheless, white property owners, neighborhood protective associations, real estate agents, and bankers increasingly restricted some areas for white residence. At the turn of the century, the all-white LeDroit neighborhood in the northwest fenced itself off from neighboring black Howard Town, whose residents protested by tearing the fence down. By 1900 blacks began to move into LeDroit

Park; and by 1915 it housed 800 middle-class and elite black families. The north-west generally became a center of Washington's black community, housing such key institutions as Howard University, Freedmen's Hospital, the Howard Theater, the prestigious Dunbar High School, major churches, many black-owned businesses, and Griffith Stadium, where baseball teams from the "Negro League" played (Reich 2006, 881–83).

In Washington, D.C., the continuing black migration eventually produced major housing shortages for black Washingtonians generally and especially for low-income blacks. These shortages caused high rents that sparked alley development and led to severe overcrowding. Some four-room alley dwellings housed four separate families who shared an outhouse and water hydrant. These conditions, along with the city's general neglect of health and building conditions in poor black neighborhoods, severe employment discrimination, and inadequate incomes, made conditions for poor migrants extremely difficult. Police brutality and frequent arrests for petty crime added to migrants' difficulties. Poor southern black migrants also confronted hostility and bias from native black Washingtonians. Natives found country migrants unso-phisticated, uneducated, and beneath them. Some sought to provide uplift, but not without condescension; others feared that whites would judge all African Americans by the newcomers' behavior. Migrants often felt uncomfortable in Washington's large, established black churches and other social organizations where middle-class blacks dominated. Migrant schoolchildren faced ridicule of their limited wardrobes and rural ways. White violence endangered black migrants and natives alike. As in many cities across the nation in 1919, a white mob, incited by newspaper stories of black criminality, attacked African Americans throughout the city; by arming them-selves in self-defense, blacks probably limited the extent of the white riot (Reich 2006, 881).

Pittsburgh

In the early decades of the twentieth century Pittsburgh became home to thou-sands of Polish immigrants, who moved westward to the newly emerging industrial steel-producing centers. Poles moving to Pittsburgh could be grouped into two cat-egories: those from Prussia who moved to America almost entirely in family units and had little intention of returning to a country where German policies made it increasingly difficult for Poles to own land, and Poles from the Austrian and the Russian sectors who were more likely to arrive in Pittsburgh as single males and either return to Europe or reconstruct families in America. While the children were growing up in Poland, Valerian D. recalled, his father had mined coal in Germany. Joseph B. was sent to Pittsburgh to earn wages for his family and eventually returned to Poland, only to see his own son leave for America.

Poles were particularly successful in establishing occupational beachheads at the steel mills of Jones and Laughlin and Oliver on the south side, at Heppenstall's and the Pennsylvania Railroad yards in Lawrenceville, and at Armstrong Cork Company, the H. J. Heinz plant, and other large industrial plants. Thus, Poles were clustered in a few industries. Valentine B. gained his first job in America on the railroad through his brother. Brothers also assisted Peter H. in obtaining employment in a foundry making castings for mines. Ignacy M. left Russian Poland in 1912 and relied on his brother to get him a position piling steel beams at the Jones and Laughlin plant. Joseph D. left Prussia for a job in a mill, procured by his wife's uncle. A cousin found Edward R. work at a machine shop. John S. followed friends from Galicia in 1909 but needed relatives to acquire machinist's work for him. Charles W. relied on relatives to gain him access to domestic work for Americans and boardinghouse tasks. The impact of this network had long-lasting effects on the Polish immigrant family. Poles were clearly more effective in obtaining work for family and friends than other immigrant groups, and as a result of kinfolk networking, young Polish workers remained attached to their families of origin and contributed most of their earnings to their parents (Bodnar 1985, 557–58).

When the United States entered World War I in 1917, European immigration ceased, creating a labor shortage that forced northern industries to begin hiring blacks. In Pittsburgh, Jones and Laughlin Steel and the Pennsylvania Railroad, among others, sent recruiters south to bring up new employees. Through a process called "chain migration," these newcomers in turn sent for friends and relatives to join them, with the result that more than 20,000 black immigrants settled in Pittsburgh in the 1910s and 1920s. In the outlying mill towns up and down the Monongahela River, hiring by Carnegie Steel plants raised the black population from 5,000 to 23,000 in Aliquippa, Homestead, Rankin, Braddock, Duquesne, McKeesport, and Clairton.

Migration altered the racial composition of the city's neighborhoods. Newcomers settled primarily in the lower and middle Hill District, the city's oldest, poorest, and most racially mixed neighborhood, located near downtown. As they did so, the previously established black community (referred to as OPs for "Old Pittsburghers"), who were more settled and a bit better off, escaped to outlying neighborhoods like Homewood, Beltzhoover, and the more prestigious upper Hill District. Whites also moved away from the newcomers, but in Pittsburgh the emergence of all-black residential areas proceeded more slowly than elsewhere. In 1920, for example, some 60 percent of blacks lived within five doors of a white family, and not until the 1930s did blacks constitute a majority of even the Hill District, the principal black neighborhood.

Racial transition also proceeded more peacefully in Pittsburgh than elsewhere. While cities like Chicago, East St. Louis, and Washington, D.C., erupted in race riots, often over maintaining neighborhood racial boundaries, Pittsburgh's Hill District was quiet. There poor blacks, Jews, and Italians lived in close proximity. They shopped together and their children attended school together, for the city's school system had been desegregated in the 1870s.

Migrants gave the community energy and vitality. Just as Pittsburgh previously had supported concert orchestras and classical musicians, in the 1920s and 1930s it became a center for jazz, nurturing such greats as Billy Strayhorn, Kenny Clarke, Art Blakey, Earl "Fatha" Hines, Roy Eldridge, and Leroy Brown, in addition to female musicians Lena Horne, Mary Lou Williams, Louise Manlt, and Maxine Sullivan. Much of this energy resulted from a synergistic fusion of old and new migrants. The older, more established migrants helped structure the new black metropolis. Robert

Vann, for example, had come from North Carolina well before World War I. In 1910, he purchased the *Pittsburgh Courier* and by the 1930s had built it into one of the country's premier black newspapers. Cumberland Posey Jr., son of the city's leading black businessman in 1900, established the Homestead Grays, one of the premier baseball teams of the Negro Leagues. And Gus Greenlee, who came up from North Carolina just before the great migration, subsequently owned the city's leading black nightclub, the Crawford Grill, as well as the Pittsburgh Crawfords baseball team, the city's other premier black baseball team.

Together, the OPs and the new migrants accomplished much. By the 1930s the Pittsburgh Crawfords and the Homestead Grays were mainstays of the Negro Leagues, the *Pittsburgh Courier* was the largest-circulation black newspaper in the country, and the Hill District pulsed with the sounds of innovative jazz performers (Reich 2006, 674).

In Pittsburgh, migrants, black or white, who entered the industrial workforce started at the bottom. But unlike their white predecessors, blacks almost never moved up. Racial discrimination explained much of this blocked occupational mobility. In addition, blacks had entered the city just as heavy industry there had begun its long-term downward slide and at the same time was modernizing and eliminating common laboring positions. Black attitudes also contributed to their blocked mobility. Many migrants regarded industrial labor as temporary work, to be done between planting and harvesting season. Therefore, they were prepared to quit should the work prove unsatisfactory, which it often did. To maintain 223 black steelworkers in 1923, for example, the A. M. Byers Company made 1,408 separate hires. Black workers had few alternatives, for they were excluded from more than half the city's trades and the rest confined them to positions as common laborers and insisted that they be paid less than union scale. A situation that was bleak during the 1920s turned disastrous during the 1930s, when a study showed that during the Great Depression more than one-third of black adults were unemployed and three-fourths were living in poverty (Reich 2006, 674).

Newark

In Newark, New Jersey, southern blacks, who had been migrating there since the second decade of the century, often experienced the same discriminatory practices they had suffered in the South. Upon arrival in the city they were forced to live in the slums of Newark's Third Ward where, according to the Negro Welfare League, "most of the dwellings were poorly heated and of considerable age. A substantial proportion of them lacked lighting facilities, inside toilets, and running water." One woman described the arrival of a black family from Alabama in 1919. The man, his wife, and seven children were paying $14 a month for three rooms, "the central room perfectly dark." A white family who preceded them paid only $9 for the apartment, but "The landlady downstairs said quite explicitly that she charges these people $14 because they were colored" (Fleming 1985, 194).

In 1930, a study by the Urban League reported that blacks were 5.5 percent of the population of New Jersey, but 3.5 percent of the gainfully employed, and 25 percent of the relief load. "White folks were yelling their heads off because there were so many blacks on relief," commented Harold Lett, the executive secretary of the league. But union membership, particularly in the skilled trades, was closed to them. Simultaneously, numerous industries began leaving Newark for the lower-taxed suburbs.

Between the two wars segregation was the order of the day for blacks in Newark. Real estate agents and property owners continued to force blacks into Newark's ghetto, where they endured substandard housing and other forms of economic deprivation. They were not accepted in white restaurants, they sat in separate sections of the city's movie houses, and they were barred from public swimming facilities. Newark was by no means the only New Jersey city to follow these patterns. E. Frederick Morrow, who was born and grew up in Hackensack in the 1920s, wrote the following in a memoir of his youth:

The only difference between the slave era and then [the twenties] was the fact that physical slavery had been abolished, but all the mental and spiritual and philosophical attitudes developed in slavery toward the Blacks remained. The whites were adamant in fostering and retaining the status quo, which meant inequality in every facet of community life. On the other hand, the Negroes had been so brainwashed, and had become so weary from the burdens and toil of life, that most accepted the inevitability of second-class citizenship.

Morrow recalled in bitter detail the uproar caused when his sister applied for a job in the public school system. Almost every white organization in town, from the Daughters of the American Revolution to the Knights of Columbus, rose in protest. The Ku Klux Klan marched through Hackensack in a fiery night parade. For Morrow, the saddest part of the story was the reaction of the town's black community. They were as vociferously opposed to Nelly Morrow's hiring as the whites, claiming they did not want their children taught by an "inferior" teacher (Fleming 1985, 193–95).

URBAN AND RURAL EXPERIENCE

In the Middle Atlantic region, only a person who lived on a farm or in a country town before 1920 could appreciate fully the complete revolution in country and small-town life that took place in the next few decades. The life of the rural community changed little between about 1820 and 1920; it changed significantly in the next few decades thanks to the automobile and truck and the improved roads reaching from farm to town, and to radio, electricity, and the motion picture. It is hardly possible to overemphasize the role of the automobile and truck and the accompanying hard-surfaced highway in revolutionizing life on the farm and in the neighboring town or small city. Until after World War I the horseless carriage remained something of a curiosity outside the larger centers of population, where the more wealthy toyed with it as a luxury. Henry Ford changed all this with the "Tin Lizzie," produced at a low cost and available to the person with average income. By 1920 motorized transportation was no longer a curiosity, but a practical method of transportation, and in Pennsylvania, 10 years later, Governor Gifford Pinchot started building the hard-top roads that lifted the farmer's automobile out of the dust and mud. By 1940, roughly, the average farmer in just about any part of Pennsylvania was reasonably sure of all-weather use of his car or truck. A trip to even a distant town could now be made in hours rather than as an all-day jaunt.

Any farm family could now see the new motion picture "palace," with its vigorous piano accompaniment of the silent pictures that flickered across a screen showing the perilous adventures or the comic actions of their favorite stars of the films. Such occasions, naturally, were special events of the week, but almost any time the farmer needed something from the village he could drive the few miles in a few minutes to get it. Life was never the same in the farm community after the coming of the automobile. It was a new and mobile life upon which some oldsters looked askance, especially when the automobile hearse replaced the slow horse-drawn vehicle in taking the deceased to their graves.

Contact with towns and in turn their contact by motor truck transportation with larger cities meant many changes. New sources of supply for a variety of foodstuffs such as fresh vegetables, fruits, and meats, which were common in city markets even earlier, began to appear in country stores by the 1930s. The home garden in town or country lost some of its appeal as the new supplies of canned or fresh vegetables and fruits appeared. Easy access to town dramatically changed patterns of life in the rural Middle Atlantic region. Most clothing could now be purchased in town or city stores, and the best in fashions was as available to the farmer and his family as to any city dweller.

Electricity followed upon the heels of the automobile as a major force revolutionizing life on the farm in the Middle Atlantic region. For example, in Pennsylvania by the 1940s, surveys indicated that well over 100,000 out of 170,000 farm homes had the advantages of electricity. This meant the coming of refrigeration and the home freezer, replacing home canning and the cold cellar. It meant the lighting of farm homes with electricity and soon brought, as they were developed, the appliances of an electrical age into the farmhouse as well as the town and city home. It meant in many homes an electric water supply system rather than pumping by hand the ton of water a day it is estimated most farm housewives used. The "typical" farm kitchen of 1940 was a far cry from that of 1920, thanks to electricity, and it was likely to be thoroughly modern. The man of the house also made use of the new source of power in lighting and equipping the barn with labor-saving devices.

Farm life changed also in the area of communication. The telephone came to rural Pennsylvania after 1900, mainly through the growth of community cooperatives, which built the lines and organized the central switchboard. It was not much before 1930 that the United and Bell commercial telephone companies adequately served the hinterland.

But the greatest revolution of all in terms of enriching the farm home and its cultural and entertainment outlook was radio. By 1945, 90 percent of all farm homes in Pennsylvania had radio. It could be operated with batteries, which enlarged its use by the thousands. Radio caught on quickly because even earlier the ordinary phonograph with its wax disks had brought into remote homes the best as well as the ordinary in music, comedy, and general entertainment. When television, after World War II, brought the picture along with the sound, the revolution in a farm environment, once largely isolated from the outer world, was complete.

The automobile enlarged and changed the farm community by making it possible for people to come together more easily and readily for a variety of purposes. The strictly country school gave way to the consolidated and larger school located in town or in some central location to which children could be transported from a wide area by school bus. By 1960, the one-room school had all but disappeared in Pennsylvania. The country church also became a victim of the ability of people to attend a larger church in town. In 1947 a study of a typical northern Pennsylvania rural county showed that less than 15 percent of the remaining churches could be called country churches and less than 16 percent of the schools were of the country type. By 1960, out of over four hundred farm organizations not more than 10 percent held meetings in the country. Even the Grange hall was apt to be in town; here also were located the veterans' organizations and just about every other social and civic group. Only the Amish country held any longer to "old ways" of farm life.

The educational horizons of the farm folk of Pennsylvania were also deepened and broadened by the new era of communication and transportation. By 1940 Grange membership was well over 60,000 in Pennsylvania, with some seven hundred active Granges. A variety of other state farm organizations developed after 1900 as those concerned with special aspects of farming such as potato growing, keeping bees, or breeding certain types of livestock perfected their associations. A Pennsylvania Country Life Association was founded in 1936 and the Society of Farm Women in 1910. By 1916 a Pennsylvania Federation of Farm Organizations was in operation, which finally became the State Council of Farm Organizations.

The county fair, with some aid from the state, continued to grow and to exert educational influence as well as provide entertainment. Going to the fair had become a great annual event in the life of most farm families of the Middle Atlantic region, even in the days of dirt roads and the horse and buggy, or the surrey with the fringe on the top. The entire family packed food for lunch and dinner and often drove several miles to attend the fair. There products of the farm were exhibited for prizes, and the latest in farm machinery and equipment displayed by their manufacturers, while harness racing and horse racing, acrobatics and other grandstand shows, and a midway carnival offered fun and excitement. Going to the fair was usually a dawn-to-dusk day of fun and frolic.

Oddly enough, the automobile finally weakened the smaller country fairs because people were able to travel farther to see finer attractions at the larger fairs. Radio also helped break down the strictly country fairs, and larger and better-financed fair associations in such cities as Reading, Allentown, and York began to present as their grand attraction elaborate stage shows featuring radio personalities. The old Pennsylvania State Fair expired before 1900 and was not revived until 1921. Eight years later a State Farm Show building was authorized at Harrisburg to be operated by the State Farm Products Show Commission. It grew quickly into the nation's largest farm exposition, held annually in January and attended by thousands of persons each year. Here the showing of farm products for prizes and the sale of the prize livestock to the highest bidder were combined with a fabulous display of farm equipment and machinery without rival anywhere else in the country, but without the side show and midway common to the typical state fair. The annual Farm Show also provides a meeting time and sounding board for all of the statewide farm organizations and associations. Hundreds of farm youth take an active part in Farm Show exhibits and activities.

Expansion of the Rural Free Delivery (RFD), started in 1896, was another aid to broadening farm life. Parcel post was added in 1913, bringing mail-order service to the farm home. The RFD brought newspapers and magazines to the farmer's doorstep almost as quickly as to the town or city dweller. By 1912, a survey indicated that hardly a farm home was without a daily newspaper and one or more magazines. The famous monthly *Farm Journal* made its home in Philadelphia in 1877 and became a favorite farm magazine throughout the region. The *Country Gentleman*, as a member of the Curtis family of Philadelphia magazines and a more literary product, was also widely read in Pennsylvania. The *National Stockman and Farmer*, founded in Pittsburgh in 1877, was another regional favorite. In 1928 it merged with the *Pennsylvania Farmer*, founded in 1912. The new combined magazine soon became the most distinctively Pennsylvanian farm journal. The weekly Williamsport *Grit* and the old-fashioned country weekly, published usually at the county seat, were staples in any farm mailbox, along with a daily newspaper of the region.

The State Agricultural Extension Service began in 1892. It was expanded in 1907. Headed by Alva Agee in the School of Agriculture at Pennsylvania State University, generally known as Penn State, and given federal support by the Smith-Lever Act in 1914, it opened another new era in the education of the farmer. John Hamilton, Pennsylvania farm leader and onetime U.S. Secretary of Agriculture, worked hard to secure this legislation. By 1922 a system of County Agricultural Extension Associations was organized, each headed by an expert in agriculture trained at Penn State and known as the county agent. Home economics was quickly made a part of the system of extension services, and specialists from the university traveled across the state lecturing and instructing as well as demonstrating improved farm and home practices. The Extension Services in 1914 began to organize rural youth into the famous 4-H clubs (Head, Hands, Heart, and Health), which carried on various special projects of their own selection. By 1940, there were over 1,500 4-H clubs with a membership of over 21,000.

Organized instruction in agriculture in the schools was first in the form of nature study and dates back to 1889, when a Pittsburgh teacher started taking classes out into the fields. Penn State offered nature study by correspondence by 1900, and in 1904 at Waterford the first rural high school course in agriculture was started. By 1911 the state was requiring it to be taught in all township schools, and two years later a vocational agriculture department was created in the Department of Public Instruction. In 1917, federal aid was forthcoming through the Smith-Hughes Vocational Education Act, which included home economics and industrial trades and skills. By 1940 rural high schools were commonly presenting courses in improved farming and home economics with state and federal aid. Students in these classes in 1928 founded the Future Farmers of America, which two years later achieved statewide organization. Such advances in farm training, as well as in the general liberal education of farm youth, were forwarded by the growth of the consolidated schools, of which there were only eight in all of Pennsylvania in 1900. By 1940, there were some 700, and a full 4,000 one-room schools had disappeared in the short span of 40 years. The number continued to decrease in the next 20 years as larger and finer consolidated schools appeared, many of which represented jointures, bringing together several neighboring rural or small-town districts, which pooled resources with the encouragement of increased state aid for teacher salaries, transportation of pupils, and modern buildings.

Despite the truly revolutionary and profitable changes in the life of the Pennsylvanian farmer, it was not a land of milk and honey for every one of them. Actual farm poverty existed in certain areas of Pennsylvania by 1930, and other farmers were not doing very well. In the first place, the average per capita income of all Pennsylvania farmers in 1929 was less than one-half that of nonfarmers. This meant that large numbers of farmers were failing entirely to reap any major benefits from the economic growth of the whole of Pennsylvania. The years from 1900 through World War I were rather prosperous ones for most Pennsylvania farmers, and all estimates agree that the average farm family enjoyed a surplus in income as matched against outlay for improving the farm home or investing in more land or machinery. The postwar depression brought down the price of farm products sharply, and many a farmer who had bought more land or machinery, or possibly an automobile, on credit found it hard to make ends meet. Basically, as the years passed the cost of operating a successful farm mounted by thousands of dollars, mainly because of increased use of expensive machinery. As early as 1933 Governor Pinchot noted, "Farmers are daily losing homes in large numbers by reason of foreclosure of mortgages." A year later, 12 percent of the state's farm families were on relief rolls. New Deal measures in Washington helped farmers in debt through loans from the Farm Security Administration.

Many farmers could hardly be helped by such measures because the land they had farmed for years was now incapable of profitably producing crops. Fully 6 percent of all of the farms in the state in 1934 were judged to be submarginal in terms of the ability of the farmer to make a living. In some areas in northern and western Pennsylvania the percentage was as high as 40. This led some farmers to turn to dairy and livestock, and by the late 1950s livestock and livestock products constituted the largest source of farm income in Pennsylvania. Vegetable growing also began to increase as market gardening to supply increasing demand in the cities. Heinz Company in Pittsburgh, one of the largest food processors in the world, also increased demand for local vegetables. Grain, however, ceased to be a leading crop, a far cry from the previous century when Pennsylvania was still considered the breadbasket of the nation (Stevens 1964, 300–305).

Urban areas of the Middle Atlantic states grew rapidly in the first half of the twentieth century, and the demands of an enlarged city population produced a sharp quickening of the emergence of the modern city. Improved paved streets and walks, street lighting, better police protection, a good water supply, adequate sewage and sanitation, even city parks became a must, and every city in the Middle Atlantic region moved rapidly to secure these improvements. The pressures created by the growth of the cities began to reach peaks in the early 1900s. One of the first problems that caught up with urban centers of the Middle Atlantic region was sanitation and sewerage and their relation to the water supply. By the early 1900s, the need for community action on health and sanitation was evident as Pittsburgh, Philadelphia, Baltimore, and other large cities of the region were afflicted with epidemics of typhoid. The next few decades witnessed notable development of sanitation and public health facilities in these cities. Slowly but surely the modern town and city began to take shape, and by the end of World War I most urban areas had a modern infrastructure in place. As the century approached its halfway point, new problems faced the urban centers of the Middle Atlantic region, such as population flight to the suburbs and deterioration of the inner city (Stevens 1964, 306–7).

ANIMAL HUSBANDRY AND HUNTING AND FISHING

Before 1900 any advocate of what was then a very new idea, namely conservation of natural resources, was a prophet crying in the wilderness. The idea of a national park system had been born in 1872 when Congress made the Yellowstone country a national preserve as a natural wonder. President Grover Cleveland talked a little bit about conservation, and President William McKinley rather forgot it. President Theodore Roosevelt made conservation a national issue in 1901, and Pennsylvania's Gifford Pinchot, as head of the nation's Forest Service, began to restrict the exploitation on an unlimited basis of not only timber but coal, mineral, and water-power sites on federal lands. Even earlier, in Pennsylvania, Dr. Joseph T. Rothrock, a native of McVeytown and a physician and surgeon by profession, in 1877 had addressed with great eloquence the American Philosophical Society in Philadelphia on the importance of conservation, and in 1886 he founded the Pennsylvania Forestry Association. In 1887 the state established a Forestry Commission, and 10 years later the Assembly voted funds to start the first 40,000 acres of state forest. By 1904, Pennsylvania, though it still was a leading lumbering state and the lumber industry cut timber without much regard to conservation, had over 400,000 acres of state forest, which would later grow to over two million acres. Gifford Pinchot returned to head the state forest program, taking over where Rothrock had left off. Together, Rothrock, Pinchot, George Wirt, and many others moved the forest conservation program ahead.

Conservation of water resources was an area in which Pennsylvania developed leadership when in 1905 it created a commission to study the problem. Out of this grew a progression of laws that brought the basic control of this vital resource under state controls. In 1922, Pennsylvania entered into a cooperative agreement with Delaware and later with other neighboring states and the federal government to regulate and control the water supply, represented by the Delaware River.

Conservation has broader meanings today than earlier; Pennsylvania was in front in developing many of these ideas. By 1896, the once-lush game lands of the state had disappeared and conservationists began to be aware of this, with the result that in that year a start toward state game conservation began. Many people resented this as an interference with private rights, but in 1903 a license to hunt game was required for nonresident hunters. The first game refuge was set up in 1905, and since that time an active State Game Commission began developing conservation of Pennsylvania's once-vanishing wildlife to a point where it compared favorably with other states. By mid-century, the commission had over 978,000 acres of game lands. The Fish Commission established in 1949 began as the Board of Fish Commissioners and developed an extensive program of propagation and distribution of fish in Pennsylvania's streams, which added greatly to the conservation of stream and recreational facilities.

Not all of the work in conservation had been done by government. Since 1931 the Western Pennsylvania Conservancy in Pittsburgh began acquiring thousands of acres to protect the land's natural beauty and to develop it for public use and conservation. Several thousand acres were presented to the Commonwealth for use in state park developments in western Pennsylvania.

The land itself is so basic a resource that by 1930 Congress was impelled to authorize a nationwide study of the evils of soil erosion. As early as 1901, Pennsylvania State University, in cooperation with the United States Department of Agriculture, had started a study of soil conditions throughout Pennsylvania. As land was denuded of timber by unregulated lumbering, the problem became more acute with every decade. Under the federal legislation the university began a more active study of soil conservation, and demonstration projects were in operation in Indiana and Armstrong counties by 1934 to show how to control erosion. Two years later federal benefits were authorized for farmers who would adopt soil conservation measures, and in 1938 the Pennsylvania Assembly authorized the creation, on a voluntary basis by vote of farmers themselves, of Soil Conservation Districts. Since at least 10 percent of the state's farmland was by then submarginal, these measures were badly needed. Building dams on small streams to check flood waters, tree planting to control loose soil, strip and contour farming rather than plowing in the old-style straight furrow, which invited rain to wash soil away, and careful crop rotation were methods used to conserve the land (Stevens 1964, 309–11).

Intellectual Life

As in other areas of the country, Progressive reform became the leitmotif of intellectual life in the Middle Atlantic region in the first half of the twentieth century. Reform movements urged improvement of education, especially at the primary and secondary level, and reform changed the nature of health care. Advances in technology also influenced intellectual life in this era as improvements in printing created a proliferation of mass-market magazines, which catered to various readers' specific tastes and interests. Even children became a target in the highly competitive and productive age of mass-market publishing. Many of the more literary publications of the nineteenth century could not survive this new approach to literary tastes. Like the rest of the nation, the Mid-Atlantic region also benefited from the communication revolution created by the new radio and film industries. But in the Mid-Atlantic region radios were not merely listened to but produced as well. This section will explore the changes that Progressive reform and new technology precipitated in the intellectual life of the Middle Atlantic.

EDUCATION

Improving primary and secondary education was for many policy makers and parents a critically important element not only in inculcating family values, training people for work, and socializing young people to a law-abiding life, but also in the achievement of the more positive goal of increasing the general welfare of the nation. When the United States began to mobilize for war in 1917, standardized intelligence testing of army recruits revealed a shockingly high percentage of men who appeared to be of substandard intelligence. These rudimentary tests and statistics confused intelligence with education and took no account of the quality or availability of education for the recruits, but the results led to a call for wide-ranging educational reform.

After 1915, across the Middle Atlantic states, teacher-training standards were raised, research in learning skills and styles increased, the school year lengthened, and the minimum legal dropout age was raised. In an effort to improve standards of education, in 1919 and 1921 the Middle Atlantic Association of Colleges and Schools established the Commission on Higher Education (CHE) and the Commission on Secondary Schools (CSS), respectively. The commissions established the concept of peer evaluation in the region and contributed to the evolving collegiality between the two levels of education. The Commission on Higher Education was located at Columbia University and the Commission on Secondary Schools at the University of Pennsylvania. The two commissions created standards and protocols to accredit their institutions. Initially, only four-year colleges and universities and traditional high schools were offered accreditation. Visits by accrediting agencies to schools were short, conducted often by only one person, and often very prescriptive in nature. Institutions were required to submit periodic review reports and host special commission visitors. Information sought from the institutions was quantitative, and denial of accreditation was often based on a single issue.

During the early years, the association's discussions on the standardization of academic credentials led to the creation of the College Board and the Carnegie Unit as ways to assure quality of academic offerings and the trustworthiness of the participating institutions. Accreditation, the ultimate and current mission of the association, was introduced. In the years that followed, accreditation in the Middle States region and around the country defined the characteristics of quality in American secondary and higher education. The Middle States Association concentrated its efforts on accreditation activities. The original objectives of the association, which had concentrated on the critique of American education, shifted to national organizations of educational specialists (http://www.msache.org/).

In 1900, only about 7 percent of the Middle Atlantic region's children between 14 and 17 years old attended high school; by 1915 that figure had doubled. In Pennsylvania the curve of high school attendance continued on roughly that path until 90 percent were in school at mid-century. School attendance laws became more strictly enforced, and children who thought about skipping school faced more numerous and more efficient truant officers. In urban areas of the Middle Atlantic region kindergarten for five-year-olds was introduced, and more training in the trades and vocational skills was included in the curriculum. By 1930, 90 percent of all grade-school-age children were attending school, up from approximately 75 percent in 1920. But as of 1940, half of the Pennsylvanians living in rural areas had not gone beyond 8.5 years of education.

In Delaware, the school system of the first decades of the twentieth century resembled those of the Deep South more than those of its Middle Atlantic neighbors. Outside of Wilmington and a few incorporated towns, the typical Delaware school was a one-room, clapboard building, where one teacher taught all the students with no particular attention paid to differences in age or skills.. The schools suffered from years of neglect; they were dark, poorly heated by potbellied stoves, and the sanitary facilities consisted of a usually decrepit outhouse. Teaching materials such as books, charts, and maps were generally lacking. The teachers were scantily paid and untrained. The landowners who controlled the state legislature kept the school tax low and arranged that it fell most heavily on tenants, on the grounds that tenants sent more children to public school than landowners did. Change did not come until the 1920s when the state's largest industrialist, Pierre du Pont, moved by a 1919 citizens' report that denounced the "little red schoolhouses" of Delaware (Strayer, Engelhardt, and Hart 1919), decided to take the issue of educational reform into his own hands. Du Pont mobilized his vast financial and political power in the state to launch a major overhaul of the educational system. His contributions to improving public education in Delaware fell into two areas: replacing antiquated one-room school houses with consolidated buildings, and creating a well-financed, professional, statewide board of education that could establish standards and enforce them (Hoffecker 1977, 110–11).

In the urban Middle Atlantic region, immigrant parents often made great financial sacrifices to send their offspring to private, usually church-sponsored schools. During this era, the Philadelphia Catholic school system became the second largest in the country behind only Chicago. Philadelphia was virtually unique in the 1920s and 1930s for its extensive system of regional diocesan-run, tuition-free central high schools. They created a model that was later copied throughout the country. During the period of the diocese's most rapid growth, priests built twice as many schools as churches. In the single year of 1925, construction proceeded on 60 major school buildings. This rapid growth meant uneven quality, haphazardly trained teachers, and makeshift crowded classrooms with occasionally more than a hundred children in a class. But it remained remarkable how good these Catholic schools could be, especially once the runaway growth settled down in the 1930s. Philadelphia Catholic schoolchildren generally performed well on standardized tests. For example, West Philadelphia Catholic won the 1924 University of Pennsylvania award for the high school whose graduates received the highest freshman grades, and Roman Catholic High School received honorable mention. Graduates in the top three-quarters of Hallahan Catholic High School for Girls were automatically admitted to Penn. At the same time state education officials were waging a campaign of petty harassment against the Catholic school system of Philadelphia. While they had no trouble getting into the University of Pennsylvania, Hallahan graduates who wished to attend the local state teachers college had to take makeup classes, and the state officials refused to accredit any Catholic school (Morris 1998, 184).

On the other hand, the public school system of Philadelphia lagged behind other cities in the early decades of the twentieth century. After completing a survey of a dozen major American municipalities in 1909, Superintendent of Schools Martin Brumbaugh concluded "not one of them presents such [terrible] conditions as are present in our city." Philadelphia schools were so crowded and facilities so inadequate that one-third of the students were on half time and over 1,700 were on a waiting list (Weigley 1982, 546).

The expansion of college enrollment in America that occurred in the 1920s—from 341,000 in 1920 to 754,000 in 1930—was predominantly a middle-class phenomenon at nonelite universities. The education of these students was broader than it had been for their predecessors. At nearly all colleges and universities, increasing student enrollment and growing faculties led to a greater assortment of courses offered. Sociology, political science, engineering, marketing, art, drama, physical education, and other new offerings joined the traditional curriculum of history, literature, mathematics, and classics. In 1920, 532 PhDs were awarded; 10 years later almost four times that figure (2,024) were granted.

For the wealthy, admission to elite eastern colleges and universities mattered most, and the moneyed usually had the edge over those who might have been more intelligent but were not of the right class. These same elite schools regularly excluded or imposed quotas on "new" immigrants and Jews, sometimes excluding them completely. Other universities discriminated less, but almost none admitted black students, regardless of their circumstances. In the Middle Atlantic region, blacks could obtain a college degree at such historically black colleges as Cheney State Teachers College and Lincoln College in Pennsylvania, Morgan State College in Maryland, Delaware State College, and Howard College in Washington, D.C.

Although hindered by de facto segregation, some black urban high schools in the Middle Atlantic region made great strides in the early decades of the twentieth century. For example, Douglass High School in Baltimore catered to the black middle class in that city, and more than one-third of its graduates continued on to college. Its distinguished alumni included musician Cab Calloway, civil rights activist Clarence Mitchell, and Supreme Court Justice Thurgood Marshall (Chapelle 2000, 194).

LITERATURE

Although the radio helped kill off more than 200 daily newspapers, the daily and the weekly newspaper survived as a form of media and still occupied a significant place in Americans' daily lives. The newspapers that survived and thrived after World War I offered a form of reading material in addition to news, advertisements, and features that was to become a part of the everyday life of most reading Americans, even if they could barely make out the English language. Comic strips, which may have saved some papers from extinction, were introduced in 1895 when Richard Outcault's *Down Hogan's Alley* was first published. The strip's main character, the "Yellow Kid," inspired toys, games, and other goods in much the same fashion that an earlier comic creation in book form, the Brownies, had. *The Katzenjammer Kids* (1897), *Happy Hooligan* (1899), *Alphonse and Gaston* (1899), *Little Nemo* (1905), *Krazy Kat* (1910), *Bringing Up Father* (1912), and others appeared, and each snagged a loyal following. As their titles suggest, many poked fun at immigrant groups, and these probably had minimal attraction for the subject group. There was enough diversity in most papers' strips to provide white readers with the chance to snicker at others, especially African Americans, who were usually lampooned if they appeared at all.

After World War I many papers published a "comic page" that included older humorous strips and new dramatic strips such as *Gasoline Alley* (1919), *Little Orphan Annie* (1924), *Tarzan* (1929), *Dick Tracy* (1931), *Mandrake the Magician* (1934), *Prince Valiant* (1937), and *Rex Morgan, M.D.* (1945). *Little Orphan Annie* was the most popular drama strip of the 1930s, and Annie and her mutt also appeared in two movies and had their own radio show. Politically conservative in its message, the strip characterized the unemployed as lazy and content with relief. Aggressively antiunion, Little Orphan Annie's creators consistently mixed stories of their heroine's trials with barely concealed assertions that workers should stop striking, go back to work, earn their keep, and shut up.

Newspapers were the most common reading matter in most Americans' lives, but magazines increasingly began to occupy American reading time. Magazine circulation reached 80 million in 1930, according to an independent survey conducted by the Audit Bureau of Circulations in 1934. There was a slight drop in the mid-1930s, but by 1942 circulation had risen to over 100 million. The new and successful magazines of the era such as *Time*, *Reader's Digest*, *Esquire*, *The New Yorker*, *Fortune*, and *Life* joined established periodicals such as the *Saturday Evening Post*, *Harpers*, *The Ladies' Home Journal*, *Good Housekeeping*, and pulp fiction and self-help magazines such as *True Story* and *Physical Culture*. The slicker urbane qualities of most of the newer magazines (*Reader's Digest* was the exception) appealed to the white middle class and to middle-class aspirants. In Philadelphia, the Curtis Publishing Company's flagship magazine, the *Saturday Evening Post*, suffered after the stock market crash. The magazine's folksy rural nostalgia perhaps seemed inappropriate as farmers went bust in a cloud of dust.

Time was first published in March 1923. Its irreverence and slick—or smug—tone and its departmental organization (like that of a university) were designed to appeal to the affluent and the urbane. The magazine's popularity grew steadily through the 1930s; its predominantly Republican and upscale philosophy appealed to a large chunk of the middle class. By the end of 1924 *Time* had 70,000 subscribers; by 1930, 300,000; and by 1937, 650,000. Founded in 1922 by DeWitt Wallace, *Reader's Digest* hoped to provide readers with articles that would be uplifting. Essentially conservative in political stance and, as the title indicated, digested, the little magazine was composed of articles culled and excerpted from other periodicals. Less nostalgic and not as folksy as the beleaguered *Saturday Evening Post*, the *Digest* sold well and consistently increased its circulation and profits.

Home workshop and do-it-yourself magazines were popular in the 1920s and 1930s. They brought suggestions and instructions for household jobs to eager readers who had time on their hands, not enough money to pay professionals to do the work, and desire for a new way to make a few bucks. Throughout the pages of these magazines were countless come-ons for the would-be small independent businessman, who was promised a pile of income from fixing locks, radios, small engines, and nearly everything else imaginable. The December 1935 issue of *Modern Mechanix* magazine, for example, contained 90 ads for job opportunities or education that could bring a new and steady (a key word) source of income, and 76 ads for all other sorts of consumer products. In addition there were 19 "self-help" ads promising solutions to everything from blemished skin to physical weakness. Perhaps the most far-fetched was the full-page ad for the "new uncrowded industry" of raising giant frogs. Sponsored by the American Frog Canning Company of New Orleans, the ad promised that a "backyard pond starts you" on the way to "make big profits."

Shown here is a 13-frame comic strip from the 1920s in which Little Orphan Annie falls asleep while reading an adventure book about prehistoric times; the strip shows her adventures when transported through a dream to the era of cave dwellers and dinosaurs. Library of Congress.

In addition to "smart" magazines, *Reader's Digest*, and do-it-yourself magazines, sensational and marginally risqué periodicals also had booming sales throughout the era. These sexually suggestive and sometimes implicitly violent mass-market magazines owed much to the success of the *Police Gazette*, whose quickly tattered issues piled up in barbershops, saloons, pool halls, and other male-oriented places. The number and circulation of these magazines expanded after the professional strong man and health-obsessed Bernarr MacFadden launched *True Story* in the 1920s. The genius of *True Story* was its cross-gender appeal, especially to women, who had only limited public access to salacious literature until MacFadden's efforts.

True Story and magazines like it were formulaic in their articles and in their visual appeal. Like *Physical Culture*, the covers often depicted beautiful young women showing enough skin to be suggestive without getting the magazine pulled from the shelves. The stories, alleged to be true and "stranger than fiction," were generally moral tales of naive good women confused and hurt by a complex modern (i.e., urban) world, much like the dynamic of soap operas. A fall from original grace often occurred, and punishment was certain: shame, ostracism, and, in more extreme cases, loss of a spouse or even death. So effective was the *True Story* formula that by the late 1920s advertisements in all sorts of magazines—including proper periodicals such as *Ladies' Home Journal*—used the confessional style.

During the Depression years, women's magazines published articles on amateur dressmaking, more efficient housecleaning, and cheaper cooking in greater numbers than they had before the crash, but they carried little information about going into business for oneself. Instead, the ads and the articles centered on child rearing and the potential embarrassment of dirty clothing, dirty children, or a dirty house. Reinforcing traditional gender roles, these middle-class magazines offered a higher-end counterpart to the moral tales of the more working-class-oriented confession magazines.

Confessional, mechanics, and smart-set periodicals replaced many of the upright literary journals and compendiums that had been vital since the nineteenth century but that had been steadily losing readers since 1900. By 1940 such venerable titles as *Literary Digest, Review of Reviews, The Outlook, Judge, Delineator, Century, World's Work, Scribner's, Forum*, and *Women's World* were gone, many after as much as a half-century of publication. Their tone of uplift and literary appreciation was rendered superfluous in a culture that traded on condensed books and articles and the "quick hit" of the newsmagazines. Many of the expired magazines were victims of their moral tone of restraint, an unfashionable position in the postwar era of automobiles, increasing sexual openness, and resistance to prohibition (Green 2000, 198–202).

The literary magazines also lost ground to the libraries, which expanded their services in the 1920s. Not only were library buildings built and enlarged, some public libraries filled trucks with books and sent them on the road to small towns and hamlets. Pennsylvania became a leader in developing traveling libraries. As late as 1938 it was estimated that fully 85 percent of rural Pennsylvanians remained without any library service. Five counties had no public library at all, and nine had a single library at the county seat. Attention to improving this situation began after 1920, and increased state aid to county libraries made possible the mobile library unit. Books could also be borrowed by mail from the State Library (Stevens 1964, 304).

Mail-order book clubs centered in the Middle Atlantic area were established in the 1920s to bring less expensive editions of great and popular books to the country and city, thereby increasing sales and, as some book club magnates hoped, a more thorough and widespread knowledge of the classics in the United States. The classics probably fared better than they might have without these efforts at mass marketing and greater reader accessibility, but popular books of the era were usually of a type other than that of a college literature course. In 1925 and 1926, the best-selling nonfiction book in the United States was Bruce Barton's *The Man Nobody Knows*. Barton, who in 1928 became a founding partner in the eminent advertising firm Barton, Batten, Durstine, and Osborn, described Christ as a businessman trying to make his way through the world, a theme that in the prosperous 1920s found many takers. Tales of the Old West and mystery novels were consistently popular fiction genres. Zane Grey's stories of lone lawmen continued to sell long after his death in 1936. Dashiell Hammett's *The Maltese Falcon* (1930) sold well (as did most of Hammett's other works), and in 1933 Erle Stanley Gardner published the first of his Perry Mason mysteries *(The Case of the Velvet Claws)*.

Harvey Allen's *Anthony Adverse* was a fiction best-seller in 1933 and 1934, but the sales of Margaret Mitchell's thousand-page saga of the Civil War South, *Gone With the Wind* (1936), surpassed the sales of any novel that preceded it within a year of its release. *Gone With the Wind* was both a love story and a nostalgic tale of preindustrial, agrarian America that evaded the problems of racial inequality in the Old South. Mitchell's work also probably offered some solace and encouragement to white Americans struggling with the effects of the Great Depression because it showed the brave face of southerners torn by the Civil War but forcefully promising to rebuild.

Some of the artistically and financially successful fiction of the era did confront the problems of class differences, the shallowness of the consumer culture, and the poverty, suffering, and struggle to survive of ordinary people. F. Scott Fitzgerald probed the first two issues in *This Side of Paradise* (1920), *The Beautiful and the Damned* (1922), and *The Great Gatsby* (1925). Sinclair Lewis found American business and small-town culture wanting in *Main Street* (1920) and *Babbitt* (1922). By the 1930s, with the deepening of the Depression, many novelists fixed their attention on the real and mythical farmer, unthreatening foreign peasant cultures, and the poor. Much of this popular literature reveals intellectuals searching for answers to the Depression and the culture and values of the common people, or the "folk." Pearl Buck made millions (most of which she donated to care for the destitute) and won the 1932 Pulitzer Prize for *The Good Earth*, her tale of peasant life in China, and Erskine Caldwell's novel about the plight of southern sharecroppers, *Tobacco Road* (1932), sold well. John Steinbeck's *The Grapes of Wrath* (1939) chronicled the lives of the Joad family, "Okies," blown off their land in the Dust Bowl and fighting to survive the lean years as migrant laborers in California. It was an immediate success in the literary marketplace, as well as in its movie version, which was directed by John Ford and released in 1940. Common to nearly all these literary efforts was a sense of individual responsibility and a belief in the need for personal rather than systemic changes to produce a more equitable society. Even the more "radical" or at least politically left works, such as *The Grapes of Wrath*, still ultimately concentrated on the family as the bulwark against hard times.

The sense of individual responsibility and heroism—and a lack of faith in the economic and political system—also informed elements of a new form of literature that hit the stores, streets, and newsstands in 1929. Comic books built upon the success of newspaper comic pages and were immensely popular among children and many adults, some of whom would not admit it. George Delacorte's tabloid, entitled simply *The Funnies*, was probably the first of the genre, although it lasted only 13 issues. But its successors, including *The Shadow* (1931), *Detective Comics* (1937), *Superman* (1938), *Batman* (1939), and tales of other superheroes that appeared by 1940 were successful for, in some cases, more than 50 years. Many of the most profitable and long-running comic books were not "comic" at all, but were dramatic stories that defined many of the social and economic problems of the Depression and war years in simplistic terms and provided solutions that ignored constitutional rights such as due process of law and habeas corpus.

Nearly all of the comic book heroes were men, and nearly all were outsiders. Only Wonder Woman broke the gender line, and her uniform—a strapless, tight bodice, shorts, and high-heeled boots—showed lots of skin, thereby mixing the message of her heroic, crime-fighting athleticism. Superman, the first of the Action Comics heroes (1938), was an alien from another planet, and many others of the genre were technological creations and mutations with superhuman powers. Often disguised to fit in with everyday life and usually operating in a large impersonal city, they represented wish-fulfillment fantasies of readers caught in a civilization that seemed neither beneficent nor responsive to the efforts of ordinary humans. Western comic book heroes, like the Lone Ranger and Gene Autry on the radio, were able to whip the bad guys through a combination of intelligence, initiative, and good intentions and, after some fisticuffs or a good fight, won the day. Their civility and sophistication in an otherwise uncivilized world also served to their advantage. As in radio dramas and detective fiction, the ordinary lawmen and the judicial system in superhero comic books were unable to cope with the evils around them (Green 2000, 202–4).

In literature old and new, Philadelphians made reputations for themselves and a limited local coterie. Agnes Repplier was counted the best of America's essayists. A. Edward Newton's *Amenities of Book Collecting* in 1918 and his subsequent popular essays on the joys of books made the check-suited, red-tied manufacturer of electrical equipment an international figure. Contributing to the creation of Philadelphia genre works were Francis Biddle with *The Llanfair Pattern*, Struthers Burt in *Along These Streets*, and William C. Bullitt with *It's Not Done*. Both Biddle's and Bullitt's books, on the theme of love of a lower-class girl by an upper-class man, titillated Philadelphians who thought they could recognize the characters. Owen Wister's *The Virginian* turned up as a silent film in 1920, and in 1929 was remade with Gary Cooper, Walter Huston, and a soundtrack. Joseph Hergesheimer supplied a pair of bestsellers, *Three Black Pennys* and *Java Head*, to the roster of writings by Philadelphians. George Kelly brought home a Pulitzer Prize in 1925 with his play *Craig's Wife*. At about the same time Arthur Huff Fauset and some other men and women, students or recent graduates from the University of Pennsylvania, began to publish *Black Opals* (1927–1928), Philadelphia's first black literary magazine since 1909. (Up to this time the blacks, more than any other of Philadelphia's minorities, expressed in writing, in the theater, and in music their sense of self and of their own community.) Fauset was a writer—his "Symphonesque" had won the O. Henry Memorial Award in 1926—who turned publisher. Edward W. Bok, an editor, who began to write after he retired from the *Ladies' Home Journal*, produced *The Americanization of Edward Bok* in 1921 and *A Man from Maine*, a biography of his father-in-law Cyrus H. K. Curtis, publisher of the *Ladies' Home Journal* and the *Saturday Evening Post* (Weigley 1982, 592–93).

The Middle Atlantic state of Maryland produced America's most important social critic of the first half of the twentieth century, H. L. Mencken. He was born in 1906 into the Baltimore bourgeoisie, and despite his rise to international fame, stayed in it throughout his life. He spent all but five years of his life in the family's row house. He had the appetites of the Baltimore bourgeoisie that he often ridiculed. He loved good heavy food, good beer, fairly good whiskey and wine, and good company, preferably male. He had the values of the bourgeoisie, which included work before play and save for tomorrow, and he had their prejudices, which he flaunted in his articles and books while others tended to keep them hidden (Bode 1977, 174–75). Mencken's most important literary contribution was his work titled *The American Language*, which was a study of how the English language was spoken in the United States. Among popular audiences he was best remembered for his satirical reporting on politics and society. He was especially critical of southern mores. His best-known commentary on this subject was his report on the 1925 Scopes trial, which found a young biology teacher guilty for teaching evolution. Mencken is credited with naming this event the "Monkey Trial." Mencken also published a literary satirical magazine in the 1920s called *American Mercury*.

Another important literary figure from the Middle Atlantic region was Malcolm Cowley of Pittsburgh. From 1929 through 1944, Cowley was the assistant editor of the *New Republic*. Also an important essayist, Cowley's introduction to an edited collection of William Faulkner stories titled *The Portable Faulkner* was probably the most important factor in the resurgence of interest in Faulkner's work in the 1950s.

COMMUNICATION

In the first decades of the twentieth century, communication became as important to the modern economy as transportation. Advertising was well known as a means of communicating to potential customers the availability of products long before the turn of the century, but what was not even foreseen in 1900 was the coming of such new advertising media as the radio and later television. These two communications media not only created new industry through the manufacture of sets and their components, in which Pennsylvania shared richly, but also revolutionized the ability of industry to attract the consumer's attention with a message about a product. The growing development of mass distribution has been influenced more largely perhaps by mass-media advertising than even by advances in transportation, for the simple reason that it is mass desire for goods that makes possible their mass production and distribution. The story of the birth of radio in Pittsburgh in 1920 at station KDKA has been told. In a few years there were more than a hundred local radio stations in the state, filling the airwaves not only with music and lectures, but also with advertising messages.

Other communications media played a part in revolutionizing business and the economy in the twentieth century. All of them were invented and in use before 1900, but their influence upon the economy had been slight. The telephone became increasingly valuable as a business aid, making it possible to conduct business over long distances by the simple expedient of placing a phone call. The role of the typewriter, and especially its adaptation to business machines of various types, has been material in the growth of mass production and distribution in the modern economy. It helped on the side to create a whole new world of employment for women, whose appearance in most business offices earlier than 1900 would have created consternation, if allowed at all. Even photography as further developed by George Eastman had its place in the changing economy, because advertisers found out quickly the truth of the old adage that "a picture is worth a thousand words." Photography was so important to modern industry that the Bethlehem Steel Company, as one example, had an entire building at its Bethlehem headquarters to house a completely modern photographic production laboratory and plant, serving the needs of this large corporation.

All of these new communications media were important to Pennsylvania because in many instances Pennsylvanians helped to create and develop them, and also because they helped to revolutionize the economy of the state through changing the nature of business, and even creating important new industrial developments as part of the state's economy to supply the needs of the new media. Atwater Kent, for example, was a pioneer in manufacturing radios. Atwater Kent radios were found in more homes than any other single make in the early days of radio. This enterprise in Philadelphia later formed the basis for the large Philco Corporation, a major manufacturer of radio and television, which in turn was absorbed by the Ford Motor Company. The Westinghouse complex of electrical manufacturing firms in Pittsburgh played a large role in not only starting commercial radio broadcasting, but also in experimenting with and improving the manufacture of both radio and television products. The Sylvania Company also developed largely through meeting the needs of radio and television (Stevens 1964, 340–41).

HEALTH AND MEDICINE

Public health issues for the bulk of the white population largely concerned three important phenomena: the increasing number of hospitals, the growing professionalization of physicians, and the great influenza epidemic of 1918–1919. Between 1900 and 1920 the number of hospital beds in the United States doubled, as cities and universities built new facilities and expanded older structures to accommodate both the burgeoning urban populations and the more sophisticated medical training of physicians. In addition, the Progressive ethos of top-down reform and its commitment to good health as a necessity for the preservation of American (that is, Anglo-American) culture stimulated the expenditure of public monies for both more efficient city governments and more efficient delivery of health care and, Progressives hoped, less disease. Clothing fashions and recreation alternatives and attitudes were additional important elements in the development of a new interpretation of health and its importance and may have been the catalysts that transformed a half-century of professional and quasi-professional complaints about Americans' physical condition into altered behavior. By 1920, the successful man was depicted in advertising and other forms of popular culture as slender, clean-shaven, and slickly groomed, a stark contrast to the turn-of-the-century identification of corpulence with success. For women, the ideal body form of the Gilded Age—rounded, corseted, and bustled—evolved first to that of the cinched but active "Gibson girl" and, by the 1920s, to the boyish-bodied flapper or streamlined body of the movie queen and the athlete.

From the late nineteenth century onward the problems of "softness" and "nervousness" had been a plague that had bedeviled middle-class men and women. Sport and the "strenuous life" ideology promulgated by Theodore Roosevelt and others, dietary reform, and various medical and quasi-medical treatments were applied with vigor and hope. The Boy Scouts were formed in 1911 after the English model; Girl Scouts and other such groups soon followed. In addition to the cures for the real or imagined diseases conjured by ad men and manufacturers, exercise and fitness activities became cures for weary desk-job Americans and their wives and children. Sun tanning became a fad in the 1920s, and the bronzed complexion replaced white skin as a mark of beauty and health. "Nature's restorative" contained vitamin D in its ultraviolet rays, and it was not long before the panacea manufacturers came out with an assortment of ultraviolet and violet ray machines in (usually) black-clad boxes filled with glass tubes in various shapes to massage the allegedly healthful rays all over the body. Civilization may have consigned one to a desk and may have processed the vitamins out of canned foods, but science and technology (or their bowdlerized offshoots) promised to bring back the healthful aspects of nature when one could not partake of the outdoors or of sport. Cereals, vitamin supplements, laxatives, irradiated milk and dairy products, and the hidden benefits of common foods were answers.

Medical education had become more structured and rigorous as early as the 1870s, when Daniel Coit Gilman at the Johns Hopkins University and Charles Eliot at Harvard University undertook the reorganization of American medical training, hoping to rescue it from the unlicensed and inconsistent efforts of the past. Formal training that included laboratory work and extended training beyond the classroom characterized the profession, and by 1900 nearly all of the nation's medical schools followed the Harvard-Hopkins example. As a result of increased emphasis on rigorous science, hospitals in the post–World War I period changed from being rest places for the poor to diagnostic and care centers where people went to be cured. With more hospitals and more sophisticated diagnostic tools, physicians were treating more patients with greater success than before. For physicians the growth of hospital care and better diagnostic tools meant longer hours, and less of them out of the office on house calls. In 1929, the typical Philadelphia physician's workweek was more than 50 hours long, but only 6 of those hours were spent on visits. The rest were spent in the office, hospitals, and clinics. But there was a dark side to the expansion of medical knowledge and technology. The poor were largely deprived of medical care, because there were few if any ways to deliver treatment that did not require them to pay. Because many lived perilously close to the edge of existence, most of the poor had to do without the shining successes of modern medicine (Green 2000, 178–79).

Material Life

The material world of the average person living in the Middle Atlantic region of the United States changed radically over the period of the first decades of the twentieth century. For example, people of the Middle Atlantic region (as other regions) were eating quite differently in 1940 than they had been in 1899. One reason for this was the new emphasis on scientifically based diets, but a far more interesting cause was the influx into the region of European immigrants who brought with them their own dietary traditions and recipes, some of which (like spaghetti) became permanent parts of the typical American diet.

Like other regions, in the first decade of the twentieth century, the infrastructure of the Middle Atlantic region strained under the challenge of the massive influx of immigrants. But unlike other regions, the largest cities of this area did not witness a proliferation of tenement houses for the poor. The alternative in cities like Philadelphia and Baltimore was the modest row house, which made owning or renting a small but comfortable house a possibility even for poor workers. Electricity changed the lives of Americans and also created new needs for electrically powered gadgets. Many of these new products, like the radio and phonograph, were manufactured in the Middle Atlantic region.

Finally, new technology brought new modes of transportation, and Middle Atlantic cities like Philadelphia, Baltimore, and Pittsburgh created massive nets of rail travel to connect outlying areas of their regions to the cities' jobs and access to shopping districts that held the latest wonders of the new technological age. This section will explore how various forces, especially technology, immigration, and science, altered the material lives of the people of the Middle Atlantic region.

FOOD

Families in the Middle Atlantic region shared in the revolution that the typical American diet underwent between 1915 and 1945. The spearheads of the great change were the advocates of the "new nutrition." The goal of their crusade was to convince Americans to jettison the greasy meat-and-potatoes diet that had been popular for decades in favor of a "balanced" program of fruits, vegetables, carbohydrates, and proteins. The critics were most successful among the middle and wealthy classes, but the "new nutrition" also affected the diet of the poor to a limited extent.

Changes in Americans' eating habits were intertwined with efforts to analyze and improve Americans' overall fitness and the delivery of health care to the population. Technological changes in the production and preservation of foods and the attempts of producers to consolidate their operations and rationalize the marketplace led to an alliance of science, medicine, and business that produced both hucksterism and innovation. Vitamins and minerals, fiber and temperance, malnutrition scares and created "diseases" were part of a drive to build a healthier America, fit for the struggle to survive in war, economic downturn, and the socioeconomic marketplace. Healthy food was considered a fundamental building block in the edifice of health and medicine that was altering Americans' lives in this era, from birth through death.

In 1915, most of the white Anglo-Saxon middle class and wealthy equated good cookery with English foodways, which included roasted joints and fowl with heavy gravies, raw oysters, piquant relishes, scalloped side dishes, loads of butter and sugar, fruited sauces, and lots of sweets. In the Middle Atlantic region, the cultural pride and nostalgia for old England and colonial America that had been evident in literature, architecture, and furniture styles for at least a quarter of a century reinforced this equation and stalled the work of health and dietary reform. In 1923, when breakfast cereals were already in their heyday, the magazine *The Nation* commissioned proponents of regional cuisine to come up with a list of "home dinners" typical of the regions of the United States. In Baltimore, Chesapeake Bay oysters, terrapin Maryland style, and roasted wild duck were noted. Roast pork and sauerkraut were the favored foods of Pennsylvania Germans.

Other foods that could be added to the list of Middle Atlantic regional foods include Maryland soft-shelled crabs and crab cakes, shoo-fly pie of the Pennsylvania Dutch country, the Philadelphia soft pretzel, a contribution of the early German immigrants, and the Philly cheesesteak. According to local legend the cheesesteak (rarely called that in Philadelphia) was invented in the late 1920s by Pasquale Olivieri. Business was not doing well at Olivieri's South Philadelphia hot dog stand, so he decided to make lunch for himself. He had a slab of steak that he could not cook on the hot dog grill. So he sliced it thin, then put it on the grill, added some onions for taste, and put it onto a hot dog roll. Pasquale (better known as "Pat") never got a bite because a cab driver drove by, smelled the sandwich, and asked how much? He didn't know what to charge, so he charged a nickel. The cab driver supposedly said, "Hey . . . forget about those hot dogs, you should sell these." It was not until 20 years later that cheese was added to the sandwich by a long-time employee, Joe Lorenzo, who was tired of the usual sandwich and added some cheese.

Some changes in the diet of the middle class came from abroad, from ethnic enclaves in Middle Atlantic cities like Philadelphia, Pittsburgh, and Baltimore. Italy's status as an ally during World War I helped broaden the popularity of pasta dishes with tomato sauce, especially spaghetti. So popular had the latter become that by the 1930s the tableware and houseware designer Russell Wright successfully marketed a spun-aluminum "spaghetti set." Red sauce, as Italians had long known, could also be a meat stretcher, and the World War I–era Food Administration and economy-minded Americans promoted the dish as healthy and patriotic. Women's magazines were full of recipes for spaghetti and its nearly infinite variations.

By the 1920s, major changes in the production and distribution of processed foods helped remove the stigma attached to them, if not necessarily the quality problems of earlier years. Food became very big business. Between 1914 and 1929, capital investment in the food industry more than tripled, making it the largest American manufacturing industry. Growers and manufacturers formed institutes and associations to promote their goods and their particular foods and became the second-largest purchasers of newspaper advertising in the 1920s. "New" foods were introduced, or at least marketed as such to a national and largely middle-class audience. The food-processing industry also became more mechanized, as assembly lines and machines replaced hand operations in slaughterhouses and commercial canneries, and prices of many goods dropped (Green 2000, 156, 160). In the Middle Atlantic region, New Jersey made a significant contribution to the processed food industry when in 1897 John Dorrance developed the technology necessary to condense soups for canning. With this discovery he launched Campbell Soup Company of Camden.

HOUSING

In the early twentieth century, both immigrants and natives bought houses in the Middle Atlantic region, but immigrants seemed to have sacrificed or saved for the purchase in greater numbers than their incomes might have suggested. By the late 1920s, 40 percent of all first-generation immigrants, including nearly 50 percent of all Poles, 40 percent of all Italians, 54 percent of all Czechs, and 45 percent of all Lithuanians, were homeowners, but 29 percent of all second-generation immigrants and only 19 percent of all native-born Americans owned houses. In Philadelphia, immigrant home-buying was the norm rather than the exception. The influx of immigrants into Philadelphia at the turn of the century did not have the same negative housing effect that it did on other major cities, with their overcrowded tenements and large single-family homes turned into multifamily dwellings. Perhaps the most important single factor in creating the differences remained in architecture. Instead of being a city of jammed-together multifamily tenements packed with renters, Philadelphia and Baltimore remained cities of endlessly repeated row homes, most of them single-family dwellings, and many of them owner-occupied. In 1920, 45 percent of Pennsylvanians owned their homes as compared to 30 percent in New York and 38 percent in New Jersey, the two neighboring states.

Financing a house often required sacrifice and some fancy footwork. Jews often formed their own construction and finance companies, and they tended to build and live in urban apartments, rather than in single-family homes. Perhaps because of their encounters with discrimination in Europe and the United States, many valued investment in businesses more highly than in real estate, because the former was more easily liquidated than the latter. Other immigrant groups opted for single-family or occasionally multiple-family residences, often financing them by having the entire family working to meet the demands of the mortgaging system of the era.

The typical mortgage available between 1915 and 1935 was for between five and seven years and for 50 to 60 percent of the cost of the house. The principal was not usually paid off in this period, and borrowers had to negotiate another loan with the original or a new bank when the first loan term had elapsed. At this time a bank could refuse a borrower a new loan and demand cash payment of the rest of the principal. Borrowers could try to find a new lender, but what usually occurred was that the next loan was offered at a new and generally higher interest rate—often as high as 18 percent payable in three years. Borrowers who agreed to the terms of a loan could not be slow in making payments; missing two monthly payments usually meant the bank foreclosed and all was lost. Ethnic groups often felt the sting of discrimination in their negotiations, and even if they didn't, they usually had to contend with bankers who were unfamiliar with their language and customs. Many ethnic groups in the Middle Atlantic region formed their own loan associations to try to gain some measure of control or at least comfort with the process. By 1916, there were, for example, 74 Polish American associations lending money to others of Polish descent.

The Depression stimulated a radical change in traditional housing financing. President Franklin D. Roosevelt's New Deal created the Home Owners Loan Corporation (HOLC) and the Emergency Farm Mortgage Act in 1933 to protect people from foreclosure. Forty percent of all eligible Americans applied for assistance, with great regional variation. Between 1933 and 1935 the HOLC lent more than $3 billion for more than one million mortgages. The HOLC also introduced a new mortgage form—the self-amortizing, 20-year mortgage with uniform payments. The Federal Housing Administration (FHA) became law on June 27, 1934. The FHA did not lend money, but insured loans so that banks could make more of them. It also set up new guidelines for mortgages, allowing up to 93 percent of the principal to be borrowed, to be paid back at a fixed interest rate for 20 years or longer, amortized over the entire period. It established minimum standards for construction of new houses and the condition of older houses and required objective inspection of properties to be financed. Nationally, the results of the legislation were astonishing. Housing starts and sales, at 93,000 in 1933, leapt to 332,000 in 1937, 399,000 in 1938, 458,000 in 1939, 530,000 in 1940, and 619,000 in 1941.

The federal government also backed housing projects for low- and middle-income families in the 1930s. In 1933 the Housing Division of the Public Works Administration began construction of 21,000 units in 49 projects in cities throughout the nation. In 1939, north of Wilmington, Delaware, the FHA sponsored Edgemoor Terrace, a 400-unit, housing development. At $5,150 the six-room houses were not cheap, but the down payment was only $550, and the monthly payment of $29.61 was less than the rents many in the area were paying. Lenders required a guarantee of steady work, which was a problem for many potential borrowers.

FHA standards and administrators' attitudes sometimes impeded efforts of the working class and the poor to borrow for housing in inner cities. Appraisal techniques and standards favored white suburbs and discouraged renovation of older homes in established neighborhoods, especially Philadelphia-style row houses that were deemed too crowded and too close to the street. Those who lived in tenement apartments in cities, in decaying frame or row houses, in company houses, in cabins and other small rural buildings, or, for the most destitute, in cardboard or scrap wood and metal shacks, were left out of FHA benefits.

Most working-class apartments and housing had minimal storage and few rooms. Kitchen cabinets and closets were virtually nonexistent: They were too expensive and there was usually no room for them even if there was enough money. Typical rooms had open shelves, pegs, boxes and trunks that doubled as seats, an occasional chest of drawers, a table, a cookstove, a washtub, a few chairs, beds and mattresses, an inexpensive record player (by the 1920s), and a used sewing machine. Few of these homes had running water, and almost none had running hot water. John Parracini, from near Scranton, Pennsylvania, lived in a boardinghouse with few comforts. There were "no carpets . . . no rocking chair . . . , no couch, just common wooden chairs." He remembered "a great big table, and benches on each side of the table, and a great big kitchen." With little storage and often no icebox until the 1930s (when the advent of refrigerators made them outmoded and cheap), working-class women relied on street vendors and small grocery stores to supply food for daily cooking.

For the working class, the kitchen served many functions in addition to cooking. It was a social area: courting couples could spend time and friends could sit around a table and talk, play cards, or otherwise socialize. Margaret Byington described a typical working-class kitchen in Homestead, Pennsylvania, in 1910: "On one side of the room was a huge puffy bed, with one feather tick to sleep on and another for covering; near the window stood a sewing machine; in the corner an organ—all these besides the inevitable cook stove upon which in the place of honor was simmering the evening's soup. Upstairs in the second room were one boarder and the man of the house asleep. Two more boarders were at work" (Green 2000, 97–98).

Black Americans in urban areas almost always had to live in segregated neighborhoods in the most dilapidated structures and with the fewest municipal services. Many of these houses were in the alleys that connected the streets with the interior spaces of city blocks, where once stables and carriage sheds had stood. As automobiles replaced horses, these buildings were converted into or replaced by two- and three-story multiple-family residences. The small open spaces between the buildings and alleys were often full of debris, because hard-pressed families often sent children and adults to scavenge the city for metal to be resold, as well as for wood and coal for heating and cooking. For many African Americans, the urban alley apartment or house, in cities like Baltimore and Washington, had one or two more rooms but less yard space than the former slave cabins or other houses in the country that many had left.

Black families with enough money to live in better housing had difficulty doing so because of racial prejudice. Segregated accommodations were the norm all over the country. Rebecca Taylor, in a 1980 interview, noted that "when I came to Plainfield [New Jersey] I discovered that Plainfield was as segregated as the South. . . . I didn't see any difference, because the theatres were segregated, the hospitals were segregated, the churches of course." The Federal Housing Administration, organized to protect homeowners and make mortgages easier to obtain, used an appraisal system that discriminated against black loan applicants and against borrowers seeking mortgages for houses in integrated neighborhoods. The 1939 *Underwriting Manual* succinctly stated its prejudicial position: "If a neighborhood is to retain its stability, it is necessary that properties continue to be occupied by the same social and racial classes."

The interior condition of segregated houses varied from the barely tolerable hovel to the immaculate abode of Washington, D.C.'s famous "Aunt Jane," whose youngest daughter began each school year with 26 clean, pressed dresses. Used furniture and appliances, recycled fruit and milk crates, and inexpensive or free secular and religious prints—especially calendars—decorated many of these homes. In a 1946 publication examining Washington, D.C. alley apartments, sociologist Marion Ratigan found many homes and apartments furnished "with only a mattress on the floor, a kerosene burner and a small pan . . . no table, no dishes, not even a cup," and a few appointed with "Biedermeyer and Hepplewhite chairs, a pier-glass table and a Governor Winthrop desk, filled with such treasures as a Cappi della Monte [sic] plate, a Meissen group, odd pieces of Wedgwood and Sevres china, hobnail and milk glass, and innumerable figurines and dolls" (Green 2000, 98–100).

Between the rural house or cabin and the urban house and tenement was the middle ground of the middle class—increasingly the suburb. Real estate development, especially tract housing, expanded as entrepreneurs in the 1920s began to use more effectively the technology of mass production in home building, and the demand for middle-income housing grew as the middle class increased in number. Moreover, the expansion of public transportation and the advent of the cheap automobile opened up large and hitherto impractical sites for housing.

For decades the wealthy had maintained homes in both the city—the seat of business and high culture—and the country or the seashore. But with the opening of the vast landscape around the cities to the streetcar and the automobile, the best of both could be had by those in the middle of the socioeconomic spectrum. In the late nineteenth century, the streetcar had opened up lands along its lines; by the 1920s the automobile opened up the spaces in between the streetcar tracks for development.

Lot sizes in new developments were generous by urban standards, averaging approximately 3,000 square feet in older streetcar suburbs and 5,000 square feet in automobile suburbs. The suburbs also offered the middle class exclusivity; restrictive covenants were often attached to deeds to shut out those few Jews, African Americans, Mexican Americans, Irish, Italians, Asians, and other immigrants who had the money and desire to move out of the city to the suburbs. The suburban ideal was white, Anglo-Saxon, and northern European, and sometimes only Protestant.

Fundamental to the development of suburbs were the new transportation arteries created to get in and out of the city. At the time of the stock market crash, plans were on the drawing board in Philadelphia to build seven routes to bypass the center city. Elsewhere, the Delaware River Bridge connected Philadelphia and Camden in 1926 and the George Washington Bridge spanned the Hudson River between New York and New Jersey in 1933. Parkways, traffic circles, timed traffic lights, bridges, and tunnels were constructed with what seemed to be dizzying speed. In the end these projects did speed traffic flow and decrease congestion for a while. But they also helped hasten white middle-class flight to the suburbs in the 1920s, thereby forming concentric rings of metropolitan settlement, with the poorest people living near the center.

Middle-class settlement patterns, improved roads, and the pervasiveness of the automobile brought about the growth of suburban shopping centers between the world wars. Only eight shopping centers were built by 1945, a result of the Depression and World War II's tightening of money for such projects. All were built in affluent suburbs like Upper Darby and Ardmore, Pennsylvania (1927 and 1928), and Shillington, in Arlington, Virginia (1944), an upscale suburb of Washington, D.C. Merchants figured that the suburban middle class was a more profitable market, and that suburban land was still cheap enough to build both stores and free parking lots. The suburban shopping center could also be pitched as safer.

In 1915, typical middle-class housing in towns and cities was large and multistoried. Three floors and 3,000 square feet of living and storage space (not including a basement) were realistic expectations for the growing class of mid- and upper-level managers and bureaucrats and their families. Ornamented neoclassical and American colonial-style buildings with expansive windows and generous residential lots (60 or 80 feet wide by 150 or more feet deep) were grander than previous generations could have hoped for. Mass-produced machine-made decorative devices, from carved interior paneling to stained glass by the running foot, made it possible for many middle-class Americans to build and buy what had once been available only to the upper end of the merchant class.

Most people living in these residences were white, Anglo-Saxon or northern European, and Protestant. With smaller families (three, four, or five children, according to the census tabulations of 1900–1940) and a commitment to more space for each child, the typical middle-class home consisted of a downstairs parlor, a living room, a library or den, a dining room, a kitchen, storage closets, and a small lavatory. Upstairs were bedrooms and a full bath, and for a small and declining number, servants' quarters (if they were not on the third floor). The attic was the primary storage area. Basements were for the heating system, coal storage if necessary, tools, and some food storage. For the middle class, who profited most by the building boom of the 1920s, oil-fired, forced-air central heating was common. People living in immigrant, working-class, and poor areas could not afford central heating until after World War II. Most middle-class homes were equipped with interior bathrooms, running water, and gas hookups for ranges. By the 1920s, nearly all suburban and urban middle-class homes were electrified throughout, and electric household tools and appliances—fans, vacuum cleaners, irons, lights, and some clothes washers—were commonplace.

There were some regional distinctions in the architecture of middle-class housing. Stone "farms" and "rambling" country houses appeared in Pennsylvania. But while the decoration and historical style of these houses differed, the arrangement of spaces was in most cases that of the middle-class form described earlier. Kitchen designers embraced the new styles and materials, adding glass doors and shelves to kitchen cabinets, and successfully promoting chrome-plated tubular steel chairs for the kitchen eating areas in the 1940s. Glass manufacturing giant Libby-Owens-Ford's "Day After Tomorrow Kitchen"—a takeoff on the 1939 New York World's Fair's motto "The World of Tomorrow"—was almost entirely made of glass and featured an appliance-filled area that resembled an innovation in fast-food service popular in the era, the Automat. So popular was the all-glass kitchen that they produced three of the models and moved them to department stores across the United States for 15 months in 1944–1945. Like the glazed, stainless steel, and enameled surfaces of other kitchens, the glass kitchen signified "sanitary" and "scientific."

The bathroom was similarly changed by the cultural demands of sanitation and science. By 1915, the bathtub was transformed from the footed cast-iron heavyweight to the molded and recessed (but still heavy) double-shelled enameled tub. With a standard length of five feet, house designers developed the compact bathroom, often only five feet wide. In it were the tub (set across the wall farthest from the door), a small enameled sink, and a toilet. The whole room was in some cases covered with white or, later, pastel tiles. The bath as appendage to the bedroom—certainly a desired architectural device from the bath-fixture manufacturers' point of view—was recommended if not necessarily adhered to by builders and homeowners since about 1915. Well-heeled Americans installed baths with bedrooms as a matter of course by the 1920s, perhaps reflecting the influence of hotel layouts and small but posh urban apartments.

By 1940 mail-order merchants offered a complete set of bathroom fixtures for $70, well within the reach of the steadily employed working class. The middle class, searching for ways to distinguish itself from the less affluent working class, had since the late 1920s turned from pure white to colors and color coordination in the bath. The color-coordinated ensembles of bathroom fixtures, bed and bath linens, kitchen cabinets and utensils, appliances, and even automobiles and auto interiors were, if not new ideas, new applications of an old idea, to be used to assert class distinction.

In the early 1920s the choices in bath linens were limited to white with the occasional red or blue piping. Cannon began marketing matching colors and different styles of linens (at a premium) in 1924. Martex introduced its fashion lines in 1926, including patterned towels as well as colors. By the late 1920s the "ensemble" idea had been picked up by manufacturers of other household goods for the bath and kitchen. Standard Plumbing Fixtures introduced 10 shades in its line, including red, gray, avocado, orange, black, pink, and blue. Crane, Kohler, American Sanitary Manufacturing, and C. F. Church broadened their palettes. Church offered toilet seats in "nine pastel shades and nine sea-pearl tints."

Previously, white had ruled the modern bathroom. White had meant clean and orderly, as in laboratories, hospitals, and clinics. But the pressures of class aspiration and exclusivity had helped devalue the meaning of whiteness, at least in the bath, and to a lesser extent the kitchen. Colors meant money beyond the necessity for buying the goods. Colors also meant fashionability and "smartness," that irreverent snobbery that insisted (perhaps with the nervousness of class uncertainty) that one was above the common worker or petit bourgeoisie. The "smart" people could ignore the overkill of whiteness; they assumed cleanliness for themselves and did not have to prove it.

For many middle-class Americans, art deco and art moderne—the avant-garde styles of the era—were unacceptable in home furnishings, other than for appliances and accessories such as lamps, and art objects such as "dancing lady" statuettes and cosmetic cases. Such homeowners remained most comfortable with the forms, styles, and designs that were derived from English, French, arts and crafts, and American colonial styles. Academic and voguish critics winced at "colonial," "French," or

"Tudor" style pieces that resembled nothing ever imagined in those cultures, but to their owners these variations and combinations represented "culture," civilization, economic success, and the pleasure of the new. Mail-order catalogs and retail outlets abounded for the willing consumer, loaded with new factory-made goods for the home.

It was in the graphic and visual arts of the era, and in advertisements and product packaging in particular, that nearly all Americans were likely to encounter line and form denoting speed and industry. Here products were pitched as new or modern, and chic. Art deco and art moderne also appeared as decoration on or in large-scale commercial buildings, railroad trains (by 1934), and automobiles (by 1932). Even Borax hand soap took on the curvilinear look of streamlining and the angular and attenuated look of art moderne (Green 2000, 105–7).

CLOTHING

In urban areas in the Middle Atlantic region, as elsewhere during the first decades of the twentieth century, the middle-class manager came into prominence. He brought with him his own distinctive style of dress. White-collar workers' socioeconomic aspirations and egos depended on their ability not only to maintain their material way of life but also to advance to higher-paying jobs. But the chance of moving up also carried with it the possibility of falling back, and white-collar workers' anxiety levels were constantly in flux, whatever their situation. Subjective judgments by superiors determined success and failure in the business office, and conformity in nearly all aspects of work life became highly valued. Typical "successful" middle-class male dress included the dark business suit and tie. The suit was best if it was double-breasted with wide lapels and padded shoulders. With the ideal slim-hipped body, the man so dressed appeared to be even broader in the shoulders than he was, thus sending the signal that he was an aggressive athletic type not to be trifled with. Fedoras, not boaters, were the required headgear for these men, and their hats covered hair slicked straight back with no part. The body as streamlined machine had no facial hair. That was either for the old-timers of the nineteenth century (who were allowed their beards because of the poor shaving technology of the day) or perhaps for "alien reds."

Critics and the young of the 1920s exaggerated distinctions between generations in matters of sexual practice, but there were significant generational differences in clothing preferences. In the 1920s, young women rejected shoe-length skirts, choosing above-the-knee hemlines and rolled stockings. Loose chemises replaced the corseted clothing that emphasized a matronly bust and hips. Bobbed hair, which some critics derided as an invitation for men to "take liberties," was in vogue, in lieu of long, upswept, and pinned hairstyles. Amply endowed women flattened their breasts with elastic girdle-like apparatuses or simply bound them to give a more boyish flat-chested appearance. By the 1930s, with the sobering impact of the economic Depression, most of the presumed wildness and boyish enthusiasm of the young had vanished. Fashions accentuated rather than flattened breasts, double-cup, underwire brassieres were fashionable, and the motherly figure again returned as the ideal. Fitted waistlines on women's dresses returned, skirt and dress hemlines fell to about one inch above the floor, and padded shoulders were common by 1940. The "sweater girl," a 1940s euphemism for a busty woman in a tight sweater, was further proof of the return of the bosom as a marker of womanhood, although some critics thought such garb was a distraction for men, especially in the workplace. The fashion changes suggest a more serious approach to the role of women and especially motherhood than in the 1920s. Middle-class men in and out of work wore conservative dark suits if they could. Skimmers and boaters were not much in evidence after the crash, except among some of the very wealthy who not only missed getting hurt by the Depression, but in some cases actually profited from it.

One happy prospect for the worriers about American fitness was the alteration in the nature of fashionable clothing that had taken place by 1915. The stiff corset, the bustle, and the voluminous skirts of the nineteenth century gradually faded from popularity until by 1915 they were uncommon. The expansion girdle still firmed up and occasionally packed in both women and men with more around the middle than they cared to reveal in their dress, and women office workers still wore long black skirts and white blouses with stiff collars and black ties (men's uniforms were similar—black or dark suits with white shirts and ties), but heavily boned clothing was disappearing from most women's wardrobes. The new sexuality among the young, even if only in talk, and the acceptance of the desirability of pleasurable sexuality in marriage meant that men and women more than ever fretted about their body shape and size, hoping to conform to the models of ideal form defined by the adolescent youth culture that was so powerful in the 1920s.

Cosmetics sales dramatized the increased concern for a new youthful and healthy beauty. The cosmetics industry did $180 million worth of business in 1930. There were 40,000 beauty parlors in operation in that year, eight times as many as in 1920. For men the pressure to be active and youthful was also intense. Their new heroes were not captains of industry with ample girths, bearded faces, and fat cigars, but actors such as Douglas Fairbanks and, to a lesser extent, Rudolph Valentino, slender clean-shaven "suaves" who got the girl. William Howard Taft at 350 pounds was the last corpulent president to serve; he was replaced in 1912 by the lean Woodrow Wilson. By the mid-1920s, the desirability for slender bodies among the middle class and wealthy became an obsession (Green 2000, 176–77).

TECHNOLOGY

In the Mid-Atlantic region, as in the rest of the country, electricity became the great technological phenomenon changing household dynamics in the first decades of the twentieth century. In 1907, only 8 percent of American homes had electricity, but within five years that figure had doubled. By 1920 it had more than doubled again: 35 percent of all American homes had the new power. By 1941, the U.S. Bureau of Labor Statistics estimated that 80 percent of all American residences were wired. At first, most homes were wired only for lights. In 1912, 16 percent of the population

The Emergence of Modern America, World War I, and the Great Depression, 1900–1940

lived in houses with electric lights. Electric lights replaced the dimmer, smelly, dirty, and dangerous open flame of kerosene lights and appealed to Americans ever fearful of fire. They also eliminated cleaning lamp parts, snipping wicks, and cleaning the soot left by the lamps. By 1920, technological breakthroughs in the development of resistance coils for toasters, hot-water pots, and hair-curling tools, as well as in the improvement of small electric motors for vacuum cleaners, washing machines, and refrigerators, spurred many homeowners to have additional wiring installed.

Between 1910 and 1920, one-piece electric motor-driven vacuum cleaners, sewing machines, and clothes washers were on the market, and the price of electricity was falling. Electric mixers (essentially eggbeaters with motors) and food grinders could be had by the end of World War I. After 1915 refrigerators powered by a small electric motor integrated into the food storage component were popular. Only electric ranges were slow to take hold of middle-class consumers' imaginations and wallets. Where natural gas was available, gas ranges remained far more popular than their electric counterparts because they had been available with oven thermostats since 1915, when the American Stove Company introduced them. In the 1930s, when the reliable, inexpensive electrostatic thermostat made electric cooking and baking more easily controlled, electric ranges captured a larger part of the market.

The middle and wealthy classes constituted almost the entire market for these appliances before World War II. Their enthusiasm for these machines relegated the eggbeater, the washboard, the wringer, the gas light, the kerosene light, the cast-iron pressing iron, the carpet beater, and the coal or wood cookstove to the attic, basement, secondhand store, summer cabin, hunting camp, or junk pile. For the working class, these were still the tools of housework and would remain so for most until after 1945.

Early twentieth-century appliances were expensive and designed for use by servants. They looked like smaller versions of the large industrial machines that performed similar functions. But by 1915, as the servant population dwindled, appliances took on a more furniture-like appearance, albeit with the streamlining associated with science, technology, and the "future." Advertisements stressed that the new machines were "mechanical servants," doing the work almost by themselves. Of course they were nothing like the automata the ads implied them to be. The myth of the mechanical servant was an effective strategy for those who never had servants or could not afford them. The wealthy still employed servants after World War I, and the hired help used the machines.

By 1920, running water was a standard convenience for most middle-class urban and suburban homes. On farms the hand pump in the kitchen and outside provided the water, because many rural homes had no electricity to run pumps until the mid-1930s. By 1930, hot and cold running water and self-fired hot-water heaters were the norm for the urban middle class and wealthy.

In the Middle Atlantic region, as elsewhere, poorer Americans in cities and the country still did most of their housework the old way until after World War II. Washday meant heating a boiler full of water on a coal or wood range, rubbing clothes on a washboard, turning a hand wringer, and hanging clothes on a drying rack or clothesline. Rose Popovich, who did the laundry of 12 boarders, recalled that her family "didn't have no washing machines. We did it by hand. I used to stand on a box to reach the washboard so that I could do some socks. I was only six years old. . . . A woman in those days never thought of having laundry done without boiling it. You had these stoves with four plates on them and you burned wood and coal here. Then you heated your boiler up on top of the stove and you boiled those clothes." The clutter and confusion and danger of washing in cramped working-class homes was captured by Margaret Byington in her 1910 study of Homestead, Pennsylvania. "The kitchen, perhaps fifteen by twelve feet, was steaming with vapor from a big wash tub set on a chair in the middle of the room. The mother was trying to wash and at the same time to keep the older of her two babies from tumbling into the tub of scalding water that was standing on the floor."

The poor, who had little or no access to running water and very limited heating facilities, used commercial laundries when they could scrape the money together. These laundries provided a range of cleaning services, from "wet wash," which was picked up wet, carried home, and dried and ironed, to "finished," which included ironing and folding. Commercial launderers enjoyed their best days in the 1920s. Gross receipts in 1929 were twice those of 1919. The electric washer and iron, as well as the Depression, brought the laundry back to the house until a brief renascence of commercial laundering occurred during the economic boom that followed World War II. Technology also altered the final step in laundry—ironing. Westinghouse began to promote its electric irons as early as 1909, stressing the relative ease of continuous ironing with an instrument far lighter than the cast-iron pressing gear of the past. Gone was the constant reheating of heavy irons on a hot stove or range; gone too was the imprecise switching of irons to keep the temperature hot enough to press but cool enough to avoid scorching, because now thermostatic controls kept the heat at a more or less constant level. By the early 1940s the continuous rotation ironer, or "mangle" (perhaps so named because of what it might do to one's hands if caught), was on the market for those who wanted to be seated while pressing large linens, a task that may have been less common before the machine was mass-produced and inexpensive.

Keeping floors and carpets clean was a constant battle. Since most roads and driveways were dirt or stone, dust was continually blowing around from the action of the wind or vehicles. Horses remained an important source of transportation for many people until the end of the Depression, and therefore horse manure (which dried quickly and became dust-like because of the normal incomplete digestion of the animals) was an additional problem.

As in other appliances for the home, the compact electric motor created a new machine—the vacuum cleaner—out of an old form, the carpet sweeper. In 1915, the American Hoover Suction Sweeper Company began production of a machine that changed little in appearance for 20 years. An upright apparatus with a small motor mounted directly over the sweeping brushes, the Hoover looked industrial and was marketed as a tool that did a better job cleaning, but did not necessarily save time. Montgomery Ward introduced a cheap ($19.45) portable machine in 1917 in the company's catalog. By the mid-1930s manufacturers had hired industrial designers to repackage the essential machine in a shell that sent the signal of "new," "more efficient," and "better," although there were no technological alterations. Henry Dreyfuss redesigned the Hoover 150 in 1936, and the Hotpoint 500 was repackaged in 1937 (Green 2000, 62–65).

Technology altered Americans' activity in all areas of work, home, office, factory, forest, farm, mill, and mine, but it did little to ease uncertainty and may have even exacerbated it. Housework chores and expectations expanded, and women faced louder clamoring from critics in the popular media, the church, and government about their responsibilities for their families' success as breadwinners or students. Manufacturing and extractive industry workers confronted more powerful machines that were often more dangerous than older tools, not only because of their size and power but also because management swelled production demands to meet the potential of the tools, to pay off debt incurred acquiring them, and to garner more of the market. Office machinery made it possible to complete some clerical jobs more quickly, but the tools did not alleviate the workloads of secretaries, clerks, and stenographers. Salesmen and managers had telephones and automobiles at their disposal to pursue clients more vigorously but also faced pressure to expand the geographic area in which they competed. New technology, moreover, could do nothing to prevent economic collapse.

After World War I in Philadelphia, Baltimore, Pittsburgh, and other cities of the Middle Atlantic region, all new houses were expected to be lighted by electricity and were wired as a matter of course. The wiring of older homes kept electricians busy as the demand for better lighting and the new appliances—irons, toasters, cleaners, and radios—grew. One of the most important of Philadelphia's new companies, the Atwater Kent Manufacturing Company, made that city a center of radio manufacturing. Two other inventions destined to change significantly the domestic habits of her householders, the electric refrigerator and the electrically operated oil burner, also came on the market in the 1920s but caught on rather slowly, possibly because of their cost. To serve all of its customers, particularly the Philadelphia Rapid Transit, the "El," trolley lines, the new subways, and the railroads, who were then electrifying their suburban lines, as well as businesses and homeowners, the Philadelphia Electric Company built new generating stations, expanded old ones, and developed a new hydroelectric plant at Conowingo, Maryland (Weigley 1982, 597).

Electricity also made the miracle of the radio possible, and Pennsylvania played a pioneer role in its development as well as the development of motion pictures and the phonograph. All of these means for bringing information, enlightenment, and entertainment to people in scattered areas were more fully developed in the decades after 1900. The best in music, as well as pure entertainment without regard to any special cultural values, could be brought to the most humble home by recordings. The movie theater blossomed in even the smallest town and by 1920 was within reach of most farm people as well as villagers who sought views of a larger world. Then came radio. Marconi developed wireless telegraphy, and in Wilkes-Barre, Pennsylvania, a Catholic priest, the Reverend Joseph Murgas, hit upon a method of wireless communication through use of a rotary spark gap for transmission, which he patented in 1905. Dr. R. A. Fessenden may well have developed a radio telephone by 1906; at least a Pittsburgh company was formed to exploit it. The vacuum tube already had been invented, and in 1906 this led to a radio-type tube.

In East Pittsburgh a youthful Westinghouse technician named Frank Conrad was broadcasting on his wireless telephone the government time signals from Arlington, Virginia, and while waiting for the signal decided to play his phonograph for his own amusement. Acting on an impulse, he decided to move it to his microphone and to broadcast his records. It was not long before he was getting requests not only for more music but even special recording requests. Conrad may well have become the very first "disc jockey." Westinghouse sensed the possibilities in this idea and took the trouble to erect a broadcasting studio and station. On November 2, 1920, those listening on the tiny crystal receivers of the time heard the historic message, "This is the Westinghouse Radio Station KDKA, Pittsburgh," and listened to the election returns in the Harding–Cox presidential contest. A year later KDKA began its first broadcast of Pittsburgh baseball, though the announcer was not allowed in the park and had to report using field glasses from a nearby high building. The age of radio was at hand, and in the next few years thousands of farm and village homes, as well as those in smaller cities, were given a new dimension in the reporting of the events and personalities of the outside world, along with entertainment and music of great variety formerly known only to those fortunate enough to be able to buy tickets to theaters in a larger city (Stevens 1964, 300).

Early commercial AM radio stations in Philadelphia radio history shared the 833 frequency in 1922. Those stations were Strawbridge and Clothier's WFI, Thomas Howlett's WGL, the Gimbel Brothers' WIP, and John Wanamaker's WOO. Other early call letters in the 1920s included WCAU and WDAR. Many stations changed dial positions in the early years. By the 1940s, the AM radio dial had taken a more definitive shape.

Young woman listening to her portable radio on the beach at Atlantic City, New Jersey, in 1922. Library of Congress.

A woman using an early twentieth-century radio with headset. Library of Congress.

The radio connection to Philadelphia also touches the receiver side. RCA is still a popular brand name in consumer electronics, and its history goes back to Philadelphia as well. But RCA is not the only receiver manufacturer that called this area home. Two other important radio companies, Atwater and Philco, also began in Philadelphia.

RCA was the exclusive radio sales agent for the four largest electrical manufacturing companies: General Electric (which had bought American Marconi), AT&T, Wireless Specialty Apparatus, and Westinghouse. These four companies owned nearly every practical patent for radio, made most of the commercial equipment, manufactured vacuum tubes, and had strong ties to international companies. Through the 1920s, RCA did not actually manufacture anything itself, but rather had its name on products made by the four partner companies.

The first radio receivers to carry the RCA brand name were the Radiola models. The Radiola I, a crystal set, was manufactured in 1923. The wooden case opened on two sides. The front lid exposed the tuning control and connections for the antenna and headphones. The rear compartment provided a space to store the owner's headphones. The Radiola II was a similar unit but used two tubes in the tuning section.

Founded in 1902 and originally created to build small electrical items and automobile parts, the Atwater Kent Manufacturing Company began making radio components in 1922. The first models were breadboard styles, built on wooden planks. By 1924, the company began selling radios in wooden cabinets. From 1925 to 1927, the company sponsored the Atwater Kent Radio Hour. As was the case with many companies, Atwater Kent was unable to survive during the Depression and closed in 1936.

In 1906 the Philadelphia Storage Battery Company was founded to build batteries and power supplies. In the early 1920s battery sales began to decline until a new market appeared: radio receivers. In 1927, the company began manufacturing radio receivers. In 1930 Philco led the industry in radio receiver sales and remained one of the top radio sellers through the 1950s.

Until radio burst upon the leisure and educational scene, music in Americans' lives came from live performances or from phonographs. Pianos and organs were still popular among those who could afford them, but the parlor organ had been declining in popularity since 1900. More common in middle-class homes was the pianola, or player piano. Introduced in 1898 by the Aeolian Company, within 25 years "automatic" pianos accounted for 50 percent of all pianos produced in the United States. The phonograph was introduced on a mass scale at the turn of the century (Green 2000, 196).

TRANSPORTATION

Perhaps the most powerful single influence changing America after 1900 was the continuing revolution in transportation and communication. It can be called continuing because the railroad, the telegraph, and the telephone already were a revolution; it not only influenced the Middle Atlantic region's economic life directly, but indirectly led to great new industrial developments centered outside the state and helped eventually to undermine the industrial supremacy the region had once enjoyed.

The country was ready for the automobile and the airplane by 1900. Mechanical know-how had already invented a horseless carriage. The raw material needed for the transportation innovations had been developed in the Middle Atlantic region, but production sites of the final products would move westward. The petroleum industry, founded in Pennsylvania, had reached a point at which gasoline and lubricants were available, the former having been a waste product in the industry's earlier days. The birth of the

The Burlington *Zephyr* arriving at the station in East Dubuque, Illinois. Library of Congress.

aluminum industry in Pittsburgh had resulted in the new metal so badly needed to expedite heavier-than-air transportation. Improvements in making steel made it much more useful in building a satisfactory automobile.

The great transportation revolution had begun in the nineteenth century with the railroad, but by the turn of the century this industry had reached its peak. In Pennsylvania, railroad mileage had just about doubled from 1875–1900, but only about a hundred miles of additional track was laid in 1900. Pennsylvania railroads carried that year 478,684,683 tons of freight, of which more than half was listed as "products of mines." These were vastly improved railroads, thanks mainly to George Westinghouse, and railroads continued to improve; but by 1915 they had ceased to grow. It was not until 1934 that American railroads made any further improvement other than possibly larger and heavier freight cars, and this came about in the development of the modern "streamliner," the famous *Zephyr* for passenger service, first used on the Burlington out of Chicago. Those railroads that provided more modern and comfortable passenger service bought cars newly designed and built by the Budd Company in its shops near Philadelphia. The nearby Pennsylvania Railroad did not avail itself of this pioneer facility in developing a modern approach to passenger traffic. A gradual abandonment after World War I of short lines, as well as elimination of passenger trains on even mainline operations, gradually but surely reduced both passenger and freight service in Pennsylvania to a minimal level so far as many local communities were concerned.

The Middle Atlantic region's connection with the development of the automobile is easily overlooked, but it could have been revolutionary in its consequences had not a young mechanic named Henry Ford chanced to live in Michigan. Gasoline was first produced commercially in Pennsylvania, and some of the pioneer experiments in this country with an automotive vehicle were made by the Duryeas while living in Reading, Pennsylvania. A lot of people tinkered with the idea. Early automobiles were built by blacksmiths and machinists who improvised from just about anything and assembled the parts into a working machine. As late as 1912, Philadelphia, Pittsburgh, and Reading were leading cities for building or assembling automobiles, and now long-forgotten names such as the Chadwick, the Dragon, and the Pullman were well-known names for horseless carriages. The Autocar Company, a by-product of a Pittsburgh venture in automobile building, began building automotive and commercial vehicles about 1908 and soon became a major manufacturer. The Mack Truck Company was launched in Allentown and went on to become a major designer and manufacturer of heavy truck equipment down through to the day of trucks powered by diesel. The Electric Storage Battery Company in Philadelphia was also one of the pioneers in manufacture of automobile batteries and became a leader in the field. In Williamsport, Lycoming Motors enjoyed a position as a well-known builder of both automobile and airplane motors. James W. Packard, a Lehigh University graduate in mechanical engineering, was one of the half-dozen outstanding figures in the early evolution of automotive engineering in the country. Just how much the technological advances in making steel and aluminum in Pennsylvania steel mills contributed to the automobile as well as the airplane is usually forgotten, but the rapidity with which the nation took to the road on wheels and to the air in planes depended in no small degree upon these advances developed in the Middle Atlantic region.

The art of forging and welding aluminum had been so advanced by 1930 that entire structures could be shaped from it. New ways of heat-treating steel and revolutionary advances in making alloys of steels, along with electric welding, equally revolutionized the use of steel in automotive transportation for frames, bodies, engines, and other parts. These basic raw materials for both the automobile and the airplane continued to be produced to a larger extent in Pennsylvania than in any other state or region. But when Henry Ford made the simple, standardized Model T Ford in 1908, the automobile industry was lost forever to Pennsylvania.

The same situation might have prevailed in the development of the airplane. Samuel P. Langley, after going to Washington's Smithsonian Institute from Pittsburgh's Allegheny Observatory, missed by about three years becoming the inventor of the airplane in 1903. He did, however, make many contributions to the science of flight. As it was, Pennsylvania's leading role in aviation development was played by William Piper Sr. in developing the small, light passenger aircraft, which became famous in peace and war as the Piper Cub, or the "flying jeep." Piper's enterprise began at Bradford, Pennsylvania, in 1930, and then moved to Lock Haven and soon became national in scope. Some seven thousand of these planes were built and used in World War II.

The geography of the Middle Atlantic region, with its hills and mountains, hardly suited it for the experimental development of airplanes. Indeed, in the early days of transcontinental airmail, which started in 1924, and air passenger service, which began in 1930, Pennsylvania's rugged Alleghenies with their tricky air currents were feared by all as the most hazardous portion of the route.

Public pressure for better roads on which to operate the growing flood of cars and trucks throughout the Middle Atlantic region was almost instantaneous. In 1911, the Pennsylvania legislature took the lead in the region by authorizing a state highway system that took over and maintained 8,835 miles of roads. This did not convert dirt roads to superhighways overnight, and as late as 1931 the state highway system included only a little more than 13,000 miles of improved highway. Gradual improvement also took place in city and town streets to get the car and truck on firm paving. A real revolution took place in Pennsylvania after 1931 when Governor Gifford Pinchot fulfilled his promise to "take the farmer out of the mud," and by 1933 the state had improved over 8,000 miles of rural road. These were the famous "Pinchot roads," which, while narrow and winding because they were built at the least possible cost, gave rural Pennsylvania what was without doubt the best country highway system in the region if not the nation. The average miles of improved highway in Pennsylvania by the 1930s were more than twice the national average per population, and as of 1934 over a million private passenger cars were registered, and some 7,000 certificates as public carriers were issued to operators of trucks and commercial vehicles. In short, by 1930 a genuine revolution in automotive transportation had been wrought.

The impact upon the economy and the life of the people was real and growing. Farmers could now move their products to ready markets with greater facility and economy, and the motor truck was starting to compete with the railroad as a common carrier. In 1940 the first link was completed in the famous pioneer Pennsylvania Turnpike, running from the Harrisburg area to within some 20 miles of Pittsburgh at Irwin. Built by a new type of highway authority set up by law in 1937 as the Pennsylvania Turnpike Commission, bonds were sold to finance the modern four-lane turnpike, and tolls were collected from its users as the means of paying off the debt. Started in 1938, the first link was opened October 1, 1940, as "the first long distance highway in America to be constructed without cross traffic at grade anywhere, and with all modern transportation necessities incorporated in its design." A Philadelphia extension of 100 miles was authorized in 1940 and completed 10 years later. A further western extension authorized in 1941 for 67 miles to the Ohio border was opened in December 1951 (Stevens 1964, 333–36).

In contrast to Pennsylvania, Delaware's major roadway improvements came as a result of private, not public, enterprise. Not surprisingly for the state, a du Pont, T. Coleman, conceptualized and constructed Delaware's first cross-state highway. "I will build a monument a hundred miles high and lay it on the ground," he boasted. He planned to construct the highway along a right of way 200 feet wide that would have separate lanes for trolley tracks, pedestrians, horse-drawn traffic, and

The cover of the June 13, 1938, issue of *Time* magazine showing Charles Lindbergh, Dr. Alexis Carrel, and the heart pump devised by Lindbergh. The two men collaborated on a book titled *The Culture of Organs* (1938). The cover was painted for *Time* by S. J. Woolf. Library of Congress.

both high-speed and low-speed motorized traffic. In 1911, the Delaware state legislature authorized du Pont's Boulevard Commission and granted it the power of eminent domain. Not everyone in Delaware was persuaded that this seeming act of philanthropy was for the best. Some farmers suspected his motives and refused to accept his condemnation authority. The state Supreme Court decided in du Pont's favor, however, and the road was built. The well-engineered road quickly won converts by including such concepts as building the road near towns rather than through them, thus creating a convenience without the congestion of major roads traveling through town. When completed, the DuPont highway, as it was called, became the spine of a statewide system of roads that changed life in Delaware. Not only did the number of cars proliferate in the 1920s and 1930s, but also the trucking industry played an increasingly important role in the state's economy. In 1924, the state registered 6,061 trucks; by 1940 the number had risen to 15,000. By the latter date trucks were hauling a million crates of poultry along the DuPont highway, plus thousands of bushels of peaches, cantaloupes, strawberries, potatoes, and other crops annually (Hoffecker 1977, 57–58).

In the Middle Atlantic region, most blue-collar workers walked or, if it was available, took mass transit to work. A 1934 survey of Pittsburgh workers revealed that 28 percent walked to work, 48.8 percent rode streetcars, 1.7 percent rode the commuter railways, and 20.3 percent drove cars to their jobs. As in most cities and suburbs, public transportation was accessible to the working and middle classes, although in the mid-1930s as many as one-third of the working class lived near enough to the job to walk, or were so poor they had to do so. Commuter railroads linked some suburbs to center cities, often stretching 40 or 50 miles out from the city limits. Middle-class commuters who chose not to drive were the mainstay of the commuter rail lines. These rail lines continued to be popular until after 1945, when a combination of taxation and federal support for auto roadways and airports signaled a precipitous decline to near disappearance for the commuter rails. For intercity transit, the passenger railroad was still the most common form of transportation, and the most dependable. The majority of the African Americans who made the Great Migration northward in the 1915–1945 period did so on the train, although Jim Crow practices confined them to the noisiest and most polluted cars (at the front), did not permit them to purchase food in transit, and prevented them from securing sleeper cars even if they had the money.

Approximately 40 percent of the eastern urban working class in the mid-1930s took the streetcar to work. But even as they were getting accustomed to or continuing a family tradition of getting up, dressing, grabbing breakfast, and hotfooting it to the streetcar, the routine was changing before their eyes, although they probably did not know it until word leaked out that the line was closing. One day the cars simply stopped coming, sometimes with no warning. In the 1920s and 1930s, many of the streetcar lines were going into bankruptcy or were being bought up by auto manufacturers, who closed them. Fare hikes were usually met with hostility and sometimes boycotts, and the rights to a line or to build a new one cost too much in graft and investment for the enterprise to be profitable for many businesspeople. The number of miles of streetcar track peaked at nearly 73,000 in 1917 but declined steadily until

1948, when 18,000 remained in service. General Motors bought up bankrupt street-car lines, tore up the tracks, and replaced the streetcars with rubber-tired vehicles, much to the discomfiture of many of the riders. City planners viewed streetcars as old-fashioned and applauded such moves. The number of streetcar riders plummeted from an apex of 15.7 billion riders in 1923 to 8.3 billion riders in 1940. Electricity as a power source for transportation was being replaced, and with great speed, in the 1920s by the power of the gasoline engine. Rather than powering the transportation of people, electricity assumed a central role as illuminator (replacing oil-based kerosene) and communication medium.

Automobiles were beginning to change the appearance of Philadelphia's streets and the regulations governing their use. In 1920, Christopher Morley could write a newspaper column celebrating Ridge Avenue, where a farmers' market still flourished, as the "stronghold of the horse," but in the same year the *Ledger* was carrying advertisements of agencies like the "Firestone Ship by Truck Bureau," urging Philadelphia businessmen to ship by truck. Big cities were learning to cope with a new kind of traffic. Philadelphia banned parking along major streets in 1922 and designated some 200 city streets as one-way thoroughfares shortly thereafter. In 1924 the city tried to control traffic on Broad Street by installing a master light in City Hall Tower. It did not work out as hoped, and the less spectacular "wooden policemen" at street level were substituted. The Philadelphia Rapid Transit Company (PRT), with an eye to holding on to its present customers and possibly attracting new ones, installed parking lots at either end of the Frankford–69th Street Elevated–Subway Line, locally known as the "El." At 69th Street western suburban travelers to and from the city transferred to suburban rail and bus lines. The rail lines, which traversed the western suburbs of Philadelphia's "Main Line" and the southwestern suburbs that reached almost to the Delaware state line, survived the national onslaught against electric rail lines and continued to serve residents of those areas into the twenty-first century (Weigley 1982, 588–89).

Political Life

Along with its notoriety for conservatism and dullness, Philadelphia, the largest city in the Middle Atlantic region, carried a reputation for political corruption into the twentieth century as well. Articles on "election frauds," "political bandits," the "Republican Tammany," and the "sad story of Philadelphia" appeared with embarrassing frequency in national periodicals. In his famous investigation of municipal corruption for *McClure's Magazine* in 1903, Lincoln Steffens found that "Other American cities, no matter how bad their own condition may be, all point to Philadelphia as worse—'the worst-governed city in the counry.'"

In Delaware the du Pont family ran politics as they seemingly ran everything else in the state. As the new century opened the du Ponts, particularly Pierre T. and Alfred I., used their power to usher in an era of Progressive reform that included modernizing its schools, roads, and welfare system. Throughout the first half of the twentieth century the du Ponts used the family's wealth and prestige to interfere in state affairs, but generally such interference benefited Delawareans. This history created a unique political attitude in the state of "Let the du Pont's do it." This mindset among the people of Delaware resulted in a lack of involvement in the political life of the state in the first half of the twentieth century (Hoffecker 1977, 207).

GOVERNMENT

New Jersey politicians resisted the wave of reform that swept through the rest of the Middle Atlantic states at the turn of the century. For example, while most states chose to pass antitrust laws, New Jersey passed laws that specifically authorized holding companies. These giant combines were less susceptible to antitrust prosecution and were uniquely suited to issuing large amounts of common stock, which simplified the takeover of smaller companies. By the turn of the century, Standard Oil of New Jersey had absorbed the oil industry under the generous provisions of the state laws. Politicians rationalized that lenient corporation laws hurt only strangers and persons not living in New Jersey, and the money received from corporations paid the expenses of state government, thus avoiding a state income tax. Given this attitude, politics and big business became fast bedfellows in New Jersey. The Republican political boss William Sewell, believing that what was good for the Pennsylvania Railroad was good for New Jersey, held court in the Pennsylvania Railroad building in Camden.

In 1900, when U.S. senators were still chosen by the legislature, New Jersey was represented by John Dryden, president of Prudential Life Insurance, and John Kean, chief executive of Elizabethtown Gas and Light Company. When Thomas Mc Carter, the state attorney general, resigned in 1903 he became head of Public Service, a holding company that soon dominated gas, electricity, and inner-city transportation in much of the state. When Public Service obtained franchises to run its trolleys along city streets, citizen groups asked the attorney general to test the legality of these franchises, but they were ignored. It was difficult to break the stranglehold of the corporations because they had powerful spokesmen in both major political parties who worked closely with political bosses, who controlled the state and county nominating conventions (Fleming 1985, 146–52).

LAW, CRIME AND PUNISHMENT, AND REFORM

At the turn of the century Pennsylvania led the country in prison reform, while its neighbor Middle Atlantic state, Delaware, clung to its antiquated criminal code that included corporal punishment. Between 1900 and 1942, 1,604 prisoners, 22 percent of Delaware's prison population, received whippings with cat-o'-nine tails. Of those who received this punishment, 66.2 percent were black. Last used in 1952, the whipping post was not officially removed from the penal code until 1972 (Hoffecker 1977, 128–29).

In the early years of the twentieth century the nationwide trend toward municipal reform brought renewed hope to Philadelphia reformers. Encouraged by the Progressive achievements of cities like Toledo, San Francisco, New York, and Cleveland, the leaders of the Municipal League launched a new attack on local corruption in the fall of 1904. At several mass meetings of business and professional men, the "Committee of Seventy" was created to war against election abuses and municipal mismanagement. The *North American,* which had become the city's most zealous reform newspaper under the editorship of Tioga County native Edwin Van Valkenburg, optimistically called it "the most logical and inherently the most powerful [reform movement] that has yet been opposed to the confederation of evil that rules the city."

Maryland also came under the influence of the reformers of the early twentieth century. In response to a great February 1904 fire that had destroyed much of the downtown, Baltimore mayor Clay Timanus, a Republican businessman, convened a General Public Improvements Conference to plan and determine the future of the downtown section. Neighborhoods, business groups, charitable agencies, and city planners all sent delegates. The group produced a program of development that received support from all interests in the city and as a result sewers, parks, school facilities, paving, fire equipment, and the city's water supply all improved.

As in other cities of the Middle Atlantic region, women's suffrage had long been an issue in Baltimore. Not limiting their campaign to voting rights, suffragists were involved in the wider reform movement and worked for clean water and streets, pure food and milk, playgrounds, and better schools. Proponents of public health programs supported the establishment of public baths, where people whose houses had no running water could bathe and wash clothes. Social reform was a major component of Progressive programs in cities throughout the Middle Atlantic region and the nation.

The last great effort of Baltimore reformers before the outbreak of World War I was a new charter designed to increase still further the efficient operation of the city government. Although the charter was rejected in 1910 by the state legislature, its provisions all became law during the post–World War I years. In 1918, Baltimore won home rule, and a merit system was instituted for civil service jobs. In 1922, the city council was revamped (Chapelle 2000, 174–76).

Reform finally came to New Jersey in 1910 when the Republican Party had been weakened by an internecine struggle between bosses and reformers. Republican bosses had defeated the reform movement, but it was a Pyrrhic victory that left the party crippled in the upcoming gubernatorial election. Smelling victory, Democratic leaders chose college president Woodrow Wilson as their candidate. As president of Princeton, Wilson led a widely publicized fight for democratization, to be achieved largely by curriculum reform and the abolition of aristocratic eating clubs. Although defeated by conservative alumni, he had gained a national reputation as a reformer. He became a much-sought-after public speaker, and from this forum he warned against regulation of public utilities as well as attempts by the federal government to regulate corporations. He seemed a safe candidate to the bosses, but during the campaign he railed against boss rule in New Jersey and once elected produced a wave of reform legislation, including election reform laws designed to break the backs of the bosses. In addition he pushed through a public utilities law establishing a three-person commission to regulate rates, and a workman's compensation law. The tidal wave of reform made Woodrow Wilson and New Jersey bywords for a new era, and people began calling Woodrow Wilson a serious contender for the presidency. Wilson won the nomination and the presidency two years later. When questions about his political experience rose, he commented that "anyone who did not get a complete political education in a year or two of New Jersey politics would be advised to seek another line of work" (Fleming 1985, 157–58).

WAR

In the Middle Atlantic area, Philadelphians, like most in their region, watched with concern as Germany overran the brave Belgians, and after the invasion of Belgium, the city's sentiments rapidly grew more sympathetic to the Allies. Public meetings protested the reported atrocities against the Belgian people, and hundreds of thousands of dollars were raised for Belgian relief. Still, there were few loud cries for war. Even after the sinking of the *Lusitania* in May 1915, whose death toll included 27 Philadelphians (Paul Crompton's entire family of eight went down with the ship), the local press called for calmness and deliberation. Three days after the sinking, President Wilson made a scheduled address at the old Convention Hall in honor of 4,000 newly naturalized citizens. More than 20,000 heard him make the famous statement that "There is such a thing as a man being too proud to fight. There is such a thing as a nation being so right that it does not need to convince others by force that it is right." The rousing ovation given his remarks seemed to indicate that many Philadelphians agreed with his views.

As the war progressed and events brought increasing American support for the Allies, protests came from Philadelphia's German Americans, socialists, and Quakers. The local branch of the German-American Alliance campaigned for a better understanding of the Fatherland's position and vigorously opposed sending munitions to England and France. Socialists urged strict neutrality and later opposed the draft. The Quakers found wide support for their antiwar stand until the United States officially became involved in April 1917. Despite the decision of the Yearly Meeting of Friends to oppose any participation in the war, many individual Quakers supported the war effort, and some went off to fight and more to serve in the noncombatant ambulance corps.

When all-out mobilization came, the variety of industry in the "Workshop of the World" enabled Philadelphia to make substantial contributions to the procurement program. Ship construction, on the decline before the war, rapidly escalated to meet the needs of the Atlantic supply line. Organized as the Delaware River District under the Emergency Fleet Corporation, the Philadelphia area built 328 ships, which amounted to 20 percent of the tonnage constructed by the United States under the wartime program. All the major yards—including the oldest, Cramp's—participated in the emergency fleet construction, but the center of activity was a new yard at Hog Island. Considered one of the greatest achievements of the mobilization program, the new yard arose out of 947 acres of swampland at the end of 1917 in a matter of months. When finished, its 50 shipways employing 30,000 workers made it the largest shipyard in the world. The first keel was laid on February 19, 1918, and the first ship was launched on August 5, 1918. By the end of the war a new ship came down its ways every four working days. A total of 122 cargo and transport vessels went to sea from Hog Island under the emergency program.

Philadelphia's largest single manufacturer before the war, the Baldwin Locomotive Works, also became a valuable component of the industrial mobilization. In addition to more than 5,000 locomotives of various types, Baldwin also manufactured artillery shells and railroad gun mounts. The Ford Motor Company made all the steel helmets used by American troops in its 10-story plant at Broad and Lehigh. Seventy-five percent of all the leather used in military boots, saddles, and shoes came from Philadelphia tanners. David Lupton's Sons made trench mortars; Fayette R. Plumb, Inc., manufactured trench tools and bolo knives; Jacob Reed's Sons made uniforms. Few Quaker City manufacturers went uninvolved in the production for war.

Philadelphia women became almost as caught up in war service as the men. They took over jobs of men called to the armed forces; they worked for the Red Cross; they organized Liberty Bond Drives; and they busied themselves in dozens of other ways. Knitting socks, ear bands, sweaters, and gloves for the doughboys became a major operation. The city's S. B. and B. W. Fleisher wool manufactory provided most of the yarn. The first woman to enlist in the U.S. navy was Philadelphian Loretta Walsh. Eventually, more than 2,000 women from the city served in various branches of the services. Others joined the Women's Land Army to work on farms and to cultivate vacant lots. Their "liberty gardens" contributed significantly both to morale and to food resources. The city suffered serious shortages in both food and fuel as the war wore on. Schools and many business establishments closed their doors during the winter of 1917–1918 because of insufficient coal supplies. There were numerous instances of mobs raiding coal cars on railroad sidings to obtain fuel for their homes. Philadelphians were urged by public officials to conserve fuel and food supplies by observing "Heatless Mondays" and "Wheatless Mondays and Wednesdays."

Despite the shortages and inconveniences, the city's patriotic fervor and support for the war effort remained high. The three major Liberty Loan campaigns were all oversubscribed. (Schoolchildren could win a captured German helmet by getting family subscriptions.) The Liberty Sing Movement, a popular phenomenon throughout the metropolis, brought thousands of people together in public to sing patriotic songs. The chief coordinator of most of the civilian activities was the Home Defense

Committee, formed by representatives from business and civic organizations even before the United States entered the war. Hundreds of volunteers contributed thousands of hours to the various projects under its auspices.

Unfortunately, some patriotic fervor became misdirected and disordered. Like much of the rest of America, the City of Brotherly Love experienced a rash of anti-German hysteria and intolerance. Constant rumors abounded about German spies and enemy plots, very few of which had any basis in fact. Perhaps the most far-fetched plot had enemy aliens planning to buy up all condensed milk to starve American babies. Many instances of anti-German intolerance were so extreme as to be humorous. German measles, for example, became "Liberty measles" for the duration. Even Black Forest Christmas legends and customs were considered unpatriotic. "It is seldom that one hears, at this time, the name of Kris Kringle," observed a *Philadelphia Bulletin* editorial in December 1917; "the name of Santa Claus has also been put under a war ban by many."

Other acts of intolerance by misguided patriots were vicious and destructive. Statues of Goethe, Schiller, and Bismarck in the city were painted yellow or defaced in other ways. Some patriotic groups campaigned for the suppression of the German press and language. Mayor Thomas B. Smith suspended all city advertising in German-language newspapers. Federal agents raided the offices of the Philadelphia *Tageblatt,* and five of its staff were indicted for treason. Although they were later acquitted of the treason charges, they were found guilty of violating the Espionage Act. The climax to the wartime intolerance came in May 1918. Against the pleas of many educators, including the U.S. commissioner of education, the Philadelphia School Board voted to end the teaching of the German language in the public schools.

While some citizens of Philadelphia were busy fighting an imagined German threat at home, thousands of its sons marched off to fight the real enemy abroad. Of the total of 60,000 men called to arms from the city, almost 7,000 served in the Twenty-Eighth Division, known as the "Iron Division" (Weigley 1982, 557–61).

Recreational Life

THE MIDDLE ATLANTIC
STATES

|

OVERVIEW
DOMESTIC LIFE
ECONOMIC LIFE
INTELLECTUAL LIFE
MATERIAL LIFE
POLITICAL LIFE
RECREATIONAL LIFE
RELIGIOUS LIFE

ENTERTAINMENT

In the Middle Atlantic region as elsewhere, Americans found new and varied means of entertainment in the new century. One important form of entertainment was the new music, especially jazz. Theatrical presentations with themes of realism, rebellion, and sexuality also drew large crowds. Baltimore both before and after World War I was a good theater town. Leading actors and musicians performed before large audiences in the city's numerous theaters. At the turn of the century, at least eight theaters were thriving in Baltimore. The two leading playhouses were the Holliday Street Theater, housed in the 1872 structure, which survived until 1927 when it was razed to make way for War Memorial Plaza, and Ford's Grand Opera House, which opened in 1871 with a performance of *As You Like It* and closed 93 years later with *A Funny Thing Happened on the Way to the Forum*. For many years a family business, Ford's Theater brought stars like George M. Cohan, Edwin Booth, Helen Hayes, Maurice Evans, and Tallulah Bankhead to Baltimore. When movies were new, Ford's screened big features like D. W. Griffith's *The Birth of a Nation* in 1915 and Cecil B. DeMille's *Ten Commandments* in 1925. Under the ownership of Morris A. Mechanic, Ford's remained the only legitimate theater in town until well after World War I.

At the turn of the century, vaudeville was America's most popular form of entertainment. For an admission price of from 25 to 50 cents, audiences went to shows of varied taste and quality. Some of these shows were considered risqué, while others were produced for the entire family. Among the more daring acts were those produced by James Kernan, a noted philanthropist who contributed generously to projects such as construction of a crippled children's hospital. At Kernan's Monumental Theater, women danced in tightly fitting corsets, and Hawaiian-style hula dancers provided entertainment that revealed parts of the female anatomy not normally seen in public. Kernan also owned the Maryland Theater, where he offered a more "refined" vaudeville, which he himself censored to assure that it was acceptable for women and children. National celebrities appearing at Kernan's theater included Ethel Barrymore, Lillian Russell, and Al Jolson. In addition to singing, the shows offered a variety of entertainment including jugglers, bicyclists, acrobats, and performing animals. Among the animal shows, those including elephants and horses were the most popular. After 1904, the theater also included motion pictures, which were integrated into the live shows. As enthusiasm for vaudeville entertainment waned in popularity in the second decade of the twentieth century, the Maryland Theater turned exclusively to movie entertainment. It survived as a movie theater until 1951 when it was destroyed by a fire.

This fate was typical of most vaudeville theaters. For example, the Lyceum, built in the 1890s in the fashionable neighborhood of 1200 North Charles Street, originally featured amateur performances. It also contained a little bar and smoking room beneath the lobby, and the first few rows offered guests comfortable sofas in place of wooden theater chairs. The unique setting caught the attention of a vaudeville syndicate that purchased the theater and brought in nationally famous acts, which included George Arliss, Blanche Bates, and George Fawcett. During World War I the Lyceum offered a mixture of road shows, musicals, vaudeville, and films. In the early 1920s, when audiences began to lose interest in legitimate theater, offerings like *White Cargo* and *Seduction* continued to attract audiences seeking the sensational. The police gave the theater good publicity when they arrested some of the performers and charged them with indecent exposure. The next show, *Getting Gertie's Garter*, was a sellout. In 1925, the Lyceum burned down (Chapelle 2000, 191–92).

Philadelphians also enjoyed the entertainment of vaudeville, which in its heyday offered such stars as Lillian Russell, George M. Cohan, Mae West, McIntyre and Heath, and Philadelphia's own W. C. Fields. Most of them appeared at some time on the stages of the two main vaudeville houses in the city, Nixon's Grand at Broad

Street and Montgomery Avenue or B. F. Keith's at Chestnut and Eleventh Streets. In the post–World War I era, vaudeville's chief competition, the movies, became increasingly elaborate and prosperous. At the East Market Street Theater or one of a dozen other new and large motion picture houses, the moviegoer might see Mary Pickford's latest film or one of Mack Sennett's two-reel comedies. Connoisseurs of the can-can choruses and daring dancers with the seven veils could find burlesque at the Casino or Trocadero (Weigley 1982, 534).

As filmmaking technology improved, movies proliferated and drew even larger crowds. By 1920 Baltimore's biggest movie houses, the New, the Hippodrome, and the Victoria, each averaged 30,000 spectators weekly. The Hippodrome also served as a venue for the newly popular big bands. Among the more popular bands in the Baltimore area were the Municipal Band and the Colored Municipal Band. Both of these performed summertime concerts in the city's parks.

In the 1920s, Baltimore's segregated society led to the growth of a widely celebrated black entertainment district along Pennsylvania Avenue, where the spirit of the Harlem Renaissance thrived. On the 1300 block of Pennsylvania Avenue, the Douglass became the focal point of entertainment. Throughout the 1920s and 1930s, this theater featured the most popular big band leaders of the era including Eubie Blake, Count Basie, Cab Calloway, and Duke Ellington. In the 1920s, the Douglass changed its name to the Royal, and due to its growing fame the area became one of Baltimore's most famous night spots. Smaller clubs sprang up nearby, and, because of their proximity to the famous Royal, they too could offer big-name entertainment. Gamby's, The Ritz, and the Comedy Club, where owner Willie Adams introduced Redd Foxx, all drew crowds. The Royal continued its popularity though the 1960s, and the stage that once provided a venue for stars such as Eubie Blake, Cab Calloway, Count Basie, and Duke Ellington gave way to Nat King Cole, Dizzy Gillespie, and Billie Holiday in the post–World War II era and then to the Platters and James Brown in the 1960s until its demise in 1965. Pennsylvania Avenue meant more than theaters and clubs. A YMCA was located nearby, as well as the black-owned Penn Hotel, where the famous entertainers appearing in venues along Pennsylvania Avenue usually stayed. Businesses that catered to blacks also opened stores along the avenue. As black customers found themselves unwelcome in many of the big downtown stores, they turned more and more to the avenue shops. From the 1930s through the 1950s, the Pennsylvania Avenue Merchants Association sponsored an Easter Parade (Chapelle 2000, 192, 194).

For those seeking more family-type entertainment, there were amusement parks. In the Philadelphia area families packed shoebox lunches and took the northwest trolleys out to the Willow Grove Amusement Park. Still another diversion became accessible to the average man when Philadelphia's first public golf links opened at Cobbs Creek in May 1916.

In the post–World War I period for Americans in the Middle Atlantic region, especially the middle class, going on vacation became an important form of entertainment. There were few paved roads between major cities until the limited number built in the 1920s were finished. The traveler who left the city on a long trip had to be intrepid. Maps of rural America were virtually nonexistent, and road signs were scarce. It was easy to get lost and completely turned around. Mechanics and filling stations were widely scattered and difficult to locate before the advent of roadside advertising signs in the late 1920s. Bridges could be rickety, with no standards of construction or inspection to at least give the impression of safety. Many were built in the distant past and were meant for the slower and perhaps lighter weight of the horse and carriage. Even in mountainous areas guardrails were the exception rather than the rule. Albert Maltz wrote of a particularly harrowing stretch of West Virginia road in 1935: "From Gauley to Weston is about a hundred miles of as about as difficult mountain driving as I know—a five-mile climb to the top of a hill, then five miles down, then up another. The road twists like a snake on the run and for a good deal of it there is a jagged cliff on one side and a drop of a thousand feet or more on the other."

Working-class Americans seldom took a vacation. Often throughout the 1920s and certainly in the 1930s periodic layoffs had already given workers too much time off. Even if times were good, many were afraid to take, or suspicious of accepting, a vacation. "A lot of guys," according to Pennsylvania steelworker and union organizer Louis Smolinski, "would never take a vacation because they thought they were doing the company a favor." Distrustful of management, these workers wanted to neither save the company money nor turn their backs by being away. In other cases there was no opportunity. Stanley Brozek knew that "the company never offered you a vacation. My dad started working in 1899 and never got one until 1936. What was the purpose of giving him one? It was to discourage him from joining the union" (Green 2000, 217–19).

FILMS

American enthusiasm for motion pictures began taking shape in the 1890s. More than even the radio, the movie industry contributed to breaking down regional differences and creating a national culture. Within a few years, middle sized and large cities all had nickelodeons offering 15- to 20-minute programs composed of a potpourri of unconnected black-and-white scenes that included brief presentations of dancing, travel scenes, speeding locomotives, and re-creations of historic events. Nickelodeons were slower to be established outside of urban areas, but companies such as Cook and Harris High Class Moving Pictures Company of Cooperstown, New York, used portable projection equipment to bring at least occasional two-hour shows to hundreds of small towns in the Middle Atlantic United States, as elsewhere, until nickelodeons began to appear in towns with as few as a thousand residents.

Even before the turn of the century, Pennsylvanians helped perfect the motion picture. In 1895, the first stereographic photographs were produced in Philadelphia by William F. Langenheim, and in 1893 Rudolph Hunter was probably the first person to build a motion picture projector. A Silesian immigrant to Philadelphia, Sigmund Lubin, may have been the first person to grasp the commercial potential of the motion picture. He established the first motion picture production studio in this country in Philadelphia. He also built a motion picture theater at the National Export Exposition in Philadelphia in 1899 (Stevens 1964, 249–50).

Short films were the rule until 1915, when D. W. Griffith broke with past practice and produced the first full-length feature film, *The Birth of a Nation*. Popular among whites for both its racist rendering of the history of the United States and for its new sense of staging and photography, the film was a huge success. The film industry capitalized on Griffith's technical innovations and developed a star system of readily identifiable players who were larger than any of their roles. In the 1920s, the movie industry moved west to California, and the impact of the Middle Atlantic region on filmmaking became minimal. Like the rest of the country, however, Americans in the Middle Atlantic flooded the new palatial movie theaters or the transformed vaudeville houses and helped to make filmmaking the leading entertainment industry in the country.

SPORTS

Baseball

In Philadelphia, baseball fans had more to cheer about than at any other time in the city's history, as the years from 1910 to 1915 brought a succession of championships to one or the other of the two local teams. The Athletics, who had won their first American League pennants in 1902 and 1905, took the title again in 1910, 1911, 1913, and 1914 behind such stars as "Home Run" Baker, "Chief" Bender, Eddie Plank, and Eddie Collins. They won the World Series in 1910, 1911, and 1913. The Phillies, with a roster including future Hall of Fame pitchers Grover Cleveland Alexander and Eppa Rixey, and the home-run hitter Clifford "Gavvy" Cravath, emerged briefly from obscurity to win the National League championship in 1915.

The opening of Shibe Park in April 1909 gave the Athletics the most modern baseball stadium in America. Accommodating 30,000 spectators, it was the first of the great concrete-and-steel arenas that were indispensable in the transformation of a boys' game into a big business. The more penurious Phillies—one of the National League's less well-financed teams—remained content with old-fashioned wooden fences and seats at the Baker Bowl, which had a capacity of 18,800. Even the increasingly shabby Baker Bowl, however, helped give Philadelphia leadership in the accessibility of its ballparks to public transportation. Shibe Park, at the northeast corner of Twenty-First Street and Lehigh Avenue, and the Baker Bowl, on the southwest corner of Broad and Lehigh, were both close to the convergence of the Pennsylvania and Reading Railroad lines and their North Philadelphia stations, as well as to trolley lines (Weigley 1982, 634–35).

The game also changed, making it a more enjoyable show for the fans, though not always for the pitchers. The new "lively" balls flew farther when they were hit and more balls were used in an average game. Previously, a ball that remained in the ball yard was used until it was the consistency of an orange; throwing out severely abraded or softened balls made it easier for a hitter to drive pitches great distances and harder for the crafty pitcher to make his offerings "do tricks"—dipping or curving crazily and sharply. The rule makers also banned "doctored" pitches—the spitball, the mud ball, the emery ball, and others—although pitchers did (and still do) throw them on the sly. The result of all this was more runs and more home runs. In 1914, all Major League teams combined hit 384 home runs; in 1920, 631; in 1925, 1,167; and in 1930, 1,565.

The fans loved it, and they especially loved, or feared, Babe Ruth, the game's towering figure between the wars. In 1919, Ruth broke a record that had stood for 35 years when he hit 29 homers. The following year he hit an astounding 54, and the New York Yankees attendance doubled. In 1921, he hit 59 into the seats, drove in 170 runs, scored 177 times, and had a batting average of .378. No one had ever hit like that before. In 1927 he hit 60 home runs (more than each of 12 teams managed to produce) and accounted for 13 percent of all the home runs hit in the Major League season. He had enormous appetites for food, strong drink, and women, but moralists could not touch him because he had a genuine soft spot for children. In 1930, he made the princely salary of $80,000, more than President Herbert Hoover. The situation bothered few Americans because, like Ruth when questioned about it, they figured that the slugger "had a better year." Semiprofessional and amateur teams abounded in most towns and cities of the Middle Atlantic region. Some represented industries hoping to parlay support of the club (with equipment, uniforms, and league fees) into support for the company's interests. Others were sponsored by

---

📷 *Snapshot*

African American Baseball in the Middle Atlantic Region

Silas Simmons held an old photo in his ancient hands. It was a picture of the 1913 Homestead Grays, a primordial Pittsburgh-area baseball team that played before the Negro Leagues were even born. His mind, Simmons said, needed time to connect the faces to positions to names. He was entitled to the delay; next month, he will turn 111 years old.

Simmons, known as Si, was born on Oct. 14, 1895. He played at the highest level of black baseball while a boy named Satchel Paige was still in grade school.

Having grown up in a central Philadelphia row house on 17th and Bainbridge Streets, Simmons was a left-handed pitcher who was signed by the nearby Germantown Blue Ribbons, a well-regarded team. He said he started pitching for the Blue Ribbons at age 16 or 17, meaning 1912 or 1913. Box scores and articles from *The Philadelphia Inquirer* describe the 5-foot-10 Simmons as routinely striking out 10 or more batters while getting a hit or two a game.

Simmons had difficulty remembering all the teams he played on. While unable to explain in detail, he indicated that players, particularly pitchers, were often picked up by other teams for brief stretches, so he might have played select games for other teams as well. (Experts confirmed that this practice was commonplace.) Researchers have uncovered box scores and game recaps with his name from many years throughout the 1910's and beyond.

Two box scores from 1926 show Simmons pitching in relief for the New York Lincoln Giants of the Eastern Colored League. He also played at least one game for the Negro National League's Cuban Stars in 1929. "I had a good curveball and a good fastball," said Simmons, who added that he was paid about $10 a game. He said that in his prime he might have been good enough to play in the major leagues, but did not consider asking for a tryout. "It was useless to try," he said.

"A lot of good black players, but they couldn't play in the league," he continued.

So that was it. After Jackie Robinson came up, they found out how good they were and started recruiting. You have to give them a chance to play.

Negroes had a lot of pride. They felt like baseball, that was the greatest thing in the world for them. You had some great players in those days. Biz Mackey, Pop Lloyd, Judy Johnson, Scrappy Brown, the shortstop. We played against all those players.

Simmons ended his baseball career soon after 1929. He had five children and settled into life as a porter and eventually as an assistant manager at Rosenbaum's Department Store in Plainfield, N.J. He retired to St. Petersburg in 1971 and lived with his second wife, Rebecca, until she died seven years ago. Having outlived his children, he moved into Westminster soon afterward.

From: New York Times, *September 26, 2006.*

churches, synagogues, ethnic clubs, and groups such as the Knights of Columbus, the American Legion, the Boys Clubs, the YMCA, and the YMHA. So central to town life was baseball that it was only slightly less important than world-shaking events (Green 2000, 221–22).

Football

In the Middle Atlantic region football at the high school and college level became extremely popular, and some of the nation's best teams came out of this region. Probably the most unlikely football heroes of the era were the young men who played for the Carlisle School in Pennsylvania, a school whose mission was to transform Indians into citizens with cultural values of white middle-class Americans. Although not academically considered a college, Carlisle played against and defeated the top college teams in the country, and under the leadership of the legendary coach Pop Warner the Carlisle Indians revolutionized the game with such innovations as the long forward pass, the double wing, and the hidden ball trick. Carlisle also produced one of the greatest players of the game, Jim Thorpe. Probably the highest moment in the school's football history occurred in 1912 when it played and defeated a West Point team led by Dwight Eisenhower, proving that in a fair battle the Indians could defeat the army (Jenkins 2007, 283–85).

Basketball, Bowling, Tennis, Golf, and Boxing

Basketball was a popular winter sport for both men and women soon after its invention in 1891. By the 1920s, the quintessentially urban game was played all over the country. High schools and colleges were the centers of organized basketball, and at least at the high school level, both boys and girls played. (There were some variations in the rules for the sexes—girls normally played with six players on a side, and few schools sponsored interscholastic competition for girls.) The college game had a substantial following but received media coverage that was modest in comparison to that afforded football, crew, and baseball. Teams of urban universities that either did not play football or that awarded the autumn game only slight attention were the exceptions to this pattern.

As popular as basketball was, bowling was the winter sport that attracted the greatest media coverage and participation among white urban Americans. The season stretched from early autumn until late spring, and the newspapers were full of charts of scores and averages and details for the duration. Both men and women and some mixed teams played, and the sport offered employment to countless young boys, who dodged the flying pins, gathered them up, and reset them.

Introduced in the United States in the latter half of the nineteenth century, tennis gained adherents gradually and steadily throughout the first decades of the twentieth century. Equipment was relatively inexpensive and readily available at local stores or through the mail, and by 1930 many cities had built public courts, some of them lighted for night play. The game's primary audience, however, was the white, primarily Anglo-Saxon elite, and these players dominated amateur and professional tennis. It was primarily a country-club sport, with English roots. The game had decorum and a white-only dress tradition that operated as a barrier to nonelites. Helen Wills Moody, Fred Perry, and Bill Tilden were the most prominent players of the era, especially when they represented their countries in the Davis or Wightman Cup championships. *Time* magazine put Australian Jack Crawford on the cover of the September 4, 1933, issue of the magazine and devoted six columns of dense text to the summer's amateur matches and important players.

Like tennis, golf in the United States between 1915 and 1945 was essentially a tale of the achievements and the sporting life of a tiny minority of primarily affluent white men. It was (and is) a sport that required a large amount of carefully managed and highly maintained acreage, and therefore a great deal of money. In spite of these elite trappings, its amateur and professional stars stimulated some media coverage and interest among Americans who could not breach the gates of the clubs where most of the rounds were played.

A few cities opened municipal courses for the general public as early as 1900, and caddies—usually working- or middle-class boys—sometimes got a chance to play. Thus, when Boston schoolboy champion and caddie Francis Ouimet defeated Britons Harry Vardon and Ted Ray to win the U.S. Open Golf Championship in 1913, it made national news and stimulated a considerable amount of popular interest in the game (Green 2000, 225–26).

In the first half of the twentieth century Merion Cricket Club, in suburban Philadelphia, became one of the great gems of the golf world. Founded in 1865 and one of America's oldest sporting clubs, Merion Club members played a number of sports including cricket, croquet, and lawn tennis. They also played golf but sought a championship course worthy of its venerable standing in American sporting society. To design the new course in 1911, the club selected a 32-year-old member named Hugh Wilson. Wilson was a Scottish immigrant who brought a talent for golf with him when he came to America. As an 18-year-old Princeton University freshman, Wilson won the first club championship at Aronimink Golf Club in 1897, one of Philadelphia's leading clubs.

Wilson traveled to Scotland and England to study the great links courses. Upon his return he set about adapting the wonders he saw to a cramped piece of property on the Main Line of suburban Philadelphia. When he was finished in 1912, his new East Course would be stuffed into only 126 acres of land (some golf courses use more than 300 acres). Wilson imbued his new course with 120 steep-faced, Scottish-style bunkers, which came to be known as the "white faces of Merion." Wilson's bunkers would influence generations of architects.

Wilson also dipped into his notes from the British Isles to create the distinctive red wicker baskets to mark the holes instead of flags. The wicker baskets were once common in Britain, where they could be seen from any angle in the high winds and would not give away any secrets of that wind's effects to the player. The wicker baskets became a tradition at Merion Golf Club, where they were woven on the premises in the maintenance shop. If a ball became lodged into the inverted basket, the player removed the ball without penalty and placed it on the edge of the hole. Hugh

Wilson would go on to design most of Philadelphia's first public golf course, Cobbs Creek, and helped at Pine Valley Golf Club, but he died at age 46 and was never able to pursue his new vocation of golf architecture. The East Course at Merion Golf Club remains the only complete course that the amateur designer ever authored.

The East Course was tested by America's best golfers almost immediately. In 1914 the U.S. Amateur championships were held at the East and West (old) Courses at Merion. There would be two rounds of qualifying play before individual matches determined a champion. There was a surprise leader after the first round on the West Course—a chunky 14-year-old from Atlanta, Georgia, named Bobby Jones. Jones led the field with a 74, which included a putt he knocked past the hole, off the green, and into a brook. Speedy greens have remained a hallmark of Merion Golf Club ever since. Walter Hagen, a great professional of the deftest touch with a putter, once putted too boldly and watched his ball roll down a slope, off the green, and into the street and out-of-bounds. Jones, "the Kid from Dixie," got his first taste of competitive golf on the East Course the next day. He shot an 89. His two-day total still qualified for match play but was dusted by reigning champion Bob Gardner in the quarter finals. Eight years later Bobby Jones returned to Merion and won the first of his record five U.S. Amateur titles. But it was his last appearance in Philadelphia that entwined the history of Bobby Jones and Merion forever.

In 1930, Bobby Jones had already captured the U.S. Open, the British Open, and the British Amateur, so when he came to the U.S. Amateur at Merion he was chasing unprecedented history, the completion of the grand slam of golf, or the "impregnable quadrilateral" as it was colorfully known. Jones performed splendidly, sweeping through his matches and winning the grand slam. He left the course under a phalanx of marines protecting him from the well-wishers in the immense gallery and promptly retired from golf at the age of 28. The last competitive hole (save for a few ceremonial appearances in his own tournament, the Masters) Bobby Jones ever played was the 11th at Merion's East Course. A plaque commemorating one of golf's historic moments is placed on a large stone to the left of the 11th tee (http://sc.essortment.com/meriongolfclub_rlxs.htm).

Boxing had been on the nether edge of society for as long as anyone could remember—full of shady characters, liquor-laced hoodlums, and dives into the canvas for a few bucks. The sport became more attractive to white audiences when Jack Dempsey, a tough and avuncular white fighter, defeated the black heavyweight champion, Jack Johnson. Johnson was a flashy fighter who provided black fans with a national hero who successfully competed against white men in a segregated society. But he frightened and outraged the racist white American majority with his expensive lifestyle, his refusal to be submissive to whites, and his penchant for white women lovers. After Johnson was defeated, Dempsey and Gene Tunney, the literate champ who quoted Shakespeare, erased some of the back alley slugger reputation of the fight game, although attending the battles was still a testing affair for the uninitiated. Before Dempsey's reign, attendance at a prizefight by the middle class and the wealthy was a rare sight. But by the mid-1920s, due to some shrewd marketing by promotional wizard Tex Rickard, boxing, which had been banished to the western states since the turn of the century, returned to the East and the "swells" and their female companions paid fashionable prices for the finer seats. In 1926, the city of Philadelphia hosted the heavyweight championship fight between Jack Dempsey and Gene Tunney at the Sesquicentennial Auditorium. Tunney, the gentleman champion who modeled his heroics after the *Three Musketeers'* D'Artagnan, read Shakespeare, and fashioned himself as a literary critic, made following the brutal sport acceptable among those who had considered themselves too refined for pugilism.

Among the regular boxing crowd, nearly everyone was impressed with Dempsey, the "Manassa Mauler." But Dempsey had not fought since September 1923, when he destroyed the Argentinean Luis Firpo in what one sportswriter described as the "greatest fight since the Silurian Age," and no champion had ever gone as long without defending his   crown. Some sportswriters speculated that the champion's years of inactivity would not serve him well if he decided to fight again. Among boxing fans, however, his years away from the ring seemed to have increased the proportion of his image, and those who actually gave Tunney a chance were laughed at.

On the day of the fight, September 23, both men traveled to Philadelphia. Tunney used the trip to gain a psychological edge over Dempsey, for he covered the 80-mile journey from Stroudsburg to Philadelphia in a plane piloted by stunt flier Casey Jones. In an age when only brave men and fools traveled by air, Tunney's act was a public warning: neither air nor Dempsey frightened him. Dempsey's trip from Atlantic City was more conventional but with more drastic results. Upon arriving in Philadelphia, he was queasy, his legs were rubbery, and he broke out in a rash. Later evidence pointed to food poisoning, and even if his adrenalin would carry him into the ring, his strength would not sustain him.

Only a handful of people on the night of September 23 knew of Dempsey's condition. What interested the mass of people who came to Philadelphia for the fight was the event itself. Actually, it was more than an event; it was a happening in the fullest sense of the word. Under overcast skies, as the temperature dropped to the lower 40s, people from every walk of life filed into the Sesquicentennial   Stadium.

📷 Snapshot

Dempsey-Tunney Fight, Philadelphia, July 23, 1923

The first round started as everyone expected it would, with Dempsey rushing Tunney, throwing left hooks. Tunney, who, after all, enjoyed Shakespeare more than fighting, was content to parry Dempsey's blows and back pedal. Sensing that his opponent was afraid to throw punches, Dempsey began to pressure Tunney even more. For Tunney it was a dream come true. Overconfident, Dempsey was doing just as Tunney planned; the champion, who fought by instinct and not by plan, was falling into Tunney's trap. Suddenly, as Dempsey launched another left, Tunney stepped in toward the champion and snapped off a straight right hand. Even high, though, the punch hurt. Dempsey staggered back, sagging a little, and then clinched, trying to gain time for his head to clear. Few in the crowd realized what had happened. Everyone knew that Tunney had won the round, and most cheered accordingly. But nobody knew how much the punch had taken out of the champion. Sitting in his corner between rounds, breathing smelling salts, Dempsey later said he thought, "I'm an old man."

For the first time in his life, he drew pity from a fight crowd. Mixed with the sympathy, however, was respect. On the wet canvas, Dempsey could not get enough traction to land a knockout blow, and a knockout was his only chance for victory. Nevertheless, he did not quit. The tenth round serves as an example. After touching gloves, Dempsey, with the urge of the old Dempsey still upon him, even if the effectiveness was gone, went on the offensive. He rushed blindly, although eagerly, it seemed, only to miss. When the bell ended Dempsey's futile efforts, there was no question about who had won the fight. Dempsey did not win one round.

He had lost, but in losing he achieved a dignity that was to become legendary. After the decision was announced, Dempsey, sick and unable to see, hugged Tunney. "All right, Gene," he said slowly. "All right, good luck."

Estelle, his wife did not like boxing, and Dempsey did not believe a wife should see her husband fight. After learning the outcome she reached Dempsey by telephone, and asked, "What happened, Ginsberg?" Dempsey's answer was as good an explanation for why a fighter loses as has ever been advanced. "Honey," he said, "I just forgot to duck." (Roberts 1979, 226–32)

Gene Tunney down for the famous "long count" in his championship bout with Jack Dempsey at Philadelphia on September 23, 1926. The Granger Collection, New York.

Newspapers reported that 135,000 people paid to attend. The fight grossed $1,895,733. Both figures were records for all sporting events, not just for boxing. Millions more people listened to the fight on the radio. All of America, it seemed, was interested. Baltimore editor H. L. Mencken had described the crowd at the Dempsey-Carpentier fight as "well-dressed, good-humored and almost distinguished." The gathering at the Dempsey-Tunney affair was that and more so. The celebrities at ringside included Secretary of the Treasury Andrew Mellon, Charles M. Schwab, Percy Rockefeller, Vincent Astor, William Randolph Hearst, Joseph Pulitzer, Anthony J. Drexel Biddle Jr., W. Averill Harriman, Harry Payne Whitney, Kermit and Archie Roosevelt, Florem Ziegfeld, and Babe Ruth, as well as every major sportswriter in the country. Looking over the crowd, promoter Tex Rickard remarked, "I ain't never seed anything like it" (Roberts 1979, 229).

Tunney was first in the ring. Handsome, dressed in a scarlet-trimmed blue robe with the Marine Corps emblem on the back, Tunney received an uproarious cheer. A few minutes later, Dempsey climbed through the ropes. Philadelphia rules required a fighter to be clean-shaven, so the champion was without his usual two-day growth. The fight went exactly as Tunney had planned. The agile boxer eluded the awkward and brutal charges of Dempsey and peppered the champion with short quick jabs. Dempsey did not win a single round.

If press reaction is indicative of the American temper, then Americans had finally accepted the commercialistic nature of professional boxing. The moral position of the sport and the harmlessness of attending a prizefight was a second social issue settled by the match. No longer were women criticized for watching two men box, and the voices of reformers and religious leaders against boxing were surprisingly quiet during the entire affair. By 1926, Americans realized that professional boxing was here to stay. Many people may have secretly resented the fact, and still more may have been openly envious of a fighter's wage, but no one felt compelled any longer to try to reverse the irreversible (Roberts 1979, 228, 234–35).

GAMES

The most popular board game ever devised was created in the Middle Atlantic region. In 1934, at the height of the Depression, Charles B. Darrow of Germantown, Pennsylvania, showed what he called the Monopoly game to the executives at Parker Brothers. They rejected the game due to what they described as "52 design errors." But Mr. Darrow wasn't daunted. Like many other Americans, he was unemployed at the time, and the game's exciting promise of fame and fortune inspired him to produce it on his own. With help from a friend who was a printer, Darrow sold 5,000 handmade sets of the game to a Philadelphia department store. People loved it! But as demand grew, he couldn't keep up with all the orders and came back to talk to Parker Brothers again. This time Parker Brothers accepted his idea. In its first year, 1935, the Monopoly game became the best-selling game in America.

HOLIDAYS, CELEBRATIONS, AND FESTIVALS

For Christians, the most important home and church intersection occurred at Christmas. For centuries an important holiday for Roman Catholic, Russian Orthodox, and Greek Orthodox families, Christmas was not celebrated by American Protestants in the Middle Atlantic states with much fanfare, if any, until the middle of the nineteenth century. By the early twentieth century, however, feasting, drink, presents, and gifts to the poor were entrenched in the region as well as throughout the country. The Germans had introduced the Christmas tree by the 1850s, and printers such as Louis Prang had met the demand for Christmas cards in the late nineteenth century.

In Baltimore's Little Italy religious festivals were major events. The two largest events celebrated the feast days of St. Anthony and St. Gabriel. St. Anthony's festival on June 13 began in 1904. It celebrated the day that devotees believe St. Anthony stopped the flames of the great Baltimore fire at the edge of Little Italy. The procession on the feast of St. Gabriel of Abruzzi began in 1920 shortly after the Italian saint was canonized. The canonization had special meaning for Baltimore Italians because many families in the city traced their roots to Abruzzi (Chapelle 2000, 160).

A holiday season tradition in Philadelphia that began in the colonial era and continues to the present is the Mummers Parade on News Year's Day. Informal merrymaking and customs that can be traced back to the colonial era were incorporated into the parade by 1901 when it became a city-sponsored event. While the Swedes and Finns greeted the New Year by visiting neighbors and shooting guns, the English and Welsh celebrated also by visiting, but added the reciting of standard rhymes and enjoying refreshments.

On New Year's Day, 1909, mummers parade on Broad Street in Philadelphia. Library of Congress.

The Germans added the Belsnickle, an early Pennsylvania German forerunner of Santa Claus, who spawned additional comic masqueraders. Revelers enjoyed shooting in the New Year as well as riding through Tinicum and Kingsessing, the southern and western sections of the city, disguised as clowns. Today's Mummers Parade also had some beginnings in nineteenth-century traditions as Philadelphia's Carnival of Horns drew thousands of costumed characters celebrating with a myriad of noisemakers to the area of Eighth and South Streets. Southern plantation life also made significant contributions to Philadelphia's New Year's Day event. Not only does its contribution include "Oh! Dem Golden Slippers," the parade's theme tune composed by Philadelphian James Bland in 1879, but evidence indicates that the famed "Strut" may have been a possible offshoot of the popular nineteenth-century cakewalk dance.

Until the 1900s, almost all masqueraders wore makeshift apparel. However, spirit and imagination provided probable motivations for the revelers to join together in associations to raise money for more elaborate New Year's costumes. The Chain Gang, the earliest club for which there is evidence, was established in 1840, followed by the Golden Crown Club in 1876 and the Silver Crown Club in 1877. String bands were organized in the early 1900s, with Trilby the first to parade in 1902, but not until 1906 did the bands compete. Bart H. McHugh, a Philadelphia theatrical producer and publicity agent, is credited with the idea for a city-sponsored parade. By the 1930s New Year's clubs had united for the purpose of encouraging and promoting the tradition of Mummery and presenting an organized body to the city when dealing with parade matters. (http://www.phila.gov/recreation/mummers_ History/ Golden_Slippers/golden_slip).

Religious Life

RELIGION AND SPIRITUALITY

In the Middle Atlantic region, as in the rest of the country, organized religion played a distinguishable and significant part in the everyday lives of most Americans, even if they only went to their place of worship occasionally. In addition to their functions as places for prayer, marriages, christenings (or brises), communions (or bar mitzvahs), and funerals, churches and synagogues were social gathering places. Most offered their members the chance to participate in organized events, clubs, picnics, and potluck suppers, and in times of trouble many churches and synagogues provided free food and shelter. One Polish immigrant boy remembered that "church was almost a second home to us. I mean we never miss[ed] a novena or any service at all." But others fell away from the fold. Another immigrant's husband "stopped going because you just get so much of it. . . . My oldest son also enlightened me when he was sixteen and gradually we stopped going altogether."

It is difficult to discern any marked differences in the pattern of religious life in the Middle Atlantic region in the twentieth century from those common to the nation as a whole. An exception might be Pennsylvania, which continued to maintain a diversity of its religious life, established from colonial days, and to boast a large number of churches relative to its population. Urbanization brought pressures to bear upon all religious faiths in the Middle Atlantic region as churches in urban areas began to face certain social problems to which religion could or should be applied. Progressive religious leaders both spiritual and lay became concerned more and more with the social gospel and social education, which applied religion to everyday life and to its social rather than purely individual and spiritual problems. Churches in urban communities engaged in social and educational endeavors within and without the church edifice that were not only unheard of in early days but continued to be frowned upon by many a conservative church member. Among these were supporting the Boy Scouts and Girl Scouts, cooperating and leading in developing recreational facilities for youth, and helping to organize senior citizens.

While city churches grew in size of congregations and magnificence of buildings and support, the typical rural church so common to early Pennsylvania suffered a continuing decline. Only the Plain People of the Pennsylvania German country held to their old ways in the face of the revolution in transportation and modern ways of life, and even these ways, dating from colonial times, were shaken.

Even though traditional Protestant churches offered aid to black migrants, newcomers from small towns tended not to join Philadelphia's established black churches. These migrants, when they did go to church, preferred to commune with people they knew. This led to the establishment of numerous Pentecostal, holiness, and spiritual churches, including evangelical Baptist churches. Within the denominational structure of the African Methodist Episcopal church, the experience of Mother Bethel African Methodist Episcopal Church is illustrative. Robert J. Williams, pastor at Mother Bethel, reportedly distributed leaflets in the South encouraging southerners to move north. His effort did expand membership somewhat, but the southern migrants for the most part sought a more evangelistic preaching style than that desired by Mother Bethel's established community. Rather than encouraging the migrant population at Mother Bethel Church, board meetings of older members convened to consider resolutions governing their members' movements, gatherings, and expressions within the church (Reich 2006, 665–66)

The religious faiths that had established themselves in early Pennsylvania remained a dominant feature of the state's religious life. Pittsburgh and western Pennsylvania still were very much a center of Pennsylvanian Presbyterianism, despite the great growth of the Roman Catholic Church in urban mining and industrial centers. The areas settled by the early Germans were still the citadels of the Lutheran and Reformed churches. The Lutherans became in numbers the largest single Protestant denomination in the state by 1926. The Baptist Church was strong in Philadelphia, and in many parts of rural Pennsylvania. The Methodist Church emerged after 1900 as one of the leading Protestant denominations in the state, and Pennsylvania was second only to Texas as a Methodist stronghold. The United Brethren and Grace Evangelical churches, both founded in Pennsylvania, merged into a single organization with considerable strength.

The new immigration, predominantly Catholic and Jewish, but also Eastern Orthodox, brought to a close the "Protestant consensus" under which the nation had developed since its founding. In Philadelphia the most venerable of the Protestant denominations was the Society of Friends, but by 1880 less than 1 percent of the Quaker City's population was Quaker. Their numbers continued to decline in the last decades of the century, until by 1900 there were only 16,000 Friends in the Orthodox and much larger Hicksite Yearly Meetings, and most of these lived outside the city. The plain dress and plain speech of the Quakers had all but disappeared by this time and, although many in the two branches of the society still regarded each other with "holy abhorrence," a gradual easing of the separation was beginning. More important, perhaps, were the divisions within the two groups as they sought to reconcile their disciplines to "worldly" challenges on all sides.

The Quakers declined numerically in relation to other faiths, but Philadelphia and southeastern Pennsylvania remain something of the "capital" for the few thousand Quakers, who exercise an influence far greater than numbers might indicate through their fine private schools and colleges, such as Haverford and Swarthmore, and the American Friends Service organization based in Philadelphia. The same is true of the Moravians, who continue to maintain their center of learning and church government at Bethlehem. The German sects, the Mennonites and the Amish, are no longer limited to Pennsylvania, and indeed there are more in Ohio and Indiana. The rural Pennsylvania German countryside is still the center of influence for these two groups, which have held more closely to their old ways than any other religious group in America. The Roman Catholic Church experienced a great growth after 1900 and by 1937 could claim about 40 percent of the entire church membership in Pennsylvania. The largest center for Catholicism in the Middle Atlantic region was Philadelphia, which in the first half of the twentieth century was the third-largest archdiocese in the country after New York and Chicago (Stevens 1964, 322–23).

An alien anthropologist landing in a working-class Philadelphia parish in the 1930s or 1940s would know instantly the centrality of religion to the lives of the inhabitants. The rows of neat brick houses were invariably centered around, and dwarfed by, an imposing cluster of granite buildings, the Catholic church, always of neo-Gothic design, built to the scale of a medium-sized cathedral, the parish school, sometimes even a high school, the rectory, the convent, one or more annexes for meeting rooms, and perhaps even an auditorium. Few contemporary religions could match Catholicism's hold on the faithful. In Philadelphia parishes, particularly those comprising mostly second- and third-generation American families, attendance at Sunday Mass hovered around 90 percent. Almost all Catholic children went to parochial elementary schools, and almost two-thirds went to Catholic high schools. It was not uncommon for the majority of adults to belong to parish organizations like the Sodality and Holy Name Society. The lay turnout at annual retreats was numbered in the 10s of thousands. Special devotions like the Forty Hours' vigil for the Blessed Sacrament—people worshipped in round-the-clock shifts—were always crowded. In one parish, between 8 and 10 thousand people turned out for Monday-night novenas for almost 20 years.

Triumphal-era American Catholicism was a highly formal, even mechanistic creed, enshrouded in mystical elements and ritual, combining to a remarkable degree theological rigor and a high degree of abstraction with practical religion that was intensely personal and emotional. Catholics were drenched in powerful, sometimes gory images: the pathetic figure of Jesus staggering through the Stations of the Cross; God the Father, implacable and austere, arriving in a burst of light on Judgment Day; the Blessed Mother, a refuge in adversity, the always-ready intervener, pleading mercy for undeserving sinners; and a whole litany of benign presences: St. Christopher for travelers, St. Jude for lost causes, St. Anthony for lost objects, a personal guardian angel. To outsiders, the Latin Mass was Kabuki theater—static and incomprehensible, medieval mumbo-jumbo. That millions knelt unprotestingly through the Mass Sunday after Sunday confirmed secularists in their conviction that Catholics were inert hordes.

But the details of the Latin hardly mattered to a lifelong Catholic. The stately cadences of the Mass were carved deep in neural pathways and had a clear dramatic structure. There was an introduction and a flurry of practical business—the readings, a short sermon, the collection—followed by the hush of growing tension approaching the Consecration; then the striking tableau, the Mass's emotional high point, as the priest, vestments flowing, held aloft the bright Host to the silver pealing of the altar boy's bell. Shuffling into line for Communion eased the solemnity, and then came a buzz of housekeeping—wiping the chalice, putting away the hosts. The tempo of the priest's prayers picked up; the rustle in the congregation increased; people in the back rows, with a quick genuflection and sign of the cross, would begin slipping out of the church; thoughts fled to everyday matters. The total experience—the dim lights, the glint of the vestments, the glow of the stained-glass windows, the mantra-like murmur of the Latin were mind-washing. They calmed the soul, opened the spirit to large, barely grasped presences and purposes. For a trembling moment every week, or every day if they chose, ordinary people reached out and touched the Divine.

The extremely high status of the priest facilitated organization in the Catholic Church. Within the sharply defined community that was Catholic Philadelphia, hardly any occupation ranked higher. "In matters of all importance," the priest was considered "the best-posted and ablest man" available; and, in truth, despite the narrowness of the seminary curriculum, a priest was far better educated than his parishioners (Morris 1998, 174). The accepted priestly image was almost wholly positive, at once wise, hypermasculine, warm, athletic, jovial—Father's jokes always brought down the house. Any fire or major disaster brought squad cars sirening up to rectories so priests could administer the last rites. (Because ministers and rabbis could not absolve sins, there was no point rushing them to the

A Russian Orthodox Church in the anthracite region of Pennsylvania. Library of Congress.

scene.) The mystery of the priest's calling reinforced his rank. Poems were written about the beauty of a young priest's hands—he was supposed to take particular care of them—for only he, at the altar every day, held in his hands the power of converting bread and wine into the true, the actual, Body and Blood of the Savior. The vow of celibacy, instead of making a priest an object of skepticism or derision, as it sometimes did in Latin cultures, elevated him above the common run of men, identified him as a person of unusual control and discipline, someone in touch with higher things, a man with a clear mind and a focused life.

No other high-status profession was as accessible to ambitious young men from Catholic blue-collar families. A good high school record in the right courses, a competitive mark on the entrance test, and a persuasive recommendation from a pastor were all that was required. Families were supposed to pay tuition, but modest means were never an obstacle (Morris 1998, 174–76).

The Episcopal Church was strongest in southeastern and western Pennsylvania among the more wealthy elements in the population. The Russian and Greek Catholic churches, and the Polish National Church, had a place in the mining and steel manufacturing areas. Pennsylvania's Jewish population grew steadily in the first half of the twentieth century, and nearly half of them resided in Philadelphia. Other strong Jewish communities existed in Pittsburgh and Harrisburg. Regardless of where and how it was expressed, throughout the first half of the twentieth century, religious life in the Mid-Atlantic region remained a vibrant part of everyday life.

WORLDVIEW

In the first half of the twentieth century, the Middle Atlantic region included some of the most important industrial and commercial centers of the country such as Pittsburgh, Philadelphia, and Baltimore, and at the same time some of the most important agricultural centers of the country, such as western New Jersey, Pennsylvania, and western Maryland. Those who lived in this region represented the oldest of the European immigrants, the German and Scotch Irish, and some of the newest immigrants from eastern and southern Europe. The black population was represented by descendents of antebellum free blacks as well as recent migrants from the South. Despite the diversity of the region, all who lived there held certain values in common. The majority were Christians who continued to look to their churches for support and community in addition to spiritual sustenance. And for the most part despite their differences in economic class, they held or aspired to bourgeois values, which esteemed thriftiness, moderation, honesty, moral behavior, a male-dominated family, and a belief in progress in time through hard work and perseverance.

FOR MORE INFORMATION

Books

Black, Brian. *Nature and the Environment in 20th-Century American Life*. Westport, CT: Greenwood Press, 2006.

Bode, Carl. *Maryland: A History*. New York: W. W. Norton and Company, 1977.

Bodnar, John. *The Transplanted: A History of Immigrants in Urban America*. Bloomington: University of Indiana Press, 1985.

Chapelle, Suzanne. *Baltimore: An Illustrated History*. Sun Valley, CA: American Historical Press, 2000.

Fleming, Thomas. *New Jersey: A History*. New York: W. W. Norton and Company, 1985.

Green, Harvey. *The Uncertainty of Everyday Life 1915–1945*. Fayetteville: University of Arkansas Press, 2000.

Hoffecker, Carol E. *Delaware: A Bicentennial History*. New York: W. W. Norton and Company, 1977.

Jenkins, Sally. *The Real All Americans: The Team that Changed a Game, a People, a Nation*. New York: Doubleday and Co., 2007.

Kyvig, David E. *Daily Life in the United States 1920–1940: How Americans Lived Through the Roaring Twenties and the Great Depression*. Chicago: Ivan R. Dee, 2002.

Lewis, David L. *District of Columbia*. New York: Norton Publishing Company, 1976.

Morris, Charles. *American Catholic*. New York: Vintage, 1998.

Reich, Steven. *Encyclopedia of the Great Black Migration*. Westport, CT: Greenwood Press, 2006.

Roberts, Randy. *Jack Dempsey: The Manassa Mauler*. Baton Rouge: Louisiana State University Press, 1979.

Stevens, Sylvester. *Pennsylvania: Birthplace of a Nation*. New York: Random House, 1964.

Strayer, George D., N. L. Engelhardt, and F. W. Hart, eds. "General Report on School Buildings and Grounds of Delaware." *Bulletin of the Service Citizens of Delaware* 1 (3), 1919.

Weigley, Russell. ed. *Philadelphia: A Three-Hundred Year History*. New York: W. W. Norton and Company, 1982.

Articles

Bodnar, John, Michael Weber, and Roger Simon. "Migration, Kinship, and Urban Adjustment: Blacks and Poles in Pittsburgh, 1700–1730." *Journal of American History* 66, no. 3 (December 1979): 548–65.

Lears, Jackson. "The Way We Live, The American Way of Debt." *New York Times Sunday Magazine*, June 11, 2006, 13.

Web Sites

"History of Merion Golf Club." http://sc.essortment.com/meriongolfclub_rlxs.htm.
Middle States Association. http://www.msache.org.

4

THE SOUTH

Overview

In the first decades of the twentieth century, no section of the country maintained its regional identity more strongly than the South. Faced with replacing a social and economic system that had developed over centuries, white southerners in the post–Civil War era constructed a strict system of apartheid, political disenfranchisement, farm tenancy, and convict labor that almost replicated the abolished slave system. Instead of mutilation and whipping, lynching and burning became the coercive forces that maintained the new social and economic structure.

A strict caste system was also established that prescribed certain work to be exclusively for blacks and other work the domain of whites. Throughout the first half of the twentieth century the South remained the poorest and least educated region of the country. Agriculture continued to dominate the economy, yet significant industrialization in textile, cigarette, and steel production grew, especially in North Carolina and Alabama. During the war years 1914 through 1918 the price of cotton rose to historic highs, generating a small boom for the southern economy. The war years also witnessed the first major migration of blacks and poor whites out of the South and into cities of the North. The black migrants carried their culture, including blues music and jazz, with them, which was eagerly taken up by white musicians in cities across the North. The 1920s brought prosperity to most of the country, but to the South it brought the boll weevil, which destroyed cotton production in the early 1920s. Later in the decade the great Mississippi flood swamped millions of acres of farmland and built property in the South.

Throughout the 1920s and into the ensuing decades, religion, especially evangelical Protestantism, continued to have a strong hold on a large number of southerners. They embraced the most fundamental doctrines of their faith, even passing laws that made it illegal to teach scientific facts that contradicted the Bible. Education in the South also lagged far behind the rest of the nation. Not only did the South spend less per capita on education than any part of the nation, but also the decision to segregate blacks from whites even in school demanded that the already meager funds had to be divided to support a dual educational system, which remained unequal in distribution of the inadequate funds available.

For much of the 1920s, Florida escaped the economic doldrums of the rest of the South and shared in the country's economic boom. Thanks to the railroad, and then the airplane, tourism in Florida flourished, and in the early 1920s land values skyrocketed. In describing the mid-1920s Florida land boom, Mark Sullivan in *Our Times* wrote, "All of America's gold rushes; all her oil booms; and all her free land stampedes dwindled by comparison with the torrent of migration pouring into Florida in the early fall of 1925." But the prosperous 1920s ended abruptly for Florida when a devastating hurricane in 1926 gave people pause, and land values came tumbling down. The rich continued to come to south Florida, however, and by the early 1930s, the money they spent in restaurants, hotels, and other vacation resorts helped south Floridians pull themselves out of the Depression. Not all Floridians fared as well. The great railroad that Henry Flagler built went into receivership after the Labor Day hurricane of 1935, and in that same year the city of Key West declared itself bankrupt.

As the Great Depression cast its economic pall over the country, most southerners were already suffering economic calamity. However, that same Depression brought President Franklin Roosevelt's New Deal, which improved the lives of many southerners, especially those living in the Tennessee Valley, where electricity began running into houses for the first time. Despite improvements to the South brought on by the New Deal, such as rural electrification and farm subsidies, as World War II approached, much of the region languished in poverty and locked into patterns of racial segregation and one-party rule.

Domestic Life

FAMILY LIFE

Despite changing values regarding family life, marriage, and divorce, most southern states, because of religion, strong tradition, and a male-dominated culture, refused to allow divorce or maintained extremely restrictive laws against it. One exception to this rule was Arkansas, which relaxed laws and reduced residency requirements to compete with Nevada, Idaho, and Oklahoma as migratory divorce destinations. Although more women and children worked outside the home in the South than in any other region, the practice did not necessarily divide the family because often mother and children worked in the same location, whether in a small factory or an agricultural field. The Depression years did not have as immediately shocking an impact on southern families as it did on those of the urban North and Midwest. Many families in the South were already living at a subsistence level when the Depression arrived, and novel activities for urban families, such as home canning, pickling, baking, sewing clothes, and even smoking meat had always been part of daily life in southern families.

MEN

The autobiography of Will Percy, one of a long line of a family of southern writers, gives much insight into the white male culture of the delta South in the first decades of the twentieth century. On the surface (and surfaces matter in an honor-bound society), Will Percy embodied the ideal of an upper-class white Mississippian. A lawyer and a decorated veteran of World War I, Percy epitomized the role of the paternalistic planter who looked after "his" black workers and praised sharecropping as a mutually beneficial economic system of race relations because it was like "family." He was a community leader who openly—and courageously—opposed the Ku Klux Klan and populist racial hatred, while adhering to his own racism, a patronizing worldview that assumed black people needed whites like himself. But in other ways—ways that imparted a tension in his autobiography—Will Percy felt less of an honorable man than he wanted to be. He did not feel he lived up to the hearty, bluff, physical manliness valued by his own family, especially by his father. As a young man, Will recalled, "drunkenness made me sick, gambling bored me, rutting per se, unadorned, I considered overrated and degrading. In a charitable mood one might call me an idealist, but, more normally, a sissy."

Will Percy carried on a conversation with his father, past the grave. The pressing urgency of honor-bound manly life made this easy—even imperative—to do. Will imagined that having him as a son "must have been difficult for Father" because Will was not "all boy, all sturdy, obstreperous charm." His father, a man of "sunshine and strength," a man who did love gambling and drinking, impressed people because "his hardy vices" were obvious and all the more admirable because "merely under control." Will Percy, too, tried to control his own, less robust vices by the terms of honor, and thus became two men. One was private, tender and imaginative; the other, which he showed to the family and the world, embraced a "moral strength, love of stability and tradition, and reverence for Stoic principle," which he did not hesitate to impose on everyone younger, weaker, or more dependent than himself (Percy 2006, 239; Stowe 1996, 138–43).

Historically the southern white male was regarded as an unchallenged patriarch, the strong respected provider, and the mainstay of southern society. The traditional image of chivalrous southerner was centered in the white southern father's devotion to family, tradition, and race. At the same time the South was often celebrated as a region that stressed the so-called "masculine traits," defined by violence, a proclivity toward the military, and hawkish attitudes toward war.

The legendary southern white father was much like the southern gentleman of myth: well educated and genteel, with a firm and commanding personality, which demanded deference from all family members and from lesser whites and blacks.

Thus the myth of southern fatherhood had a distinct class bias. While not all scholars agree, some have argued that this patriarchal status established by the planter class in antebellum times continued into the next century and was even imitated by poor whites and blacks.

Popular literature often characterized the lower-class white fathers as drunken, irresponsible, and lazy, and black fathers as usually absent or nonexistent. The characterization of black fathers was probably more true in urban areas than in rural ones. Whereas towns and cities offered protection and domestic jobs for black women, black men were excluded from jobs other than those associated with farming. On the other hand, in the rural South, where most blacks lived in the first decades of the twentieth century, black men almost always headed landowning and tenant families. And in rural areas of the South, sociologists found the black patriarch ruling his family very much as did his white counterpart (Wilson and Ferris 1989, 1106).

WOMEN

As with other areas of southern history in the early twentieth century, daily life for white women turned on race, religion, class, and location. Where one lived, country or town, mattered. So too did the social connection formed by church, work, and family. Women functioned in a strongly paternalistic society where their roles as wife and mother were clearly defined and unalterable. Writing in 1895, Senator Benjamin "Pitchfork" Tillman of South Carolina argued that men in other parts of the nation should look to his state, where lack of divorce prevented men tired of their "skinny and shrunken wives" from going after "some young and buxom girl," where lynching made it "dangerous to monkey with men's womankind," and where an unwritten law allowed "men to shoot men who slept with their wives and daughters—the best law to protect women's virtue I ever heard of" (Clinton 1993, 613). Most middle-class white women in the South accepted the status quo. For example, in Georgia, Mildred Rutherford, president of her state's chapter of the Daughters of the Confederacy, complained as follows:

Women who are working for [women's suffrage] are striking at the principles for which their fathers fought during the Civil War. Women's suffrage comes from the North and the West and from women who do not believe in states rights and who wish to see Negro women using the ballot. I do not believe the estate of Georgia has sunk so low that her good men can not legislate for women. (Clinton 1993, 612–13)

On the other hand, in 1930 in Atlanta, Georgia, a small group of southern women organized the "Association of Southern Women for the Prevention of Lynching" (ASWPL) to renounce the horrors done in their name. Jessie Daniel Ames, a Texas-born southern woman active in suffrage and interracial reform movements, led the movement. She and 12 founding members established the ASWPL as an arm of the Atlanta-based Commission on Interracial Cooperation, an organization working for racial harmony. The ASWPL's founders, all active in Protestant churches and interracial organizations (they were later joined by members of Jewish women's groups), wanted to prevent lynching by educating southern whites about its causes and prevention. They were convinced that lynching was sanctioned murder, and the result of a "false chivalry," by which white men committed onerous crimes against blacks in the name of protecting white women's virtue.

Although rural southern life maintained a rugged masculinity, women provided a vital social and economic presence. Not only did the countrywoman perform all the functions of mother, nurse, family counselor, and spiritual leader, she was as well spinner and weaver, knitter, seamstress, quilter, fruit and vegetable preserver, butcher, and supplemental field hand. Women also tended the livestock and maintained the vegetable garden, which contributed significantly to the family diet. As late as 1930, women worked on farms in the South more than in any other region of the nation. Southern countrywomen also kept track of kinships and relatives and remembered ancient folk rhymes, ballads, party games, and the ingredients and applications of folk remedies as well as recipes. Women were also responsible for maintaining a semblance of religion and social refinement in the rural South. Although the rural southern family remained strongly patriarchal in nature, the mother provided the social and human ties that bound the family together (Wilson and Ferris 1989, 9).

In the South, from 1900 through 1920, married women both black and white worked more often outside the home than their counterparts anywhere else in the United States. The high work rates of southern women can be explained by the unusually large numbers of black women in the workforce. Rural black women typically entered field labor at a young age, and those living in towns moved into domestic employment. Black women usually remained at work after marriage because of the poverty of their families and the demand for their labor. As the mill economy expanded in the early twentieth century, white women, single and married, entered the workforce. Daughters often joined mothers at work and, whether they were field hands, tenant workers, or mill hands, southern females labored together with family members long after employment had segregated families in other regions of the nation.

The growth of the urban South, with commercial, financial, and manufacturing centers, created jobs for white women as clerical workers, sales clerks, and factory operatives. During the 1920s, the South felt the effects of the technological and bureaucratic transformations that reshaped America. Growing corporations and commercial establishments such as banks enlarged their record-keeping functions and redefined office tasks in ways that created great demand for female clerical help. Because office work demanded specific skills, the new female workers differed dramatically from the farm and mill workers who had learned their skills through childhood employment and on-the-job training. Since few white women from mill towns or tenant farms had the education to compete for such jobs, and racial prejudice and their lack of education kept black women out of store and office employment, the new workforce came largely from the homes of white craftsmen, shopkeepers, landowners, and other groups who had been able to secure secondary education for their daughters. Middle-class black families produced the clerical workers for black-owned businesses. Turnover was greater in these professions than in traditional areas of female employment because a vast majority of female clerical workers and professional women—unlike farm workers, domestics, and mill hands—retired from the labor force upon marriage.

During the 1920s and 1930s, light manufacturing and labor-intensive services such as commercial laundries opened and closed in response to changes in local economies and the national economy. By the end of the 1930s, industrial and agricultural employment among women had declined markedly. The mill town, the garment factory, and the tenant farm persisted in the South, but none fully recovered the tenacious hold they had had on women's lives in an earlier era (Blackwelder 1989, 76–77).

CHILDREN

Child labor in fields and factories persisted in the South long after urbanization and Progressive reform movements had diminished it elsewhere. The wages of children who entered into degrading competition with their parents varied considerably, but indicative of the low wages for children is the record of textile mills in North Carolina that paid 10 and 12 cents a day for child labor. In most cases the pay went directly to the father. The workweek averaged about 70 hours for children, as it did for men and women. In 1887, Alabama had passed a law limiting a child's factory workday to eight hours, but the law was repealed in 1895 at the demand of a Massachusetts company that planned to build a large mill in the state. Children in Alabama went to work before dawn and did not return home until well after sunset. Children of eight and nine years of age could be seen as late as 9:30 at night finding their way home with little lanterns. Illiteracy among mill village children was three to four times that among white children at large, and only about one in five of Alabama mill village children between the ages of 6 and 15 attended school.

By the turn of the century, Samuel Gompers and the American Federation of Labor had campaigns for child labor legislation underway in Alabama, Georgia, and the Carolinas, where 90 percent of the children in southern textiles were employed. Protestant ministers, women's clubs, and humanitarian groups joined the effort. It took more than 12 years of struggle for child labor laws to be passed, and by any standards they were rather weak. By 1912, all southern states had adopted an age hour limit and some sort of prohibition against night work for children, but the minimum age limit was only 12 and a child could work up to 60 hours a week. Furthermore, an investigation by the Federal Bureau of Labor revealed that the age limit laws were openly and freely violated. Reform groups, organized labor, and ministers put up a valiant effort to get stronger laws to protect children, but in the face of the interests of northeastern capital and southern mill owners, their efforts remained fruitless, and effective laws regulating children in the southern textile mills would not be passed until the New Deal era (Woodward 1974, 418–20).

In addition to work, illness and infectious disease had a debilitating effect on the social and intellectual development of children in the South. Hookworm probably represented the most reprehensible of these primarily childhood ailments. Some health reformers even described it as the single germ of southern backwardness. A major effect of the southern hookworm campaign was that rural school modernizers became convinced that the health of schoolchildren and their school environment were related to the process of learning. Regional poverty and underdevelopment, which had seemed to nineteenth-century southerners to be inevitable products of fate and providence, were, by the turn of the twentieth century, regarded as environmental. Almost gleefully, reformers blamed hookworm infection for southern under-education. The debilitating effects of the parasite made many older children "likely to drop out altogether with the minimum amount of education which their opportunities offered." The "widespread prevalence" of hookworm weakened the "bodies and minds" of schoolchildren, declared Virginia state school officials. Infected children became "easily fatigued," and unable to study with interest. Even with the teachers' determined involvement, these officials feared that children with hookworm made "poor progress" and probably left school uneducated. Another reformer declared that ill health and ignorance weakened the "race generation after generation, always tending to produce a condition of physical, intellectual, economic, and moral degeneracy."

The new consensus that environment shaped health, which in turn determined educational progress, received additional confirmation in a flood of studies—many of them subsidized by the Rockefeller Sanitary Commission—that demonstrated the alarming extent of hookworm infection among southern rural schoolchildren. Increasingly, however, these studies, rather than confirming that hookworm constituted the single "germ" of southern inertia, pointed instead to many other sources of debility and inactivity. Surveys of school hygiene conducted by health officials in Alabama, South Carolina, Tennessee, Georgia, and Florida documented the wide extent of parasites such as hookworms, but they also revealed a pattern of malnutrition, disease, and dental problems as well as a variety of other "defects" among southern children. In every instance investigators concluded that unhealthful conditions adversely shaped the educational experience.

In 1914, a systematic survey of health conditions in the schools located in the Virginia Piedmont, published by the U.S. Bureau of Education and sponsored by the Rockefeller Commission, examined the physical characteristics of schoolchildren, the health conditions of school facilities, and their effect on the educational performance of children. This study concluded that it was necessary to create a better physical setting for public education in an environment that would make possible children with "rosy cheeks and bright eyes" rather than "pale faces and vacant stares," healthy arms and legs rather than "thin and bloodless ones," and brains enriched by rich blood rather than a "watery stream poisoned by a leech-like, moth-born parasite." The survey recommended that the first objective of school reform should be to help children be responsive, healthy, and alert. The machinery necessary to achieve these results, argued the report, must be had "at any cost," for at stake was the "future of our Southland."

By reinforcing environmental effects in school modernization, the hookworm campaign encouraged far-reaching structural changes in southern rural schools. A major goal of public health reform was to ensure that every schoolhouse in the South had a sanitary privy, and this became a symbol of the triumph of rural school modernization. Reformers hoped that establishing sanitary privies would provide a model for sanitation in the rest of the community. They believed that schools, which previously had been centers of infection in most of the rural South, could instead become models of modern hygiene. A veteran of the hookworm campaign put it bluntly: If schools lacked facilities for the sanitary disposal of human waste, how could modern sanitation be "inculcated in children from homes who from time immemorial have ever used the woods and fence corners?"

The hookworm plague among children in the South created a subtle but profound revolution in southern life. For the first time the federal government, with help from private foundations, intruded (albeit in a positive way) into the private lives of families in the South, and the vehicles of this intervention were their own children (see the sections on Intellectual Life and Health and Medicine) (Link 1988, 623–42).

PETS

Southerners kept pets, but they were more likely to express concern about the practical and material value of animals, and less likely to express concern about right and wrong treatment of animals. On the other hand, many southerners were likely to form strong emotional attachments to individual animals, especially dogs that displayed special talents for hunting or protection.

Although individuals and household members developed strong attachments to dogs and treated them with affection, they almost always evaluated them on the basis of their working ability. Once unable to work, however, dogs were not discarded; rather they were "retired" and allocated a special status in the household. Despite the affection southern dogs received, whether working or retired, they were expected to reside outside the house.

In the South cats were kept as pets less frequently than dogs. But where they appeared, usually in rural areas, they were also expected to work for their living. The most common southern felines were barn cats, whose main purpose was rodent control. Often in the South, pigs, cattle, sheep, and chickens were treated as family pets until they became food. From time to time, however, an especially endearing food animal might receive a reprieve and become a permanent member of the family (Wilson and Ferris 1989, 1233–34).

Economic Life

WORK AND WORKPLACE

Workers in the South for the most part were excluded from the technology-driven manufacturing and wage boom of the first two decades of the new century. In 1880 per capita annual income in the South stood at $376. At the end of the economic boom of the 1920s it was $543 for nonfarm workers and $183 for farm workers, or an average of $363. As bad as the economy was at the end of the nineteenth century, it was worse at the end of the 1920s. A majority of southerners engaged in the physically strenuous work of farming. Although tractors were used on most dairy farms, mules provided the power elsewhere, where the most commonly seen equipment was the animal-drawn plow. A lack of capital in the South prevented large landowners from paying cash to their workers, and it also thwarted poor farmers' efforts to buy land or even seed and equipment. Therefore, landowners and poor farmers entered into tenancy agreements. Landlords provided farmland, seed, mules, tools, housing, food, and other necessities, and in return landlords received half the corn and cotton the tenant farmer produced. In this situation, no tenant earned enough to escape the cycles of debt and poverty that marked cotton tenancy, and as the cotton economy slowly deteriorated in the 1920s and 1930s, the grip of misery grew tighter.

Up until World War II, the plantation landlord and the tenant farmer dominated the nation's perception of the South. They became symbols of the region's poverty and cultural backwardness and exemplified the paternalism, exploitation, and social-class dimensions of southern agriculture. There were two socioeconomic levels of sharecroppers, and they were defined by the farmers' contributions to production and their need for subsistence credit. Some tenants, for example, owned their own mules and equipment and also bought their own seed and fertilizer. In these cases their portion of the crop could be as much as two-thirds or three-fourths. On the other hand, those sharecroppers who possessed nothing and could only supply their labor fared much worse. Dependent on credit for nearly all living necessities, and working under much supervision, they ordinarily received no more than half the crop, from which the landlord deducted costs for "furnishings" and interest.

In the chronically depressed southern agriculture of the early twentieth century, tenancy increased steadily as many farmers lost their land. In 1930, when tenancy peaked, there were 228,598 cash tenants, 772,573 sharecroppers, and 759,527 other tenants (mostly share tenants) in 13 southern and border states. In areas where staple-crop production dominated the agricultural economy, tenant farming was most common. In 1937, the President's Committee on Farm Tenancy estimated that 65 percent of all farmers in the Cotton Belt and 48 percent in tobacco regions were land tenants or sharecroppers. This comprised nearly one-half of the southern farm population of 15.5 million. Approximately two-thirds of southern tenants were white, but among the lowest tenant group, the numbers of whites and blacks were about equal.

Southern tenancy created a culture of rural poverty. Tenants and sharecroppers received some of the lowest incomes in America, rarely clearing more than a few hundred dollars per year, and often, especially in years of low crop prices, tenant farmers received no net income at all. Consequently, rural southerners continued to live at the bottom of the national scale. Cotton and tobacco tenants worked in the fields and lived in pine-board cabins that lacked window glass, screens, electricity, plumbing, and even wells and privies. Thousands of families were without common household furnishings, stoves, mattresses, or adequate clothing and shoes.

The poorest sharecroppers subsisted on a diet that relied heavily on salt pork, flour, and meal. Owning no cows or poultry and tending no gardens, they seldom consumed milk, eggs, or fresh vegetables. Malnutrition compounded wretched living conditions to make chronic illness a major feature of rural life, as malaria, pellagra, and hookworm infection stunted the development of children, shortened lives, and lowered the economic productivity of the poor (Wilson and Ferris 1989, 6–7).

Tenant farmers had certain colloquialisms and errors in grammar that were almost universal and gave the regional language a dialect more distinct than any other region of the country. Some of the more obvious were: double and sometimes triple negatives, "done" and "seen" used as past tense, "ain't" and "ary," occasionally "haint" and "nary," "like" used as a conjunction, and "don't" with the third person singular. Idioms and unusual word usages were abundant. For example, the next-to-youngest child was always the "knee baby," no matter how old. "Evening" was afternoon, which differed from "night," which was from supper onward. Menopause was "when nature leaves." Midwives were referred to as "grannies." If a person had a bad reputation a tenant farmer might say "He's got a lot of mess to him." Tenant farmers also often began sentences of opinion in a self-effacing manner; for example: "I reckon," "It seems like," or "I allus say." "Studyin" invariably meant thinking about, and "fittin tah" or "fixin to" was universally used instead of "I am planning to" or "I am going to" (Hagood 1939, 68).

One of the familiar figures of southern rural lore was the tight-fisted landlord who kept all accounts, charged exorbitant interest on advances, and took over his tenants' cotton for debts. Since he held almost all local political and economic power in his hands, a planter could impose whatever terms he pleased on a sharecropper, and often, to ensure his own profit in lean times, he would cut even deeper into the shares of the tenant farmer, who had no recourse—either political or judicial—to oppose the planter's injustices. Moreover, tenants had little security on the land. They worked under year-to-year verbal agreements, which allowed landlords to dismiss tenants who were disruptive or questioned the system. Or landlords could simply dismiss workers without notice when crop demand lowered.

Consequently, sharecroppers accustomed themselves to moving on the average of once every two years. This resulted not only in an unstable life for the family but also for the places they lived. For without permanent residents who would take a civic interest in the community, there was little likelihood that there would ever be pressure for good schools, public health, or other services. The forced mobility of tenant farmers also contributed to the general public view that poor tenant farmers were shiftless and rootless. During the Great Depression, initial New Deal agricultural policy made the plight of the tenant farmer even worse. The acreage-reduction contracts of the Agricultural Adjustment Administration (AAA) decreased labor needs and, in effect, encouraged landlords to dispense with tenants to avoid sharing government payments with them. Not until 1937 with the passing of the Bankhead-Jones Tenancy Act—providing $85 million in loans, spread over three years, "to help tenant farmers buy their own land, animals, seed, feed, and machinery," as well as help existing landowners to rehabilitate their properties—did some relief come to the tenant farmer in the South.

In the decades after the 1930s southern agriculture underwent revolutionary changes in technological development, the most remarkable of which was the mechanical cotton picker, which came into general use during World War II and made the most labor-intensive aspect of cotton farming obsolete. The mechanization of southern agriculture was a major cause of the great postwar exodus of the rural poor from the land and, in many cases, from the region.

Natural disaster also played a great role in transforming the life of workers in the agricultural South in the first decades of the twentieth century. In 1892, the boll weevil, a small cotton-eating beetle, crossed the Mexican border into Brownsville, Texas. By 1915, it had reached Alabama and by the early 1920s had populated the entire cotton South. This small insect, which bored into cotton plants and turned the cotton boll black, rendering

---

📷 *Snapshot*

A South Carolina Sharecropper Remembers the Boll Weevil

"Speakin' of de war time, after de war gits over and de sojers come home, hit look lak ever'thing go wrong on de place. Mister Oscar, he had helt and helt all our cotton till de price go down to nuttin' in 1921, and then he sell. Half de time, dat year, all on de place went hongry. So I say one day to Jake, 'Jake, dis ain't gwine do; us'll have to plant some peas lak dat man from 'way out yonder—Doctor Kinhap, I believe dat he name—egvised de farmers to do. Miss Jane, she say she want us to plant peas. But Mister Oscar say, 'un-uh', he don't want nothin' but cotton planted on de place; dat he in debt and hafter raise cotton to git de money to pay wid. So when dat win' begin to blow all dem thunder clouds out de wes', 'long 'bout July, I tole Jake hit a bad sign. Sho' nuff dar did come trouble, 'long 'bout Augus' and September. De boll weevil come des lak dat doctor man from 'way out yonder say he'd come. And, bless yo' life, dat bug sho' romped on things dat fall."

Miss Jane, she tried to git him to plant sumpin' in place of cotton, but he say, 'un-uh, des lak dat time she want him to plant peas. And one day he went down to Columby and gived a mortgage on de place and bought mo' gewano dan ebber befo'. When me and Jake was haulin' hit home, I say to Jake one day, 'Jake, dis gewano don't smell lak hit grow cotton on dat lan' up home.' Anyway, Mister Oscar had us haul it out and put hit down in de fields and plant cotton on hit. De cotton come up and started to growin', and, suh, befo' de middle of May I looks down one day and sees de boll weevil settin' up dere in de top of dem little cotton stalks waitin' for de squares to fo'm. So all dat gewano us hauled and put down in 1922 made nuttin' but a crop of boll weevils. And de very same thing happen agin de nex' year.

From: American Life Histories: Manuscripts from the Federal Writers' Project, 1936–1940.

---

it worthless, devastated southern cotton fields in the early 1920s. The boll weevil proved to be a relentless and unstoppable enemy to the cotton farmer. Total cotton production in 1921 plunged to scarcely more than half of 1920's output, and while the price per pound rose by a fourth that did not compensate those individuals whose family farms had been completely ravished by the insect. Not until 1924 did cotton production return to 1920 levels, and by that time many small farmers had been ruined and cotton's domination of the southern agricultural economy had ended. Most had to leave the land for textile mills or for the long trek up to northern cities. The economy of some areas was completely transformed as a result of the boll weevil invasion. In the town of Enterprise, Alabama, for example, the citizens erected a monument to the boll weevil. Although it destroyed the cotton economy of the area, it forced the people of Enterprise to diversify their crops and develop small industry to ensure that they would never be at the mercy of the caprices of a single-crop economy (Wilson and Ferris 1989, 6–7).

The great flood of 1927 also contributed to the troubles of an already economically devastated South. The waters had begun rising as a result of prolonged and heavy rainfall across the country's midsection. This overflow eventually found its way to the Mississippi. Man-made levees protected cities that lay north of the juncture with the Ohio River, but south of the juncture of these two great rivers the force of the water broke levees in Mississippi and Arkansas, flooding over 2.3 million acres and

A commercial district partially submerged by floodwaters in 1927. Library of Congress.

affecting more than 170,000 people. Over five million acres were eventually inundated in those two states. At some points on its southward flow, the Mississippi grew to over one hundred miles wide. To spare New Orleans, levees on the opposite side of the river were dynamited, and as a result more than 6.2 million acres of rural Louisiana ended up under water and more than 250,000 Louisianans felt the impact. Until recently, the great flood of 1927 was considered the greatest natural disaster in the history of the country, and it affected the region of the country least able to resist such a disaster. The Red Cross counted over 600,000 displaced persons, and as many as 500 lives were lost. Only a massive federal government effort involving over 333,000 volunteers and 1,400 paid workers, coordinated by Secretary of Commerce Herbert Hoover, kept the death toll from reaching into the thousands.

Because of the boll weevil and the flood, the Depression had already come to the South before the great national economic collapse of 1929–1932. Recognizing the dire straits of the southern economy, the New Deal economists paid special attention to the area. In addition to the Agricultural Adjustment Act (AAA), which paid southern farmers (as well as farmers in the rest of the country) to curtail production of staples such as cotton, the New Deal pushed through legislation to create a regional electrical program. While electric lights had been beaming and electric appliances humming throughout America in the 1920s, much of the South had remained dark and unwired. Very few electric lines found their way into the South, leaving that region even further behind than the rest of the country. One of the most important acts of the first hundred days of the Roosevelt administration was the creation of the Tennessee Valley Authority (TVA). Under the TVA, the government took control of dams and munitions factories built along the Tennessee River. These facilities were turned into providers of low-cost electricity and fertilizers for the river's watershed. It also provided thousands of jobs to a severely underemployed region and promoted regional economic development, which included fertilizer production, planning, and even bookmobiles to bring learning to the back country.

Outside the farm, textile mills provided the greatest opportunity for work, but wages and conditions remained abysmal (see the sections on Material Life and Manufacturing). As in other areas of southern life, the workplace was dominated by attitudes toward race. The caste system, the color line, and the new spirit of racial aggression were strongly felt in labor relations and in trade unions. Caste sanctioned a division of labor into white men's jobs and black men's jobs. Sometimes aided by employers' policies of hiring, sometimes encouraged by politicians, white labor kept up an unremitting pressure to drive blacks out of the better-paid, more attractive work, and further down in the job hierarchy. While at the end of the Civil War black artisans were said to have outnumbered whites by five to one, they made up only a small proportion of the labor force in most crafts by 1890. From that time to 1910 blacks held their own fairly well in some of the crafts. Between 1890 and 1910 the total of black male workers in all nonagricultural pursuits increased by two thirds, but this was to be explained by the great expansion of "Negro-job" industries— sawmills, coal mining, and railroad construction and maintenance. The increasing mechanization of tobacco manufacturing converted many "Negro jobs" into "white work," and broke what had once been almost a black monopoly. The mounting employment of white women, and the more rigid segregation of races this always implied, also eliminated black workers in other industries. Early in the twentieth century there was much comment upon the disappearance of blacks from trades they had traditionally monopolized, or very largely so. "It is possible now," wrote one southerner in 1904, "to live in New Orleans as free from any dependence on the services of Negroes as one could be in New York or Boston."

The story of Clarence Dean is illustrative of the plight of the black worker in the South. Dean started as a "scrapper" at the Sloss-Sheffield Steel and Iron Company in Birmingham, Alabama, in 1933. For 12 hours each day, Dean, a wiry 18-year-old, directed the flow of molten iron as it poured out of a blast furnace and ran down a trough into pig-iron molds. "It was a man-killer," he said later, referring to the 150-degree temperatures around the blast furnace. "You'd be wet from the time you hit the clock." But the heat bothered Dean less than the job discrimination in the furnace department. He was promoted to "lineman," the worker who put the iron into the pig molds, and years later to "trough man," but he stopped there in the department's ultimate "black" job. Dean coveted the position of "iron pourer," the leader of the furnace crew. He knew that the iron pourer was a white man's job, but nevertheless he pursued it. "What about me trying out on pouring iron?" Dean asked his supervisors. "We ain't going to give niggers no white folks' jobs," they replied. Through the years Dean trained white workers to be iron pourers. "They'd tell me, 'Clarence, take care of Mr. Sam, take care of Mr. Robert.'" And that is where Clarence Dean remained until the early 1960s, when, as a result of a federal order against job discrimination, he was finally promoted to a job he had coveted and for which he had been qualified for over 30 years.

Clarence Dean's story underscores the centrality of race to the experience of workers in Birmingham, the South's leading industrial city in the twentieth century. It represented a situation faced by thousands of blacks there, and by many more in other places. To understand its meaning one must examine what happened when Birmingham workers formed powerful unions during the 1930s and 1940s, for the building of unions influenced the careers of both Clarence Dean and Jim Crow, but with strikingly different results. The unions gave white workers new power to enforce job discrimination, thus severely curtailing black opportunities. The gains made at blacks' expense provided whites with a clear economic stake in preserving racial discrimination. Clarence Dean's career parallels the experience of black workers throughout the South (Norell 1986, 669–94).

TRADE AND MARKETS

In the first half of the twentieth century, no institution in the rural South had more influence on the economic, political, and social life of the people than the crossroads store. These small enterprises, which sprang up in the postbellum rural South, were usually started by a nonsouthern merchant who arrived in the area with commercial skills not attributable to the typical rural southerner. In the post–Civil War South these entrepreneurs found ways and means of exchanging goods and services with a minimum of cash, which remained scarce in the postwar South. The storekeeper used his northern connections to keep the store stocked. State laws that made liens against crops possible also provided the merchant with a means of providing credit in small amounts to the thousands who had no other means of obtaining it. The store served everyone's needs regardless of race or status.

The southern country store remained more thoroughly connected to local economy and culture for a far longer period than in any other part of the United States. Three intersecting factors created this phenomenon. First of all was the sheer geographic isolation of the rural southern community, secondly the cyclical nature of the cash crop economy, which made credit necessary, and finally, in the rigidly segregated South, the country store provided the only space where a necessary interaction of the races could occur.

The country store provided everything necessary for material daily life. The store usually included an array of goods that ranged from clothes, to canned grocery goods, to hardware supplies. After 1920, more often than not a gasoline pump could be found out in front of the store. When someone was born, married, or died, the store provided the items needed for these rituals of life and death. The country store was no orderly department store; its goods were not likely to be very systematically arranged and displayed. Almost everything was to be found behind something else.

Sunday afternoon at a country store in Gordonton, North Carolina, in 1939. Note the kerosene pump on the right and the gasoline pump on the left. Rough, unfinished timber posts have been used as supports for the porch roof. The brother of the store owner stands in the doorway talking to Negro men sitting on the porch. Library of Congress.

The architecture of the store usually resembled that of a barn. Additions were made as needed. A wing or shed added on one side might be used for machinery, tools, and other heavy items, along with kerosene for home lamps. Another wing might store seed, fertilizers, stock feed, horse collars, ropes, chains, and general hardware. The merchant often had an office in the rear of the store, where the books were kept. This is also where the merchant would meet with those who wanted to go over their accounts or seek more credit. The office also served as a reception room for the regional jobber or drummer, who took orders for the store and controlled delivery. The drummer was much more than a salesman; he was a local attraction, who brought news and opinions from the outside and a fund of racy stories sure to go the rounds. Often the country store had the only telephone in town and thus became the immediate contact point with the outside world.

In the absence of a doctor or pharmacist, the local merchant often made diagnoses and prescribed medicines from his store's own pharmacopoeia, which might include such remedies as Lydia Pinkham's Vegetable Compound, castor oil, or elixirs for colic or coughs. The store also operated as a general gathering place every day except Sunday, when the local church took over that role. Social life of the community centered around the local country store. Stories were told, and local news was shared. Notices of jobs or items for sale were posted. In the summer, men gathered on a hot day outside the store to loaf, whittle, play checkers, or pitch horseshoes and to comment on the attractions of passing women. In the winter, men and boys, and sometimes a few women, sat around the potbellied stove swapping yarns, arguing politics or religion, and recounting details of farming operations. There was a philosophy present in the assumptions underlying this talk called a "cracker-barrel philosophy." The country store with its southern flavor continued well into the twentieth century and can even be found in some contemporary small towns. However, the value of these stores today is more nostalgic than practical. The goods inside are more likely to be local craft or souvenir items for sale to passing tourists rather than the necessities of life offered a half century ago (Wilson and Ferris 1989, 16–18).

Up until the 1940s, the country store represented the economic focal point for 75 percent of the South's population. But the remainder of southerners who lived in the cities witnessed the emergence of an urban marketplace, as expanding economies attracted northern capitalists to the region's cities. Birmingham's steel industry, for example, grew so rapidly that by the 1920s it became recognized as the "Pittsburgh of the South," and in Nashville aggressive bankers expanded local insurance companies throughout the mid-South to make Union Street the "Wall Street" of the South. The emergence of new urban markets in the South, however, did not continue unbroken in Nashville, Birmingham, or any other city of the South. The Great Depression hit southern cities hard. Except for Miami, urbanization in the South declined, and market activity slowed in the 1930s amid low agricultural prices and regional poverty, while the exodus to northern cities continued. Sustained development of urban markets in the South, which had an encouraging start in the 1920s, would have to wait until the post–World War II era to realize its full potential (Miller and Pozetta 1989, 2–3).

CASTE AND CLASS EXPERIENCE

In the post–Civil War era, the transition from slavery to caste as a system of controlling race relations went forward gradually and tediously. Slavery had been vastly more than a labor system, and the gap that its removal left in manners, mores, and rituals of behavior could not be filled overnight. During the three decades of the post–Civil War era, whites created a system of apartheid, political disenfranchisement, and economic oppression that left most southern blacks, although free from slavery, in a state not much better than their antebellum situation. By the last decade of the nineteenth century segregation was firmly in place throughout the South, and this new order would endure until well after World War II. The new southern racial order, which relegated blacks to second-class citizenship, was bolstered by discriminatory legislation as well as systematic violence, especially the practice of lynching, which sent a strong message to the black community of the South not to challenge white supremacy. The message was clear: crimes by blacks against whites, whether murder or rape or even trivial behavior deemed "uppity," would be punished swiftly and brutally. Also blacks were aware that even if they followed the white supremacist code, they could be the target of a lynching incited by a false charge. In 1923, in Rosewood, Florida, for example, an entire black town was burned to the ground and several blacks lynched and many more murdered in a riot that was instigated by a white woman who accused a black man of beating her, when in fact the beating had come from a white man with whom she was having an extramarital affair.

The National Association for the Advancement of Colored People (NAACP) began campaigning during World War I for a federal law against lynching, and antilynching bills passed the House in 1922 and 1938, but they failed to overcome filibusters by southern senators. Lynching would not become a federal offense until the passing of the Civil Rights Act of 1964.

Through the first half of the twentieth century, life in the South remained highly segregated. Two separate societies developed that had very little in common except for location and occasional unequal interaction. The Civil War and Reconstruction had abolished slavery but had not ended the strict two-tiered society that became written into law and custom throughout the South. Land ownership remained overwhelmingly in the

NAACP pickets protest the practice of lynching at the Crime Conference in Washington, D.C., on December 11, 1934. Library of Congress.

hands of the whites. Within the white community social status varied with land-holding and possessions, but even the lowliest white enjoyed a standing higher than any black.

Acceptance in the South of immigrant Catholics occurred slowly if at all in the first decades of the twentieth century. In the 1910s, for example, Georgia demagogue Tom Watson vilified Catholicism by reference to the same stereotypes used to denigrate blacks. "The African belief in the conjure bag is a progressive state of mind," claimed Watson, "compared to Roman Catholic belief in saints that secure tenants for vacant houses." The Ku Klux Klan also focused its venom on the same groups, as torchlight parades of Klansmen lit the black and Irish ghettoes of many southern cities. By the early 1920s Catholics in Georgia organized a statewide educational and propagandist group, "The Catholic Layman's Association of Georgia," to fight Georgia natives. But any hopes southern Catholics had of changing the prejudice against their religion dimmed in the 1928 election when the candidacy of Catholic Al Smith raised new cries against papist designs on the country, and Smith became the first Democratic presidential candidate since Reconstruction not to sweep all the South's electoral votes.

Italian immigration sent shockwaves through portions of the South, which had always existed in an either/or white or black society. These new olive-skinned kinky-haired arrivals from Europe shook age-old racial theories. In Tallulah, Louisiana, in 1899, five Sicilian men were lynched, ostensibly because of a dispute over a goat, but really because they had violated the protocols of racial interaction. These men had committed the error of socializing on an equal basis with blacks with whom they lived and worked. Other immigrant groups, including the Cuban cigar workers in Florida, German farmers in the Piedmont and Shenandoah region, Greek spongers in the Florida fishing village of Tarpon Springs, and others made their home in various regions of the South and all brought their unique traditions that added to the flavor of southern culture, but none probably upset the racial sensibilities of white southerners as much as the ambiguously pigmented Sicilians of Italy (Orsi 1992, 314).

Variations on race and social organization complicated the predominant biracial categories of southern life, especially in the peripheries of the South such as the Gulf states and New Orleans, which had a history of foreign immigration, Indian survival, and multireligious identities. In Florida, for example, Seminole Indians continued to live with indifference toward Euro-American life. In 1821 the United States took

A segregated water fountain in Oklahoma City, Oklahoma, in 1939. Photograph by Russell Lee. The Granger Collection, New York.

possession of Florida and immediately began a campaign to eradicate the Native Americans living there. Through three bloody wars the Seminoles, in alliance with African Americans who had fled plantations and set up independent tribal communities in Seminole territory, successfully resisted conquest by the U.S. military and inflicted numerous wounds on the country, making the Seminole wars the bloodiest Indian wars in the nation's history. Finally on May 10, 1842, a frustrated President John Tyler ordered the end of military actions against the Seminoles. At that time over $20 million had been spent, 1,500 American soldiers had died, and still no formal peace treaty had been signed. The Seminoles quietly retreated into the hinterland and wet wilderness of south Florida.

In the 1880s, when the wars were over and the Seminole survivors and their descendents finally had been left alone to get on with their lives in south Florida, the U.S. government once again sent agents to approach them—to count them, coerce them into government programs, and "civilize" them. Despite their small numbers, they had not died out as many had predicted; indeed, they were increasing in numbers. Into the early twentieth century, the government's Indian agents sent despairing letters to Washington, reporting: "They are satisfied, happy, and contented with their mode of life and unanimously in favor of continuing therein." But not all of the world beyond Lake Okeechobee and the Big Cypress and the Everglades was content to let them continue their particular "mode of life" (http://www.seminoletribe. com/tribune/40anniversary/history.shtml). With the explosion of white settlement in south Florida that began as a trickle in the late 1800s and turned into a flood by the 1920s, the intervention of several groups of "Friends of the Seminoles" and of the state and federal governments now became an ironic necessity for the "protection" of the Seminoles. Lands were set aside in Immokalee ("im m—kl" or "my home" in Miccosukee) and Big Cypress, in Brighton, and in Dania (now Hollywood). It would take until the 1970s for all these scattered parcels to be consolidated and taken into federal trust as Seminole reservations. Only much later, in the 1980s, would a fifth reservation, at Tampa, be created. In 1996, a sixth, Fort Pierce, was added.

In 1913, the U.S. government appointed a special commissioner to the Seminoles and opened the first Seminole Agency, in Miami. Directed by the Bureau of Indian Affairs (BIA), a part of the U.S. Department of the Interior, the agency moved to Fort Myers in 1917 on the premise that it would be closer to the Seminoles' villages. But by the mid-1920s, the people also were gathering on the lower East Coast and the agency was relocated to Dania, between Fort Lauderdale and Hollywood. Around 1942, the BIA Seminole Agency returned to Fort Myers but, in late 1950, the Dania office was reestablished where it remains to this day, in the heart of the Hollywood Reservation, near the intersection of Stirling Road and U.S. 441.

During the tenure of these government agents, there never had been any question of their exercising control, much less leadership, over the people. The time-honored internal system of medicine men and women and clan elders continued to function, even though it operated among fewer people than in past years and in isolated camps rather than in large communities. "Government" still meant essentially the same thing that it had meant for many generations. It meant the guidance of tradition, the word of the elders, freedom of choice, and the right to search, in councils, for consensus. By the middle of the twentieth century, however, events in the outside world once again caused the Seminoles to seek among old traditions for new responses, and the movement toward a unified political authority began.

In 1946, the U.S. Congress passed a law permitting American Indian tribes to file claims against the U.S. government for losses suffered through treaties broken or lands lost to the United States. Less than a year later, the Florida Seminoles filed their petition with the federal Indian Claims Commission. Rather than any attempt on the part of the U.S. government to provide justice, this was a part of a larger move to finalize claims and end the government's relationship with the tribes. As another element of the larger process, in the 1950s, so-called "Termination Acts" were debated in Congress. These acts designated certain tribes to which Congress felt they owed no further debts; therefore, they could be "freed from federal supervision and control." The Florida Seminoles were among them (http://www.seminoletribe.com/tribune/40anniversary/history.shtml).

In addition to the Seminoles, other villages and reservations of tribes who resisted the great removals of the nineteenth century dot the landscape of the South. In North Carolina in 1838 during the Great Removal, about 1,000 Cherokee Indians retreated into the mountains of their homeland and refused to be relocated. After the federal government granted recognition to this group in the late nineteenth century, they became the largest reservation in the South, and as the new century unfolded they began to cater to tourists to maintain their economic independence. In Mississippi, a small group of Choctaws also resisted removal, and as the new century opened they had survived an ill-fated alliance with the Confederacy as well as economic hardship to become the largest Indian tribe in the South. Although outstanding agriculturists, the Choctaws' activities were rather unromantic, and they have received little attention from travelers or scholars. The Lumbee Indians of North Carolina also resisted removal, and they remain the largest federally unrecognized tribe in the United States. From the 1890s through World War I the Lumbees went to Georgia to work in the turpentine industry, but at the end of war they returned to their homeland in North Carolina to farm cotton, corn, and tobacco (LaFarge 1956, 230–33).

URBAN AND RURAL EXPERIENCE

Until World War II, 75 percent of southerners lived in rural areas and engaged in a life dominated by their agrarian economy. They lived without electricity, and their social, economic, and political lives were encompassed by the local church and the country store. If their children went to school—which was only opened for a few months a year—it usually meant a long walk of several miles to a poorly lit, damp, and uncomfortable one-room schoolhouse. It is little wonder that for people living in the rural areas of the South "going to town" was cause for celebration.

The interior of a little red schoolhouse with teacher and students in Crossville, Tennessee, c.1933. Library of Congress.

For the most part—with the exception of Birmingham, which became a major steel producer—southern cities remained more commercial than industrial and more tied to agriculture than their counterparts in other regions of the country. Major inland cities like Atlanta, Memphis, and Nashville began to grow in the early twentieth century, but New Orleans maintained its role as the region's dominant urban area. For southerners living in the city an ethos of boosterism and commercialism, which emphasized economic growth, new technology, local loyalty, and progress, prevailed. Chambers of commerce appeared in large and small towns alike. Throughout the South, developers and speculators built office buildings, stores, and theaters. Railroad stations, hotels, theaters, YMCAs, government office buildings, and churches—rather than grand office buildings—usually silhouetted the skyline.

After 1920, thanks to automobiles and buses traveling on newly constructed roads, rural southerners would come to town to shop and to enjoy the luxury of the new elegant air-conditioned movie theaters being built throughout the urban South. Because of their small size, religious objections, and the high cost of renting films from distributors, small rural towns of the South had fewer theaters than any other region of the country, and therefore a trip to the movies became an exceptional experience for rural southerners. The major film producers had built magnificent palaces in the 1920s to show their films and, even in smaller cities of less than 100,000, entrepreneurs had imitated the style set by the big five film companies. Therefore, for the small cost of a ticket, poor southerners could appropriate for a short time some of the acknowledged symbols of wealth that the theaters had adopted, such as plush carpets, air conditioning, chandeliers, upholstered seating, and obsequious ushers.

Although southern cities felt less of an impact in the late nineteenth century from foreign immigrants than their northern counterparts, a number of ethnic groups did make their way South, leaving their influence on a number of southern cities. The Irish were a key part of the workforce and politics in Memphis, New Orleans, and Richmond. Merchants of Jewish ancestry were an important force in business and politics in Atlanta and Montgomery. Near the end of the century, Italian immigrants flocked to New Orleans. In the first decades of the twentieth century the proportion of foreign-born citizens declined in all major southern cities, and this trend continued through the first four decades of the twentieth century (Wilson and Ferris 1989, 1436).

ANIMAL HUSBANDRY AND HUNTING AND FISHING

Southern dairy production changed surprisingly little from the late nineteenth century until World War II. During that era, all across the region many small farmers kept and milked a few cows, separated the milk, fed the skim to the hogs, made their own butter, and sold surplus cream in town or shipped it on the railroad to market. Along with the sale of eggs, this trade remained one of the few farm activities that produced a small but steady cash flow. The 1930s witnessed the development of a number of small cheese manufacturing plants. Also, better roads brought motor truck carriers to formerly remote areas to pick up whole grade B milk from small unspecialized producers.

In the early 1900s chickens also provided a small but steady cash flow to farmers, who always maintained a small flock for their own use. Consequently, the rural population of the South remained largely self-sufficient in terms of supplying its chicken and egg needs. In the 1930s a more modern system began, as specialized poultry farmers began growing 10,000 to 20,000 birds every six or seven weeks and selling them to agribusiness firms, which slaughtered, dressed, packed, and then transported the poultry in refrigerated cars across the nation (Wilson and Ferris 1989, 28, 34).

By 1910 most southern states had joined the rest of the nation in enacting trespass and game laws, which made market hunting and sale of wild animals illegal. State agencies empowered wildlife agencies to monitor populations of species defined by law as game and determine how and when these species were to be hunted. Southern distinctiveness in hunting stemmed from a peculiar combination of traits found in the region. Although the myth of a plantation lifestyle continued on restored plantations, where privileged participants hunted for quail

---

📷 *Snapshot*

Fried Squirrel or Rabbit

Squirrel and rabbit are two of the finest and most tender of all Southern wild meats. Both should be decapitated and dressed immediately after shooting. After skinning, wipe the carcass with a cloth dipped in scalding water to remove loose hairs. Both squirrel and rabbit can be fried like chicken for a different but delicious dish.

    4 squirrels or rabbits
    Vinegar to cover
    Cold water to cover
    Flour to coat
    Salt and black pepper
    Shortening for frying
    4 tbsp. flour
    2 cups sweet milk

After the animals are cleaned, rinse and soak them in vinegar for 1 hour. Then soak them in cold water for 3 hours or overnight. This soaking helps take the wild taste out of the meat and tenderizes it at the same time.

Cut the meat into pieces and dredge them in flour seasoned with salt and pepper. Brown the meat slowly in hot shortening in a heavy skillet until brown on both sides. Add the 4 tbsp. flour and milk, stirring often to mix well. Cover the skillet tightly and cook over lowest heat until the meat is tender (about 30 minutes), turning once and basting several times. Serves 4.

We ate a good bit of game. We always had all the fish we wanted, and my dad was a hunter, so we'd have ducks and quail and occasionally squirrel and sometimes rabbit—the rabbit was my request. We had quite a bit of game, which at that time was not a problem because it was plentiful. We were always careful not to kill when the young were coming on. We usually hunted on Saturday afternoons or early in the morning. Sometimes we'd have duck for Sunday dinner, and I can't remember having fish any way but fried. —Benjamin B. Ferrell

From: Strickland and Dunn 2002, 57.

and deer and took part in colorful pageants at the exclusive hunt clubs, most rural southerners hunted out of necessity.

In the first half of the twentieth century, southern youngsters—at least the 75 percent who lived in rural areas—were taught at an early age to hunt by fathers or close relatives. Guns were treasured possessions passed from father to son. Hunting was a masculine activity, and responsibility not only to kill but also clean and cook the game usually fell on the men. While the wealthy hunted quail and deer on their plantations, the poor supplemented their low-protein diet by killing squirrel, possum, and rabbit (Wilson and Ferris 1989, 1230–31).

Fishing offered an integral form of recreation and livelihood in the South. It was predominantly a masculine activity passed along from one generation to the next. It fulfilled a need to provide a private challenge, as success or failure was the individual's alone. The type of fish or seafood caught depended on the region. The coast of Florida was known for its red snapper, while Georgia and Louisiana were noted for their shrimp. The most common freshwater fish in the South were catfish, trout, and bass, but every region had its local "pan fish" known as bream, perch, shell crackers, or blue gills, depending on the region in which they were fished. Despite their difference in name, these small fish all suffered the same fate once caught. They were dipped in a cornmeal mixture and cooked in a boiling pot of oil (Wilson and Ferris 1989, 1119–220).

Intellectual Life

SCIENCE

Southern universities promoted little original scientific research outside of the agricultural fields. Relying principally on the provisions of the 1862 Morrill Federal Land Grant Act to fund any increase in scientific instruction, intended to support agricultural education, southern public universities hired faculty to teach a broad range of courses in horticulture and animal husbandry, to conduct research related to these fields, and to provide extension services. Scientific disciplines not directly related to producing knowledgeable farmers, however, frequently languished. With the passage of the Hatch Act in 1887, which established a national system of agricultural experimental stations, and the Smith Lever Act in 1914, which financed extension of those stations, Congress expanded the federalization of agricultural research and education, begun with the Morrill Act. The effects of these acts on the South were important. First of all they helped remove the southern prejudice against "book farming." As the father of the extension system, Seaman Knapp, said, "What a man hears, he may doubt; what he sees he may possibly doubt; but what he does he can not doubt" (Graham 1990, 200–221). Secondly, the extension schools laid the foundation for the agricultural revolution that would occur in the South in the post–boll weevil era, when the South made great strides toward crop diversification and mechanization. Finally, during the New Deal era, farm extension representatives protected the rights of sharecroppers and tenants as they made decisions on acreage allotments and cash payments and on the fair cash distribution between the sharecropper or tenant farmer and the avaricious landowner.

In the post–World War I era, southern institutions of higher education grew and improved. They went beyond the scope of agriculture and were able to attract well-educated faculty. Consequently, the number of competent scientists in the South slowly increased. Their origins varied. Some were southerners who chose to pursue their careers in the region of their birth. Others, armed with advanced degrees from universities outside the South, discovered that the slowly expanding southern schools offered them a good starting point in their careers. In addition to an influx of young men who had postponed their college education to serve in the armed forces, the growth and improvement of high schools funneled more students into the region's colleges. Furthermore, farsighted professional educators such as David Crenshaw Barrow at the University of Georgia and Edward Kidder Graham and Harry Woodburn Chase at the University of North Carolina utilized increased funding from philanthropic, legislative, and alumni sources to change their institutions into true universities with a new emphasis on research and community service. This expanded the role of the southern university in the life of the region.

The Tennessee Academy of Science, in an attempt to combine service to the community with funded research, adopted a novel approach to encouraging scientific research. In 1925, Society president Scott C. Lyon suggested the establishment of a biological research station at Reelfoot Lake, a remote area of swamp, marsh, and open water invaded only by an occasional fisherman and a few adventuresome biologists. While such outposts had become an integral aspect of the outreach program of many state universities, no state academy of science had considered such an ambitious undertaking. Six years later, the state legislature set aside 10 acres and a dilapidated building for the use of the academy and, quite uncharacteristically for parsimonious southern legislatures at the time, granted $2,500 "for expenses." Thanks to the volunteer labor of academy members and continued state financial support, the Reelfoot Lake Biological Station became a reality. Individual researchers and entire classes used the facility. Summer seminars attracted faculty and graduate students, and academy members assembled there for formal and informal meetings. In 1939, an entire issue of the academy's journal contained papers generated by research at Reelfoot Lake, and single papers appeared in almost every issue.

The turbulent era of the Great Depression was a difficult time to begin costly projects, as the state academies discovered. However, the financial turmoil also motivated southern scientists to utilize their expertise to benefit the South. Keenly aware of the economic difficulties of the region, many of them joined state boosters in advocating industrialization as the panacea for the South's problems. Realistically, they knew that without such economic development the financial support necessary for first-class institutions of higher education and related research facilities would never materialize.

In 1931 the Alabama Academy of Science made a concerted effort to attract industrial scientists into their organization and elected George J. Fertig, a scientist employed by the Pittsburgh Testing Laboratory (located in Birmingham), as its president. Fertig claimed that with the South's "temperate climate," "abundant rainfall," and "many raw materials of industry," scientists should turn their attention to research that would encourage industrial development and thus aid the region economically.

The Tennessee Academy reacted in a similar manner. In 1933 it sponsored a symposium focusing on the recently created Tennessee Valley Authority. At the seminar A. E. Parkins, professor of economic geography at George Peabody College, maintained that in addition to water power the state should publicize its timber, limestone, marble, and mineral resources. Paraphrasing the vision of regional planners that the valley development area would be "dominated by small industrial centers each with well-kept factories, neat clean homes, schools, churches, and community houses," he agreed that "low taxes, low rents, home-grown food, wholesome home and community life, modest but sufficient incomes, ought to fit the Valley population to weather future depressions and adversities such as frequently befall human beings."

Such dreams of the future, however, did not materialize so easily. Since the end of the Civil War and through the first decades of the twentieth century, southerners, in their quest for new industry, had consistently promised low taxes, a cheap labor supply, and inexpensive utilities. While such a policy did induce low-paying factories to locate in the South, it failed to attract high-technology, research-oriented industry and thus established a "self-reinforcing pattern of slow growth wherein the potential for social and political disruption was minimal" (Smith 1988, 619). Southern scientists would have to await the post–World War II boom for the sort of economic development and research facilities that they coveted.

Southern scientists displayed keener foresight when they spoke out on behalf of conservation of the region's natural resources, especially when a particular incident caught their attention. In 1923, the North Carolina Academy of Science (NCAS) voted to cooperate with the Virginia Academy of Science (VAS) in "securing the conservation of a selected part of the [Great] Dismal Swamp," a wildlife haven on the border between the two states that appeared to be threatened by real estate developers who proposed that the area be filled in and thereby rendered "useful." In 1929, the VAS resolved to fight the Virginia Public Service Company's efforts to construct a dam at Goshen Pass, a scenic gorge in the Appalachian Mountains. While the academies' contributions to the resolution of these issues are difficult to assess, the Great Dismal Swamp was not drained and filled, and Goshen Pass remains in its natural state.

Both the Tennessee and North Carolina academies expressed continuing concern about foresting operations in the Appalachian Mountains. In 1935, they formally protested what they viewed as the "apparently ruthless and unnecessary destruction of thousands of trees and shrubs by overzealous Civilian Conservation Corps workers." Between 1938 and 1941 the North Carolina Academy successfully petitioned the United States Forest Service to dedicate Black Mountain as a natural area in perpetuity. It also requested that the federal government purchase a "primeval forest" near Highlands for the same purpose, but this wooded haven eventually lost its timber to voracious nearby sawmills.

The Conservation Committee of the NCAS designated itself as a natural resources "watchdog" with crusades that involved the wood duck; wild venus flytrap plants, which evidently were being spirited out of the state illegally; and stream pollution. Perhaps the academy's most satisfying victory came much later, in 1953 and 1954, when it helped to save Crabtree Creek Park, located between Raleigh and Durham, from being covered by airport runways. A successful lobbying effort, mounted by a variety of organizations including the academy, convinced the U.S. government to build Seymour Johnson Air Force Base further east, near Goldsboro (Smith 1988, 597–622).

EDUCATION

A southern educational revival ushered in the new century, but the tasks before the reformers of that generation loomed large. On every measure—per pupil expenditure, length of school terms, teacher preparation and salaries, conditions of schools, attendance and graduation rates—the gap separating the opportunities and performance of black and white children was marked—and the gaps separating southern schools from those in many other parts of the nation were pronounced as well.

By 1900, compulsory attendance at a public or private school was universal outside the states of the old Confederacy, where it was practically nonexistent. As late as 1904, only Tennessee and Louisiana had laws that restricted children under 12 from working. Not until after World War I did states such as South Carolina, Georgia, and Mississippi adopt even weak school attendance policies. These laws met with mixed reactions. When a law was passed in North Carolina making school attendance compulsory for children between the ages of 7 and 14, many parents rebelled. "The government can't tell a man what to do with his children unless its gonna [sic] take over the feeding and clothing of them too." Some parents complained that school kept their children from doing their chores. Whenever I want my children to do something one mother complained, "they say 'I got to study for two testies [sic] tomorrow.'" On the other hand, a father thought the law was a good thing because "some people would not give their children an opportunity to go to school if they were not made to do so." An illiterate mother felt that it was important for her children to go to school, "for a person without education nowadays ain't looked on no better than a dawg [sic]." About 10 percent more nonwhite than white children did not attend school at all due to the woeful conditions of schools for African Americans in the segregated South.

Local boards set school standards, and in some areas of the South the school year was as short as three months. In the rural South, most students went to a school that had only one teacher, and students often had to walk a mile or more to reach these schools. The schoolhouses themselves were usually one-room cabins that leaked when it rained and were cold in the winter. Often there were no desks and children sat on roughly hewn wooden benches. Often school would be canceled because conditions inside the schoolhouse were unbearable. Because teachers were paid around $25.00 a month and the term lasted from three to five months a year, they all held other jobs the rest of the year as housekeepers or farm helpers. With teachers who were usually only a little better educated than their students, the curriculum was limited and determined by gender.

Both boys and girls learned the basics of arithmetic, spelling, and reading, but girls also learned housekeeping and cooking while the boys took a class in agriculture. One mother was pleased that her son was enthused about his agricultural course because maybe it meant he would stay on the farm and help out, instead of moving away as he threatened. In the 1920s, school consolidation came to many areas of the South, and with it an improvement in curriculum and school conditions. But the new schools also brought insecurity and instability to the lives of rural southerners. One mother objected to the consolidated schools where her farm children mixed with town children. As a result her children were making unreasonable demands, such as sandwiches made with white bread instead of cornbread. Or another objected that the children were gone all day because of the distance of the school, which demanded a long bus ride. Others objected to the "badness" they learned from the city children on the bus and at school. One mother complained that town children talked back to the teacher, and her children were picking up that bad habit and bringing it home and talking disrespectfully to her.

Also at the consolidated schools rural children for the first time met children who did not have to work at home, had fine clothes, went to the movies, and did not mind their parents. Consolidation, which was designed to bring children closer together, simply served to remind rural children how different they really were (Hagood 1939, 152–53).

The segregation of schools in the South taxed meager resources even more, as each county had to set up a dual system. Most teachers had only a high school education themselves, and the stock of schoolbooks and equipment was meager. The defining factor of education in the South in the first half of the twentieth century was segregation by race, which invariably meant black schools were woefully underfunded. Often, school boards diverted money intended for black schools to their white counterparts, and blacks were forced to get by with whatever residual funds might remain. New instructional materials invariably went to white schools, while the outdated and worn out went to the black schools.

These discriminatory actions were fought vigorously though not always successfully by southern black citizens. For example, in 1880, black citizens in Augusta, Georgia, under the leadership of the famous educator Richard Wright, managed to get Ware High School established as the public high school for blacks. Almost immediately the white-dominated school board initiated a series of ongoing attempts to close the high school. In 1897 after the *Plessy v. Ferguson* decision, which validated southern segregationist policy, and after black disenfranchisement, Ware High School was finally closed. Blacks took the issue to the Supreme Court but were rebuffed by that body in the *Cumming et al. v. Board of Education of Richmond County* case. Ignoring the racist motivation of the decision to close the school, the Supreme Court said that it could see no discrimination. Furthermore, the Supreme Court stated that education was an issue for the states to manage, not the federal courts. Despite the board's contention that the school's closing was temporary and reversible when black enrollment and the system's finances improved, the school was not reopened for almost 40 years.

In the post–World War I era, blacks of Atlanta organized politically to establish a high school for their children. Although banned from Democratic Party primaries, they could vote in local special elections, and they mobilized to do so to defeat school funding measures proposed by white school boards and white parents. Finally, to get the votes necessary for passage of the budget, the white school board agreed to build a black high school. The name of the school, Booker T. Washington, was significant. The board wanted and succeeded in installing a mainly industrial curriculum, despite pressure from black citizens for a more diversified course of study. The Augusta and Atlanta episodes show how secondary education for blacks in the South was almost nonexistent. Blacks were not completely deprived of high school

Table 4.1 Southern School Statistics, 1900–1930

	Literacy (10 Years of Age and Older)							
	1900		1910		1920		1930	
	White (%)	Black (%)	White (%)	Black (%)	White (%)	Black (%)	White (%)	Black (%)
United States	5.7	4.5	3.7	4	2.5	2.9	1.5	16.3
Alabama	15.2	7.4	10.1	0.1	6.4	1.3	4.8	26.2
Arkansas	11.8	3.0	7.1	6.4	4.6	1.8	3.5	16.1
Florida	9.0	8.4	5.2	5.5	3.1	1.5	1.9	18.8
Georgia	12.2	2.4	8.0	6.5	5.5	9.1	3.3	19.9
Kentucky	13.9	0.1	10.7	7.6	7.3	1.0	5.7	15.4
Louisiana	20.4	1.1	15.0	8.4	11.4	8.5	7.3	23.3
Mississippi	8.1	9.1	5.3	5.6	3.6	9.3	2.7	23.2
N. Carolina	19.6	7.6	12.3	1.9	8.2	4.5	5.6	20.6
Oklahoma	8.1	7.0	3.5	7.7	2.4	2.4	1.7	9.3
S. Carolina	13.9	2.8	10.5	8.7	6.6	9.3	5.1	26.9
Tennessee	14.5	1.6	9.9	7.3	7.4	2.4	5.4	14.9
Texas	5.1	8.2	3.3	4.6	2.2	7.8	1.4	13.4
Virginia	11.4	4.6	8.2	0.0	6.1	3.5	4.8	19.2

Sources: Abstract of the Twelfth Census of the United States, 1900 and 1910, Government Printing Office, Washington, DC, 1912, p. 245; *Abstract of the Fourteenth Census of the United States*, 1920, Government Printing Office, Washington, DC, 1923, pp. 432, 434; *Statistical Abstracts*, Government Printing Office, Washington, DC, 1933, p. 43.

Table 4.2 Annual Expenditures per Pupil in Southern States, 1912–1913 and 1928–1929

	1912–1913		1928–1929	
	White	Black	White	Black
Alabama	$8.50	$1.49	$37.50	$7.16
Arkansas	7.89	2.62	26.91	17.06
Florida	14.75	3.10	78.25	10.57
Georgia	9.18	1.42	31.52	6.98
Kentucky	8.63	6.45	25.27	25.77
Louisiana	16.60	1.59	40.64	7.84
Mississippi	8.20	1.53	31.33	5.94
N. Carolina	6.69	2.50	44.48	14.30
Oklahoma	16.29	12.20	40.48	20.83
S. Carolina	9.65	1.09	52.89	5.20
Tennessee	8.32	3.94	46.52	31.54
Texas	10.89	7.50	46.71	39.66
Virginia	10.92	3.42	47.46	13.30
Average	$10.50	$3.76	$42.30	$15.86

Source: Monroe N. Work, *The Negro Year Book*, 1914–15 and 1931–32. Tuskegee Institute, 1915 and 1933, 232, 223.

studies, however. Many of the private black colleges established after Reconstruction had preparatory departments where black youngsters could get the essentials of a secondary education.

White-dominated school boards of the South did not prevent elementary schooling for black children. But the public elementary schooling that was provided was meagerly financed and usually took place in facilities that were substandard by any definition. Thus, schooling for blacks in the first half of the twentieth century was a largely dismal exercise at every level. Throughout the South, poor black parents supplemented the meager public resources available to them, and black teachers labored heroically under dismal conditions. Only the efforts of historically black colleges such as Fisk University, Hampton Institute, Morehouse College, Spellman College, and Atlanta University, to name several, mitigated the situation and provided a foundation for black intellectual pursuits and a fund for social improvement (Urban and Wagner 2003, 151–53).

Until his death in 1915, and in his legacy thereafter, Booker T. Washington remained central to the growth and purpose of black education, especially in the South. Born into slavery in Virginia in 1856, Washington emerged as the nation's foremost black leader in the post-Reconstruction era. In his 1901 autobiography, *Up from Slavery*, Washington recounted his struggle to escape poverty, obtain an education, and achieve dignity and respectability as a black man in a nation tightly controlled by whites. Ambitious and hardworking, Washington was 16 when he enrolled in

Hampton Institute in 1872. Hampton had been founded by General Samuel Chapman Armstrong, whose missionary parents in Hawaii had taught him to adhere to the principles of the Puritan ethic. Washington absorbed Armstrong's teachings, which emphasized patience, respect for lawful authority, the doctrine of self-help, and the wisdom of gaining and applying the skills and attitudes that would enable one to acquire land, own a home, and provide for one's family.

Washington left Hampton convinced that for black Americans to achieve success, they must develop a sense of racial pride, become responsible citizens, and engage in useful service. In 1881 Washington went to Alabama to organize a secondary and normal school that became Tuskegee University. There he made the work ethic and pragmatic outlook that had been instilled in him the cornerstone of the new institution's educational philosophy. At a time when education was considered by many to consist of acquiring an acquaintance, no matter how slight, with the classical languages and belles lettres, Washington emphasized the dignity of labor and the value of skilled trades.

Admirers applauded Tuskegee for teaching blacks marketable skills that would enable them to become self-sufficient. Along with Hampton, Tuskegee became the model of black higher education most favored by white philanthropists. By the turn of the century, new financial backers such as Andrew Carnegie, the John D. Rockefellers, Sr. and Jr., and the trustees of the General Education Board (founded in 1901) also praised Washington's practical approach and funneled support to Hampton, Tuskegee, and their offshoots.

Many blacks also revered Washington, who was seen to have great acceptance among influential whites, including presidents Theodore Roosevelt and William Howard Taft. Over time Washington became a master at courting the favor of powerful white people and accommodated himself, at least outwardly, to the segregated system that had taken root in the South and in other parts of the nation. Instead of lashing out openly at racial discrimination, Washington chose to work behind the scenes to improve conditions for African Americans. In his public persona, he emphasized the necessity for decency and fair play and encouraged southern blacks to "cast down your bucket where you are" and create a better life through hard work and education. Behind the scenes, however, Washington quietly financed some of the earliest court cases against segregation and in other ways worked to decrease the injustices being done to his race. With scheming that rivaled that of any political boss, Washington developed a network of associates into the "Tuskegee machine" and maintained his power through patronage and shrewdness. As Louis Harlan has pointed out in his excellent biography of Washington, the man was much more complex and enigmatic than he appeared to be when highlighted in the public sphere.

The event that catapulted Booker T. Washington into national prominence (and controversy) and that earned him the label as the great accommodationist occurred in 1895. Addressing a biracial audience at the Cotton States Exposition in Atlanta, Washington insisted that the great majority of his race had little or no interest in social equality, but rather sought goodwill and the opportunity to improve themselves and be of greater service to society. Washington won great applause from the whites who agreed with his pronouncement that "in all things that are purely social we can be as separate as the fingers, yet one as the hand in all things of mutual progress."

Booker T. Washington's perceived willingness to postpone civil and political rights in favor of economic opportunity evoked criticism from some blacks and whites who thought that it encouraged discrimination and in fact retarded economic progress. William Monroe Trotter, the editor of the *Boston Guardian*, a black newspaper, for example, editorialized in 1902 that Washington's acceptance of black disfranchisement was "a fatal blow . . . to the Negro's political rights and liberty." Ida Wells-Barnett, a crusading editor whose Memphis newspaper office was destroyed by a mob in 1892, criticized Washington's virtual silence on the subject of lynching at a time when the practice was near an all-time high in the southern states.

No critic offered a more searching and potent challenge to Washington than did William Edward Burghardt Du Bois. Washington offered him a position in mathematics at Tuskegee, but Du Bois turned it down, having already accepted an offer to teach classics at Wilberforce University in Ohio. After two years at Wilberforce and a year-and-a-half stint at the University of Pennsylvania, working on what became the classic *The Philadelphia Negro*, Du Bois was invited to Atlanta University in 1896. There, for the next 13 years, he and his graduate students in sociology undertook an in-depth study of "the Negro problem" in the South.

As Du Bois probed and exposed the wretched conditions and injustices that defined black peonage in the South, he became increasingly critical of Washington's equivocations on political rights, his submissive concessions to southern caste discriminations, and his narrowly materialistic conception of black education. The rupture between the two black educators became public with the publication in 1903 of Du Bois's *The Souls of Black Folk*. In a chapter titled "Of Mr. Booker T. Washington and Others," Du Bois took direct aim on Washington's public posture of submission and silence on civil and political rights. Du Bois termed Washington's "Atlanta Compromise" a complete surrender of the demand for equality and a ploy to win the esteem of whites that had resulted in his becoming the "most distinguished Southerner since Jefferson Davis, and the one with the largest personal following."

Du Bois found Washington's advocacy of industrial education particularly distasteful and harmful. He accused Washington of preaching a "gospel of Work and Money" to such an extent that the higher aims of life were almost completely overshadowed. In an essay titled "The Talented Tenth," Du Bois wrote the following:

If we make money the object of man-training, we shall develop money-makers but not necessarily men; if we make technical skill the object of education, we may possess artisans but not, in nature, men. Men we shall have only as we make manhood the object of the work of the schools—intelligence, broad sympathy, knowledge of the world that was and is, and of the relation of men to it. This is the curriculum of that Higher Education which must underlie true life.

For Du Bois, the classics, humanities, and social and physical sciences held the knowledge of most worth. The "talented tenth" of the race, the leadership cadre, should be educated, not trained. Despite Du Bois's emphasis on the "higher education of selected youths" and Washington's concern for industrial education for the masses, in actuality both men were seeking leadership of and influence over "the talented tenth," or the black intelligentsia. Whereas Washington wanted to persuade prospective teachers, editors, ministers, and businessmen to guide the race's social development along the self-help and accommodationist lines he favored, Du Bois advocated leadership by a more assertive and articulate class of college-educated men and women like himself.

Du Bois's more aggressive stance led him to confer with other black leaders who favored vigorous resistance rather than accommodation to racism. A series of strategy-planning meetings at Niagara Falls beginning in 1905 led to the formation in 1909 of the National Association for the Advancement of Colored People (NAACP). In time, this group and other civil rights organizations pried open the doors that had denied equal access and treatment to one-third of the South's population.

In the short term, Washington prevailed in his argument with Du Bois, mainly because he was the recipient of millions of dollars from white philanthropists who favored Washington's emphasis on technical skills and service, which fit the designs of the philanthropic empire that sought to impose corporate dominance over American life. With the ear of powerful white philanthropists, Washington was able to get money to support Tuskegee and other schools he endorsed and to deny funds to rivals who threatened Tuskegee's interests. Although generous, these grand donations also served to reinforce the existing racial and class structures.

Mary McLeod Bethune (1875–1955), another leading black educator at the time, chose a third path. She recognized the need for advanced education for minority women and made improvement of African American women's education and socioeconomic status her lifelong commitment. She was born in Mayesville, South Carolina, and was educated in a mission school (Scotia Seminary) and in the Moody Bible Institute. Bethune taught in Florida and Georgia from 1897 to 1903. She founded the Daytona Educational and Industrial Training School for Negro Girls in 1904. Combining the practical with the intellectually uplifting, she created a curriculum that included reading, writing, spelling, arithmetic, cooking, cleaning, sewing, and religion. She maintained her school with financial support from white liberal tourists from the North and blacks and whites in the community. Bethune often had her students sing in tourist hotels to raise funds for the school. In 1923, the school was merged with Cookman Institute of Jacksonville, Florida. Bethune was president of the new Bethune Cookman College from 1904 to 1942 and from 1946 to 1947. Recognized nationally as a leader in education, she used a variety of prestigious national positions to advance the cause of African American education.

In the first half of the twentieth century, with few exceptions, universities in the South remained segregated. And as the new century opened, white schools in the South struggled. Merely staying open in some cases was a great accomplishment for southern colleges, while those in the North began to prosper. Universities such as Princeton and small colleges such as Lafayette in Pennsylvania enjoyed handsome endowments that enabled them to establish large-scale programs. In addition, schools that concentrated on engineering and other scientific fields, such as the

Massachusetts Institute of Technology (MIT), emerged to train a new generation of specialized professionals.

In the South, only the state universities of Virginia and North Carolina offered the doctoral degree prior to the turn of the twentieth century. Other schools throughout the region initiated master's programs in the sciences and strengthened scientific offerings in the undergraduate curriculum. In 1888, the Georgia Institute of Technology opened in Atlanta. Founded at the behest of Henry Woodfin Grady and others who espoused the New South Creed, Georgia Tech operated on the "shop culture" approach rather than that of the "school culture"; that is, it "placed greater stress on practical shop work and produced graduates who could work as machinists or as shop foremen, but who were not well prepared for engineering analysis or original research" (Smith 1988, 603). MIT, on the other hand, "stressed higher mathematics, theoretical science, and original research." Given its orientation and its extremely low faculty salaries, Georgia Tech could not attract prominent scientists to its campus. While the curriculum was broadened during the Progressive era under the leadership of Kenneth G. Matheson, not until World War I did Georgia Tech blossom into a truly modern institution (Smith 1988, 603).

LITERATURE

In the first half of the twentieth century American literature came into its own, and southern writers made an important contribution to this newfound notoriety. Among the most famous were William Faulkner, Thomas Wolfe, Flannery O'Connor, and Carson McCullers, who used the peculiarities of their region for settings and themes that although localized had universal meaning. Also significant were the so-called Fugitives, a group of poets and writers at Vanderbilt University who lamented the passing of an older South and the invasion of modernism.

In the rural South reading material was scant. In the house of a tenant farmer one might find children's schoolbooks, the Bible, and a few farmers' magazines such as *The Progressive Farmer* scattered about. Many houses also considered the Sears Roebuck Catalogue as part of their reading material. Catalogs were designed for hours of fireside reading, with woodcuts and flamboyant descriptions to encourage cover-to-cover browsing. Rooted in the principle of "never omitting the obvious," the description of the "Long Range Wonder Double Barrel Breech Loading Hammerless Shotgun, the World's Wonder" totaled some 3,000 words. If there was not something among the stereoscopes and bicycles, buggies and mackintoshes, dry goods, furniture, and gramophones to catch the buyer's fancy, the final testimonials, glowing recommendations of satisfied customers, and most convincingly the famous money-back guarantee usually did (Hagood 1939, 70–71).

In the first half of the twentieth century, southerners preferred historical novels, especially those that romanticized the glory and gentility of the antebellum South. Often referred to as the "Moonlight and Magnolias" genre, it was an art taken up mainly by women. Mary Johnston, who wrote more than 20 historical novels, penned significant portrayals of both the antebellum and postbellum South. Her *Miss Delicia Allen* (1933) was a classic story of aristocratic grace and romance on a Virginia plantation, and *The Long Roll* (1911) remains one of the best popular treatments of the impact of the Civil War. In 1936 the publication of *Gone With the Wind* confirmed the ascendancy of this romanticized view of the South. Margaret Mitchell's incredibly successful novel relied on stock settings and stereotypes to mythologize the Old South, and her description of the Reconstruction era affirmed the belief that the antebellum era was one of aristocratic gentility lost forever. Standing in stark contrast to this view was William Faulkner, who created his own fictional world in Yoknapatawpha County, based on his own experience of life in Mississippi. His novels exposed the foibles, peculiarities, material struggle, and spiritual and emotional conflicts of the South in which he grew up. On the surface his stories seemed to be simple local yarns, but the universality of the human themes and emotions explored in his work won him international acclaim, including a Nobel Prize (Wilson and Ferris 1989, 862).

HEALTH AND MEDICINE

Beginning at the turn of the century, public health officials moved to fill the vacuum created by failures of the private medical sector. Quite apart from the humanitarian duty to help diseased people, the public health movement in the South rose from the self-interest of whites who required improved health care and more sanitary living conditions for blacks. Black illnesses threatened not only white health but also white pocketbooks. Philanthropic foundations became staunch allies of public health officials in the struggle to safeguard the nation's health, and the South, as the most needy section of the country, was a prime target for organized charity. Before World War I the Rockefeller Foundation in particular worked with federal, state, and local health officials, first to combat hookworm and then to stamp out pellagra. Between 1909 and 1914, the Rockefeller Sanitary Commission led a region-wide campaign designed to eradicate hookworm infection in the South. After almost a year of operation, the campaign's most effective instrument became the dispensaries, or free demonstration clinics that were experiments in health care for the indigent. The dispensaries transformed the campaign from a program of eradication to a program of education. With a strong emphasis on exhortation and persuasion, they were modeled on the evangelical revival and sought to attract rural southerners to a new concept of public health. These clinics were successful in public relations, but they failed to eradicate hookworm disease.

Although for the most part unsuccessful in eradicating the disease, these campaigns inspired a wide range of policy changes in the progressive South. For example, Rockefeller agents early on graphically documented the problem of soil pollution. Surveys had demonstrated that only slightly more than half of all southern rural schools had privies. Many of these privies, probably most of them, did not meet sanitary standards because of improper construction and drainage. These same surveys further demonstrated that careless privy construction posed major health hazards. A study of the rural schools of Lauderdale County, Alabama, found that water samples from 19 out of 20 schools contained fecal matter. Almost as soon as they detected the presence of hookworm, health reformers urged the construction of sanitary privies and the education of rural southerners about their proper use and maintenance. The widespread construction of sanitary privies in the rural South depended on the commitment of the health and educational bureaucracy. In several states school and health officials introduced expanded regulations that strongly encouraged or even required the construction of state-approved privies. In some states the impetus came at the local level. In 1910, for example, the Rowan County, North Carolina, Board of Education agreed with reformers that hookworm disease was "contagious wherever soil pollution is allowed" and that many of its rural schools were "breeding-places for the disease" (Link 1988, 623–42).

When one thinks of public health service one usually thinks of help coming to people in need, but this was not always the case. In the mid-1930s, a group of doctors from the U.S. Public Health Service teamed with local doctors in Alabama to try to understand the syphilis disease. The unknowing subjects of their experiment were black men living in Macon County, Alabama, near Tuskegee Institute. The "Tuskegee Study," as it came to be called, involved a substantial number of men, 399 who had syphilis and an additional 201 who were free from disease to act as controls. All of the syphilitic men were in the late stage of the disease when the study began. The Public Health Service (PHS) sought to discover the effects of syphilis on untreated black men. The 399 syphilitics and the 201 controls believed that they were receiving treatment for "Bad Blood," a term used by rural blacks to describe various ailments, while the PHS carefully denied treatment—even after penicillin became available. The PHS deceived the men into submitting to painful spinal taps, both by calling them a special examination and also by completing them quickly before word of their severity spread through the black community. In return for a meal, the survivors submitted to a yearly PHS exam at the Tuskegee Institute hospital to determine the progress of the disease. Those who passed away were brought to autopsy in return for burial expenses. Local doctors cooperated fully with the PHS and did not offer treatment, and the PHS shielded the men from a statewide venereal treatment program in the late 1930s. Throughout the entire program, which lasted 40 years, no physician raised the question of morality, and few physicians questioned the obvious flaws in the program (Daniel 1981, 303–4).

Material Life

FOOD

In the rural South processed food was slow to reach the poor white and black tenant farmers, who could hardly afford such an expense anyway. Many rural southerners' diets continued to consist of little more than ground cornmeal made into mush or bread, fried salted pork, molasses, and, in season, local greens. Freshwater fish including brim, perch, and catfish, which southerners fried in cornmeal, provided protein, as did fried squirrel, rabbit, and other small mammals that southerners trapped or hunted. Fried rounds of cornbread called hushpuppies usually complemented a fried fish meal. The origin of the word *hushpuppies* has various theories, but a common one in Georgia and North Florida is that while frying the fish in an outside oil pot, the person cooking the fish would throw bits of cornmeal that had fallen off of the fish at the dogs who were howling at the smell of the frying fish. Thus the term *hush puppy*. Around the turn of the century flour began to supplement cornmeal with more frequency as the large flour mills of the Midwest began to produce white flour at a price that even the poorest farmer could afford. This innovation brought one of the most important changes to the southern diet to occur in decades, as flour biscuits became as common on the southern table as corn bread.

The lack of variety in the southern diet, especially the lack of fresh vegetables and fruits, caused pellagra, which resulted from a lack of niacin in the system. This deficiency can be caused by either a lack of green leafy vegetables or a diet with too much corn. Given what rural southerners were eating, both of these causes could be attributed to the deficiency.

In the early 1900s chicken began to challenge pork as the most common meat eaten in the South. For the poorest farmers, however, chicken remained a luxury and therefore became a popular Sunday dish, often served to visitors, including the local preacher. Humorous tales about the preacher's love for chicken abound in both black and white folklore.

Corn remained an important vegetable. Even for breakfast—in the form of cornmeal mush—it maintained its ubiquitous presence on the southern table well into the mid-century. Other important vegetables in the southern diet included cowpeas, sweet potatoes, okra, turnips, and mustard greens. Unlike their northern neighbors, southerners ate the turnip's greens, not its roots. Cowpeas were of many varieties including black-eyed peas, crowder peas, whippoorwills, and tiny lady peas. The water in which these peas was boiled was never thrown away but rather became "pot liquor" into which cornbread was either dunked or crumbled.

In the South the preparation of pork, particularly hams and barbecue, was clearly related to place. For exam-

---

📷 *Snapshot*

Breakfast in the South

Breakfast in the South was one of the most important meals of the day *because* it sustained family members through a hard morning in the fields or a long walk to school. I don't remember the time we would get up in the morning as far as the clock was concerned. We didn't have an alarm clock; Mama just had her inner clock set. Mama always got up first, and she always built the fires. Then she would get us children up; we girls helped with breakfast. We would usually set the table and put the preserves and syrup out while Mama was getting breakfast ready.

We always had hot biscuits, butter, syrup, and preserves, and we usually had bacon, sausage, or ham, and eggs. If we had bacon or sausage we would have cream gravy with our biscuits, but if we had ham, we poured red-eye gravy over the ham. Usually Mama would put the meat on to fry first and then start the coffee—now I'm talking about boiled coffee—and she always put cold water in the coffee pot to settle the grounds. Then she did the gravy and eggs. Then she would start the biscuits. We always had hot biscuits; Papa had to have his hot biscuits. She waited to put the biscuits in last so there would be a hot fire in the oven. I can still hear Mama coming into the room and saying, "Go get your papa up. I'm putting the biscuits in the oven." That was Papa's cue to getup. He would get to the table right when the biscuits were being taken out of the oven. Papa always had a big tumbler of buttermilk with every meal, including breakfast. We drank sweet milk. —Mary Lowry

From: Strickland and Dunn 2002, 15–16.

Snapshot

Weekday Meals in the South

Southern tradition says, "Buttermilk at dinner, sweet milk at supper." And sometimes that was all there was for a meal, but most Southerners were fortunate enough to eat well off the land when they worked hard and planned carefully. Dinner—the noon meal—often consisted of foods left over from Sunday dinner or from breakfast. . . . In the winter, dried beans or peas, carefully winnowed and stored months before, sweet potatoes taken from beneath their insulating bed of straw and dirt, some cold-hardy greens, bread enhanced with that wonderful mixture of sorghum and butter, and maybe something sweet—a fried pie made with dried peaches—were supper staples. Weekday dinners and suppers in the old South were often meatless except, of course, for the salt pork that flavored almost every cooked vegetable. —Dr. Herman Benthul

From: Strickland and Dunn, 2002, 31.

ple, the practice of curing hams by hanging them for six months was most common in Virginia or central Kentucky. Barbecue became so closely tied to place that its method of preparation was integrated into local ritual. In North Carolina, for example, it had to be cooked so long that it fell apart, and it was supposed to be served in shreds in a sandwich. In south-central Kentucky, barbecue consisted of pork shoulder, bones-in, dipped in a peppery sauce and served on slices of white bread. In parts of Texas, sausage links were barbecued. Parts of the South preferred other meats to pork for their barbecue. Texans, for example, ate barbecued beef brisket, and in western Kentucky, mutton was the preferred meat.

Natural environment and local culture have produced a number of very distinctive regional cuisines in the South. The most popular of these was Louisiana's Cajun style, which includes the liberal use of various sorts of peppers, pepper-based sauces, onions, garlic, rice, and beans (Wilson and Ferris 1989, 545–46).

DRINK

The preferred drink in the South among "refined people" was sweet tea. The best way to make it is with sunshine. Sweet sun tea is made in a clear jar with two quarts of water, into which are placed five teabags, and the jar is then allowed to set in the sun for about two hours. With a cup of sugar it becomes sweet tea. The beverage of choice among the not-so-refined, especially the men, was moonshine. It was made in a variety of ways and usually done under the light of the moon to avoid the sheriff's interference, thus the name moonshine.

Another drink that began in the South but soon became America's most popular refreshment was Coca Cola. One fervent admirer called it the "holy water of the American South," and William Allen White once called it the sublimated essence of all that America stands for. John S. Pemberton, known as "Doc," concocted Coca Cola in 1886, primarily as a hangover cure. Soon after inventing it, he sold the patent rights to Asa Candler for $1,750, who in turn sold it in 1919 to the Coca Cola Company for $25 million. At the time it was the largest financial deal in the history of the American South. The prime mover of the 1919 transaction was the banker Ernest Woodruff. His son Robert (1889–1985) took over the company in 1923. Until World War II, when the Coca Cola Company decided it had a patriotic duty to get Coke to thirsty servicemen abroad, the drink was chiefly marketed in the United

States. After the war its fame spread internationally and it became a symbol of the United States as recognizable as the American flag. Asa Chandler briefly flirted with the idea in 1900 of Coca Cola cigars and Coca Cola chewing gum, but until the 1950s the company remained strictly a one-product enterprise.

> **📷 Snapshot**
>
> **Sunday Dinner**
>
> Almost everyone—except perhaps the cooks—looked forward to the traditional Southern Sunday dinner. This was the special meal of the week when favorite dishes requiring extra cooking time and attention as well as cherished ingredients like plenty of cream, butter, white sugar, and eggs were prepared by the women: fried chicken, mashed potatoes, creamed corn, cakes, and pastry desserts—pies or fruit cobblers. Understandably, eating during the rest of the day was light. . . maybe a watermelon in the middle of the afternoon, and milk and corn bread at supper. The large amount of cooking for Sunday dinner not only made that meal special for guests, but also provided leftovers for the week, when labor in the fields and around the farm prevented elaborately cooked meals. —Gertrude McDonald
>
> *From: Strickland and Dunn 2002, 69–70.*

HOUSING

The basic housing style found throughout much of South was the shotgun house—one room wide, one story tall, and several rooms deep (usually three or more), with its primary entrance in the gable end. These houses allowed air to pass freely through the house, thus offering some relief in the long, hot southern summers. The perpendicular alignment of the shotgun house breaks with the usual Euro-American pattern, in which the gables are on the sides and the entrance is on the facade or long side. Although gable-entry houses occur in some parts of central Africa, the shotgun house is a New World hybrid that developed in the West Indies and entered the United States via New Orleans in the early nineteenth century. The shotgun house was popularized in New Orleans, first seen there definitively in 1832, though there is evidence that houses sold in the 1830s were built 15 to 20 years earlier. They were eventually built heavily throughout the South, because their great length allowed for excellent air flow, while their narrow frontage increased the number of plots that could be fitted along a street.

Shotgun houses were most popular before widespread ownership of the automobile allowed people to live farther from businesses and other destinations, and when building lots were kept small out of necessity, 30 feet (9 meters) wide at most. An influx of people to cities, both from rural areas in America and from foreign countries, all looking to rapidly fill emerging manufacturing jobs, created the high demand for housing in cities. Shotgun houses were thus built to fulfill the same need as row houses in northeastern cities. Several were usually built at a time by a single builder, contributing to their relatively similar appearance.

A well-known theory for the shotgun house's popularity over other available styles of housing was that in New Orleans and some other cities, property tax was based on lot width; thus, a shotgun house would minimize property taxes. But the most compelling reason was probably its cheap construction cost and superior natural air-cooling qualities, in a time long before air conditioning. The many later variations suggest adaptation to conditions not present when the shape was first used, showing that its flexibility probably contributed to its popularity. The rooms of a

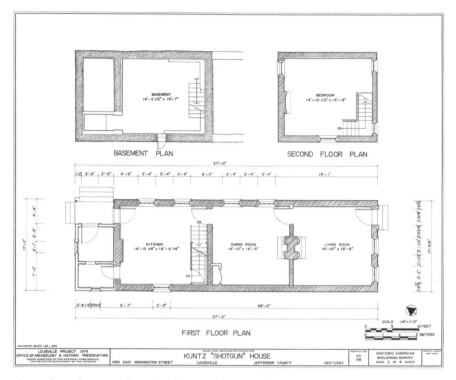

BASEMENT
14'–2 1/2" x 15'–7"

UP

BASEMENT PLAN

BEDROOM
14'–10 1/2" x 16'–0"

DN

SECOND FLOOR PLAN

57'–0"

KITCHEN
14'–10 1/4" x 16'–6 1/4"

DINING ROOM
14'–10" x 14'–9"

LIVING ROOM
14'–10" x 14'–9"

57'–0"

FIRST FLOOR PLAN

SCALE: 1/4"=1'-0"

LOUISVILLE PROJECT 1974
OFFICE OF ARCHEOLOGY & HISTORIC PRESERVATION
UNDER DIRECTION OF THE NATIONAL PARK SERVICE,
UNITED STATES DEPARTMENT OF THE INTERIOR

DRAWN BY: BAYER LEE, 1974

KUNTZ "SHOTGUN" HOUSE

1401 EAST WASHINGTON STREET   LOUISVILLE   JEFFERSON COUNTY   KENTUCKY

SURVEY NO.
KY
119

HISTORIC AMERICAN
BUILDINGS SURVEY
SHEET 2 OF 4 SHEETS

Floor plan of a typical single shotgun house with bathroom. The shotgun was the most popular house style in the American South from the 1860s to the 1920s. Library of Congress.

shotgun house are lined up one behind the other; typically a living room is first, then one or two bedrooms, and finally a kitchen in back. Early shotgun houses were not built with bathrooms, but in later years a bathroom with a small hall was built before the last room of the house, or a side addition was built off of the kitchen. Some shotguns may have as few as two rooms. Chimneys tended to be built in the interior, allowing the front and middle rooms to share a chimney with a fireplace opening in each room. The kitchen usually has its own chimney.

Other than the basic floor layout, shotgun houses have many standard features in common. The house is almost always close to the street, sometimes with a very short front yard, and a porch. The purpose of the entire house is to create a breezeway throughout the house. The purpose of the porch is to allow the hot air to cool slightly before entering the breezeway. In some cases, the house has no front yard and is actually flush with the street or, if there is one, the sidewalk. The original steps were wood but were often replaced with permanent concrete steps.

Folklorist John Michael Vlach suggests that the origin of the building style and the name itself may trace back to Haiti and Africa in the 1700s and earlier. The name may have originated from Africa's Southern Dahomey Fon area term *to-gun*, which means "place of assembly." The description, probably used in New Orleans by Afro-Haitian slaves, may have been misunderstood and reinterpreted as "shotgun." Folk etymology and oral tradition assert that the word comes from the design of the house, which would allow a person to shoot a shotgun through the front door and hit something out the back door without disturbing anything in the house.

The theory behind the earlier African origin is tied to the history of New Orleans. In 1803, there were 1,355 free blacks in the city; by 1810 blacks outnumbered whites 10,500 to 4,500. This caused a housing boom, and as many of both the builders and inhabitants were Africans by way of Haiti, historians believe it is only natural they modeled the new homes after ones they left behind in their homeland. Many surviving Haitian dwellings of the period, including about 15 percent of the housing stock of Port-au-Prince, resemble the single shotgun houses of New Orleans. This theory is now widely accepted by historians.

In the 1920s and 1930s, the rapidly expanding middle class and the enormous mobility offered by the automobile began a movement outward from the cities into newly developing suburbs. Until this movement to new unpopulated areas, southerners usually found themselves in houses dominated by the tradition and natural environment of their region. That meant a house of one or two stories with shaded porches and breezeways that allowed for the free flow of air to provide some relief from the long hot summers that usually began in April and lasted through October. The most popular nontraditional architectural design to invade the South in the 1920s was the bungalow style, which synthesized precedents from many sources without mimicking any. These houses were basically wooden with masonry complements such as porches, chimneys, piers, and retaining walls. The style has low lines and generous roofs with broad sloping overhangs. Windows are commonly short and grouped together to take advantage of breezes. Floor plans flow from one space to another, which renders a feeling of openness. Typically, circulation was through the living room, which often had a large fireplace. Although originating in California, the style was available throughout the country. Even the Sears and Roebuck catalog carried California bungalow house plans for the meager price of five dollars. Southerners embraced this style, which had been designed for a similar climate, and it was built throughout the region for middle- to low-income housing, in small towns and large. One can readily date the period of growth and expansion of certain sections of cities by the presence of whole groups of these bungalows in a neighborhood. One such subdivision is Riverside in Miami, along west Flagler Street.

Art deco design, which celebrated the new age of the machine and utilized the newly discovered designing possibilities of poured concrete, was first used in large office buildings and then in large residences and apartment complexes. In the 1930s Miami Beach, which was experiencing a building boom due to its rising status as a vacation resort, was inundated with art deco enthusiasts, who gave the area the largest concentrated collection of this style in the country. Not only hotels, but two- to four-story low-cost apartment buildings of similar design sprang up nearby to provide housing for hotel and restaurant employees.

In the early to mid-twentieth century, revivals became a popular architectural form for middle-class southerners. Renaissance and colonial revival styles were the most common. In the 1920s along the rapidly expanding southeastern coast of Florida, the neo-Italianate, a revival of the Italian villas of the Mediterranean, dominated the newly developed cities of George Merrick's Coral Gables and Addison Mizner's Boca Raton in South Florida (Wilson and Ferris 1989, 56, 99–103).

CLOTHING

In the final decades of the nineteenth century and increasingly throughout the twentieth century, the South experienced trends in women's fashion that characterized the entire nation. Hemlines rose and fell; waistlines shifted, disappeared, and reappeared. Areas of focus moved from head to bosom to leg and back again; the model type moved from the "Gibson Girl" to the "New Look" and ultimately the "American Look" characterized by egalitarianism, freedom, comfort, casualness, and action. These varied fashion trends reflected and facilitated change toward an increasingly homogenized national lifestyle. Some women's styles in the South, however, remained distinctive, especially in the rural area and the mill towns. Mills in the upland South provided inexpensive ready-made clothing, but shirts and dresses were frequently made at home from the white or print cotton sacks that staples such as rice and flour were packaged in. Women in this area often wore men's shoes. The nineteenth-century view of women lingered into the twentieth. Consequently, some of the more radical styles of the 1920s that seemed to threaten the virtue and place of women were met with resistance. Religious leaders, newspaper editors, and public officials openly denounced styles such as the slit skirt of 1913 and the flapper look of the 1920s.

Southern men's clothing remained relatively unchanged in the first decades of the twentieth century, although among workmen in the South there was a growing preference for bib overalls. Specific occupations required specific clothing. For example, carpenters, cobblers, tailors, and blacksmiths all had distinctive work aprons, and street vendors often wore colorful clothing that distinguished them to passersby. Southern blacks preferred clothes of bright colors and bold design. Although poor, most blacks tried to maintain at least one set of "Sunday go to meeting clothes," which they kept cleaned and pressed for church services and other special occasions (Wilson and Ferris 1989, 613).

Although the "American Look" reigned supreme, local and sectional variations created practical responses to differences in climate and status. The clothing needs of a south Georgia farmer's wife, for example, were far different from those of an office worker in Atlanta. A female sociologist studying white tenant women in the mid-1930s noticed a prevailing fashion mode: "the cotton dress, faded and otherwise in fairly good condition, a well worn and usually ragged sweater in cool weather, no hose, shoes out at the toes and run over at the heels." Although she saw no women barefoot in winter, she noticed many went without shoes in the summer. Variations from the mode were numerous, she noted, but not without limitations. No woman wore a dress more elaborate than a ruffled cotton house frock, none had high heels, and very few used makeup or nail polish. The best-dressed woman of the group wore a clean dark blue broadcloth dress with a prim starched collar, embroidered apron, silk hose, and two-toned saddle sport shoes. At the other end of the spectrum were women with ragged and torn dresses and several in overalls. In summer she noted that it was evident that a few wore no underwear, but in the winter none was without some sort of heavy wrap, even if it was an old worn-out man's overcoat (Hagood 1939, 67).

MANUFACTURING

By the end of the nineteenth century, southern iron made its most successful incursion in a hard-fought struggle for sectional dominance. From their first visits to the South ironmasters of the North believed that certain southern advantages—

abundant ore, proximity to seaports, and cheap labor— might prove decisive in making the South dominant in the iron and steel industry. A delegation that included Andrew Carnegie toured the coal and iron districts of the South in 1889 "to spy out the land." Carnegie declared that "the South is Pennsylvania's most formidable industrial enemy" (Woodward 1974, 127–28). By the end of the nineteenth century, the South was producing far more pig iron than the entire nation produced before the Civil War, and investment in blast furnaces was mounting faster than in any northern state.

In addition to the iron industry, the South took the lead in several phases of the second Industrial Revolution, which dominated the last years of the nineteenth and the first decades of the twentieth century. The most important single mechanical innovation in the South was the cigarette machine invented by James A. Bonsack, a young Virginian still in his teens, and patented in 1880. And other southern inventors added numerous devices for packing, bagging, labeling, and processing tobacco. New men, uninhibited by the traditions and complacency of the old order, William T. Blackwell, James R. Day, Julian S. Carr, R. J. Reynolds, the Dukes, and their kind, were of the breed that had seized control of beef, petroleum, and steel in the North. The leader was James Buchanan Duke. "I had confidence in myself," he declared. "I said to myself, 'If John D. Rockefeller can do what he is doing for oil, why should not I do it in tobacco.'" "Tobacco is the poor man's luxury," he observed, thereby announcing the foundational principle of several southern fortunes and religious endowments based on the processing and selling of a harmful habit-forming weed (Woodward 1974, 309).

As the new century began, Duke began his plan to imitate Rockefeller's feats in oil. In 1901, he fused his Continental Tobacco and American Tobacco companies into Consolidated Tobacco, and he was well on his way to bringing the entire industry under his control. He had also purchased the patent for Bonsack's cigarette machine. Duke had taken quite a gamble, for there were many forces that stood in his way. In the South every state but Louisiana either had or was planning legislation against the use of cigarettes. The growing consensus at the time was that cigarettes were harmful. In 1907, several business owners announced that they were refusing to hire smokers, causing the *New York Times* to comment that "Business . . . is doing what all the anti-cigarette specialists could not do." And, in 1906, in Kentucky, an angry group of farmers formed the "Night Riders," who donned hoods and rode horses out to terrorize other farmers who sold tobacco to Duke's price-gouging American Tobacco Company. They burned barns and fields and even lynched some who sold their product to Duke. By 1911, Duke's American Tobacco Company controlled 92 percent of the world's tobacco business. But in that same year the Supreme Court ordered the dissolution of his company. Duke remained steadfast and, despite numerous setbacks, events would soon alter the fate of the tobacco industry.

In 1917 the United States entered World War I, and the army command became convinced that cigarettes would distract soldiers from other more serious vices like whiskey and women. General George Pershing declared, "You ask me what we need to win this war. I answer tobacco as much as bullets. Tobacco is as indispensable as the daily ration; we must have thousands of tons without delay." Duke's most popular

A Lucky Strike cigarettes ad from 1929. The Granger Collection, New York.

brand, Bull Durham, launched an advertising campaign that announced, "When our boys light up, the Huns will light out" (www.journalstar.com/articles/2005/05/22/Sunday_am/doc428 b981453c7e539709681.bat). Resistance to cigarettes collapsed, as those opposed to sending cigarettes to the doughboys were accused of being traitors. As a result of this campaign, an entire generation of young men returned from military service addicted to cigarettes, and thanks to the war and aggressive new marketing strategies, the 1920s witnessed the cigarette's triumph over the cigar, pipe, and snuff as the most popular form of tobacco consumption.

Although southerners liked their tobacco, cigarettes were slow to catch on in the region. Shortly after the Civil War, Virginian Samuel Schooler remarked that he knew the man he was looking at was an outsider as he "knew he did not belong about here—he was smoking a cigarette which is unheard of in these parts." Up through World War I in the South, the preferred use of tobacco was in the form of snuff, a finely ground tobacco in powder form that was inhaled through the nostrils. Southern boys returned from the war with the new cigarette habit, and cigarettes soon challenged cigars and snuff as the preferred form of tobacco inhalation. But old habits die hard, and snuff remained popular, especially in the rural South. Although snuff remained popular, those who identified with the New South, particularly those in the cities, took up the modern habit of cigarette smoking.

The dramatic elements in the rise of the southern cotton mill gave the movement something of the character of a crusade. The successful competition with New England, the South's old political rival, the popular slogan, "bring the factories to the fields," and the organized publicity that attended every advance, combined to enshrine the cotton mill in a somewhat exalted place in southern history. The cotton textile industry in the South traced its roots to pre–Civil War days; however, the industry did not really take off until the late nineteenth century. A report on the cotton-textile industry published in 1900 stated, "The growth of the industry in the South is the one great fact in its history during the past ten years." The number of mills in the South grew from 161 in 1880 to 400 in 1900, which represented an increase of 67.4 percent in the 1890s. A great number of the new mills, moreover, were equipped with more up-to-date machinery than the mills of the old textile regions. The first factory operated entirely by electricity was located in the South, and many improvements first found their way into the country through that region. The increase in the number of mills revealed only a fraction of the expansion. In the four leading states of North and South Carolina, Georgia, and Alabama—in which virtually all the increase took place—the average number of spindles per mill increased from 3,553 in 1880 to 10,651 in 1900. In total number of spindles the same states rose from 1,195,256 in 1890 to 3,791,654 in 1900, or an increase of 217 percent in the 1890s.

Both the historians and the promoters of the cotton-mill campaign held that the movement was motivated by "moral incitement" and became "a form of civic piety" in the South. While the incentives common to most industrialization were admittedly present, especially the promise of cheap labor in the highly competitive and cost-sensitive textile industry, "the moral considerations" played a large part in the southern campaign to bring textile manufacturing to the South. Profits mattered and mill owners did well. In the early years of the movement, according to the census report of 1900, "the return upon investment in southern cotton mills has greatly exceeded that upon factories in the North."

But the possibility of cotton mills raising the standard of southern living explained the public zeal that, in the Carolinas, Georgia, and Alabama, converted an economic development into a civic crusade inspired with a vision of social salvation. Not only did this process occur in the efficient chambers of commerce of cities like Charleston, Atlanta, and Charlotte, big newspapers, and among northern visitors and settlers, but even more typically in isolated Piedmont towns. Old market villages of a few hundred citizens, which had drowsed from one Saturday to the next since the eighteenth century, were suddenly aflame with the mill fever and "a passion for rehabilitation." Stock was often subscribed in small holdings. Early mill executives came from backgrounds as lawyers, bankers, farmers, merchants, teachers, preachers, doctors, and public officials. City dailies and country weeklies devoted columns to the crusade, and itinerant evangelists added the theme to their repertoire. "Even machinery was wrapped with idealism and devotion," according to one account.

Much was made by mill promoters of the philanthropic motive of giving "employment to the necessitous masses of poor whites." Undoubtedly this motive was sincere in some cases. Its force, however, is somewhat diminished by evidence submitted by the promoters themselves. Francis W. Dawson of Charleston, one of the most forceful propagandists for cotton mills, wrote that employment in the mills subjected the poor whites "to elevating social influences, encourages them to seek education, and improves them in every conceivable respect." In the same editorial he stated that in South Carolina there were at that time "2,296 operatives, upon whom 7,913 persons are dependent for support. The amount paid out in wages monthly is \$38,034" (Woodward 1974, 134). Noble intentions aside, in reality during the first decade of the twentieth century the average worker and dependent earned an income of a little over 12 cents a day, necessitating entire families, including women and children, to work in the mills together. By 1929, that salary had increased to \$12.94 a week, but in the Northeast the same amount of work earned \$19.82 a week, or about 52 percent more. And by the time of the Great Depression many had lost faith in the redemptive power of the mills. Typical of the attitudes of southerners toward mills was that of one sharecropping woman who in 1932 believed it would make no difference who was elected president, because the Depression had been caused by machines displacing men from jobs (Hagood 1939, 59; Woodward 1974, 131–40).

As rising debt and falling cotton prices forced families into mill towns, they did their best to bring as much of their world as possible into their new environment. A typical mill village contained a three-story brick factory often designed in Greek revival or neo-Roman style, creating a visual statement of the noble ambitions of the owners. Near the factory was the company store, the superintendent's house, and the factory-built church. Throughout the rest of the town were three- to four-room worker houses. In contrast to the extravagantly designed factory building, these houses were wood frame vernacular style, often shotgun houses. Around each house was a space for a vegetable garden and, as they had on the farm, families worked together in the factory. Children depended on their families for security and protection, while parents depended on children to work and contribute their earnings to the family. Village members depended on and helped each other. One person recalled that her village was "one big community"; families gathered together for hog killing in late summer or early fall and they shared common pasture land for cows and pens for their hogs. If someone was sick other villagers brought food to the family and even took up collections for a family in need. The benefits of a tight community also had its drawbacks because everyone knew everyone's business, and the town maintained rigid standards to which everyone had to adhere. It was not uncommon for a divorced women or a woman with an illegitimate child to be forced to leave town. One of the greatest adjustments to village life was the change in the pace of life from the natural rhythms of the sun and the seasons to the rigidity of factory time.

The factory owner was often a person of high ideals and hopes of lifting up his economically and socially deprived workers. Factory owners' attitudes created a paternalistic society in which the factory owner not only provided the church, the teacher, and a visiting doctor, but he might also send a supervisor through the streets at night to tell everyone to be in bed after nine o'clock. Workers accepted this paternalism when they wanted it, for example, company-sponsored baseball teams and schools, but they rejected that which they didn't want, such as cooking and child-rearing classes. Workers went to the factory early in the morning to spend 10 to 12 hours in a poorly ventilated, noisy, and dusty environment. The lint that fell onto their clothes and hair marked them as mill workers, and the cotton dust that filled their lungs marked them for an early death. The worker's most powerful protest before the establishment of unions in the 1930s was moving out. Factory workers often packed up and moved on to another mill town if they heard there were better wages, a kinder supervisor, or better living conditions, or they had felt slighted for some reason by their current employer. Created with the promise of redeeming the South, the mill villages, while in fact creating places of employment for displaced farmers, never quite arrived at their goal. After the boom of the World War I years, the decline in the cotton supply, the shortening of women's dresses in the 1920s, and the opening of textile factories outside the United States, put the mill villages into an economic depression long before the rest of the nation. Unlike the rest of the nation, the mill villages never recovered fully (Hall 1979, 245–86).

In the new century mining began to play a major role in the new industrial South. Many new mining towns sprang up and others grew into cities because of the mines. Birmingham was an example. In the 1880s, it was described as "a staring, bold, mean little town: marshes and mud roads everywhere and shallow pine shacks and a box car for a depot, and gamblers and traders from and over the globe." By 1900, it boasted a population of 38,415. The rapid growth of coal mining in Kentucky, Virginia, Maryland, Tennessee, Alabama, and Arkansas attracted thousands of southern farm workers to these areas in search of work and a better life. Three decades into the new century, that promise still eluded them. Workers and their families found themselves practically imprisoned in towns controlled by the mine owners. Miners had to trade at the company store where prices were higher than at outside stores. To work they had to sign agreements called "yellow dog contracts," by which they agreed not to join a union or take part in any demonstration against the company. Denied the right to organize, they remained virtually in the custody of the company officer, who often was deputized by the county sheriff.

Most miners in the South on the eve of the Great Depression lived in unspeakable poverty, with a hovel for shelter, the poorest of clothing, a poor diet, no sanitation, and little medical attention, all of which led to early death. The average life expectancy

Coal mining scene, near Bluefield, West Virginia, showing four men with a railcar full of coal at the mine entrance. Library of Congress.

of a worker after entering the mines was 15 years. Life was especially precarious in smaller mines, which in the struggle to survive neglected basic safety precautions. Carelessly hung electric wires and neglected slate roofs caused many deaths that could have been prevented if precautions had been taken. Dampness and poor ventilation resulted in lung disease caused by the daily inhalation of coal dust, and by the age of 35 a young man was already a wheezing invalid crippled by partially collapsed blackened lungs. Working hours varied, as miners were paid by the carload of coal. A fully loaded car brought from 35 to 50 cents. A lucky miner was able to load three to four carloads a day, but sometimes the foreman sent him home after one, and after loading the car he had to clean up the slate and dirt in his work station, and for this he received no pay. In mining towns there were usually more workers than needed; therefore, the mine owners gave all the men a few days' work rather than a few men full-time work. This enabled the mine owners to keep the workers' wages from getting higher than the amount owed to the commissary.

In the Depression year of 1932, the average miner made $30 a month; thus, the deductions from his pay left him only around $15 a month for family necessities such as food and clothing. At the end of each month the worker was a little more in debt to the company store. The miner usually was forced to take his pay in highly inflated company scrip that was only good at the company store. If his month's statement showed that he earned $35, in reality he only had made about $25 inasmuch as prices at the company store were 25 to 100 percent higher than chain store prices. When the inflated scrip ran out, often long before the end of the month, his wife had to "draw" on scrip from the company store, and by payday the miner generally discovered that he had drawn all his earnings. Barbershops and movie theaters also accepted scrip at 20 to 30 percent above the price for cash. Many companies made more profit off their store than they did the coal mine, and some operated mines simply to have renters and customers for their stores.

The miners' homes were usually poorly constructed shacks closely set in a row along hillsides or creek bottoms. The worst were without plaster, running water, toilets, or sanitation facilities of any kind. Cracks in the walls were covered with newspapers and plastered with a flour and water mixture. Water was carried from springs or roadside creeks, and outhouse toilets were built over a creek or over a slope in the back yard. The cow, if the miner was fortunate enough to own one, was stabled either next to the house or under it, if it was built on stilts on a hillside. For the miner who succeeded in becoming a foreman, conditions were somewhat improved. He may have had running water in his house, solid walls, a door that shut tightly, and a small front yard.

Many miners maintained vegetable gardens to supplement their diet. Food was always a problem. Compelled to pay exorbitant prices at the commissary, it was difficult to maintain a healthy family diet. Corn bread made from meal and water was a common part of the diet, as well as potatoes either fried or mashed. In Kentucky, pumpkins that local farmers raised for livestock were often donated to miners for food when there was a surplus. In growing months, miners' wives foraged for greens, and for weeks these greens, eaten with fat meat and corn bread, provided the main meal of the day.

Even with New Deal legislation such as the Wagner Act, which established workers' rights to organize, and the Guffey Act, which protected the price of coal, the miners' struggle for better working conditions and pay was not easily won. Coal mines were struggling in the 1930s and were not in a position to grant many demands. Competition within the industry had increased, because too many mines had been opened and there was new competition from other energy sources, specifically oil and gas. Idleness caused chronic restlessness, and the danger of the work when it was available spread bitterness also. Workers attempted to renew their struggle with management in the mid-1930s under the leadership of John L. Lewis, president of the United Mine Workers Union (UMW).

Supported by pro-labor legislation of the New Deal, John L. Lewis, as head of the newly formed Congress of Industrial Organizations, had led successful strikes in the auto and steel industries, but under the dire conditions in the coal industry and due to Lewis's own management style, a solution for the miners did not come as easily. It would not be until after World War II that mine workers would see an improvement in their conditions (Couch 1934, 361–73).

On the eve of the Great Depression, the five leading southern states in manufacturing were North Carolina, Virginia, Alabama, Tennessee, and Georgia. Although cotton remained the most important industrial product, southern iron and steel plants concentrated chiefly in Alabama, Tennessee, and West Virginia had advanced remarkably, producing products valued at $396 million on the eve of the Great Depression. Alabama reported 21 steel mills with 11,630 workers, ranking the state fifth in the country in iron production. Other industries in the South included the cottonseed oil industry, primarily in Texas, and the furniture industry in North Carolina, Tennessee, and Virginia. In the north Florida panhandle the paper industry also began developing around the turn of the century and continued to grow through the post–World War II era (Couch 1934, 80–92).

TRANSPORTATION

In the first decades of the twentieth century, the South had fewer automobiles per capita than other parts of the country. Mules still provided the power on every black farm and most white ones. However, by the 1920s trucks were hauling increasing amounts of goods, and by the 1930s buses linked many towns that had heretofore been isolated. Getting to market, going to church, or gathering for special occasions became easier as roads improved and motorized transport replaced foot- and mulepower as the ways to get around. Along the waterways, boats, barges, and ferries remained important for moving crops, goods, and people. Railroads also continued as vital links across the region.

Despite the backwardness of transportation in the South, in the most southern area of the United States, in an era that marveled at engineering wonders such as the Brooklyn Bridge and the Panama Canal, Henry Flagler built a "Railroad to the Sea," which would be called the "Eighth Wonder of the World." Flagler, the son of a minister, realized his dream of becoming rich when in 1867 he partnered with a young John D. Rockefeller, and along with Samuel Andrews they formed the Standard Oil Company. At 57, Flagler became impatient with the daily routines of the very successful company and sought new outlets for his creative genius. He found the project of his dreams in Florida. In 1885, Flagler wrote a close friend, "I believe, we can make St Augustine the Newport of the South" (Akin 1991, 116). St. Augus-

This undated photo shows a passenger train crossing Knight's Key Bridge in Florida. Library of Congress.

Mr. H. M. Flagler and his party leave the first train to arrive at Key West, Florida, on the Oversea Florida East Coast Railroad in January 1912. Library of Congress.

tine had fascinated Flagler from the time of his first visit with his ailing wife, Mary Harkness Flagler. He dreamed of transforming the ancient Spanish colonial village into the finest resort town on the East Coast. He hired the prestigious architectural firm of Career and Hastings to design hotels, to enhance the Spanish ambiance of the town.

Soon the town, which had no adequate hotels when Flagler first arrived, boasted the grand Ponce de Leon Hotel (mentioned in *The Great Gatsby*), then considered one of the finest hotels in America. From St. Augustine Flagler moved down the coast, building hotels in new resort areas and constructing a railroad along the way to provide transportation for the wealthy clientele, mostly his New York business associates who began to winter in Florida during the Gilded Age. By 1895, Flagler's Florida East Coast railroad had reached the new town of Miami. But the journey did not end there. With the announcement of the building of the Panama Canal, the 74-year-old Flagler saw new opportunities and began planning the building of his railroad to Key West, the closest American port on the Atlantic side of the canal. The biggest project of the age was building Panama Canal, but to many Americans the second largest project was the Florida East Coast Extension, and it also captured the attention of the United States and the international public. When the project began in 1905, engineers estimated that the line could be completed in eight years. But due to hurricanes, mosquitoes, and various unanticipated problems connected with the logistics of building 128 miles of railroad over the ocean, it took over 11 years to finish the project.

On January 22, 1912, Henry Flagler stood on the platform of his private railroad car as the Key West crowd below gave him a tumultuous welcome. The citizens of Key West, isolated for so long off the tip of Florida, now felt united with the mainstream of American commerce, and the oft-maligned Flagler, wealthy Standard Oil pioneer and Florida East Coast developer, now felt his much criticized business decision vindicated. The Key West extension, often referred to during its construction as "Flagler's Folly," was now being dubbed the "Eighth Wonder of the World." Flagler died a little over a year after realizing his greatest accomplishment.

He did not live to see the financial collapse and demise of his cherished

J. R. Parott, H. M. Flagler, and others at the opening of Florida Keys Railway in 1912. Library of Congress.

project. Cargo entering the Caribbean from the Panama Canal never was transferred to Flagler trains in Key West as planned. Lack of adequate storage facilities at Key West kept products on their ocean vessels until they reached their northern destinations. The train did bring tourists and products to Key West, but never at the rate to make a profit. In 1935, a hurricane destroyed much of the ailing line and proved to be its death blow. The Florida East Coast Railroad went into receivership and the federal government bought the entire right of way for a fraction of what it had cost to build. Using the roadbed and bridges as a base, the federal government built a roadway to Key West, which opened three years later. Cars that travel to Key West today still travel over the roadbed created by Flagler's workers in the early 1900s, and if one gazes out onto the water, the bridges that once carried trains out to sea can still be seen.

Political Life

GOVERNMENT

During the late nineteenth and early twentieth centuries, the region solidified its reputation as "the benighted South," "the Nation's Number One economic problem," and the home of race-baiting demagogues. Political scientist V. O. Key, after examining the politics of the period, stated, "The South may not be the nation's number one political problem, as some northerners assert, but politics is the South's number one problem." Key identified the failures of southern politics with the fact that there was no viable Republican Party, leaving the Democrats in control of a one-party system. As Key explained, "in the confusions and distractions of one-party politics broad issues of economic philosophy are often obscured or smothered by irrelevant appeals, sectional loyalties, local patriotism, personal candidacies, and, above all, by the specter of the black man." More fundamentally, Key emphasized the success of white elites in the black-belt plantation counties, who impressed "on an entire region a philosophy agreeable to its necessities and succeeded for many decades in maintaining a regional unity in national politics to defend these necessities." Although often challenged, socioeconomically privileged whites of the black belt emerged victorious from the crucial political crises in southern history and were the primary architects of the system of white supremacy and black disfranchisement upon which the one-party system rested. Normally allied with town merchants, businessmen, and industrialists, plantation-oriented whites induced other groups within southern society "to subordinate to the race question all great questions of the day." They largely succeeded in doing so until the Depression of the 1930s forced public figures to face squarely the need for economic development and relief.

In *Origins of the New South*, C. Vann Woodward notes the "paradoxical combination of white supremacy and progressivism" and suggests that the Progressive movement failed to fulfill "the political aspirations and deeper needs of the mass of people." In the South, because of issues of race, Progressivism did not fit to the characteristics of the national movement. In general Progressives divided into two wings, the stronger of which was a rural-based antitrust movement that sought to defend local values, while the other was "urban-based, professional-minded, bureaucratizing and centralizing" in thrust. Some historians depict segregation and disfranchisement as the "seminal" Progressive reforms, and they locate substantial continuity between populism and Progressivism and stress white consensus on "the great race settlement of 1890–1910."

Other historians contend that southern Progressivism was a reaction to lower-class insurgency that threatened the Democratic Party's domination of political power in the South. Democratic elites responded with a "revolt against democracy" that sought "the stabilization of society, especially the economy, in the interests of the local established powers, at the expense of the lower strata of society in the South, and sometimes at the expense of out-of-state corporations." The leading proponents of this program of disfranchisement and reform were plantation elites who "bore striking resemblances to antebellum 'patricians.'" Despite the varying interpretations of the government and politics of the South in the first half of the twentieth century, the underlying issue of all politics remained a white consensus that the black population should remain disenfranchised, segregated, and politically emasculated. With few exceptions, southern whites successfully created this reality, which was not broken until after World War II.

LAW, CRIME, AND PUNISHMENT

A tendency toward violence has been one of the character traits most frequently attributed to southerners. In various guises, the image of the violent South confronts the historian at every turn: dueling gentlemen and masters whipping slaves, flatboatmen indulging in rough-and-tumble fights, lynching mobs, country folk at a bear baiting or gander pulling, romantic adventurers on Caribbean filibusters, brutal police, panic-stricken communities harshly suppressing real and imagined slave revolts, robed night riders engaged in systematic terrorism, unknown assassins, church burners, and other less physical expressions of a South whose mode of action is often extreme. The image is so pervasive that it compels the attention of anyone interested in understanding the South. When one loyal southerner was asked by a probing Yankee why the murder rate in the South was so high, he replied that he reckoned there were just more folks in the South who needed killing.

More sophisticated theories point to other reasons. During the first half of the twentieth century, southern society had a larger proportion of lower-status occupations, so that the same factors that caused people in lower-status occupations in the North to be more violent had a proportionately greater effect on the South. In the same way, the agricultural nature of southern life also contributed to the pattern of southern violence. Poverty is also a logical factor to suspect as the underlying cause of the South's pattern of violence, for informal justice operated most often where formal legal structures were not so prevalent or firmly in place. Ignorance and racial fears, long formed by stereotyping, also underlay the South's habits of violence. A final possible reason could be the South's homogeneity. As some sociologists have pointed out, conflict is more passionate and more radical when it arises out of close relationships. The closer the relationship, so the reasoning goes, the greater the affective investment, the greater the tendency also to suppress rather than express hostile feeling. In such cases, feelings of hostility tend to accumulate and hence intensify (Hackney 1969, 906–25).

The resurgence of the Ku Klux Klan in the 1920s also contributed to violence in the South. Riding a wave of anti-immigration feelings and fear among the lower and lower-middle class of the erosion of morality, and the threat of blacks, the Klan, with its promise to protect American values, emerged in the South and elsewhere as a powerful social and political force in the 1920s. In addition to picnics and parades that celebrated America, the Klan took it upon themselves to restore morality to the country. At various times they whipped wayward husbands, drove women of ill repute out of town, banished those whom they deemed as unscrupulous businessmen (often Jews), and kept blacks under control through intimidation and violence. The fiercest of Klan activities in this period was their practice of lynching, which occurred often and in various places throughout the South.

In the first half of the twentieth century in the South, the most overt and horrific display of southern violence was public lynching. For many African Americans growing up in the South in the late nineteenth and early twentieth centuries, the threat of lynching was commonplace. The popular image of an angry white mob stringing a black man up to a tree is only half the story. Lynching, an act of terror meant to spread fear among blacks, served the broad social purpose of maintaining white supremacy in the economic, social, and political spheres. In some parts of the South, such as the Mississippi Delta, hardly a black person lived who did not know of a lynching at some time in the area. Author Richard Wright, who was born near Natchez in southwest Mississippi, knew of two men who were lynched—his step-uncle and the brother of a neighborhood friend. In his book *Black Boy*, he wrote: "The things that influenced my conduct as a Negro did not have to happen to me directly; I needed but to hear of them to feel their full effects in the deepest layers of my consciousness. Indeed, the white brutality that I had not seen was a more effective control of my behavior than that which I knew."

Although the practice of lynching had existed since before slavery, it gained momentum during Reconstruction, when viable black towns sprang up across the South, and African Americans began to make political and economic inroads by registering to vote, establishing businesses, and running for public office. Many whites—landowners and poor whites alike—felt threatened by this rise in black prominence. Foremost on their minds, some whites espoused the idea that black men were sexual predators and wanted integration in order to be with white women. Lynchings were frequently committed with the most flagrant public display. Like executions by guillotine in former times, lynchings were often advertised in newspapers and drew large crowds of white families. They were a kind of vigilantism in which southern white men saw themselves as protectors of their way of life and their white women. By the early twentieth century, the writer Mark Twain had a name for it: the United States of Lyncherdom.

Lynchings were covered in local newspapers with headlines spelling out the horrific details. Photos of victims, with exultant white observers posed next to them, were taken for distribution in newspapers or on postcards. Body parts, including genitalia, were sometimes distributed to spectators or put on public display. Most infractions were for petty crimes, like theft, but the biggest one of all was looking at or associating with white women. Many victims were black businessmen or black men who refused to back down from a fight. Headlines such as the following were not uncommon:

"Five White Men Take Negro into Woods; Kill Him: Had Been Charged with Associating with White Women" went over the Associated Press wires about a lynching in Shreveport, Louisiana.

"Negro Slain By Texas Poss: Victims Heart removed After His Capture By Armed Men" was published in *the New York World Telegram* on December 8, 1933.

"Negro and White Scuffle; Negro Is Jailed, Lynched" was published in the *Atlanta Constitution* on July 6, 1933.

"Alabama Negroes Lynched; Mob Takes Them from Officials" was published in the *New York Times* on September 30, 1919.

Newspapers even printed that prominent white citizens in local towns attended lynchings, and they often published victory pictures—smiling crowds, many with children in tow—standing next to the corpse. In the South, an estimated two or three blacks were lynched each week in the late nineteenth and early twentieth centuries. In Mississippi alone, 500 blacks were lynched from the 1800s to 1955. Nationwide, the figure climbed to nearly 5,000. Although rape was often cited as a rationale for lynching, statistics now show that only about one-fourth of lynchings from 1880 to 1930 were prompted by an accusation of rape. In fact, most victims of lynching were political activists, labor organizers, or black men and women who violated white expectations of black deference, and were deemed "uppity" or "insolent." Though most victims were black men, women were by no means exempt. In 1923, whites burned the moderately prosperous black town of Rosewood, Florida, to the ground, killing scores of men and women in the process. Their excuse was that the town was harboring a black man who had beaten a white woman. Facts later revealed that the culprit was a white man whom the alleged victim was trying to protect.

According to black journalist and editor Ida B. Wells, who launched a fierce antilynching campaign in the 1890s, the lynching of successful black people was a means of subordinating potential black economic competitors. She also argued that consensual sex between black men and white women, while forbidden, was widespread. Thus, lynching was also a means of imposing order on white women's sexuality. Wells, who would later help found the National Association for the Advancement of Colored People, was forced to flee Memphis after her offices were torched in protest of her antilynching and civil rights efforts.

With lynching as a violent backdrop in the South, with Jim Crow as the law of the land, and with the poverty of the sharecropper system, blacks had no recourse. This triad of repression ensured blacks would remain impoverished, endangered, and without rights or hope. Whites could accuse at will, and rarely was a white punished for a crime committed against a black. Even for those whites who were opposed to lynching, there was not much they could do. If there was an investigation, white citizens closed ranks to protect their own, and rarely were mob leaders identified (American Experience. http://pbs.org; *Bill Moyers Journal* "The Legacy of Lynching" www.pbs.org/wgbh/amex/till/peopleevents/e_lynch.html)

Blacks also suffered violence during times of labor unrest. Often during strikes, white employers would hire blacks desperate for work to replace striking white workers. The thought that blacks were stealing their jobs augmented racial hatred, and whites reacted with violence. For example, during a nationwide railroad strike in 1912, the introduction of black strikebreakers in New Orleans led to a riot that left six dead, and during the same strike in Macomb, Mississippi, three black strikebreakers were killed. Another railroad strike in 1922 resulted in the death of one striker and six black strikebreakers.

In the antebellum period, a penal system in the South had been practically nonexistent. After the Civil War, the state was suddenly called upon to take over the plantation's penal functions. Penal officials thought they found a solution with a system called "convict labor," which put prisoners to work throughout the South. The South's "penitentiaries" became great rolling cages that followed construction camps and railroad construction. In areas such as north Florida, hastily built stockades were built deep in forests or swamps to provide labor for turpentine mills. This system was such an obvious throwback to slavery that it ignited the moral outrage of the country, and, beginning in the first decade of the twentieth century, reform groups across the country pressured the southern states to reevaluate their penal systems. One by one the states changed. Georgia abolished the system in 1908, and by 1917 Mississippi, Arkansas, Louisiana, and Florida had done likewise. In place of convict labor, southern states established road prisons where inmates—including those who had only committed misdemeanors—were sentenced to obligatory work building new roads. In 1924 in Georgia, which was not unlike other southern states, 95 percent of those on the road gangs were black. Southern Progressives became strong advocates of the prison road gang system, as it seemed an adequate way of fulfilling their apparently conflictive goals of uplifting the prisoners through creative work projects and at the same time controlling their black population. Reformers applauded the work, which put prisoners in the open air exercising and breathing freely. Despite enthusiasm for the new system, the reality remained that conditions and treatment of prisoners in these road prisons were deplorable. Furthermore, the fact that the majority of the prisoners were black emphasized the reality that the system was inextricably linked to southern racism (Wilson and Ferris 1989, 1495–96).

WAR

The onset of a seemingly remote war in Europe set in motion forces that would have great consequences for daily life in the South. The most immediate impact was a sharp economic downturn caused by reduced cotton trade with Europe. The collapse of the cotton market, which in the mind of southerners was caused by the English naval blockade, initially caused financial hardship and also conjured memories of the Civil War blockade, creating hostility toward the Allies in the South. Even as the United States moved closer to war, many prominent southerners eschewed the martial tradition of their homeland and urged President Wilson to maintain the country's neutrality. Several southern politicians opposed the president's preparedness program and a few southern congressmen even voted against his declaration of war.

Despite their skepticism about the war, once America was involved, southerners, along with most of the nation, threw themselves wholeheartedly into the effort. Both culturally and ethnically the white South had strong ties to Great Britain, and the British enhanced those ties by purchasing huge amounts of cotton, which rejuvenated the sagging southern economy. Moreover, the strong military tradition of the South beckoned them to the patriotic call to arms in 1917.

The war eventually provided a great stimulus to the southern economy. Textile factories worked overtime providing jobs and money to mill workers, and southerners were able to avoid limits on the price of cotton at a time when the government was placing price controls on commodities. The war also accelerated fundamental changes in the South's economic structure. The seeds for an era of regional development and electrification would be planted when the government began the construction of explosives and chemical nitrate plants in the South. The plant they built at Muscle Shoals, Alabama, served as a model for the Tennessee Valley Authority.

Military service also diminished the provincialism of the thousands of southerners who left home to serve in the military. It also changed the attitudes of those who remained at home, as the South saw the construction of numerous bases in their region, and along with the bases came young men from every region of the country. The presence of so many Yankees, westerners, and midwesterners in their midst forced southerners to think differently about themselves and the stereotypical images they held of "outsiders."

These demographic shifts caused much stress for many southerners, as the number of lynchings increased markedly during the war years. And for one of the first times in their post–Civil War history, blacks retaliated against white violence in kind. For example, in Houston, Texas, a black army unit responded to racial harassment by killing 17 white civilians. The war also caused social upheaval in the South by stimulating the first stage of the great black migration, as southern blacks lured by the promise of jobs and racial equality moved in great numbers to northern cities. Women were also touched by the war. In addition to losing brothers, husbands, and sons on battlefields, they saw other political changes stimulated by the war that brought them the vote in 1920. Wartime fervor also fueled the Prohibition movement, which gave southern women a long-sought goal: prohibition of the sale of alcohol. Although not as drastic as the Civil War, which still lingered in the South's collective memory, World War I also brought great changes to many aspects of southern life (Wilson and Ferris 1989, 672–73).

Recreational Life

SPORTS

The South shared with the rest of the nation the enthusiasm for college football. Although southern universities and colleges lagged far behind in academic standards, their football teams were the pride of the region, for they competed effectively with the best teams in the nation. In an attempt to bring some coordination to the rules governing college play, various regions established athletic conferences. The oldest was the Big Ten in the Midwest, but other regions soon followed them. The Southern Conference was formed on February 25, 1921, at a meeting in Atlanta. Fourteen institutions from the 30-member Southern Intercollegiate Athletic Association (SIAA) reorganized as the Southern Conference. Those charter members included the universities of Alabama, Auburn, Clemson, Georgia, Georgia Tech, Kentucky, Maryland, Mississippi State, North Carolina, North Carolina State, Tennessee, Virginia, Virginia Tech, and Washington and Lee. Athletic competition began in the fall of 1921. In 1922, six more schools—Florida, Louisiana State, Mississippi, South Carolina, Tulane, and Vanderbilt—joined the fold. The University of the South joined the ranks in 1923, Virginia Military Institute in 1925, and Duke University in 1929. Since then, a series of membership changes have occurred, with 42 institutions having been affiliated with the league at some point. The league has undergone two major transitions during its history.

The first occurred in December 1932 when the Southeastern Conference was formed out of the 23-school Southern Conference. The league's 13 members west and south of the Appalachian Mountains reorganized to help reduce the extensive travel demands that were present in the league at the time. In 1936, the Southern Conference invited the Citadel, William and Mary, Davidson, Furman, Richmond, and Wake Forest to join the membership. Since then, the Atlantic Coast Conference also formed out of the old Southern Conference.

Although baseball was played in every city in the South, there were no Major League teams. The favorite Major League teams for many southerners in the 1930s were the Browns and the Cardinals, both of St. Louis. Not only were these teams the closest geographically to the heart of the South, but, given their proximity, it was often possible at night to hear broadcasts of their games on the radio. In the 1920s and after, for two months of the year, February and March, when spring training began, Floridians could see real Major League stars up close. Most cities, even small towns, had their own baseball teams. Often they were sponsored by local industry. Eduardo Gato Cigar Company, for example, in Key West, not only outfitted a team but built a stadium and also paid for his team to travel to other Florida cities and Havana to play. Blacks in the South also played baseball, but as in the rest of southern life, they were excluded from participation on white teams. Segregation laws throughout the South even prohibited blacks from playing on most fields. Despite these limitations

Frank Lockhart in his new Stutz Blackhawk Special in 1928. Library of Congress.

blacks formed their own semiprofessional and amateur leagues throughout the South, and baseball prospered in the black community. In the first half of the twentieth century, blacks also had their own professional leagues, but like their white counterparts, the Major League during this era eschewed the South and concentrated its franchises mostly in the Midwest.

Auto racing, the sport most identified with the South, began in 1902 when crowds gathered along the hard flat beach between Ormond and Daytona in Florida to watch Alexander Winton's "Bullet" outrace Ransom Olds's "Pirate" by seconds. The next year the Ormond Beach Hotel sponsored a winter festival, which culminated in a race sponsored by the American Automobile Association. From that time until the mid-1950s racing enthusiasts and participants gathered to watch races on the beach, which became known as the Daytona Beach Road Course. The first stock car races were held on the beach in 1936, and they continued there until the 1950s, when Daytona built an inland racetrack.

The South also laid claim to the country's premier horse-racing event, the Kentucky Derby. Kentuckians had been racing horses since the late eighteenth century, but the race that brought the state national attention did not begin until 1875, the year that owners of the Churchill Downs racecourse established the Kentucky Derby as a feature race. In 1894 the owners built the grandstand that became the symbol for the race. Since that time, the race has gained national, even international attention, and every spring horse-racing enthusiasts focus their attention on Louisville, Kentucky, the home of Churchill Downs and the Kentucky Derby. In the 1920s, horse racing also came to Florida when a track was built in Hialeah for the enjoyment of the wealthy Palm Beachers. Through the 1920s, 1930s, and 1940s the elegantly landscaped horse track with its palatial grandstand track would host the wealthiest families of America, who would leave their mansions in Palm Beach and embark in their personal parlor cars on the train, which ran directly from Palm Beach to Hialeah Track.

MUSIC

Perhaps no other region of the country has contributed more to American music than the South. And although blues and jazz have been well integrated into the national musical scheme, country music continues to remain regionally identified with the South. This music was played in every hamlet of the South, but with the invention and spread of radio, the fountainhead of country music became Nashville, Tennessee. Since 1925, WSM Radio's *Grand Ole Opry* in Nashville has featured country music acts on its stage for live Saturday night broadcasts. This program introduced the nation to most, if not all, of the greats of country music. To this day, membership in the *Opry* remains one of a country music artist's greatest ambitions.

The most influential group at the *Opry*, and probably in country music history, remains the Carter Family. They changed the character of what was then more commonly called "hillbilly" music by switching emphasis from hillbilly instrumentals to vocals, and making scores of their songs part of the standard country music canon. They also created a style of country guitar playing known as "Carter-picking," which became the dominant technique for decades. Along with Jimmie Rodgers, the Carter Family were among the first country music stars. Comprising a gaunt, shy gospel quartet member called Alvin P. Carter and two reserved country girls—his wife Sara and their sister-in-law Maybelle—the Carter Family sang a pure, simple harmony that influenced not only the numerous other family groups of the 1930s and the 1940s, but folk, bluegrass, and rock musicians such as Woody Guthrie, Bill Monroe, the Kingston Trio, Doc Watson, Bob Dylan, and Emmylou Harris, to mention just a few.

It is unlikely that bluegrass music would have existed without the Carter Family. A. P., the family patriarch, collected hundreds of British/Appalachian folk songs and, in arranging these for recording, both enhanced the pure beauty of these "facts-of-life tunes" and at the same time saved them for future generations. Those hundreds of songs the trio found around their Virginia and Tennessee homes, after being sung by A. P., Sara, and Maybelle, became Carter songs, even though they were folk songs and in the public domain. Among the more than 300 sides they recorded are "Worried Man Blues," "Wabash Cannonball," "Will the Circle Be Unbroken," "Wildwood Flower," and "Keep on the Sunny Side." The Carter Family's instrumental backup, like their vocals, was unique. On her Gibson L-5 guitar, Maybelle played a bass-strings lead (the guitar being tuned down from the standard pitch) that is the mainstay of bluegrass guitarists to the present. Sara accompanied her on the autoharp or on a second guitar, while A. P. devoted his talent to singing a haunting though idiosyncratic bass or baritone. Although the original Carter Family disbanded in 1943, enough of their recordings remained in the vaults to keep the group current through the 1940s. Furthermore, their influence was evident through further generations of musicians, in all forms of popular music, through the end of the century.

Another important member of the *Grand old Opry* in the early years was Roy Acuff. The *Opry* began as a show with primarily part-time artists who used the show to promote their live appearances throughout the South and Midwest, but with the help of Roy Acuff, the professionalism of country music became established at the *Opry*. By 1933, Acuff formed a group, the Tennessee Crackerjacks, in which Clell Summey played dobro, thus providing the distinctive sound that came to be associated with Acuff (and later provided by Pete "Bashful Brother Oswald" Kirby). Acuff married Mildred Douglas in 1936, and that same year he also recorded two sessions for ARC (a company controlling a host of labels, later merged with Columbia). Tracks from these sessions included two of his greatest hits: "Wabash Cannonball" (featuring vocals by Dynamite Hatcher) and "The Great Speckle Bird."

Making his first appearance on the *Grand Ole Opry* in 1938, Acuff soon became a regular on the show, changing the name of the band once more to the Smoky Mountain Boys. He won many friends with his sincere, mountain-boy vocal style and his dobro-flavored band sound and eventually became as popular as Uncle Dave Macon, who was the *Opry*'s main attraction at the time.

During the 1940s, Acuff's recordings became so popular that he headed Frank Sinatra in some major music polls and reportedly caused Japanese troops to yell "To hell with Roosevelt, to hell with Babe Ruth, to hell with Roy Acuff" as they banzai-charged at Okinawa. These years also saw some of his biggest hits, including "Wreck on the Highway" (1942), "Fireball Mail" (1942), and "Night Train to Memphis" (1943).

ENTERTAINMENT

For many southerners, important forms of entertainment were visiting, porch sitting, and eating together on Sunday afternoons. For the less devout there was also music, dancing, and drinking moonshine. A uniquely southern contribution to this form of entertainment was the juke joint, which has given us the word *jukebox*, and was also the birthplace of the music form known as the "blues." There are two words or terms that are closely related today, namely, *juke joint* (a small inexpensive café mainly in the southern states) and *jukebox* (an automatic coin-operated phonograph). The term *juke joint* undoubtedly came first, because it was brought into the daily language in the South by the African Americans decades before the first coin-operated phonograph was demonstrated to the mainly white populations of the big northern cities. The juke joints were from the very beginning normally located next to the cotton fields and owned by the white owner of the fields. In a few cases, however, the café could also be leased to a longtime loyal old laborer, who could no longer work as hard as before (http://www.jukebox-works.com/historyTerm.htm).

During the 1920s, these rural weekend establishments were often run by a local bootlegger or by someone selling

Saturday afternoon in a beer and juke joint in Clarksdale, Mississippi, in 1939. Library of Congress.

his product. They provided musical entertainment in homes or in abandoned share-cropper houses as a means of selling food and corn liquor for profit. Juke joints also contributed to the formation of one of the country's most enduring and important cultural legacies: the blues. If the Mississippi Delta was the cultural crucible that birthed the blues, then the juke joint was the kiln where the musical fires burned brightest. For black Delta sharecroppers, isolated by a lack of transportation, singing and listening to the blues provided a social outlet and a "pressure valve" to vent the week's stress.

"Sometimes they'd just drive that tractor up there and jump off and go on in there," one man recalled, remembering his mother's Charleston, Mississippi, joint. "[You'd] see a lot of tractors, mules and stuff. As long as you on the plantation, you could drive the tractor anywhere you want." Irene Williams, "Mama 'Rene" to locals, ran the Do Drop Inn in Shelby, Mississippi: "The juke joints, to me, enable the peoples to go out and ventilate. When you work hard, you're tense. . . . Not able to pay bills, not able to buy the amount of groceries that you need to buy. Not able to do a lot of things that you want to do. And when you go to these places you're able to ventilate and let off the stress, and you're able to cope the next week with your problems better." In the lawless days of early Delta culture, that blowing off steam would often get violent. Legendary slide guitarist Robert Nighthawk sang about the darker side of Delta nightlife. In one song, "Goin down to Eli's," he decides he's going to kill his woman whom he caught dancing in the local juke joint. He knows he'll go to jail, but he decides he'd rather be in prison than be worrying about his woman cheating on him.

Chester Johnson remembered: "If you stayed there till about 10 o'clock and didn't nothing happen, you better go on home. 'Cause from about 11 o'clock on there's gonna be some shootin' going on. Some guy's gonna whoop his old lady about dancing with somebody." Despite the occasional violence, and the obvious liquor law violations in dry Mississippi, juke operators and their patrons had little to fear from local law enforcement. "You paid that man to sell that whiskey," James Alford, manager of Smitty's Red Top Lounge in Clarksdale, Mississippi, said. "They didn't say it like that, but that's all they were doing—paying the sheriff or the chief of police or whoever would let you sell" (http://www.steberphoto.com/articles-1.htm).

HOLIDAYS, CELEBRATIONS, AND FESTIVALS

Special occasions in the South were often celebrated ritualistically with home-cooked meals with families and friends. Thanksgiving, Christmas, New Year's, weddings, and parties required special cooking and often long-term preparation. A large hen or rooster, straggling into the winter, was the obvious choice for holiday chicken and dressing, but many special occasion dishes required that rural southern families make that rare trip into town to purchase foods that signaled the holidays: apples, oranges, a coconut, light corn syrup, marshmallows, cocoa, raisins on the stem. A midwinter apple or orange was such a treat that many children appreciated them as gifts at Christmas.

Pecans, hickory nuts, and black walnuts added to the variety and interest of holiday fare. Most southerners also grew a few rows of popcorn specifically for Christmas, out of which came popcorn balls, made with sorghum, and popcorn for stringing around the freshly cut Christmas tree. The prevalence of rich, fruit-laden dishes that characterize special occasion southern cooking represented a celebration of life in the dead of winter, a recognition that luxury was possible even in hard times, because people had planned and worked hard to have the stored and store-bought goods. Parties and weddings, too, generated their share of fancy cooking, such as taffy parties or box suppers, designed to acquaint young men and women and to give those who were sweet on each other a chance to subtly make their designs public. Thanksgiving, as one southern woman remembered, didn't mean different food, but just more of the same thing:

We always did have lots of company, so Mother would take two big old fat hens and make dressing. She sure could make good dressing.

Mother never did cook anything the day before except at Christmas and New Year's and special days like that. She always made 3 or 4 kinds of fruitcake, and she had a big tin can—I guess it must have been ten gallons—and she'd put those fruitcakes in it and put the top on it and let it set for a long time. At Christmastime, we always had a ham and a variety of vegetables to go with it, but I've seen as many as four meats on a table. We grew everything, you know, and canned all our food, so we didn't have to buy anything but coffee and sugar and flour. So we'd have all those canned foods—vegetables and relishes and what all. We always had lots of pies at Christmas, and when I learned how to make fudge, I'd do that, and there were plenty of good pecans to go in it. For dinner on New Year's Day, we'd eat just about the same thing we had for Christmas except black-eyed peas, which always were eaten for good luck. We always had plenty of company on special days, because my mother would always set such a table, and all the relatives liked to come and fill up. Lots of times company didn't even let Mother know they were coming, just dropped in, but I never did see her get up and add to the dinner but one time. But I had to do the dishes, so I just wanted to boot those people out sometimes. It was like the grand hotel. (Strickland and Dunn 2002, 99–100)

One of the great celebrations in the Gulf Coast South was Carnival. The Gulf Coast Carnival absorbed Caribbean, Latin America, Native American, and African Caribbean traditions and created a celebration of food, festival, party, and parades that transcended class and race. The Carnival festival followed the Catholic liturgical calendar; thus, festivities began on January 6, the Feast of the Kings, and ended on Mardi Gras or Shrove Tuesday, the day before the penitential 40 days of Lent. The Carnival season could be as short as three and a half weeks or as long as two months, depending on the Easter date. During Mardi Gras the streets were filled with parades of colorful floats on which sat members of the various "krewes" who had spent the previous year designing the floats. As they wound their way through the streets, krewe members rewarded spectators with beads, trinkets, and candies thrown from the float. Various krewes sponsored different parades, which always ended in a grand party. Krewes, which had traditionally been made up of the economical and historical elite of the city, celebrated varied themes. For example, the Zulu parade of New Orleans, "krewed" by the black middle-class and elite community, began in 1909 as a reaction to white stereotypes of blacks as savages. Mocking those white stereotypes, Zulu members dressed in grass skirts and "wooly wigs," put on blackface, and threw rubber spears and decorated coconuts to the crowds. Since the early nineteenth century, various krewes have included comic cowboys, Indians, and various mythological themes. Despite the variety of themes, they all reflected the will to celebrate the triumph of joy over sorrow (Wilson and Ferris 1989, 1230–31).

Religious Life

RELIGION AND SPIRITUALITY

In the ranks of southern Protestantism, regionalism thrived most conspicuously. Forty years after Appomattox, 3,500,000 of 6,200,000 white church members in the South still belonged to three explicitly southern denominations: the Southern Baptist Church, the Methodist Episcopal Church South, and the Southern Presbyterian Church. Most others held membership in locally independent congregations unaffiliated with episcopate, presbytery, conference, or convention. A 1910 religious tract titled *The Fundamentals* laid out the essentials of fundamentalism, which insisted on the literal accuracy of the Bible as God's word. Fundamentalism was embraced by various theological seminaries as well as by a number of highly successful evangelists and prominent public figures. The rural homogeneity of the South, little disturbed by immigration, industrialization, new intellectual currents, and all the other forces that were elsewhere transforming society made the South the battleground for fundamentalism.

Fierce sectarian debate often obscured a consensus on fundamentals. On such precepts as heaven and hell, God and Satan, depravity and redemption, there was little dispute. Few southerners doubted the literal authenticity of the scriptures or the ever-presence of God in human affairs. For example, in 1905 a committee of the Southern Presbyterian General Assembly attributed a series of railway accidents to the operation of trains on Sunday. "So long as the nation shows such utter disregard for His authority," the committee declared, "so long may we expect the continued repetition of these and other so-called accidents."

Ecclesiastical isolation from the rest of the nation fostered regional accommodations between church and society. Thus, in the late nineteenth century, as racial distinctions in secular spheres were being drawn more sharply, southern Protestants regrouped into all-white and all-Negro denominations. The Mississippi State Baptist Convention of 1891 insisted that "they [blacks] are distinct, for their good and our's [sic]. To do otherwise is to inflict an evil on them and to raise an insurmountable barrier to success." "Theories of race were as much a part of Southern Baptist thinking as the Virgin Birth or the Second Coming," one student declared.

In a region lacking adequate resources either for public education or ministerial training, church leadership did not necessitate intellectual acuity. Episcopalians and

Presbyterians required a seminary degree for clerical ordination, but other denominations often prescribed nothing more than a call from God. Baptist congregations administering ordination seldom demanded formal schooling. Southern Methodists asked only that candidates be familiar with the Bible, "the ordinary branches of an English education," and two of John Wesley's sermons, "Justification by Faith" and "The Witness of the Spirit"; preachers thus licensed "on trial," however, had to complete a four-year correspondence course before final ordination. In 1907, the Nashville *Christian Advocate* lamented that many Methodist clergymen were "totally ignorant" of twentieth-century civilization. As late as 1927, only 4 percent of Southern Methodist clergy were seminary graduates, only 11 percent had college degrees, and approximately 32 percent had no schooling beyond the elementary level. Nor was there often time in the pastor's crowded routine for extensive independent study. A survey published in 1923 estimated that more than one out of three southern clergymen served four or more churches. Even so, many shared the experience of a Navarro County, Texas, preacher who had to "raise a little cotton" to supplement his clerical earnings. A Baptist leader complained that Baptist rural churches had won for themselves "the pitiful distinction of paying an average wage which is less than a capable field laborer now earns."

Many were indifferent to the lack of education among their ministers. One observer wrote, "whenever the day comes that the Methodist Church requires a college course as conditional to admittance to the [ministry], that day will sound the death-knell of the Church." "Send out men whose hearts are hot with love to God," he urged, " . . . and the Holy Ghost will use them to the pulling down of the strongholds of sin and the upbuilding of the kingdom of God." The Baptist *Christian Index* approvingly likened the reaction of a congregation to an "earnest" extempore preacher to that between steel and flint, "the sparks fly in all directions."

Despite such sentiment, Southern Methodists and Baptists both sponsored theological seminaries, the Methodist theological school at Vanderbilt University and the Southern Baptist Theological Seminary, in Louisville. Southern Presbyterians sponsored four seminaries: Union Theological Seminary (Worsham, Virginia), Columbia (South Carolina) Theological Seminary, Southwestern (Tennessee) Theological Seminary, and the Louisville Theological Seminary. With the exception of Vanderbilt, all lacked substantial endowments or other reliable sources of revenue. And all had to contend with a stifling popular distrust of scholarship. Where academic inquiry intruded into the realm of faith, ancient myth was often acclaimed over present truth. And the strongest prevailing myth was fundamentalism.

What evoked the greatest wrath among fundamentalists were attacks on a literal interpretation of the book of Genesis, which by the beginning of the twentieth century occurred with great frequency. By 1900, most non-fundamentalist theologians had accepted Darwin's theories as fact and could agree with James Wilson, professor at the Columbia School of Theology, who argued that evolution could be reconciled with a "not unreasonable interpretation of the Bible," and that evolution could be construed as "God's plan of creation." Southern fundamentalists stood firmly against this accommodation of religion to scientific fact and remained steadfast in their conviction that Adam came from dust, not from any other species (Bailey 1963, 618–35).

The most spectacular head-on clash between southern fundamentalism and science took place in Dayton, Tennessee, in 1925. The Tennessee legislature, sympathetic to fundamentalist views, adopted a law banning the teaching of Charles Darwin's evolutionary theories in public schools. This led to a challenge by the American Civil Liberties Union (ACLU), which came to the defense of John Scopes, a high school biology teacher accused of breaking the law. The trial that ensued pitted the famous defense lawyer Clarence Darrow against perennial presidential candidate and recent Florida real estate tycoon William Jennings Bryan. The trial ended with Darrow cross-examining Bryan and mockingly pointing out the discrepancies between fact and reality in the Bible. Nevertheless, the jury found Scopes guilty and made him pay a nominal fine. Bryan died within a week of the trial. Some speculated it was the intense heat, but others thought it was the humiliation he suffered in Dayton, Tennessee.

Newspapers and magazines eager for a show in the age of "ballyhoo" characterized the trial as a circus and gave the impression that though Scopes was convicted, the victory went to modernism, which had shown up the ignorance and naiveté of the southerners' simple faith. In fact, the advocates of fundamentalism continued to rule local and state school boards in the South and evolution was off limits in many schools. Town boosters and Progressives bemoaned the image of the South as a land of ignoramuses, as H. L. Mencken described them, but most southerners remained firm in their belief in Scripture and suspicious of science as the final say on the meaning of human life.

Despite living in the most economically challenged region of the country, the Protestant churches of the South paid little attention to Christian teachings in the context of the economically devastated society to which they preached. If little attention was given to newer theological interpretations, even less was given to the application of Christian teachings to the social milieu. A Baptist historian finds that editors of Baptist journals in the southeastern states failed during this era "to perceive any relation between Christian morality and economic justice."

In 1900, a study sponsored by the Georgia Baptist *Christian Index* concluded that the majority of the poor,

the submerged tenth, the begrimed masses who swarm in the slums and wretched tenement houses of our large cities, some of whom are also found in the smaller towns and even in the country, are dissipated, vicious, wicked and immoral. Many reformers of the day teach that, if you improve their surroundings and educate them, you can lift them up. Far be it from us to discourage any efforts along this line of work; but what these people need is to be made over again. There is but one power in the world that can do this, and that is the gospel of the Son of God.

Essentially, religious thought in the South had changed little since the era of frontier revivalism. An almost single-minded emphasis on individual regeneration remained. Sermons abounded in expositions on salvation, the joys of heaven, and the

A 1937 photo of Zora Hurston demonstrating a voodoo dance. Library of Congress.

horrors of hell; often they were a recital of the clergyman's "personal emotional experience and nothing else." A Baptist leader complained, "with gratifying but all-too-few exceptions, our country preachers confine themselves largely to evangelistic sermons." In an address before the Southern Baptist Convention in 1899, George W. Truett, pastor of the Dallas First Baptist Church and a renowned pulpit orator, belittled ministers who expounded "philosophy, or science, or culture, or worldly wisdom." Popular hymns warned of the uncertainty of human existence. A hymn in the official Southern Methodist *Hymnal* cautioned as follows:

Death rides on every passing breeze,
And lurks in every flower;
Each season has its own disease,
Its peril every hour!

A selection in the Southern Baptist *Hymn and Praise Book* warned as follows:

That day of wrath, that dreadful day,
When heav'n and earth shall pass away
What pow'r shall be the sinner's stay?
How shall we meet that dreadful day? (Bailey 1963, 618–35)

Churches in the South were devoid of ornamentation. In the first half of the twentieth century, these plain white clapboard church facades dominated the southern landscape. Sunday church attendance was an all-day affair, with no time for other secular activity. Southern Protestants who went to these services heard a strong folk mix of biblical fundamentalism, emotional conversion experiences, and periodic spiritual rejuvenation. The minister was an important member of the community and ever-present at the important rituals of birth, marriage, and death.

Although their churches were usually stark and humble, southern Protestants did find ways to express their faith to the world. As roads began to wind their way through the rural South in the 1920s and 1930s, travelers witnessed a new form of evangelization emerging in the South, the roadside message. Urban Christians may have had their grand churches, but in the rural South the sign—usually with no more than a terse "Jesus Saves" (anything more might have suggested uncertainty)—in the 1920s became an important southern icon that carried a basic truth upon which a stable life could be built.

After kinship, religion was the most important value in southern black life. In the antebellum South, religious expression was often a stifled or a secretive affair carried out under the suspicious and watchful eye of a white man. After emancipation, religious separation in the South became formalized as freedmen left their former masters' churches to establish their own houses of worship. Black Christian images of God differed greatly from what antebellum whites emphasized. African American Christianity celebrated Moses and the Israelites' deliverance from Egypt, and they envisioned a God more like African deities. The black religious South in the twentieth century included such practices as ecstatic trances and spiritual possession. This sometimes took the form of talking in tongues and always involved movement, loud singing, and dancing. Some black churches influenced more by the Catholic traditions of Caribbean blacks expressed belief in hags, witches, and hoodoo priests, who celebrated rituals that combined Catholic practices with ancient African worship. These churches flourished as an underground alternative religious system that in many ways ran counter to traditional Protestant Christianity. In the rural South those who had intimate knowledge of hoodoo or voodoo were called doctors. These doctors had the power of life and death over people whether they believed in voodoo or not. Zora Neale Hurston related a story of a hoodoo doctor in Florida who gave power to a woman to kill a man who had disgraced her daughter. Thanks to the hoodoo incantations, the woman was able to kill the culprit simply by shooting an image of the man. The voodoo doctors were usually older men and women who had apprenticed under earlier practitioners.

The more traditional black churches in the South continued to provide leadership in the black community from the time of emancipation through the civil rights movement of the mid-twentieth century (Wilson and Ferris 1989, 136–37, 492–93).

Whether black or white, southern churches provided spiritual solace and social security in an ever-changing world. And so in the first half of the twentieth century, the South remained a land of piety and tradition. "There is no part of the world in which ministers of the Gospel are more respected than in the southern states," a distinguished Methodist editor declared, and he doubted whether there was "another territory of like area beneath the sun, where there is a stronger, better faith in the Bible, where the Sabbath is better observed, where a larger per cent of the people attend church, and where virtue in womanhood and honesty in manhood are more common and command a better premium." A preoccupation with individual repentance, a dogged insistence on biblical inerrancy, a tendency toward overt expression of intense religious emotions: these legacies of frontier revivalism still held a primacy. Of this most southerners were proud (Bailey 1963, 630–35).

SECULAR RITES OF PASSAGE

In the South, folk belief, customs, and superstitions related to childbirth endured well into the twentieth century. These traditions were an amalgamation of Native American, African American, and Euro-American folk remedies and beliefs. From conception though gestation, delivery, and postpartum, many southern families sought to ensure the health and intelligence of babies and the safety of mothers through a strict adherence to ritual based on folk culture.

For example, many southerners believed that it was possible to determine or control the sex of an infant at conception through certain acts performed by the parents. Some southerners believed that a baby boy was assured if the father kept a leather string in his pocket during conception. The side to which the female turned following intercourse (to the left for girls and the right for boys) was also believed to be effective in determining the sex of an infant. Other folk beliefs surround the gestation period of pregnancy, such as the notion that the pregnant female who crossed a threshold or began to climb stairs using her left foot would have a girl, but if she started with her right foot, it would be a boy.

One of the oldest beliefs about childbirth maintained that events occurring to the mother during pregnancy had important consequences for the baby. For example, if a pregnant women experienced fright, was deprived of cravings, or had contact with certain people or animals, the child in her womb could be affected. Women were told to only look at beautiful things during their pregnancy. Even a child's disposition could be determined during the gestation period. The belief was that a disagreeable mother would have a disagreeable child. Or if a mother looked on a dead baby while pregnant, her own child would be stillborn. Naming the baby or calling its selected name before birth could have similar fatal consequences.

Herbal teas were offered to the woman to hasten labor, and if that failed pepper was blown in the mother-to-be's face. An almost universal technique used to reduce pain during labor consisted of placing a sharp instrument—a knife, scissors, an axe—on or under the pillow or bed of the laboring woman "to cut the pain." Other pain remedies included herbal tea such as chamomile or even the southern refreshment of choice, Coca-Cola. Southerners believed it was inappropriate and even a bad omen for the father to be present at the birth, although in some areas of the South the presence of the father or some article of his clothing was often utilized to transmit male strength to the female in labor. One of the most persistent and widespread beliefs about childbirth in the South, especially among blacks, was about the psychic powers of babies born with faces covered with a veil or caul, the membrane of the amniotic sac. The belief prevailed that these babies possessed the power to foresee the future and to see and hear ghosts. The delivery phase of the birth process ended with the careful and traditional disposal through burning or burial of the placenta, membranes, and cord. These disposal methods were believed necessary for the future well-being of infant and mother (Wilson and Ferris 1989, 464–65).

SACRED RITES OF PASSAGE

Although the rest of the nation was turning more and more to funeral homes to direct mourning and burial of the dead, in the South the old practice of wrapping and rapidly burying the corpse remained the standard well up to the 1940s. Southern ministers comforted mourners at the grave with visions of an anthropomorphic eternity. Ideas of "heavenly recognition" conjectured that earthly friendships would be renewed after death and that "pastors will meet their dear flocks there and rejoice with them." The editor of the Methodist Raleigh *Christian Advocate* visualized the "hosts of the redeemed gathering about the great White Throne.... They are clothed in garments of white, with crowns of rejoicing upon their brows, and golden harps suspended on their arms, and palms of victory in their hands." Another North Carolina clergyman wrote that "it is sad to say farewell to those who are dying; but how sweet to think of greeting [them] on the eternal shore of rest, sweet rest." Other sacred rituals that remained peculiar to certain sects among the southern Protestants included snake handling, foot washings, and total immersion at baptism.

MORALITY

Perhaps because it had so little else to give its people, the South nurtured in them a generous and often obsessive sense of the past. The rest of the country might be committed to commercial expansion or addicted to the notion of progressive optimism, but many people in the South, even if they cared to, were unable to accept these dominant American values; they had been left behind, they were living on the margin of history—a position, they believed, that often provided the sharpest perspective on history. Southerners believed that their sense of tradition, cultivated from youth, gave them manners and morals that were superior to the rest of the materialistic, mongrelized nation. They did not have the material advantages of the rest of the country, but they took comfort in their spiritual and moral superiority. Fundamental Protestantism, segregation of the races, manners, and cultivation of personal relationships in the South, as opposed to rising Catholic influences in the North, racial mixing of the people, and the depersonalizing experience of the big northern cities, were objective facts that convinced white southerners of their moral superiority.

SACRED SPACE AND SACRED TIME

Sacred space and time became one in the South during their camp meetings, sometimes called revivals. Although camp meetings had been generally supplanted by more decorous indoor services, most southern congregations still sponsored special evangelistic campaigns each year. In the rural South, the revival season began in July and August, after the crops were laid by. And when it arrived, it became the major focus of the entire community. Religious newspapers devoted lengthy columns to revivals. A few reports published in 1900 are illustrative. A South Carolina dispatch related that they had been in a village that had "just passed through one of the happiest revivals that has ever been conducted in that section of the coast country." The pastor of the Dalton, Georgia, Methodist Church announced that "for three weeks, during a downpour of rain day and night, the greatest revival Dalton ever had has been going on" and that "practically the whole city [is] revived." A participant in an East Macon, Georgia, revival wrote, "I never saw such a meeting. It looked as if the entire community had professed conversion." The Lexington, Mississippi, Baptist Church likened its revival to "a cluster of rich grapes. We crushed them and drank the sacred wine and by faith inhaled the fragrant spices of the 'empty tomb.'"

At Union Baptist Church, in Tippah County, Mississippi, the service that was to conclude a revival ended "with a good old-time handshaking while the membership sang, with feeling, 'Amazing Grace,' with chorus, 'We'll all sing Hallelujah.' The interest was so marked . . . that it was thought best to continue the meeting." A report from the Hermansville, Mississippi, Baptist Church described their revival as a "spiritual earthquake." Luxora, Arkansas, Methodists felt they were "on high ground, having just closed one of the most successful meetings ever held in the county"; in that same state a report from the little town of Nashville declared that "our whole community was moved and touched" by a series of evangelistic services. From Texas came an account of a Methodist revival on the Glenwood charge, near Fort Worth, where "there was evident the 'old time power,' as Christians were made happy."

Where religious passions surged to a high tide, revivals were often protracted. In 1900 Methodist revivals at Tracy City, Tennessee, and Scottsville, Kentucky, lasted three weeks, while Russellville, Arkansas, Methodists were "blessed with a great meeting, which continued more than three weeks." Another meeting at Dalton, Georgia, continued three weeks and then was extended for "another week at least." The Knoxville Highland Avenue Methodist Church entered its sixth week of revival services in February 1900, "with added enthusiasm and zeal." And, in July 1904, the pastor of the Cherokee Avenue Baptist Church, at Gaffney, South Carolina, reported "almost a continous [sic] revival for the past two months." But the New Orleans *Christian Advocate* complained in 1900 that "most meetings have closed too soon to get great in gatherings."

Normally revivals were evaluated according to the number of conversions, although other results were not overlooked. During one east Tennessee revival, "many old neighborhood feuds" were said to have been settled. A Baptist revivalist in a turbulent area of southeastern Mississippi, "where they kill men and threaten preachers" and where the meeting house "had the sign of buckshot about the door that stole the life of a man," hoped he had been "at least some help" in promoting tranquility. A revival report from Fairmont, South Carolina, told of only one addition to the church, but rejoiced that "the church was strengthened spiritually."

Revivals, or camp meetings, as they were sometimes called, continued through the twentieth century. In the 1920s, the Klan, in an attempt to fortify their claims of a religious dimension to their crusades, helped promote and organize many camp meetings. And in the late 1930s as electricity arrived, artificial lighting systems replaced the great lightwood fires that used to light up the night. Despite these changes, throughout the decades revivals remained basically the same. They were a time when the unchurched were brought into church fellowship, hearts were warmed by the words of a visiting evangelist, local feuds were reconciled in the name of Christian fellowship, and the community was purged and revitalized for the forthcoming trials of winter. In the 1920s, a number of scandals involving corrupt evangelists brought ridicule on this southern tradition of revivalism, but the significance of the camp meeting to the continuity of community in the rural South cannot be underestimated (Bailey 1963, 632–34).

WORLDVIEW

The South has traditionally served as a counterpoint to the American way of life, because it seemed to differ from the North in a number of aspects. In the first half of the twentieth century, southerners had a greater sense of history than northerners, a greater attachment to place, and more deferential social customs. By all reports southerners placed more emphasis on personal relations and on ascribed statuses than did northerners. Not only did white southerners prize political and social cohesion, but also by most measures the South was more homogeneous than the other regions of the country (Hackney 1969, 906, 925).

In the first half of the twentieth century, regional consciousness remained stronger in the South than in any other part of the United States. This "historical lag" is the source of whatever is most distinctive in southern thought and feeling. After its defeat in the Civil War, the South could not participate fully and freely in the "normal" development of American society—that is, industrialism and large-scale capitalism arrived there later and with far less force than in the North or West. By the Reconstruction period New England's regional consciousness was in decline and by the turn of the century the same was true for the Midwest, which never developed a strong sense of regional consciousness comparable to the South, New England, and the West in literature, art, and politics. But the South, burdened by its history of defeat, felt its sectional identity most acutely during the very decades when the United States was becoming a self-conscious nation. While the other regions submitted to dissolution and began to mold into a single national identity, the South worked desperately to keep itself intact. Through an exercise of will, it insisted that the regional memory be the main shaper of its life.

Perhaps because it had so little else to give its people, the South nurtured in them a generous and often obsessive sense of the past. The rest of the country might be committed to commercial expansion or addicted to the notion of progressive optimism, but the South, even if it cared to, was unable to accept these dominant American values; it had been left behind, it was living on the margin of history—a position that often provides the sharpest perspective on history. For this reason possibly the South's greatest contribution to the country in the first decades of the twentieth century was its writers. They remained among the few Americans who could view the dominant bourgeois myths of materialism and progress with a detached critical eye, and who could evoke a spatial dimension or view that evoked another America, dominated by preindustrial mythology (Howe 1951, 357–62).

FOR MORE INFORMATION

Books

Akin, Edward N. *Flagler: Rockefeller Partner and Florida Baron.* Gainesville: University of Florida Press, 1991.

Couch, W. T., ed. *Culture in the South.* Chapel Hill: University of North Carolina Press, 1934.

Hagood, Margaret Jarman. *Mothers of the South: A Portraiture of the White Tenant Farmer Woman.* Chapel Hill: University of North Carolina Press, 1939.

Hall, Jacquelyn Dowd. *Revolt against Chivalry: Jessie Daniel Ames and the Women's Campaign against Lynching.* New York: Columbia University Press, 1979.

LaFarge, Oliver. *A Pictorial History of the American Indian.* New York: Crown Publishers, 1956.

Miller, Randall, and George Pozetta, eds. *Shades of the Sunbelt: Essays on Ethnicity, Race, and the Urban South.* Boca Raton: Florida Atlantic University Press, 1989.

Percy, Will. *Lanterns on the Levy: Recollections of a Planter's Son.* Baton Rouge: Louisiana State University Press, 2006.

Strickland, Laurie, and Elizabeth Dunn. *Old Time Southern Cooking.* Gretna, LA: Pelican Publishing Co., 2002.

Sullivan, Mark. *Our Times: The United States 1900–1925.* New York: Charles Scribner, 1927.

Urban, Wayne, and Jennings Wagoner. *American Education: A History.* New York: McGraw-Hill Companies, 2003.

Wilson, Charles Reagan, and William Ferris, eds. *Encyclopedia of Southern Culture.* Chapel Hill: University of North Carolina Press, 1989.

Woodward, C. Vann. *Origins of the New South 1877–1913.* Baton Rouge: Louisiana State University Press, 1974.

Articles

Bailey, Kenneth. "Southern White Protestants at the Turn of the Century." *American Historical Review* 68, no. 3 (April 1963): 618–35.

Blackwelder, Julia Kirk. "Race, Ethnicity, and Women's Lives in the Urban South." In *Shades of the Sunbelt: Essays on Ethnicity, Race, and the Urban South,* ed. Randall Miller and George Pozetta, pp. 75–91. Boca Raton: Florida Atlantic University Press, 1989.

Clinton, Catherine. "Stars and Bars Feminism." *Reviews in American History* 21, no. 4 (December 1993): 612–16.

Daniel, Peter. Review of *Bad Blood: The Tuskegee Syphilis Experiment* by James Jones. *Journal of Southern History* 48, no. 2 (May 1981): 303–4.

Graham, Robert Charles. Review of *Taking the University to the People: Seventy-five Years of Cooperative Extension* by Wayne D. Rasmussen. *Journal of Economic History* 50, no. 1 (March 1990): 200–221.

Hackney, Sheldon. "Southern Violence." *American Historical Review* 74, no. 3 (February 1969): 906–25.

Hall, Jacquelyn Dowd, Robert Konstadt, and James Leloudi. "Cotton Mill People: Work, Community, and Protest in the Textile South." *American Historical Review* 91, no. 2 (April 1986): 245–86.

Howe, Irving. "The Southern Myth and William Faulkner." *American Quarterly* 3, no. 4 (Winter 1951): 357–62.

Link, William A. "Privies, Progressivism, and Public Schools: Health Reform and Education in the Rural South, 1909–1920." *Journal of Southern History* 54 (November 1988): 623–42.

Norell, Robert. "Caste in Steel: Jim Crow Careers in Birmingham, Alabama." *Journal of American History* 73, no. 3 (December 1986): 669–94.

Orsi, Robert. "The Religious Boundaries of an In-Between People: Street Fest and the Problem of the Dark-Skinned Other in Italian Harlem, 1920–1990." *American Quarterly* 44, no. 3 (September 1992): 313–47.

Smith, Nancy Midgette. "In Search of Professional Identity: Southern Scientists, 1883–1940." *Journal of Southern History* 54, no. 4 (November 1988): 597–622.

Stowe, Steven. Review of *The House of Percy: Honor, Melancholy, and Imagination in a Southern Family.* by Will Percy. *Reviews in American History* 24 (March 1996): 138–43.

Web Sites

Almind, Gert J. "Jukeboxes." http://www.jukeboxworks.com/historyTerm.html.

American Experience. http://pbs.org. *Bill Moyers Journal* "The Legacy of Lynching" www.pbs.org/wgbh/amex/till/peopleevents/e_lynch.html

American Life Histories: Manuscripts from the Federal Writers' Project, 1936–1940. http://www.americanmemory.gov.

Journal Star Archives. http://www.journalstar.com/articles/2005/05/22/Sunday_am/doc428b9 81453c7e539709681.bat.

Steber, Bill. "Juke Joints." http://www.steberphoto.com/articles-1.htm.

Wickman, Patricia. "Seminoles." http://www.seminoletribe.com/tribune/40anniversary/history.shtml.

5

THE MIDWEST

Overview

In 1900, the century changed, but life for most midwesterners in many ways remained much the same as it had been since the end of the Civil War. The Victorian family model of father, mother, and children (more in the rural areas and less in urban settings) that had developed in the previous century was firmly intact as the new century opened. People still traveled from one place to another by walking, by horse, or by trains that were powered by steam, or in the cities by trolleys using the new power source, electricity. Newspapers and books remained the primary source of news and information, and entertainment came in the form of live shows. Rural and small town children usually attended school in a one-room schoolhouse, while schoolchildren in the cities went to public or parish schools organized in the Lancastrian method of neatly aligned rows of desks and strict discipline. Most food was purchased fresh, and, except for flour and other cereal products, some processed meats, and canned goods, most foods were still purchased locally. The federal government remained distant, and politics remained local and almost wholly a concern of—and run by—men.

But most of the midwestern world on which the sun shined on January 1, 1900, would be greatly transformed over the next 40 years. In fact, the events of the first four decades of the twentieth century made the nineteenth-century boasts of material progress seem quaint. In the ensuing decades the automobile and airplane not only revolutionized travel but also changed people's concepts of space and time like nothing had since the railroads of the mid-nineteenth century. Electricity expanded from solely industrial and commercial to private use, and people bought appliances, conveniences, and home entertainment media that their grandparents never could have dreamed possible.

Government also began to change the lives of the people in dramatic if also erratic ways. During World War I, for example, the federal government rationed or controlled food, drink, and travel, and regulated production in factory and field, and at the end of the war the government told Americans that alcohol was bad for them and they could no longer expect alcoholic beverages to be produced, distributed, or sold legally in their country. At the same time, state and local governments established work rules, set wages, regulated public conveyances, inspected foods, conducted hygiene and other public health programs, controlled public utilities and set their rates, laid down zoning rules, and in general made daily life more scheduled and managed than it had ever been, especially in urban areas. To many, these reforms and regulations seemed overly intrusive, yet when the economic devastation of the Great Depression reduced many people to hopeless poverty and despair, they were glad to see the government bring order into their lives. Federal programs that supported farm prices, helped the dispossessed recover a lapsed mortgage, put people back to work, provided safety nets in the form of pensions and workers' compensation, brought electricity to rural areas, and saved the banking system all persuaded many Americans to look to government as a source of inspiration, information, and improvement when the great American capitalist machine could not. And as a result of the Great Depression, most Americans began to understand the benefits of a government that concerned itself with improving their quality of life.

From 1900 to 1929, industrial development grew at a dizzying rate, especially in the Midwest. Led by the new automobile industry, the burgeoning steel conglomerates, and food processors, the Midwest exploded with industrial development, which swelled the population of the older cities and created many new ones. Workforces increased, and the relative standard of living climbed, though many industrial and agricultural workers suffered from harsh working conditions and low wages. Leisure time increased, as did the number of workers seeking recreational outlets. The entertainment industry led by movies, sports, and radio became massive capitalist enterprises. Religion also went through numerous transformations in this era as the dominant Protestant denominations of Midwest America dealt with the powerful appeal of Pentecostal and holiness movements and faced the massive immigration of European Catholics, Eastern Orthodox, Jews, and others in the late nineteenth and early twentieth century. Along with the European migration, blacks from the South began their trek northward and transformed many of the cities of the Midwest both demographically and culturally. In many ways, the period from 1900 to 1940 remade the Midwest to such a degree that Americans worried about losing their old ways to modernism, immigration, and governmental regulation, and they fought back with appeals to religious fundamentalism, nativism, racism, and a political rearguard action against Progressivism and the New Deal.

Domestic Life

As the new century unfolded, forces evolved that radically altered the Victorian family model fabricated in the nineteenth century. The automobile, consolidated schools, youth clubs, birth control, changed expectations of marriage, migration, and women entering the workforce all contributed to the modification of the definition and role of family in the first decades of the twentieth century.

Men continued to perceive themselves as the principal breadwinners of the family, and they measured their worth in their ability to support their families and, when able, their communities. Women also made great strides toward economic independence in this era, and in 1920 they realized the long-sought goal of enfranchisement. Families became smaller, especially among the middle class. In urban areas, more attention was paid to children, and, as the century evolved, children became more educated. A child who would not be expected to complete more than six years of education in 1910 was finishing high school by the 1920s. Various immigrant and ethnic groups resisted women's economic independence and political empowerment, but changes in the national culture and economy had their effects on assimilating many women into wider expectations of social autonomy.

The Depression, with its high unemployment and home mortgage foreclosures, brought unprecedented pressures on families, but most survived. Although the family underwent many changes in this era, the concept of family continued to define the fabric of American life. This section will explore those changes and adaptations that families made over the first four decades of the twentieth century.

FAMILY LIFE

By the 1920s in the Midwest, more people both urban and rural were marrying younger. There were many factors motivating young people to marry. Aside from encouragement by the community to marry soon after graduating from high school, there was also the availability of factory jobs, which allowed a young man to avoid a prolonged apprenticeship and still obtain employment with a salary that could support a family. There also existed increased employment opportunities for wives to supplement family incomes. The relatively greater ease of dissolving marriages, the diffusion of knowledge regarding birth control, and the growing tendency to engage in leisure-time pursuits as couples rather than groups also contributed to lowering the age at which people married. The typical middle-class family structure in the Midwest, as in other parts of the nation, consisted of a married couple and their unmarried children.

Middle-class Protestant weddings in the Midwest usually included of a brief ceremonial exchange of pledges by a man and woman before a duly sanctioned representative of the community, usually either a judge or a minister. This ceremony, very largely religious in the 1890s, became for the Protestant middle class increasingly secularized in the new century. Just before the turn of the century, 85 percent of the local marriages were performed by a religious representative and 13 percent by a secular agent, while in 1923 those performed by the religious leaders had fallen to 63 percent, and secular weddings had risen to 34 percent. Such trends worried the clergy. A prominent minister in a midwestern city, for example, reported to sociologists Robert Lynd and Helen Merrell Lynd in their study of *Middletown* (Muncie,

Indiana) that the increase in divorce in the new century was largely due to the secularization of the marriage ceremony. He believed that taking marriage out of the sanctity of the churches relaxed the obligations one partner had toward the other in respect to their relationship.

The choice of a mate in marriage was nominally hedged by certain legal, religious, and traditional or customary restrictions. Interracial marriage, for example, continued to be legally prohibited in most parts of the Midwest. Laws also prohibited marriage with an insane person, an imbecile or epileptic, a person having a transmissible disease, or, within certain limits, with a male who had been a public charge, a person whose former marriage had not been dissolved, a person under the influence of liquor or narcotics, or a man under 18 or a woman under 16 years of age. Religious requirements varied somewhat from one religious group to another, but generally concerned two main points: first, nominal prohibition by Catholics of marriage outside the Catholic Church and a corresponding though weaker sentiment among Protestants against marriage to a Catholic; and second, varying but somewhat lessening emphasis upon the permanency of marriage, whereby a few religious leaders refused to remarry a divorced person. Some ministers would refuse to marry persons living in "open [sexual] sin," though the marriage ceremony was commonly regarded as the accepted means of regularizing such individuals (Lynd and Lynd 1929, 112–14).

Once married, the newlyweds usually left the homes of their parents at once and began to make a home of their own; the bride symbolically confirmed her new identity by dropping the last name of her father for the name of her husband. Financial support of the wife by the husband, sexual fealty to one partner only, and sufficient mutual consideration that excluded cruel treatment, sufficient "sobriety" and "morality" to avoid charges of "habitual drunkenness" and "criminal conviction," and the desire and the ability to have children—all represented the minimal expectations of marriage. Theoretically, among native-born Americans, love—the mysterious attraction of two young people for each other—was seen as the only valid basis for marriage. In some states, as a corollary to this belief, loss of affection after marriage, previously an unacceptable reason for legal separation, in the mid-1920s became recognized as sufficient cause for divorce. Commenting on the increasing divorce rate, social columnist and advisor Dorothy Dix pointed out the following:

The reason there are more divorces is that people are demanding more of life than they used to . . . in former times . . . they expected to settle down to a life of hard work . . . to putting up with each other. Probably men are just as good husbands as they ever were, but grandmother had to stand grandpa. For he was her meal ticket and her card of admission to good society. A divorced woman was a disgraced woman. . . . But now we see things differently. We see no good purpose is achieved by keeping two people together who have come to hate each other. (Lynd and Lynd 1929, 128)

Along with rising divorce rates, a decline in births also brought changes to the middle-class family structure in the first decade of the twentieth century. The primary reason for the declining birthrate was the increase in the use of birth control among middle-class families. The male condom was the most frequently used form of birth control, although diaphragms were increasing in use. The 1920s and 1930s also witnessed a decline in parental authority over children as the automobile and school-centered activities began to draw children away from the family core.

While middle-class white families struggled with issues such as divorce, family size, and the loss of control over their children, the newly arriving black families from the South struggled with survival. Up until the second decade of the twentieth century, although life in the rural South had many difficulties, family ties and tradition kept southern blacks close to their roots. But during World War I, the immigrant labor supply from Europe had dried up, creating employment possibilities that were heralded in attractive articles written by the *Chicago Defender* and other black papers. These same papers used biblical metaphor in beckoning southern blacks north by extolling the advantages of living in the "promised lands" of Chicago, Detroit, Cleveland, and other industrial cities. At the same time the arrival of the boll weevil in the South began to push blacks from their traditional home. Such factors caused the emotional and cultural ties that had held blacks in the South to begin to disintegrate, and the Great Migration north began. Large midwestern cities, which absorbed much of the movement, were strange and forbidding to black families who had lived seemingly forever on Mississippi Delta plantations or in small southern towns. Men in worn, outmoded suits carrying battered baggage and women clutching ragged, barefooted children crowded into the Midwest's large urban train stations.

Upon arriving, they hopefully looked for a familiar face. Every Sunday at train stations throughout the Midwest, migrants would mingle with local blacks who went to the station to meet a friend or a relative or just to see who had arrived from their hometown. Often there was no familiar face to depend on, and the family had to make it on their own. The first few days for a newly arrived black family were terrifying. Eventually they would find the "Negro section" of the city, where housing was scarce and ordinary conveniences were often lacking. Many black families who could not afford the high rent took in lodgers to share the burden. Sometimes they took in lodgers even when the added income wasn't necessary. The lodger might be a newly arrived migrant relative or a friend down on his luck. Regardless of the reason, the family structure often differed greatly from the Victorian model of middle-class America (Spear 1967, 147–49).

For most white middle- and many working-class families of the Midwest, the first decades of the century were relatively comfortable. For the newly arriving black families, even those who did not immediately experience economic improvement, at least there was hope. This era of modest prosperity and hope for most families came crashing down at the end of the 1920s when the Great Depression arrived. One immediate impact of the economic collapse was a further drop in the birth rate, which had already dropped below three children per family by the 1920s. Consequently, the generation born in the 1930s represented the smallest population increase in the history of the United States. During the Depression years, socializing with nonfamily members also declined, because the cost of going out or entertaining at home became prohibitive (Kyvig 2002, 226).

Franklin Roosevelt was elected president in 1932, promising a New Deal for Depression-riddled American families, which meant that midwestern families began to feel the impact of a socially involved federal government to a degree they had never before experienced. For example, to save families from losing their homes to foreclosure, one of the immediate acts passed by the Roosevelt administration with the support of a compliant Congress was the Home Owners Loan Corporation. On the day the corporation opened for business in Akron, Ohio, a double line of applicants stretched three blocks down Main Street. Eventually the Home Owners Loan Corporation would refinance one of every five homes in America (Kyvig 2002, 233).

MEN

As the new century unfolded, many middle-class men still clung to the social ethics of the Victorian model. They gained their manly identity through their occupations and were expected to work hard and be good providers for their families. Away from work, the family and home were the centerpieces of their life. Many blue-collar workers also accepted these values, which advocated sexual continence, work before pleasure, temperance, and punctuality. Men who supported capitalism believed such conduct was required to get ahead in the marketplace, to keep one's job in the workshop, and to become an independent master. Many working men believed that Victorian behavior would help revitalize their own culture of productivity through an emphasis on brotherhood and mutual cooperation. As a counterpoint there also existed a bachelor subculture that rejected piety, sobriety, sexual abstinence, and steady work.

In addition to saloons, favorite gathering places for working-class men were poolrooms and bowling alleys. Although at these venues the variant aspects of male culture converged, a survey in 1913 of 806 working men found that the majority of those who frequented billiard parlors were single and born in the United States or Great Britain. They were mainly transportation workers, clerks, or in domestic or personal service. While men with short workdays were the most likely to visit poolrooms, these halls also took up a large proportion of the discretionary time of those who worked 11 or more hours a day. There was also a very strong correlation between income for workers earning less than 35 dollars a week and use of the poolroom. There were probably more billiard parlors than any other commercialized entertainment except perhaps the movies.

In addition to poolrooms, bowling alleys, often associated with saloons, also provided a cheap and readily accessible male entertainment. Banned in large cities of the Northeast for several years because of its close association with gambling, bowling prospered in the Midwest. Because of the considerable gambling connected to the sport and because alleys were often located in the basements of saloons, bowling was not regarded as a respectable sport for women, and the proprietors of bowling alleys were closely associated with the male bachelor subculture (Riess 1991, 74–77).

Some historians have found that males of all classes at the turn of the century expressed a "national urge to be young, masculine, [and] adventurous" and rebellious against the "frustrations and sheer dullness of an urban industrialized culture" (Marsh, 1988, 165). They use this male image to explain the rise in popularity of boxing and football in the early decades of the century. While there is much truth to this generalization, others have suggested that during the first two decades of the twentieth century, a different male image emerged, especially in the newly developing suburban areas. This new male created an original model of masculine domesticity. Although this suburban male did not share household duties with his spouse, he did take up increased responsibilities for bringing up children, especially sons, by teaching them and taking them on trips. A domestic male would also be more inclined to make his wife, rather than male cronies, his regular companion on an evening out. And while he might not dust the mantel or make the bed, he would take a significantly greater interest in the details of running the household and caring for his children (Marsh 1988, 165–66).

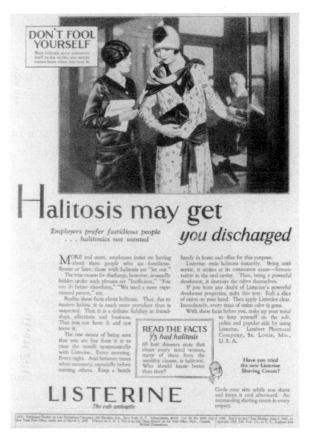

This anti-halitosis advertisement for Listerine antiseptic mouthwash appeared in the July 5, 1929, issue of *Life* magazine. Library of Congress.

For the most part, middle-class men eschewed the gathering places of the working class, and many found male companionship in clubs founded to promote their own business interests. Eventually, the members of these organizations became less concerned with creating business contacts than with improving the communities in which they lived. Leaders in this movement toward charitable fraternal organizations were midwestern men. In 1915, for example, the first Kiwanis Club was organized in Detroit, Michigan, with the purpose of promoting the exchange of business among the members. However, even before the Detroit club received its state charter, the members were distributing Christmas baskets to the poor. By 1919, after lively debate over the club's mission, the organization officially became dedicated to community service. In 1917, Chicago businessman Melvin Jones established the Association of Lions Clubs with the belief that local fraternal business clubs should expand their horizons from purely professional concerns to the betterment of their communities and the world at large. In addition to earmarking specific fundraising projects to aid local charities, these fraternal organizations provided low-cost life insurance for their members, giving them the peace of mind that their families would be economically secure even if they died.

Catholic men joined the Knights of Columbus, which, like non-Catholic fraternal organizations, did charitable work in their communities, offered low-cost life insurance programs, and provided scholarships for deserving students. In Chicago, the Knights also took on the additional work of caring for delinquent boys (Shanabruch 1981, 189). Midwestern Knights also supported a vigorous public education program, which combated the lingering forces of anti-Catholicism in that region (Fisher 2000, 100).

Black men also subscribed to the cultural code that men had the responsibility of being providers for their family. That need was often the final and most compelling motive for making the decision to travel north. With much of white life closed to them, black males created their own space for expressing concern for the economic and social well-being of the community by building social and fraternal lodges and making them the center of community activities. Most important of these male organizations were the Prince Hall Masons, which traced their history back to the late eighteenth century. Membership in black Masonic Lodges transcended class, as men were measured by their virtue, not their pocketbooks. In addition to the Prince Hall Masons, most black communities included another male organization known as the Knights of Pythias. These lodges fulfilled the male aspiration to provide not only for their own families but also the larger black community. The lodges provided benefits for sickness or death in an age when few blacks carried insurance. They also established scholarships for promising young people.

Another important gathering place, particularly for black men, was the barbershop. The black-owned barbershop provided a space where black men aired their opinions and debated issues. The barbers who presided over these shops were usually important community leaders. Black barbers, in contrast to their white counterparts, melded their trade into a close-knit network, which enabled them to provide their customers with information about jobs and housing. In 1916, for example, Robert Horton, a barber from Mississippi, recruited nearly 40 men and women to join his family in a migration club that secured a discount for travel to Chicago, where he established a barbershop in his new city that became a gathering and information center for migrants from Mississippi (Reich 2006, 60).

In summary, the male culture of the Midwest, regardless of class or race, judged itself by men's ability to be good providers for their families, and when able, to extend their concern to their immediate community. They also left to women domestic responsibilities of household management and child rearing, and when possible, the majority of working-class men continued to prefer to pass their leisure time in the company of other men.

WOMEN

In their study of the "typical American" community, sociologists Robert and Helen Merrell Lynd discovered that "Middletown" (Muncie, Indiana) husbands, when talking frankly among themselves, were likely to speak of women as creatures purer and morally better than men but at the same time as relatively impractical, emotional, unstable, given to prejudice, easily hurt, and largely incapable of facing facts or doing hard thinking. One group of the city's "most thoughtful men" agreed that "there's something about the female mind that always short circuits a general statement into a personal criticism." A school official, approached regarding the possibility of getting a woman on the school board, replied, "with only three people on the board there isn't much place for a woman." Another group of "prominent Middletown men" also agreed that "Woman is the most unselfish creature on earth within her family, but with outsiders she is quick to imagine snubs to her family, bristle up, and become unsocial."

According to the Lynds' study, Middletown wives appeared in part to have accepted the impression of them that many of their husbands maintained. The mottos of two of the city's women's clubs ("Men are God's trees, women are his flowers," and "True womanliness is . . . the greatest charm of woman") suggested little change from the prevailing attitude reflected in the title of a commencement essay in 1891, which affirmed that "Woman Is Most Perfect When Most Womanly." At a local political dinner, the talk at one of the tables turned to women's smoking, and a woman politician said with an air of finality: "Women have to be morally better than men. It is they who pull men up or cause their downfall." Women, on the other hand, were frequently heard to express the opinion, accompanied by a knowing smile, that "Men are nothing but big little boys, who have never grown up and must be treated as such" (Lynd and Lynd 1929, 117–19).

If "Middletown" reflected the continuity of cultural values in the small-town Midwest, the large cities and their suburbs revealed significant social changes underway in the first decades of the twentieth century. As the new century opened, more women entered the workforce than ever before, and World War I propelled the movement of women into the workplace and became an important force in altering gender relationships not only in the Midwest but also throughout the country. In the 1920s the number of women in the Midwest working outside the home doubled, and they comprised 21 percent of all wage earners. Still, for the most part, women remained concentrated in low-paying and low-status jobs. These included clerical positions, store sales, teaching, and nursing.

A major issue that emerged for women in the new century in the Midwest and elsewhere was their rights as women in the workplace. During World War I when women entered new occupations because the men left to join the army and navy, unions and individual rank-and-file members often objected. The locals of the Amalgamated Street and Electric Railway Employees in, Chicago, Cleveland, and Detroit in 1917 and 1918, for example, fought the entry of the hundreds of women who became streetcar conductors. The male unionists maintained that women workers could be difficult to organize, even though in the past they had organized themselves and even participated in strikes. The result was that trade unions did not take women seriously as workers and for years the AFL (American Federation of Labor) refused to spend money for organizing low-paid women workers.

By 1920, a majority of women in the United States lived in cities and towns, rather than on farms. Yet even at that date literally thousands of women who worked for wages were in farming. Until the end of the nineteenth century, for example, almost half a million women were employed on farms, a figure that included only those who were actually paid for their work, or worked as farmers or planters. It did not include the millions of women who were farm wives, whose work in the home might be onerous and almost unending and who in addition might work for days or even weeks in the fields, especially at particular times in the annual cycle of farm work. Because wages were not paid for this labor in the home and in the field, it was not counted in the census figures on women's work. The great majority of women farm workers (that is, laborers) who were paid were black. In 1900, for example, there were 440,000 black women farm workers and 290,000 white ones. By 1930, the number of white women in agricultural labor (primarily as farmers) was still rising, reaching 345,000 that year, but at that date the number of black women had fallen to 420,000. This change reflected the migration of black families to midwestern cities like Detroit and Chicago, a trek that had begun during World War I and continued through the ensuing decades.

Under slavery, black women had generally worked in the fields, and during the late nineteenth century only in the South were white women used to working in the fields, mirroring, no doubt, the greater poverty of southern farmers after the Civil War. A survey made in 1921 of some 900 families in Nebraska, for example, showed that only 12.5 percent of white women ever worked in the fields. Even when a Midwest farm wife did not work in the fields, her job was a heavy one, as it had been on the frontier or during an earlier and less developed stage of American agriculture. By the early years of the twentieth century, whatever may have been the attitudes of farm wives earlier, to many women life on the farm seemed dull, draining, and disadvantageous. The benefits of city life were now evident to all farm people through magazines, catalogs, newspapers, and other means whereby city culture spread into the countryside. Especially in the eyes of women, the contrast between town and the individual homestead farm became more evident than at any other time in the country's history. In fact, there was sufficient discontent among farm women in the early twentieth century for the Department of Agriculture in 1913 to conduct a survey of attitudes among 55,000 correspondents on farms. Many of the farmers' wives wrote in directly, recording their attitudes and those of their neighbors. As one Iowa woman wrote, women want to feel "that they are partners in fact with their husbands and not looked upon as subordinates." In her opinion "the worst feature of farm work is too much work and too little pleasure. . . ." The main cause for dissatisfaction of farm women in the Midwest was their isolation. "The fathers get so accustomed to the mother staying at home they seem to forget that they might enjoy a little rest and recreation," the Iowan complained. "And the mother gets so accustomed to it she, too, seems to forget she is human."

A woman who lived on an admittedly "splendid" 320-acre farm in Minnesota with "unlimited opportunities" still found her situation almost intolerable "on account of being so shut off from the outside world." Women have to stay home, she noted, while the man "is less subjected to the monotonous drudgery than is the woman." A similar comparison of the life of the farmer and that of the farm wife was made by another farm woman: "The hardest phase of country life for the women in my neighborhood is the monotony, with no means or opportunity for any social life whatever." Even where there was no fieldwork, as a woman from Michigan made clear, work in the home could be backbreaking. "We do not feel so very much ne-glected by the department [of Agriculture] as by our men." Even on wealthy farms, with good and expensive equipment, "the women must still do the work much as their mothers before them did" (Degler 1980, 406). The Michigan woman explained as follows:

There are no modern conveniences such as water in the house, bath, modern lights, vacuum cleaners, etc., and often not even such inexpensive things as an oil stove, fireless cooker, washing machine, gasoline iron, bread mixer, and many such small items which help so much to lighten the women's work; while the men have all the modern machinery and farm imple-ments their work requires. (Degler 1980, 406)

The woman writing this report did not blame the men for selfishness or even indifference; rather, she ascribed the problem to men's lack of recognition of the large amount of work performed by farm women. A Colorado woman suggested "the department should educate the farm men to the necessity of labor-saving devices for the household. Improvements in the farm home seem to fall behind improvements on the farm" (Degler 1980, 406).

Regardless of how arduous and demanding of time and effort the life of the farm woman may have been, it was always possible to combine work and family on a farm. Both occupations took place at the same site, as it were. When work for women moved outside the home, however, women who could most readily follow it were those without family responsibilities or those who had no husband or no income. By the early years of the twentieth century, although the great proportion of married women did not work outside the home, there was a sufficiently large number of mar-ried women who did, for whatever reason, that the combining of home and work was neither novel nor rare (Degler 1980, 400–411).

During the 1920s women also entered into social spaces that were formerly the ex-clusive domain of men. In the 1920s, for example, many midwestern women made, sold, and drank liquor in unprecedented fashion. Decades later, a woman recalled the many evenings she donned her flapper finery and headed to the dance halls where she and her friends shimmied to jazz tunes and slipped outside to share a pint of moonshine. Until the advent of Prohibition, drinking in small midwestern towns was governed by clearly defined and understood social rules. Saloons were male preserves and reflected the ethnic and occupational strata of the community. Any woman who drank in a saloon was assumed to be a prostitute at worst, "loose" at best. When reputable women drank, they did so at home. Prohibition rattled these traditional patterns. It curbed some drinking, but more significantly, it changed the drinking habits of youth and women. Prohibition accelerated the advent of het-erosocial nightlife as new watering holes welcomed young couples and groups of women, as well as men.

Prohibition also allowed ethnic groups and women to capitalize on the under-ground economy by launching new businesses in the manufacturing and sale of li-quor. Women cooked liquor on the kitchen stove to supplement the family income.

Husbands and wives running "moonshine joints" and "home speaks" competed with saloons hastily converted into soft drink parlors. A few women operated bustling roadhouses. In the 1920s, gray-haired mothers appearing in court on bootlegging charges confounded judges and juries, whose previous contact with female criminals had been almost exclusively with prostitutes. In all aspects of the liquor business, women moved into spaces that had once been reserved exclusively for men. Prohibition allowed women to rewrite the script of acceptable public behavior and to transform one arena of commercial leisure bounded by rigid gender roles.

There is great irony in Prohibition. The law had, in effect, created a vacuum of rules, and women exploited the opportunity to slip into niches in the economy of liquor production, distribution, and consumption. Women had been in the vanguard of the Prohibition movement, a movement designed to restrict male behavior by abolishing the vice-ridden retreat of the saloon and curbing male drinking. Yet, a decade after legislative success, some of the very same women led the campaign for repeal of the 18th Amendment, having concluded that some kind of regulated liquor trade was preferable to moral anarchy. Much to their dismay, during Prohibition, drinking had become an equal opportunity vice. True, many saloons closed their doors forever and the consumption of alcohol did decrease. But during Prohibition, men and women reconstructed social drinking habits, and the greatest change was women's newfound penchant to belly up to the bar. Unforeseen by proponents and opponents, Prohibition effectively created new social spaces in speakeasies and nightclubs; this allowed a redefinition of sex roles in one of the most gender-segregated arenas of leisure—getting together for a drink. Behavior followed structural change. Public drinking was not on the list of rights demanded by twentieth-century feminists. Indeed, the seemingly frivolous activities of young women in the 1920s dismayed feminists, who saw them divert energy from politics. Nevertheless, the reorganization of drinking did increase women's autonomy. Whether they spent an evening drinking and dancing with their boyfriends, husbands, or members of their ladies clubs, doors that had been closed to them now opened in welcome. Prohibition provided women with new economic opportunities, greater choices of public leisure, and a chance to broaden the definition of reputable female behavior (Murphy 1994, 174–76).

When the Great Depression brought an end to the boom of the 1920s women felt the economic pressure in many ways that were determined by their gender. Among women who before the Depression were employed outside the home, the wave of layoffs hit them first. Employers, when making layoff decisions, showed preference to keep men on as the principal breadwinners and let women go. For those women who did not work outside the house, their home was their domain, and by 1933, many were threatened with the loss of the focus of their lives as over 40 percent of home mortgages fell into default. Sometimes under the pressure and humiliation of economic failure, families simply collapsed. Desertion rates soared in the 1930s as many husbands simply abandoned what they considered to be hopeless situations and many women were left alone to deal with the problems of maintaining a semblance of family order. Patterns of consumption reveal some of the difficulties facing women. While overall food sales declined, challenging women to become more creative with fewer resources, the sale of items such as scotch tape soared as women tried to repair household items rather than discard them. Almost half of the families in America survived the Depression years without losing their jobs or their homes, but for the women in the families of the other half who did, daily life became a serious struggle. Women did whatever they could to keep their families together. Many women stood in lines at garbage dumps to salvage some edible food for their family. Some took in wash and sewing, others cared for children in their homes, while others sought relief from private and public welfare agencies (Kyvig 2002, 226–28). For some the New Deal policies of direct relief, home loans, and public works saved their families; others would have to wait until World War II restored prosperity to the economy and their lives. But for many women, the Depression marked the end of their lives as they knew it and they would never recover what they had lost.

CHILDREN

In the Midwest as other areas of the country, parents considered the education of the young to be one of their foremost responsibilities, and for most people their religious faith remained a philosophical guide for child rearing. A mother who was prominent in the educational work of a medium-sized midwestern city stated in a forum on child rearing, "I believe there is no boy problem. Children are not a problem but a joy. We can trust them and God will lead them." Most of the papers given at the mothers' council tended to deal in generalities. For example, "The duty of parents is to make their children realize the sacred duty of every man to vote, to exercise the political sacrament of the ballot." In the case of working-class families, in answer to every question in regard to children, mothers of the working class would answer by such blanket explanations as "the cause of that is sin or the devil and the only remedy is salvation" (Lynd and Lynd 1929, 178).

In the first decades of the new century the responsibility of child rearing fell mainly on the parents, but increasingly the burden became shared with school, church, and youth organizations, both secular and nonsecular. In the new century in cities and towns, when a child turned six, the community became involved with the child's education. As children entered high school, a number of activities began to draw them away from the home. Aside from various clubs at school, there were the Boy Scouts, the YMCA, and the YWCA.

Catholics of the Midwest maintained their own schools and their own clubs. As a Catholic alternative to the YMCA and YWCA, for example, the Chicago Catholics under the leadership of auxiliary Bishop Bernard Sheil organized the Catholic Youth Organization (CYO) in 1930. Sheil founded the CYO also because he recognized that young urban Catholics were being drawn away from the church by the competition of such exhilarating pleasures as drinking, fighting, and womanizing. He feared that the church, along with family and schools, apparently had lost its historic function as an agent of socialization and had little relevance to the needs of young Catholic males in the 1920s and 1930s. Sheil wanted to find a way to bring the young men back into the fold. The Catholic Church's concern over the protection of its young in America dated back to the mid-nineteenth century, when it created parochial schools to counter Protestant influence in the public schools. In the early 1900s, when most Catholics were unassimilated new immigrant stock, bishops worried that adult-directed boys' organizations like the YMCA and the Boy Scouts would undermine the faith of good Catholics by promoting the values of the Protestant core culture to the detriment of their own religious heritage. In fact, Sheil exaggerated the danger, for the Protestant-oriented YMCA and Boy Scouts drew few Catholics to them and were designed for rural American youth coming to the cities more than for immigrants. In any case, most immigrant families could hardly afford to allow children to spend time in clubs of any kind or even school. Their labor was too valuable. Also, among some immigrant cultures, schooling beyond learning catechism and basic literacy and arithmetic was deemed superfluous, even dangerous to cultural norms and family needs.

Still, as the second generation of children of immigrants grew up and as older Catholic populations such as the Irish and Germans continued to be city dwellers, such organizations as the CYO played larger roles in organizing youth activities. Sports were especially appealing to boys. The CYO began operations in 1931 with a huge boxing tournament and a 10-team basketball league. Sheil emphasized boxing because it appealed to poor working-class youth—the precise group he wanted to attract to the CYO. The CYO became an important training ground for boxers, three of whom made the 1936 Olympic team. The CYO differed significantly from Protestant-inspired youth athletic clubs in that the CYO reflected a Catholic perspective that did not fear the influence of women as teachers of older boys, as the late Victorians had. And the CYO used sport not to build manly, healthy, and physically muscular Christians but rather to save souls. Also, in the pre–World War II years, the CYO always served a heterogeneous lower-class Catholic clientele, while Protestant boys' groups started with a homogeneous middle-class WASP (white Anglo-Saxon Protestant) population. CYO branches were soon established all over the country and by 1940 reached 150,000 Catholic youth. Besides boxing, the CYO sponsored a baseball league and for years the biggest basketball association in the United States (Riess 1991, 101–2).

PETS

Although Pennsylvania (see Chapter 2, The Northeast) led the way in protecting stray animals, a second wave of humane organizations emerged around the turn of the century. This new group included the Chicago Anti-Cruelty Society, established in 1899. As in other parts of the country, the Midwest experienced an explosion of interest in house pets, particularly dogs, during the Victorian age, and at the turn of the century enterprising Chicagoans found ways to capitalize on the new money-making opportunities generated by pet enthusiasts. Taking advantage of the growing market created by people who kept their dogs indoors most of the time, one Chicago seller promised dog couches that had "a very smart finished appearance in complete harmony with the interior décor." Also by the mid-1930s, dog treadmills were being designed for apartment dogs that did not get enough exercise outdoors. As more people bought smaller breeds that were unaccustomed to the colder climates of northern cities of the upper Midwest, a Chicago entrepreneur offered "coat style" dog sweaters made to order, woolen dog blankets, and rubberized rain slickers with small rubber boots (Grier 2006, 308). All this reflected the trend toward anthropomorphizing pets and making them part of the family, especially in middle-class homes. Attitudes toward the purpose of keeping and the treatment of animals also distinguished rural from urban America, especially in the farm-rich areas of the Midwest.

Economic Life

In the first half of the twentieth century, the Midwest became the industrial center of the United States. Taking advantage of the transportation infrastructure provided by the Great Lakes and the railroads, the abundance of cheap labor, and the open space of the Midwest, the industrial giants of the country settled into the Midwest. New factories sprang up in every city in the upper Midwest, and where there were no cities, such as along the southern shore of Lake Michigan, corporations created them. The myriad of unskilled jobs generated by the new industries created a new industrial working class, and along with them tensions of class and race, which would follow any large and rather hurried concentration of people from diverse backgrounds. The population explosion and the rapid development of technology in the cities also made divisions between urban and rural life more obvious than they had ever been in the country's history. Generally those working and living on farms, until well into the 1930s, did not experience directly the technological marvels occurring in the cities, and by 1930, the small family farms seemed almost to stand as memorials to a world left behind by an urban population that within one generation had shifted velocity from the speed of a horse to that of an airplane.

WORK AND WORKPLACE

The Midwest workplace became the venue for the greatest industrial innovations of the first half of the twentieth century. These new industries began and remained in the Midwest for the first half of the century. This revolution started with the automobile in 1901, when Ransom Olds of Lansing, Michigan, began producing a car for the middle class.

Even though the curved-dash Oldsmobile cost a mere $650, it remained out of reach to many living on an average income. In 1906, another midwestern automobile maker, Detroit's Henry Ford, began building a reliable four-cylinder 15-horse-

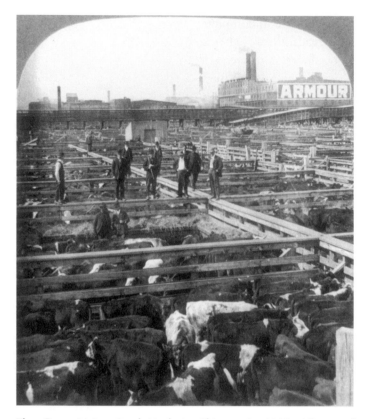

The Great Union Stock Yards in Chicago in 1909. Library of Congress.

power car intended for the middle-class market. The $600 Model N Ford was deluged with orders, and Ford was soon producing 100 Model Ns a day. In 1908 Ford announced the production of the Model T and by 1914 had reduced its cost to $490. Ford's greatest innovation was the replacement of individual construction crews with the moving assembly line. At the same time that Henry Ford was promoting the Model T, another Detroit businessman, William C. Durant, busied himself collecting small independent automakers, including Buick, Oldsmobile, Cadillac, and Chevrolet. He also purchased control of parts makers Fisher Body and Charles Kettering's Electric Starter and Battery Company. Together, these small companies would become General Motors Corporation. In 1919, awash in World War I profits, Durant also established the General Motors Acceptance Corporation as a means of financing his automobiles, and within two years, half of all automobile buyers, instead of paying cash for their cars, were entering into credit purchase agreements. By 1926, 75 percent of all car purchasers bought their car on credit, which expanded dramatically the population that could afford to buy automobiles. Credit buying also altered buying habits, as more drivers began to eschew the economically reliable but unchanging Model T for the more expensive but colorful and ever-changing styles and optional luxuries of General Motors cars.

New "scientific" production methods emerging in the Midwest not only contributed to the creation of new industries like the automobile, but they also transformed the working space of more traditional occupations. Before the turn of the century, for example, cleaning and preparing meat had been a skilled trade, but this craft also came under the influence of the rationalization of the new industrial order. By 1890, the assembly line, or rather the disassembly line, had been introduced to the meatpacking industry. From that time on, all that was needed to be a meatpacker was a strong back and the ability to do simple repetitive tasks. A laborer could spend an entire day for months at a time slicing jowls off hogs as their carcasses were drawn past them on a moving chain. After putting in nine very chilly hours at the plant, life was little better at home for many workers. In Chicago, these "factories" became an important and sometimes permanent stopping place for many immigrants who lived with their families in a dismal area called "the Back of the Yards." Houses were squalid frame buildings of varying sizes. They were divided into family dwelling units with as many as 12 people living in the same house. All the houses had running water, but there was usually only one toilet set in the hall between the housing units. Bathtubs were scarce; over 90 percent of the dwellings were without them. Despite such terrible conditions, stockyard workers remained unorganized.

As Saul Alinsky pointed out, "the packers froze and suffered side by side in the factories, but on the street they hardly spoke to one another" (Alinsky 1969, 80). Bonus systems established by Swift Meat Company also set workers against each other. It was not uncommon to see one person stab the hand of another with a fork to grab pieces of meat that could be trimmed more quickly. With so many forces pulling them apart, it took meatpackers longer than other industrial workers to organize for better pay and work conditions. It was not until the fall of 1939 that the Packing Workers Organizing Committee (PWOC) of the Congress of Industrial Organizations (CIO) organized a majority of workers, thereby forcing the meatpackers to recognize the union. This union victory could not have succeeded without the help of Bishop Bernard Sheil, who convinced the mostly Catholic immigrants

> ### 📷 *Snapshot*
>
> **Scene from a Meatpacking Plant As Described in Upton Sinclair's *The Jungle* (1906)**
>
> It was a long, narrow room. At the head there was a great iron wheel, about twenty feet in circumference, with rings here and there along its edge. Upon both sides of this wheel there was a narrow space, into which came the hogs at the end of their journey. . . . It [the wheel] began slowly to revolve, and then the men upon each side of it sprang to work. They had chains which they fastened about the leg of the nearest hog, and the other end of the chain they hooked into one of the rings upon the wheel. So, as the wheel turned, a hog was suddenly jerked off his feet and borne aloft.
>
> At the same instant the car was assailed by a most terrifying shriek. The shriek was followed by another, louder and yet more agonizing—for once started upon that journey, the hog never came back.
>
> Meantime, the men upon the floor were going about their work. One by one they hooked up the hogs, and one by one with a swift stroke they slit their throats. There was a long line of hogs, with squeals and lifeblood ebbing away together; until at last each started again, and vanished with a splash into a huge vat of boiling water.
>
> The carcass hog was scooped out of the vat by machinery, and then it fell to the second floor. It was then again strung up by machinery, and sent upon another trolley ride; this time passing between two lines of men, who sat upon a raised platform, each doing a certain single thing to the carcass as it came to him. One with a swift stroke cut the throat; another with two swift strokes severed the head, which fell to the floor and vanished through a hole. Another made a slit down the body; a second opened the body wider; a third with a saw cut the breastbone; a fourth loosened the entrails; a fifth pulled them out—and they also slid through a hole in the floor. There were men to clean the carcass inside, to trim it and wash it. Looking down this room, one saw, creeping slowly, a line of dangling hogs a hundred yards in length; and for every yard there was a man, working as if a demon were after him. At the end of this hog's progress every inch of the carcass had been gone over several times; and then it was rolled into the chilling room, where it stayed for twenty-four hours, and where a stranger might lose himself in a forest of freezing hogs. (Sinclair 2003, 30–31)

that the Church supported their right to demand a just wage. After a successful summer of organizing by the PWOC, the industry accepted the demands of the PWOC and the meatpackers were on their way to better working and living conditions.

The rapid rise of new industries such as the automobile in the Midwest stimulated an economic boom that lasted through the 1920s. At the end of this boom, the average per capita income for nonfarm workers in the Midwest was $854 and for farm workers it was $262. The Great Depression, however, put the brakes on this unprecedented prosperity for the unskilled worker. In Chicago, in 1931, in the depths of the Great Depression, a survey found that unemployment had reached 50 percent in the all-important manufacturing sector. African Americans suffered even more. In Chicago, blacks made up only 4 percent of the population, but they represented 16 percent of the jobless. African American women, often employed as domestic help in white middle-class families, were the first to lose their jobs as the economy took a serious downturn. Already by January 1931, African American female

A 1903 view of Chicago showing State Street, looking north from Madison Street. The Granger Collection, New York.

unemployment in Chicago had reached 58 percent; in Detroit it was 75 percent, and 51 percent in Pittsburgh. Because the economic depression was primarily a capitalist indus- trial collapse, wage earners in the largest cities remained the hardest hit. In the rural areas of Ohio, for example, unemployment stood at 12 percent, while in Cleveland it reached 23.7 percent in the late 1930s. At the height of the Depression, authorities in the city of Detroit, deciding they could no longer afford the luxury of a zoo, ordered the slaughter of its animals to feed the hungry people of their city.

The arrival of Franklin Roosevelt and the Democratic majority into Washington in 1933 stimulated a number of changes in the depressed American economy. Government public work projects designed to give the unemployed jobs, federally insured home finance programs, and rural electrification were just a few of the programs that directly affected midwesterners. Beer brewers of the Midwest were also grateful to the new lead- ers in Washington, because one of the very first acts passed made the brewing of beer (albeit 3.2 percent alcohol content) legal again. Being able to drink a beer and go back to work in a brewery gave millions of people throughout the Midwest, and the rest of the country, the feeling that the government was taking direct and prompt action to improve their lives (Kyvig 2002, 221–24, 293).

TRADE AND MARKETS

Since the nineteenth century, Americans had become accustomed to buying at the local store on credit, but the credit buying of big-ticket items such as cars, initiated by William Durant of General Motors, soon spread to other areas of the American economy and revolutionized buying and marketing in the 1920s. Soon everything from cars to washing machines and vacuum cleaners could be bought for a little down and small monthly payments. Clever advertising campaigns orchestrated by companies led by teams of behavior psychologists quickly transformed luxuries like automobiles into necessities, cigarettes into health and beauty aids, bad breath and body odor into curable afflictions, and cereal into a breakfast staple.

Nowhere could the rhythms of the pulsating marketplace of the new century be better measured than in Chicago's downtown area. The daily influx of commuters reflected the commanding importance of the Loop in metropolitan Chicago. Its most glittering attractions were the department stores along State Street. Marshall Field's was easily the most famous enterprise, with a floor area of nearly 40 acres in its new buildings, 45 display windows, and 50 elevators. It was, as a national magazine observed in 1907, "more than a store. It was an exposition, a school of courtesy, a museum of modern commerce" (Mayer and Wade 1969, 218).

But it had its rivals. Down the street was Carson, Pirie Scott Company's store. Louis Sullivan had designed the building and made it one of the landmarks of the "Chicago School" of architecture, and energetic entrepreneurs had made it a serious competitor of Marshall Field's. Mandel Brothers was on the same side of State Street, and the Boston Store was across the street just a little farther south. Chicagoans and those visiting the city could also shop at The Fair, Rothschilds, Siegel, Cooper and Company, and Stevens stores, all among State Street's retail giants. "These huge establishments are from twelve to fifteen stories high," wrote two astonished visitors, "and contain every possible article of trade, from watches and boot laces, to the most exquisite art treasures and priceless gems. Anything, indeed can be purchased there, even real estate and country houses." Comparing these department stores with the best in France and England, they declared Chicago's to be "larger and, if possible, more complete in scale, more daring and perhaps more fantastic in their display" (Mayer and Wade 1969, 220).

The Loop had something for every taste. Along Michigan Avenue, just east of the Loop proper, elegant shops catered to the "carriage trade" with the latest fashions from Paris and New York. The wholesale produce market ranged along South Water Street, north of the Loop. Just inside the Loop to the west, LaSalle Street contained the city's major financial institutions. At the head of the canyon rose the Board of Trade, emblematic of Chicago's domination of the nation's grain exchange. Banks and financial institutions lined both sides of the street, their austere classical facades bulging with the driving energy that had made them the commanding force in the financial affairs of the Midwest. In this expensive setting, Burnham and Root's Rookery Building was a special gem.

Few other large cities had so concentrated their central functions. "Within an area of less than a square mile," wrote City Club secretary George E. Hooker in 1910, "there are found the railway terminals and business offices, the big retail stores, the wholesale and jobbing business, the financial center, the main offices of the chief firms of the city, a con-

A 1905 view of Chicago showing Madison Street, looking east toward Lake Michigan from State Street. The Granger Collection, New York.

siderable portion of the medical and dental professions, the legal profession, the city and county government, the post office, the courts, the leading social and political clubs, the hotels, theatres, Art Institute, principal libraries, the labor headquarters, and a great number of lesser factors of city life." He noted by contrast that in New York these features were "scattered from the Bowery to 59th Street, a distance of five or six miles," and in London from "Oldgate Pump to Victoria Station, a distance of four or five miles" (Mayer and Wade 1969, 218–26).

Other Midwest cities also boasted sophisticated downtown shopping areas located within the heart of their cultural and commercial life, which thrived in the first decades of the twentieth century. In Detroit, for example, throngs of people filled Woodward Avenue to shop at Hudson's, the tallest department store in the country, which stood near the palatial Public Library and Art Institute. Clevelanders boasted of their Arcade building on Euclid and Superior Avenues. Greatly influenced by King Vittorio Emmanuel II's Grand Galleria in Milan, the glass-domed, iron-framed building served as the commercial center of downtown Cleveland in the first part of the twentieth century. In later years, some referred to it as America's first shopping mall.

An innovation in marketing that developed in the Midwest around the turn of the century was the great mail-order houses led by Sears Roebuck and centered in Chicago. Mail-order houses had begun before the turn of the century, but their great growth was made possible by two innovations: Rural Free Delivery, which arrived in 1896, and parcel post, which began in 1913. Mail-order houses supplied customers in literally every town and on every farm in America with a greater variety and volume of things in common use than any other merchant in the world. They sold by mail everything from a paper of pins to a nine-room house. They received as many as 200,000 letters a day and sold upward of 100,000 different kinds of articles, including food, clothing, implements for farming, decorations for houses, tools for barns, and even the houses and barns themselves.

CASTE AND CLASS EXPERIENCE

The sense of community that had existed in small midwestern towns through the turn of the century began to erode in the new century. Community cohesion perceptibly wore down as the small cities of the Midwest grew up in the post–World War I era. More and more people were identified by the neighborhood in which they lived, their occupation, and what they owned. Tensions increased between the well-to-do and the not-so-well-off. The further one moved down the social line the less they felt like they "belonged" to the community. High unemployment among young people and the willingness of impoverished workers to take low-paying jobs lowered the overall wage scale, and during the Depression years the prospect of upward mobility seemed improbable. During these years the economic gap between the 3 of 10 residents who identified with the upper class and the 7 who did not grew even wider.

Business owners and managers ran the small towns in the Midwest. This class controlled the educational system, civic institutions, churches, government, and the local newspaper. This class also provided the bulk of charitable funds and the tax revenues. The well-to-do accepted as traditional their responsibility to care for destitute women, children, and the disabled, but tended to think of economic hardship as the result of an individual's flaws and therefore found it hard to grant relief to able-bodied males even when jobs were simply not available (Lynd and Lynd 1929, 494–95).

During the World War I years, the large cities of the Midwest, particularly Chicago, Cleveland, and Detroit, began to experience the first wave of black migration from the South. An offer from an agent, an encouraging letter from a friend in the North, or the appeal of the militant black press, coming after years of smoldering discontent, sparked the final decision to migrate. Through these media, tenant farmers and sharecroppers, displaced by agricultural reorganization or disastrous floods, or merely weary of their marginal economic status and the proscriptions of the southern caste system, learned of the opportunities that awaited them in Chicago, Detroit, Cleveland, Toledo, and elsewhere in the industrial Midwest. Each southern black who chose to migrate made a highly personal decision, but he was frequently influenced by the power of mass suggestion. Wherever African Americans gathered, particularly in the country towns of the South, the North became the principal topic of conversation. Jeremiah Taylor of Bobo, Mississippi, for instance, was resigned to his farm until one day his son came back from town with the report that folks were leaving "like Judgment day." Taylor went to town, skeptical, and came back determined to move north. As friends departed, many persons went along just because "it seemed like everybody was heading that way." A woman in Macon wrote to her friend in Chicago: "May, you don't no how much I miss you. . . . it is lonesome here it fills my heart with sadness to write to my friends that gone [sic]. . . . May, now is the time to leave here. . . . if I stay here I will go crazy" (Spear 1967, 136).

The early migrants had only vague notions of what they might expect at their destinations, and they often headed north with visions of fantastic wages and unbounded liberty. Moreover the image of the North filtered south through the promises of agents, the glowing letters of friends, and the appeal of the African American press. It took on a mythical quality that gave to the migration an almost religious significance. The rhetoric of the migration was highly charged with biblical imagery such as "The Flight out of Egypt," "Bound for the Promised Land," and "Going to Canaan." For example, a party of migrants from Mississippi held a solemn ceremony when their train crossed the Ohio River.

The profound changes that took place in the Chicago black community between the 1890s and 1920 had both internal and external dimensions. On the one hand, they were the result of the mounting hostility of white Chicagoans. Whites grew anxious as a growing black population sought more land and better housing; they feared job competition in an era of industrial strife when employers frequently used blacks as strikebreakers. Whites also viewed black voters as pawns of a corrupt political machine. All these fears were accentuated by the rise of a racist ideology in the early part of the century that reinforced traditional antiblack prejudices. On the other hand, blacks were not passive objects in the developments of the early twentieth century. Their response to discrimination and segregation, the decisions their leaders made, and the community activities in which they engaged all helped to shape the emerging black community. The rise of Chicago's black community resulted from the interplay between particular trends in the development of the city and major currents in African American life and thought.

The increasing physical separation of Chicago's African American community from the rest of the city was but one reflection of a growing pattern of segregation and discrimination in every major midwestern and northern city that received African American migrants from the South in the early twentieth century. As the black community grew and opportunities for interracial conflict increased, so a pattern of discrimination and segregation became ever more pervasive. Perhaps the most critical aspect of interracial conflict came as the result of black attempts to secure adequate housing. In Detroit, for example, where promises of jobs in the lucrative auto industry gave that city the second-largest black population in the urban Midwest (behind Chicago), white real estate agents, developers, bankers, and insurance agents used a variety of mechanisms from restrictive covenants to redlining to bar African Americans from all but a handful of inner city neighborhoods. Blacks who managed to break through the businessmen's barriers often met violent resistance from white homeowners. In 1925 alone, white mobs attacked five black families who had dared to move across the color line. Once neighborhoods were segregated, so were public schools and many other public spaces such as theaters, restaurants, and amusement parks. City officials ignored the needs of the largest African American area, a desperately overcrowded ghetto known as Black Bottom, while an almost exclusively white police force ran roughshod over the district's residents (Reich 2006, 249–50).

In Cleveland also, mass migration of blacks from the South led to residential segregation, and all-black pockets became evident by 1917 in the vast district running astride Cedar and Central Avenues. Because black housing options were constrained by low wages and the opposition of white residents in outlying districts, the World War I influx precipitated a severe housing shortage. Although a small number of black southern migrants succeeded in recreating a semi-rural subsistence living in a handful of outlying enclaves, the overwhelming majority became trapped in the emergent Cedar Central ghetto, which, by 1930, had a population density twice the city's average. Landlords divided single- and double-family houses into numerous kitchenette apartments and charged disproportionately high rents, while the less fortunate World War I migrants lived in garages, storefronts, even boxcars. The new arrivals in Cleveland also suffered discrimination from the long time black residents, who had formed business alliances and political ties with prominent whites. The northern-born "old elites" looked down on the new southern migrants and feared that they might jeopardize their own hard-earned status within the economic, political, and social community of Cleveland (Reich 2006, 201).

As white hostility almost closed the housing market to blacks in the major cities of the Midwest and created a physical ghetto, it also limited the opportunities for blacks to secure desirable jobs and gain access to public facilities. African Americans in the midwestern cities, as elsewhere, were largely confined to the domestic and personal service trades and were unable to gain even a foothold in industry and commerce. In Chicago, for example, in 1900, almost 65 percent of black men and over 80 percent of black women worked as domestic and personal servants, while only 8.3

percent of the men and 11.9 percent of the women were engaged in manufacturing (and most of the women so employed worked in their own homes as dressmakers and seamstresses). In 1910, the pattern remained the same. Over 45 percent of the employed black men worked in just four occupations: porters, servants, waiters, and janitors. And over 63 percent of the women were domestic servants or laundresses (Spear 1967, 20–30).

In Detroit those who found employment in the auto industry brought home paychecks larger than they had ever dreamed of in the South, but discrimination in the workplace relegated black workers to the most demanding and dangerous jobs in the auto plants. At the Dodge Brothers plant, for example, blacks were restricted to the spraying room, where they spent their days inhaling toxic clouds of paint particles (Reich 2006, 248).

In both 1900 and 1910 in the midwestern cities, more blacks were engaged in the professions than their numbers would warrant, but these were concentrated in professions that required relatively little formal training such as in music, the theater, and preaching. Relatively few black Americans could be found in the legal, medical, and teaching professions, and those who were served an almost exclusively black clientele in the racially segregated ghettos. A large portion of those blacks employed in manufacturing, trade, and transportation were unskilled laborers. Although blacks could find some decent homes on the fringes of their traditional neighborhoods, the core of the "black belt" remained a festering slum. In these areas, between 1900 and 1915, the lines were drawn in the struggle for housing. Racial tensions ran high along such contact points, and in some midwestern cities these tensions erupted into full-scale racial war.

Such injustice could not continue without reaction. Before 1915 in various cities there were several preliminary skirmishes that set the pattern for future, and more serious, confrontations. As in other cities of the Midwest, southern blacks flocked to East St. Louis in the early 1900s in search of job opportunities. By 1916 the city's African American population accelerated so rapidly that by the end of that decade black migration outnumbered the rate of European migration. The resulting tensions over jobs and housing led to a riot in 1917 that left 39 blacks murdered by rampaging white mobs and nine whites killed in retaliation (Reich 2006, 732).

The strongest blow to racial tranquility occurred two years later in the summer of 1919. On July 27, the south side of Chicago exploded after a stone-throwing incident on a beach led to the drowning of a black youth. When police ignored blacks' charges that white men had stoned a young boy to death for having crossed into the white part of the beach, a crowd of blacks attacked several white men. In response, after dark, white gangs beat, stabbed, or shot 38 blacks who had been walking through white neighborhoods. This instigated a race war in which 2 people died the first day and over 50 were injured. The following day white gangs assaulted blacks leaving the stockyards. Mobs pulled blacks off streetcars and kicked and beat them. Blacks retaliated by attacking whites who worked in black neighborhoods. The following night white rioters raided black neighborhoods, firing shots into their homes from automobiles. During this, the worst night of the terror, 20 people were killed and hundreds were injured. The next five days were the worst the city had known since the Great Fire. Fighting, shooting, stabbing, and pillaging left scores injured and over a half-dozen dead. Mobs pulled blacks from streetcars, bands of rioters roamed neighborhoods, homes were sacked and burned.

Finally the governor sent in the troops. Peace was restored, but the scars could not be easily erased, for the grim affair left deep wells of guilt and remorse, hate and bigotry. Worse still, conditions did not change, and the ghetto continued to expand and fester. Five days after the riot the *Chicago Tribune* editorialized, "So long as this city is dominated by whites there will be limitations placed on black people. A rebellion by Negroes against facts which exist and will persist will not help." A white minister was even more explicit. "I believe in segregating the blacks for their own good as well as the good of the whites." The Kenwood and Hyde Park property owners associations responded with demands for a conference to deal with the "promiscuous scattering of Negroes throughout the white residential districts of our city."

The following year, as black leaders refused to accept "segregation by mutual consent" as proposed by white neighborhood associations, bombs exploded in homes of those blacks who refused to remain restricted to the worst neighborhoods of the city. Between January and March 1920, eight bombings of homes were recorded. Blacks of Chicago, unlike most European immigrants, had no hope of escape from their ghetto. Forever marked by color, their only hope for success existed within a rigidly defined and severely restricted ghetto society. No physical wall encircled the black belt of Chicago or any other black ghetto in the Midwest, but an equally impervious wall of hostility and discrimination isolated blacks from the mainstream of life. Another half-century would pass before blacks could expect fair, just, and equal access to decent housing, economic activity, and all that comes with a dignified life. It took a revolution in law, politics, conscience, and civil rights to bring that expectation into being (Spear 1967, 147–66).

The mass migration of blacks from the South and Jews and Catholics from Europe to the predominantly white, Protestant, medium-sized towns of the Midwest caused the resurrection of the Ku Klux Klan, a formerly southern phenomenon. Those who feared the changes to their community brought about by newcomers saw the Klan as a defender against the wave of unwelcome and uncertain change perpetrated by the arrival of so many new and different people. One member proclaimed, "This great country of ours is American, thank God! We make our boys and girls live here twenty-one years before we allow them to vote, and we ought to do the same with all foreigners." The Klan also attacked what they viewed as the "Catholic menace" rising in their midst. One woman, on being asked about her membership in the Klan, responded, "It's about time [to join] the other good people and [do] something about the Catholic situation, the Pope is trying to get control of the country." She warned that the "Klan will overcome this [Catholic] menace."

One Klan member defended the organization's anti-Semitism by declaring, "We are charged with being against the Jew, [but] we are against no man," he declared. "Jesus Christ is the head of the Klan. The Jew is not for Him and therefore the Jew has shut himself out of the Klan." In explaining prejudice against blacks, a Protestant preacher resorted to the Bible and declared that "God Almighty has commanded us, that we should not mix our blood. We must protect our womanhood," he warned. Although the Klan reinforced discrimination against blacks, Catholics, and Jews throughout the Midwest, the practice of discrimination (at least in the case of blacks and Jews) was also supported by a public policy that continued to advocate segregation, protected neighborhoods' self-proclaimed "rights" of exclusion, and still had not revoked the Supreme Court's flawed principle established in 1893 of separate but equal (Lynd and Lynd 1929, 483–85).

Native Americans in the first half of the twentieth century also suffered from an official policy of discrimination. Just before the beginning of the twentieth century, in 1890 at Wounded Knee, South Dakota, Sitting Bull and a band of Sioux were massacred by federal troops. This event, according to Indian historian Alan Josephy, marked the completion of the white man's conquest of the Indian in the United States. Aside from a few Sioux reservations in the Dakotas and small Chippewa reservations in northern Wisconsin, by 1900 there was little in the Midwest that recalled the Native peoples who once dominated the region.

By the 1920s, federal policy had reduced many Indian tribes to a scandalous level of poverty. Indians received little or no education and were treated as wards of the state, incapable of self-government or making decisions for themselves. Whatever revenues the tribes received from land sales were dispersed, with virtually none of them going to assist the Indians to create sound foundations for the development of the human and economic resources of the reservation. The situation demanded reform. In 1924, as an acknowledgment of the nation's gratitude to Indians who had volunteered for service in the armed forces during World War I, the Snyder Act conferred citizenship upon all Indians. Two years later a special group under Lewis Meriam investigated Indian conditions for the Department of the Interior and proposed a sweeping list of reforms, including a halt to allotments, which—in an attempt to promote assimilation—distributed Indian reservation lands to individual Indian families. This practice had brought about a drastic reduction of reservation land and was finally recognized as one of the prime causes of Indian impoverishment and continued demoralization. The Wheeler-Howard Act, better known as the Indian Reorganization Act, stemming from the Meriam Survey and administered by Indian Commissioner John Collier, brought an end to the allotment policy, encouraged tribal self-government, extended financial credit to the tribes, began an improvement in educational and medical facilities, restored freedom of religion for Indians, and promoted a revival of Indian culture. Despite these efforts by the government to alter the pattern of injustice, on the eve of World War II, conditions of Native Americans in the Midwest, as elsewhere, remained deplorable (Josephy 1969, 342, 350–52).

URBAN AND RURAL EXPERIENCE

In the early twentieth century, large midwestern cities became characterized by the ethnic and racial diversity of their people and neighborhoods. According to the 1920 census, Illinois contained over 650,000 foreign-born males, most of whom lived in the Chicago area. In Michigan, 10 percent of the population was comprised of foreign-born males, most of whom lived in the Detroit area; and in Ohio 6 percent of the population was made up of foreign-born males, most of whom lived in the Cleveland or Cincinnati area. The great black migration to midwestern cities also added to their ethnic diversity. Chicago was home to 110,000 blacks, Detroit 44,000, and Cleveland 35,000. In the large urban areas of the Midwest blacks and European immigrants comprised 20 percent of the population in 1920. These groups tended to cluster in their own separate sections of the city, creating numerous ethnically distinct neighborhoods with their own bakers, butchers, taverns, mortuaries, parishes, synagogues, and churches.

Due to the variety and number of disparate cultures and national backgrounds, no single ethnic culture dominated the culture or politics of these midwestern cities, though several groups were largely excluded from it by reason of prejudice, poverty, ignorance, or cultural dispositions discouraging civic involvement. Except for the African Americans, whose movement was restricted by zoning laws, white intimidation, and violence, ethnic clustering began to break down by the end of the 1920s. This trend was encouraged in a time of urban prosperity and rapid growth, which provided improved housing possibilities in farther reaches of the city and suburbs, an excellent public transportation system, a growing number of chain stores, and attractive commercial districts. Mass commercial entertainment, including radio, vaudeville, motion picture theaters, and professional baseball teams, drew people out of their neighborhoods and into a common urban experience. At the same time, the closing of immigration from eastern and southern Europe, due to new federal legislation establishing nationality quotas, meant the immigrant and ethnic populations already in the Midwest, as elsewhere, did not get the steady influx of newcomers necessary to reinvigorate Old World cultures in America, and most of these groups gradually assimilated into American life.

Electricity created the great divide between urban and rural life in the first decades of the twentieth century. By 1920, 85 percent of urban dwellings were electrified, while only 10 percent of rural areas enjoyed the benefits of electricity. Twenty years later, even after the New Deal rural electrification program had begun, 95–99 percent of homes in cities such as Chicago, Kansas City, Cleveland, Dubuque, and Toledo were electrified, but the percentage of homes in rural areas with electricity ranged from 10 percent in rural Missouri counties to 76 percent in some parts of rural Wisconsin, with most rural midwestern areas hovering around 45 percent. Rural Americans, especially women, understood from magazines and mail-order catalogs what they were missing by not being connected to electric lines. Without an electric pump, water had to be hauled from well or stream to the house for bathing, cleaning dishes, and laundry. Heating of water and cooking of food had to be done on a wood- or coal-burning stove. In addition, risk of a fire in the house due to coal- or wood-burning heating devices was always greater than it was with electric heat. The lack of electricity also denied the rural family forms of entertainment that city dwellers were beginning to take for granted by the mid-1920s, such as the radio and the motion picture theater. Also, reading was limited to daylight hours. The gulf between urban and rural life would not be bridged until after World War II, when rural electrification would become commonplace (Kyvig 2002, 66–68).

Midwestern farmers also ate differently than their urban cousins. While urban dwellers began to make use of the rapidly developing variety of commercially processed foods, midwestern farmers depended largely on what they could raise themselves and what was in season. Whereas canned and, to a lesser degree, frozen products made vegetables and fruits available all year round in the city, on the midwestern farm these foods were limited to the "summer diet," while the winter diet centered around smoked or salted pork, storable grains such as wheat and corn, potatoes, beans, and dried fruit (Kyvig 2002, 108–9).

In the farmlands of the Midwest the Great Depression came much earlier than it did to the city. By the mid-1920s the agricultural depression of the postwar era had the agricultural Midwest in its grip. Those who had incurred debt to purchase land and equipment in the war boom found themselves deep in unpayable debt. Some farmers lost their land to mortgage-holding banks. Drought hit the area hard from 1934–1936, driving farmers deeper in debt. By 1940, as many as 52 percent of farmers in some areas were tenants farming on rented land. In reaction to worsening farm conditions in the Midwest, many enlisted into Milo Reno's Farm Holiday Association. Reno, from Oskaloosa, Iowa, called on farmers to withhold their products from the market to drive up food prices and focus attention on the plight of the farmer.

Midwestern farmers' lives began to improve in the mid-1930s when the New Deal's agricultural policies began to take effect. The Rural Electrification Administration, for example, brought light and convenience appliances into their lives, and the Agricultural Adjustment Act helped them realize some of Milo Reno's economic objectives by establishing price supports for staples and access to credit. With the help of the federal government most midwestern farmers endured the economic crises of the 1920s and 1930s and continued their rural lifestyle. Despite the many perceived cultural and social advantages of urban life, people in the country were not anxious to abandon their life for the city during a depression. According to the U.S. census, the proportion of urban to rural population remained relatively unchanged in the upper Midwest until after World War II.

ANIMAL HUSBANDRY AND HUNTING AND FISHING

While the lower Mississippi Valley was recovering from the great flood of 1927, lower midwestern and western farmers were beginning to suffer a drought that would last well into the 1930s. The prolonged drought centered on western Kansas, eastern Colorado, and the panhandles of Oklahoma and Texas. The severe drought in this area, along with the strong winds that characterized the region and the farming that had loosened the topsoil, turned most of the area into what came to be called the "Dust Bowl."

This tragedy was more than simply a natural disaster with human social implications. It was, rather, the result of economic activity in the region that had begun around the turn of the century when farmers began to wrestle the land away from ranchers. The southern plains, which experienced very little rainfall and averaged

The drought of the early 1930s caused thousands of farmers in the lower plains of the Midwest to abandon their land in search of better opportunities farther west. Library of Congress.

winds of 10 to 20 miles per hour daily, was a land devoid of trees and large vegetation. Grass was the only plant that thrived in the area. As one farmer noted, "Grass holds the earth together." Denied woods, which provide traditional building products, resourceful farmers used the sod they were tearing up for planting to build houses. In the bare dirt that remained behind, the farmers planted wheat, which did not have the same earth-holding qualities of grass. During World War I, the price and demand for wheat rose, and farmers tore up more sod, which they replaced with wheat. The demands of food had sown the seeds of wheat and of disaster. It only took a long drought, such as occurred in the early 1930s, to bring the Dust Bowl calamity to the southern grass plains.

From 1932 onward windstorms swept the powder-dry soil a thousand feet into the air and created huge black blizzards that blotted out the sun and left a thick dirt residue in their wake. In May 1933 alone, dust storms removed an estimated 300 million tons of plains soil and deposited it along the eastern United States from the Great Lakes to Washington. In 1934, a single storm produced a dust cloud that reduced visibility from the Rockies to the Great Lakes and from the Canadian border to Oklahoma.

The storms worsened in 1935, with several deaths by suffocation reported. Respiratory problems became common throughout the Midwest, and physicians reported epidemic proportions of cases of pneumonia. The problem did not subside until 1939, when substantial rainfall over the previous three years began to reduce the Dust Bowl problem. Meanwhile, the farmers and tenant workers had abandoned the dust-choked plains. The population in the region was reduced by 34 percent between 1935 and 1937. So many people left this area that the region did not recover its population until the 1960s. Those who left, mostly for California, found little relief there, as the great agribusinesses developing in the area exploited the newcomers as migrant laborers.

Indian peoples experienced the boom and bust years of the 1920s and 1930s variously depending on location and economy, but most Native peoples were already impoverished by negligent and inefficient management of Indian Affairs programs, which cheated them out of already meager allotments, and by the lack of education and opportunity on reservations. The federal government did abandon the old policy of trying to convert Indians into "Americans" by breaking down tribal culture and breaking up tribal resources. But neither federal nor state governments did much to help Indians during the hard times of the Depression. Indians in the Midwest and plains states who lived near water supplemented their meager diets by fishing. In the lakes of Minnesota and Wisconsin, salmon, pike, and other food fish were harvested by Indians throughout the year

> **📷 Snapshot**
>
> **Life in the Dust**
>
> Everybody's going to leave this country. Boom is over. Wheat blowin out. Dust storms getting darker and darker. Everybody running and shooting and killing. Every body fighting every body else. These little old shacks like this, they're bad, no good for nobody. Lots of kids sick. Old folks [too].
>
> This is the final battle! Armageddon! This dust blowin so thick ya cain't breathe, cain't see the sky, that's the scourge over the face of the earth! Men too greedy for land an for money and for the power to make slaves out of his feller man. Man has cursed th' very land himself! (Woody Guthrie, *Bound for Glory*, 1983, 186, 188)

or for as long as the weather permitted. Treaties with the federal government guaranteed Indians year-round fishing, which annoyed sport fishermen who viewed year-round Indian fishing as injurious to their interests (Green 2000, 165–66).

Intellectual Life

Philanthropic gifts to museums and universities from those whom the new industries made rich elevated significantly the intellectual life in the Midwest in the new century. The new University of Chicago became home to some of the country's most important scholars, and the contributions at the school ranged from innovations in education and philosophy to the creation of the first controlled atomic reaction. Midwesterners also read newspapers that proclaimed themselves to be the world's greatest—though such boasts reflected midwestern boosterism rather than factual realities based on circulation, social, or cultural influence—and they listened to radios that not only brought them entertainment but news and commodity prices. This section will explore some of the innovations in science, education, literature, and communication that transformed the life of midwesterners and the rest of the country in the first half of the twentieth century.

SCIENCE

In an age that celebrated inventors and innovators as practical scientists, the Midwest gave the country some of the most renowned inventors of the early decades of the twentieth century. Probably the most popular of all in the first decade of the twentieth century were the Wright Brothers, who, in their bicycle shop in Dayton, Ohio, created the first successful heavier-than-air flying machine. Elmer Sperry, who was born in New York, moved to Chicago at the end of the nineteenth century and became a professional inventor in the first decades of the twentieth century, claiming over 350 patents. He made major contributions to the technology of electric light, electric railways, electric automobiles, batteries, and, probably most important of all, gyroscope guidance, which made control and stabilization of airplanes possible. Henry Ford of Michigan adapted the scientific principles of mass production to the automobile and provided Americans with an affordable car (Hughes 2004, 56–58, 84–85, 185–86).

While the Midwest reveled in the accomplishments of its practical scientists, in the late 1930s theoretical scientists at the University of Chicago were exploring the possibilities of atomic energy. Enveloped in great mystery and secrecy, the work of these men, drawn from all over the world, including refugees from totalitarian countries, was in some ways the most crucial struggle of World War II. For it was thought that Germany was close to success in creating a bomb that would dwarf all others and put the world at the mercy of the Nazis. The only safety rested with winning the scientific race, and beating the enemy to the decisive weapon.

The big breakthrough came on Friday, December 2, 1942. Late in the morning Enrico Fermi, the great Italian physicist who directed the construction of the experimental atomic reactor, was ready to take the fateful step. "We all knew this was the real test," Arthur Compton wrote later. "The Geiger counters registering the neutrons from the reactor began to click faster and faster, until their sound became a rattle. 'Throw in the safety rods,' came Fermi's order. Immediately the pointer moved back toward zero. The rattle of the counters fell to a slow series of clicks. For the first time, atomic power had been controlled and stopped." After a moment's pause, "someone handed Fermi a bottle of Chianti and a cheer went up. Outside on Ellis Avenue students and faculty and passersby moved briskly through the unpleasant, chilling winter air unaware that a few hundred feet away the 'Atomic Age' had begun" (Hughes 2004, 394–95; Mayer and Wade 1969, 370).

EDUCATION

In the first decades of the twentieth century a revolution in education originated in the Midwest. It began when the great philosopher of education John Dewey accepted a position on the faculty at the University of Chicago in 1894. Dewey's use of scientific experiments to link his ideas to his social interests was leading him into the philosophy of "pragmatism." Dewey and other early pragmatists believed that ideas, like biological organisms, survived and evolved according to their ability to interpret and guide real-world events. Pragmatism was an ideal philosophy for a man who wanted to make a difference in the world, and John Dewey was such a man.

Dewey was appointed to the newly established and richly endowed University of Chicago as head of its Department of Philosophy, which also included the fields of psychology and pedagogy. This multifaceted department allowed him to combine all of his developing interests under one academic umbrella and to have a major voice in all that would occur in each of the three fields. As a condition of his coming to Chicago, Dewey made it clear that his department needed a laboratory school for educational experimentation. Enrollment in Dewey's school grew quickly as its fame spread throughout national academic and professional circles. Dewey's work received even more publicity when Francis Parker's teacher-training school, recently detached from the control of the Cook County political apparatus, also became part of the university. Parker's school functioned as a teacher-training laboratory, while Dewey's school continued its mission as a testing ground for educational principles. When Parker died, the two schools were combined to form a School of Education with Dewey as the head. Dewey proceeded to lay out the intellectual foundations of his educational efforts in a series of books and articles.

For Dewey, the school itself was a social institution, a part of society, and needed to be consciously organized as such. In Dewey's formulation, learning was a natural by-product of concrete social activities. So, by organizing schools like other social institutions, Dewey believed learning would lose the abstract quality that permeated so much of the academic study that went on in schools in curricular terms. This meant aligning school experiences with the real-life occupational and democratic experiences of the surrounding society. Students and their teacher formed this real-life curriculum cooperatively. Together with a commitment to scientific methods and principles, this meant that the school functioned both as a learning laboratory and as a vehicle for the improvement of a democratic society. Dewey did not assume that a child-oriented curriculum meant abandoning traditional subject matter. Rather, he saw his program as an occasion for reorganizing traditional subjects to fit the needs of both children and society. Although child-centered, it still took the children from where they were to where the educators wanted them to be. Thus, for Dewey, teachers had to have knowledge of both children and subject matter to orchestrate the most productive blending of the two. The activities that constituted Dewey's curriculum were intended to improve the classroom society and, thereby, to improve the larger society of which they were a part.

Another important leader in pedagogy in the Midwest at the time was Ella Flagg Young, whose pedagogical progressivism was aligned with Dewey's views, despite the fact that she operated in a quite different environment from that of the philosopher. She spent almost her entire adult life in the public schools of Chicago. After teaching and traveling for a number of years, Flagg went to work in the Chicago school system, as principal of the city normal school. Her graduate studies, her European experience, and her long years in the schools made her an ideal candidate for this position. She had a unique ability to combine theory with practice, and she also had a long record of positive contacts with the teachers of Chicago. Her views of the dignity and importance of teachers made her the friend of classroom teachers and, potentially, the enemy of administrative Progressives, who sought to mechanize the teachers' role in the new top-down form of school management. She brought these beliefs to bear on the curriculum and staff of the normal school where she served until 1909, at which time she was chosen as superintendent of the Chicago schools.

Young dedicated her energies to collegial teacher-administrator relations. While a school principal, she had founded a club for her teachers where they could come for discussions of school affairs. This club soon became a movement, and Ella Flagg Young clubs flourished in most elementary schools of midwestern cities. Later, as an assistant superintendent, she founded a teachers' council in her district, a body that was to advise her in her administration of the schools. She had a long, cordial relationship with the Chicago Teachers Federation (CTF), the association founded to link the elementary teachers throughout the city with each other.

Neither Dewey nor Young were victorious in the battles they fought. Public education emerged from the Progressive era more influenced by the organizational reforms of centralization and curricular differentiation advocated by administrative Progressives than by the pedagogical alterations sought by Dewey or the empowerment of teachers sought by Young. Pedagogical Progressives such as Dewey and Young made significant headway in experimental and laboratory schools and had a substantial influence over many teacher-training institutions, all of which resulted in less rote memory work and more experiential learning for many students. However, the followers of Dewey and Young had little success in dislodging the traditional teacher-dominated, subject-centered curriculum that characterized most public and many private school classrooms, and for the most part students in the classroom continued with the rigid teaching system of the previous century, only now the classrooms and the teachers who worked in them were part of a streamlined, bureaucratic school system. Administrators were firmly in control of their teachers and deferential to their boards. A modernized educational apparatus had been firmly installed in the nation's urban schools (Urban and Wagoner 2003, 221–28).

At the beginning of the twentieth century in the rural Midwest, children averaged eight years of schooling, and in 1939 the 2.1 million Chicagoans who were born before World War I typically had a limited education. Four percent had never been to school, another 7.5 percent had attended fewer than five years, 60 percent had no more than an eighth-grade education, 75 percent had not finished high school, fewer than 10 percent had attended college, and less than 5 percent had completed college. Those statistics for both the rural and the urban Midwest would change radically for those born after the war. From 1920 to 1940, with the introduction of compulsory education laws in the upper Midwest, averages increased, especially in the number of high school graduates. According to U.S. census statistics, the number of young people in school at the age of 17 in 13 midwestern states grew by an average of 80 percent from 1920 to 1940. States in the Midwest where young people remained in school longest included Illinois, Michigan, Ohio, Indiana, and Wisconsin. In the latter the increase of

This Wisconsin schoolroom with its fixed desks in straight rows was typical of the early twentieth century. Library of Congress.

students in school at 17 years of age rose by 148 percent from 1920 to 1940 (U.S. Census).

The school, like the factory where many of these children would spend their adult lives, was a thoroughly regimented world. Immovable seats in orderly rows fixed the sphere of activity of the child. Bells divided the day into periods. There were study periods in which children learned lessons from textbooks, followed by recitation periods when they told the teacher what the book said. The rapidly industrializing Midwest demanded an educated population, which these schools provided. But the education went beyond academics to include a socialization of children to the regimen and order of the clock-driven industrial world.

Initially, the consequences of the Great Depression were slow to be felt in the public schools, particularly in the urban public schools. For example, city school systems actually had slightly larger budgets in the 1931–1932 school year than they had in 1930–1931. By 1932–1933, however, the situation was becoming critical, with several large cities in the Midwest and elsewhere on the verge of bankruptcy. In the Depression's initial stages, city school systems responded with a variety of cost-cutting strategies such as increasing class size and closing small schools. Business "efficiency," a watchword in schools since the early twentieth century, was now emphasized even more. Administrators and school boards embraced detailed budgeting as a way to stretch the dollars spent on public education. Inevitably, teachers' salaries, which comprised approximately 75 percent of most school budgets, became a target of budget cutters, and teacher layoffs and salary cuts became commonplace.

Additionally, many urban school districts launched campaigns to cut the "fads and frills" from school programs. This usually began with the elimination of programs such as night schools, summer schools, kindergartens, and playgrounds, and then spread to nonacademic subjects such as music, art, physical education, and industrial education, as well as to programs for the physically and mentally handicapped.

Perhaps the most notorious example of Depression-era cutbacks in urban public schools occurred in the city of Chicago. The Chicago situation was dangerous even before the onslaught of the Great Depression, with school and other tax revenues being gutted in the 1920s by poor collection procedures and skimming on the part of corrupt politicians. The arrival of the Great Depression exacerbated the situation and led to a full-blown crisis. In April 1931, the school board claimed that it no longer had the funds to pay its teachers. In the next two years, Chicago teachers were paid for only four of their nine months of work. To make matters worse, their payment was not by check but, instead, by a warrant that was redeemable for less than its face value. All this took place in the midst of a taxpayers' strike led by real estate interests but supported by many of the city's small property owners. Action by the city's mayor resulted in a symbolic victory for the teachers and the schools when he discharged from the city payroll a lawyer whose firm had represented the taxpayers' association. The mayor also intervened to prevent teachers from being arrested for not paying taxes on their vehicles and arranged in March 1932 to have them paid the wages they had earned in December 1931.

In 1933, the board of education announced that it would reduce expenses as its contribution to solving the schools' financial problems. This reduction resulted in abolishing all junior high schools, closing the city's junior college, cutting the number of kindergartens by one-half, reducing the number of physical education teachers, abolishing all coaching positions, reducing the numbers of music teachers and supervisors, making elementary principals responsible for two schools, eliminating manual arts and household arts from the elementary schools, suspending all textbook purchases, closing all school swimming pools, and abolishing the position of dean in the high schools.

The response to these massive cuts was a protest rally attended by 25,000 Chicagoans. However, the rally failed to get the attention of the school board members and, subsequently, many citizens sought court injunctions to stop the cuts. The court did not grant these injunctions, and the cuts were implemented. The result was that in September 1933, 300 kindergarten teachers, 455 junior high teachers, and more than 600 elementary teachers lost their jobs. The remaining teachers found their class sizes and course loads increased substantially.

Although the mayor was unable to help the teachers who had been laid off, he was successful in obtaining a loan from the federal government to pay the remaining teachers a portion of the salaries they were owed. The situation then stabilized, though at a level of service far beneath what had been offered previously. Further stability came later in the decade as the state government moved to increase its contribution to school funding and, thus, decrease school dependence on local property taxes. This was particularly important because property values, both in Chicago and in the rest of Illinois, had decreased by over a third from 1927 to 1935.

The Chicago situation resulted in an upsurge of union sentiment on the part of the teachers. While Chicago's teachers had participated enthusiastically in organizing teachers' unions in the early twentieth century, their various local unions had fallen victim to the antiunionism that characterized America during the business-dominated 1920s.

A less contentious, and more representative, situation existed in Detroit schools during the Depression. In contrast to the situation in Chicago, Detroit's schools and teachers underwent a much less tumultuous upheaval. Few if any teachers lost their jobs, teachers were usually paid on time, their salaries were not cut severely, and the school program remained relatively untouched. In Detroit, the mayor supported the schools in their battle for loans from the business community, and school board members resisted attempts to lay off teachers, cut salaries, and abolish programs. Finally, Detroit's superintendent was much more interested than his Chicago counterpart in maintaining educational quality and was more politically adept at maintaining existing levels of services. Although there were some salary cuts for teachers, they came only during the depths of the Depression. Despite an attempt to eliminate art, music, physical education, manual training, and home economics from the curriculum, a movement that had been successful in Chicago, the school board refused to accede and thereby preserved the existing curriculum. The board's reluctance to cut back was due in no small part to a large and active coalition of civic groups who defended these modern subjects.

A large part of Detroit's success in weathering the Depression was attributed to the actions of wealthy board members whose loyalty to the public schools outweighed their own immediate economic interests. Although most board members came from the same economic background as those wealthy businessmen who sought to cut property taxes and thereby severely reduce public school programs and teacher salaries, they placed their long-term loyalty to public education over their immediate economic interest. The wealthy board members in Detroit acted much more responsibly than the political hacks on the board in Chicago. Even this relatively positive action in Detroit had long-term negative consequences. For in the end, the school board's economic decisions in the Depression years put business interests firmly on the side of the cost cutters, which effectively ended the business-labor alliance that had supported the schools so effectively since the Progressive era.

While Chicago and Detroit offer alternative examples of urban districts' ability to weather depression conditions, the situation in rural districts was more uniformly negative. Even before the Depression, rural schools featured the lowest-paid teachers, the shortest school terms, the oldest and most inadequate facilities and equipment, and the highest rates of student absence. Depression-era conditions intensified these problems and thereby increased the gap between urban schools and their rural counterparts. Property taxes, the source of almost all rural school revenues, were particularly hard hit by an avalanche of farm failures and their accompanying financial devaluation.

In addition to this upsurge in rural economic distress, there was an increase in rural birthrates, particularly in the poorer southern states. This placed a heavier burden on rural schools already faced with decreasing revenues. In addition to making the usual cuts in personnel and salaries, many rural areas simply closed their schools during the height of the Depression. An urban district, even when facing cuts of up to one-third of total revenue, was in a far better position to absorb such a reduction than was a rural district that started with only a fraction of the revenue of its urban counterpart (Urban and Wagoner 2003, 258–60).

LITERATURE

Thanks to the electric light bulb, the increase in leisure time, and higher literacy rates, reading became more popular in the first decades of the twentieth century than it ever had been. Magazines and newspapers flourished, and in the 1920s a new form of marketing literature, the Book-of-the-Month Club, was born. The Literary Guild soon followed it. Although begun regionally, these two companies soon were selling books by mail nationwide and contributing to the developing national culture. *Reader's Digest*, founded in 1922, contained a brief, easily readable compilation of articles from various sources and thereby provided the reader with a broad spectrum of contemporary ideas, albeit from an ethically and politically conservative point of view. Advice books also became very popular in the 1920s. Advice columnists and writers such as Emily Post taught proper etiquette both at home and in the world of business. The popularity of self-improvement literature continued into the next decade. The most popular book of this type in the 1930s was written by Dale Carnegie,

An engraver working on the *Chicago Defender* newspaper, 1942. Library of Congress.

who instructed Americans on *How to Win Friends and Influence People*.

Newspapers continued to provide primary reading fare for most midwesterners. Every major city published at least two major dailies, which filtered out into the surrounding rural areas. Among the most popular and influential were the *Chicago Tribune*, the *Detroit Free Press*, the *Detroit News*, the *St. Louis Post-Dispatch*, the *Milwaukee Journal*, and the *Cleveland Plain Dealer*. Blacks in the Midwest, no matter what city they lived in or near, read the *Chicago Defender*. Founded by Robert S. Abbott on May 5, 1905, and heralding itself as "The World's Greatest Weekly," the *Defender* had become, by the advent of World War I, the nation's most influential black weekly newspaper, with more than two-thirds of its readership base located outside of Chicago.

During World War I, the *Chicago Defender* waged an aggressive (and successful) campaign in support of the Great Migration movement. This movement resulted in over one and a half million southern blacks migrating to the North between 1915 and 1925. In subsequent years the *Defender* provided first-hand coverage of events such as the Red Summer Riots of 1919, a series of race riots in cities across the country. It campaigned for antilynching legislation and for racially integrated sports. The *Defender* also provided an important outlet for black literature. Included among its contributors in the 1920s and 1930s were Walter White and Langston Hughes. It also published the early poems of Pulitzer Prize–winning poet Gwendolyn Brooks. With its promotion of black literature, its up-to-date reporting on issues that affected black Americans, and its leadership in political and social campaigns that benefited black Americans in the first half of the twentieth century, the *Defender* became, if not in name certainly in fact, the national literary and cultural journal of black America (Grossman, Keating, and Reiff 2004, 248).

COMMUNICATION

In an age of technological wonders none could surpass the radio for the influence it had on the daily lives of Americans. On May 19, 1922, the age of commercial radio in the Midwest began when two socially prominent young Chicagoans and radio enthusiasts—Thorne Donnelley and Elliott Jenkins—formed Midwest Radio Central, Inc., and started WDAP as an experimental station. The first broadcasts originated from the Wrigley Building, where people complained that they had an "erratic effect" on the famous tower clock. The first programs that those fortunate enough to have receivers could hear were talks, weather reports, and three concerts a week. In that same year in July, after a tornado damaged the antenna at the Wrigley Building,

WDAP moved its studios to two handball courts on top of the Drake Hotel. The station had only one microphone, which was occasionally carried downstairs to the Drake ballroom to allow listeners to enjoy live dance music from Jack Chapman and his orchestra. This became midwesterners' favorite program, as Chapman's programs increased the volume of station mail from 200 to 800 letters received a day.

In 1923, midwestern farmers began hearing regular updates on the prices of their products when the Chicago Board of Trade purchased WDAP from Donnelley and Jenkins. In that same year radio captured the imagination of Colonel Robert Mc-Cormick, who marveled over the "the little box that picks up sounds from the air." And soon his newspaper, the *Chicago Tribune*, was in the radio business. Using the call letters WGN (for World's Greatest Newspaper) the station expanded its service through the region. Soon midwesterners were listening to events live in their living rooms that previously they could only read about in their newspaper. In addition to news, weather, and commodity prices, WGN broadcast myriad live events, including the Democratic and Republican Party national conventions of 1924, the Loeb-Leopold murder trial sentencing, political debates, college football, Major League Baseball, and the Indianapolis 500. Even the Scopes "Monkey Trial" came live through the radio into homes throughout the Midwest.

Other Midwest newspapers also embraced the new radio technology. On August 20, 1920, the *Detroit News* began to operate a radio station for listeners in Michigan and claimed to be the first newspaper in the world to run a radio station. In May 1922, the *Milwaukee Journal* sponsored its first radio program on Milwaukee's first radio station, WAAK, which was owned by the Gimbel Brothers Department store. Then in June 1927, the Federal Communications Commission assigned the newspaper the call letters WTMJ, to stand for *The Milwaukee Journal*. They used their new station to sell newspapers. Milwaukee residents listened to the WTMJ Orchestra and Bill Carlsen's orchestra. Carlsen was later hired by WTMJ and went on to become Wisconsin's most widely known radio and television weather forecaster.

In 1924, a new Chicago radio station, with the assigned call letters WBBX, began broadcasting under the ownership of Sears. Despite the assigned call letters, Sears first broadcast the station under the call letters WES (World's Economy Store). An immediate hit, the station kicked off a grand opening from a broadcast station in Chicago's Sherman Hotel using new call letters—WLS (World's Largest Store)—days later. The station broadcast farm and weather reports, music, tips for housewives, and evening entertainment. *The National Barn Dance*, heard on Sunday evenings, became the most popular radio program in the Midwest.

In 1926, Freeman Gosden and Charlie Correll created a new form of radio entertainment when they premiered the *Sam and Henry Show*, a comic drama about African American life on the south side of Chicago. The show would soon become known as *Amos 'n' Andy* and would remain the most popular of all radio shows throughout the 1930s and 1940s. In 1928, WGN introduced radio advertising on a show called *Radio Floor Walker*. The mostly musical variety show had commercials interspersed throughout the presentation. Listeners complained so much about the barrage of advertising that WGN created a new format, the "single sponsor program," which became the common format throughout the golden age of radio.

Father Charles Coughlin addresses a large Cleveland rally in 1936. Library of Congress.

In 1928, William Lear invented the first car radio, and in 1929 WGN began interrupting programs to carry police bulletins to officers in their squad cars and to the listening public as well. This experiment would lead to police radio systems, which were implemented in the following decade. By the 1930s the radio had become a common household item. *Fortune* magazine surveys in 1937 and 1938 found that listening to the radio had become the nation's most popular pastime, edging out moviegoing and far surpassing reading.

Individual listening habits varied widely, but in any case, whether the listener was a Chicago worker or a farmer's wife, radio reduced the sense of personal isolation. The worker could listen to an ethnic station offering traditional music from his homeland, the Midwest farmer might listen to commodity price quotations or weather reports, and his wife might listen to a recipe show or soap opera. In any case, radio brought a variety of information and entertainment into the home, allowing people an escape from their daily routine and a chance to feel that they were connected to others as part of a vast unseen audience (Kyvig 2002, 71–90).

By far the most important and influential radio personality emanating from the Midwest in the 1930s was Father Charles Coughlin. A Roman Catholic priest in Detroit, Coughlin began his radio career in Detroit in the 1920s defending his faith against attacks by the Ku Klux Klan. In those days his calm mellifluous voice appealed to a common sense reason that attracted a large national audience. In the decade that followed, as his audience grew so did his ambition. Funds from enthusiastic listeners flowed into his coffers, and he was soon broadcasting weekly to a national audience from his newly constructed Little Flower Shrine in suburban Detroit. His broadcasts gradually changed from sermons to political treatises. He told his listeners that the reason for the Depression was rooted in a conspiracy by international bankers, mostly Jewish, in his calculations, and he advocated government control of banks. He had supported Roosevelt in the 1932 election, but when the president did not adopt his banking recommendations, Coughlin broke with the Democrats and formed his own National Union party, which in addition to a political agenda carried strong anti-Semitic undertones.

Many Catholics in America innocently listened to Coughlin's treatises on politics and religion and did not grasp the implications of his anti-Semitism, but others did. Forming a group called the Christian Front, these mostly young male bigots launched a campaign of hate against the Jews. Their plans to rid the country of Jews included overthrowing the national government. Most Coughlin fans doubted these allegations against his more virulent followers, but their skepticism was tempered when they read in the morning papers of January 14, 1940, that the Federal Bureau of Investigation (FBI) had uncovered a Christian Front plot in New York City to seize the ammunition in the National Guard Armory and launch a revolution against the United States. Even those who scoffed at the absurdity of such a plan shuddered when they discovered that those who would be the first line of defense against such an attempt, including the head of the National Guard in New York and many police captains, sympathized with the movement. Coughlin supported the Christian Front throughout their trial, and after this final flight from reality, Coughlin was silenced by his bishop, and he quietly retreated from the national scene. But for a short while this midwestern radio priest captured the imagination of a group of fanatics who certainly gave Jews reason to worry whether the atrocities against their brothers and sisters in Europe might not be repeated in their own American towns.

Material Life

Material life in the Midwest was modified by geography and recent history. Food consumption was varied, ranging from the ethnic meals that could be found in the restaurants and homes of immigrant neighborhoods in the cities to the farm produce that dominated meals of the Midwest farmer. Housing varied also. The most popular house in the Midwest was the single-family bungalow, but for the thousands of black and white migrants from the South and immigrants from Europe, this was a dream not in their reach, and they lived in overcrowded substandard housing in neighborhoods long since abandoned by the middle class. Some realized their dream; others had to pass it on to their children.

Manufacturing dominated the economic and often the social life of midwesterners in towns and cities. Most wage earners in the urban Midwest worked in a factory system, and the farmers in the region produced their grains for major food manufacturers. Although the automobile had come into vogue in this era, mass transit still remained the major mode of transportation for the rapidly growing population of the Midwest, and railways laced the cities and countryside, connecting neighborhoods, regions, and major cities to each other. This section will review these and other major changes that occurred in material life in the Midwest over the first four decades of the twentieth century.

FOOD

Midwest farmers' diets depended largely on what they raised. Most farm families processed their own food. Home canning increased among farmers after 1917, and the farm price crash of the post–World War I period reinforced this tendency. Up until the 1940s, in rural areas with no access to ice or no storage facilities, farmers dug vegetable kilns, usually underground, or cellars into which the vegetables were placed in layers separated by straw. If a spring was nearby, a shed might be built over it to provide cool storage for dairy products, which were packaged in crocks and wooden boxes. In any case, chances for contamination by bacteria were good, and many rural Americans caught periodic diseases that affected their digestion and drained their stamina. Smoked or salted pork was the common meat product eaten at the rural table.

In urban areas of the Midwest the diet of the new commercial age predominated. Processed foods from cans often made up the evening fare. Technological and organizational revolutions made it possible for giant meatpackers in the Midwest such as Armour and Swift to dominate the tinned meat market, solving the problem of meat storage in the home. While factory workers and common laborers usually carried their lunches from home, the noontime meal for the urban office worker in the postwar era was often taken at one of the new fast-food restaurants emerging in the Midwest. White Tower, White Castle, and Toddle House led the way in affordable quick-serve lunches and dominated this market in the Midwest. In the immigrant neighborhoods of the urban Midwest, the odor of native foods that emanated from homes and local restaurants could be smelled in the late afternoon hours. In terms of eating, the midwestern urban workers, who suffered from time to time from unannounced layoffs even before the Great Depression, did not fare as well as their neighbors on the farm. In 1923, a typical laid-off worker in Muncie, Indiana, trying to feed his family on five dollars a week, would spend two dollars on the cheapest cuts of meat and three dollars for the rest of the food, which would consist of bread, potatoes, and beans.

Given the changing population that brought new cultures and habits to the urban areas, and the rise of industry in the Midwest, which left little opportunity for the leisurely eaten lunch at home, eating habits and foods consumed changed greatly from what they had been just a decade before the turn of the century.

For the Indians of the plains and Midwest, changing food habits over the decades had placed them in a severe nutritional crisis. Before white domination in their area, Indian diet had been dependent on the low-cholesterol meats of the buffalo, the deer, and the elk. But by 1927 a study showed that the staple food of the Sioux reservation in South Dakota consisted of "grease bread," or white flour bread or biscuit dough fried in fat. Potatoes or beans were the only vegetables most tribes consumed, and squash and tomatoes were eaten by only a few. Inhabitants of the reservations in South Dakota consumed virtually no green vegetables, fruits, milk, eggs, butter, or cheese. Meat came from monthly government rations of 25 to 40 pounds of beef per family per month. Theoretically, this allotment might have been sufficient, but those not on the ration rolls usually moved in and ate with the recipients of the meat until it was gone, usually in about two or three weeks. For the remainder of the month the diet consisted of grease bread (Green 2000, 68, 165–66; Lynd and Lynd 1929, 62).

HOUSING

In the 1920s in a typical midsized midwestern city, researchers Robert S. and Helen Merrell Lynd discovered that single-family homes accommodated 86 percent of the population, semi-detached units another 10 percent, and various sorts of apartments 4 percent (Lynd and Lynd 1929, 93). In larger cities such as Chicago different patterns emerged, and the housing density, especially near the center of the city, was more immediately visible. To avoid the congestion, the wealthy, who had lived in exclusive neighborhoods along the shore of Lake Michigan south of the center of the city moved to large tracts of land outside this area, while those with modest but regular incomes occupied old houses or newer apartments in once-fashionable areas. Many residential districts near downtown continued to be overcrowded, with too many people for every room, too many families for every house, too many buildings for every block.

A visitor to the city could not get far from the Loop of downtown Chicago without encountering block upon block of two- and three-story houses and three- and four-story flat buildings, which compressed a great deal of humanity into very small spaces. Newspaper editors and reformers continually sought to touch the public conscience by exposing the social consequences of high-density housing in the heart of the metropolis. Yet, in one sense, this perspective was deceiving, because it obscured the important fact that Chicago was predominantly a city of middle-class homes and that the great growth in the metropolis took place in the outer zones. In the six years between 1910 and 1916, for instance, the population living within four miles of the corner of State and Madison Streets remained stationary at about 1,000,000 persons, while the number in the area from four to seven miles out jumped from 460,000 to 1,076,000; and in the belt from seven to ten miles from the center, the increase was from 180,000 to 332,000.

Among the most spectacular residential changes of the period was the shift of Chicago's social elite to the "Gold Coast" on the near north side. Presaged by Potter Palmer's move to Lake Shore Drive in the 1880s, the exodus from "the Avenues" became a stampede after 1893. Mansions on the south side sold for a fraction of their original cost. A house at Prairie Avenue and Eighteenth Street that cost over $200,000 sold for $25,000; another, one of the finest in the city, that cost $150,000 in 1870, went for $36,000 in 1909. On the west side, Ashland Boulevard met the same fate. As the new generation built lavishly along the lakefront or erected sumptuous townhouses along Astor and North State, the old baronial structures fell to the new landlords, who divided up the spacious buildings into small apartments and converted coach houses into multifamily dwellings. Those who stayed watched sadly as the most fashionable neighborhood in Chicago slipped into slumdom.

This residential change seemed even more abrupt because, to the west of the fine old south side neighborhoods, many of the newcomers were southern blacks. Although still only about 2 percent of the population in 1910, the African American population increased rapidly in the next decade. Soon black neighborhoods that had been limited to the areas just south of Sixteenth Street moved south along both sides of State Street almost to Fifty-Fifth Street. The center of black Chicago was the corner of Thirty-First and State, where business and professional people had their offices. Another large black neighborhood grew up on the west side bounded by Lake Street, Ashland, Austin, and Warren Avenues, but it did not yet have all the characteristics of the "black belt" farther south, because other immigrant groups still lived in the area.

Everywhere blacks moved, the grim specter of segregation followed. "The color line as it appears in the Chicago housing problem is too important to be overlooked," Sophonisba Breckinridge and Edith Abbot wrote reluctantly in 1912. They concluded that although the majority of Chicagoans believed in fair play, the attitude toward the Negro was formed by a minority. "And today they [the minority of whites] not only refuse to sit in the same part of the theatre with him and to let him live on the same street with them or even in the same neighborhood. Even where the city administration does not recognize a black 'ghetto,' the real estate agents who register and commercialize what they suppose to be universal race prejudice are able to enforce one in practice" (Mayer and Wade 1969, 252).

African American housing bore the marks of this discrimination throughout the urban Midwest. Poor blacks lived in houses that were small and mainly frame. Originally designed for single families, they were now occupied by several. Few blacks owned their own homes, and because they could not move elsewhere there was little incentive for landlords to maintain the properties. A survey in Chicago in 1913 found only one-quarter of the buildings in good repair; a third still had outdoor toilet facilities. Despite these conditions, rents for poor blacks generally ran about 25 percent more than similar housing for poor whites. Similar results could have been recorded in East St. Louis, Cleveland, and Detroit.

Midwestern cities had large immigrant populations, many of whom lived among their own immigrant groups in subdivided houses or apartments. If the annual income was less than $2,000, the family had little choice other than an apartment in a large building, but those with greater resources preferred flats because of what one visitor called "the restless characteristic of city life." The new buildings hugged the streetcar and elevated lines, giving the breadwinner quick access to the job downtown or in industrial areas. Mixed in, too, were individual houses. Some were large and spacious, if not pretentious. Others were modest, the result of thrift by "mechanics" or skilled craftsmen. With the help of "building societies," these workers were able to save enough money to buy their own homes. By the turn of the century, thousands of laborers had emerged from the most crowded blocks to move to the newer, more pleasant residential streets. The "bungalow"—usually a one-story floor plan with a living room, dining room, kitchen, two bedrooms, and a single bath—became the typical single-family house in the Midwest for people with a modest income.

Immigrant life in these districts centered more on the family and neighborhood than on the central city. Although their life in America had diluted many old customs, it was still possible to maintain a strong cultural flavor with their national parish church, shops and restaurants serving ethnic fare, and religious festivals wherever a critical mass of a particular immigrant group formed. Nearby shops fulfilled daily needs, and the growth of retailing at major traffic crossings reduced the dependence on downtown. Schools and churches increasingly became the focus of organized social life as other competing forms were excluded. In middle-class areas taverns and saloons were kept out by use of "local option" and "no licensing" laws. Even second-generation immigrants were willing to forgo the "corner club" for the propriety of the residential neighborhood. Thus, in cities of the Midwest, every year, second-generation immigrants moved from the overcrowded, centrally located neighborhoods into the middle-class world beyond. These areas occupied a wide belt around the densely inhabited residential and commercial core, thinning out toward the municipal limits and fading into nonurbanized areas or suburban settlement. The lots were larger, the buildings more substantial, and the people fewer (Mayer and Wade 1969, 252–62).

At the turn of the century the midwestern mail-order house, Sears, Roebuck and Company, created an innovation in affordable housing by selling through its catalog high-quality, low-cost, prefabricated houses. From 1908–1940, Sears, Roebuck and Company sold more than 100,000 of these homes through their mail-order "Modern Homes" program. Over that time Sears designed 447 different housing styles, from the elaborate multistory Ivanhoe, with its elegant French doors and art glass windows, to the simpler Goldenrod, which served as a quaint, three-room and no-bath cottage for summer vacationers. (An outhouse could be purchased separately for Goldenrod and similar cottage dwellers.) Customers could choose a house to suit their individual tastes and budgets.

Sears was not an innovative home designer. Instead, Sears was a very able follower of popular home designs, but with the added advantage of modifying houses and hardware according to buyer tastes. Individuals could even design their own homes and submit the blueprints to Sears, which would then ship off the appropriate precut and fitted materials, putting the homeowner in full creative control. Modern Home customers had the freedom to build their own dream houses, and Sears helped realize these dreams through quality custom design and favorable financing.

The process of designing a Sears house began as soon as the Modern Homes catalog arrived. Over time, Modern Homes catalogs came to advertise three lines of homes, aimed for customers' differing financial means: "Honor Built," "Standard Built," and "Simplex Sectional." Honor Built homes were the most expensive and finest quality sold by Sears. Attractive cypress siding and cedar shingles adorned most Honor Built

A reproduction of a page from the Sears, Roebuck and Company mail-order catalog "Book of Modern Homes" is shown in front of an original catalog-bought house in Glasford, Illinois, in 2006. Trisha and Michael Robertson's home was originally purchased for $725 through a Sears, Roebuck and Company mail-order catalog in 1909. From 1908 to 1940, Sears sold an estimated 60,000 to 70,000 mail-order homes through its catalog. AP Photo/(Peoria) *Journal Star,* Fred Zwicky.

exteriors. Depending on the room, interiors featured clear-grade (i.e., knot-free) flooring and inside trim made from yellow pine, oak, or maple wood. Sears's catalogs also reported that Standard Built homes were best for warmer climates, meaning they did not retain heat very well. The Simplex Sectional line, as the name implies, contained simple designs. Simplex houses were frequently only a couple of rooms and were ideal for summer cottages.

The ability to mass-produce the materials used in Sears homes lessened manufacturing costs, which lowered purchase costs for customers. Not only did precut and fitted materials shrink construction time up to 40 percent, but Sears's use of "balloon-style" framing, drywall, and asphalt shingles greatly eased construction for home buyers. Balloon-style framing systems did not require a team of skilled carpenters, as previous methods did. Balloon frames were built faster and generally only required one carpenter. This system used precut timber of mostly standard 2 by 4s and 2 by 8s for framing. Precut timber, fitted pieces, and the convenience of having everything, including the nails, shipped by railroad directly to the customer added greatly to the popularity of this framing style.

Before the invention of drywall, builders used plaster and lathe wall-building techniques, which again required skilled carpenters. Sears homes took advantage of the new home-building material of drywall by shipping large quantities of this inexpensively manufactured product with the rest of the housing materials. Drywall offered advantages of low price, ease of installation, and added fire-safety protection. It was also a good fit for the square design of Sears homes.

During the Modern Homes program, large quantities of asphalt shingles became available. Alternative roofing materials included, among others, tin and wood. Tin was noisy during storms, looked unattractive, and required a skilled roofer, while wood was highly flammable. Asphalt shingles, however, were cheap to manufacture and ship, as well as easy and inexpensive to install. Asphalt had the added incentive of being fireproof.

Sears helped popularize the latest technology available to modern home buyers in the early part of the twentieth century. Central heating, indoor plumbing, and electricity were all new developments in home design that Modern Homes incorporated, although not all of the homes were designed with these conveniences. Central heating not only improved the livability of homes with little insulation but it also improved fire safety, always a worry in an era when open flames threatened houses and whole cities. Indoor plumbing and wiring for electricity were the first steps toward modern kitchens and bathrooms. Sears's Modern Homes program stayed abreast of any technology that could ease the lives of its home buyers and gave them the option to design their homes with modern convenience in mind (http://www.searsarchives.com/).

MANUFACTURING

In the first decades of the twentieth century the Midwest developed into the largest and most diversified manufacturing region in the country. Many of the familiar giants appeared at that time, some by mergers, and others by sheer growth. The Illinois Steel Company, and later Carnegie-Illinois, became part of the U.S. Steel Corporation in 1901; most of the suppliers of agricultural machinery in the region joined the newly formed International Harvester a year later. Near Milwaukee, Wisconsin, Allis Chalmers Corporation manufactured bright orange tractors that were seen on farms throughout the Midwest. In Cincinnati in the early 1900s the Crosley brothers, Powell and Lewis, who manufactured a small economy car and the nation's first push-button radio, became the city's largest employer and remained so until the 1940s.

Chicago's traditional leadership in such areas as meatpacking and food processing continued. The men's clothing industry, which had accounted for 8 percent of the country's output in 1879, produced 18 percent by 1914. At the turn of the century, printing and publishing establishments employed over 20,000 people, and Chicago was second only to New York in both areas. Smaller manufacturing firms flourished in these and other industries, most congregating in multiple-storied buildings on the fringes of the central business district where they could take advantage of Chicago's excellent transportation facilities and be close to a large metropolitan labor force.

In the Midwest, manufacturers introduced the organized industrial district idea to the United States. Under this scheme, the district acted like a residential developer, assembling land, laying out streets, and installing utilities. It often also provided architectural engineering and financial services to the industrial clients; occasionally the district even furnished dining facilities and executive clubs. But most of all it brought together compatible business enterprises and created an attractive environment that most companies could not readily provide themselves. One of the first of these was the Central Manufacturing District, which developed a square-mile tract of land north of the Union Stock Yards on both sides of the south fork of the south branch of the Chicago River. Organized in 1890, it could promise its clients the same excellent freight facilities enjoyed by the stockyards. The section filled up rapidly with light manufacturing and distribution establishments. By 1915 the district was ready for its second enterprise, the Pershing Road Tract, immediately to the west. It, too, flourished and was ready for government use in World War I.

In Lake County, Indiana, another industrial complex developed when the federal government constructed an artificial lake front harbor and a canal to accommodate new steel, chemical, and refinery plants. Eventually, Indiana Harbor Canal would handle over 20 million tons of cargo a year and would become the leading petro-

Two "top women" at the U.S. Steel plant in Gary, Indiana, wear oxygen masks for their work cleaning the tops of 12 blast furnaces. Their job is one example of many taken over by women while American men were serving in World War II. Corbis.

leum shipping port on the Great Lakes. To find room for expansion, companies soon filled newly made land out into the lake along the south shore.

Farther east along the Lake Michigan shoreline were sand dunes that, to an industrial-minded observer in 1900, appeared bleak and forsaken. An early surveyor found that the face of the country looked like "some powerful convulsion had torn the earth asunder and thrown it up into sand peaks, leaving the cavities to be filled up with the lake and marshes." Yet to U.S. Steel, scouting about for a site for a new, modern plant, the site seemed ideal for development. The very remoteness of the place required that the corporation create not just a factory complex but a new city as well. The Pullman strike of 1894 had soured many businessmen on the desirability of "model towns." Far from producing a contented and productive labor force, Pullman's experiment had bred bitterness and resentment. The "most perfect city in the world" had become just another industrial town with its ordinary problems magnified by frustrated hopes when the Pullman Company refused to listen to workers' complaints during the depression of the 1890s. But U.S. Steel had no option; major facilities would require a large working population and all the installations and public services needed to sustain it.

However reluctantly, the company went into the city-making business, naming their urban creation Gary, Indiana, after the chairman of the board, Elbert H. Gary. A. F. Knotts, attorney for U.S. Steel, who was formerly employed by the Pullman Company, was determined to avoid the mistakes of his previous employer. Most of all he wanted to keep away from company housing, which he thought brought such woe to Pullman. Gary was more a gigantic tract development than a model town. The choice sites along the lake went into industrial plants and a harbor. A few blocks were reserved for public buildings, and others were set aside for institutional use. The rest was laid out in the conventional grid pattern. The utilities provided for a population of 200,000, and the names of the projected main business streets, Fifth Avenue and Broadway, reflected the pretensions, if not the scope, of the project.

Gary was incorporated on July 17, 1906. By December it had 10,000 inhabitants. Two months later, the first steel poured from the new furnaces. In its way, Gary was the country's first "instant city," although it never matched the grand expectations of its founders. For a long time, however, it was essentially a "company town," an appendage to the immense steel complex at the tip of the lake.

TECHNOLOGY

The electric revolution had a great effect on the industrial life of the urban Midwest. The assembly lines at Ford Motor Company's River Rouge plant ran on electricity, and in Muncie, Indiana, Ball Brothers Glass Manufacturing Company adopted electrical bottle-blowing machines to turn out as many glass jars with 8 workers as previously it had required 210 skilled workers and their assistants to make. The impact of electricity in the midwestern rural areas was far less. By 1920, 47 percent of urban dwellings had been wired, but only 1.6 percent of farm dwellings. During the New Deal, the Rural Electrification Act of 1935 made low-cost loans available, which made electrical production and distribution in rural areas possible. In rural America the growth after this law was meteoric. By 1940, a third of American farms had electrical power, and 10 years later 90 percent of American farms had electrical power. The other great technological innovation of the first third of the century, the telephone, was seen as less a necessity. In midwestern urban areas such as Muncie, for example, domestic telephone use actually declined from 1926 through the Depression year 1936 (Kyvig 2002, 66–69).

TRANSPORTATION

In midwestern cities, as elsewhere, mass transit remained the crucial catalyst for expansion. The cable car, which had been so important in the 1880s and 1890s, quietly gave way to the electric street railway and the elevated train. Some of the old cable lines hung on, and in Chicago, for example, it was not until 1906 that the final epitaph was written. "State Street bade an unregretful farewell to the last cable train of the Chicago City Railway," the *Tribune* noted wistfully. "Groaning and decrepit it rattled and bumped around the Loop for its last performance at 1:35 A.M. The train consisted of a battered grip-car and a twenty-year-old trailer."

New electric street railway systems soon laced most cities of the Midwest, and in urban areas nearly everyone was within easy walking distance of some line. The route pattern was rectangular, with service along nearly every section-line street, some half-section streets, and most of the major diagonal arteries. The bitter competition for franchises so characteristic of the earlier period diminished; for example, in 1913 the city council of Chicago put the entire system—nearly 1,000 miles of track—under the management of the Chicago Surface Lines, thus creating what Chicagoans claimed to be the largest unified street railway system in the world. Its volume of traffic reached 634 million fares in 1913. By 1929 that figure soared to nearly 890 million. Chicago serves as a model, but throughout the Midwest, public transportation systems that created a mobile workforce stimulated the development and expansion of manufacturing cities more than any other single force.

For example, after 1913 Clevelanders commuted from their new suburb of Shaker Heights on streetcar lines, built by Oris P. and Mantis J. van Sweringen ("the Vans") to serve their new residential development. From 1913–1915, the Vans built most of the rail sections east of Shaker Square, routing streetcars to downtown Cleveland via existing tracks of the Cleveland Railway Company. Later, they built the grade-separated "rapid transit" section between Shaker Square and downtown Cleveland, for faster service. This opened in two stages, first in 1920 to East 34th Street, then in 1930 to the new Terminal Tower, which the Vans built as Cleveland's main railroad station.

The growth of cheap, reliable mass transportation made possible the "segregated city," with special areas devoted to residence, manufacturing, commerce, service business, and government. Gone were cities of "mixed use," where manufacturing, business, and residence were intermingled. Now a central business district, a streetcar suburb in the city, an industrial section, and working-class neighborhoods became the norm. The mass transit systems also connected people to entertainment such as amusement parks and baseball parks, located strategically along or at the end of the line. Paradoxically, the mass transit systems that connected the city also divided people, as racial and economic segregation went hand in hand with the transformation of the uses of urban space.

Most people in the cities embraced mass transit as an accessible and affordable means of expanding their available space. One exception to this rule was St. Louis. Although mass transit plans were discussed, the infatuation with the automobile (St. Louis was the first city to have a gas station, and the first automobile accident was recorded there) prevented serious rapid transit implementation. Instead, in 1912, St. Louis became one of the first cities to create a comprehensive automobile traffic plan complete with tree-lined parkways, benches, and streetlamps. The City Commission created the plan in hopes of alleviating congestion in the downtown business districts and reclaiming blighted downtown areas. Other midwestern cities also accommodated automobiles and trucks by widening streets and providing for on-street and off-street parking. Cities also installed signs and traffic lights to regulate flow and encourage movement of people and goods. Developers hitched their fortunes to the auto age by buying up areas away from fixed-rail service to promote new automobile-driven communities.

In 1922, J. S. Nichols of Kansas City, Missouri, opened his Country Club Plaza to serve as the business district for a large-scale residential development. It featured paved and lighted parking lots. In the 1930s and 1940s, Sears and Montgomery Ward set up large free-standing stores with on-site parking away from the centers of big cities. This new age of shopping was no longer dependent on ready access to mass transit. The shift to an auto-dominated urban and suburban culture took time, and although the Depression of the 1930s slowed the process for a while, the New Deal public works programs implemented in those years built roads and bridges that provided further infrastructure that later sped the dominance of automobiles and trucks as the principal means of transportation after World War II.

When Barney Oldfield climbed into a monster automobile built by Henry Ford in 1903, he said, "It might kill me, but they will say afterward that I was going like hell when she took me over the bank." Ford had built the car to win a race and $28,000 in prize money. But his dream was not to join the wealthy enthusiasts and sportsmen who up to that time had been the only ones interested in the new invention called the horseless carriage. Ford, the midwestern farmer's son, had a dream to build a car for the people. The money and notoriety he would gain from winning a big race with a big prize would put him on that path. By 1908, Ford had done it. He built a car that would sell for a price that people with average incomes could afford, and the automobile revolution was underway. In 1913, he created the first moving assembly line, and as production increased he dropped the price of each car. The car that initially sold for $950 in 1908 sold for $360 by 1915.

In 1906, Woodrow Wilson, president of Princeton University, remarked that nothing would spread socialism in the United States faster than the automobile. It offered, he said, a picture of the arrogance of wealth for all to see. Thanks to Ford, the story of the automobile did not turn out as Wilson envisioned. By 1920 the car for many had become a necessity. When a woman was asked how she could own a car and not a bathtub, her response was "you can't go to town in a bath tub." Although trains and buses would remain essential to the travel infrastructure of the Midwest, automobiles would become a fundamental factor in the transformation of the living habits of middle-class America throughout the region. Drive-in restaurants, movies, suburban shopping centers, and the suburbs themselves owed their rapid development in the first half of the twentieth century to the automobile.

Will Durant, another automobile pioneer who was more entrepreneur than inventor, brought another innovation to the industry. In 1919, after consolidating a number of small automobile companies into the giant General Motors, he used his abundant supply of capital generated from war profits to create the General Motors Acceptance Corporation (GMAC), the first commercial credit company in America. Now people of modest income had an alternative to buying Ford's dependable, economical, but boring Model T. With a little down and a little a month they could step up to one of General Motors' colorful and powerful models. G.M. operated under the principle of planned obsolescence, a production and marketing strategy that emphasized measured change in engineering and style, which encouraged customers to buy new "improved" models rather than hold on to the older ones.

At the beginning of the century, interurban lines began to connect major metropolitan areas of the Midwest. The history of these lines goes back to the mid-nineteenth century when, in 1850, the Aurora Branch Railroad made connections with Chicago. By the 1870s, seven interurban electric lines either entered Chicago or connected with surface and elevated lines at the edge of the city. At the edge of the Chicago lines, in turn, tracks connected to enter the other major cities of the Midwest, including Detroit, Milwaukee, and St. Louis. Most of these interurban lines survived the initial impact of the automobile, and well into the mid-twentieth century these trains provided transportation for people traveling from one midwestern city to another (Mayer and Wade 1969, 206–8, 250; Kyvig 2002, 29–30).

Political Life

The rapid growth of midwestern cities at the turn of the century brought demands for new infrastructures such as telephone lines, electric lines, and public transportation, which required large amounts of money and invited the corruption that money can bring. In the early decades of the century most cities of the Midwest had to deal with a flood of corruption in local government that within two decades would rise to the level of the White House during the Harding administration. Often political parties ran on a platform no more substantial than the pledge to "throw the bums out." The best that political parties could say in many cities was that they were less corrupt than the other guys. During this era, a group of political activists emerged, mostly professional and mostly middle class, who called themselves Progressives. They tried to bring honest and sound government to the cities by professionalizing the administration of the cities through the appointment of a city manager and the establishment of citizen oversight groups, such as public utilities commissions.

In the 1920s, midwesterners witnessed a rise in organized crime, as the illegitimate business of beer and liquor sales became the domain of criminals. Although other cities throughout the country suffered the same fate, the midwestern city of Chicago, because of its infamous citizen Al Capone and the bloody gang wars fought by him, received the reputation as being the gangland capital of America. At the same time in the late 1920s and 1930s, in an odd cultural juxtaposition, bank robbers became folk heroes to a population feeling cheated by large corporations and banks. These issues flavored the public life and helped shape opinions of midwesterners in the first decades of the twentieth century. They created a public opinion that on one hand was cynical about political life, yet on the other hand yearned and hoped for and believed in the possibility of reform.

GOVERNMENT

Political dialogue in the Midwest in the first two decades of the new century, as in much of the rest of the country, was dominated by Progressivism. Progressives embraced the cause of honesty and efficiency in government, a concern that led to a variety of reforms of state and local government. A group of reform mayors, including Hazen Pingree of Detroit, Thomas Johnson of Cleveland, Samuel E. "Golden Rule" Jones of Toledo, and Socialist mayor Emil Seidel of Milwaukee, successfully attacked corrupt machines and provided efficient municipal services such as mass transportation, water, and electrical power. In Detroit, Progressive urban reform preceded the new century. It began with the administration of Hazen Pingree, who served as mayor of that city from 1890 to 1897. Pingree's career embodied the two models that Progressive reform movements throughout the Midwest would follow. First was structural reform, which stemmed from middle-class values and assumptions, which emphasized businesslike efficiency and honesty in government, and social reform that displayed sympathy for immigrant and working-class conditions and attempted to attack the causes of these conditions rather than the symptoms. While in office, Pingree championed municipal ownership of utilities, better government service, home rule, tax equalization, social welfare programs, improved schools, and more public parks and baths. In contrast to most reform governments, Pingree's administration depended on the immigrant and labor votes as his power base, which contradicted many assumptions that reformers' power base remained in the middle and upper middle class (Mohl 1970, 286–87).

In Cleveland, Tom Johnson, although a successful businessman with numerous property interests, advocated taxing wealthy businesses and property owners to generate funds for much-needed improvements in the city. Milwaukee Socialists led by Victor Berger, who would become the country's first Socialist representative in Congress, sought to reform the legacy of the Industrial Revolution on the local level. Progressivism and Socialism had different leaders and spoke different languages, but were, in many ways, remarkably similar in practice. Socialists rejected the Progressive idea of government regulation of industry. Instead, they sought to replace the capitalist system with a planned economy of state-owned industries that would protect workers from business monopolies. Until that time came though, Socialists supported measures that were quite similar to the Progressives. Like Progressives, Milwaukee Socialists also advocated cleaning up neighborhoods and factories with new sanitation systems, municipal ownership of water and power systems, community parks, and improved education systems. Many of these goals were realized when in 1910 Milwaukeeans elected Emil Seidel the first Socialist mayor in the country. These urban ventures in what reformers approvingly called "gas and water socialism," or in Milwaukee "sewer socialism," encouraged many Americans to accept the principle of government regulation of necessary services.

The most important Progressive victory at the state level came in 1900 when Robert M. La Follette defeated the Wisconsin political machine to win the governorship. Once elected, La Follette called on experts at the state universities to draft reform legislation. By the time La Follette had finished his three terms in 1906, Wisconsin had enacted a system of business taxation and regulation and social services that led Progressive president Theodore Roosevelt to call the state "the laboratory of democracy." By 1915, Wisconsin not only had passed a direct primary law but also raised taxes on railroads and other corporations, established a railroad regulatory commission, enacted a law controlling lobbying, inaugurated a state civil service system, and adopted a state income tax. La Follette's success in Wisconsin became a model for other Progressive victories elsewhere in the Midwest. A number of governors, most notably Albert Cummins of Iowa, later joined La Follette in the U.S. Senate to form a Progressive core in that otherwise formidable bastion of conservatism (Harrell, et al. 2005, 788–90).

Progressive reform did not permeate every city of the Midwest, as those Americans who read Lincoln Steffens knew only too well. In a series of exposés on city government at the turn of the century, Steffens reported on corruption in major cities in the United States. Of the seven cities he pointed out as particularly corrupt, five of them were in the Midwest. Describing St. Louis, he told his readers that it remained in 1901 "the worst-governed city in the land." He pointed out that in St. Louis corruption came from the top. Formerly the best citizens, the merchants and big financiers, used to rule the town, he pointed out, and they ruled it well. But a change had occurred, and he lamented that public spirit had become private spirit, public enterprise had become private greed. He wrote of St. Louis:

Public franchises and privileges were sought, not for legitimate profit and common convenience, but for loot. Taking selfish interest in public councils, the big men misused politics. The riffraff, catching the smell of corruption, rushed into the municipal assembly, drove out the remaining respectable men, and sold the city—its streets, its wharves, its markets, and all that it had to the now greedy businessmen and bribers (Steffens 1957, 163).

As for Chicago, Steffens reported that the city was

First in violence, deepest in dirt; loud, lawless, unlovely, ill-smelling, irreverent, new; an overgrown gawk of a village, the 'tough' among cities, a spectacle for the nation. With resources for a magnificent system of public parking, it is too poor to pave and clean the streets. They can balance high buildings on rafts floating in mud, but they can't quench the stench of the stockyards. The enterprise which carried through a World's Fair [in 1893] to a world's triumph is satisfied with two thousand five hundred policemen for two million inhabitants and one hundred and ninety-six square miles of territory, a force so insufficient (and inefficient) that it cannot protect itself, to say nothing of handling mobs, riotous strikers, and the rest of that lawlessness which disgraces Chicago. (Steffens 1957, 164)

In Kansas City, Missouri, government was controlled by the Tom Pendergast machine. Big money was made illegally in this town because Thomas J. Pendergast, lever of the crooked Democratic machine, let it happen. With a baronial presence—masquerading as a fine Catholic benefactor of the city since early in the century—he literally owned the town. Under him were an alliance of crooked magistrates, attorneys, sheriffs, policemen, aldermen, businessmen, poll hackers, and stooges who jumped immediately so as to not anger Pendergast. His chief lieutenant was Mafia-backed John Lazia, a product of the town's "Little Italy," and who served to enforce the decrees of "Tom's Town." Through much of the first half of the century elections often would be won on the simple promise of cleaning up city hall, but that rarely occurred. Despite the gains of Progressives, local politics in many parts of the Midwest remained a rough-and-tumble world where only the strongest survived (http://www.crimelibrary.com/gangsters_outlaws/outlaws/floyd/3.html).

LAW, CRIME, AND PUNISHMENT

Prohibition, which went into effect on January 16, 1920, stimulated the rapid growth of organized crime, which in the ensuing decades would become woven into the fabric of American society. Prohibition liquor sales became another means, along with drugs, prostitution, and even legitimate services such as laundry, by which money flowed from upper- and middle-class communities into the neighborhoods and purses of the poor. Because of middle- and upper-class patronage of speakeasies and purchase of illegal alcoholic beverages, Prohibition opened up a new criminal occupation with less risk of punishment, more certainty of gain, and less social stigma than traditional criminal activities. Mobsters even became popular culture heroes. As illustrated by the following quotation, Al Capone, the famous Chicago gangster who was invited to be among the official welcoming committee when Benito Mussolini visited Chicago, saw his criminal activities as providing a public service:

If I break the law, my customers are as guilty as I am. The only difference between us is that I sell and they buy. Everyone calls me a racketeer. I call myself a businessman. When I sell its bootlegging. When my patrons serve it on a silver tray on Lake Shore Drive, its hospitality. (Gossop 2007, 164)

Besides supplying a public demand, organized crime also stimulated the economy of a number of legitimate businesses. Floral shops, truck mechanics, restaurateurs, undertakers, and lawyers all benefited from the activity of these extralegal entrepreneurs. A more lasting effect on the economy was their participation in labor-management relations, which entrenched organized crime in unions for many years after the end of Prohibition.

The city of Chicago under Capone became a stronghold of organized crime, but Chicago did not have a monopoly on this enterprise. Every major city in the country had a story, if not as dramatic, at least similar to Chicago's. Crime syndicates did not begin with Prohibition, They rose to power through the saloons, gambling houses, and brothels of the nineteenth century, but crime in Chicago took a large step toward organization in the early twentieth century under Big Jim Colisimo, a poor Italian immigrant who rose from waterboy on a railroad gang to famous Chicago restaurateur. His road to success was paved by politics and crime. Through astute organization of the voters in his neighborhood, Colisimo became a precinct captain. Once inside the political fraternity of Chicago, he could operate illegitimate services without fear of legal recrimination. He opened a string of brothels, the profits of which provided capital for his famous restaurant, Colisimo's Café, which achieved national fame and received famous visitors such as Enrico Caruso and George M. Cohan.

Although he was rapidly turning legitimate, small-time racketeers were constantly harassing Colisimo, and so he sent for his nephew Johnny Torrio of New York, head of the famous Five Points Gang. Once in Chicago, Torrio protected Colisimo, but he used his clients' connections to establish his own political and criminal hegemony. In late 1919, recognizing the potential financial boom that would arrive with Prohibition, Torrio tried to convince Colisimo to get in on the ground floor of the bootlegging business. Colisimo laughed at the idea of bootlegging and told Torrio to "stick with the women" (i.e., prostitution).

On May 11, 1920, five months after the Prohibition era began, Colisimo died from multiple gunshot wounds. The murderer was never discovered. Some said it was a jealous wife, others surmised that it was small-time racketeers, and still others suspected that Torrio's apprentice Alphonse Capone did it. But Torrio, who shed the most tears at the funeral, protested, "We wuz like brothers." Colisimo's funeral was the first of the gangland funeral extravaganzas that would become commonplace in the 1920s. The honorary pallbearers included three judges, an assistant state attorney, a member of Congress, a state representative, and nine aldermen. With a custom-made casket and magnificent floral tributes, the cost of the funeral came to $50,000, which Torrio paid.

Now in complete control, Torrio set his plan for expansion. To launch his start in the beer industry, he partnered with a well-known legitimate brewer, Joseph Stentson. Stentson brewed the beer, and Torrio handled distribution. He also brought the Italian Alky cooking guild under his complete control. Immigrants had been producing alcohol in the backrooms of tenements and selling it wholesale to bootleggers for decades. The Italian distillers organized themselves under the Unione Siciliano. The Unione, once a legitimate voting bloc in the Italian community, had by 1920 become synonymous with the Italian underworld.

Italians hardly monopolized crime. There were German gangs, Irish gangs, Jewish gangs, and others. But in several cities Italian gangs gained universal prominence, and in the popular mind they became synonymous with organized crime. Several factors contributed to Italian success in this highly competitive business of organized crime. Italians had a deep loyalty to family and clan tradition. They also possessed a fierce partisanship toward group laws as opposed to outside regulations, and a dislike and contempt for government, an attitude that they had brought with them from Italy. Their failure to integrate into the rest of the society also brought them closer together. Finally and most importantly, they brought with them from Italy a *padrone* system, which demanded unfettered loyalty to their local leader and provider.

Torrio efficiently organized these various clan groups into the most powerful criminal organization the country had known up to that time. He understood there were other non-Italian gangs who would never come under his control. Therefore, he organized Chicago and Cook County into small kingdoms. Each leader promised not to invade the other's territory. The leaders even met periodically at Torrio's restaurant, The Four Deuces, to discuss differences and to ensure peace.

Despite Torrio's efforts, there remained too much suspicion, which eventually precipitated major fissures in the pact. The first was with the Irish gangster Dion O'Bannion, who had risen from newspaper boy to small-time burglar to florist and leader of one of Chicago's most important gangs. His flower shop was across the street from Holy Name Cathedral on North State Street at Superior Street, where he had served as an altar boy. He wore specially tailored suits that concealed three revolvers. He was quick-tempered, crude, undiplomatic, and lacked the cool savvy of Torrio. In 1924, Torrio offered to combine enterprises with O'Bannion, but the Irish gangster refused. He did not want any part of Torrio's brothels, which he considered immoral. On November 10, 1924, the first incident in what would be called the "Bootleg Battle of the Marne" occurred when three members of Torrio's Unione Siciliano shot and killed O'Bannion in his own flower shop. Torrio thought removing O'Bannion would bring harmony to the underworld, but he was wrong.

Unwilling to risk his life, and happy with the $50 million dollars he had made in the first four years of Prohibition, Torrio fled with his wife to a villa in Italy. He turned his entire organization over to his deputy Al Capone, who waged a vicious and uncompromising war against O'Bannion's successors. The war culminated on February 14, 1929, in the vicious machine-gun murder that became known in local folklore as the St. Valentine's Day massacre. Capone's men, disguised as police officers, entered a garage on Clark Street that was a known O'Bannion gang hangout. The "police" told the gang members to put their hands up and face the wall. Supposing a typical police shakedown, they complied. In the next moment machine guns filled the room with bullets, smoke, noise, and blood, and the O'Bannion gang members lay dead on the floor.

The gruesome execution of several of his enemies ended gang resistance against Capone and his empire. Capone continued to work the rackets, brothels, and speakeasies and rapidly became a multimillionaire. Capone's control of the city was so tight that in the autumn of 1928 Frank Loesch, president of the Chicago Crime Commission, went to Capone (not the police or the mayor's office) to ensure legitimate elections, and the elections turned out to be the cleanest and fairest in 40 years. By this time, however, Capone's days as a free man were numbered. An Internal Revenue Service (IRS) investigator, Elmer Irey, had built a case against him that was strong enough to convict him on tax evasion charges. Capone was sentenced to 11 years in prison and a $50,000 fine. He spent the larger part of his sentence in Alcatraz, the harsh prison in San Francisco Bay, where it was discovered in 1938 that he suffered from an advanced case of syphilis. After his release, he spent the last years of his life at his south Florida estate on Palm Island, Miami Beach, where he lived as a feeble recluse dying of advanced neurosyphilis in 1947 at the age of 48.

In addition to organized crime, the Depression years also saw the emergence of a number of criminals who, with the tools of their trade, a submachine gun and a fast car (preferably a Ford Model A), acted as independent entrepreneurs in the underworld of crime. Their victims of choice were the banks, but they were not beyond robbing a roadside store for groceries, gas, or a pack of cigarettes. Among the criminals that dominated the headlines of the Midwest were John Dillinger in Indiana and Illinois, "Pretty Boy" Floyd in Ohio, Missouri, and Oklahoma, and "Baby Face" Nelson in Illinois and Minnesota. Despite their differences and distinctive habits, they shared the love of fast cars, machine guns, bank robberies, and the knowledge that they would probably die young. Unlike most criminals, whom normal law-abiding citizens would hold in disdain, these Depression-era gangsters became folk heroes

A re-enactment of the 1929 St. Valentine's Day massacre from the film *The St. Valentine's Day Massacre*. Library of Congress.

to many. Perhaps this was so because they created public personas as down-home folks who were caught in a struggle with the impersonal forces of finance and law enforcement. Americans who had lost their savings to a failed bank or their possessions to a sheriff's sale or knew somebody who had suffered that fate felt an odd camaraderie with these often psychopathic criminals.

REFORM

At the turn of the century, despite rampant political corruption, Chicagoans could boast of a number of reform movements, which served as models for the rest of the country. In 1894, William T. Stead, an English editor and Christian socialist, issued a challenge to Chicagoans with his sensational exposé of social conditions in the city, *If Christ Came to Chicago*. Stead described graphically the plight of the workers, the savage brutality with which their aspirations were crushed, and the corruption and indifference of Chicago's leaders. "If Chicago is to be the Capital of Civilization," he wrote, "it is indispensable that she should at least be able to show that every resident within her limits enjoyed every advantage which intelligent and public-spirited administration has secured for the people elsewhere."

Stead's widely read book struck a responsive chord. Progressive reformers, churchmen and women, and people resentful of the dirt, noise, pollution, and corruption in the city pushed for reform on every front from clean water to clean streets to clean government. Reform activity in Chicago, the largest city in the Midwest, characterized the middle- and upper-class nature of most reform movements occurring throughout the region and the United States at the same time. Typical of such groups was the Civic Federation, headed by many of Chicago's most prominent businessmen and their wives, who dabbled in social reform. Committed to the city's current economic structure and at the same time to the idea of class conciliation, the federation made noteworthy efforts to provide systematic relief for the needy, improve housing and sanitary conditions, and drive the grafters and boodlers from City Hall.

Others paid less attention to structural reform and immersed themselves in social reform. Jane Addams, for instance, and the remarkable women she enlisted at Hull House, knew through personal experience the problems of alienation and exploitation faced by Italian and Slavic immigrants who huddled in Chicago's west side tenements. Addams and her followers established settlement houses (the most famous of which was Hull House) where the poor received child care services, a needed meal, job and housing information, and a myriad of other services otherwise inaccessible to the poor. By means of surveys and reports on housing, work, and sanitary conditions, the settlement house also informed other Americans of the intolerable physical and social conditions that mired immigrants and working-class urban dwellers in dirt, poverty, and alienation from American norms. Motivated in part by the work of Addams and her followers, many middle- and upper-class women in cities throughout the Midwest contributed to efforts to establish settlement houses for the working class and immigrants and through them received their first taste of public life and civic responsibility.

By the turn of the century, some five hundred women's clubs in the United States boasted over 160,000 members, and through the General Federation of Women's Clubs, they funded libraries and hospitals and supported schools, settlement houses, compulsory education, and child and women labor laws. Eventually they moved beyond the concerns of home and family to endorse controversial causes such as women's suffrage and unionization. To that list the National Association of Colored Women added the special concerns of African Americans.

In the first decades of the twentieth century, the newly emerging Jewish community of Cleveland remained instrumental in reform in that city. Indeed, the Jewish community even took over a Protestant organization, the Council for Educational Alliance, when it was on the brink of collapse. The Jewish community also pioneered in the establishment of a system for unified fundraising that benefited numerous charitable agencies in the city. The reform movements in both Cleveland and Detroit reflected a dynamic multicultural movement, which contradicted the historic model of reform being driven primarily if not exclusively by the elite WASP middle and upper class (VanTassel and Grabowski 1986, 6–9).

American educational reformer John Dewey. Library of Congress.

Another important midwestern reformer was Clarence Darrow. Already known nationally as the "people's lawyer," Darrow brought to the reform movement a searching critique of the American industrial system. Other midwestern reformers include Thorstein Veblen, who sought to revise classical economic theory, and John Dewey, who formulated a philosophy of education designed for the new industrial age (see the sections on Intellectual Life and Education).

Religion entered the campaign for social reform with men like Graham Taylor of the Chicago Commons settlement house, who combined practical knowledge of the plight of the poor with a strong belief in the Social Gospel. Catholic priests throughout the industrial Midwest, armed with the social encyclical *Rerum Novarum*, reminded the immigrant workers of their parishes that they had a God-given right to live and demand wages that allowed them to support their families in dignity. Influenced by the Catholic personalist philosophy of Peter Maurin and the work of his follower Dorothy Day in New York, in the 1930s, groups of young Catholics established Catholic Worker Houses of Hospitality in cities throughout the Midwest including Cleveland, Detroit, Milwaukee, St. Louis, and Chicago where the poor could come for shelter, a meal, information, or simply a few moments respite from the harsh world of the Depression 1930s. As this discussion implies, reform in the first decades of the twentieth century took on many forms, and motivation varied from those who wanted to reform a system they felt to be basically sound to those who wanted to overturn the entire social structure of the country.

WAR

When on April 2, 1917, President Woodrow Wilson asked Congress for a formal declaration of war against Germany, normal life in the Midwest as well as the rest of the nation underwent numerous convolutions. None had their lives changed more drastically than those young men who received notice that they had to go to war. To supply the million men deemed necessary to fight the war, Congress early in May 1917 passed a draft bill, and President Wilson declared June 5, 1917, as registration day. Ray Stannard Baker's wide-flung, high-powered propaganda campaign to make the day a festival and patriotic occasion succeeded in stirring up a national sentiment that dispelled or intimidated any remaining reluctance to the draft. To the polling places went 10 million young men. Each set down the data required—name, address, age, physical features, occupation, and reason, if any, for exemption. Each received a small green card certifying his registration. Without disturbance anywhere, almost one male out of every five in the country had shown his readiness to be tested for the army. The next step was to create a lottery that would determine who out of the 10 million would be sent to fight in Europe (Sullivan, V 1933, 302).

Almost three million were drafted; another two million volunteered. Most were white and young, between the ages of 21 and 31. Some 20,000 women served as clerks, telephone operators, and nurses. In a nation of immigrants, nearly one draftee in five was born in another country. Training often aimed at educating and Americanizing ethnic recruits. In special development battalions drill sergeants barked out orders while volunteers from the YMCA taught American history and English.

Mexican Americans and African Americans volunteered in disproportionately high numbers. Blacks quickly filled out four all-black army and eight National Guard units already in existence. They were also granted fewer exemptions from the draft than their white counterparts. Only 10 percent of the American population, blacks comprised 13 percent of the draftees. Southern Demo-

---

📷 Snapshot

You're in the Army Now!

In the following excerpt from *Our Times,* Mark Sullivan describes the lottery as it unfolded on the morning of July 20, 1917, in Washington, D.C.

A distinguished group of Senators, Representatives and High Army officers gathered in the public hearing room of the Senate Office Building around a large glass bowl containing 10,500 black capsules with numbered slips inside. Rarely has human eye been so privileged to see fate engaged in concrete functioning, the gods of the machine in operation. The gods for once made a formal ceremony of their distribution of destinies, Secretary of War Baker was to draw the first capsule, Senator George Chamberlain of Oregon, next in hierarchical order, was to draw the second, Representative S. Hubert Dent of Alabama the third, Senator Warren of Wyoming the fourth, and so on through a long list of minor gods.

At 9:49 A.M. Secretary of War Baker, blindfolded, put in his hand and drew out a capsule—it was number 258. Flash powder boomed, cameras clicked, reporters sprang for the door. By telephone and telegraph the number "258" sped over the country to waiting newspaper presses, to stock tickers, to crowds standing before bulletin boards of Draft Offices. In each of the 4500 local villages and precincts across the country any man with the number 258 was chosen to fight—he had to now go to camp or show cause why he should be exempt.

The lottery went on until after two the following morning; one blindfolded man took out the capsule, three tellers verified the number, and six tallymen recorded the list, one on a large blackboard which was photographed and reproduced on front pages everywhere. That day there was more excitement throughout the country than on the day of declaring war, for the lottery told each registrant how close he was to battle. War in general had become war personally. (Sullivan, V 1933, 304–5)

crats in Congress had opposed training African Americans in arms, fearful of the prospect of putting arrogant strutting representatives of black soldiery in every community. Consequently, the majority of blacks in the armed services remained in support roles. However, four regiments of the all-black 93rd Division brigaded with the French army were among the first Americans in the trenches and among the most decorated units in the army.

On the home front many Americans reacted to the propaganda against Germany with a personal hate campaign against Germans in this country. Sauerkraut became liberty cabbage, frankfurters became hotdogs. German dogs were tortured and killed. The Midwest, which had become home to many Germans in St. Louis, Cincinnati, Chicago, Milwaukee, Minneapolis, and St. Paul, became especially susceptible to this nativistic patriotism. In Chicago, for example, a German practice of walking with friends or sweethearts in Grant Park was forbidden as Germans were prohibited from areas (such as parks) where large numbers of people gathered. And throughout the Midwest as well as the rest of the nation German American institutions came under attack. Although merely cosmetic, some discrimination was hateful. The names of schools, foods, streets, and towns were often changed, and music written by Wagner and Mendelssohn was removed from concert programs and even weddings. Physical attacks, though rare, were more violent. German American businesses and homes were vandalized, and German Americans accused of being "pro-German" were tarred and feathered and, in at least once instance, lynched.

The most pervasive damage was done to German language and education. German-language newspapers were either run out of business or quietly chose to close their doors. German-language books were burned, and Americans who spoke German were threatened with violence or boycotts. German-language classes, until then a common part of the public school curriculum, were discontinued and, in many areas, outlawed entirely. None of these institutions ever fully recovered, and the centuries-old tradition of German language and literature in the United States was pushed to the margins of national life and in many places effectively ended (http://rs6.loc.gov/learn/features/immig/german8.html).

Recreational Life

Baseball, movies, sports clubs, and taverns made the city the place to be for entertainment in the first decades of the twentieth century. As the working class increased, so did the number of people searching for recreational outlets in the small amount of free time they had. As the demand for entertainment grew, so did the entertainment industry. Sports and movies were the main benefactors of this new market demand. Movies have been discussed elsewhere, but this section will show how sports and music became entwined into the lives of Americans and even became a means for European immigrants to enter into the cultural milieu of their new home, and how black migrants from the South used their music to make a significant contribution to American culture.

SPORTS

Diverse ethnicity dominated the sports of the cities of the Midwest. One of the few new immigrant groups that came to America with any organized sporting heritage at all, the Bohemians, established themselves in heavily Czech neighborhoods in Chicago, St. Louis, Milwaukee, and Cleveland. In 1862, as part of a romantic resistance movement against the ruling Austrians, Bohemian nationalists had organized the Sokol movement. Its philosophy, modeled after the German *turnverein*, sought to develop nationalism and strong bodies and minds for the future revolution. The Sokol tradition in America went almost as far back as in Bohemia; a unit was established in St. Louis in 1865. The primary goals of American Sokol units were to promote physical culture and to encourage newcomers to identify with their fellow Bohemians and their language and culture. By 1900 there were 184 units in the United States, mostly in the Midwest. The members were mainly working class or small merchants who were freethinkers. Hostility between freethinkers and devout Catholics eventually caused the latter to organize their own Sokols.

The Sokol hall was normally one of the largest buildings in a Bohemian neighborhood, and the center of its cultural and social life. It often housed the community's major recreational institutions like the Czech theater and choral societies. Sokols sponsored annual gymnastic exhibitions and family holiday outings that would include Sokol drills and folk dancing. The Sokol leaders met the challenge of attracting the interest of the American-born by organizing Sunday Bohemian baseball leagues for them. This got the youth involved in the Sokol and encouraged them to sustain their ethnic identity. The quality of play was quite high; by 1910, several Chicago Bohemians had made the Major Leagues. Their achievement was a source of great pride in the community, even among non-baseball fans.

Baseball by the turn of the century was well on its way to becoming America's national pastime. Urban politicians played an influential role in professional baseball from its earliest days. However, unlike boxing and horse racing, which operated under severe legal constraints and social opprobrium, baseball did not need to circumvent antigambling laws or operate in violation of the penal codes. The national pastime, the preeminent commercialized spectator sport in the city and its surrounding area, was regarded as a clean, exciting game. Club owners cultivated public images as selfless, civic-minded businessmen who sponsored teams out of a concern for the public welfare.

In reality owners were usually profit-oriented businessmen, typically professional politicians or friends or business allies of politicians, just as involved in urban politics as other sports entrepreneurs. Although not all executives were members of urban political machines, in cities that had powerful bosses, teams were often affiliated with their organizations. Political connections helped club owners in a variety of ways, such as providing protection against interlopers, obtaining inside information, obtaining public lands at reduced prices, and securing preferential treatment from the municipality. These services greatly enhanced the security and profitability of an entrepreneur's investment in baseball.

During the first three decades of professional baseball, when teams came and went with great regularity, nearly all major and minor league clubs had direct or indirect connections to urban politics. Ted Vincent examined the occupations of 1,263 officials and stockholders and found that nearly half were politicians, including 50 mayors, 102 state legislators, and countless judges, councilmen, and police commissioners—in sum, mainly professional politicians trying to profit from a new business venture in a field disdained by old money, while picking up votes from fans who were grateful to them for sponsoring a popular entertainment. A number of politicians, especially those who founded new teams, were also civic boosters. The first all-salaried team began in the Midwest. The Cincinnati Red Stockings, organized in 1869 by local boosters under the leadership of businessman and politician Aaron Champion, used sports to publicize their hometown. The team was a great success on the field, going undefeated in 1869 (56–0–1) and winning its first 25 games a year later before suffering its first loss. The club did a great job advertising the Queen City (Cincinnati) but only broke even at the box office. Its example encouraged the formation of at least four other fully salaried teams in 1870, including the Chicago White Stockings, a club backed by leading business and political leaders who also wanted to use baseball to publicize the sophisticated and progressive character of their city (Riess 1991, 194–95).

By 1893, the National League was on sound economic footing, and in 1901 the American League formed. Attendance in what became known as the big leagues doubled between 1901 and 1908, and Major League owners made very substantial profits. Between 1901 and 1911 the Chicago White Sox, owned by former player and manager Charles Comiskey, a son of a former Chicago city councilman, earned over $700,000. Across town, the Cubs were also making large profits. At the end of 1905, sporting goods tycoon and ex-player Albert G. Spalding sold the team to Charles W. Murphy for $105,000. Charles P. Taft, whose brother was secretary of war, financed the purchase. In the following season the new owners made $165,000. Between 1907 and 1913 their earnings reached $810,000, about an 800 percent return on their original investment.

Major League Baseball's success in the early decades of the century helped to alter the physical space of the cities where they played. In Detroit, at the corner of Michigan and Trumbull, on April 12, 1912, 26,000 fans crammed into a newly renovated ballpark for opening day. It was one of many new baseball venues that would rise up in the first decades of the twentieth century. Urban fans coming to games often had never seen such an expanse of open green space (consequently, across the nation baseball stadiums were always referred to as parks). Paul Sommerkamp, the Cincinnati Reds public address announcer, captured the sensation of fans entering these glamorous monuments to baseball. "There it sat," he wrote, "in kind of a dilapidated neighborhood, like a jewel. It was sort of an oasis. You'd walk up through the portals to the seats. The sight of that bright-green grass would hit you, and you'd think you'd walked into another world" (http://www.crosley-field.com/).

In Chicago, the owner of the White Sox, Charles Comiskey, decided that his team needed a new steel and concrete ballpark. In 1909, he bought a piece of land that had once been the city landfill to construct his ballpark. Construction on the ballpark began on February 15, 1910. It was completed in just five months and was named White Sox Park. Within the decade every Major League city in the Midwest had a new baseball park, and Chicago had two.

In 1918, the two leagues played a 130-game schedule, and total attendance barely topped three million. Planning another short season and fearing continued losses in 1919, many owners lowered salaries further and slashed expenses. Although the aura surrounding owners like Connie Mack, and to a lesser extent John McGraw, had declined during the 1910s, that of Chicago White Sox owner Charles Comiskey continued to shine. After his club won the 1917 World Series, an article attempted to demonstrate how the "Old Roman" had "won a fortune and whole army of personal followers through enlightened business methods." In 1919, with the war over and Babe Ruth in ascendance, baseball attendance had mushroomed to record levels, generating dramatic profits for the owners without comparable rewards for the players. Comiskey through shrewd business acumen was able to afford to buy a team that included the best players of the decade, including Eddie Collins and "Shoeless" Joe Jackson. But Comiskey's tight purse strings also left players convinced that although they were the best at what they did, they were being paid the same as the worst in the league. After Comiskey's White Sox won the American League pennant, the players found themselves in a position as World Series participants to capitalize on their accumulated resentments. Several of the players conspired with gamblers to fix the Series, and others through their silence became complicit in the plot. After the fix was discovered, the disillusionment of a generation of fans was captured by a young boy who ran up to Shoeless Joe Jackson and pleaded, "Say it ain't so Joe!"

In the end Comiskey's primary sin rested not so much with his employment practices, as abysmal as they may have been, but with his subsequent efforts to protect his team and investment by covering up the scandal and undermining the prosecution of the participants. Neither Comiskey nor the White Sox, at least during his lifetime, ever recovered from the devastation of 1919. Forty years would pass before the White Sox would win another pennant, and almost 90 years before they would win a World Series. Comiskey was, by all accounts, broken by the scandal. Although he died a wealthy man in 1931, his estate totaled far less than it might have had the scandal not occurred. The priest who delivered his funeral sermon attributed his death to "a broken heart" (Tygiel 2000, 61).

In 1934, at the height of the Depression, the Cincinnati team, on the verge of bankruptcy, was bought by millionaire industrialist Powell Cros-

FATIMA
TURKISH BLEND
CIGARETTES
"NO GOLD TIPS BUT FINEST QUALITY"

Special Offer

On receipt of 40 "FATIMA" Cigarette coupons, we will send you an enlarged copy (size 13 x 21) of this picture (without advertising) or of any other picture in this series (National League and American League teams). This picture is mounted, and ready for framing. Write plainly your name and address, stating picture desired.

PREMIUM DEPARTMENT
Liggett & Myers Tob. Co.
7th Ave. & 16th St., New York City, N.Y.
FACTORY NO. 25 SECOND DISTRICT OF VA.

A Fatima cigarettes coupon for a portrait of the 1913 Chicago White Sox. Library of Congress.

ley. His ownership not only changed the name of their field from Redland Field to his own, but also changed the game in ways that secured its survival during the Depression and its continued success thereafter.

Baseball aficionados always claimed that baseball was tailor-made for radio. Although ball games were included among some of the first broadcasts, the marriage between the two was not obvious from the start. From the beginning, many owners had feared that accessibility to baseball on the radio would reduce ticket sales, and during the Depression years, when baseball attendance took a deep downturn, many owners blamed it on the radio. Some teams even prohibited the broadcast of their games in hopes of reviving ticket sales (Tygiel 2000, 99). Crosley, the owner of several radio stations and the manufacturer of the famous push-button radio that bore his name, was convinced otherwise. Seeing baseball as a means of selling radios and promoting his team, he announced that all games of the Reds would be broadcast. To announce the games, he introduced Red Barber, who would become a legend among radio broadcasters. From that point on, the union of baseball to radio was secured. Crosley brought another innovation to the game when in 1935 he convinced the skeptical owners to allow him to install lights and play the game at night. James T. Golden of the Cincinnati *Enquirer* remembered that special evening when fans for the first time saw Major League Baseball under the lights:

The field showed up in a more uniform light, green and tan, than it does in daytime. . . . What clouds there were were so thin that the ball, when it flew high, shone through them like a bald head in a steam room. And when there was no mist, the sphere stood out against the sky like a pearl against dark velvet.

From 1901, which begins the modern era of baseball with the establishment of two major leagues, until 1940, five Major League teams have played and continue to play in four midwestern cities. From 1901 until 1940, these teams together won 28 pennants and 13 World Series. And fans in those midwestern cities were able to root for some of the greatest that ever played the game: Ty Cobb, Eddie Collins, and Cy Young, to name a few. The teams established in these cities, the Chicago Cubs, the Chicago White Sox, the Detroit Tigers, the Cincinnati Reds, and the Cleveland Indians, have continued to be among the most successful and stable in Major League Baseball (Tygiel 2000, 60–62).

After baseball, football also emerged as a great spectator sport in the early decades of the twentieth century. Unlike baseball, people had much more interest in the collegiate game in this era than the professional one, and the midwestern colleges fielded some of the best teams in the country. All but one of the major teams of the Midwest were organized in a conference that became known as the Big Ten. The original members organized in 1895 included University of Chicago, University of Illinois, University of Michigan, University of Minnesota, Northwestern University, Purdue University, and University of Wisconsin. Indiana University and the University of Iowa were admitted in 1899. Ohio State joined in 1912. Chicago withdrew in 1946 and Michigan State College (now Michigan State University) was added three years later in 1949. Football in this era became the social focal point of every fall weekend at colleges of the Midwest as students, alumni, and local supporters descended on campuses where hundreds of thousands of dollars had been spent building football stadiums that could hold up to 80,000 fans.

Over the first decades of the twentieth century major rivalries developed among the Big Ten schools themselves and between some of the more important programs such as Michigan and the biggest schools in the East, which at the time included West Point, Penn State, and a number of what later became known as the Ivy League schools. As the decade of the 1920s unfolded, however, the biggest football program by far belonged to independent Notre Dame, a small Catholic college located in northern Indiana. By bringing innovations to the game such as the inclusion of the forward pass as an integral part of the game; by producing skilled players who in addition to being good athletes provided good newsprint, such as George Gipp and the "Four Horsemen"; and by winning more games and championships than any other college team, the small midwestern school became the darling not only of their alumni, but also of working-class Catholics throughout the country who included themselves among the "subway alumni" of Notre Dame.

Professional football attempted to ride the coattails of the collegiate game into popularity, but up until the early 1930s it had little success. In 1920, the American Professional Football Players Association (APFA) was formed. Of the 19 teams that comprised the league in 1921, 17 were located in the Midwest. In 1922, the APFA changed its name to the National Football League (NFL) and the Chicago Staleys changed their name to the Bears. That year marked the beginning of the NFL, and of the 14 teams that formed the first NFL, 13 were from the Midwest. Team location in the first years made the Midwest the center of gravity and birthplace of professional football. The roots of the NFL are midwestern, and the two oldest franchises, the Chicago Bears and the Green Bay Packers, are from that region. Each of these teams owed their endurance to the ingenuity of their pioneer owners George Halas and Curly Lambeau, respectively. In 1919, Lambeau was able to get financial backing for uniforms and salaries for players from the Indian meatpacking company where he worked. With this financial backing, Lambeau picked up college stars from all over the country, plus some unknowns who turned out to be "greats." In 1929, tiny Green Bay won the first of three straight national professional football championships, pacing stalwarts from New York and Chicago in league standings (the playoff system began in 1933). The 1929–1931 title teams featured all-time pro greats like Red Dunn, Verne Lewellen, Cal Hubbard, Bo Molenda, Jug Earp, Mike Michalske, Johnny (Blood) McNally, Bill Kern, Arnie Herber, Clarke Hinkle, Lavvie Dilweg, Tom Nash, Milt Gantenbein, and Hank

American football coach Knute Rockne when he was captain of the Notre Dame football team in 1913. The Granger Collection, New York.

Bruder. In many games, players would play for almost the full 60 minutes. These teams were hailed all over the country as some of the greatest ever.

In 1925, George Halas, owner of the Chicago Bears, was desperately seeking a special gate attraction to help draw attention not only to his team but also to the National Football League as a whole. University of Illinois running back Harold "Red" Grange, who ran with ghostlike speed and elusiveness, seemed to be the answer. Although college stars rarely turned to pro football in those days, Halas and his partner Dutch Sternaman pondered just how much Grange could do for their team. Grange, who worked as an ice deliveryman during his college summers, agreed to play for the Bears. On Thanksgiving Day, 1925, just 10 days after Grange's last college game, 36,600 fans filled Wrigley Field to see Red's pro debut against the Chicago Cardinals. Up to that time that crowd represented the largest to see a professional football game. Ten days later more than 70,000 packed New York's Polo Grounds to see Red and the Bears take on the New York Giants. From that day, the success of Halas's Bears and professional football was assured.

In an age that witnessed the birth of big-business professional spectator sports, midwestern cities led the way by providing the birthplace for professional football and the venue for some of professional baseball's most successful franchises. Professional sports, while bringing notoriety to midwestern cities, also provided a basis for community for the otherwise ethnically and culturally diverse and divided people of the urban Midwest.

MUSIC

In the 1920s, amid the misery of the highly segregated life on the south side of Chicago, a musical synthesis that would come to be known as the Chicago blues developed. The blues form, which originated in the Mississippi delta in the post–Civil War era, was first popularized about 1911–1914 by the black composer W. C. Handy. The poetic and musical form of the blues first crystallized around 1910 and gained popularity through the publication of Handy's *Memphis Blues* (1912) and *St. Louis Blues* (1914). Although instrumental blues had been recorded as early as 1913, the blues became a national craze when Mamie Smith recorded the first vocal blues song, *Crazy Blues*, in 1920. The blues influence on jazz brought it into the mainstream and made possible the records of blues singers like Bessie Smith and later, in the 1930s, Billie Holiday.

In the 1930s and 1940s, blues artists in Chicago added electric guitars, saxophones, and drums to the traditional guitar and harmonica of the Mississippi delta blues, and a number of important record companies, including the famous Chess Records (in the late 1940s) captured these sounds and distributed them nationwide. There are

Jim Thorpe on a 1984 U.S. postage stamp. The Granger Collection, New York.

Chicago bluesman Muddy Waters. Library of Congress.

thousands of Chicago blues artists who can still be heard in blues joints around Chicago, particularly on the south side and at the House of Blues in downtown Chicago. Although there were thousands of blues men and women in Chicago, only a relative handful have gained national fame. Among them are Howlin' Wolf, Sun Seals J. B. Hutto, Muddy Waters, Sonny Boy Williamson, and Willie Dixon. Their music has influenced such well-known stars as Paul Butterfield, Fleetwood Mac, and the Rolling Stones. Although blues were and are played throughout the nation, the Midwest contributed most to the developing sound of the blues. Blacks brought the music from its origins in the Mississippi delta up through the Mississippi River cities of Memphis and St. Louis, and over to Kansas City, up to Chicago. In each of these cities, something new was added. For instance, in Kansas City a fast style of playing with a piano accompaniment called "Boogie Woogie" was added to the repertoire. Since its proliferation in the early part of the century, blues music has continued to influence every form of American music from rock to hip hop to classical (Lloyd 1968, 69–70; http://www.history-of-rock.com/blues.htm).

ENTERTAINMENT

In the early decades of the twentieth century Chicago typified, though on a larger scale, the kind of entertainment one might find in the urban Midwest. Just south of Van Buren on State Street, the penny arcades, cheap saloons, burlesque palaces, and tawdry vaudeville beckoned to the tourist and the unwary. A little farther away the vice district operated around the clock without much official interference, indeed often with police collusion. For those seeking higher things, there were theaters on Randolph Street, the Art Institute, the Public Library, and Orchestra Hall along Michigan Avenue, and numerous bookstores and art galleries scattered about downtown.

The Coliseum on South Wabash provided a convenient site for all kinds of large civic affairs. Throughout the country it was famous, because both political parties had chosen it several times for national conventions. But Chicagoans knew it best at this time as the site of the notorious annual First Ward balls staged by the amiable and corrupt "bosses" of the central city—"Hinky Dink" Kenna and John "The Bath" Coughlin—to raise money for the Democratic organization. On these joyous occasions, the city's political swells mixed with masses at the levee, and thousands would frolic far into the night. In 1908, one reporter counted 2 bands, 200 waiters, 100 policemen, 35,000 quarts of beer, and 10,000 quarts of champagne. All this was easily consumed before the hosts "sent for reinforcements." "It's a lallapalooza," said city boss Hinky Dink Kenna with measured understatement. "All the business houses are here, all the big people. Chicago ain't no sissy town," he declared (Mayer and Wade 1969, 224).

Religious Life

In the early twentieth century, religiously the Midwest could be divided into two major groups, the Protestants who dominated rural and small town areas and the Catholics who formed majorities in the larger urban areas. By the 1920s, Jews entered the mix in the midwestern cities of Chicago, St. Louis, Cleveland, and Detroit. Although Catholics and Protestants represented by far the largest groups, they by no means represented two unified institutions. Protestants were torn by their views of the modern world and Catholics by the cultural differences they brought with them from Europe. While membership declined among most mainline Protestant groups in the 1920s and 1930s, white pentecostal and evangelical congregations grew. Catholics, meanwhile, remained steadfast in their faith. One major reason for Catholic allegiance was that the Church remained a familiar institution in a new and strange world. Despite myriad theological and cultural differences, all religious groups worried about the antireligious trends of modernity that pulled their young away from their religious roots. This section will explore religion in the Midwest and its influence on the habits and morals of the people of the region.

RELIGION AND SPIRITUALITY

Outside of the major cities of the Midwest, where immigrant Catholics represented the largest single religious group, evangelical Protestant denominations and Lutheran churches dominated the rural areas and small to medium-sized towns and cities. The evangelical Protestantism practiced was loosely linked to the capitalist materialist myth embraced by most Americans. The Lynds in their study of an average-sized city in the Midwest found the following statements quite indicative of the religious perspective of the people: "I believe in prayer because of experiences," remarked an active member of Rotary. "A couple of years ago everybody told me not to buy [a material essential in his industry]. Experts said to me, 'Trim your sails. It sure is a time to sit tight.' Well, my judgment was against it, but just the same I went ahead and bought fifty carloads—and in ten days it went up 50 per cent in price.

Now, I don't mean that God said, 'There's Jim in Middletown. I'll help him out,' but somebody guided me, and I think it was Him. That's why I believe in prayer." When the high school Bearcats were playing for the state basketball championship, those unable to attend the game assembled in the high school auditorium to hear the returns. A minister conducted the meeting, opening it with prayer, and as the tension grew during the game, a senior class officer prayed, "Oh, God, in thee we entrust this win. Jesus, wilt thou help us!"

One midwestern Protestant minister observed that for many the gospel of faith was predominantly preached in contrast to the gospel of works followed in everyday living. As an example he cited the minister of a well-to-do church who, during a period of dire unemployment, prayed, "O Lord, care for the 3,000 unemployed in this city and raise up friends to them. Set the factory machines going that [they] may again have work." In the 1920s, townspeople of the Midwest often gathered, as some sociologists noted, every Sunday in an ethnically homogeneous group that gave emotional and spiritual support to their own material and social position in the community (Lynd and Lynd 1929, 371–76, 402–4).

But the image of class and religious solidarity of one midwestern town does not belie the tensions that welled beneath the apparently united front of Protestantism. In the upper Midwest, as in the rest of the northern states, the tensions of modernism versus fundamentalism tore at the unity of the Protestant denominations. This was particularly true among members of the Northern Baptist Convention and the Presbyterian Church. Until 1925, conservatives controlled the denominational boards and agencies in both churches, but there was a growing concern that liberals had undue influence on the missions supported by the churches. In the early 1920s conservatives conducted minor purges of liberals, and in 1925 moderates, disenchanted by the increasingly caustic tactics of the fundamentalists, deserted the conservative alliance. Both the Northern Baptists and the Presbyterians suffered defections, but by the end of the decade they both had joined the Methodists and the Episcopalians in tolerating, if not promoting, more modernistic views of Christian theology (Harrell, et al. 2005, 870–71).

Despite the fact that during the Depression years of the 1930s most mainstream Protestant churches lost members, the spirit of religion remained strong. Protestant churches that escaped declining membership during the Depression were those that emphasized local and regional leadership and reinforced traditional values. Conservative churches in the Midwest and elsewhere were the hardiest survivors of the Depression, and during these times of hardship, millions of Americans remained intensely loyal to their local churches. Despite public ridicule of fundamentalists during the 1920s caused by (among other peculiarities) their stubborn defense of creationism, the 1930s witnessed the beginning of a shift in American Protestantism toward conservative evangelical churches. In 1942 a poll conducted by *Fortune* revealed that 82 percent of Americans believed in a God who "rewards and punishes after death" (Harrell, et al. 2005, 937).

Catholics in the big cities, representing for the most part a diverse immigrant population, faced different challenges than their predominantly native-born Protestant counterparts. The membership in the Catholic church in the Midwest, and especially in its larger dioceses of Chicago, Milwaukee, St. Louis, Detroit, and St. Paul represented for the most part a multiplicity of ethnic groups that became advocates for a Church that more closely characterized the Church they remembered in their home country. During the nineteenth century in Chicago, for example, the Germans sought and received a German auxiliary bishop, the Poles and other central Europeans established their own ethnic parishes, and in St. Paul the Germans bought land for their own ethnic cemetery. The greater heterogeneity and strength of nationalist groups in the later nineteenth and early twentieth century made the problems of nationalist aspiration even more acute.

Responding to the needs of immigrants was not a problem that suddenly appeared at the end of the nineteenth century and vanished at the beginning of the new century. The hierarchy of the Catholic Church was called upon to acknowledge the uniqueness of each ethnic group as soon as enough people of one nationality existed to organize a lobby for special treatment or demand a voice in ecclesiastical affairs. That the Catholic Church survived the storm of immigrant nationalism is remarkable. It might have been deemed unreasonable to expect that one institution could withstand the centripetal force generated by more than 20 nationalities. Yet its bishops and archbishops, without benefit of successful models, brought unity out of potential chaos. The Polish National Church in Chicago was the only schismatic break, and it made but limited progress. Unlike Lutheranism and other Protestant groups north and south that broke into denominations, the Catholic Church maintained its ecclesiastical and spiritual unity and prospered. For European peasants, the Church was an integral part of life. It was their mediator with the supernatural and a center of community life. When these people came to America, it remained the only recognizable public institution that gave them a sense of community and belonging. The sacrifices that immigrants made to build schools and churches reflected their commitment to and their need for the Catholic Church. As Protestant membership diminished in the 1920s and 1930s the Catholic churches grew and thrived under the leadership of "bricks and mortar" bishops who built Catholic institutions of learning, worship, social service, and health care throughout the major urban areas of the Midwest.

As a church of the working class, the Catholic Church defended the interests of its constituency. Church leaders realized that supporting the workers' struggle for a just wage was not only a moral responsibility but also the best means to counteract the influence of radical organizations whose economic theories were based on what Catholic leaders considered atheistic materialism. Unlike its counterparts in Europe, the Catholic Church in the Midwest was not bound by a self-serving commitment to repressive regimes or repressive social and economic policy. Throughout the Midwest parishes set up labor schools to explain to workers their rights to organize and to demand fair wages as outlined by the great social encyclical *Rerum Novarum*. When workers in the major cities of the Midwest engaged in labor battles in the 1930s with big steel and later with the auto industry, they found the Church on their side. A group of young Catholics in Chicago, calling themselves the Chicago Catholic Workers, even opened a soup kitchen at the Great Republic steel strike of 1937 and published a paper that presented the strikers' point of view when their grievances were ignored by the mainstream press. In 1930, in St. Paul, the Catholic archdiocese opened a free clinic for needy children, the first established by a privately owned hospital in Minnesota. And in the same year, the archdiocese sponsored a Catholic conference on industrial problems, at which was discussed the ethical aspects of labor, wages, and employment. Unlike some of their Protestant counterparts, Catholics did not accept the idea that wealth or poverty was a result of divine approbation; they viewed them as temporal problems that needed to be solved by material means.

Like Catholics, Jews in the Midwest represented for the most part an immigrant population. Due to the rising anti-Semitism in central Europe, the Jewish population in the Midwest as well as the rest of the country experienced a rise in the early 1930s. The total Jewish population in the midwestern cities of Chicago, Detroit, and Cleveland numbered just under 60,000 in 1916, but due to immigration and births, that number increased to over 650,000 by 1936 (http://www.thearda.com). Like Catholics, many American Jews continued to live in enclaves. Although most sent their children to public schools, they maintained their own school systems and felt very strongly about resisting the homogenizing, assimilationist pressures of American society. In 1925, a Chicago rabbi asked the following questions:

What will become of our children? Do we want them to grow up men and women who have an understanding of the problems of life, who know the history of their ancestors, who are proud Jews, and who will be a credit to us? Our children are running away from us. . . . Let us build houses of worship, social centers and Hebrew schools and let us provide the means for the coming generation to learn and to know. (Harrell, et al. 2005, 870)

Many Protestant ministers and Catholic priests could have expressed similar sentiments. And their words would have been received in earnest by many Americans who in the 1920s and 1930s had embraced religion as a refuge from the modern world of constant change and turmoil.

WORLDVIEW

Midwesterners in the first four decades of the twentieth century comprised a diversity of groups that included southern migrants both black and white, European immigrants of myriad cultures and religions, and native-born midwesterners with one or more generations behind them. Despite the diversity of origin, tradition, and religion, these midwesterners, both new and old, shared certain views.

In the first decades of the twentieth century, the midwestern economy expanded, with new farmland and new industries that promised unlimited and unrestricted opportunities. The region represented the renewal of the American myth (as old as the nation) of a new, more natural world unhampered by a corrupt artificial order. Whether they had come from the remnants of the broken slavocracy of the South, the new financial plutocracy of the Northeast, or the corrupt aristocracies of Europe, they (or their parents) had escaped a world of unnatural artificial order, which had maintained wealth exclusively for the privileged. Midwesterners optimistically believed that in the natural order of things, honesty and hard work would be rewarded. These beliefs gave midwesterners, despite their various differences, and despite the prejudices experienced by many, a common sense of optimism, belief in fair play, and a naive sense of superiority, which created an isolationist worldview that would continue until the attack on Pearl Harbor in 1941 ended the illusion that they could remain unaffected by the outside world.

FOR MORE INFORMATION

Books

Alinsky, Saul. *Reveille for Radicals*. New York: Vintage Books, 1969.

Degler, Carl. *At Odds: Women and the Family in America from the Revolution to the Present*. New York: Oxford University Press, 1980.

Fisher, James T. *Catholics in America*. New York: Oxford University Press, 2000.

Gossop, Michael. *Living with Drugs*. Burlington, VT: Ashgate Publishing Company, 2007.

Green, Harvey. *The Uncertainty of Everyday Life 1915–1945*. Fayetteville: University of Arkansas Press, 2000.

Grier, Katherine C. *Pets in America: A History*. Chapel Hill: University of North Carolina Press, 2006.

Grossman, James, Ann Duskin Keating, and Janice Reiff, eds. *The Encyclopedia of Chicago*. Chicago: University of Chicago Press, 2004.

Guthrie, Woody. *Bound for Glory*. New York: Penguin Books, 1983.

Harrell, David Edwin, Edwin S. Gaustau, John B. Boles, Sally Foreman Griffith, and Randall Miller. *Unto a Good Land: A History of the American People*. Grand Rapids, MI: William B. Eerdmans Publishing Company, 2005.

Holli, Melvin. *Reform in Detroit: Hazen Pingree and Urban Politics*. New York: Oxford University Press, 1969.

Hughes, Thomas P. *American Genius: A Century of Invention and Technological Enthusiasm 1870–1970*. Chicago: University of Chicago Press, 2004.

Josephy, Alvin M. Jr. *The Indian Heritage of America*. New York: Knopf, 1969.

Kyvig, David E. *Daily Life in the United States 1920–1940: How Americans Lived through the Roaring Twenties and the Great Depression*. Chicago: Ivan R. Dee, 2002.

Lloyd, Norman. *The Golden Encyclopedia of Music*. New York: Golden Press, 1968.

Lynd, Robert S., and Helen Merrell Lynd. *Middletown: A Study in Modern American Culture*. New York: Harcourt Brace and World, 1929.

Mayer, Harold, and Richard Wade. *Chicago: Growth of a Metropolis*. Chicago: University of Chicago Press, 1969.

Reich, Steven A. *Encyclopedia of the Great Black Migration*. Westport, CT: Greenwood Press, 2006.

Riess, Steven A. *City Games: The Evolution of American Urban Society and the Rise of Sports*. Chicago: University of Chicago Press, 1991.

Shanabruch, Charles. *Chicago's Catholics: The Evolution of an American Identity*. Notre Dame, IN: University of Notre Dame Press, 1981.

Sinclair, Upton. *The Jungle*. Tucson, AZ: Sharp Press, 2003.

Spear, Allan. *Black Chicago: The Making of a Negro Ghetto 1890–1920*. Chicago: University of Chicago Press, 1967.

Steffens, Lincoln. *Shame of the Cities*. New York: Hill and Wang, 1957.

Sullivan, Mark. *Our Times: The United States 1900–1925: Over Here 1914–1918 V*. New York: Charles Scribner's Sons, 1933.

Tygiel, Jules. *Past Time: Baseball As History*. New York: Oxford University Press, 2000.

VanTassel, David, and John J. Grabowski, eds. *Cleveland: A Tradition of Reform*. Kent, OH: Kent State University Press, 1986.

Urban, Wayne, and Jennings Wagoner. *American Education: A History*. New York: McGraw-Hill Companies, 2003.

Articles

Marsh, Margaret. "Suburban Men and Masculine Domesticity, 1870–1915." *American Quarterly* 40, no. 2 (June 1988): 165–86.

Mohl, Raymond. Review of *Reform in Detroit: Hazen Pingree and Urban Politics* by Melvin G. Holli. *American Quarterly* 22, no. 2 (Summer 1970): 286–87.

Murphy, Mary. "Bootlegging Mothers and Drinking Daughters: Gender and Prohibition in Butte, Montana." *American Quarterly* 46, no. 2 (June 1994): 174–94.

Web Sites

Association of Religious Data Archives (ARDA). http:// www.thearda.com.

Crime Library. http://www.crimelibrary.com/gangsters_outlaws/outlaws/floyd/3.html.

Geostat Center: Historical Census Browser. http://fisher.lib.virginia.edu/collections/stats/histcensus/php/county.php.

German Immigration. http://rs6.loc.gov/learn/features/immig/german8.html.

History of Chicago. http://www.encyclopedia.chicagohistory.org/.

History of Crosley Field, 1912–1970. http://www.crosley-field.com/.

History of the Blues. http://www.history-of-rock.com/blues.htm.

Library of Congress, Prints and Photographs Division, FSA-OWI Collection, Library of Congress. http://www.americanmemory.org.

Sears Archives. http://www.searsarchives.com/.

6

THE SOUTHWEST AND ROCKY MOUNTAIN WEST

Overview

In this chapter, the Southwest includes the states of Arizona, New Mexico, and Texas, while the Rocky Mountain West comprises Montana, Colorado, Utah, Wyoming, and Idaho. As the twentieth century opened, two of the states of the Southwest had not yet entered the Union; and, with the exception of Colorado (1876), the Rocky Mountain states had just entered the Union within the previous decade. Until the post–World War II era, these sections of the country remained relatively underpopulated, with migrant families from the Midwest and East and immigrants from Europe and Asia mingling with the older Mexican and Indian cultures of the region. After experiencing rapid growth in the early 1900s, New Mexico's and Arizona's growth slowed down to a rate only a little above the national average. The exception was Texas. Stimulated by the oil boom from 1920 to 1940, the population of Texas grew by 37 percent to almost four million people. Growth in the equally underpopulated Rocky Mountain West over the first four decades of the twentieth century was also slow. Only Colorado, energized by a thriving mining industry, surpassed the one million mark by 1940. Populations in each of the other Rocky Mountain states hovered around 200,000 at the beginning of the century and the half million mark by 1940. The least populous state was Wyoming, which began the century with 92,000 people and expanded to 225,000 by 1940.

Although the newest region of the United States, some of the oldest cultures in the hemisphere lived there. Some Pueblo Indians, for example, still lived in towns that had been continuously inhabited since the twelfth century. The Mexicans with Euro-Indian ancestry traced their cultural roots to native peoples of centuries past and to the sixteenth-century Spanish encounter. The impact of these ancient cultures could still be felt in the early twentieth century. The Indian population remained the largest in the country and for the most part fixed in their traditions, and in the Southwest, Catholicism remained the dominant religion.

Oil dominated and propelled the economy of Texas in the first half of the twentieth century, though agriculture and ranching remained important. But limited resources and population in the other states of this region restricted their commercial and economic growth. In Arizona and New Mexico, tourism stimulated by the natural wonders of the area and the rich cultural tradition of the native peoples became the most important industry, while Colorado and other Rocky Mountain states depended on mining and agriculture to maintain their economies. As immigrants and white Americans from other regions began to migrate to the West, three major cultures—Indian, Mexican, and Euro-American—converged, sometimes commingled, and sometimes conflicted. Mexican dietary habits changed, and they learned enough English to survive in the workplace. Many "Anglos," as non-Mexican whites were called, greeted their friends with a *"Buenos dias"* or said good-bye with *"Hasta luego,"* and they learned to enjoy Mexican food and to appreciate the benefits of adobe construction. At other times, Mexicans (even those with American citizenship) were expelled from the region; and some Native Americans, like the Apache, suffered from loss of their land and means of livelihood.

Left out of this cultural mix for the most part were the Pueblo Indians, who managed to maintain farming and herding economies that remained peripheral to the larger American economy until well into the twentieth century. The Pueblos resisted the dynamics of the invading cultures and in many ways, including religious worship and dietary and dwelling habits, lived much as they had for the previous thousand years. This is in contrast to the Navajos who, as the twentieth century unfolded, began to feel the increasing pressure of white social and political encroachment on their way of life (White 1991, 237). But neither Indians nor Mexicans nor Americans could avoid the impact of world events. The economic boom of the pre–World War I and then the World War I years brought thousands of Mexicans across the border where they were welcomed by a labor-hungry region. When the economic downturn of the following decade turned into an economic collapse, these same Mexicans suddenly became unwelcome. Other events of the first half of the twentieth century also affected the region. When the automobile became the darling curiosity and then the necessity for Americans, these regions, like other parts of the United States, began a massive highway building plan. People of the Southwest and Rocky Mountain West also listened to the radio and enjoyed playing sports such as golf and football, which were rapidly becoming national fixations.

In the 1920s, children of the Southwest and Rocky Mountain West, as in other sections of the country, left their little one-room schoolhouses behind and took buses to the larger, more efficient, more specialized consolidated schools. Like Americans everywhere, the people of these regions witnessed changes in technology, education, even in the habits and complexions of the people they met every day as the new twentieth century brought a whirl of transformation that many could hardly understand, much less absorb.

This section will explore the dynamics created when distinct cultures, new technology, and new politics converged in the Southwest and the Rocky Mountain states in the first decades of the twentieth century. Confronted with this upheaval, the various peoples of the Southwest and Rocky Mountain West assimilated what they found beneficial in other traditions while trying to preserve the integrity of their own unique cultures.

Domestic Life

FAMILY LIFE

In the rural Spanish American homes of the Southwest, during the early twentieth century, the family still continued to be a strong primary group under paternal authority. In the villages, the Catholic Church served as the focal point of social activities as well as religious worship. For recreation, the young and old alike enjoyed feast days, dances, wedding parties, school functions, and political rallies. The virtues of those communities have been well described by John H. Burma in his 1949 article in *Social Forces*, which he concluded with this summary:

In a day of almost cut-throat competition, the rural Spanish-American village represents a non-communist form of co-operation between persons who live and work in a compact social group. Here a real social consciousness, even if limited in scope, shines out to the larger individualistic society.

English was spoken in the school, but it remained the only place in the village community in which English was used. The resort to Spanish among family members and in neighborly greetings was regarded as an expression of regard for the old traditions; yet, the language of the street had become a corrupted oral Spanish composed of persistent archaisms and new fused forms, with an English word injected here and there for the modern innovations. While the Spanish-speaking people were borrowing English words to enlarge their vocabulary in a multicultural world, the English-speaking newcomers were also injecting some Spanish words into their conversation (Perrigo 1971, 381–82).

The Pueblo Indians of the Southwest used passive resistance and a deliberate policy of trying to exclude outside influences that might destroy their way of life in order to retain many of the traits of their original family culture. The Pueblo communities remained closely knit units in which, for the sake of solidarity and welfare of all, the individual was subjected to the group. Parents treated their children gently and permissively but threatened them with punishment from spirits if they misbehaved. Pueblos were monogamists. Marriage involved little courtship and scant display of emotion. Within the Pueblo all domestic affairs were responsibilities of extended families or households. These units included an old couple and a number of their children. Each nuclear family of the household unit was separated from the others by having one or two rooms or even a separate house to itself in the same area of the pueblo.

Frequent interaction of its members, cooperative work in numerous tasks, and the sharing of food characterized the household. Preparation and eating of food was normally done separately by each nuclear family, but frequently one member of the household would spend a day with the older couple, help them prepare their meal, and eat there as well. The building of houses, as well as the addition or repair of rooms, was done together, and during that time all lived and ate together in the home of the nuclear family that was benefiting from the task. Other activities such as planting and the harvesting of crops were also household tasks. All members worked together on such tasks.

Special sacred rituals such as attending the death of a member of the household also brought the extended family into cooperative action. The funeral rites, including a feast celebrated four days after death, were prepared and shared by all members of the household. Other ceremonial occasions also brought all members of the household together. All shared in the preparation of food for the various festivities, which lasted from one to three days. In winter, the home of the senior couple was the place where nuclear families gathered for the evening meal to gossip and listen to old folktales.

The Pueblos maintained marriage patterns and customs established in earlier times. Marriage with first cousins was prohibited regardless of household affiliation. Initially a newly married couple could be undecided whether to identify with the wife's or husband's household. A number of factors might influence the choice, the most important being the amount of property that was offered to the couple. In theory land and houses were owned by the village, but the distribution of land was based on inheritance.

Upon the death of the senior couple, the position of household leadership was sometimes assumed by the oldest married son or daughter. In the few cases of separation or divorce that occurred, the spouse who changed household allegiance returned to his or her natal household and gave up all rights in the former spouse's family. In the event of the death of a spouse in a childless marriage the surviving spouse gave up all rights within the household and returned to his or her original household. If there were children, the surviving spouse remained in the household with all rights intact. However, if the spouse remarried, he or she had to leave the household. For this reason, if there was a remarriage, it usually occurred within the same household. By maintaining these closely knit interdependent familial communities, the Pueblos successfully resisted intrusion from outside cultures and influences and well into the twentieth century were able to maintain a lifestyle ordered by traditions hundreds of centuries in the making (Josephy 1969, 161–62; Dozier 1960, 156–57).

For the Navajos, the basic social unit was the nuclear family. Society was matrilineal, with the position of women very strong and influential in all phases of social, economic, political, and religious life. Married couples usually, though not always, built their houses or "hogans" near that of the wife's mother, but a married man kept strong ties with his own mother's family. Extended families, composed of husband and wife and unmarried children, together with married daughters and their husbands and children, all usually lived near one another and formed a cooperative unit whose members worked together in farming, herding, and house building (Josephy 1969, 173).

The transient nature of life in the mining towns of the Rocky Mountain West did not create an environment supportive of the Victorian model of family life prevalent in the established communities of other parts of the country. At the turn of the century in the camp towns of the Rocky Mountain West, prostitutes, gamblers, and saloon owners existed as a kind of antithesis or replacement for what most middle-class Americans considered a family-based community. Prostitutes might have formed a community among themselves, or a community of sorts might have developed among prostitutes, their pimps, and their customers. Western myth often pretends that such commitments did form. In these myths prostitutes have hearts of gold. They nurse the sick and contribute to charity, and men in the bordellos pay for sex but have real affection for those who sell. Most of the men who populated these towns shared a common belief in the Victorian moral order, in which community revolved around domesticity and the home and in which "true" women were pure and pious, managing the home as a haven from the world. But in the mining camps these ideals remained largely absent. As a result, as one observer in Montana wrote, "Men without the restraint of law, indifferent to public opinion, and unburdened by families, drink whenever they feel like it, whenever they have the money to pay for it, and whenever there is nothing else to do" (Nugent 1999, 159). Bad manners followed and profanity was a matter of course. Miners tolerated this half-world because they believed that they would only reside there temporarily. Far from envisioning a future spent outside familiar community boundaries, they intended to reenter those traditional communities as wealthy men.

The lack of stable family life in the camp towns drew the attention of reformers led by merchants (who saw stable, family-based communities as a key to financial success) and the missionary impulse of Protestant women in the West that took the conventional female virtues of piety, purity, and domesticity and made them subversive. Eventually as towns grew and became more stable, men did settle down and marry "true women" who eventually established domestic tranquility. Prospectors' camps soon were abandoned, but hard-rock industrial mining towns lasted, where soon women and children became more evident. Teachers and housewives decidedly outnumbered prostitutes and dance hall girls. The working man and his family were what are called today social conservatives; in an Irish Catholic town, like Butte, Montana, for example, this was certainly the case. Wives created homes as havens; husband and wife were head and heart of the home, as traditional marriage theology prescribed. It actually worked that way in a great many cases (Nugent 1999, 159).

But the bordellos and saloons of the West remained as a counterpoint to stable family life throughout the twentieth century. What made bordellos and saloons notable in the West was not their existence, for they existed throughout the country, but their centrality to early social life in the towns of the new West. These places would not retain their eminence as towns developed, but neither would they disappear, and they remained as a constant counterpoint and threat to the ideal of domestic tranquility (White 1991, 305–6).

One group of migrants to the West that was able to secure stable family structures was the Mormons. Since the mid-nineteenth century when they first moved West, Mormons were able to create cohesive, homogenous, family-based communities centered around the church. The Mormons cooperatively built schools, canals, irrigation ditches, meeting houses, and homes. By the beginning of the twentieth century the Mormons had developed over 500 communities stretching from Alberta, Canada, to the Mexican border and from Bunkerville, Nevada, to San Luis Valley,

Colorado. These communities continued to thrive well into the twentieth century (White 1991, 301–2).

WOMEN

At the beginning of the twentieth century men continued to outnumber women in the West. In New Mexico, men outnumbered women by a ratio of 17 to 10 and in Arizona by a ratio of 4 to 1. The numbers were even more lopsided in Colorado. Even though the numbers were uneven, men depended upon women to provide for the families by preparing meals, raising chickens, making butter and milk from the family's dairy cow, growing a garden, keeping the home clean, and making or mending clothing. When necessary, women assisted men in the fields by walking behind the plow planting, cultivating, or harvesting (Bakken and Farrington 2003, 318–20).

Women were also scarce in the western mining towns. In 1900, in the two largest industrial mining centers—Butte, Montana, and Colorado's Cripple Creek—the ratio was 3 men to 2 women. In an economy that drew a disproportionately male population, women found a narrow set of options. Because there were vastly more men of marriageable age than women, particularly among migrant miners, women tended to marry young. They were likely to be considerably younger than their husbands, who had to delay marriage until they had the skills and commanded the wages needed to support a family. Given age differences and occupational diseases and underground dangers of mining, wives tended to outlive their husbands. They had to support their families when their husbands were sick or disabled and after they died.

Whether they had to work outside the home or not, women's conditions varied with the success of mining organizations. The Western Federation of Miners (WFM) and the United Mine Workers of America (UMW) began to organize miners around the turn of the century. Although women's wages were lower than union men's wages, mining town women benefited both directly and indirectly from organized labor. Women in union towns depended on higher wages commanded by union men, and on union services like sick and death benefits. Although women's conditions improved somewhat with the arrival of the unions, their lives in the first decade of the twentieth century were nonetheless hardly secured or leisured. Women grew vegetables in arid mining camps at high altitudes, preserved food, cooked on wood-burning stoves, made clothing, and did laundry for extended households. Few had running water and so had to haul it from an outside well and heat it for cooking, cleaning, and for baths for men covered with grime from the mines. Women also cared for the young, the old, the sick, and the infirm.

Mining town women's options varied by class, race, and marital status, and by whether they labored at home, earned "respectable" wages, or sold sex and companionship. Regardless of age or marital status, in the paid workforce, or in their households, all women cooked, cleaned, laundered, sewed, waited on tables, and provided companionship for men. Whether they were paid and what they were paid for distinguished reputable women from those who were considered disreputable.

Before the 1920s, few respectable married women performed public wage work, and most of the larger mining communities accommodated segregated red light districts. Married women and widows might earn money and remain respectable in the privacy of family households. Many kept boarders or did laundry for single men, especially when illness struck or unemployment jeopardized men's wages. Single women could work in the respectable marketplace as waitresses, laundry workers, domestic servants, and clerks. A small number found professional opportunities as teachers or nurses. Though numerically few, proportionately more women worked as doctors and lawyers in the West than in other parts of the nation, because gender was not a handicap in an area that had a desperate need for people with professional skills. Often, however, the largest group of women wage earners consisted of those who sold sex, companionship, drinks, and dances throughout the mining West.

As mining industrialized, more women joined the male majority in towns that offered steady work, union wages, schools, and sufficient stability to support families. However, as minerals were depleted in western towns, mining companies shrank and their populations aged. In the 1930s, the Great Depression closed many mines, but a number of closed former mining towns like Aspen Park City, Breckenridge, and Telluride became ski resorts and tourist destinations. These enterprises, like the older mining communities, offered women low-paying service work in hotels and restaurants. In this way, women's labor connected the late nineteenth- and early twentieth-century mining towns to the later twentieth-century tourist boomtowns of the West (Bakken and Farrington 2003, 305–7).

Economic Life

WORK AND WORKPLACE

In the emergence of the modern Southwest, in the early decades of the twentieth century, one of the impressive changes in the landscape was the appearance of oil derricks on the silhouette of the skyline in many localities. Oil had been discovered quite early in Texas, but full capitalization of that resource had been delayed until more uses for oil could create a greater demand. After 1900, an unprecedented market for the "black gold" was created by the conversion of heating plants from coal- to oil-burning furnaces, the increase in the number of automobiles and trucks, the development of the diesel motor, the progress of aviation, and the utilization of more and more petroleum-based products. As the price of oil increased, "wildcat" prospecting became frenzied; eventually several Texas oil companies emerged as industrial giants. In the oil boom Texas climbed quickly to first place in the Union and continued to hold that leadership. The initial area of rich production was the Spindle Top

The Beaumont, Texas, Spindle Top oil field. Library of Congress.

field near Beaumont, which opened in 1901. Within the next few years other fields were tapped near the Gulf Coast. A major oil strike occurred at Ranger in 1917, followed by the development at Big Lake in 1923 and the discovery of the rich Yates pool in 1926 in the valley of the Pecos River. From there, exploration successfully ventured northward on the high plains, and the annual production of 257 million barrels put Texas in first place among all the states in 1928. Another boom followed in 1930, when the richest field yet found was opened in eastern Texas. Soon "black gold" was being pumped out of 19,000 new wells, and the area of successful drilling continued to expand. By 1930, the 90,000 wells in Texas were producing nearly half a billion barrels, or one-third of the petroleum output of the United States.

The oil boom had far-reaching effects. Wherever new fields were opened, new towns mushroomed immediately and became the centers of feverish land sales at speculative prices. They also attracted a concentration of shops for the assembly and repair of equipment that in turn attracted people looking for work from other regions of the country. Such rapid growth in Texas had a negative impact on the people that settled there. For this spectacular expansion preceded the construction of good roads, the provision of adequate protection against fire, and the adoption of proper police and sanitary measures. Trucks broke down, fires raged out of control, disease threatened to become epidemic, and crime increased disproportionately.

Eventually the Texas Rangers and local vigilance committees established order in the oil camps, and then the newcomers rebuilt the towns and obtained improved roads. As orderly development emerged in the fields, the center of financial activity shifted to Houston, the "oil capital." There, after the port had been improved and a ship canal had been built, the oil companies erected their refining plants. Wealth from this new industry also built several skyscrapers where the oil tycoons maintained their offices. This absorption of the leading citizens of Houston in the accumulation and protection of their fortunes made many of them very conservative in politics. On the other hand, the petroleum industry also had a progressive influence, in that the taxes levied upon it contributed immensely to the building of good public schools and colleges throughout the state.

Many of the oil fields also produced natural gas, which Texans soon accepted as a convenient fuel. As early as 1910, a pipeline was laid from the Petrolia field to Dallas and Fort Worth; and after 1927 when the Panhandle gas fields were tapped, more distribution systems were built. By 1940, one-half of the households in the state were consumers of natural gas. Pipelines were laid into 16 other states, and Texas began producing 42 percent of the natural gas of the United States. Due to the abundance of this fuel in Texas, Americans across the nation were learning to heat and cook with gas.

Among other mineral products, Texas had risen to first place in the Union in the processing of asphalt, another product brought into demand by the use of motor vehicles. Texas also stood near the top in the production of sulphur, salt, cement, helium, and gypsum.

From Texas, exploration for oil extended into the neighboring states of New Mexico and Arizona, and in the former some rich fields were found. The first to be opened, in 1922 and 1923, were the Hogback and Rattlesnake fields on Navajo lands in San Juan County and the Artesia field near Carlsbad. In 1926 and in 1929, others came in at Hobbs and Eunice. As soon as refineries were built to serve those fields, production increased steadily but not spectacularly. New Mexico and Arizona never came close to rivaling Texas, nor would oil

> ### 📷 *Snapshot*
>
> **Everyday Setting: Spindle Top, Texas**
>
> Without warning, the level plains of eastern Texas near Beaumont abruptly give way to a lone, rounded hill before returning to flatness. Geologists call these abrupt rises in the land "domes" because hollow caverns lie beneath. Over time, layers of rock rise to a common apex and create a spacious reservoir underneath. Often, salt forms in these empty, geological bubbles, creating a salt dome. Over millions of years, water or other material might fill the reservoir. At least, that was Patillo Higgins's idea in eastern Texas during the 1890s.
>
> Higgins and others imagined such caverns as natural treasure-houses. Higgins's intrigue grew with one dome-shaped hill in southeast Texas. Known as Spindletop, this salt dome—with Higgins's help—would change human existence.
>
> Texas had not yet been identified as an oil producer. Well-known oil country lay in the Eastern United States, particularly western Pennsylvania. Titusville, Pennsylvania introduced Americans to massive amounts of crude oil for the first time in 1859. By the 1890s, petroleum-derived kerosene had become the world's most popular fuel for lighting. Thomas Edison's experiments with electric lighting placed petroleum's future in doubt; however, petroleum still stimulated boom wherever it was found. But in Texas? Every geologist who inspected the "Big Hill" at Spindletop told Higgins that he was a fool.
>
> With growing frustration, Higgins placed a magazine advertisement requesting someone to drill on the Big Hill. The only response came from Captain Anthony F. Lucas, who had prospected domes in Texas for salt and sulfur. On January 10, 1901, Lucas's drilling crew, known as "roughnecks" for the hard physical labor of drilling pipe deep into Earth, found mud bubbling in their drill hole. The sound of a cannon turned to a roar and suddenly oil spurted out of the hole. The Lucas geyser, found at a depth of 1,139 feet, blew a stream of oil over 100 feet high until it was capped nine days later. During this period, the well flowed an estimated 100,000 barrels a day—well beyond any flows previously witnessed. Lucas finally gained control of the geyser on January 19. By this point, a huge pool of oil surrounded it. Throngs of oilmen, speculators, and onlookers came and transformed the city of Beaumont into Texas's first oil boomtown.
>
> The flow from this well, named Lucas 1, was unlike anything witnessed before in the petroleum industry: 75,000 barrels per day. As news of the gusher reached around the world, the Texas oil boom was on. Land sold for wildly erratic prices. After a few months over 200 wells had been sunk on the Big Hill. By the end of 1901, an estimated $235 million had been invested in oil in Texas. This was the new frontier of oil; however, the industry's scale had changed completely at Spindletop. Unimaginable amounts of petroleum—and the raw energy that it contained—were now available at a low enough price to become part of every American's life. (Black 2006, 1–2)

have the cultural and economic impact on those states that it did in Texas (Perrigo 1971, 327–28).

In Oklahoma, oil started flowing just before statehood in 1907. The Phillips brothers made their first strike at Bartlesville, in 1905, and were in on many others, forming Phillips petroleum, later the sellers of Phillips 66—named after the highway built in 1917. Strikes in Cherokee, Creek, and Osage lands sent oilmen scrambling to persuade the Indians to sign leases and allow drilling to begin. The Osages, who controlled their own mineral rights by treaty, found themselves to be among the "richest people in the world," receiving $12,400 per head by 1923. Tulsa proclaimed itself, justly enough, the "oil capital of the world" with 800 oil companies and 140,000 people by 1930. Many were transient or seemed so. Herbert Feis, the future state department official and historian, visited Tulsa in 1923 and saw "crowds of men" on "the street corners day and night who looked as if they had just come to town with no place to go." Many were in khaki shirts, army breeches, and high boots—ordinary dress of the oil fields and plains. "The oil industry, is, after all," Feis observed, "one which keeps its people on the move without notice. Often after the first rush, workers traveled with wives and children who showed up in school any day, at any point in a semester." Companies moved their employees whenever and wherever their skills were needed, all over the oil patch (Nugent 1999, 198).

Cheap oil stimulated further economic development. Among the western states, Texas ranked first in manufacturing industries. The timber resources in the eastern part of the state, which previously had been drawn upon in the early production of lumber, now were utilized more and more in the manufacture of pulp and paper. After 1911 this trend was stimulated by the invention of a process for the making of sulphate paper from the fiber of yellow pine; and by 1940 the annual return from all forest products, including paper pulp, was near $50 million. Another early industry, flour milling, also had expanded with the growth of the state; so that by 1940 it, too, had attained an annual production valued at about $50 million. A third early industry that had continued to grow rapidly was meatpacking. By 1940 it was yielding a gross return about as much as that of flour milling and timber processing combined. Likewise, textile manufacturing, which had originated before 1900, continued to grow, especially in the Dallas area.

The manufactured products of Texas, worth only about a quarter of a million dollars in 1910, had grown 20 years later to a figure of approximately one and one-half billion dollars. Attracted by this newly developing wealth, Americans from other regions moved to Texas. In the early decades of the twentieth century the state's population grew by 37 percent, most of which came from other regions of the United States. Only the Great Depression of the 1930s temporarily slowed this meteoric growth.

Arizona and New Mexico, although producers of mineral ores, were less favorably endowed in other conditions required for great growth of manufacturing industries. The cost of transportation to distant markets was prohibitive except for specialized light goods, and the population of the two states was not large enough to provide much of a local market. Moreover, most cities in these states lacked abundant electric power at low commercial rates and did not have the supply of water essential for many large industries. Not until after World War II, when young men who had been stationed in training bases near Albuquerque returned to the region to live, were there sufficient workers and consumers to support manufacturing (Perrigo 1971, 333–34).

In the final decade of the nineteenth century, Arizona had the last gold-mining revival it was to see until the Depression of 1929. In the 1890s, new gold deposits were discovered in Yuma and Yavapai counties, where the Congress and Octave mines in the Date Creek Mountains and the King of Arizona, Fortuna, and Harqua Hala in the Yuma County desert all enriched their owners. The Mammoth, north of

Tucson, also became important at this time. New milling methods and development of the cyanide process aided production in the new mines as well as in the old but also added to the polluting effects of the mining.

At the beginning of the century the rising price of copper made that mineral more attractive than gold or silver to speculators. Nevertheless, Arizona's production of gold and silver increased with the development of these new large copper mines, due to the fact that many copper ores contain large amounts of the precious metals. In the early to mid-1900s copper ores yielded 70 percent of the state's silver production and from 40 to 50 percent of the gold.

The increase in the price of gold in 1933, plus Depression conditions and their effect on copper, resulted in a renewed interest in the gold fields and prospecting. However, while production from these sources increased, lode gold mining remained a minor industry in Arizona. The greatest stimulus to Arizona's copper industry came from outside the region. As more and more Americans discovered the benefits of electricity, the demand for the vehicle that delivered this new product, copper, increased exponentially. During this period Arizona's annual production grew from 800,000 pounds valued at $9,000,000 in 1874 to the peak of 830,628,411 pounds valued at $146,190,600 in 1929.

Another important industry that developed in Arizona in the first decades of the twentieth century was tourism. More and more Americans, liberated by their new automobiles from the restrictions of distance, came to discover the majesty of the Grand Canyon and the other natural wonders of the state. Of all the businesses dedicated exclusively to the tourist trade, the lodging of visitors was probably the most important; and of the thousands of tourist courts, fine hotels, sanitariums, and guest homes, the guest ranches were regarded as most characteristic of the state. By the 1930s there were more than 300 "dude ranches" in Arizona. Some had large herds of ranging cattle and only a few guests, while others had many guests and just enough cattle to keep the visitors entertained. Still others dispensed entirely with the cows and specialized in swimming pools, tennis, and relaxation in the sun. But because guest-ranching developed more or less fortuitously from a combination of bad times in the cattle business and the eagerness of visitors to live on a real ranch, many dude ranches still retained the cowboys, horses, and atmosphere of the old-time western ranches.

Most of the forests of Arizona, about 12 million acres, were set aside in the early twentieth century as national forest land. They became invaluable to the state for recreation and for the conservation of water, soil, and game; in addition, they yielded between four and six million dollars in lumber annually. Practically all of the wood was taken from the 3,607,000 acres of commercial saw timber. And in the first decades of the twentieth centuries Americans looking West were attracted to jobs in the lumber mills of Arizona cities such as Flagstaff, Williams, and McNary.

Although Arizona's economy depended on its agriculture, mining, lumber, and visitors, less than half its employed population was engaged in occupations specifically connected with those basic sources of wealth. Of the 165,000 gainfully occupied persons, 38,700 were employed in agriculture; 17,600 in extraction of minerals; 2,000 or more in lumber; and several thousand in occupations devoted principally to accommodating visitors. That left more than half the working population engaged in other trades and professions—19,600 in wholesale and retail trade; 17,000 in building, manufacturing, and mechanical industries; 13,000 in professional and semiprofessional occupations; and 16,000 in transportation.

Primarily a vacation land and a producer of raw materials, a large part of Arizona's energy has always been spent in maintaining its lifelines, the channels of interstate traffic and commerce connecting it with the rest of the world. The state had few factories. Those it did have were chiefly concerned with the production of materials used in the basic industries, or commodities and novelties for local markets—for example, dynamite, fruit and vegetable crates, saddles, wood novelties, canned milk, grapefruit, and vegetables. Some grain was milled; some meat was packed; some cotton was ginned; and some hides were tanned. But hardly a pound of Arizona cotton and wool was spun within the state, beyond what was used in Indian blanket weaving; and not an ounce of Arizona copper was fabricated there, except a few handhammered novelties made from metal refined in other states.

When Arizona entered the Union in February 1912, the rights of workers were written into the new state constitution. For example, the constitution prohibited the use of a labor blacklist, and it also contained provisions for employers' liability and workmen's compensation. This constitution encountered powerful opposition, both at the time it was written and during the course of ratification. Arizona nevertheless became a state under it in 1912, a clear indication that the working men of the territory were represented by effective leadership.

The skilled railroad workers were the earliest to organize in Arizona. The engineers and trainmen established the first lodge of the Railroad Brotherhoods in Douglas about 1883 and branched out rapidly. Until the turn of the century they represented practically every member of their craft in the territory. The Arizona Brotherhoods developed with their national organizations into well-organized and powerful unions, which the railroad operators soon recognized and bargained with. Once their strength was built up in the territory, they never lost it. The objectives of the brotherhoods sprang from their determination to secure safety, tenure, and increased wages, and their program to decrease the large number of accidents on the railroads brought them into active participation in federal, and sometimes state, politics. In 1903, for example, they succeeded in getting the Arizona Legislature to pass an act forbidding the working of trainmen for more than 16 consecutive hours (Perrigo, 1971 330–31, 342–43, 351–52).

The miners' unions, which sprang up in the Rocky Mountain West more or less spontaneously out of the dangerous and semifeudal conditions existing in most of the early mining camps, had neither the influence nor the central organization of the Railroad Brotherhoods. Most of them were connected with the Western Federation of Miners, but they functioned as independent unions. Strikes were frequent and were characterized by the militancy of the miners and the refusal of the operators to bargain with their employees in any way except as individuals. By the end of the nineteenth century and well into the twentieth, western miners waged armed warfare in open class conflict with their capitalist adversaries.

This war began in 1892 when armed miners confronted the gunmen of mine owners in the mining towns strung out along the canyons of the Coeur d'Alene River of Idaho. The Mine Owners' Protective Association (MOA) had hired Pinkerton and Thiel detectives to infiltrate the local miners' union and, allegedly, to act as agents' provocateurs. One of these detectives, Charles A. Siringo, actually became secretary of the Gem Miners' Union local.

The Coeur d'Alene strike had begun when the MOA reduced wages. The miners walked out, and the owners, vowing never to hire a union man, set out to break the union. They perfected a set of tactics that would become increasingly common over the next two decades wherever the unions com-

Five miners in a lead mine in the Coeur d'Alene region of Idaho, 1909. Library of Congress.

manded significant local support. Knowing local officials to be unsympathetic, the mine owners, while maintaining their own armed force of guards, claimed that local authorities could not preserve order and appealed to the governor of the state for militia. If the governor refused, the mine owners turned to the federal government and courts for marshals and, if possible, troops.

Such tactics proved effective in Coeur d'Alene. Although initially peaceful, angry miners, frustrated over the length of the strike and the federal injunctions that the mine owners obtained against them, took up arms in July 1892. They assaulted the Frisco and Gem mines, destroyed the Frisco mill, and captured all the guards and scabs. They then marched on the Bunker Hill and Sullivan mines, and, after capturing the company's ore concentrator, which had cost $500,000, they secured the dismissal of all the scabs there. The fighting left six men dead.

The miners had won a Pyrrhic victory. The MOA now easily obtained a declaration of martial law. Six companies of the Idaho National Guard marched in and made wholesale arrests of union members and of local businessmen and lawyers who sympathized with the union. The soldiers herded more than 300 men into crude stockades or "bullpens." Eventually, in 1893, the United States Supreme Court overturned the convictions of those who were found guilty of crimes rising out of the strike, but by then the MOA had largely broken the union.

One of the greatest achievements of the mine owners in the late 1890s and early twentieth century was their success in driving a wedge between middle-class and working-class members of the mining towns. Many of the people in the bullpens of Coeur d'Alene in 1892 had been merchants and lawyers who had backed the strike. Middle-class men and women who sold the miners goods and provided services often sympathized with their customers. Such support became rarer and rarer in the late 1890s and the early twentieth century. Labor violence in many places became not just a struggle between laborers and their employers but also a struggle between classes that convulsed communities.

Two strikes at Cripple Creek, Colorado, illustrated the changing relations between the workers and the middle class. At Cripple Creek in 1893 the miners' union fought a bitter and violent strike when mine owners attempted to increase the working day in the mines from 8 to 10 hours. Armed miners confronted armed deputies, with casualties on both sides. The miners seized mines, banished scabs, and dynamited one mine. The miners, however, obtained significant middle-class support. Governor Davis Waite, in one of the few cases in which a state government proved sympathetic to striking miners, helped negotiate a settlement and used the state militia to prevent further violence rather than breaking the union. When the strike ended, Cripple Creek returned to normal. Both business and the miners prospered.

The second strike came a decade later. It arose because the Western Federation of Miners (WFM) was an industrial union pledged to protect not only the underground miners who were victorious in 1893 but also the less skilled and more vulnerable mill and smelter workers. The 1903 strike arose over the refusal of the Colorado Reduction and Refining Company to allow the WFM to organize its mills. The WFM and the underground miners of Cripple Creek backed the smelter workers, and a strike ensued.

The strike was long and complicated, but bitterly antiunion mill owners defeated the WFM because they could rely on an antiunion governor to send troops and because the miners gradually lost the support of the local middle class. Governor J. H. Peabody of Colorado twice dispatched the militia to Cripple Creek over the protests of local officials. They came the second time not to preserve order but, in the words of their commander, "to do up this damned anarchistic federation." In "doing up" the WFM, militia officers refused to obey court orders or honor writs of habeas corpus. But the critical blow to the union was the rise of a local Citizens' Alliance. As the lengthy strike progressed, merchants found it impossible to extend any more credit to miners. The union then opened cooperative stores, a move that alienated local shopkeepers. This dispute gave conservative elements in the community an opening, and by the end of August they had organized the Citizens' Alliance, with largely compulsory membership among local businessmen. The Citizens' Alliance operated as a vigilante organization and was determined to break the union and the strike. By March 1904, members of the Citizens' Alliance had begun forcibly deporting union leaders and strikers from the town.

The conflict exploded in a series of ugly incidents in June 1904. That month, shortly after nonunion men reached a railroad station to board a train, someone blew up the railroad depot, killing 13 men. The Citizens' Alliance blamed the WFM; the WFM blamed agents provocateurs hired by the mine owners. But initiative lay with the Citizens' Alliance, whose members forced, at gunpoint, the resignation of the sheriff and other local officials sympathetic to the WFM. The militia and the Citizens' Alliance then began the wholesale arrest and deportation of union members, while Cripple Creek employers introduced a permit system designed to deny employment to all union workers. The Citizens' Alliance broke the union, but in doing so they in effect also broke themselves. Two years later Cripple Creek had nonunion miners and lower wages, but business was stagnant, buildings were vacant, and real estate values had declined by half. Wealth continued to pour from the mines, but merchants of towns learned too late that they indeed lived not off the mines but off the miners.

The Cripple Creek strike was only one of a series of violent confrontations that shook the West at the turn of the century. Throughout the West striking miners faced federal troops and

A bird's eye view of the 1896 fire at Cripple Creek, Colorado. Library of Congress.

state militia as well as small private armies of gunmen hired by the mine owners. Although the WFM bore the brunt of the violent conflict with employers, the conflict extended beyond the hard-rock mines. One of the bloodiest incidents occurred in 1917 in the coal mines of Ludlow, Colorado, that were owned by John D. Rockefeller. After a bitter strike in which the wives and daughters of the largely Greek, Slavic, and Italian miners played as active a role as did their husbands, strikebreakers, militia, and deputies attacked the tent colony that strikers had erected after their eviction from company housing. The strikers resisted, and, as the battle raged, the attackers set fire to the tents. The attack killed 39 people, including 2 women and 11 children who suffocated in a pit underneath a burning tent.

The Ludlow Massacre was particularly notorious because so many women and children were among the victims, but neither attacks on armed strikers nor murders of union organizers were unusual in the first years of the twentieth century. Nor were they confined to mining. They occurred also in the lumber industry. The Wobblies (the nickname given IWW members) in particular developed, and reveled in, a fearsome, if largely unwarranted, reputation. They often preached industrial sabotage but rarely practiced it. They were more often the victims of violence than its instigators. Armed gunmen hired by the employers, militia, federal troops, and vigilantes from citizens' alliances repeatedly assaulted IWW (International Workers of the World) organizers. In Butte, Montana, in 1917, for example, vigilantes lynched Frank Little, a one-eyed, part-Indian, antiwar Wobbly organizer, and in the lumber mill town of Everett, Washington, in 1916 local vigilantes fired on a boatload of arriving Wobbly organizers. A gun battle ensued in which five Wobblies and two deputized vigilantes died and at least 51 others, mostly Wobblies, were wounded (White 1991, 346–50).

The IWW attracted the fierce loyalty of the migratory workers of the West, who were in many ways the backbone of the western extractive economy. They cut timber and worked in sawmills, built and repaired the railroads, harvested the crops, and worked the less skilled jobs available in the mines. Most of these workers were semiskilled or unskilled. In the Southwest many of them were nonwhite, but in the late nineteenth century, particularly in the Rocky Mountains and in the Pacific Northwest, many were European immigrants. They moved from job to job because their work was often by its very nature seasonal, and long bouts of unemployment in the mines and mills interrupted their working life. Between jobs, migratory workers were the men who rode the rails looking for work. If they were lucky, they traveled in empty boxcars or gondolas; if not, they suspended themselves beneath the cars, where they hurtled along 10 inches above the roadbed. William Z. Foster, who became head of the American Communist Party, had been a western migratory worker; so, too, for a period, was William O. Douglas, the future Supreme Court Justice. Usually single, often foreign-born, and owning little beyond what they carried with them, these men were an alienated and potentially revolutionary segment of the western working class.

The Wobblies survived because they understood the nature and the needs of the migratory working force whom the AFL (American Federation of Labor) organizers usually ignored. Wobbly union halls became dormitories, social clubs, mess halls, and mail drops for migratory workers. Wobbly union cards became a pass to ride the trains unmolested. The social network the Wobblies created explains how the IWW could hold worker loyalty despite the nearly constant defeats Wobbly unions endured.

Ironically, one of the few successful strikes the Wobblies organized in the West led to their demise. Capitalizing on long-standing worker discontent with long working hours, horrible conditions, and low pay, the Wobblies virtually shut down the Washington and Idaho timber industries in the summer of 1917. The strike, however, took place in a nation at war. The United States had just entered World War I, and the armed forces demanded timber for cantonments, railroad cars, and ships. But above all, they needed Sitka spruce for the biplanes of the period, and Sitka spruce was available only in the Pacific Northwest. The government jailed the union leaders.

The Wobblies returned to work but continued the strike on the job. They acted as if they had been granted an 8-hour day, quitting work after 8 hours or putting in only 8 good hours in a 10-hour day. They engaged in ingenious slowdowns and sabotages. They crippled lumber production nearly as effectively as if they had gone on strike. The government attempted to pressure lumbermen to concede the eight-hour day, but it failed. To procure necessary production, the government organized the Loyal Legion of Loggers and Lumbermen and demanded membership from all those who wished to work in the woods; the government also delegated 25,000 troops, the Spruce Production Division, to work in the woods as needed. In exchange for breaking the union and disciplining the workers, the government mandated, and the lumbermen accepted, an eight-hour day for the industry. The loggers had won their central demand, and reforms in working conditions and wages followed; but the government had, nonetheless, broken the Wobbly unions and jailed their leaders. Between 1917 and 1919, Idaho, Washington, California, Oregon, and other states passed criminal syndicalism laws aimed at the Wobblies. The laws made illegal membership in any organization "advocating crime, sabotage, violence or unlawful methods of terrorism" as a means of accomplishing reforms.

With the end of the war, fear of Bolshevism swept the nation following the Russian Revolution; and this fear brought the Wobblies under renewed attack. In 1919, American Legionnaires attacked a Wobbly hall and lynched Wesley Everest, a Wobbly and a war veteran with a distinguished record. This killing was part of a more general reaction against labor radicalism that followed World War I. As the government arrested and deported many radical leaders, others, including IWW leader Big Bill Haywood, jumped bail and fled to the Soviet Union (White 1991, 293–94).

Unions attracting less attention than that of the miners, but influential in their trades and localities, were organized in the printing and building trades and among the barbers, bartenders, gas and steam fitters, boiler makers, and other skilled workers. In agriculture—where the farm field workers were nearly all Mexicans, and the range hands were cowboys with a tradition of individual action and loyalty to the "old man"—there was no organization.

The depression of 1921 was another setback for labor, but by 1925 the American Federation of Labor was again making gains in many trades. In agriculture, effective AFL unions were formed among the fruit and vegetable packers, the aristocracy of labor in this field. But 1929 brought retrenchment again, and for several years unemployment overshadowed all other problems. Organizations unaffiliated with the AFL began to grow among the unemployed. In 1934, a hunger march on the Arizona capitol at Phoenix, followed by a strike among relief workers for more adequate relief, received much publicity and met with drastic opposition from civil authorities. By 1935 union activity had again increased. One of the AFL's outstanding accomplishments was the solid organization of the lumber workers around Flagstaff, McNary, and Williams, Arizona, where the industry employed Mexican, black, and white workers.

In 1935 the Congress of Industrial Organizations (CIO) also became active in the West. Many of the fruit and vegetable workers withdrew from their AFL union to form branches of the United Cannery, Agricultural, Packing and Allied Workers of America, a CIO organization that organized among all agricultural workers. Of the farm laborers in Arizona, for example, in the 1920s and 1930s some 20,000 were Mexicans, migratory workers, or dispossessed farmers from the Midwest, who were seasonal workers earning an average annual income estimated at $259. The CIO also took over two miners' locals, at Bisbee and Oatman, in the 1930s and over the next few years carried on a vigorous organizing campaign in most of the mining and smelting towns of the West (Works Progress Administration 1940, 100–101).

In areas of the Southwest, the old Spanish American villages had long been battered by disintegrating influences; yet the people, especially those of the older generation, persisted in occupying many of them. Their ancestors had had access to grazing lands on the mesas as well as possession of their own irrigated fields in the valleys. By application of their ingenuity and hard labor in the frugal use of their limited resources, Southwest Indians once had maintained a village life, which had been nearly self-sufficient in its economy and eminently satisfactory in its social relationships. In the nineteenth century, after the abolition of primogeniture, the family of a deceased landowner divided his fields among his direct heirs. A tract of land that once grew food for a family was cut up into narrow strips of only a few acres each for the families of sons and grandsons. Simultaneously the villages lost ownership of much or all of the co-op lands. By the beginning of the twentieth century, as the land base of the village economy dwindled away, many of the men supplemented their meager income by leaving the community several months annually to work in the beet fields of Colorado or in local mines or ranches or in railroad construction. Many moved their families to neighboring cities where they found employment, and some of them became successful proprietors of business establishments. Even so, they retained possession of small tracts of land in remote villages and returned frequently for visits, where the pull of family ties and relatives remained strong.

The early twentieth-century subsistence-based economy of the Rio Grande Pueblo Indians of the Southwest remained, as it had for centuries, largely agricultural. Agricultural produce was raised in irrigated gardens, which surrounded the village. These gardens consisted mainly of corn, but wheat and beans remained important secondary crops. Melons introduced by the Spanish in a number of varieties were also an important part of the diet. Cleaning and upkeep of the irrigation canals from both the Rio Grande and its tributaries remained important activities of the Rio Grande Pueblos.

An Indian plowing his land on the Sacaton Indian Reservation in Arizona in the early twentieth century. Library of Congress.

In the villages of the more western Pueblo Indians, the Hopi for example, there were no permanent streams or water supplies, and successful farming depended on the exigencies of the weather. Rainfall in that area was less frequent (often fewer than 10 inches a year), and when it fell, it often did not fall where it was needed. In this environment religion was thoroughly integrated into the workplace, and the Hopi created a complex ceremonialism, which emphasized the magical control of the weather. Farming in the western Pueblo regions required no complex system of canals, terraces, or dams. Corn, melons, and beans were planted in alluvial fans or on the banks of dried streams (arroyos). Rain in the summer brought floodwaters that swept over the fields and provided the essential moisture for the planted crops. Farming was a hazardous occupation for the Hopi Indians because there was little and insufficient rain, and when it came, it often caused uncontrollable floods, which often uprooted or buried growing crops in sand. The Hopi farmers thus planted several fields to guard against loss from flood and relied on magical rites to bring about just the proper amount of moisture to ensure a harvest (Perrigo 1971, 378–80).

CASTE AND CLASS EXPERIENCE

Westerners usually divided the nonwhites in the West into four divisions: the Indians, the Mexicans (as they called both Mexican Americans and Mexican immigrants), the "Mongolians" (as they called the Chinese and some Asians), and blacks. Until lumped together by whites, none of these groups except, perhaps, blacks had ever thought of themselves as a single race. Mexicans, far from considering themselves a single race, had subdivided themselves according to racial distinctions of their own. The creation in the white American mind of an Indian race also imposed homogeneity on a people who usually considered themselves as made up of numerous distinct peoples or nations. The Chinese similarly had many divisions of their own and were, in any case, as ethnocentric as any white American. They thought of themselves as a superior people and would never have lumped themselves into a single race with other Asians.

As used in the West, the concept of race created a confusing system of classification. Sometimes it seemed to rest on biology, using, for example, skin color and other features to distinguish Indians as a single group. At other times, however, racialists described people who were of mixed descent as a single race. The many blacks who had some white ancestry were still black. Mexicans were a mixture of people of Native American, European, and African descent; but racialists lumped them together and labeled them as a single race. This confusion of criteria illustrates how much race was a cultural construction and not simply a recognition of any biological "facts."

Having created races, racialists could then ascribe characteristics to them, which were demeaning and derogatory. According to the ruling racialist mythology, for example, both Indians and Mexicans were dark, dirty, without morals, incapable of sexual restraint, cruel, vindictive, and lazy. Racialist stereotypes could easily be joined to sexual stereotypes. Whether condemned as sensual and lascivious or as ugly drudges, nonwhite women had to bear unfavorable comparisons to Anglo-American "true" womanhood. Racialists distinguished between racial groups according to both their particular mix of undesirable traits and their usefulness for whites. Thus, "useful" Mexicans and blacks often ranked ahead of "useless" Indians. At other times, "brave" Indians ranked ahead of "cowardly" blacks and Hispanics.

Not all whites accepted the tenets of racialism. Virtually all early twentieth-century white Americans were racially prejudiced—that is, they thought that nonwhites were inferior to whites. But racialism was more than mere prejudice. It was an assertion that not only were nonwhites inferior but they were permanently inferior. God and nature had doomed them to be either the servants of whites or to disappear. Many whites rejected racialism's assertion that nonwhites were permanently inferior people whose only choice was between extinction or underclass status. Instead they believed that "inferior" peoples could, with help, redeem themselves by imitating white Americans. Racial differences for these assimilations were neither innate nor permanent. They gave these differences a distinctive cultural interpretation.

The Christian reformers who governed U.S. Indian policy in the late nineteenth and early twentieth centuries, for example, did not seek either the biological extinction or the permanent subordination of Indians. Instead they sought to destroy the Indian customs that they thought were the cause of Indian inferiority. Having taught Indians "proper" American values and gender roles, the larger society could assimilate them just as it assimilated European immigrants. For the reformers, assimilation was the alternative to extermination, and they argued that it was the proper course by drawing on both democratic ideology and Christian morality.

If either the racialists or the reformers had been able to achieve their goals, the distinctive social arrangements of the western United States would have proved unnecessary. If the racialists, for example, had succeeded, they would have simply eliminated nonwhites or reduced them to permanent servitude. If the assimilationists had succeeded, they would have eliminated any separate identity for western minorities. But in fact neither racialists nor assimilationist reformers proved able to succeed completely in their plans. Racialism ran into serious problems when nonwhites failed to fade away or accept subordination as predicted (White 1991, 320–21).

By 1900, the Southwest and the Rocky Mountain West had emerged predominantly Anglo-American in population and culture. Yet these regions also had acquired some large and influential minority groups. The ancestors of two of these groups, first the Indians and then the Spaniards, had in turn been the majority people who once had regarded this land as their own. They had sought strenuously to keep it that way, but the great infiltration by others had transformed them into minority status; and then they were joined by more recent minority accretions: the African Americans, the Asian Americans, and the Mexican Americans. All of them had contributed much of the labor that had transformed the Southwest and the Rocky Mountain West so remarkably in the brief span of one century. Meanwhile, either overtly or unconsciously, all had also made some cultural contributions.

Indians officially became a minority group in 1924, when the granting of citizenship theoretically terminated their inferior status as "wards," or "stepchildren." Since 1887, assimilation had been attempted under the provisions of the Dawes Act, but, because the individual allotment of land as authorized by that act could not be carried out effectively in this semiarid climate, most of the reservation land remained undivided. A family could not live by farming 160 acres of rock and cactus; therefore, a majority of Indians remained under tribal management and tried to maintain a pastoral economy. In some instances, as in the case of the Pima, the lands were distributed, but more often the reservation pattern was modified only by the sale or lease of some of the land to ranchers, followed by the purchase of additional acreage for the reservation by the federal government (Perrigo 1971, 371–72).

Although most Indian communities managed to maintain a diminished land base, they faced numerous economic challenges and changes. Some Indians attempted to link their communities to the larger economy through farming, but these efforts largely failed. Most Indians by the early twentieth century had learned to scrape together a minimal living by mixing hunting, fishing, gathering, and gardening with casual labor and payments from the federal government. These payments represented money owed Indians under treaties, funds won in land settlement cases, or rent from allotments leased to whites. When all else failed, the government would provide rations to those in desperate need. Taken together, these sources of income managed to sustain most Indian communities in abysmal poverty. Indians became at once the poorest and the most dependent of western minorities. Most Indians escaped integration into the dual labor economy, but the price was economic marginalization. By the early twentieth century most reservations had no functioning economy at all. By 1900, conditions on the reservations had degenerated badly, in part due to misunderstanding that fostered errors in reservation management and in part due to negligence that permitted exploitation of the Indians. In New Mexico, Arizona, and southern California, a few boarding schools had been provided, but they too often left the children to be maladjusted and unhappy when they returned to their family homes. Consequently, after 1892 some government-supported schools were opened on the reservations. Such marginalization necessarily meant disaster for many Indian communities.

Strong Indian communities remained in the Southwest among the Navajos and Pueblos, but at their worst, southwestern reservations, like many more reservations elsewhere in the West, could become sinks of misery. By the twentieth century, for example, the Jicarilla Apaches on their high, mountainous reservation in New Mexico had attained a level of suffering as deep as that found anywhere in the West. The government had allotted the reservation, and whites soon gained access to most of its prime resources. White squatters and homesteaders claimed the best agricultural land, and officials leased the Jicarillas' winter grazing lands to Anglo and Hispanic herders. The government sold off part of the reservation's timber and deposited the proceeds in noninterest-bearing accounts in the federal treasury.

Until drought hit in the mid-1890s, the Jicarillas survived by combining food rations, annuity payments due them by treaty, some livestock raising, and handicraft production. A few obtained jobs in the Indian police, the only regular jobs available at the agency. But with the drought the Jicarillas' herds died, and the Indians nearly died with them. Their population fell from 815 in 1900 to 588 in 1920. They lived on corn tortillas and black coffee. The government responded callously. In 1911, officials cut Jicarilla food rations in half. Poorly housed and poorly fed, the Jicarillas sickened; by 1912 an estimated 75 percent of the tribe had tuberculosis, and the disease made it even harder for the Jicarillas to end their free fall into misery. Even when temporary work became available, about 61 percent of the Jicarilla men were too sick to take advantage of it. Those who could work found that their employers routinely paid them less than non-Indians for equivalent work. In such circumstances the community became difficult to sustain (White 1991, 324–25).

In 1926, the U.S. Department of the Interior authorized the Institute for Government Research to make a survey of conditions on the western reservations. Published in 1927, the "Meriam Report," as it was named, called attention to the deplorable conditions prevailing on the reservations and the inferior services rendered by the Bureau of Indian Affairs. Schools were inadequate, salaries were too low, living quarters were wretched, health services were substandard, the death rate of Indians from tuberculosis was several times higher than that of the nation-at-large, and some of the reservations actually faced a state of emergency.

In 1929, a new commissioner of Indian affairs, Charles J. Rhoades, a banker and scholar, undertook alleviation of the social ills revealed in the Meriam Report.

Before the end of his term of office, in 1933, he had obtained an increase in appropriations and a reorganization of the administrative service. By that time, however, the Great Depression had made the plight of the Indians even worse. Simultaneously the economic catastrophe had installed in Washington, D.C., a new administration with a passion for experimental reforms. The next appointee as head of the Indian Bureau was John Collier, a social worker who had edited *American Indian Life* magazine and had long been a scathing critic of past practices. Collier immediately inaugurated sweeping reforms. He ordered that the bureau should employ qualified Indians, that no more reservation land should be sold, and that henceforth the emphasis should be upon providing day schools instead of boarding schools. Then he secured a congressional appropriation for emergency relief and another one for support of an Indian Civilian Conservation Corps. The next year, 1934, he obtained the enactment of the Indian Reorganization Act, which contained these provisions: that no further distribution or alienation of tribal land would be permitted; that the existing reservations should be enlarged by purchase of contiguous areas; that the tribes should be given assistance in the drafting of constitutions providing for their own local government; that they should be authorized to establish business corporations; that the Congress would create a revolving fund from which loans could be granted for improvement of production on the reservations; that Indians should be prepared for positions of leadership among their own people; that they should be encouraged to revive their traditional cultural practices; and that this new program would be effective for each tribe only after it had been accepted in a referendum by the tribe.

Immediately, most of the tribes of the West voted for acceptance of their "New Deal," although the largest, the Navajos, failed to adopt a constitution because their experience had made them skeptical about promises emanating from the Bureau of Indian Affairs. They continued to be governed by a traditional tribal council, which was recognized by the Congress in an act adopted in 1950. The tedious drafting and adopting of a constitution, which placed responsibilities for management upon the Indians themselves, with the government agents functioning as advisers, followed acceptance by other tribes.

Then the tribes obtained loans for the opening of cooperative stores, the development of their craft industries, the drilling of wells, and the improvement of farms and livestock. New emphasis was placed upon day schools, 32 of which were opened on the Navajo reservation alone by 1937. The encouragement given to the Indians to prepare for leadership resulted in the employment of more Indian teachers, so that by 1940 one-fourth of the teachers were Indians. Adult education was also promoted and bilingual textbooks were prepared. Likewise, the health service was expanded by means of an increase in appropriations to four million dollars by 1936 (Perrigo 1971, 372–73).

The northward flow of migrants from Mexico had begun during World War I when crossing the border was restricted only by qualifications as to age, health, literacy, and means of support. During the war years even those restrictions were disregarded so that by 1920, 250,000 Mexicans had crossed into Texas, 62,000 had come to Arizona, and 20,000 had moved into New Mexico. After the war the increased demand for cheap labor tripled those numbers. During the Depression, as jobs became scarce, Mexicans and Mexican Americans became targets of discrimination for local authorities throughout the West. Authorities argued that they were concerned about the possibility of having to care for expanding numbers of indigents. During this decade tens of thousands of Mexicans were deported, including native-born Americans of Mexican descent.

Although not in numbers that equaled their movement to the Midwest and Northeast, southern blacks also migrated to the West in the first decades of the twentieth century; they followed the population of roughly 1,600 black cowboys who had migrated to Texas and Oklahoma in the post–Civil War era, the more than 25,000 black soldiers (buffalo soldiers) who had been stationed there between 1866 and 1917, and the few who had come west to find their fortunes and then remained in places like Helena, Montana, where there were over four hundred African Americans, descendents of those who had first come there during its gold rush and remained to operate restaurants, hotels, and retail stores, some becoming rather substantial as early as the 1880s (Nugent 1999, 389).

Many blacks migrated to the cotton fields of Texas. Despite the sorry conditions, the Texas Cotton Belt actually indulged in less prejudice than did the Deep South; and in the western communities of the state, where blacks were not very numerous, they generally were well treated. As a rule the African American leaders of that era were inclined to be patient and to place their hope in vocational education, more of which was made available after 1912 by the founding of junior colleges for black Americans. Through those years Texas had two race riots, both in 1919. After fighting for democracy elsewhere, many blacks who had served their country in World War I were determined to carry the struggle for democracy into their own neighborhoods. The whites in Texas sensed this awakening and were determined to squelch it, and open clashes with loss of lives occurred in both Houston and Longview in that one year. In the 1920s, terror again took over in that state, as the newly resurrected Ku Klux Klan resorted to the burning of property and the flogging or hanging of "uppity" blacks. By that time, too, a new way of nullifying the black vote had been devised. Insisting that their party was a private association that could restrict membership, the Democratic Party of Texas excluded blacks, thus preventing them from voting in Democratic primary elections, in which the winning candidates nearly always were selected in the general election.

Nevertheless, blacks were steadily gaining in economic status and increasing in numbers. By 1930, the 850,000 blacks there comprised close to 15 percent of the total population of the state. Although about two-thirds of them were small farmers, and one-eighth of the total were still sharecroppers, those who had broken such bonds now accounted for the ownership of 23 percent of the total number of farms. The 38 percent who dwelt in the cities had employment in business and manufacturing. By 1930, the African American community of the Southwest supported 4,000 churches, six junior colleges, two senior colleges, numerous adult evening classes, and several welfare associations (Perrigo 1971, 385–86).

In the Rocky Mountain West, the ethnic variety of the early twentieth-century industrial mining towns was as great as anywhere in the United States. Bingham, in the Utah mountains, for example, had 1,210 Greeks, 639 Italians, 564 Croats, 254

Japanese, 217 Finns, 161 Englishmen, 60 Bulgars, 59 Swedes, 52 Irish, and 15 Germans in 1911. These were the top years of European immigration to the Americas, and the West received its full share. Railroad agents recruited and sold land to farm families and also recruited wageworkers. Labor "padrones," like the Greek Leonard Skliris, contracted their countrymen's labor (for a cut) to mining companies and other employers. After years of being exploited, Greek workers broke his hold in 1912.

Greeks and Italians soon outnumbered all other Europeans and Americans in Carbon County, Utah. In 1915, Greek miners in Price, the county seat, petitioned their bishop in Crete to send them a priest, and a year later young John Petrakis, with his wife, mother, and four children, arrived. A thousand miners from all over the Utah mountains greeted their train when it pulled into Salt Lake City "with a celebratory thunder of gunshots fired into the air." Men who had not seen women or children from Crete since leaving home "knelt and prayed in gratefulness, and some wept and reached gently to touch the hem of my mother's dress as she passed," writes the novelist Harry Mark Petrakis of his parents' arrival in Utah. Greeks earned a reputation as fighters for workers' rights. One, Louis Tikas, took part in the overthrow of the grafter Skliris and then gave his life in the infamous Ludlow Massacre.

In Wyoming, the Colorado Fuel and Iron Company bought up a copper camp named Hartville in 1899, and in a year the area's population boomed to around fifteen hundred. The majority were recent immigrants, led by hundreds of Italians and Greeks, scores of Swedes, English, Lebanese, Japanese, and others. By 1910, Greeks and Italians were running bakeries, grocery stores, saloons, and construction firms. Hartville had become a family-oriented working-class community. Butte, Montana, continued its maturation from mining camp to community in the first decades of the new century. The censuses of 1910 and 1920 counted about 40,000 people there, and in 1917, at the height of wartime copper demand, it was doubtless higher. Irish men and women had been arriving since the 1870s, and, as happened in San Francisco, early arrival meant easier assimilation. The Irish were not the only ethnic groups; before 1903 even more miners from Cornwall were there, and by 1910 Croatians, Germans, Italians, and Finns contributed fifteen hundred to three thousand each. Idaho also had an ethnically diverse population. In 1910, two of every five Idahoans had been born outside the United States. The predominant group was Scandinavian, but Germans, Italians, Finns, Greeks, Japanese, and Chinese also lived there. A number of black families populated and farmed the Snake River valley, while Spanish Basques herded sheep on the ranges south and west of Boise (Nugent 1999, 154, 158–59).

URBAN AND RURAL EXPERIENCE

As the new century opened, American society turned away from its rural past: the lifeways that had been part of most people's common experience in Anglo America since colonial days faced a new metropolitan future. The shift signaled a change far larger than simply a move from farm to city, from raising crops and livestock to working in factories and offices. Rather, it was a shift in lifestyles and worldviews and one that required decades to complete. The first decades of the twentieth century were the last years in American history when both cities and new farms would proliferate. New York emerged in the 1880s census as the first million-plus metropolis, to be joined by Philadelphia and Chicago in 1890. At every census throughout the nineteenth century, city people took a greater share of the American population, from 1 in 20 in 1800 to 1 in 7 in 1850 to 2 in 5 in 1900. Yet farms and farm people multiplied too. In 1913, 59,363 final homestead entries, covering 10,885,000 acres of land, were "proved up"—that is, deeded over from federal to private ownership. Never before or since did proved-up acres exceed 10 million in one year.

This parallel pattern of both farm and city growth continued to about 1913. After that cities kept developing, but rural America began leveling off. New homestead entries averaged over 83,000 every year from 1901 through 1910 but slipped to 53,000 a year between 1911 and 1915, and below 24,000 between 1921 and 1925. Fingers of new settlement probed into certain isolated areas after 1913, to be sure, but after that peak year American farms and farm population stopped expanding, stabilized for 25 years until the late 1930s, and then started to shrink and have shrunk ever since.

This of course was not evident in 1901. The western horizon was not cloudless, but there were plenty of reasons why land-seekers should have been optimistic. Vast lands remained "open," railroads were eager to sell their grants, and Congress kept inflating homestead sizes to try to accommodate the aridity of the high plains. Experts insisted that irrigation and dry farming were the answers to the devil of drought. So the frontier of settlement, stalled since the outset of the Great Plains farm depression in 1887, started moving west again. Simultaneously cities and industries proliferated. Mining, more than ever an industry involving substantial capital and wage labor, attracted migrants as multiethnic as in the Northeast. Serbs, Croats, Greeks, and others did not fear to cross the Mississippi. In Arizona, Bisbee with its mines and Douglas with its smelters, almost unpopulated in 1900, topped 9,000 persons a dozen years later. Price, Utah, attracted several thousand people. Northern Idaho communities from Lewiston to Coeur d'Alene nearly doubled their population. Mexicans and Japanese were much more visible than before 1901.

Several small towns in 1901 became cities as they easily passed 100,000 persons by the 1910 census. Salt Lake City rose from 34,000 in 1900 to more than 100,000 by 1913; and by the 1910 census Spokane had gone from 39,000 to 104,000, Oakland from 67,000 to 150,000, Portland from 90,000 to 207,000, and Seattle from 81,000 to 237,000. Several counties in California's San Joaquin Valley more than doubled their populations because of irrigated crop raising and intensive stock farming. California's "hydraulic society" had begun. Los Angeles County became the population leader of the entire West, exploding from 170,000 in 1900 to 504,000 in 1910 and nearly doubling to 936,000 in 1920.

With drought and depression behind it, the West became briefly a rare and clear case of simultaneous urban and rural growth, the dual expansion of both the very customary and the very new. This was nearly the final hour of the traditional, Jeffersonian, homestead-seeking America, yet also a time of headlong rush into a new kind of world. By the early years of the century the West was already resisting generalization. Texas was not Montana; Idaho was not Wyoming.

In the first 13 years of the century the Great Plains west of the 98th and 100th meridians truly opened up. Homesteads, railroad lines, whistle stops, grain elevators, churches, courthouses, and all the trappings of commercial farming and stock raising filled the treeless, sunbaked sea of grass from south Texas to the middle of Alberta and Saskatchewan. No part of the region lacked migrants. The most startling increases took place in Texas and Oklahoma, which between them added 1,715,000 people in 1900–1910 and another million or more by 1917. Expansion in the four plains states north of them (Kansas, Nebraska, and the two Dakotas) was also considerable: 787,000 between 1900 and 1910, and 300,000 between 1910 and 1920.

So strong was the optimism, so confident the people, so reassured were they by scientific theories of dryland farming and the possibilities of irrigation that they surged beyond the 100th meridian, beyond the 102nd into Colorado, the 103rd into New Mexico, the 104th into eastern Montana. In 1890 two giant counties occupied all Montana between Wyoming and Canada for about 125 miles west of the Dakota line. Only 7,400 people rattled around in them. By 1920 they had portioned off into 16 counties with 117,700 people settled on farms or ranches or in small towns sprinkled along the routes of the Great Northern and the Northern Pacific Railroads. None of those towns came near having 10,000 people, or ever would. Similar county chopping took place in eastern Colorado and New Mexico as scores of thousands homesteaded the grasslands and sprinkled them with little towns marked from miles away by their tall white grain elevators (Nugent 1999, 133–34).

ANIMAL HUSBANDRY AND HUNTING AND FISHING

The story of animal husbandry in the West is closely connected to the story of the treatment of Indians in the first decades of the twentieth century. At the end of the nineteenth century, parts of several Apache tribes were settled on the San Carlos Reservation in Arizona, where for many years they sickened in idleness and survived on government rations. The reservation embraced acres of good grazing land, and neighboring cattlemen argued that, since Apaches never could or would use that range, white men should have access to it. Consequently, under duress, and under the eternal threat of troops, Apaches were led to sign away about a quarter of their reservation to the cattlemen.

All the good rangeland on the remainder was leased to a few powerful cattle companies. Then, in the early 1920s, the Apaches started running some small bunches of cattle of hopelessly mixed breed on the most worthless parts of their range. The white cattlemen were only amused. Then, by the most intense efforts, the Apache cattlemen began making a little money and buying good bulls, so that their herds were working up to where they were producing presentable, saleable beef cattle. Encouraged by this modest success, the tribe refused to renew certain leases to the white cattlemen and began to expand their own operations. Immediately the pressure became heavy upon senators and congressmen and upon the Indian Bureau to force the Indians to lease to the white ranchers. The senators from Arizona showed conscience, and the Indian Bureau remained firm. By 1932 there were some 28,000 head of Indian-owned cattle grazing the range, and all the leases had been ended. Still, the cattle interests had a string tied to the whole affair, for the Apaches were not allowed to breed their own bulls.

Their herds had started with odd longhorns—some from Mexico—dairy cows, and anything they could acquire. To obtain decent "grade" beef cattle required careful breeding with registered bulls and continuous culling of off-colored cows. The production of suitable bulls demands a bull-breeding herd of registered cows and registered bulls. Otherwise, a cattle producer must buy expensive bulls from other breeders. As the big Apache operation grew prosperous, the Indian cattlemen were required to spend thousands of dollars of their profits yearly buying good sires from non-Indians.

The Indians solved their problem during the great drought of the 1930s. As a relief measure, the government bought cattle from drought-devastated ranches. Some "drought relief cattle" were issued to Indians; many were butchered and distributed as food for relief purposes. A Bureau of Indian Affairs agent appointed by New Deal Interior Secretary John Collier spotted a herd of registered heifers that were due to be bought before the creatures starved to death. The heifers were quietly shipped to the San Carlos Reservation. They were in such miserable condition that nobody thought twice about them. On the Apache grass they prospered, and suddenly the cattle interests were presented with something done and finished: the Indians had a registered bull-breeding herd, and in a short time the San Carlos cattlemen would begin selling registered bulls to white cattlemen (La Farge 1956, 242–43).

In the Southwest and Rocky Mountain West in the first decades of the twentieth century, the sportsman could find a plentiful supply of big game. Bison were rapidly becoming extinct, but brown and black bear, mountain lion, deer, elk, and other species of big game were found and could be hunted in season. In Arizona, the mule deer, so called because of its long ears, was the principal big-game animal of the region and was found nearly everywhere except in the Navajo country in the northeastern section of Arizona. More than 15,000 (comprising the largest single herd of mule deer in the United States) roamed the Kaibab forest, north of the Grand Canyon. The largest bucks weighed up to 240 pounds dressed and carried antlers with a spread of from 30 to 40 inches. The little Arizona whitetail, seldom weighing more than a hundred pounds, was more numerous but also more elusive and was found only in rough, brushy country. Certain Arizona business firms offered prizes to the hunter bringing in the first deer as well as the heaviest buck of the season.

Of the six indigenous species of cloven-hoofed animals found in Arizona by the first white settlers, the elk alone became extinct. But imported stock, preserved through supervision and protection, were to be found on the Mogollon Plateau. Additional stock released in the Hualpai and Bill Williams mountain areas brought the number of elk in the state to between three and four thousand head by the late 1920s. Elk hunting was revived in 1935, and during the 1936 open season 85 bull elk were taken. Special permits were required for elk hunting.

The only wild bison or buffalo of the Southwest were found in Arizona in House-rock Valley, in the north-central part of the state, where a short hunting season was permitted under closely restricted conditions. Many hunters sought bear as well as deer on the Mogollon Rim. The state's most predatory animal, the mountain lion, could be hunted year-round. The great cats were usually found in the roughest and most brush-covered country, where deer were plentiful. Since a mountain lion would commonly destroy no fewer than 50 deer in a year, the killing of one lion meant saving the lives of hundreds of deer. Occasionally, the jaguar, called *el tigre* by the Mexicans, drifted in from Sonora, but, unlike the mountain lion, the jaguar could seldom be treed.

Hunting mountain lion and bear on horseback, with a pack of dogs, was a sport that was truly western. The hunter, racing at breakneck speed over rough and broken ground with the roar of dogs in his ears, experienced an unforgettable thrill.

An American bison, 1909. Library of Congress.

Numerous species of smaller game also attracted the sportsman to the Southwest. The wild turkey, the largest of American game birds and classed as big game, could be found throughout the northern pine and oak area of the West. Various species of duck, snipe, and other waterfowl inhabited the lakes and streams, including green-winged and blue-winged teal, mallard, widgeon, redhead, and goose. White-wing pigeons, quail, and doves were hunted as well as jack rabbits, for which there was no closed season limit.

The development of dams and aqueducts in the West in the first decades of the twentieth century created an increasing number of artificial lakes, which were stocked with fish and provided ample opportunities for the game fishermen. A string of beautiful lakes below Flagstaff and the big bodies of water from the Salt River irrigation system offered good fishing for bass as well as numerous other varieties (Works Progress Administration 1940, 132–33).

For centuries the buffalo, or more properly the North American bison, had provided Native Americans of the West with both food and material to make clothing, shelter, and weapons. However, by the turn of the century, this animal became the last fur bearer to suffer near extinction. The discovery that buffalo hides could be turned into a cheap leather suitable for making machine belts, together with the expansion of the railroad across the West after the Civil War, sealed the bison's fate. The wholesale slaughter of the buffalo eventually abated from lack of targets, but killing continued for a while on a retail basis, with hunters like Theodore Roosevelt who rushed off and paid for the privilege of hunting a trophy before it was too late.

Others, however, sought to save the pitiful remnants of the species. Some ranchers started private herds. William Hornbaday, of the New York Zoo, organized the Bison Society; and George Bird Grinnell, the editor of *Field and Stream,* worked to protect the small group of bison in Yellowstone from poachers. By the beginning of the twentieth century, the buffalo moved from being a commodity to a symbol of the American West, gracing American coins and appearing in Wild West shows. Such symbolic status became the last refuge from extinction open to this animal, whose uniqueness, size, and power caused Americans to endow it with a special national meaning (Milner, O'Connor, and Sandweiss 1994, 246–48).

Intellectual Life

EDUCATION

In the Rocky Mountain West, the availability of schools and teachers varied widely. In the late nineteenth century, Nevada had only 38 schools, or about 7 for every thousand school-aged children, while at the same time the figures for Montana and Nebraska were among the highest in the nation. In general western states did well in placing urban children into the classroom and poorly in putting rural children into schools. Because western population was sparse, fewer taxpayers provided for schools than in the East, thus increasing individual tax burdens. Between 1880 and 1920 the West spent more per capita on education than any other region.

The widespread perception that male schoolteachers in the West took the job because they were "too lazy to work, hadn't the ability to gamble and . . . couldn't scrape a little on the fiddle" created particular opportunities for women teachers. Wages, while higher than in the East, were not high enough to hold qualified male teachers. Also, under male supervision the inherent violence of the West sometimes crept into the classroom. For example, in Leadville, Colorado, the local school board had to urge the prosecuting of an instructor for "shooting at scholars." These factors contributed to a large proportion of women teachers—larger than the rest of the country—in the West. And by extending the "cult of true womanhood" to the classroom, middle-class western women in the late nineteenth and early twentieth centuries had little trouble in establishing the classroom as a domain as rightfully theirs as the kitchen or parlor. Classrooms seemed to be but extensions of the home and thus rightfully under control of women. In many areas of the West the one-room schoolhouse also became the community social center, allowing the female teacher's domesticating influence to extend beyond the students in the classroom and into the community (White 1991, 313–14).

In the territories of New Mexico and Arizona the quest for statehood served as a stimulus to the development of their educational system. As early as 1874 the legislature in Arizona had founded a system of schools with the governor presiding as ex-officio territorial superintendent; and, in 1889, a separate superintendent office was created. By that date, development funds had been provided and a uniform series of textbooks had been adopted. A university was established at Tucson. In addition, normal schools for the training of teachers opened in Tempe in 1885 and in Flagstaff in 1899. By 1910, the public schools of Arizona had an average daily attendance of approximately 20,000 pupils.

In New Mexico, the effective efforts for improvement in education began with the founding of a university in Albuquerque in 1889, and four years later normal schools were established in Silver City and in Las Vegas. Meanwhile, in 1891, the legislature had enacted an improved public school law, which created a territorial system headed by a board and a superintendent. Expenditures increased from $85,000 in 1892 to a quarter of a million dollars seven years later. Thereafter additional funds were derived from the letting of leases on nearly three million acres of land that had been obtained in 1898 as a gift from the federal government through the efforts of Harvey B. Ferguson. By 1910, the public schools in New Mexico enrolled almost 60,000 pupils.

The national trend in rural and sparsely settled regions in the 1920s was away from the local one-room schoolhouse toward consolidation, and the states of the Southwest followed this trend. In Arizona, for example, elementary and high school districts ranged in size from 5 to 100 square miles. A union high school district was composed of two or more adjacent elementary districts. Temporary "accommodation schools" were established in regions not yet organized into school districts. Bus transportation was provided for pupils in the larger districts. Reflecting another national trend in education at the time, Arizona children from 8 to 16 years old were required to attend school for not less than eight months of each year.

Elementary teachers must have completed four years, and secondary teachers five years, of college work to qualify for teaching in the public schools. Although Arizona had many sparsely settled areas in the first four decades of the twentieth century, elementary and secondary schools were available for most of its children. In 1930, 91 percent of the children between 7 and 13 years of age were actually enrolled in public schools, as compared with 79 percent in 1920.

As in other regions of the country, the educational system in the West suffered during the Depression years. In Arizona, for example, public school enrollment, which in 1930 was 103,806, decreased during the next few years. The number of public school teachers was 3,273 in 1930. But during the difficult Depression years it declined seriously, until in 1934 there were only 2,834 public school teachers working in the state. These teachers received an annual average salary of $1,637 in 1930 and $1,309 in 1934.

Reflecting another national trend, courses in home economics, agriculture, trade, and industry were provided in a considerable number of the public high schools of the West; and vocational instruction in rural areas was supplemented by the work of county farm and home demonstration agents. In Arizona, technical training in law, engineering, agriculture, music, and education was offered by the three institutions of higher education, which had a combined enrollment of 3,157 in 1934. Because of the large percentage of Mexicans and Indians in Arizona's population, "Americanization" work was an important part of the school programs.

The education of Indian children in Arizona remained under the jurisdiction of the Office of Indian Affairs in the U.S. Department of the Interior. For the year ending June 30, 1938, there were 13,000 Indian children, 6 to 18 years of age, in the state, of whom 8,000 were enrolled in Indian schools. There were several types of these schools: federal day schools, reservation boarding schools, and nonreservation boarding schools; and mission, private, and state day schools and boarding schools. A small number of Indian children were also cared for in the regular public schools. According to the 1938 annual report of the commissioner of Indian affairs, the majority of the Indian children attending school were in the federal day schools. This was in line with the general policy of the Office of Indian Affairs to strengthen family ties by allowing the child to remain at home during the school year, in distinction to the policy of former years that sought to educate the Indian children by separating them from home influence and tradition (Works Progress Administration 1940, 119–20).

📷 *Snapshot*

The Great Disaster at a Consolidated School in Texas

On March 17, 1937, the *New York Times* reported that "All of the fears of consolidation were realized one afternoon in Texas in New London, where a new consolidated school exploded and crashed in with a deafening roar, killing 500 teachers and children." The *Times* report continued, "The building was fireproof, so flames died quickly, but the strength of the blast and the massive volume of falling debris killed almost everyone inside the building instantly. Seven hundred children from nine through eighteen years of age and forty teachers were in the structure when the explosion occurred. More than five hundred students and teachers were killed, with fewer than two hundred escaping with injuries. Most of the children and teachers were gathered in the auditorium when the blast wrecked the school as though a bomb from an air-raider had found its mark." Horrified mothers who were gathered for a PTA meeting in a cafeteria three hundred feet from the auditorium helplessly watched the building collapse on their children.

Screaming hysterically, the mothers raced across the campus. With bare hands they clawed at the debris, trying desperately to reach children whose cries could be heard from beneath the crumbled structure. As darkness fell on the ruins of the school, the community center for this region of scattered oil camps and small hamlets, the campus presented a macabre scene. Sightseers crowded elbow to elbow with grief-stricken parents, watching the rescue crews at work with acetylene torches beneath floodlights from the football field and a string of electric bulbs hastily put in place above the wreckage. Alongside the tragic pile, an ever lengthening line of white sheets told the magnitude of the disaster.

The story of the disaster also led some observers to question the wisdom of putting so many children together in large schools. A *New York Times* article dismissed such fears, arguing that the new "consolidated schools are of sand and stone, have stairways of slate and cement, and are classed as fireproof." Many parents and educators agreed "the consolidated school is the antithesis of the little red school house." For rural communities, "it provides facilities held equal to those of city schools, enabling sparsely populated districts to combine in one well-equipped school." (Lindenmeyer 2005, 151–53)

COMMUNICATION

Radio found immediate and enthusiastic acceptance in the Southwest and Rocky Mountain West. The topography of mountain and desert, resulting in isolation of remote settlements, made the miracle of radio a welcome antidote for either forced or chosen solitude. In the 1920s, when the radio arrived in the West, there were still people alive who had watched the smoke signals of hostile Indians; ridden the narrow twisting roads along sheer canyon cliffs in stagecoach or on horseback; and watched the slow, tedious transformation of barren deserts into fertile valleys and gem-like cities. These survivors of a more bucolic age bridged two separate eras, and by no means the least of the changes witnessed was the coming of the radio.

In awed respect, old-timers watched the conquest of the treacherous vastness of space. Suddenly, great distance was dwarfed to virtual nonexistence and the still air became vibrant and alive with human voice. Although neither the Southwest nor the Rocky Mountain West could claim any part in the initial discoveries in regard to the radio, its subsequent interest was ambitious and aggressive. Licensed on June 21, 1922, KFAD in Phoenix became the thirty-sixth station in the entire country and was the first to be licensed in the state. Soon after, KFCB, also in Phoenix, which had been broadcasting for some time as an amateur station, was also licensed to operate.

The amateurs of Arizona assisted in radio development in the state. Amateurs were the only ones who could build or repair or understand the earlier "contraptions," and the tinkerers who knew the intricacies of the subject were men set apart and admired. From 1922 to 1924 more than 75 percent of the sets used were built by amateurs. Initially, all of the radio receiving sets were crystal sets (Works Progress Administration 1940, 129).

The two largest population centers in the area, Texas and Oklahoma, also were early pioneers in radio. In 1922, radio station KOMA went on the air in Oklahoma on Christmas Eve. The station had only 15 watts and its chief function was to rebroadcast the programming of the larger eastern cities. In Dallas, KFJZ (in 1917), WRR (in 1920), WPA, WBAP, and WFAA (all in 1922) all competed for air space. In the early unregulated days, there were virtually no rules to allow a fair distribution of the dial for broadcasters, and so in 1922, all five Dallas stations agreed to a timesharing plan on each frequency. November 11, 1928, was declared "National Frequency Allocation Day," when the Federal Radio Commission (FRC), predecessor to the Federal Communications Commission (FCC), brought organization to the dial by assigning dedicated frequencies to the strongest stations and culling out many of the small-time opportunists and enthusiasts. WBAP of Dallas was awarded a clear channel position on the dial, becoming one of only a small handful of stations in the nation that was allowed to send its signal to a reported 42 states. To honor the art of "DX-ing" (distance listening) Wednesdays after 3 P.M. were declared "Silent Night" in the 1920s, which meant that low-powered stations turned off their transmitters so that high-powered stations across the United States could be easily received on anyone's dial (http://www.knus99.com/amlist.html).

Material Life

FOOD

Canning, inventive packaging, and advertising were changing the dietary habits of many Americans in the early twentieth century, but for Mexican Americans in the Southwest, their diet remained much the same as it had for centuries. It consisted mainly of corn-based breads, beans in various forms, and meat, usually chicken or pork, which was highly spiced to disguise hints of putrefaction. The Mexican American diet consisted of a variety of foods and dishes that represented a blend of pre-Columbian and Spanish cultures. The typical Mexican diet was rich in complex carbohydrates, provided mainly by corn and corn products, beans, rice, and breads. The typical Mexican diet contained an adequate amount of protein in the forms of beans, eggs, fish, and shellfish, and a variety of meats, including beef, pork, poultry, and goat. Because of the extensive use of frying as a cooking method, the Mexican diet was also high in fat. The nutrients most likely to be inadequately provided were calcium, iron, vitamin A, folacin, and vitamin C.

Traditionally, Mexicans ate four or five meals daily. The foods eaten varied with factors such as income, education, urbanization, geographic region, and family customs. With emigration to the United States, major changes occurred in the Mexican American's diet. Healthy changes included a moderate increase in the consumption of milk, vegetables, and fruits, and a large decrease in the consumption of lard and Mexican cream. The introduction of salads and cooked vegetables increased the use of fats, such as salad dressings, margarine, and butter. Other less healthy changes included a severe decline in the consumption of traditional fruit-based beverages in favor of high-sugar drinks. Consumption of inexpensive sources of complex carbohydrates, such as beans and rice, also decreased as a result of acculturation. In addition to the negative impact on the health of this population, these dietary changes also adversely affected the family's budget when low-priced foods were replaced with more expensive ones.

Eastern and midwestern migrants to the West brought their own dietary habits with them and, as mentioned earlier, these habits had an impact on both the Mexicans who had recently moved into the area and on those who had called the region home for generations. But the Mexicans also influenced the dietary habits of their northern neighbors, as Americans became introduced to the flavor of chili, frijoles, and tortillas. Remaining outside of this culinary cultural mix were the Pueblo Indians, who remained steadfast in their diet of locally grown foods including corn, beans, and melons.

HOUSING

The most typical architecture of the Southwest was that based on the adobe designs of the Pueblo Indians. The Pueblos dwelt in adobe residences that usually sat atop mesas or plateaus. These adobe houses were single- or multistoried structures with apartment-like rooms; the buildings, made of adobe or stone, were either rectangular, square, or oval and rose in terraced tiers overlooking a plaza. At the turn of the century the largest Pueblo was that of the Zuni, which was inhabited by some 2,500 people. There are at least two Pueblo Indian towns, Acoma and Orqibi, that date back to 1150 A.D., making them the oldest North American towns in existence. In the twentieth century the Pueblos added glass windows, wooden doors, and factory-made furniture to their ancient adobe homes.

Harvey Houses of the West

Fred Harvey was just 15 years old when he emigrated to the United States from Liverpool, England. He first worked as a dishwasher in New York for just $2 per day. Saving his money, he soon moved on to New Orleans, where he worked again in the restaurant business, learning the trade from the ground up. In 1853, he moved to St. Louis, Missouri. Six years later, he and a partner opened a restaurant in St. Louis. His partner soon left Harvey to join the Confederacy and the restaurant closed.

Harvey took a job at the St. Joseph, Missouri, post office. From there he sorted mail for the first railroad post office in Leavenworth, Kansas. The connection with the railroad changed his fortune.

During this time, the young entrepreneur noticed that the lunchrooms serving rail passengers were deplorable, and most trains did not have dining cars, even on extended trips. The custom at the time was to make dining stops every 100 miles or so. Sometimes there would be a restaurant at the station, but more often than not, there was nothing to feed the famished travelers. The dining stops were also short, no longer than an hour, and the passengers were expected to find a restaurant, order their meal, and get served in this short amount of time.

Harvey saw an opportunity to return to the restaurant business. He opened his first restaurant in the Topeka, Kansas, Santa Fe Depot Station in 1876. Leasing the lunch counter at the depot, Harvey's business was an immediate success. Impressed with his work, the Atchison, Topeka and Santa Fe soon gave Harvey control of food service along the rail line. The Harvey Houses along the Santa Fe route became the first chain restaurants. At its peak, there were 84 Harvey Houses. They continued to be built and operated into the 1930s and 1940s.

In the Southwest, Fred Harvey hired architect Mary Colter to design influential landmark hotels in Santa Fe and Gallup, New Mexico, Winslow, Arizona, and at the South Rim and the bottom of the Grand Canyon in the 1910s and 1920s. The rugged, landscape-integrated design principles of Colter's work influenced a generation of subsequent western American architecture.

After World War I, when people began to travel in automobiles, the company began a gradual decline. However, once again they adapted, moving away from full reliance on train passengers. Soon they began to package motor trips of the Southwest, including tours of Indian villages and the Grand Canyon.

During the Depression, the Harvey Company suffered along with the rest of the nation, as no one could afford to travel. However, the trend was reversed with the commencement of World War II. Suddenly the trains were filled with troops and the Harvey Houses began to feed them. (http://www.legendsofamerica.com)

In the Rocky Mountain and Great Plains West, the idealized agrarian image of Currier and Ives's late nineteenth-century western farmers' homes reflected eastern sensibilities, not western reality. Often during the first months of settlement, some families lived in lean-tos, or even canvas-topped carts or wagon boxes. In the plains areas the lack of lumber made people look to other building materials. Houses were often scooped out from the sides of creeks, with front walls of sod. Once families could build more substantial houses, cultural influences became apparent, such as the differences between the Yankee and the southern tides of settlement. The well-built southern-style log cabin had a breezeway through the center, while Yankees built two-story wood frame houses. Less affluent people of the West often lived in wooden shacks reinforced with an additional coating of tarpaper nailed to board walls, Without insulation this construction barely provided sufficient shelter against the blizzards of the Rocky Mountain winters (Milner, O'Connor, and Sandweiss 1994, 297).

In the period between World War I and World War II suburban sprawl in major western cities stimulated a new western architectural design called the ranch house, which in the post–World War II era dominated American home design. The ranch home originated in southern California. It was the particular work of San Diego architect Cliff May, who was inspired by nineteenth-century haciendas, with their rooms opening onto wide porches and interior courtyards. By the early 1940s, the design began showing up in architects' plan books. The very name evoked myth. "When we think of the West," a writer in an architectural design book mused, "we picture to ourselves ranches and wide open spaces where there is plenty of elbow room." The ranch house sought to capture this feeling with its horizontal orientation, low-slung roof, rooms flowing one to the other, picture windows, and sliding glass doors inviting residents outdoors to the patio and the barbecue grill. The ranch house conjured up dreams of informal living, ideal weather, and movie star glamour. In the early post–World War II period the rest of America became captivated with the western ranch house. In Levittown, New York, the first great post–World War II suburb, ranch houses commanded a 20 percent premium over the Cape Cod style (Hine and Faragher 2000, 526–27).

A Fred Harvey eating house and Santa Fe Station in Chanute, Kansas, c. 1900. Library of Congress.

TRANSPORTATION

Government subsidies and a rash of enthusiasm after the Civil War to connect the entire country by rail sparked an explosion of railroad construction in the Southwest and Rocky Mountain West in the last decades of the nineteenth century. The Atlantic and Pacific Railroad Company, for example, with a land grant subsidy of more than 10 million acres along the 35th parallel in Arizona, began to lay its tracks westward across the territory in 1882. By 1890 or soon afterward, all the important mining centers of the West had railroad service.

After the quiescent depression years of the 1890s, the railroads again began laying track and platting towns prodigally throughout the West—from 1901 to 1913 usually 50 to 100 new miles of track a year. In 1905 alone, the railroads had constructed 300 new miles of track and platted nearly 40 new towns. The Northern Pacific, confident that farmers would keep coming, started selling tracts no larger than 320 acres. The Great Northern not only promoted irrigation and dry farming but also backed the "good roads" movement, the campaign in the Midwest and West to create a network of all-weather paved roads. The railroads also sent demonstrator trains to educate settlers in home economics and better farming methods, and in 1911 they began sponsoring dozens of demonstration farms.

In the 1920s, the railroad industry, as it had in other parts of the country, reached its peak in the Southwest and Rocky Mountain states. From that decade onward it suffered from sharp competition with newer forms of transportation. Considerable retrenchment began to take place after 1930, and many branches ceased operations in that decade. Railroads continued to be important, but after World War I they no longer led the way west or anywhere else. The story of Coburg, Montana, typifies what happened in the 1920s to country towns that the railroads had called into existence, only to be snuffed out later by weather and economics. Coburg began life as a railroad siding on the Great Northern line in the late 1880s. By World War I, 50 families lived there in an apparently successful settlement. Life was not plush; a dry summer in 1918 turned into a brutal winter for both cattle herds and for homesteaders huddled in tarpaper shacks. Still homesteaders kept arriving, and banks kept extending credit well into 1921. Then came a sharp national recession. Credit dried up; land auctions proliferated. By the late 1920s all that remained of Coburg were the train depot, the hotel, a storage building, and an isolated shack or two. Everything else had been burned, torn down, or hauled away. The railroad pulled out in the 1930s, and by that year Coburg was no more. Where once there was a farmstead on every 320 acres, there was not a sign of human habitation in 200 square miles (Nugent 1999, 183–84).

At the turn of the century, when there were still plenty of people in the West who had never seen a railway train, an automobile was unloaded at the Southern Pacific depot in Tucson. Dr. Hiram W. Fenner, who had ordered it, fiddled with the contraption until it got up steam, and finally drove gingerly through the tremendous crowd in the first automobile to enter the territory. The remarkable record of the West in catering to sportsmen, nature lovers, and sightseers was achieved by taking advantage of automobile transportation. As early as 1905 a few courageous men in each state owned automobiles, but at that time they were able to travel only on a few local roads of dirt and gravel radiating from the larger towns.

The first cross-country car trips occurred in the next decade, but they were not for those with shallow pockets. Auto travel required plenty of time and money and a vehicle more substantial than the Model T Ford, the utilitarian car that had introduced the middle class to the wondrous world of the automobile. A frequent traveler to the West in the earliest era of automobile travel recalled, "The tourists of 1913 to California were prosperous Eastern types, the mainstays of the big hotels—bank directors, corporation presidents, young bloods without hats and in white flannels talking golf, polo and motor cars, elderly ladies of comfortable embonpoint with lorgnettes and lapdogs" (Nugent 1999, 179). Many of these early adventurers kept accounts of their journeys, which were sometimes published and then read by thousands of Americans who, at the time, could only dream of such an adventure.

Alice Huyler Ramsey, for example, started out in 1909 with three women friends in a Maxwell automobile from New York. Forty-one days later they arrived in San Francisco. They crossed the Mississippi River on a bridge of "wooden planks and just wide enough for passing." The Iowa mud almost defeated them, and after 13 days of

An advertisement for the Southern Pacific Railway showing a new streamlined train, the interior of a dining car, and maps of four routes of the Southern Pacific, 1937. Library of Congress.

slogging they put the Maxwell on a freight car for the last hundred miles to Omaha. As they crossed Nebraska their nemesis was sand. Not a road was paved, and the "highway was a mere trail into Cheyenne as it crossed ranches and hills." Ranchers, not expecting much auto traffic, had fenced in the range with gates that "we had to open and close as we passed through. After a harrowing climb over the Sierras' cliffs and switchbacks, on a road heavy with sand [and] in truth not an automobile highway [but] an old wagon trail," they reached the ultimate West, the Golden Gate (Nugent 1999, 179).

As the cars became more numerous, the counties and states improved some of the roads; and in 1916 the federal government inaugurated a program of matching funds for the development of an interstate system of improved and numbered highways. Annually more and more of the state roads were incorporated into that system. In 1919 Beatrice Larned Massey drove 4,154 miles in 33 days from New York to San Francisco via Chicago, Yellowstone Park, Salt Lake City, and Reno, together with her engineer husband and another couple in a Packard twin-six touring car. The Masseys carried all manner of cables, towlines, spark plugs, tire pumps, wrenches, and other auto first aid equipment. They also took along their tennis rackets and golf clubs, but no camping equipment, because they intended to stay in good hotels. Conditions had improved since Ramsey's trip. Utah had some real cement roads, and California, "the beautiful land of sunshine and flowers had miles of good roads smooth as marble with no dust" (Nugent 1999, 180).

With the close of World War I, motorists clamored for better highways, and the road-building programs in the western states as well as the rest of America began in earnest. The exclusivity of the automobile excursion westward waned rapidly in the 1920s when the newly developed national highway system made cross-country trips almost commonplace. By 1929, the national highway network and mass-marketed cars, as well as intercity buses and trucks, had in little more than a decade transformed auto travel to the West from an upper-class preserve to a fairly common experience. In the 1930s travel books such as Ramsey's and Massey's changed into guidebooks, from accounts to be read for vicarious pleasure by the fireside to lists of tips for soon-to-be travelers. Car travel was available to the masses by the 1930s, permitting many thousands to drive west to California on U.S. 66 to escape the farm depression closing in on the Midwest.

In January 1910, 11 planes, 3 dirigible airships, and several free balloons were exhibited at Los Angeles at the first international meeting of fliers on American soil. The following month three of these aviators came to the Southwest on a barnstorming tour. The "Men-Birds," as they were called, made their first flights in Arizona at Phoenix, and thousands of awe-stricken spectators crowded into the capital city to see them. Tucson, not to be outdone, also arranged for a Man-Bird exhibition by Charles K. Hamilton, one of the three performing in Phoenix. Tickets were sold for the spectacle, and to prevent gate-crashing, aviator Hamilton was required to take off and land in a very small field surrounded by a high board fence. In his flimsy and awkward ship, Hamilton accomplished this feat, which modern airmen would pronounce absolutely suicidal, three times; and the newspapers reported that "despite a stirring breeze he attained the terrific speed of 40 miles per hour."

In 1911, Robert G. Fowler broke the world's sustained flight record by flying from Yuma to Maricopa without stopping—165 miles in 206 minutes—and Cal P. Rogers, trying to top the transcontinental flight record, reached Tucson 27 days after he left New York. Both of these flyers had difficulty in landing at Tucson, and as the word was passed among aviators, the airships that visited other southwestern towns passed right over the Old Pueblo. But Tucson was air-minded enough to establish the first municipal airfield in the United States—one of such dimensions that Tucsonians could say in triumph, "If that isn't big enough for them to land, we'll rent the county."

Regularly scheduled passenger and express plane service into Arizona was begun late in November 1927, when the Aero Corporation of California inaugurated a triweekly line between Los Angeles, Phoenix, and Tucson. The schedule became a daily one about a year later. Planes also stopped at Winslow and at Boulder Dam (Works Progress Administration 1940, 115; Perrigo 1971, 347).

THE SOUTHWEST AND ROCKY
MOUNTAIN WEST
|
OVERVIEW
DOMESTIC LIFE
ECONOMIC LIFE
INTELLECTUAL LIFE
MATERIAL LIFE
POLITICAL LIFE
RECREATIONAL LIFE
RELIGIOUS LIFE

Political Life

GOVERNMENT

Progressive politics emerged on the national scene dramatically and swiftly in 1901 when an assassin's bullet felled President William McKinley and thrust Theodore Roosevelt into the White House. America's western frontier past fascinated the new president, and he feared that the closing frontier might endanger the nation's democratic heritage. As president he believed himself to be in a position to protect what he viewed as the country's frontier legacy by conserving America's natural resources and preserving the remnants of a vanishing wilderness landscape where one could recover the "vigorous manhood" that the "rough riders" of an earlier day had enjoyed as a birthright. Gifford Pinchot, head of the forest service, shared Roosevelt's vision, and with the president's support he crafted conservation policies in the West that would directly affect the daily lives of western Americans who hoped to turn the vast resources of their region into immediate financial profit.

The most striking proof of Pinchot's influence came in 1905, when Roosevelt transferred 63 million acres of forest reserves, the great majority of them in the West, from the Interior Department to the Agriculture Department and placed them under Pinchot's control as the head of the renamed U.S. Forest Service. More than any other agency, the Forest Service epitomized Progressive-era conservation. Pinchot and his followers committed themselves to promoting professional management, believing that only those with scientific expertise should decide how best to use forest resources. They feared that a hunger for quick profits might tempt corporations and private landowners to cut the forest more rapidly than it could replenish itself. Politicians might be wooed too easily by local constituencies eager for rapid development, no matter what its cost. Only a scientific forester—so the argument ran—could know enough and be disinterested enough to look after the long-term interests of people and forests alike.

To produce this new style of government manager, Pinchot relied on the new schools of forestry, all more or less inspired by German traditions, that were appearing at Cornell, Michigan, and Yale (the latter financed by a gift from Pinchot's father). Young men—and they were all young men in the early years—who hoped to become foresters received their training from these schools and then made their way into the Forest Service to be inculcated with the values it represented. Energized by an elite esprit de corps and a vision of disinterested public service, the young foresters fanned out across the western landscape with a goal of managing public forests so that frontier abundance could be saved from scarcity and could last forever.

Like other Progressives, Pinchot, Roosevelt, and their followers strongly believed what the historian Samuel P. Hays has called "the gospel of efficiency." For Progressives the greatest villain was the waste of resources that prevented "the people" from enjoying their fullest use. Pinchot liked to borrow and extend Jeremy Bentham's famous utilitarian principle as the central goal of conservation: "the greatest good for the greatest number for the longest time." To waste resources, to use them inefficiently, was to steal from future generations. The correctness of this principle seemed so self-evident that it was hard for conservationists to see their opponents as anything other than venal and corrupt. The Progressives believed that short-sighted landowners, dishonest bureaucrats, domineering monopolists, and craven office-holders all had bad motives for putting their own interests above the public good.

There was, inevitably, a darker side to this vision of scientific management. Despite their democratic rhetoric, their apparent defense of the people and democracy against monopoly and corruption, the Progressive conservationists were suspicious of many democratic institutions. They tended to look more toward executive authority than toward the legislature to enact their reforms, and they saw the good of the whole (by which they often meant well-to-do middle-class easterners like themselves) as being more important than the special concerns of individual constituencies. Progressives preferred expert knowledge to the messier judgments of public debate. They generally preferred centralized authority and decision making to local control. Pinchot's Forest Service was notable for the decentralized organization of its district system but ultimately derived its authority from Washington rather than from local communities. In pursuit of what they saw as democratic ends, the Progressives sometimes thought it necessary to circumvent democratic means.

And so it was perhaps inevitable that Roosevelt and Pinchot should come into conflict with people who did not share

President Theodore Roosevelt, left, and Gifford Pinchot stand on the deck of the steamer *Mississippi* during a tour of the Inland Waterways Commission, 1907. Library of Congress.

their vision. Among those who opposed the expanding system of national forests were senators and representatives from the western states and local citizens, who saw more and more of their local landscape being removed from development and placed under Forest Service control. The conflict came to a head in a famous confrontation in 1907. Congress sought to limit Roosevelt's ability to withdraw western land from settlement by passing an appropriations bill that required the president to have congressional permission before creating any new national forests in Colorado, Idaho, Montana, Oregon, Washington, and Wyoming. The list included the most heavily timbered states in the nation and the ones most hostile to Washington's control. All were in the West. Roosevelt had no choice but to sign the bill, but the night before doing so, he ordered the creation of new national forests on 16 million acres of western lands. These "midnight forests" enraged western congressmen and perfectly expressed the mingled idealism and arrogance that typified conservation during the Roosevelt years. The conflict between western property holders and developers on one side and conservationists on the other continued on throughout the twentieth century.

Many westerners railed against government interference in land management, but they wholeheartedly supported federally funded reclamation projects such as the Newlands Act, which created the Bureau of Reclamation. Although numerous water diversion projects existed throughout the West before massive federal involvement, Progressive engineers were the first to promise water as a consistent resource. Beginning with the construction of the Roosevelt Dam in Arizona in 1911, the federal government throughout the century has played a major role in western land policies, which continue to affect the daily life of those living there. From the time of its initial proposal, the Progressive concept of using federal dollars to guarantee water for agrarian users was viewed as a blessing by westerners. Although many in the region opposed government regulation of timber and mining industries, they welcomed government programs that brought new sources of water, without which daily life in many areas of the West would have been impossible.

Aside from their conflict over land management, the West responded enthusiastically to Progressivism, particularly to the call for regulation of the railroad and other corporations and to increased participatory democracy. As historian Arthur Link has pointed out, "The most distinctive feature of western progressivism was its passion for more democratic anti institutional political reforms. . . . they were more common than anywhere else in the nation." In the West the first wave of reform often came at the municipal level, where local civic leaders would lead a campaign to eradicate a corrupt machine government in league with utilities and other corporations doing business with the city, replacing the ousted powers with a reform mayor. This is what occurred in Denver, for example, where the reform coalition included the wealthy activist Josephine Roche and two men who went on to national prominence, George Creel and Judge Ben Lindsey. Of all western cities, however, it was Galveston, Texas, that made the greatest contribution to urban Progressivism. In reaction to the local government's incompetence in the face of a terrible hurricane and tidal wave that ravaged the city in 1900, killing at least 6,000 people, Galveston instituted a businesslike city commission form of government that soon became a model for cities throughout the country.

On the national level the West stood in the vanguard of Progressivism. In 1904, Republican Theodore Roosevelt carried every western state except Texas, and in the 1912 race the progressive Democrat Woodrow Wilson took every state in the Southwest and Rocky Mountain West except Utah. The region also produced a number of Progressive leaders on the national stage. Among them were Hiram Johnson of California, George Norris of Nebraska, William Borah of Idaho, and Francis Newlands of Nevada. In addition to conservation, already discussed, the West figured largely in two other major facets of national Progressivism: women's suffrage and Prohibition.

Before 1917, the only states that had granted suffrage to women were in the West, and the region also pioneered in females holding public office. Mary Howard of Kansas, Utah, became the first female mayor in the country, and Jeannette Rankin of Montana the first congresswoman. Miriam "Ma" Ferguson of Texas and Nellie Taylor Ross of Wyoming became the first women governors in 1925. Although Ferguson was a stand-in for her husband, Ross won the office outright on her own.

Sociologist Edward Ross voiced conventional wisdom when he explained, "In the intermountain states, where there are two suitors for every woman, the sex becomes an upper caste to which nothing will be denied from street car seat to public ballots and public offices." Scarcity was indeed a factor, but not the only one. Frontier egalitarianism and individualism affected women as well as men. Promoters often featured the vote to lure women and families westward; and established groups like the Mormons saw women as a counterbalance to the new wave of foreign immigrants, which tended to be heavily male. Thus for a variety of reasons, some commendable and others less so, the West truly pioneered in basic political rights for women in the United States.

In the minds of many, women's suffrage went hand in hand with the Prohibition movement. As historian Norman Clark has written, "In those states where women could vote on such issues before 1919 (Wyoming, Colorado, Utah, Idaho, Washington, California, Kansas, Oregon, Arizona, Montana, Nevada, and New York) all but two (California and New York) adopted by popular vote a state law prohibiting the saloon." In fact women's organizations did attack the saloon, and various brewers' associations opposed women's suffrage. However, it is also true that some suffragists, such as westerner Abigail Scott Duniway, viewed Prohibition as a quixotic diversion and a danger to the suffrage campaign.

Nevertheless, the West (along with the South) forced national Prohibition on the wet cities of the Midwest and Northeast. First by local option, then by state vote, one state after another in the first decades of the twentieth century went dry, often with considerable turmoil. Among the earliest was Kansas, where Carrie Nation first captured national headlines in 1900 by entering a Wichita saloon wielding an iron rod and throwing rocks at a painting of Cleopatra at the bath (Milner, O'Connor, and Sandweiss 1994, 506–9).

Within the restrictions of the local, state, and federal government, the Pueblo Indians of the Southwest maintained their own governmental forms. Typical of the

Pueblo government structure in the early twentieth century was the Moiety Organization of the Tewa Pueblos. As with other Pueblos of the era, the governmental, familial, and religious structures were interrelated. The members of each pueblo were divided equally between the Winter and the Summer people. Moiety affiliation had to be confirmed by initiation. Each Moiety conducted an initiation rite every four years, the Winter group in the fall and the Summer group in the spring.

At this time both male and female children who were from 6 to 10 years old were admitted. The nucleus of the Moiety was the Moiety Association. This association was envisioned as a human being. The head was the chief or head priest; the arms were his right- and left-arm assistants, and the body incorporated the members of the association. When the head priest died, he was replaced by his right arm; the left arm moved to the right-arm position, and a new left arm was chosen by the association.

Moiety associations were responsible for all the primary religious and governmental functions of the Pueblo, which included maintenance of the annual solar and lunar calendar, organization of communal dances, coordination of purification rites conducted by the medical associations, coordination of communal hunts, coordination of warfare ceremonies, organization of planting and harvesting activities, supervision of cleaning and construction of irrigation ditches, repair and construction of pueblo courtyards for tribal ceremonies, appointment of officers to compel members of the community to participate in all government and religious functions, and installation of officers of the civil government needed to interact with outside government officials. From what can be understood about the Pueblo, it appeared that their governmental system remained the most democratic and egalitarian of government systems within a country that prided itself on the same (Dozier 1960, 152–53).

LAW, CRIME, AND PUNISHMENT

The twentieth century claimed to have a number of "crimes of the century." One of the earliest occurred on December 30, 1905, in Idaho when a homemade bomb rigged to a latch exploded as former governor Frank Steunenberg opened the gate to the front lawn of his home in the small town of Caldwell. The bombing captured the nation's attention because it involved issues that had captured the attention of many Americans in the late nineteenth and early twentieth centuries. Starting with the Haymarket bomb in 1886 and lasting through the Wall Street bombing and rash of letter bombs in 1920, Americans had been confronted for the first time with the terrorism of random killing by anarchists. In 1906, when Steunenberg became the first American assassinated by dynamite, his murder and the ensuing kidnapping of three officers of the World Federation of Miners (WFM) became a cloak-and-dagger saga of intrigue that Americans followed daily in their local papers.

A drifter, Henry Orchard, who possessed vague ties to the WFM, committed the crime. The bombing came after years of a protracted union struggle in which Steunenberg, while he was governor, had supported the mine owners. Orchard was easily fingered for the crime, because he had carelessly left crumbs of dynamite sprinkled around his hotel room and burglar tools in his trunk. After his arrest he was placed in solitary confinement and fed little for several weeks. Eventually he was invited to a sumptuous dinner including cigars and brandy with the chief investigator, James McParland. At the dinner he was explicitly encouraged to link union leaders Bill Haywood, Charles Moyer, and George Pettibonne to the crime. In return he was transferred to a private but comfortable bungalow on the prison grounds, where he resided until his death in 1954.

With Orchard's accusations in hand, McParland set out for Colorado where the union officers resided. He found Haywood in a brothel and arrested him without a warrant. He also found Moyer and Pettibone and hustled them onto a specially prepared train, back to Idaho. Making no stops for fear of being served with a writ of habeas corpus, McParland arrived in Boise, where he deposited Haywood in the death row cell previously occupied by Orchard.

While Haywood and the others waited in prison for their trial, their arrest became a *cause celebre* among radicals and socialists worldwide, including Jack London, who contributed to their defense fund and gave fiery speeches across the nation denouncing their kidnapping. Clarence Darrow came to the defense of Haywood and his associates. Initially Darrow went directly to the Supreme Court and argued that the men should be released because they were denied the right to habeas corpus and in fact had been kidnapped out of the state of Colorado. The Supreme Court agreed that the method of capturing Haywood and the others was extralegal but because they were at the present time in Idaho, they could in fact be tried. What ensued was one of the greatest show trials in western history, in which Darrow was able to win the acquittal of Haywood and his associates. The trial attracted national attention because of the terror of the original act, the dramatics in the courtroom, and the sinister actions of the government. Fear of terrorism stirred many who thought that if such a thing could happen in Caldwell, Idaho, it could probably happen anywhere, but there were others, especially those who sent their dollars to the defense fund, who worried to what degree a frightened people would allow the government to trample on their rights (Clymer 2003, 137–42).

Recreational Life

SPORTS

In addition to the sports fare typical of the United States in the first decades of the twentieth century, the Southwest had sports they could call particularly their own. With the great majority of visitors and permanent residents alike, the favorite outdoor pastime was horseback riding, which was a year-round activity in southern Arizona. Cow ponies were generally used, although almost any other kind of mount suited to the experience and desires of the individual could be obtained in the larger communities. Mule and burro pack trips, with or without the services of a guide, were especially popular in the mountain and desert sections. And a bit of amateur prospecting for gold or silver commonly added to the interest of such trips.

Guests at dude ranches often accompanied the cowhands on spring and fall round-ups and exhibited their skill in horsemanship at the amateur rodeos staged by many of these ranches. Also in the Southwest, the amateur or professional rodeo with its bronco busting, calf roping, and steer bulldogging was a prominent sporting event in nearly every community or resort.

In the 1920s and 1930s, the universities and teachers colleges of Arizona, Texas, and New Mexico were represented in the Border Conference Intercollegiate Athletic Association, The major sports sponsored by this organization were football, basketball, and track events, along with baseball, boxing, tennis, and golf.

High school teams of the Southwest competed in events sponsored by state interscholastic athletic associations. Football, basketball, and track events constituted the major conference sports. Although most competition was intrastate, some high school football teams competed with schools from other states within the Southwest region, and in the 1930s the annual Greenway Track and Field Meet in Arizona offered classified competition to local athletes from elementary schools, secondary schools, and colleges, as well as athletes from neighboring states (Works Progress Administration 1940, 131–34).

Another sport that became popular, especially in the Rocky Mountain West, was snow skiing. In this region the sport dates from the mid-1930s when the Union Pacific Railroad opened its posh Sun Valley, Idaho, resort complex, the West's first major ski facility. World War II temporarily blocked expansion, but Sun Valley's development stimulated the beginning of other ski resorts throughout the region, particularly in Colorado.

Religious Life

RELIGION AND SPIRITUALITY

In the Southwest well into the twentieth century, the Spanish Catholic roots of the region still influenced the religious culture. In Arizona, for example, according to the federal religious census of 1926, of the 153,086 Arizonans who were church members, 96,471, or 63 percent, were Roman Catholic. Spanish- and English-speaking Mexican immigrants, together with Indians, constituted the majority in this denomination.

Protestant churches were slow to develop in the Southwest. For example, there was no Protestant church in Tucson until 1878, when a Presbyterian mission was built there and used by all non-Catholic denominations. In 1881, various other denominations began building churches of their own. The Methodists with 10,571 members, the Presbyterians with 6,163 members, and the Baptists with 8,040 members became the principal Protestant denominations in the early twentieth century.

Religious beliefs and practices among the Indians were extremely complex. The Hopi responded least of all to the white man's religion and retained their ancient dances, including the curious ceremony in which live rattlesnakes are held in the dancers' mouths. While the Yuma were willing to accept some of the tenets and ceremonial forms of Christianity, many remained faithful to at least some of the most important of their old rituals. Each Easter in the Yaqui village near Tucson, and in the village of Guadalupe not far from Phoenix, the Yaqui Indians stage their Passion Play. The Papago, who were among the first to accept Christianity, perform their ancient rites each March at San Xavier. The *Chill-ko*, or harvest ceremony, and various bird songs give thanks to the gods and ask for further beneficence. The sacred songs are handed down from one generation to another (Works Progress Administration 1940, 120–22).

Terrace Homes of Hopi Indians at Oraibi on the Hopi Reservation in Arizona, c. 1903. Library of Congress.

The Spanish character of Catholicism in the Southwest also sets it apart from the Catholicism of the rest of the United States, where in the pre–World War II era the Irish dominated both the administration and the traditions of the Church. Most distinctive of the Mexican Spanish influence in the Southwest, especially in the more remote Spanish American villages, was membership in *Los Hermanos Penitentes*— a curious cult that had existed since the time of the Spanish missionaries and continued well into the twentieth century.

The group was banned in the Mexican period but that ban, along with the annoying curiosity of rude newcomers, caused the order to go "underground." The fraternal rites, including the procession during Holy Week with its carrying of the cross and moderate flagellation, were performed thenceforth in strict secrecy, and members were forbidden to write or relate to outsiders anything about their rules and ceremonies. Under those circumstances the maintenance of standardized rules became impossible. Because each chapter handed down its own procedures by oral transmission, many variations appeared in local practices. Some chapters even degenerated into mere political clubs that were maintained by their leaders for promotion of solidarity in their competition with Anglo-American rivals for election to local offices (Perrigo 1971, 395).

The turn-of-the-century Pentecostal movement had tangled roots in both the West and the South and in two interrelated beliefs. One belief emphasized "Christian perfection" or "entire sanctification," a second grace that cleansed the believer from the tendency to sin. The second belief derived from events in the book of Acts and

The most effective publicist of the Pentecostal movement was Aimee Semple McPherson. Library of Congress.

emphasized "speaking in tongues" or glossolalia. Although historians of Pentecostalism have uncovered scattered references to glossolalia during the nineteenth century, they agree that the 1906 Azusa Street (Los Angeles) revival began modern Pentecostalism. Led in part by William J. Seymour, a one-eyed black minister from the South, the rise of Pentecostalism is a little-known black contribution to white religious life. In the early days, most Pentecostal churches were integrated, but by the 1920s they had separated into primarily white or black congregations.

From Azusa Street, the Pentecostal "full Gospel" revival spread up and down the West Coast and into the rural areas of Oklahoma, Texas, and Missouri. There the Pentecostals also created yet another religio-social subculture. Their world emphasized spiritual healing, religious ecstasy, glossolalia, and general renewal. The faith demanded a strict personal morality (no cards, jewelry, cosmetics, or bodily ornamentation, and minimal amusements). Their musical imagery, which would later influence early rock and roll (for example, the song "Great Balls of Fire") called for a high degree of participation and emotional release. For many, the profession of the ministry proved a popular road to success. The democracy of the message was obvious. As one minister stated, "We did not honor men for their advantage, in means or education, but rather for their God-given gifts" (Milner, O'Connor, and Sandweiss 1994, 381). In this sense, the Pentecostals reached out to the religious needs of the common people. Not surprisingly, they manifested great strength in old populist or socialist areas of the West.

The most effective publicist of the Pentecostal movement was Aimee Semple McPherson. Reared in a Salvation Army family, McPherson arrived in Los Angeles in 1918 to establish the Four Square Gospel Church, revealed to her in a vision. A strikingly beautiful woman, she utilized the Hollywood atmosphere to turn her worship services into media productions. "Sister Aimee" also established a religious radio station (KFSG, Kall Four Square Gospel) to spread her message. From the mid-1920s to the mid-1930s, she appeared on the front page of the *Los Angeles Times* approximately three times a week. Beneath the hype and extravagance, McPherson emerged as America's first "superstar" media evangelist. She provided a national platform for the Pentecostal message, one that it would not regain until the 1970s and 1980s. By that time, the charismatic dimension of Pentecostalism had spread into Roman Catholicism, the Episcopal Church, and a number of Native American communities as well as among many televangelists.

A revival of religious conservatism occurred in the decades between the two World Wars. The rapid growth of the Ku Klux Klan, which claimed a tenuous link with right-wing Protestantism, provided the most extreme example of this religio-social backlash. Another form of repression came in the attacks on Native American faiths. During the 1920s, the fundamentalist–modernist controversy split the main-line Protestant churches into two warring camps. All of these national movements affected the West.

The Klan proved exceptionally strong in several western states, especially Colorado, Texas, and Oregon. Its anti-immigrant and anti-Catholic message drove some Catholics out of Oregon and Colorado and soured Protestant–Catholic relations in El Paso for a decade. In Oregon, militant nativists introduced legislation in 1922 that would have required all children to attend public school, ostensibly for reasons of "Americanism." The real goal was to destroy the Catholic parochial school system. Catholic resistance found ready allies from the Lutherans, Seventh-Day Adventists, and the American Jewish community as well as several liberal Episcopal and Presbyterian clergymen. In 1925, the law was overturned by the Supreme Court.

Religious suppression also found its way into the long-festering question of the First Amendment and Indian religious liberties. Through the 1920s and 1930s, Indian religious freedom was a major issue for Native Americans. In the 1920s, the debate pitted Commissioner of Indian Affairs Charles H. Burke against the reformer John Collier. In 1921, Burke issued a circular that reinforced the directive of 1883, prohibiting ceremonial dances and "celebrations" that included actions deemed improper and even harmful. As the historian Francis Paul Prucha has pointed out, this attack infuriated Collier and inspired his "campaign in support of religious liberty for Indians." The ensuing national debate climaxed in 1926 when Collier and his followers defeated a congressional bill that would have legalized Burke's position.

But the fight was not over. In the 1930s, when President Franklin Delano Roosevelt appointed Collier as commissioner of the Bureau of Indian Affairs (BIA), Collier viewed Indian religious freedom as a cornerstone of his blueprint on Indian policy. Like Burke, he issued a directive. The 1934 circular entitled "Indian Religious Freedom and Indian Culture" declared that Indians be granted "the fullest constitutional liberty, in all matters affecting religion, conscience, and culture," and that "no interference with Indian religious life or ceremonial expression will hereafter be tolerated." Reversing the centuries-old approach, Collier declared, "The cultural liberty of Indians is in all respects to be considered equal to that of any non-Indian group." At BIA schools, Collier prohibited compulsory attendance at religious services and permitted students to return home for ceremonies. Christian reformers and Christianized Indians saw Collier's circular as a step backward. Some tribes opposed the concept of religious freedom as a matter of principle: it would violate tribal sovereignty by interfering in internal tribal affairs. If the majority of a tribe, such as the Lakotas, opposed the Native American Church, for example, the tribe did not want Washington ordering it to legalize peyote. The issue of religious freedom for Indians was not resolved in the 1930s, but Collier's stand did begin to bring Indian religions under the constitutional guarantees granted to other citizens.

The fundamentalist–modernist controversy, which so disrupted the nation's Protestant churches, also had a strong western component. Two transplanted Pennsylvanians, Lyman and Milton Stewart, used the profits from their Los Angeles–based Union Oil Company to support a series of conservative evangelical causes from the 1890s forward. During the Progressive era, Lyman Stewart began to attack theologi-

The Masked Kachinas (Hopi Indian "Rain-makers") dance at the Village of Shonghopavi, Arizona. Library of Congress.

cal liberals, especially Presbyterian Thomas F. Day, who was eventually dismissed from the San Francisco Theological Seminary in 1912 for teaching higher criticism, which questioned fundamentalist views. In 1907, Stewart helped found what would become the Bible Institute of Los Angeles. He also financed the publication of William E. Blackstone's millennial tract *Jesus Is Coming,* which became the most widespread premillennial piece of literature in the world. Finally, Stewart funded the publication of *The Fundamentals* (1912–1916), a series of conservative pamphlets that are usually acknowledged as the opening shots in the fundamentalist–modernist controversy. The Stewart brothers helped inaugurate what became the most disruptive twentieth-century controversy among American Protestants. Over the years, the nation's Protestant churches began to divide along theological lines (liberal–conservative) rather than denominational ones. The sociologists Robert Wuthnow and James Davison Hunter have argued that this ever-widening liberal–conservative split lies at the heart of the post–World War II "restructuring of American religion" (Milner, O'Connor, and Sandweiss 1994, 381–84).

RITUALS AND RITES OF PASSAGE

Although converted to Christianity by Spanish missionaries, the Pueblo Indians adapted themselves to Catholic ritual only externally. Behind that convenient screen they continued to practice their own indigenous patterns of culture, including adherence to many of their ancient religious rituals. For example, the Hopi Rain Dance, in which members of one of the religious societies dance with live rattlesnakes, was held every August. Like other Pueblo ceremonies, outsiders could view the rain dance, because the Indians felt that anyone who watched with sympathy and respect was also a participant who contributed to the efficacy of the rite.

The strong attachment to such established rituals, together with the maintenance of personal responsibility to the group, the security afforded by the close-knit relationships and society of the Pueblo, and the continued observance of personal and group conduct designed to ensure harmony between the people and the supernatural world continued to protect the towns from the disintegrating influences of the surrounding non-Indian culture well into the twentieth century (Josephy 1969, 163–64).

WORLDVIEW

When the American novelist James A. Michener died in 1997, he left his papers and a large endowment to the University of Northern Colorado in Greeley. Sixty years before, the young Michener had received an offer to teach there. Anxious for a job in those Depression years, yet equally anxious about leaving his boyhood home in Pennsylvania, Michener had gone to one of his former professors at Swarthmore College for advice. "You'd be making the biggest mistake in your life," the man told him. "The sands of the desert are white with the bones of promising young men who moved west and perished trying to fight their way back East." Without prospects, however, Michener reluctantly decided he had no choice but to accept the position.

Much to his surprise, Michener fell in love with the West. "Almost all that I saw I liked," he later recalled. He was awed by the landscape—majestic buttes rising abruptly from the plains, mountain valleys crowded with blue spruce and aspen—and astounded by the irrigation systems that turned deserts into thousands of acres of melons and sugar beets. But what struck him most forcefully were the people. "For the first time I caught the fire and fury that characterizes life in the West," he wrote. "A new type of man was being reared in the West. He was taller, ate more salads, had fewer intellectual interests of a speculative nature, had a rough and ready acceptance of new ideas, and was blessed with a vitality that stood out conspicuously to a stranger from the East." Over a long career as one of the most successful American writers of the twentieth century, Michener traveled to many exotic places, but he always treasured his western sojourn. "One of the good things about my life was that I spent the formative years in Colorado and got away from an insular Eastern-seaboard perspective," he reflected in 1980. "Having had that experience, and having renewed it constantly, I built or acquired an optimism which I've never really lost." Michener spoke for many when he evoked the mythic and real power of the West (Hine and Faragher 2000, 512).

FOR MORE INFORMATION

Books

Bakken, Gordon Morris, and Brenda Farrington, eds. *Encyclopedia of Women in the American West*. London: Sage Publications, 2003.

Black, Brian. *Nature and the Environment in Twentieth-Century American Life*. Westport, CT: Greenwood Press, 2006.

Clymer, Jeffory A. *America's Culture of Terrorism: Violence, Capitalism, and the Written Word*. Chapel Hill: University of North Carolina Press, 2003.

Hine, Robert V., and John Mack Faragher. *The American West: A New Interpretive History.* New Haven, CT: Yale University Press, 2000.

Josephy, Alvin M. *The Indian Heritage of America.* New York: Alfred A. Knopf, 1969.

La Farge, Oliver. *A Pictorial History of the American Indian.* New York: Crown Publishers, 1956.

Lindenmeyer, Kristine. *The Greatest Generation Grows Up.* Chicago: Ivan R. Dee, 2005.

Milner, Clyde, Carol A. O'Connor, and Martha A. Sandweiss. *The Oxford History of the American West.* New York: Oxford University Press, 1994.

Nugent, Walter. *Into the West: The Story of Its People.* New York: Alfred A. Knopf, 1999.

Perrigo, Lynn. *The American Southwest: Its Peoples and Cultures.* Albuquerque: University of New Mexico Press, 1971.

White, Richard. *A New History of the American West.* Norman: University of Oklahoma Press, 1991.

Works Progress Administration, ed. *Arizona, A State Guide.* New York: Hastings House, 1940.

Articles

Burma, John H. "Present Status of the Spanish-Americans in New Mexico." *Social Forces* 28, no. 2 (December 1949): 138.

Dozier, Edward. "The Pueblos of Southwestern United States." *Journal of the Royal Anthropological Institute of Great Britain and Ireland* 90 (1960): 146–60.

Web Sites

"Dallas Fort Worth Radio History." http://www.knus99.com/amlist.html.

Legends of America. http//: www.legendsofamerica.com.

7

THE PACIFIC WEST

Overview

At the turn of the century, the Pacific West still remained the great frontier of America. The largest city in the region was San Francisco; Los Angeles still remained a small town with great dreams. Over the next 40 years all this would change, as the population boomed, bringing with it large buildings, bridges and roads, and massive public works projects to provide water for farms and cities. Yet much about the West would remain the same. Frontier families still lived in the Pacific Northwest without the conveniences that the rest of Americans were beginning to take for granted. The West was home to the first great national parks, which were set aside to preserve what was natural, grand, and expansive about America's self-image.

The great convergence of many varied people in such a concentrated period of time produced social, economic, and cultural clashes. These showed in various ways, but most obtrusively in the violent labor conflicts in the agricultural areas of California, as well as the mining areas of Nevada, and the lumbering regions of the Pacific Northwest. Tensions worked themselves out more subtly in politics and in education.

The free and open spirit of the frontier West provided a fertile environment for scientific investigation and educational expansion. California became home to some of the country's greatest universities and centers for the study of science and engineering, fields especially useful to the vast region needing new infrastructure, water projects, agricultural techniques, and ways to extract the mother lodes of minerals from the ground. California also became a social laboratory, where strands of Progressivism and then many of the political experiments of the 1920s and 1930s redefined public life and policy.

Because it represented novelty and excitement, the West, especially California, captured the attention of the rest of the country, and by the 1930s, with innovations in science, technology, architecture, lifestyle, and of course its film industry, the West for many Americans became the trend-setting region of the country. Improved roads in the new century and improved communication in film, radio, and print meant people could imagine being and going there. Americans also moved further west and northwest into the territories of Hawaii and Alaska in this era, where they found well-rooted indigenous cultures far different from their own. They also found new opportunities for wealth in the minerals of Alaska and the rich soil and inviting climate of Hawaii. Although Americans had been settling in the Pacific West since the early nineteenth century, the majority of Americans settling in this area had come more recently, and they considered themselves the last of the American pioneers. This section will explore the lives of those who lived in the last American frontier of the Pacific West, which in this chapter includes California, Nevada, Oregon, Washington, and the territories of Alaska and Hawaii.

Domestic Life

THE PACIFIC WEST

|

OVERVIEW

DOMESTIC LIFE

ECONOMIC LIFE

INTELLECTUAL LIFE

MATERIAL LIFE

POLITICAL LIFE

RECREATIONAL LIFE

RELIGIOUS LIFE

FAMILY LIFE

Easterners and westerners from the United States as well as easterners and westerners of the world come together in the Pacific West. Most families living in this region in the first half of the twentieth century had family and ancestors in the Midwest, in the East, and some in Asia. In the nineteenth century family patterns in the West had been distinctive; however, with the increasing flow of population to the West in the first decades of the twentieth century, the daily life of the Western family began to appear more and more like that of the East and Midwest. By the 1940s, patterns of family life originating in New England, the old South, and the Midwest had mingled with the pioneer traditions of the far West. During much of its history, the West had been little more than a series of colonial outposts, economically and psychologically exploited by the East, but with the development of metropolitan centers like San Francisco, Los Angeles, Portland, Seattle, and Denver, the West ceased to be a colonial appendage of the East, and these urban aggregations tended to exhibit the same concentric pattern of family types as in eastern cities.

Despite the characteristic urbanization of the first decades of the twentieth-century, much of the West remained rural, and as one moved away from urban centers and out into the hinterland, one could find pioneer ruggedness and self-sufficiency seldom found in the older regions of the country. For example, during the Great Depression the Jim Burns household, consisting of his wife, two sons, a housekeeper, and a family cow, survived on $200 a year on Waldron Island in Seattle's hinterland. They ate seagull eggs, fish, clams, wild nettle greens, homegrown whole wheat, and free fruit from a friendly neighbor's trees.

One distinctive characteristic of western families in the first decades of the twentieth century was their mobility and their diversity. From the Imperial Valley of southern California north through the San Joaquin and Sacramento valleys the cotton, citrus fruits, and other crops demanded seasonal laborers. A simple agrarian folk from the Middle West and Southwest, displaced by drought and the mechanization of agriculture in the 1930s, flowed west to meet this need. The fictitious Joad family, immortalized by John Steinbeck in his novel *The Grapes of Wrath*, dramatized the problems of these itinerants as they "starved" their way to California in a dilapidated truck. Says Ma Joad in a closing comment: "We ain't gonna die out. People is goin' on—changin' a little maybe but goin' right on!"

Prior to 1882, the Chinese, and later Japanese and Filipinos, moved to the American West in large numbers into the early twentieth century, and well-rooted traditional family relationships played an important role in the integration of those from Asia and the Asian Pacific into western society. Statistical studies in the 1940s showed crime among Asians varied inversely with the degree to which they were incorporated in closely integrated family and community groups. Sociologists of the era explained the low crime rate among Japanese in the first decades of the twentieth century by the clear definitions and moral discipline of the transplanted patriarchal family and by the efficiency and organization of their community. Higher crime rates among Chinese and Filipinos in these same decades were explained by the relative lack of family life, a weak community organization, and disorganizing contact with Americans.

Among the Native Americans of the Pacific Northwest, the changes in family life from the days of their great-grandparents to the generation of the early to mid-1900s were tremendous. The contrast between the relatively self-sufficient homesteads of the white pioneer in the region and the urban apartment house life of some of his grandchildren was great, to be sure, but not nearly so great as the difference between the wood plank houses of the nineteenth-century Indian and the modern bungalows of some of his descendants. In the first half of the twentieth century most Native Americans of the West remained true to their traditional cultural and family values; however, some drifted toward the Anglo-American culture. The degree to which they became disorganized in large part was determined by the intensity and character of contacts with white civilization, on the one hand, and by the source and adequacy of sustenance, on the other.

At the turn of the century, four-fifths of the adult population of Utah and one-fifth of that of Idaho was Mormon. This fact created a distinct family life in that part of the region. Desert isolation and church sanction made it possible for the early "saints" to develop a polygamous form of family life. But non-Mormon hostility, together with the monogamous backgrounds of husbands and wives, which made adjustment to a multiple-mate situation difficult, had almost eliminated the plural marriage by the early 1940s.

In the first decades of the twentieth century and up to World War II, progress on one hand and disorganization on the other characterized family life in the Pacific Coast states. The average income per family equaled the wealthiest regions of the country. The circulation of daily newspapers was higher and the number of passenger cars in proportion to population was greater than in any other geographic division. Infant and maternal mortality rates were lower, and more playgrounds were available for urban populations of the Pacific and Mountain states than for other regions. Most of the national parks were in the West, and relatively more families visited them from near points than from far. Western families spent more for recreation than eastern families of comparable income.

In contrast to these statistics, which reveal a relative degree of material comfort, at least for middle-class families living in the West, divorce rates increased as one moved west and southwest across the United States. The estimated divorce rate in the far West per 1,000 population, in 1940, was double that for the remainder of the United States. One in every 40 American divorces was secured in Reno. However, it must be remembered that in the 1920s Nevada became a migratory divorce destination when that state passed a law that permitted anyone who had resided in the state six months to divorce spouses easily. Sociologists also blamed family instability for crime rates in the region. The number of robberies and auto thefts known to the police per 100,000 population was almost twice as high as for any other region. Pacific Coast cities also led America in suicides.

Perhaps these statistics were related to the fact that in the first half of the twentieth century, families in the West were the least religiously affiliated in the United States. The highest percentage of adults not in church was found in the Mountain and Pacific states—about 70 percent for the Far West as compared with 50 percent for the United States as a whole.

In conclusion, it could be said that the western family of the pre–World War II twentieth century was more distinctly American in its characteristics than was the family of any other region. Since most families had come to the Far West from the Middle West, East, or South, often in several stages, there was more opportunity to lose European traits and acquire American ways of living. Unassimilated foreign groups could be found during this era in the West to be sure—small groups of patriotic Asians, for example—but not to the same extent as east of the Rockies. Americans in the 1920s and 1930s became notorious, as compared with the citizens of other countries, for their individualism, mobility, and frequent divorces. Americans also loved their homes, had small families, and believed in education, recreation, and hospitality. All these points became magnified in the far West.

Home ownership in this era was as high on the Pacific Coast as for any region in the country. The average size of a family household in the far West was smaller, the percentage who had completed four years of college was greater, people were considered more hospitable, especially in the hinterlands, and families spent more for recreation than in other sections. Sociologists in the pre–World War II twentieth-century America speculated that the principal problem for the average American family was how to combine compatibility and comfort with stability. Western families, with their demonstration of material success on one hand, and the spiritual crises of divorce and crime on the other, seemed to have demonstrated that they shared in that American family dilemma (Hayner 1948, 432–34).

In Hawaii, the family system was the essential element of the social structure of the islands. The main configuration was an extended family, the *ohana*. Some members of the *ohana* lived in the highland rain forest, others in the mid-level farmlands, and others on the coast. Families shared the bounty of each region. Regardless of their specific living area, *ohanas* spent the majority of their time on the coast, where families lived together in large houses (Barnes 2007, 20).

MEN

In the first decades of the twentieth century, the West remained a "man's world." In many parts of the region local custom seemed to have resisted the domestication of males that had occurred during the Victorian age in the Midwest, Northeast, and Mid-Atlantic sections of the country. Refined demeanor was not necessarily a virtue, and informality was commonplace. A Montana tourist house, for example, bore a sign that read "throw your hat on the floor and make yourself at home." In a region where a man had to prove his worth through his own abilities, personal worth carried far more value than personal connections. Class lines were less sharp, and male camaraderie was more prevalent. "A man makes friends without half trying," was the boast of many small western towns.

The popular male Hollywood film images of the 1930s and 1940s were built on this idealized western male image. Sam Spade of San Francisco—the fictional detective popularized by Humphrey Bogart—was a loner, an independent man with his own convictions and a self-created sense of honor; Gary Cooper's grave voice and homespun morality made him the most beloved male star of the decade; and Clark Gable became famous "just being myself" on the screen. It was a world that made virtues of self-prescribed morality, loyalty, ruggedness, and individualism.

Many men in the early part of the century had moved west because of the greater occupational opportunities. This was well illustrated in the western lumbering industry, which, around the turn of the century, attracted workers from the depleted forest regions of Wisconsin and Michigan. Lumbering, certainly one of the trades that displayed the masculine characteristics of the West, remained the principal economic activity of the Pacific Northwest through the early decades of the twentieth century. Until the 1930s, these loggers seldom married, but by that time, with the changes in technology that made logging operations more accessible, the peripatetic bachelors of the earlier days were largely replaced by married men. By the late 1930s, the typical logger of the Pacific Northwest was no longer an uncivilized, unwashed individual. He became, more often than not, a family man.

In the urban areas of the West, male habits of work, play, and style were similar to those of other regions. Ironically, the nationally more homogenous fashions and lifestyles of males as well as females were being determined, not in the older, more established regions of the country, but rather in the new West of Hollywood, California, where the new film industry played a major role in influencing male and female lifestyles.

WOMEN

In the first decades of the twentieth century in the hinterlands of the West, one could still find hardworking pioneer women hazarding crude kitchen and household equipment in the wilderness, which included hungry and ferocious cougars. Many of the women of the rural West mirrored the robust women portrayed by Betty Mac-

Donald in her novel *The Egg and I*. Days were long, work was hard, and housekeeping and cooking were done without the benefit of electricity or indoor plumbing.

In the more isolated coastal regions of the West such as the Olympic peninsulas, fishermen of the region spent many months at a time away from home. Consequently their women gradually took over control of the family.

In metropolitan areas of the West such as San Francisco, Los Angeles, Portland, and Seattle women's daily life became increasingly like that of the Midwest and East, and by the late 1930s western women were receiving commendation from eastern fashion leaders for stylish dressing, and Hollywood also was setting the national trends for fashion and style.

CHILDREN

Through the 1930s in the West, home delivery remained the most common birthing experience, especially for families with limited economic resources or those living outside cities. Most believed that having a baby at home could be perfectly safe with the help of an experienced midwife, nurse, or physician and a situation free of complications. Although by the 1930s a growing number of Americans understood that healthy babies and mothers needed at least the help of a trained nurse or doctor at the time of delivery, in the West, especially outside the cities, access to good care remained difficult. Mildred Kine safely had her first child at home in Boulder City, Nevada, in January 1933. Kine was part of the wave of more than 5,000 workers and their families who had moved to the area when the federal government began construction on what eventually became Hoover Dam. "I had a nurse come in and help," Kine recalled. "It was either that or go to Las Vegas, because the hospital up here was only for workmen and they didn't want to have maternity cases up there." Lillian Whalen, another Boulder resident, remembered that a local doctor also supervised many births in the town. Many local deliveries occurred, she recalled, "on the screen porches of the little houses, with the fans drifting around . . . evidently it was a healthy thing," she concluded, " because [the doctor] never lost a mother or a baby" (Lindenmeyer 2005, 34, 35).

During the industrial era, the middle classes invented childhood as a distinct phase when children should be protected from the cares of a competitive world. They believed children should play and romp freely, not only for their pleasure, but for their full emotional and physical development. Working-class children, however, were often compelled to work to help support their families. The difference between malnutrition and eating enough, for many families, was bridged through a child's wages. Karen Sanchez-Eppler comments on the industrial era, "Thus to the extent that childhood means leisure, having a childhood is in itself one of the most decisive features of class formation. The working child was, in many ways, deprived of the primary activity defining childhood—play."

In the West, as elsewhere, employment for children—and adult attitudes toward child labor—ranged widely during the industrial era. Many children worked in traditional settings, on family farms alongside their parents. Farm work was often regarded as wholesome and character-building. Juvenile delinquents and orphaned or abandoned children, in fact, were frequently sent to the countryside as workers on family farms. Many children, however, experienced farm work far differently than those who extolled it imagined. In the West, some worked long hours as itinerant laborers, picking sugar beets or dragging heavy bags of cotton. Stooping for 12-hour days under a hot sun could result in heat exhaustion or back injuries. Carrying bags or boxes of produce to weighing stations, children were expected to lift enormous loads for their sizes. A report from the Children's Bureau revealed that 70 per-

> ### 📷 Snapshot
>
> **A Woman's Life in the Pacific West Frontier**
>
> This I'll go where you go, do what you do, be what you are, and I'll be happy philosophy worked out splendidly for Mother for she followed my mining engineer father all over the United States and led a fascinating life, but not so well for me, because although I did what she told me and let Bob choose the work in which he felt he would be happiest and then plunged wholeheartedly in with him, I wound up on the Pacific Coast in the most untamed corner of the United States, with a ten gallon keg of good whiskey, some very dirty Indians and hundreds and hundreds of most uninteresting chickens. . . .
>
> "Now," I thought, " we have all the livestock warm and comfortable, surely it is at last time to fix the house."
>
> That's what I thought. It was time to plow and plant the garden. I had read that the rigors of a combination of farm and mountain life were supposed eventually to harden you to a state of fitness. By the end of those first two months, I still ached like a tooth and the only ting that had hardened on the ranch was Bob's heart.
>
> Right after breakfast one May morning he drove into the yard astride a horse large enough to have been sired by an elephant. Carelessly looping the reins over a gatepost he informed me that I was to steer this monster while he ran along behind holding the plow. All went reasonably well until Birdie, the horse, stepped on my foot. "She's on my foot," I said mildly to Bob who was complaining because we stopped. "Get her off and let's get going, " shouted the man who had promised to cherish me. Meanwhile my erstwhile foot was being driven like a stake into the soft earth and Birdie stared moodily over the landscape. I beat on the back of her knee, I screamed at her, I screamed at Bob and at last Birdie absentmindedly took a step and lifted the foot. I hobbled to the house and soaked my foot and brooded about men and animals. (MacDonald 1945, 4, 44)

cent of children working in Colorado's beet fields were physically deformed "apparently due to strain" (Lindenmeyer 2005, 38).

In the cities, street peddlers—the children who sold newspapers, matchbooks, and gum, or who scavenged for junk—comprised another class of child laborers who were often viewed romantically. These "street merchants" seemed, by some accounts, to turn work into play, roaming the streets with a familiarity and élan many adults admired. They frequented bars, gambling houses, and theaters. They gave some of their earnings to their parents but often kept some for candy and other treats.

In California, half of all teenage boys and one-fourth of teenage girls held part-time jobs. Overcrowded working-class homes in the city provided little to no space for children to play. Consequently, children flocked to the streets, some to become the "little merchants" hawking newspapers or collecting junk ("junking"), and some to play improvised games. With no other place to go, these children appropriated the streets as their own, but police officers saw such public space quite differently.

Indicative of the life of Mexican Americans and of working-class children was the story of César Chávez. Chávez, born on March 31, 1927, in Yuma, Arizona, a Mexican American community where Spanish was more common than English, typified the life of working-class children in the West. During his early childhood, Chávez's parents worked on his grandfather's ranch and in the family's small store in Yuma. The Depression eventually crushed the family's businesses, and by the early 1930s

📷 *Snapshot*

Jack London: San Francisco Newsboy

By the time I was ten years old, my family had abandoned ranching and gone to live in the city. And here, at ten, I began on the streets as a newsboy. One of the reasons for this was that we needed the money. Another reason was that I needed the exercise.

And so, at ten, I was out on the streets, a newsboy. I had no time to read. I was busy getting exercise and learning how to fight, busy learning forwardness, and brass and bluff. I had an imagination and a curiosity about all things that made me plastic. Not least among the things I was curious about was the saloon. And I was in and out of many a one. (London 1913, 23)

the Chávez family headed to California in hopes of finding work. Like most migrant farm families, everyone, even young Chávez, was expected to work in the fields. State child labor laws did not forbid the employment of entire families in agricultural piecework, even including young children like César. Lobbying by the owners of large farms and outdated cultural assumptions about children's farm labor being restricted to family chores contributed to the absence of child labor regulations in agriculture. His family's constant moves and young César's responsibilities in contributing to the family's income greatly hindered his education. By the time he entered the eighth grade, he had attended 30 different schools. At 14 he spoke little English and quit school altogether before entering high school.

A study of sugar beet workers by the U.S. Children's Bureau in 1935 showed that there were many young migrant farm workers like César Chávez in the United States. The 946 families interviewed for the study included 670 children between the ages of 6 and 16 who reported that they had worked for wages in the beet fields sometime during the past year. Among the youngest workers, 280 were under age 14 and only two-thirds had enrolled for any schooling in 1935. Workdays could be as long as 12 hours, and pay was low. Families earned a median income of only $340 for the entire year. Government officials judged that poor living conditions resulted in an "inadequate diet, insufficient clothing, poor housing, and [a] lack of needed medical service" for all workers. Some of the families in the study were of Mexican or Spanish American heritage. Families identified as "Russian-Germans" comprised the second most frequent ethnic group at 22 percent. Profits drove landowners to hire entire families, "due in part," investigators concluded, "to the fact that men with families are considered more reliable and more likely to see work through to completion than solo workers." Officials estimated that more than 15,000 children worked in the sugar beet fields each year.

Working the beet fields involved two infamous tools despised by migrants and especially dangerous for children: the short-handled hoe and the machete. The short hoe had a 12- to 18-inch handle; the machete was kept very sharp. Workers used the hoe to remove weeds from between young beet plants. The tool's short handle forced workers to stoop

Jack London, c. 1910. Library of Congress.

over. Employers believed this stance made it less likely workers would damage the beet plants, but the tool caused aching backs, and the stooped posture could cause permanent spinal deformities in children. The machete's razor-sharp, semi-curved blade was used to pick up beets off the ground and cut off their green tops. Many beet workers, both children and adults, lost fingers to the sharp machete (Lindenmeyer 2005, 56–57).

The Depression years were difficult for children of working-class families like the Chávez family. For most children, cutting back, making do, and doubling up became common phrases that characterized their lives during the country's worst economic crisis. Most American households were touched in some way by the Great Depression's hard times. Yet not every young person's family suffered economic loss during the 1930s. For example, the affluent family of Henry Barr, who was born in 1928, seemed far removed from the nation's economic slide. Henry's father held degrees from a prestigious college and law school. In the early 1920s, the elder Barr headed the San Francisco branch of a New York law firm. He left that position in 1926 to start his own business. Henry's mother had attended an elite women's college before marrying. At the time of Henry's birth the Barrs also had a four-year-old son and a two-year-old daughter. During the 1930s the family lived in what an interviewer from the University of California at Berkeley's "Oakland Growth Study" described as "a large, vine-covered, masonry house set on a terraced lot, with substantial lawn and garden." Full-time

César Chávez, 1966. Library of Congress.

nannies tended to Henry and his siblings, and the children attended schools with youngsters from similar family circumstances. Once Henry reached the upper-level elementary grades, he spent his summers at camp and enjoyed a variety of recreational activities. He received a "moderate" allowance from his parents, and from the age of 12 earned money at part-time jobs such as "gardening for neighbors, working as a stock boy, selling mistletoe at Christmas." Henry did not need the money; the jobs were supposed to instill a strong "work ethic" in the growing boy. From an early age, Henry felt he was "destined for the law," and his pathway to social and economic success as an adult was not hampered by the fact that he grew up during the worst economic crisis in U.S. history.

Henry Barr's childhood was very different from the lives of children of most Americans growing up during the Great Depression. Still, even children and adolescents like Barr, whose parents were able to shelter them from the major deprivations of hard times, witnessed the shifts in popular culture and public policy influenced by the Depression. Children and adolescents living in families that Franklin Roosevelt identified as "ill-housed, ill-clothed, and ill-fed" became the focus of New Deal efforts to ease the Depression's worst effects. Many children and adolescents growing up in families that lost income during the 1930s took part in their parents' efforts to maintain a "brave social front . . . to present to its neighbors." Some historians have speculated that such issues may not have been as important to children from families that were already poor or members of the working class before the onset of the Depression. But it appears that during the 1930s many children, especially adolescents and youth at the lower rungs of American society, were unhappy about their families' circumstances and the inequities highlighted by the decade's economic challenges. Shifts in public policy and popular culture probably contributed to this trend.

The economic problems of the 1930s shook many stable families and completely toppled the most fragile ones. The same study that included Henry Barr also uncovered stories of other children in Oakland who lived in families directly affected by hard times. The mothers of children and adolescents in the study attributed "problems with offspring, kin, friends, and community roles to lack of money and its side effects." Many other families throughout the United States would have shared this circumstance. Seventy-seven percent of American households had incomes of less than $2,000 per year (the equivalent of $30,000 in 2000). Between 1929 and 1933, the national average household income fell from $2,300 to $1,500. New Deal programs aimed at providing work relief pumped millions of federal dollars into the nation's infrastructure. Combined federal and state relief efforts kept the poorest American families from starving and also helped improve the lives of many children and adults who were not direct recipients of federal relief. But as late as 1940, 35 million American homes still had no running water, 32 percent continued to rely on outdoor privies, 39 percent did not have a bathtub or shower, and 27 percent contained no refrigeration device. From the perspective of a glass half full rather than half empty, these numbers also show that by the end of the Depression decade most children did have access to at least the basic amenities associated with growing up in modern America. The years after Franklin Roosevelt's election in 1932 brought a new attitude to Washington that included the implementation of programs that helped ease the Depression's worst effects for many children and their families. That shift was part of a new definition of modern American childhood that became embedded in law and public policy (Lindenmeyer 2005, 12–14).

Despite the infinite variations in individual circumstances, the 1930s generation shared some common features. For one, the median age in the United States had risen gradually, from 23 in 1900 to 26 in 1930, and then climbed sharply to 29 during the Depression decade. Adults simply chose to have fewer babies during hard economic times. This allowed them to focus their available family resources and energies on fewer children, thereby underscoring reformers' efforts to establish childhood and adolescence as a sheltered and protected stage of life for all American children. Life expectancy continued to rise, also contributing to the higher median age. During the Depression, children under 19 years of age formed a smaller portion of the total population than any generation to that date in U.S. history. As in the past, society depended on families to care for the economic security, psychological development, safety, and health of children. But the onset of the Depression challenged the long-held belief that families could accomplish those tasks without help from the government. This shift occurred at the same time a growing number of Americans embraced a model of ideal American childhood as a period best spent in school and protected from adult responsibilities through age 17. By 1940, public policy and popular culture recognized this ideal as the sole model for modern American childhood.

As adolescents in the West as elsewhere remained in school longer than ever before, their leisure activities became progressively distinct from those of children and adults. An important expression of their independent style and taste was music. Swing music particularly appealed to teens and youth partly because it was their own. In 1934, the 25-year-old Benny Goodman and his band introduced this new sound to a national radio audience on the New York–based show *Let's Dance*. Unfortunately for the East Coast teenagers, the Goodman band did not perform until the last hour of the 9:00 P.M. to 1:00 A.M. show. But on the West Coast teenagers heard Goodman's band in prime time. In 1935, the Benny Goodman band went on a road tour across the United States. Most people who came to the shows during the early days of the tour offered only lukewarm reception to the unfamiliar musical style. The story was different when the band reached the Los Angeles Palomar Ballroom on August 25, 1935. There Goodman and his fellow musicians received an enthusiastic welcome from young fans very familiar with the band's Saturday night broadcasts (Lindenmeyer 2005, 192–93).

Generational disagreements over musical tastes and standards of acceptable behavior preceded the 1930s. But the growing age segregation and proliferation of popular culture in the 1930s added to tensions within families. A woman from California wrote the U.S. Children's Bureau asking for parenting advice. "We are elderly parents (50 and 65)," she explained. Her daughters, age 13 and 16, were popular and had many friends. "However," the mother lamented, "we feel ignorant of how best to control their good times. We want to allow them all the liberty we can—but it is quite plain that youngsters are 'different'—the boys do not seem gentlemanly—the girls have little reserve of manner—if any. Perhaps living in the age of bathing suits has a lot to do with it." The Children's Bureau's Ella Oppenheimer sympathized and replied, "You are not alone in your difficulty in knowing how best to handle your girls. I wonder if your girls belong to the Girl Scouts? The influence of this organization during adolescence, especially, is salutary" (Lindenmeyer 2005, 194).

Group activities dominated the free time of most adolescents. Having fun with a group lowered social pressure between the sexes and was generally more inexpensive than dating. Dating could present problems for boys who had little money to spend on entertainment. Social practice dictated that males pay the evening's expenses while on a date. "Going Dutch" meant that girls would pay their own way during an evening of coed socializing. The practice was not unique to the 1930s, but it became increasingly popular among adolescents during hard times. It also took some of the pressure off a girl to provide sexual favors in exchange for a boy paying for entertainment or food.

"Going steady" was another popular dating practice. The announcement that a boy and girl were going steady meant that the two had agreed to an exclusive relationship but were not serious enough to proceed with formal engagement and marriage. A girl who went steady could enjoy consistent male companionship and still maintain a respectable reputation. She needed to avoid kissing and necking in pub-

Snapshot

A Southern Black Family Moves West, 1906

Paul Bontemps had left Alexandria armed with a railroad ticket that would allow him to go as far West as the railroad would carry him. But it was unthinkable that he should go through Los Angeles without at least stopping long enough to say hello to his relatives and friends who had migrated there from Louisiana. Furthermore, a layover in the City of the Angels provided a much-needed chance to rest and bathe and eat home cooking.

He soon decided that Los Angeles would be the place where he would rear his children. Wages for bricklayers were considerably higher in California than they had been in Louisiana. Los Angeles afforded an ample number of good nursery schools and kindergartens to choose from, and the public and private schools were nonsegregated. The city also provided excellent playgrounds and library facilities. So Paul decided to select a house in the Watts section of the city, an area where friends and relatives from Central Louisiana were already residing. Watts was a pleasant, integrated residential community with neat houses and lawns. When Paul Bontemps compared the muddy streets and Jim Crow customs of Alexandria with this bright new California neighborhood, Watts must have seemed like a heaven on earth. He found just the house for the family, one he was sure Maria would like.

"This was one of the happiest times of my mother's entire life," recalled Arna Bontemps. At last she was free of the fear she had carried in her heart since becoming a wife and mother in Louisiana, a dread that one day her husband or one of her younger brothers would be killed or maimed. Maria Bontemps did not consider returning to teaching after the family moved to California, for her daughter was still quite young. Before her marriage Maria had taught in the public schools. She was a polished young woman. Soft-spoken and somewhat retiring, Maria Bontemps divided her time between her family and her etchings. She was also an accomplished dressmaker. Before long, she had more customers than she could accommodate.

Paul Bontemps and his wife Maria worked hard to put the South as far behind them as they could. Paul Bontemps was not especially proud of his African heritage, nor of the French culture that was his, a fact that set him apart from his son and that would be a lasting source of disagreement between them. Actually, his feelings about life in Louisiana remained ambivalent, for while he considered the vestiges of his background to be a disadvantage in his new home, he always remembered Louisiana with nostalgia, asserting, from time to time, that if it had not been for the "conditions" he would never have left Alexandria. He even harbored a secret desire to go back and give Alexandria another try. But the thought of his children's future was a sobering one; it always made him glad he had left the South when he did. (Jones 1992, 29–34)

lic, but doing so in private with her steady beau was less perilous to a girl's reputation than dating several boys at the same time. During the 1930s adolescent boys and girls spent a lot of time together outside the watchful eyes of adults. Going steady was one way teens devised to self-regulate the new freedoms surrounding dating and social activities (Lindenmeyer 2005, 195–98).

A woman who grew up in Oakland, California, in the 1930s married her high school boyfriend. Several years later the woman told researchers that she and her boyfriend had used his car to neck when he brought her home at the end of a date. The girl's mother would flick the porch light on and off to signal that it was time for the girl to come in. If she did not respond right away, the girl's mother "would come out and yell and stamp her foot." The couple had a strong physical attraction for each other but waited until they married to have intercourse. But some teens did "go all the way." About one-fourth of female teens in a California study acknowledged that they had sex in high school, or at least before marriage (Lindenmeyer 2005, 14–15).

Janice Rice remembered that she "only went to high school because I had to. . . . I didn't like it, wasn't happy there at all." She felt rejected by her peers and began hanging out in dance halls where she met older men and felt "popular." Asked whether she engaged in sexual intercourse, Rice replied as follows:

Most of the time I'd go all the way, and I got in trouble. Then my mother bought me a diaphragm and made me wear it—even if I went to the movies with a girl friend, because "you never can tell." That's what I'd do with a daughter, get her a diaphragm. . . . Once you've gone all the way, it's hard to stop. . . . I didn't want to stop. . . . If they don't get it from you, they will from someone else, and you don't want that to happen. (Lindenmeyer 2005, 197)

Janice Rice had an illegal abortion while still in high school and married for the first time at age 19. Between then and age 38 she married and divorced five times. Janice was a rebellious teen and continued to resist mainstream conventions throughout her life. She was an extreme example of teen sexual experience in the 1930s, but the increase in unsupervised social activities did foster opportunities for sexual activity among adolescents. Since most did not have good access to information about birth control, it is likely that the traditional condemnation of birth outside of marriage discouraged many young couples from engaging in intercourse. In the West as elsewhere, although changing social mores in the first half of the twentieth century dictated that children be treated as children for a longer period of time, they seemed to be growing up faster than ever before (Lindenmeyer 2005, 197).

PETS

In the United States, large-scale breeding of canaries and other small caged birds for wholesaling developed during the first two decades of the twentieth century. By the 1920s, the warm climate of California proved hospitable for raising large numbers of exotics such as parakeets and zebra finches, which were once exclusively imported from Europe. In addition to raising their own exotics, western dealers also began to import birds from neighboring countries to the south. An Omaha, Nebraska, business that shipped birds anywhere in the United States offered for sale "Mexican Mockingbirds, Mexican Cardinals and Brazilian Gray Cardinals" (Grier 2006, 247).

Economic Life

Opportunities abounded in the Pacific West from the turn of the century onward. Whether it was lumbering, mining, or the grand new public works projects in damming great rivers or building infrastructure for growing cities, a person could find work in this area of the country. As the new century opened, the Pacific West also began to rival the great fisheries of the Northeast, as motorized boats made the negotiation of the rough north Pacific a greater possibility and opened up large areas of previously unfished waters. Even during the Depression years many western workers, specifically those outside of agriculture, suffered far less than their counterparts in the rest of the country.

In the rush for prosperity, racial differences did not evoke the same level of hatred that they did in other sections of the country, at least on the surface. And blacks who migrated from the South found far greater opportunities in the West with far less prejudice than they experienced in other sections of the country. World War II brought a surge of blacks westward to work in the aircraft and defense industries, and with the influx racial tensions rose. It might be said that blacks experienced less discrimination because there were more people to share discrimination with. The West was also home to thousands of Japanese, Chinese, and Mexicans, all of whom felt some of the prejudice of white Anglos, elsewhere reserved for blacks.

In addition to racial differences, there was probably no other region that experienced such pronounced differences between urban and rural life as did the West. The greatest contrasts might be found between an apartment dwelling family in the newly burgeoning city of Los Angeles and the frontier family of the Pacific Northwest. The latter until as late as 1940 still did without indoor plumbing, electricity, and the conveniences that accompanied that technology.

WORK AND WORKPLACE

At the turn of the century it was easy to make a living in the booming economy of the Pacific West. From the railroad building and gold in Alaska to the lumbering industry in the Pacific Northwest to the booming cities of California, opportunities for work were abundant. Los Angeles led the way; the construction of the Los Angeles aqueduct kept thousands employed between 1907 and 1913. To Los Angeles came the produce and products of agriculture, and packing, shipping, canning, and food processing continued to offer seasonal and regular employment. So too did transportation and shipping via two railroads, two large streetcar companies, and the fourth busiest port in the nation. With home building constant across three decades, there was an expanding job sector in the building trades. The oil industry was producing 106 million barrels a year by 1920, a quarter of a million barrels of it coming from Signal Hill south of Los Angeles. More tires were manufactured in greater Los Angeles than in any place other than Akron, Ohio, and more automobiles were being assembled than in any city other than Detroit.

In California, the hotel and tourist industry gained even further strength, along with two new economic sectors, aviation and motion pictures. An ambitious fishing industry grew up among the Portuguese in San Diego and the Japanese in San Pedro. Consciously designing itself as the Gibraltar of the Pacific, the city of San Diego wooed and secured the large and permanent presence of the U.S. Navy and the Marine Corps, and the Port of Long Beach became an important naval installation. The earlier western products such as beef, wheat, and gold continued to flow into and through California ports, but by the 1920s they were augmented by, and in some instances surpassed by, some newer ones—automobile accessories, cotton fabrics, furniture, machinery, motion pictures, tuna fish, canned and frozen vegetables, wine, and then in the 1930s and especially the 1940s, airplanes and their accessories—all produced, made, or processed in the West (Starr 2005, 182–83).

Among the new industries, that of motion picture making was unique. Film production had originated in the East, but after the production of California's first commercial film, *The Count of Monte Cristo*, in 1908, the advantages of the southwestern climate and scenery, and the lack of unions, attracted the other principal producers to Hollywood in the years from 1910 to 1912. They brought with them the actors and actresses who were to become the idols of that generation. Soon *The Birth of a Nation* (1915), produced by D. W. Griffith, was grossing millions of dollars, and the era of lavish expenditures and the creation of "stars" had dawned. In the 1920s, however, the industry provoked public criticism as a result of the scandalous conduct of some of the actors and the excessive appeal to sensuality by some of the competing producers. To forestall censorship by a government agency, the producers voluntarily employed Will H. Hays as their "czar" for the fixing of standards and the policing of the industry. This step restored at least the veneer of respectability and responsibility to the industry and revived public confidence. Soon afterward, in 1927, a remarkable technical improvement made possible the synchronization of sound with the picture, and the popular reception accorded Al Jolson in the first "talkie," *The Jazz Singer* (1927), inaugurated a new era in filmmaking. By 1930 it had climbed to a position among the top 10 industries in terms of value of product in the nation (Starr 2005, 276–78).

In California another industry that experienced phenomenal growth was electric power production. Because the power conducted on high-tension lines from distant hydroelectric plants was inadequate to meet the demands of the booming industries, gas from the oil fields was piped in for use as fuel in large steam-power plants. In the early 1920s, those plants became absorbed into three major companies, the Great Western Power Company, the San Joaquin Light and Power Company, and the Pacific Gas and Electric Company. Later in that decade the three merged into a new company that took the title of the latter, which became popularly shortened to the PG&E. By 1940 California ranked third among the states in the production of electric power, and 13 years later its output of 26 billion kilowatt hours from both privately and publicly owned facilities was second only to that of New York.

The location of flight centers in California contributed to a westward migration of the aviation industry, so that as early as 1935 the production in California plants was valued at almost $20 million. Even greater expansion came on the eve of World War II, when the government spent $150 million on aviation in California, and private investors accounted for an additional $80 million. Numerous colleges and universities, dominated by a rapidly expanding University of Southern California and the newly established University of California at Los Angeles, also sustained large payrolls and promoted study and research in science and technology useful to the region's growth and development.

Nowhere in the West was the economic boom of the first decades of the new century more evident than in the ambitious construction projects. Megadevelopers not only built large housing tracts throughout Los Angeles but also grand public structures such as the 900-room Ambassador Hotel (1919) on Wilshire Boulevard, with its wildly popular Coconut Grove nightclub; the Coliseum and Rose Bowl stadiums (1921); the Biltmore Hotel (1923) at Fifth and Olive facing Pershing Square in the downtown sector, designed in opulent Italian and Spanish Revival motifs; the Central Library of Los Angeles (1926); the California Club (1929); and the new and expanding university campuses.

By 1929 Southern California's rapid emergence as a fully materialized American space resembled a motion picture studio set. Indeed, a scene in the film *Intolerance* (1916) shot between Sunset and Hollywood Boulevards might very well stand as a paradigm for the interconnection of the nascent film industry and the rising region. Intended to depict the city of Babylon at the height of its power, the 300-foot-high set functioned, like the expositions recently concluded in San Francisco and San Diego, as a dream city of past and future (Starr 2005, 176–77, 183).

The demand for labor in this rapidly growing region created a workforce that in some industries became more militant in demanding fair pay and benefits from their employers than their counterparts to the east. Some of the most radical and most violent worker demonstrations and strikes of the twentieth century took place in the West. Workers in this region wielded more political power than workers in other regions. The West was also the center of the anarchist International Workers of the World (IWW or Wobblies) strength. One example of this power was the General Strike of 1901, which led to the formation of the Union Labor Party in San Francisco. This Union became so powerful that they were able to elect two mayors from their ranks: orchestra leader Eugene "Handsome Gene" Schmitz, president of the Musicians' Union, and Patrick Henry "Pin Head" McCarthy, president of the Building Trades Council. Schmitz was removed from office in 1907 for corruption, a conviction that was later overturned on appeal. McCarthy, who followed Schmitz in office did a more-than-creditable job as mayor until he left office in 1912 to amass a fortune in the construction industry. McCarthy's successor as mayor, the flamboyant James "Sunny Jim" Rolph Jr., maintained excellent relations with the unions of San Francisco during his tenure, which lasted almost two decades.

Los Angeles unions never fared as well as their counterparts in San Francisco. One major obstacle was *Los Angeles Times* publisher Harrison Gray Otis, who was a major power in the city and a vociferous opponent of unions. On the morn-

---

📷 *Snapshot*

Oil and the Spirit of Los Angeleos

Oil and gas came to mind when William Andrew Spalding, reminiscing about the city's mood at the turn of the century, commented on the unfailing cheerfulness of Angelenos in the face of adversity. They had seen their cattle die, their banks fail and their real estate boom collapse; they had survived earthquakes, fires, floods and the Southern Pacific, and always they had "come up smiling after each throwdown" and gone on with the business of building a metropolis.

"When an oil belt was developed within the city boundaries which seemed to bring as much destruction of values as it produced—when there was no system, no order—when oil went to waste and the gas escaped—when there was no market for the product, and the price fell to ten cents a barrel—then the people addressed themselves to solving the strange problem, this embarrassment of riches.

"They constructed storage tanks, and devised means of transportation; they invented burners, and learned how to use crude oil for steam generation and brickmaking; they learned how to utilize the crude oil in road making; they acquired the art and devised the apparatus for refining; they discovered a way for saving and utilizing the gas that had been escaping from their wells; they prospected with 'wild-cat' boring until they had extended the territory miles outside the originally developed area. In short, they established one of the greatest petroleum fields in the world. With such a record of courage, persistence and achievement, it is no wonder that Los Angeles began the new century with a stout heart and a confident air." (Weaver 1973, 55–56)

ing of October 1, 1910, in reaction to Otis's staunch opposition to a metal workers strike, union members bombed the headquarters of the *Times*. Unfortunately the victims were workers like themselves. The bombing left 20 employees dead and 17 injured. An investigation led by the well-known private detective William J. Burns soon discovered three suspects—Ortie McManigal, a radical with a taste for dynamite; James McNamara; and McNamara's brother John, an official of the Bridge and Structural Iron Workers Union. Famed attorney Clarence Darrow came to the union workers' defense, but the McNamara brothers confessed and when the trial ended, McManigal and the McNamara brothers were condemned to life sentences and some 33 union members were convicted of various degrees of complicity in the crime. The negative publicity surrounding the bombing and the trial impeded the union movement in Los Angeles for the next quarter of a century.

Two years later, in 1912, the Industrial Workers of the World (IWW) spearheaded a bitter dock strike in San Diego. The IWW already had a reputation for often resorting to violence to achieve their ends and it was this capacity for violence in fact as well as in rhetoric, that gave the union a dreaded reputation. By 1909, there were IWW locals in San Francisco, Los Angeles, Redlands, and Holtville in the Imperial Valley. Now dubbed "the Wobblies" by the *Los Angeles Times*, the IWW favored free-speech confrontations and strike actions. Between April 1910 and March 1911, Wobblies flooded into Fresno, demonstrating continuously and filling the jails to capacity.

In 1912, when the Wobblies descended on San Diego, the city leaders prepared themselves for battle. Police and vigilantes pulled incoming Wobblies off trains, took them into custody, and roughed them up, forcing them to run violent gauntlets. When a crowd of roughly 5,000 gathered outside the city jail to protest the Wobblies' incarceration, high-pressure fire hoses were used to disperse them. During the demonstration at least one detainee was beaten to death. On May 4, 1912, two San Diego police officers shot and killed an IWW member in front of the union's headquarters. At the height of the tension, Emma Goldman, the anarchist, and her companion Ben Reitman, arrived in San Diego on a lecture tour. A hostile mob gathered outside the U.S. Grant Hotel where they were staying and kidnapped the radicals. They tarred and feathered Reitman and then put him on the same 2:45 A.M. night owl train on which they had forcibly boarded Goldman.

The very next year, on August 13, 1913, a deadly riot in the hop fields of Wheatland in southern Yuba County in the Sacramento Valley created yet another IWW scare. Given the seasonal nature of harvest work in California, living conditions for migrant workers were by and large appalling. Nowhere was this more true than on the Ralph Durst hop ranch outside Wheatland. In the early summer of 1913, Durst had spread circulars throughout California, southern Oregon, and northwestern Nevada advertising harvest work on his ranch. By late July, some 2,800 men, women, and children—approximately one-third of them people of color—had flooded onto the Durst ranch in search of work. Living conditions were more horrible than usual (there were as few as eight toilet sheds for the entire workforce), and wages averaged $1.50 a day, with workers expected to pay for their own food and water (temperatures frequently soared to 120 degrees) at Durst-owned concessions.

With the help of IWW activists, a strike action was organized. Ralph Durst called in the sheriff, a posse of sheriff's deputies, and the district attorney of Yuba County. When this group confronted a crowd of workers listening to IWW activist Richard "Blackie" Ford, a bench on which some workers were standing collapsed, startling the crowd. Scuffling ensued, which led to fistfights. Someone began swinging a two-by-four as a club. A deputy fired a shotgun into the air, trying, as he later said, to sober the crowd into cooperation. Instead, more gunfire broke out, some 20 shots in all, this time from within the melee. The deputies fought their way back to their automobiles and sped off. When the crowd dispersed, five prostrate forms were revealed on the ground: the sheriff, clubbed into unconsciousness but still alive, together with the dead bodies of the district attorney, a sheriff's deputy, and two unidentified workers. The IWW fled the scene, leaving the impression that they were responsible for the violence. A manhunt ensued, with the usual round of arrests and beatings. Eventually, two IWW activists, Blackie Ford and Herman Suhr, were tried, convicted, and sentenced to life in prison.

Labor tensions continued for the next six years. On July 22, 1916, a bomb went off on lower Market Street in San Francisco in the course of a Preparedness Day parade intended to support American entry into the European war. Although no one could determine who set the bomb off—historians have concluded it was probably a German agent provocateur—a radical socialist leader by the name of Tom Mooney and his associate Warren Knox Billings were arrested, charged, and put through a near-kangaroo trial in which the district attorney used fabricated evidence and perjured testimony to win convictions and death sentences. Even though their sentences were later commuted to life, the Mooney/Billings convictions remained a rallying cry for labor and the left for the next 20 years.

In reaction to the rising tide of violence among labor organizers in the state, Governor William Stephens signed the Criminal Syndicalism Act into law in April 1919. This act declared it a felony, punishable by 1 to 14 years in prison, to advocate or in any other way to promulgate violence as a means of "accomplishing a change in industrial ownership or control or effecting any political changes." Mere membership in an organization advocating such doctrines constituted a felony. Passed at the height of the nationwide anti-Red hysteria following World War I, the California Criminal Syndicalism Act was a draconian measure specifically directed against the IWW. By 1921 40 Wobblies were convicted and serving time at San Quentin under this act, which remained law until 1968, when the Ninth Circuit of the U.S. Court of Appeals declared it unconstitutional.

During the later 1920s and 1930s numerous violent confrontations between capital and labor continued. In 1927 Mexican American field workers organized the Confederacion de Uniones Obreras Mexicanas, or the Confederation of Mexican Workers, which organized farm workers in 20 locals throughout southern California. In the Imperial Valley, 2,746 Mexican workers, with the assistance of the Mexican consul general in Calexico, formed a local of the organization calling themselves the Mexican Mutual Aid Society of Imperial Valley. In May 1928, just before the start of the cantaloupe harvest, the organization submitted a list of demands for improved wages and working conditions. Growers and civic leaders united against the action.

The local sheriff arrested the union leaders and charges of a Communist conspiracy were immediately launched. The union appealed to the president of Mexico, who protested to the president of the United States, Calvin Coolidge. The president sent a state department official to the Imperial Valley to investigate. The cantaloupe growers and state officials defeated the union in 1928, but the sheer magnitude of what had been accomplished—the organization of a Mexican agricultural workers' union—was not lost on either the growers or workers of California. The confederation promised to be an organization that would have to be reckoned with in the future (Starr 2005, 203–4).

During the Great Depression, even as California and other western states drove out Mexican and Mexican American workers, California alone was flooded with more than 300,000 Americans from the Great Plains and the Southwest, the drought- and Depression-stricken Dust Bowls of Texas, Arkansas, Kansas, Missouri, and, most dramatically, Oklahoma, whence the generic pejorative epithet for all such people, "Okies," was derived. By the middle of 1934, there were 142 agricultural workers in California for every 100 jobs. Wages plummeted by more than 50 percent. In May 1928, for example, after organizing, Mexican workers in the Imperial Valley were receiving 75 cents an hour for picking cantaloupes, but in June 1933, many of them were working for as little as 15 cents an hour.

The Communists, who had been making great inroads into unions in the early 1930s, entered this struggle. The Trade Union Unity League, a national organization chaired by William Zebulon Foster, the Communist Party candidate for president in 1924 and 1928, organized the Cannery and Agricultural Workers Industrial Union (CAWIU). When 8,000 Mexican, Filipino, Chinese, Japanese, and Sikh workers—led by the Mexican Mutual Aid Society—went out on strike in the Imperial Valley in January 1930, organizers from the CAWIU hastened to their assistance. The CAWIU activists printed thousands of leaflets in English, Spanish, Chinese, Japanese, Tagalog, and Slavonian together with a Spanish-language newsletter, and spread them via automobile throughout the Imperial Valley, provoking further organization and strike action. Empowered by the Criminal Syndicalism Act, police, sheriff's deputies, American Legion vigilantes, the district attorney, and the courts launched what by now had become the almost standard counteroffensive of Red Scare roundups, arrests, harassments, indictments, and trials. Nine union leaders were convicted of criminal syndicalism. Five of them were sentenced to 3 to 42 years in Folsom or San Quentin; another defendant was given 28 years; and the judge deported three Mexican defendants. Superior court judge Von Thompson declared that all the defendants were Communists in conspiracy to destroy the economy of the Imperial Valley, and therefore anything short of a life sentence should be considered too lenient. Two of the defendants, when released on parole in early 1933, were immediately deported to the Soviet Union.

In late July and early August 1931, the CAWIU organized a strike by 2,000 cannery workers, mostly women, in the Santa Clara Valley south of San Francisco. Once again, the local sheriff went into action, rounding up the usual suspects. Once again, an assembly of strikers was assaulted by squads of police wielding blackjacks and nightsticks, and water cannons were used to disperse the crowd. In late November

1932, CAWIU organizers turned their attention to Vacaville in Solano County, with the same scenario of confrontation, Red Scare, and arrests. All in all, the CAWIU played leadership roles in 24 agricultural strikes in 1933, including pea pickers in Santa Clara and Alameda counties, a beet strike in Ventura County, peach strikes in Fresno and Merced counties, a grape strike in Merced, and a cherry and pear pickers strike in the Santa Clara Valley.

Then in autumn 1933 Californians witnessed the largest single agricultural strike in the history of the nation: a cotton pickers strike in the San Joaquin Valley with 10,000 strikers across a 500-mile front, led in part by the CAWIU. The confrontation that followed resulted in a succession of violent clashes, arrests (300 strikers in jail by early October), the cooperation of local government with the growers, and a brilliantly organized resistance. Antistriker vigilantism reached new dimensions during the cotton strike, and it was fully legitimized by local authorities. The sheriff of Kern County deputized more than 300 growers to confer legality on their efforts to break the strike. On the afternoon of Tuesday, October 10, 1933, an automobile caravan of 40 armed vigilantes drove into the small Tulare County town of Pixley as CAWIU organizer Pat Chambers stood speaking to a gathering of strikers. Leaving their automobiles, the vigilantes approached the crowd with drawn pistols and rifles. Delfino Davila, a 58-year-old part-time consular representative of Mexico in nearby Visalia, approached an armed vigilante and pushed his rifle to the ground. A nearby vigilante clubbed Davila to the ground, then shot him to death. "Let them have it, boys!" one of the vigilantes yelled as he and the others fired into the crowd. Another striker, 50-year-old Dolores Hernandez, was killed and eight others were wounded.

The Cotton Strike of 1933 ended violently. And although the results of the strike were inconclusive, it did move California in a decidedly conservative direction on the issue of labor unrest. Over the next half-decade, the ubiquitous presence of California law enforcement officers remained constant and foreboding during a myriad of new strike actions. The American Legion also became an almost permanently mobilized vigilante force. The Associated Farmers of California, Inc., became a potent force both in the suppression of local strikes and in the state legislature, where it blocked any proposed pro-striker legislation. Its magazine, *Associated Farmer,* continued to fan the Red Scare. Extensive spy networks were established. In July 1934, at the height of the dock strike in San Francisco, Sacramento police raided the CAWIU state headquarters, arresting 24. Seventeen defendants were brought to trial on six counts of criminal syndicalism. The Sacramento Conspiracy Trial, as it came to be known, represented the most powerful courtroom counterattack to date by the California right. The city of Sacramento went into a de facto condition of martial law, with a National Guard colonel placed in charge of the police and 500 businessmen sworn in as deputies. When the trial was over—the hostile judge, the intimidated jury, the denied motions by defense attorney Leo Gallagher, the rising hysteria of the community—it was perhaps a miracle that four defendants were acquitted and that two of the convicted were recommended for probation. Eight of the convicted were sentenced to 1 to 14 years in state prison, where they languished until, after long and tortuous arguments, the Third District Court of Appeal of the State of

California on September 28, 1937, reversed the verdict and ordered the remaining defendants released (Starr 2005, 204–7).

Even as the Sacramento Conspiracy Trial was being conducted, National Guardsmen were patrolling the Embarcadero waterfront of San Francisco with rifles and fixed bayonets or manning machine gun emplacements at strategic locations or sweeping through the area in tanks. This display of force was instigated by the outbreak of the largest maritime strike—up to that point—in American history. The International Longshoremen's Association (ILA) had called the strike in protest against employer domination of hiring halls through a shape-up system of spot-hiring and the issuance of a company-controlled blue book allowing an individual longshoreman to be chosen for work. The longshoremen walked out in early May 1934, joined by other locals in Seattle, Tacoma, Portland, San Pedro (Los Angeles), and San Diego. In San Francisco other unions joined the strike in support of the longshoremen including the San Francisco Teamsters Union; the boilermakers and machinists; the Sailors Union of the Pacific; the Pacific Union; the Ship Clerks Coast Marine Firemen; the Oilers, Water Tenders and Wipers Association; the Marine Cooks and Stewards Association; the International Seamen's Association; the Marine Engineers Beneficial Association; and the Masters, Mates, and Pilots Association. The Waterfront Employers Union, meanwhile, launched plans to bring in up to 2,500 strikebreakers, to be housed in two ships offshore so as to avoid the necessity of their crossing picket lines to get to the docks.

At the center of resistance and counter-resistance were two charismatic San Franciscans. Roger Dearborn Lapham became the spokesman for the owners. This 51-year-old president of the American Steamship Company was the absolute paragon of establishment values—preparatory school, Harvard, the Bohemian and Pacific Union clubs, poker, duck hunting, golf, and a sultanic appetite for the good life. Leading the strikers was Australian-born Alfred Renton "Harry" Bridges, 34, thin, sharp-featured, terse, and sardonic, a look of feral distrust in his narrowed eyes, long suspected of Communist affiliation. The fleshy Lapham wore double-breasted suits, cuff-linked white shirts, old-school ties. Bridges wore blue denim shirts, a flat white longshoreman's cap, and heavy black canvas pants with a cargo hook hanging from the back pocket. Bridges openly welcomed Communist participation in the strike, which soon erupted into violence. In preparation for the strike, San Francisco police chief William Quinn organized an antistrike task force of patrolmen, mounted policemen, and radio cars. This force clashed with 500 longshoremen near the waterfront, prompting Chief Quinn to purchase a cache of tear gas bombs. Throughout the rest of May, police and strikers clashed frequently. On July 3, 1934, 5,000 longshoremen and their sympathizers gathered on the Embarcadero to prevent the exit of trucks from Pier 38. Later that day, at approximately 1:30 in the afternoon, police and strikers clashed at Second and Townsend Streets. The police fired into the crowd, and a striker later died from a fractured skull.

Two days later, on July 5, 1934—soon to be known as "Bloody Thursday"—police and strikers spent the morning in a full-pitched battle atop Rincon Hill near the waterfront. In a classic military maneuver, mounted police advanced up the hill behind a covering barrage of rifle and pistol fire, and longshoremen defended their position on the heights with two-by-fours and bricks and, in one instance, an oversized slingshot capable of propelling missiles at a high velocity for distances up to 400 feet. That afternoon, during a lunchtime lull in the confrontation, a phalanx of police converged on the ILA headquarters on Stewart Street, where downtown San Francisco ran into the Embarcadero. Once again, tear gas and guns were fired; 2 strikers lay dead on the street, 30 others suffered gunshot wounds, and 43 others were clubbed, gassed, or hit by projectiles. At this point, Governor Frank Merriam sent in 4,600 National Guardsmen. San Francisco workers responded with a general strike on July 15, 1934, which virtually shut down the city. At this point, with government and the strikers in a condition of total confrontation, a civic group led by newspaper publishers organized a mediation, and on July 18, 1934, the Strike Strategy Committee, over the strong objections of Harry Bridges, voted 191 to 174 to end the general strike the following day and to submit the entire dispute to the National Longshoremen's Board for arbitration.

The sheer drama of the San Francisco waterfront strike, its capacity to stimulate such a panorama of open insurrection and suppression, underscored the volatility of California, battered as it was by powerful forces on both the left and the right (Starr 2005, 208–10).

The most important strike in the West and perhaps in the entire United States in that era was the one that occurred in Seattle in 1919. The war was hardly over, it was February 1919, the IWW leadership was in jail, but the IWW idea of the general strike became reality for five days in Seattle, Washington, when a walkout of 100,000 working people brought the city to a halt.

It began with 35,000 shipyard workers striking for a wage increase. They appealed for support to the Seattle Central Labor Council, which recommended a city-wide strike, and in two weeks 110 locals—mostly American Federation of Labor, with only a few IWW's—voted to strike. The rank and file of each striking local elected three members to a General Strike Committee, and on February 6, 1919, at 10:00 A.M., the strike began. Unity was not easy to achieve. The IWW locals were in tension with the American Federation of Labor (AFL) locals. Japanese locals were admitted to the General Strike Committee but were not given a vote. Still, 60,000 union members were out, and 40,000 other workers joined in sympathy.

Seattle workers had a radical tradition. During the war, the president of the Seattle AFL, a socialist, was imprisoned for opposing the draft and was tortured, and there were great labor rallies in the streets to protest. The city now stopped functioning, except for activities organized by the strikers to provide essential needs. Firemen agreed to stay on the job. Laundry workers handled only hospital laundry. Vehicles authorized to move carried signs: "Exempted by the General Strike Committee." Thirty-five neighborhood milk stations were set up. Every day 30,000 meals were prepared in large kitchens, then transported to halls all over the city and served cafeteria style, with strikers paying 25 cents a meal, the general public 35 cents. People were allowed to eat as much as they wanted of the beef stew, spaghetti, bread, and coffee.

A Labor War Veteran's Guard was organized to keep the peace. On the blackboard at one of its headquarters was written: "The purpose of this organization is to preserve law and order without the use of force. No volunteer will have any police power or be allowed to carry weapons of any sort, but to use persuasion only." During the strike, crime in the city decreased. The commander of the U.S. Army detachment sent into the area told the strikers' committee that in 40 years of military experience he hadn't seen so quiet and orderly a city. The mayor swore in 2,400 special deputies, many of them students at the University of Washington. Almost a thousand sailors and marines were brought into the city by the U.S. government. The general strike ended after five days, according to the General Strike Committee because of pressure from the international officers of the various unions, as well as the difficulties of living in a shut-down city. The strike had been peaceful. But when it was over, there were raids and arrests: on the Socialist party headquarters, on a printing plant. Thirty-nine members of the IWW were jailed as "ring-leaders of anarchy."

In Centralia, Washington, where the IWW had been organizing lumber workers, the lumber interests made plans to get rid of the IWW. On November 11, 1919, Armistice Day, the Legion paraded through town with rubber hoses and gas pipes, and the IWW prepared for an attack. When the Legion passed the IWW hall, shots were fired—it is unclear who fired first. They stormed the hall, there was more firing, and three Legion men were killed.

Inside the headquarters was an IWW member, a lumberjack named Frank Everett, who had been in France as a soldier while the IWW national leaders were on trial for obstructing the war effort. Everett was in army uniform and carrying a rifle. He emptied it into the crowd, dropped it, and ran for the woods, followed by a mob. He started to wade across the river, found the current too strong, turned, shot the leading man dead, threw his gun into the river, and fought the mob with his fists. They dragged him back to town behind an automobile, suspended him from a telegraph pole, and took him down, and locked him in jail. That night, his jailhouse door was broken down, he was dragged out and put on the floor of a car, his genitals were cut off, and then he was taken to a bridge, hanged, and his body riddled with bullets. No one was ever arrested for Everett's murder, but 11 Wobblies were put on trial for killing an American Legion leader during the parade, and 6 of them spent 15 years in prison.

Why such a reaction to the general strike, to the organizing of the Wobblies? The following statement by the mayor of Seattle suggests that the establishment feared not just the strike itself but what it symbolized:

The so-called sympathetic Seattle strike was an attempted revolution. That there was no violence does not alter the fact. . . . The intent, openly and covertly announced, was for the overthrow of the industrial system; here first, then everywhere. . . . True, there were no flashing guns, no bombs, no killings. Revolution, I repeat, doesn't need violence. The general strike, as practiced in Seattle, is of itself the weapon of revolution, all the more dangerous because quiet. To succeed, it must suspend everything; stop the entire life stream of a community. That is to say, it puts the government out of operation. And that is all there is to revolt—no matter how achieved. (Zinn 2003, 379–80)

Out in the Pacific, labor relations were quite different. Hawaii's economy, which depended on agriculture, particularly sugar, created a planter class, which dominated the politics and the economy of the island. The high-intensity labor required could not be met by the local population, and therefore, since the mid-nineteenth century, labor had been imported onto the islands. The first workers came from the China in 1852 and the last mass importation of labor occurred in 1932 when 100,000 Filipinos arrived. The planters' power on the island left little room for labor negotiation, leaving the immigrant labor force powerless to address their deplorable wages and living conditions.

As a result of the planter practice of playing one immigrant group off against another, when labor did organize they did so according to nationality. In 1909, for example, 5,000 Japanese plantation workers went on strike because they were being paid 25 percent less than the Portuguese who were working the same number of hours per month. In retaliation, planters hired strikebreakers at twice the rate they were paying the Japanese and evicted them from the plantation. The strike was eventually broken and the Japanese went back to work at their original wage. In 1920 the Filipino Federation of Labor, under its fiery leader Pablo Manlapit, went on strike. Although the Japanese launched a new strike at the same time, they refused to coordinate their actions and they both failed. In 1924, another more violent strike also failed, but in 1935, Hawaiian workers benefited from the territorial status of the islands when they became protected by the National Labor Relations Act that passed as part of President Franklin Roosevelt's New Deal. A strike in 1937 by Filipino workers ended with the strikers receiving a 15 percent pay increase. By this time two-thirds of the workers were Filipino, so the benefits were widespread. In 1938, the International Longshoremen and Warehousemen's Union (ILWU) organized on the island and launched an organizing campaign that developed into a violent struggle. At one point in Hilo, the second-largest city in Hawaii, gunfire broke out between police and strikers, leaving 50 strikers wounded. After this event, known as the Hilo massacre, workers returned to work and

Snapshot

What Scares Them Is When Nothing Happens

The following poem by someone named Anise was printed during the Seattle General Strike of 1919 in the *Seattle Union Record,* a daily newspaper put out by labor people.

What scares them most is That NOTHING HAPPENS!
They are ready
For DISTURBANCES.
They have machine guns
And soldiers,
But this SMILING SILENCE
Is uncanny.
The business men Don't understand
That sort of weapon . . ., It is your SMILE
That is UPSETTING Their reliance
On Artillery, brother!
It is the garbage wagons
That go along the street Marked
"EXEMPT by STRIKE COMMITTEE."
It is the milk stations
That are getting better daily,
And the three hundred WAR Veterans of Labor
Handling the crowds WITHOUT GUNS,
For these things speak
Of a NEW POWER
And a NEW WORLD
That they do not feel
At HOME in.

From: Zinn 2003, 378.

the strike ended in a stalemate. But the strike established the credibility and permanence of the ILWU on the island, and when World War II ended they successfully organized the plantation workers, winning rights, wage increases, and protections long denied (Barnes 2007, 58–61).

TRADE AND MARKETS

The free-wheeling environment of the Pacific West, as well as the great diversity of the ethnic groups who had recently arrived at the turn of the century, gave many minority groups opportunities in trade and commerce they might not have enjoyed in other parts of the United States. One example is Amadeo Peter Giannini, who as a boy witnessed his father, a San Jose rancher, being shot to death by a disgruntled employee over a disputed sum of less than two dollars. Small sums could mean everything to some people, as young Giannini had learned in the most tragic way possible. Entering the family produce business in 1882 at the age of 12, Giannini was a financial success by the time he reached 30, and in 1904 he opened the Bank of Italy in San Francisco.

In May 1908, Giannini heard Princeton president Woodrow Wilson give a speech in which he complained that American banks restricted their services to the affluent. Taking Wilson's words to heart Giannini established the first Bank of Italy branch outside San Francisco, in San Jose. Another branch, in San Mateo, followed in 1912. By 1922, the Bank of Italy had a total of 62 branches "extending from Chico to San Diego." Giannini operated his banks on the theory that he could build large concentrations of capital from the small deposits of ordinary Californians. Shares in the Bank of Italy were distributed to as many investors as possible, with no one being allowed to acquire a dominant interest. Giannini also believed in making loans, provided that the recipient be a man or woman of proven character (not necessarily great assets) and be willing, in the case of a business, to accept the bank's advice as to its development.

Through Giannini's actions, the Bank of Italy helped reverse the prevailing notion that a bank loan was a privilege. Giannini's philosophy was adhered to as well by another Italian American banker, Joseph E. Sartori, who had founded the Security Savings Bank of Los Angeles in 1888. Thus, the Bank of America, as the Bank of Italy became known in 1930, was on hand for the first three decades of the twentieth century to finance the construction of homes, hotels, office buildings, and regulated public utilities in the private sector, and—especially in the case of the Bank of America—to back publicly issued bonds for construction projects such as the Golden Gate Bridge. Giannini's background in produce made the Bank of Italy/America especially adept in financing the rise of California agriculture. The bank also had significant influence on the rise of Hollywood in the same period. During the Depression, the bank's loan policy enabled innumerable farmers to keep their properties and an even larger number of Californians to refinance their homes. Because of the Bank of Italy/America, the Security Trust, and the other banks of the state (among them Wells Fargo, the Bank of California, the Anglo-California Bank, and the Crocker Bank), California remained economically independent and escaped becoming a colony of the eastern financial interests or the property of offshore investors through most of the twentieth century (Starr 2005, 187–89).

William Nickerson provides another example of a successful minority entrepreneur in the free-wheeling West. When he arrived in Los Angeles in 1920 it was just beginning to explode as an attractive place for migrants, and the importance of its African American community was growing apace. Although blacks were among the first settlers of the area and received a certain amount of recognition for that, by the turn of the century the black community was still very small and its leadership structure was weak and fragmented. Blacks in 1870 made up just 1.6 percent of the city's population, with just 93 souls. The next 30 years brought the first significant migration of African Americans to Los Angeles, so that by 1900 there were 2,131 living there, constituting 2.1 percent of the total. Although blacks were still a negligible portion of the total population, the number living there by 1900 was sufficient to create an important social and economic structure, and for a small black commercial elite to emerge.

This fact was recognized just after the turn of the century, when Booker T. Washington visited the city. Among those African American business and social leaders to greet Washington were B. W. Brown, a graduate chemist who ran a hardware store and manufactured grocery specialties; a Mr. Strickland, who was a successful butcher; M. R. Dunston, who had established a large and successful van and storage business; a Mr. Jamison, who was known as the "scrap iron king"; G. W. Holden, the "hog king"; and, perhaps most important, J. L. Edmonds, editor of *The Liberator*, the first African American newspaper in the city. Blacks had also established a rich institutional structure in Los Angeles, with five African Methodist churches and one each black Presbyterian, Christian, and Episcopal churches. Angelino blacks had also set up some 29 lodges of the major fraternal orders in the city, such as the Odd Fellows, Masons, Knights of Pythias, United Brothers of Friendship, and the True Reformers, and it may have been this fact that attracted Nickerson to the city to push his fraternal insurance program. The population of Los Angeles exploded between 1900 and 1920, growing fivefold from 102,479 to 576,673. The number of African Americans there increased from just over 2,000 to 15,579, but their percentage of the total population grew only from 2.0 percent to 2.7 percent. During the next decade, the general population of Los Angeles exploded again, to 1,238,584 by 1930, and the black population increased to nearly 39,000, 3.1 percent of the total. Thus, Nickerson was pursuing his business interests in one of the most rapidly growing cities in America. The black community there had, by the early twentieth century, begun to be concentrated in a large colony on Central Avenue, with the business section at Twenty-Second Street and Central.

J. Max Bond, in his study of blacks in the city, described the Central Avenue area at that time as follows:

Here many newcomers from Texas, Louisiana, Arkansas, Georgia, and Alabama—have settled; most of the business and professional men of the race have their offices in and are residents of this large community; here are found the business concerns of Negroes living in other communities; and here resides still a large number of the first families of Los Angeles. In the Central Avenue community, poverty and prosperity exist side by side. On every hand conservative old families are surrounded by people of a lower level of culture. (Ingham and Feldman 1994, 61)

The lure of Los Angeles for African Americans was perhaps no different than it was for other Americans. As Frank Fenton wrote in *A Place in the Sun* (1942), "This was a lovely makeshift city. Even the trees and plants did not belong here. They came, like the people, from far places, some familiar, some exotic, all wanderers of one sort or another seeking peace or fortune or the last frontier, or a thousand dreams of escape."

Nickerson secured a license to sell insurance in California and, at the same time, also got a real estate license. He rented an office for five dollars a month at 1804 South Central Avenue, in the heart of the black business district. A great need, however, was to get someone, in Nickerson's words, who was a "'live wire' to assist . . . in getting the American Mutual properly established in the state of California." This was Norman O. Houston, of whom Nickerson said, "At first I didn't think so much of this young man, but he was very insistent, so much so that I concluded to give him a decent hearing. I reasoned I needed someone with experience who could help me and was known here." Houston became the first employee of American Mutual in California, and he would be one of the founders of Golden State Insurance.

Nickerson and Houston set out to drum up business in Los Angeles. They concluded that the various African American churches would be a good starting point. Houston was made superintendent of agents, and three young men were hired as the first agents. One of the agents hired by Nickerson and Houston during these early months was George Beavers. Nickerson later recalled his first impressions of Beavers: "He was a short, stocky young fellow and wore glasses. He was quiet and unassuming. One thing I soon found out about him was as represented, he was not only a 'beaver' but of the bull dog type as well—he was a hard worker and a fighter as well." These three men would dominate the African American insurance business in California for decades to come (Ingham and Feldman, http://aae.greenwood.com/doc.aspx?fileID=IBL&chapterID=IBL-2239&path=/encyclopedias/greenwood//>).

The dreams of expanding commerce and trade in the San Francisco Bay area grew with the completion of two great bridges, which gave rise to the idea of an exposition to be built on the protruding shoals and mudflats adjacent to Yerba Buena Island in San Francisco Bay, with an airport for land-based and sea-based aircrafts. Work began in February 1936 and it took 18 months to create Treasure Island atop the shoals, and another two years to build the ambitious Golden Gate International Exposition, which celebrated emerging economic connections to Latin America and the Asia-Pacific Basin. The City Beautiful stage featured exhibition halls, courts, open spaces, and promenades, dominated by the "Court of Pacifica," from which rose an 80-foot statue of that name, intended to be placed on a promontory overlooking the bay as a westward-oriented Statue of Liberty. Unfortunately, Pearl Harbor necessitated a change in plans. The navy commandeered Treasure Island when the United

States declared war on Japan, and in 1942, with no other alternative possible at the time, the statue was dynamited (Starr 2005, 189).

CASTE AND CLASS EXPERIENCE

Ever since the early 1900s, a sector of California had been at war with the state's Japanese immigrants. This California Japanese War, as Carey McWilliams described it, was part of a larger "Yellow Peril" movement that brought with it a virulent "White California" crusade led by former San Francisco mayor James Duval Phelan, who was elected to the U.S. Senate in 1914. Upper-class Californians such as Phelan and *San Francisco Chronicle* publisher Michael H. de Young scapegoated the Japanese to please the masses. Politicians such as Phelan, in turn, took a hard line against the Japanese to please de Young and the *Chronicle*. In early 1905, the *Chronicle* led a campaign to segregate Japanese children in the public schools of San Francisco through a series of virulently racist editorials. When the school board and Mayor Eugene Schmitz put this segregation into effect in October 1906, President Theodore Roosevelt, who had recently won the Nobel Prize for negotiating peace between the Russians and the Japanese, was furious. How dare San Francisco, Roosevelt fumed, so grossly insult the proud people of Japan, the Yankees of the Pacific, long-standing American friends? Summoning Schmitz and the president of the school board to the White House, Roosevelt brokered the so-called Gentlemen's Agreement with Japan, put into effect in 1908, in which the Japanese government promised not to issue any further passports to laborers seeking to emigrate to the United States in exchange for the withdrawal of the offensive San Francisco ordinance. Roosevelt was further embarrassed in 1908 when, just as the Great White Fleet was sailing into Yokohama Harbor, the California legislature began to discuss the statewide segregation of Japanese children in public schools and a ban on Japanese ownership of land. Roosevelt took his case directly to Governor James Gillett, protesting California's contravention of national policy. The next year, 1909, saw the publication of *The Valor of Ignorance* by the Los Angeles–based soldier of fortune Homer Lea, who outlined in great detail a future Japanese invasion and occupation of the Pacific Coast.

As the White California movement gained strength, in 1913 the legislature passed the Alien Land Act, which prohibited Japanese land ownership in the state. Despite the fact that President Woodrow Wilson sent Secretary of State William Jennings Bryan to Sacramento to lobby against the bill, it became law with the support of Governor Hiram Johnson. In April 1919, as Japan sat with the other victorious allies at Versailles, California once again embarrassed the Department of State by an expansion of the Alien Land Act of 1913, which precipitated a rediscussion of segregation, and a series of viciously anti-Japanese speeches given in the U.S. Senate by James Phelan. The fact that Governor Johnson and Senator Phelan, both Progressives and otherwise involved in the reform and upgrading of California, were so determinedly anti-Japanese underscored the disquieting fact that there was an undercurrent of racism in Progressivism, which in California revealed itself in a sustained and strong anti-Japanese sentiment.

While not universal in California, these feelings nevertheless tainted a portion of the population, including elements of the Progressive upper middle class, through the 1930s. Racism thrived despite the fact that in other ways Californians demonstrated a great admiration for Japanese craftsmanship, especially in their architecture and landscape design. For example, in 1894, California obtained the Japanese Pavilion from the Columbian Exposition in Chicago and had it permanently installed in Golden Gate Park in San Francisco, where it became an instantly popular teahouse and public garden. The San Francisco department store Gump's did a thriving trade in Japanese furniture and art, and Bay Area architects adapted northern California redwood to the Japanese wood-building tradition. In southern California a generation of Japanese gardeners helped shape the horticultural aesthetics of that region. And thanks to the efforts of David Starr Jordan, the founding president of Stanford and an ardent admirer and advocate of Japanese culture, Stanford ranked second only to Harvard as the university of choice for Meiji-era students—eager to sharpen their professional and technical skills in order to help accelerate the westernization of their country. In October 1905, Jordan joined San Mateo attorney Henry Pike Bowie to form the Japan Society of Northern California. Fluent in Japanese, married to a highly placed Japanese woman attached to the Imperial Court, and a skilled painter in the Japanese style, Bowie devoted his considerable energies to promulgating the strength and beauty of Japanese culture. Even more boldly, he erected a memorial gate on his San Mateo estate to honor the valor of Japanese soldiers and sailors during the Russo-Japanese War.

The White California movement, however, had no interest in embracing Japanese culture. It represented the common, even vulgar, side of the California identity, however highly placed its leadership. It was, moreover, a racism based on envy. Japanese immigrants to California did well. They worked effectively as agricultural laborers, skillfully brokering their contracts through appointed leaders. With their savings, they rented land and started profitable farms.

In the early 1920s, Japanese women were allowed to enter the United States as "picture brides," so called because their marriages were brokered in home villages sight unseen, according to Japanese custom. The marriages and family formation resulting from the arrival of these women created a baby boom of American-born *nisei*, who were citizens and grew up fully American in the 1920s and 1930s. The window for such immigration was brief, however, and the Immigration Act of 1924 prohibited the Japanese from immigrating to the United States. Perceived as an insult in Japan, the act provoked demonstrations of protest and further poisoned the relationship between the two nations.

Even before Pearl Harbor, *Newsweek* ran an article, on October 14, 1940, warning of the threat posed by Japanese living around military installations in Hawaii and California. On the day of Pearl Harbor itself, the Federal Bureau of Investigation (FBI), assisted by sheriff's deputies, began rounding up suspected Japanese aliens in Los Angeles County. By December 9, 1941, some five hundred *issei* (Japanese noncitizens) were in federal custody on Terminal Island in Los Angeles Harbor (Starr 2005, 224–27).

Although the migration of African Americans to the urban North has held the attention of urban historians and public policy planners, for many blacks the American

West epitomized both social freedom and economic opportunity. Even when racial restrictions appeared, many black westerners persisted in the belief that the move to the West was, according to one historian, "a journey toward hope." Black westward migration took place in an environment of special challenges. Unlike south-to-north movement, migration to the West entailed greater travel distances through difficult countryside. Moreover, there was the possibility of settling among culturally different people—Mexican Americans in the Southwest, Chinese immigrants on the West Coast, and Native Americans throughout the rest of the region. Yet African American settlers willingly faced unknown dangers of the West rather than the perceptible social, economic, and political oppression of the South or East.

As black populations in western cities grew, identifiable African American communities began to emerge in the region. Beginning in the 1850s, San Francisco held the largest black population in the West until it was surpassed by Los Angeles in 1910. Blacks migrated to western cities between 1900 and 1940 to work as longshoremen, barbers, railroad porters, hotel cooks, waiters, maids, ship stewards, and cannery workers. A few professionals such as physicians, attorneys, ministers, and schoolteachers rounded out the occupational spectrum. Black communities in cities such as Denver, San Francisco, Los Angeles, and Seattle supported numerous churches, social clubs, fraternal orders, and businesses, as well as chapters of the National Association for the Advancement of Colored People (NAACP) and the National Urban League. Several black-owned newspapers, such as the *Northwest Enterprise* (Seattle), The *Montana Plaindealer* (Helena), and the *California Eagle* (Los Angeles), reported the social and political activities that occurred in these growing black communities.

Throughout the twentieth century Los Angeles had been the center of California's African American population. Black migrants to Los Angeles were attracted by its image and tangible benefits. Southern California had been touted since the late nineteenth century as a land of sunshine and opportunity for blacks from the southern states especially. This area also seemed the Promised Land of freedom from overt discrimination and oppression. As the terminus of major transcontinental railroads, Los Angeles attracted many Pullman porters, whose quarters formed a nucleus for its black community by 1900, and who provided information on where to go and what to do for blacks they met waiting at the railroads. The growing economy provided a variety of urban jobs, and the expanding racial community offered employment for its businesses and professionals. By 1920, Los Angeles was home to over 15,000 African Americans; by 1940 that number had grown to 63,774, over half of their population in California. Unlike larger northern centers of the Great Migration, movement to Los Angeles continued during the Great Depression.

African Americans initially were scattered among the general population, but by 1920 a distinct ghetto had formed along the north blocks of Central Avenue. Racially restrictive covenants became widespread after court decisions in the 1910s upheld their legality, confining most blacks to a few blocks east and west of this street. While small communities were formed in a few adjacent cities, most notably Pasadena, relatively few blacks lived outside the city before World War II. This community developed a vibrant society, anchored in churches that served as cultural as well as religious centers. Women formed several service organizations, along with a branch of the National Association of Colored Women. The Los Angeles Forum was founded in 1903 as a center for discussing civic affairs, and an NAACP branch was set up in 1913. Marcus Garvey's Universal Negro Improvement Association established a vigorous presence during the 1920s, though divided into two factions, and a National Urban League branch was formed that same decade. The community had several newspapers, of which the most prominent were the *California Eagle* and the *Los Angeles Sentinel*. Discrimination in jobs and public accommodations was common, but its impact was somewhat lessened by the fact that other minorities, especially Mexicans, Japanese, and Chinese, were similarly treated and sometimes given lower status. Although African Americans constituted only a small minority of any political district, they elected an assemblyman from Los Angeles regularly after 1918 (Reich 2006, 496–97).

During the first decades of the twentieth century, Mexican Americans represented the largest minority population in the city of Los Angeles. From 1920 to 1930 their population tripled from 33,644 to 97,116, surpassing San Antonio, Texas, as the leading Mexican American community in the United States. Despite the overwhelmingly American character of this population, they suffered terrible discrimination. Observing Mexican American life in California in the late 1930s, a sociologist commented as follows:

When a vice-principal of a high school admits that he does not urge Mexican boys to seek varied employment as other boys do because he knows that they cannot do anything more than work in the groves, there is discrimination. When a city council refuses to let Mexican-American boys and girls swim in the public plunge and when it places at the entrance of the bathhouse a red sign reading FOR WHITE RACE ONLY and when it admits through its city clerk that this is for the purpose of keeping out "Mexican" children, it is both ignorance and discrimination. (Daniels and Olin 1972, 222–23)

In the early 1930s, in a federal program that can only be described as ethnic cleansing, the government forcibly repatriated Mexican Americans along with their American-born children. Thousands of Mexicans were assembled in local train stations with their luggage and hastily wrapped belongings prior to being stuffed into crowded trains for shipment back to Mexico.

Since the turn of the century schools for "Mexicans" and schools for "Americans" had been the custom in many a southern California city. It mattered not that the "Mexicans" were born in the United States and that great numbers of them were sons and daughters of U.S. citizens. It was the custom that they were segregated at least until they could use English well enough to keep up with English-speaking children. Neither did it matter that many of them had a command of English nor that there was no legal basis for their segregation. Under a law, enacted in 1885 and amended in 1893, it was possible to segregate Indians and "Mongolians" in California's public schools. To many an administrator this included "Mexicans." This pattern was followed principally because the majority groups in the local communities wanted it done that way.

When the United States acquired California in 1848, the Indian population stood at 100,000. But the heavy influx of whites, friction with miners, ruthless massacres of Indians, and the loss of habitat and wildlife decimated the Indian population, and by the turn of the century there were probably no more than 15,000 Indians left in the state, living on eight reservations. In 1911, as recorded by Theodora Kroeber, the last "wild Indian" in the entire United States, a Yana man named Ishi from the slopes of Mount Lassen in California, gave himself up to the civilized world that had been pressing in around him. Throughout the first decades of the twentieth century the Indians of California remained extremely poor and overlooked by the state's non-Indian population (Starr 2005, 13).

Indian tribes to the north remained relatively free from white encroachment until the mid-nineteenth century. From that time, and into the twentieth century, however, the native tribes were rapidly dispossessed, placed upon reservations, and reduced in numbers. At a later period the decrease became less marked, but it continued nevertheless, partly as an actual extinction of the aboriginal population and partly as an absorption into the dominant white culture. Most of the Chinookan tribes were finally placed on Warm Springs and Grande Ronde Reservations and on Yakima Reservation in Washington; all of the Athapascan tribes on the Siletz Reservation, except the Umpqua, who went to Grande Ronde; the Kusan and Yakonan tribes on the Siletz Reservation; the Salishan peoples of Oregon on the Grande Ronde and Siletz Reserves; most of the Kalapooian peoples on the Grande Ronde, though a few on the Siletz; most of the Molala on the Grande Ronde; the Klamath on Klamath Reserve; the Modoc mostly on Klamath Reserve but a few on the Quapaw Reservation in Oklahoma; the Shahaptian tribes of Oregon on the Umatilla Reservation; and the Northern Paiutes on the Klamath Reservation (http://ca.encarta.msn.com/encyclopedia_761558216_9/oregon.html).

ANIMAL HUSBANDRY AND HUNTING AND FISHING

In the first decades of the twentieth century, the East Coast, Gulf of Mexico, and Great Lakes fisheries began to get strong competition from those on the Pacific Coast. Before 1910 only 2 percent of the national harvest of fish was landed in the Pacific. The ocean had been considered too rough for the small wind-powered craft that hauled in most of the fish in the United States. Large motorized fishing craft altered the calculus of the fishing industry so that by 1915 Pacific fleets landing salmon, sardines, and tuna were beginning to change American fish-eating habits as well as livestock-feeding practices.

The Pacific Ocean was rich in fish. One observer from Santa Cruz remembered that the schools of sardines offshore were so dense that the seabirds feeding on them formed an impenetrable black cloud just above the surface of the water. Harvesting of sardines, tuna, and salmon off California's huge coast soon enabled the state's fisheries to outproduce all other states. On any body of water, but especially on Pacific swells, landing nets flooded with fish (a grueling job by any account) was just the beginning of the labor of commercial fishing. Processing plants for canning food fish or transforming sardines and fish by-products into chicken feed employed thousands of workers yearly. By 1915 Californian A. P. Halfhill had developed the process of baking tuna in steam, then canning it. He toured the United States periodically into the 1920s promoting his "chicken of the sea" to Americans, who for a time preferred canned salmon to the newer canned tuna. By 1925 Long Beach, San Diego, and Monterey dominated the California packing industry.

West Coast Azorean men abandoned the whaling industry for the abalone camps that Chinese fisherman had left, and trolled for albacore as soon as motorized fishing vessels made the practice reasonably safe. They were joined by Japanese American fishermen in the tuna hunt. By 1920, two-thirds of the licensed fishers in San Pedro were Japanese. Japanese owned 50 percent of the 400 boats in the port and landed 80 percent of the fish.

Between 1915 and 1925, typical southern California fishing boats were big enough to hold but one day's catch, three crewmen, and a 15- to 25-horsepower engine. Their catches went to the canneries in San Pedro and San Diego, where they were processed into the canned tuna and salmon Americans had begun to integrate into their diets by 1915. Many of the cannery workers lived in tuna or salmon company housing that, like company housing in most industries, was barely more than shelter. Absent from most were running water, electricity, and much space.

By the late 1920s, Halfhill had made his point to American consumers, demand rose, and large-scale tuna fishing dominated the industry. Long boats between 95 and 125 feet long, powered by large diesel engines and with enough fuel storage area on board to enable the boats to travel up to 5,000 miles or 30 days without returning to port, revolutionized both the fishing industry and the lives of the crews. Refrigerated holds held up to 150 tons of tuna, and crew members increasingly found the cycles of their lives altered, from day-to-day trips (often long days in the summer) to sojourns at sea more akin to the great whaling voyages of the previous century. Like agricultural workers, some fishermen had been migrating annually for several years before the advent of the big tuna boats. Monterey fishermen had moved north to fish sardines in the summer or farther south to hunt tuna or mackerel, thereby spending weeks and even months away from home and family.

American fish processors, like their analogs in the wheat business, initially benefited from the outbreak of World War I. The hostilities in Europe effectively closed the North Sea to fishing, thereby eliminating one of the world's great sources of sardines, herring, and other food fish. The Western Hemisphere and parts of Europe not blockaded became markets for American fish and fish products. But after the war ended the market collapsed, especially for sardines. Prices returned to 1914 levels, and canneries up and down the American coasts closed. A moderate recovery in the industry occurred after the recession in 1920 and 1921, and the Depression had less disastrous consequences for the fishermen and canners than it had for many other American workers. In part this was because the postwar crash was so severe, and in part the diversification of canners into fish-meal livestock feed enabled them to make use of much of the 75 or 80 percent of the fish that had been wasted previously, particularly in the tuna industry. Total landings declined on the West Coast in 1930–1931 but increased for tuna and sardines (by 7 percent and 25 percent, respectively). Landings for the 12 other leading fish declined by an average of 19 percent (Green 2000, 55–56).

Pacific Coast fishing spread all the way north to Alaska, where by the turn of the century almost 700,000 cases of salmon valued at just under $2.8 million were

Snapshot

Nature Guide: A Voice for Wilderness, John Muir

"Damming and submerging it 175 feet deep would enhance its beauty by forming a crystal-clear lake." Landscape gardens, places of recreation and worship, are never made beautiful by destroying and burying them. The beautiful sham lake, forsooth, should be only an eyesore, a dismal blot on the landscape, like many others to be seen in the Sierra. For, instead of keeping it at the same level all the year, allowing Nature centuries of time to make new shores, it would, of course, be full only a month or two in the spring, when the snow is melting fast; then it would be gradually drained, exposing the slimy sides of the basin and shallower parts of the bottom, with the gathered drift and waste, death and decay of the upper basins, caught here instead of being swept on to decent natural burial along the banks of the river or in the sea.

Thus the Hetch Hetchy dam-lake would be only a rough imitation of a natural lake for a few of the spring months, an open sepulcher for the others. "Hetch Hetchy water is the purest of all to be found in the Sierra, unpolluted, and forever unpollutable." On the contrary, excepting that of the Merced below Yosemite, it is less pure than that of most of the other Sierra streams, because of the sewerage of camp grounds draining into it, especially of the Big Tuolumne Meadows camp ground, occupied by hundreds of tourists and mountaineers, with their animals, for months every summer, soon to be followed by thousands from all the world.

These temple destroyers, devotees of ravaging commercialism, seem to have a perfect contempt for Nature, and, instead of lifting their eyes to the God of the mountains, lift them to the Almighty Dollar.

Dam Hetch Hetchy! As well dam for water-tanks the people's cathedrals and churches, for no holier temple has ever been consecrated by the heart of man. (Muir, *The Yosemite*, 255–57, 260–62, as quoted in Black 2006, 35)

processed at 37 Alaskan canneries. Such intense fishing took its toll, and in 1914 Governor John F. Strong reported to the secretary of the interior on the dangerous depletion of the salmon due to the unchecked exploitation of the salmon fishers. By the 1920s, partly because of the boom associated with feeding canned salmon to thousands of troops in World War I, fishing had replaced mining as Alaska's major industry. But by then even the packers were beginning to think that there could be a problem with the supply of salmon. In 1921, Secretary of Commerce Herbert Hoover became so concerned by the salmon decline that he took the extraordinary step of recommending to President Warren G. Harding the establishment of the Alaskan Peninsula reserve. Harding created the reserve by executive order and thereafter fishing was allowed only by permit. Eventually Congress passed the White Act in 1924, which mandated that 50 percent of salmon in any stream be allowed to pass upstream to spawn. The act was hailed as a major milestone in the effort to preserve Alaska's renewable salmon resources. Regulation of coastal and inland fisheries would not be transferred to Alaska until it became a state (Borneman 2004, 290–91).

Federal regulations were also implemented to protect the natural environment of the West. By the turn of the twentieth century, the question of whether the boundaries of national parks were sacred or not was resolved in Yellowstone National Park in California in the preservationists' favor, but it loomed larger than ever in Yosemite Park. Unlike the struggle in Yellowstone, where proponents of reconfiguring park boundaries could be branded as invaders intent on the pillaging of a sublime landscape for shortsighted corporate greed, at Yosemite the far more democratic issue was the water supply for the city of San Francisco. City engineers in the early 1880s had envisioned the possibility of damming the high-walled Hetch-Hetchy Valley, situated 150 miles to the east, as the best way to solve San Francisco's perpetual water supply problem. The problem was that Hetch-Hetchy was situated inside the boundaries of the new Yosemite National Park, which had been established in 1890 by Congress after a long campaign led by naturalist and Sierra Club founder John

Muir, *Century* magazine editor Robert Underwood Johnson, and other outdoor enthusiasts.

The tradition of Americans enjoying Yosemite Park stretched back further than the date it was established as a national park. Since the end of the Mariposa Indian war in 1851, Americans had been coming by foot and horseback to the area to wonder at the magnificent Yosemite Valley. On June 30, 1864, President Abraham Lincoln signed a bill granting Yosemite Valley and the Mariposa Grove of Giant Sequoias to the state of California as an inalienable public trust. This was the first time in history that a federal government had set aside scenic lands simply to protect them and to allow for their enjoyment by all people. Ameri-

Wilderness preservationist John Muir. Library of Congress.

can visitors regarded Yosemite as a national treasure; however, for city fathers and most San Franciscans, the basic needs of a human population quite obviously were to take precedence over the preservation of wilderness, no matter how spectacular. They maintained that the public good to be gained by damming the valley for the benefit of the many people of San Francisco far outweighed the good of preserving it for the pleasure of the relatively few visitors to the site.

That John Muir did not see it that way came as no surprise. He had first come to the attention of American nature lovers in the 1870s with his writings on the natural glories of Yosemite, which proved instrumental in the designation of the region as America's second national park. More surprising was Secretary of the Interior Ethan Allen Hitchcock's refusal in 1903 to grant the right of way for the dam and reservoir to the city. Hitchcock asserted that no argument the city had made compelled him to violate the intent of Congress in reserving the area.

Led by Muir, Yosemite defenders appealed to the growing revulsion toward what many critics had long ago declared to be an excessively materialistic society. For preservationists, the proposal to flood Hetch-Hetchy Valley represented the most egregious sign of an overly commercialized, overly urbanized civilization slouching toward decadence. Muir and others condemned the proposal as an ungodly, satanic act that would destroy one of God's own "temples." Others clamored against the private interests that allegedly stood to profit from the control and sale of the water supply and the associated hydroelectric power that would be generated by the dam. Defenders of the valley also engaged the services of independent engineers, who testified that other alternative sources, outside the bounds of Yosemite, could be tapped to solve the city's water problem. Opposition came from across the country in the form of letters and telegrams from civic groups, scientists and travelers, and editorials from leading newspapers and magazines. The conservationists were initially victorious, but the proponents of the dam were persistent and politically powerful. They eventually wore down the opposition and, amidst the protests of conservationists on December 6, 1913, the Senate voted 43 to 25 in favor of the proposal, and President Woodrow Wilson signed the Raker Act that would flood Hetch-Hetchy, signaling a major defeat for the preservation movement.

The dam did not diminish Americans' enthusiasm for the park. Until 1907 they continued to come by horse-drawn wagon to wonder at the natural beauty. After that date visitors to the park began arriving on the newly built train, which increased access to the park, and its popularity as a vacation stop. Hotels sprang up and tents dotted the meadows of Yosemite. After 1913, Americans drove into the park on rugged unpaved roads and camped throughout the meadow. As enthusiasm for auto camping expanded in the 1920s, so did the number of visitors to Yosemite. Campers and nature lovers approached the one million mark by the late 1930s and surpassed that milestone for the first time in 1954 (http://www.nps.gov/yose/historyculture/index.htm).

Intellectual Life

California led the way in the intellectual life of the Pacific West. The open and free spirit of the Pacific West created an environment where experimentation could thrive. New research institutions, which would soon lead the world of science and technology, such as California Technical University, emerged in the first decades of the twentieth century. Some of the greatest discoveries of the twentieth century would be uncovered at the scientific centers of California.

Settlers from other areas would bring with them from the regions of their birth their ideas about education and plant them into the schools of the West. Western literature became a popular genre throughout the country, and many books, such as *The Grapes of Wrath* and the mystery novels of Dashiell Hammet and Raymond Chandler, became raw material for the burgeoning California film industry in the 1930s. Californians also created their own image of a healthy lifestyle, which meant a healthy diet including lots of fruits, such as grew in abundance in the Pacific West, and lots of outdoor exercise and activities in the fresh air and sun, which were also abundant in southern California. This section will explore those aspects of intellectual life in the West that distinguished it from the rest of the nation.

SCIENCE

Scientific creativity in California benefited from enterprises in geology, mining, astronomy, and aviation that proliferated in the state in the first decades of the twentieth century. At the beginning of the twentieth century electronics also emerged as yet another cause and matrix of scientific, technological, and entrepreneurial virtuosity. In the early part of the century, new inventions developed at Palo Alto, California, created an entirely new world of transcontinental phone calls, radio, television, and high-speed electronics. The person most responsible for the explosion of technological discovery at Palo Alto was Lee de Forest, who had earned his PhD in 1899 from the Sheffield Scientific School at Yale University and entered the business world as a variously employed but mainly freelance inventor. In 1910, de Forest moved to Palo Alto, where he was associated with the Federal Telegraph Company. While there, in 1912, de Forest invented a vacuum tube called the Audion that converted alternating current to direct current and functioned as an amplifier. On the day it was invented, de Forest and his colleagues amplified by 120 times the sound of a housefly walking across a sheet of paper.

After selling his Audion tube to American Telephone and Telegraph (AT&T) for $50,000 as an amplifier for transcontinental phone calls, de Forest went on to develop the Audion further, making possible the broadcast and reception of voice and music over the airways. A rival, Edwin Armstrong, a junior at Columbia University in New York, while working on the same type of vacuum tube, achieved similar—and, many would claim, superior—results. From Armstrong's and de Forest's inventions would come radio, motion picture sound, and television. De Forest himself moved to Hollywood, where he married the silent-film star Marie Mosquini and continued to invent, to take out patents, and, to the continued distress of Edwin Armstrong, to promote himself as the Father of Radio.

California also soon led the way in developing new techniques of technology for the transmission of images. Philo T. Farnsworth, a native of Utah who moved to San Francisco at the age of 21 in 1925, conducted experiments with the electronic projection of images. Setting up a laboratory in a loft in the Cow Hollow section of San Francisco, Farnsworth—with financial support from local investors and the assistance of his wife, his brother, and some assistants—soon developed a dissector tube he called the "orthicon" that allowed him, on September 7, 1927, to transmit a simple image—a black glass with a line drawn down the center—through purely electronic means and thus demonstrate the basic technology of television. Because of the need to investigate claims made by an unsuccessful patent application submitted in 1923, the U.S. Patent Office did not award Farnsworth priority until 1934. Therefore he was never able to capitalize on this recognition. However, the pattern embodied by Farnsworth—that of a self-instructed westerner bringing an important scientific experiment to conclusion in California—fit an established paradigm.

In the first three decades of the twentieth century, Stanford gave both Farnsworth and de Forest substantial backing. Stanford had developed a special niche for experts in electrical engineering, thanks in significant measure to Professor Frederick Emmons Terman, who had earned a doctorate in electrical engineering from the Massachusetts Institute of Technology (MIT) in 1924. After returning to his home in Palo Alto to recover from an attack of tuberculosis, Terman soon began teaching at Stanford where he devoted his research energies to the vacuum tube. Fascinated by the commercial possibilities of this device, which had already stimulated a whole new range of industries, Terman became convinced that Stanford University should participate not only in theoretical research relating to electrical engineering, but in its commercial implementation as well.

In 1937, Terman provided funds, laboratory access, and faculty advice to Stanford graduate Russell Varian, who had worked for Farnsworth, and his brother Sigurd as they worked on a new kind of vacuum tube designed to amplify microwave signals into an ultra-high-frequency current. On the evening of August 19, 1937, the first klystron tube, as the Varian brothers called it, was put into operation, and subsequently described in the *Journal of Applied Physics*. Work continued on the klystron tube at Stanford through the rest of the decade. When war came, it was a key component in the success of radar.

Two other Stanford graduates, David Packard and William Hewlett, were, with Terman's guidance, designing and building an audio oscillator that would generate electrical signals within the frequency range of human hearing and would, when connected to a loudspeaker, produce a high-quality tone. Hewlett and Packard formed a company, headquartered in Palo Alto in the one-car garage of the house Packard and his wife were renting, with Hewlett moving into the backyard cottage. By the late 1930s, they had perfected the audio oscillator and the Hewlett-Packard Company had made its first big sale: four oscillators to Walt Disney Productions for the enhancement of the music for *Fantasia* (1940).

Across the San Francisco Bay in Berkeley, meanwhile, a contribution was being made to the most important scientific and technological feat of the twentieth century: releasing the power of the atom. There, University of California Berkeley physics professor Ernest Orlando Lawrence, yet another Yale graduate, had invented and developed by 1931 a cyclotron that generated high-energy beams of nuclear particles that made possible the exploration of the atomic nucleus, which is to say, the ability to peer into the very building blocks of matter. After scientists unleashed the power of the atom, Americans as well as the rest of the world began to live in an entirely new universe (Starr 2005, 259–63).

EDUCATION

During the first decades of the twentieth century, as families moved westward, they brought with them ideas of education rooted in their native regions. Added to this mix of those who had come west from the other parts of the United States were those who had come east from Asia and north from Mexico. This convergence of many varied regions of the world manifested itself in the ethnically mixed classrooms of the West.

Hiroko Kamikawa, for example, born in Fresno on July 11, 1920, remembered when she was six years old, entering first grade at Lincoln Elementary, the public school located in her neighborhood. Fresno was a town of about 15,000, and like most communities of its size, it had several elementary, middle, and high schools. Lincoln Elementary reflected the social makeup of its surrounding neighborhood. In Hiroko's case that meant she attended school with children of Japanese or Chinese heritage and a few from European immigrant families. Like most children who attended school in their own neighborhoods, Hiroko knew her classmates well and felt quite comfortable in school. She was a good student and popular among her peers. Children at schools like Hiroko's Lincoln often recognized ethnic and racial differences, but these distinctions served as curiosities rather than divisions among students. Hiroko remembered one incident that illustrated this point. One day her teacher reprimanded her and two German boys for chewing gum. As punishment, Hiroko and her classmates had to stand in front of the other children and sing songs while prominently displaying on their noses the wads of gum taken from their mouths. Since Hiroko's parents spoke no English at home, she knew more Japanese than English, so she chose to sing a Japanese folk song titled "Hato Popo." For similar reasons the two boys picked a German tune. Contrary to the teacher's intent, Hiroko recalled that all three had a good time and the other students in the class enjoyed hearing the traditional folk songs. For the most part, in the Pacific Northwest, ethnically diverse classrooms were met with benign indifference on the part of the parents and curiosity on the part of the students. Don Duncan, a journalist who was a student in Seattle in the 1930s, had similar memories; he recalled, "A boy had a much rougher time if he wore glasses than if he had a non-white skin" (Thompson and Marr 2001, 20).

In response to the large number of immigrant families sending their children to public schools, by the 1930s school systems such as the Long Beach City schools in California instituted character education classes, which included subjects such as honesty, courtesy, responsibility, industry, and punctuality. The school board believed that the teacher needed to instruct pupils in what were "considered American standards, since pupils come from all types of homes, many of which do not know what these standards are" (Lange 1931, 426–29).

Throughout the Pacific West states, neighborhood schools developed in the new communities that radiated out from the major cities around the turn of the century. A common characteristic of schools in this region was their rapid growth in the first decades of the century. Beacon Hill School in Seattle was typical of the growth experienced throughout the region. Beacon Hill opened in 1892 when an electric line was built connecting the new suburb to the center of the city. Initially it was a two-room school that housed less than a hundred students where grades 1–5 were taught. By 1904 a large new building was added that housed more than 200 students in grades 1–8. By the 1930s there were almost a thousand students in the school. The gym was so crowded that students recalled they could only do stationary exercises during physical education classes (Thompson and Marr 2001, 20).

Because of this rapid growth in the region, many children went to school in "portables"—rapidly assembled wood frame buildings that served as classrooms. Meant to be temporary, often they became the only type of classroom building that many children ever knew. In addition to traditional subjects such as arithmetic, spelling, grammar, and reading, all students took required health and physical education classes. Gender also determined curriculum, as girls took classes in sewing and cooking, while boys took classes in woodworking.

In the early decades of the twentieth century, the school system of Hawaii reflected a curriculum established by an occupying power; consequently, schoolchildren in Hawaii studied subjects that were designed to acculturate them and make them useful citizens in the developing American economy. The curriculum emphasized long and heavy drills in English grammar and vocabulary as well as vocational training. The girls studied home economics in the elementary grades as well as in middle school, and the boys studied agriculture.

Paralleling these schools created by the U.S. government were the Kamehameha Schools, established in 1887 under the terms of the last will and testament of Bernice Pauahi Bishop, a direct descendant of Kamehameha the Great and last of the House of Kamehameha. Bishop's will established a trust called the "Bernice Pauahi Bishop Estate" for the maintenance of the school. The original purpose of the school was to train native Hawaiians in agricultural work so that they could compete successfully with the foreigners who were establishing a massive agricultural industry on the islands. Over the years, however, young Hawaiians demonstrated little interest in agriculture and the school developed into a well-endowed, prestigious college preparatory program (Barnes 2007, 41).

In Alaska in the early twentieth century, there were two school systems established: one maintained with territorial funds and the other through the Office of Indian Affairs. Schools were also medical centers, and a physician's or nurse's home, along with the teacher's residence was often part of the school building complex. Vocational training was the primary objective of the schools in Alaska, and young boys learned skills such as boat building, sled construction, gasoline engine repair, snowshoe making, tanning, taxidermy, ivory and wood carving, animal husbandry, agriculture, and bookkeeping. Girls studied homemaking, cooking, sewing, blanket making, and basket weaving (Cook 1934, 27).

LITERATURE

The film noir of the late 1940s was inspired by a new genre of writing, namely, the hard-boiled detective story. The San Francisco–based Pinkerton-detective-turned-novelist Dashiell Hammett, the Ernest Hemingway of the detective story, introduced the hard-boiled style in such classics as *Red Harvest* (1929) and *The Maltese Falcon* (1930), in which detective Sam Spade asked nothing of anyone and expected even less. As in the case of Steinbeck's *The Grapes of Wrath* (1939) becoming John Ford's brilliant movie of 1940, *The Maltese Falcon* became equally well known through the 1941 film directed by John Huston and starring Humphrey Bogart in one of the most riveting performances of his career.

Hammett moved to southern California in the early 1930s to work in Hollywood, as did F. Scott Fitzgerald, James M. Cain, Horace McCoy, and William Faulkner. In such figures, fiction and film coalesced. Edmund Wilson, in fact, described *The Grapes of Wrath* as the first major American novel to be written as a movie script. While most writers had their difficulties with the assembly-line techniques of the studios, their cinematic experiences strengthened their novels and vice versa. Fiction in California became tense, telegraphic, story-driven. It also began to explore more completely the life and times of the Golden State. The protagonist of Knight's *You Play the Black and the Red Comes Up* (1938) ends his story with an evocation of California as an emotionally empty place: "I could remember everything about California," he notes, "but I couldn't feel it. I tried to get my mind to remember something that it could feel, too, but it was no use. It was all gone. All of it. The pink stucco houses and the palm trees and the stores built like cats and dogs and frogs and ice-cream freezers and the neon lights around everything."

John Steinbeck's *The Grapes of Wrath*, one of the most popular books of the twentieth century, was born in the West in the 1930s. Steinbeck had reported on conditions in the field for the *San Francisco News*. While he was

A scene from Darryl F. Zanuck's 1940 production of *The Grapes of Wrath* by John Steinbeck, with Henry Fonda, Jane Darwell, and John Carradine. Library of Congress.

not formally on the left, his depiction of vigilante action against Dust Bowl migrants, most dramatically the nighttime burning of a migrant encampment ("Hoovervilles," as such encampments were called), certainly positioned his protagonists, the Joad family of Oklahoma, against a sea of troubles caused by the hostile growers of the San Joaquin Valley. Because *The Grapes of Wrath* was so successful as a documentary novel, it was taken as literal truth. Even Franklin Roosevelt referred to the Joads in one of his fireside chats as though they were actual people. On the other hand, Steinbeck outraged Oklahomans as well as Kern County growers with his depiction of the Joads and was denounced in the House of Representatives by a congressman from Oklahoma (Starr 2005, 282–83).

The West also provided material for Zane Grey's popular pulp fiction novels of cowboys, lawmen, and bandits in the Old West. One of the nation's most prolific writers, he published over 90 books. Grey used the West as a background for his easily read morality stories about men who confronted some wrong event from their past and emerged triumphant or tried to escape it and were defeated.

COMMUNICATION

Within months after radio's successful debut in Pittsburgh in 1920, Los Angeles became the first city in the West to have a commercial radio station. But the first radio station in the West originated on the campus of San Jose College in April 1909, when Charles David Herrold, an electronics instructor, constructed a broadcasting station. It used spark/gap technology but modulated the carrier frequency with the human voice, and later music. The station, "San Jose Calling" (there were no call letters), continued in an unbroken lineage eventually to become today's KCBS in San Francisco. In 1927, radio station KGFJ became the first station to broadcast 24 hours a day. An early staple of radio airtime along with sporting events, classical music, and jazz was religious services. While most radio preachers reached only a local audience, one who gained a major national following emanated from California, Aimee Semple McPherson, whose Four Square Gospel church preaching and showmanship made her seem the complete embodiment of California's novelty and eccentricity.

Material Life

In the first half of the twentieth century, Pacific westerners maintained an image that materially speaking they were living "the good life." Even migrant workers who did not fare so well, some earning less than 15 cents an hour in California agricultural fields during the Depression years, had been attracted to the Pacific West by the promise of a better material life. During the early 1930s over 300,000 Americans from the Great Plains and the Southwest states flooded into California seeking a better life. Despite the hardships of many, especially in the years of the Great Depression, the general impression remained that Pacific westerners, especially Californians, lived well, ate well, and worked prosperously.

Californians developed housing and clothing styles unique to their environment, which other Americans imitated. Problems presented by the uniqueness of their environment, especially the lack of water in certain areas, were seen as challenges, which they solved though technology, and they conquered the vastness of the geography of their area first through efficient rail systems and later through superhighways. It was good to be a Pacific westerner in the first half of the twentieth century. No problem seemed unsolvable, and nothing but brightness shined into the future. This section will explore those aspects of material life in the Pacific West that made it either envied or imitated in much of the rest of the country.

FOOD

The Pacific West contributed greatly to the changing food habits across the nation in the early decades of the twentieth century. Since the end of the nineteenth century with the development of the refrigerated car, canning, and the creation of irrigation districts, California became a foodbasket of the nation, supplying Americans with wheat, and a variety of vegetables that were previously only available locally and in the harvest months. In the new century, Americans began to eat canned asparagus, beets, tomatoes, and other vegetables, most of which came from the irrigated fields of California. Emerging health concerns and the linking of good nutrition to healthy bodies stimulated the sale of citrus fruit grown in California, as well as raisin production. California also took the lead in canning vegetables to send throughout the country. At the turn of the century 11 of California's largest canners formed an association of vegetable canners that would eventually become Del Monte, the nation's largest producer of canned food. This company eventually opened canneries in Idaho, Washington, Alaska, and Hawaii.

The rivers of Washington produced salmon that was smoked, processed, and canned and also shipped throughout the nation. Washington fisheries also contributed herring, halibut, salmon, and cod to the American diet. The salmon industry extended all the way north to Alaska (see the section on Animal Husbandry and Hunting and Fishing). In the first half of the century Washington also became the nation's largest producers of apples. During the Great Depression apples from Washington became one of

First haul of the salmon season along the Columbia River in Oregon, 1904. Library of Congress.

the icons of the era when apple growers, facing a bumper crop in 1930, shipped crates of apples eastward to the jobless. A man could buy a crate for $1.75 on credit and then sell them on the street for five cents apiece (Kyvig 2002, 225). After the American Reciprocity Act of 1874 removed the duty on sugar, Hawaii's sugar industry grew at exponential rates, creating a planter class that dominated the politics and economy of the island. Until World War II, when the economy began to move away from sugar production, Hawaii was one of America's principal suppliers of sugar. In the first half of the century pineapples became almost synonymous with Hawaii, and most of this fruit, which eventually ended up on American tables either fresh or canned, came from there (Barnes 2007, 39, 61).

HOUSING

Electric wiring at the turn of the century, along with indoor plumbing, added substantially to the cost of house construction. To keep house prices stable while adding these new technologies, builders cut costs by reducing the size and number of rooms in the average house. The most widespread manifestation of the new minimalist approach to house design was the bungalow, which first appeared in California at the start of the twentieth century and spread eastward rapidly to the Midwest. These single-storied houses had high ceilings and large windows and were surrounded by

Eight Chinese men working at a machine canning salmon, probably in Washington or Oregon, 1913. Library of Congress.

a veranda. The shaded windows and large openings made the house especially pleasing in warmer climates, but soon the bungalow was proclaimed to be a new standard of sensible and thrifty family living, and variations of the style appeared throughout the United States (Kyvig 2002, 61).

The last decade of the nineteenth century witnessed a concerted effort on behalf of San Francisco civic leaders to support the development of an architectural style that celebrated and memorialized the coming of age of the city as capital of the Far West. The city not only had the money but also the architectural expertise to realize the goal, since a new generation of architects, many of them trained at the Ecole des Beaux Arts in Paris, were establishing studios in the city. And they would be there to help San Francisco rebuild from its greatest tragedy of the century.

At 5:12 A.M. on the morning of Wednesday, April 18, 1906, the Pacific and North American tectonic plates suddenly sprang over and from 9 to 21 feet passed each other along 290 miles of the San Andreas fault. Shock waves sped across the terrain at 7,000 miles per hour. The first quake to hit San Francisco (estimated to be 8.3 on the Richter scale) shook the city in two phases for 45 seconds. Within the hour, 17 aftershocks rattled the city. City Hall and numerous other unreinforced brick buildings, together with many crowded tenements south of Market Street, collapsed instantly. Facades fell from homes, revealing furniture within. Less sturdy homes crumbled completely. Innumerable fire mains broke, impeding the work of firefighters. Within three days the central and northeast quadrants of San Francisco lay in smoldering ruins (Starr 2005, 162–63).

Miraculously, many of the buildings designed by the architects trained in Paris survived the earthquake and fire of April 1906. These architects, moreover, remained to rebuild the city between 1906 and 1909, and thus the architectural standards of the pre-quake city were observed. In the reconstruction that followed, these architects fashioned an engaging tradition of domestic design for the middle, upper middle, and upper classes.

In the newly developing neighborhoods of San Francisco—St. Francis Wood, Presidio Terrace, Seacliff—Mediterranean Revival style predominated. That style also became prevalent in the upscale community of Piedmont in the Oakland hills. At the same time, architects were transforming domestic Berkeley into a wonderland of bungalows with rustic redwood facades on the outside, and gleaming polished wood within. Unfortunately, fire would destroy many of these homes in September 1923.

With his plan for the Chicago World's Fair of 1893, Daniel Burnham had launched the City Beautiful movement, which envisioned the transformation of American cities into neo-Baroque orchestrations of broad boulevards, and grand plazas complete with fountains, statues, and Classical Revival structures. Working with local architect Edward Bennett out of a studio atop Twin Peaks, which held a commanding view of the city, Burnham submitted a plan calling for the transformation of San Francisco along City Beautiful lines. Ironically, the Burnham Report was formally filed in City Hall just a day before the earthquake of 1906. When Burnham, who was in Paris, learned of the earthquake, he left immediately for San Francisco with hopes of having a clean slate on which to design his vision of the city.

📷 *Snapshot*

Childhood Memories of the Great Earthquake

Dorothy Day, co-founder of the Catholic Worker Movement, spent her early childhood in the San Francisco Bay area. In her autobiography *The Long Loneliness* she recalled her experiences as a young girl during the fateful night of the San Francisco earthquake.

> The earthquake started with a deep rumbling and the convulsions of the earth started afterward, so that the earth became a sea which rocked our house in a most tumultuous manner. There was a large windmill and water tank in the back of the house and I can remember the splashing of the water from the tank on top of our roof. My father took my brothers from their beds and rushed to the front door, where my mother stood with my sister, whom she had snatched from beside me. I was left in the big brass bed, which rolled back and forth on a polished floor. When the earth settled, the house was a shambles, dishes broken all over the floor, books out of their bookcases, chandeliers down, chimneys fallen, the house cracked from roof to ground. But there was no fire in Oakland. The flames and cloud bank of the smoke could be seen across the bay and all the next day the refugees poured over by ferry and boat. Idora park and the racetrack made camping grounds for them. All the neighbors joined my mother in serving the homeless. Every stitch of available clothes was given away. All the day following the disaster there were more tremblings of the earth and there was fear in the air.

(Day 1952, 21–22)

While there was some support for implementing the Burnham Plan, in the immediate aftermath of the catastrophic earthquake, most civic leaders wanted to rebuild as quickly as possible and feared the delay that an entirely new city plan would demand. Therefore Burnham's plan was scuttled after a successful campaign led by *San Francisco Chronicle* editor Michael H. de Young to have the city rebuilt on its prior grid as quickly as possible (Starr 2005, 175–77).

CLOTHING

Fashion historian Jane Mulvagh noted that prior to the late 1920s, to comment on an outfit with "Whew! Pretty Hollywood" was an insult. When film producer Cecil B. DeMille ordered fashions from Paris for film star Gloria Swanson, he specifically requested theatrical exaggeration, not current couture styles. All that began to change, partially at the insistence of the stars themselves. At first Hollywood imported the French couturiers to work on film projects at the studios. Chanel, Molyneux, Lanvin, and Schiaparelli all made the trek westward. When Coco Chanel visited in 1929, she created elegant, sophisticated wardrobes for movies that ended up being shelved because of the abrupt drop in hemlines the following season. In addition, movie directors and executives discovered that many couturiers' designs may have looked stunning in person but seemed flat and unmemorable on film.

The solution was for studios to seek out indigenous talent to head up house wardrobe departments. The most famous of these designers were (Gilbert) Adrian, Edith Head, and Howard Greer. Their challenges were vastly different from those of Parisian fashion designers. Hollywood costumers, wrote Margit Mayer, "were not couturiers in the European sense; rather, they were art directors of femininity." They knew the importance of image and how to create illusion to achieve it. To optically lengthen Norma Shearer's short legs, MGM's Adrian raised the waistlines of her dresses. To disguise Barbara Stanwyck's long waist and low behind, Paramount's Edith Head constructed a belt that was wider in the front and fitted to be worn higher on the waist. Just as important to movie producers as the look of fashions on film was to avoid a repeat of the expensive Chanel disaster of 1929. Consequently, studio designers not only had to fuse style and glamour with the star's personality, they also had to make contemporary clothes that would not look outdated during the film's expected run of perhaps two years.

Studio wardrobe designers also had to be adept at period costuming. Although historical accuracy was not always a governing factor, the styling of the costumes had to be convincing. For hit movies, the influence of the costumes on mainstream fashion styles was sometimes significant. For instance, in designing costumes for *Gone With the Wind* in 1939, Walter Plunkett submitted antebellum material samples from the 1850s and 1860s to a northern textile mill for replication. As part of the agreement with the manufacturer, licensed *Gone With the Wind* cotton fabrics were widely distributed. In addition, designs of prom dresses of the following spring were replete with wide crinoline skirts. Similarly, a number of other historical-themed movies of the 1930s directly influenced what fashionable American women wore the following year. *The Merry Widow*, for example, inspired versions of the bustle in 1934. In that same year Mae West starred in *Belle of the Nineties* and revived an interest in the cinched hourglass waist. And American women began wearing capes and high collars again after the release of *Mary of Scotland* in 1936. Indeed, throughout the decades since the 1930s the impact of period movie costuming has been felt repeatedly in the American fashion arena.

In addition to inspiring revivals of historical costumes, the studio designers also influenced contemporary American fashions with stylistic interpretations that appealed to a broad spectrum of women. Joan Crawford's tailored suits with padded shoulders were a staple model for ready-to-wear makers throughout the late 1930s and into the 1940s. The tapered trousers worn by Katharine Hepburn and Marlene Dietrich were widely copied. Versions of Adrian's white satin gown, made for Jean Harlow in *Dinner at Eight*, were seen at many social events of 1933. And the men's undershirt business suffered a severe blow when Clark Gable took his off in *It Happened One Night* (1934). Some studio head designers such as Academy Award–winning Edith Head, Adrian, and Howard Greer even attained celebrity status and were as eagerly courted by advertisers as the stars they dressed.

One other West Coast influence that began to make its presence known in American fashion was the California style. Whereas New York clothiers largely conveyed an urban look in their collections, California makers emphasized sportswear. Designer names such as Cole, Koret, White Stag, and dozens of others began to promote their California origins in logos, on garment labels, and especially in advertising. At their peak in the mid-twentieth century, more than six hundred garment manufacturers on the West Coast produced about $200 million in apparel—almost one-third of the total ready-to-wear business in the United States at the time.

Although there were a significant number of dress, suit, and coat makers on the West Coast, the specialties of the larger firms were centered on sportswear, notably swimwear, slacks, and shorts. Fashion styles of slacks and shorts for most American women, though, were not broadly accepted initially, even in California. The styles of pants introduced for women by the Paris couturiers in the 1920s, particularly Chanel and Patou, were innovations of their resort wear collections. These casual types of trousers were worn by sophisticated socialites who gathered in St. Tropez, Monte Carlo, and Palm Beach to escape winter. Only gradually did the styles of menswear trousers, sailor's gobs, shorts, and pajamas begin to appeal to American women, and then primarily through sports clothing such as golf and tennis apparel. By the mid-1930s, though, slacks and shorts had become fairly common in the wardrobes of most women. Ready-to-wear makers routinely included models in slacks and shorts in their spring lines. However, the debate continued about when and where women could or should not wear pants. In 1936, *Vogue* offered the following specific advice:

In Florida and California they play golf in tailored slacks like a man's flannel trousers. But conservative Easterners say they don't like them on Long Island courses. Slacks for fishing? Yes, everywhere—from deep-sea fishing off Montauk to marlin fishing at Bimini. Slacks for boating? Decidedly yes, whether you're handling your own sail or cruising on a Diesel-engine yacht. Slacks for gardening and country loafing? By all means. And now, rumours drift about that America may take up the fashion of Continental women at Cannes—that of wearing slacks at night to dance in casinos or yacht-clubs.

By the close of the decade, though, *Vogue* acknowledged that pants were "an accepted part of nearly every wardrobe today." Most especially, the editor noted, "in California [they] go in for them wholeheartedly" (Hill 2004, 53–56).

MANUFACTURING

The first large electric companies, General Electric and Westinghouse, were geared to providing products and services on a large scale, such as street lighting and streetcars, which left a large opportunity for small manufacturers to provide electrical appliances for the home. In the West the Hotpoint Company of Ontario, California, began manufacturing home products such as the electric stove, mixers, and blenders (Kyvig 2002, 62). Over the next decades, electrical products for the home from companies such as Hotpoint would revolutionize domestic life, especially for women, who were expected to keep a much cleaner and efficient home thanks to the introduction of electric irons, washing machines, vacuum cleaners, and stoves.

Manufacturing north of California in Washington and Oregon for the most part involved the processing and packing of the rich resources of the area including lumber, salmon, and fruit, especially pears and apples. (For manufacturing in Alaska and Hawaii, see the sections on Food, and Animal Husbandry and Hunting and Fishing).

TECHNOLOGY

The technology developed in the Gold Rush for moving water across land had led to new innovations in the technology of irrigation. This same technology would also enlarge and stabilize the metropolitan infrastructure of San Francisco and Los Angeles. As the population of Los Angeles shot past the 100,000 mark in 1900, the city saw itself hurtling toward the dreaded day when it would have to increase its supply of water or decrease its supply of settlers. With limitless growth a basic tenet of their booster faith ("Big Is Good, Bigger Is Better, Biggest Is Best"), Angelenos began to cast about for new sources of water. They had enough to slake the thirst of about 250,000 residents. They were then thinking in terms of two million.

Fred Eaton, an engineer and a former mayor (1898–1900), had explored the possibility of building an aqueduct to tap the melted snow flowing from the eastern slopes of the Sierra Nevada into the Owens River some 250 miles north of Los Angeles. He persuaded William Mulholland, the municipal water department's superintendent and chief engineer, to look into his scheme. Eaton also had the foresight to file a claim in his own name for much of the river's surplus flow and for land that could be used for dams and reservoirs.

After rattling across the path of the proposed aqueduct in a mule-drawn buckboard, Mulholland pronounced the project feasible and put a price tag on it of something in the neighborhood of $24,500,000. In July 1905, *Los Angeles Times* editor Harrison Gray Otis sprang it on his readers with the headline "Titanic Project to Give City a River." Two months later the city's voters approved a $1,500,000 bond issue to acquire Owens Valley lands and water rights, including the Eaton options. An additional bond issue of $23 million was passed in 1907, and work began on what the press called "the Panama Canal of the West."

No American city had ever faced such an engineering challenge. The 233-mile aqueduct had to pass over foothills, through mountains (its 142 separate tunnels totaled 52 miles), and across the Mojave Desert. But before Mulholland's 5,000-man army could lay a foot of conduit, a 120-mile railroad had to be built to carry heavy machinery into the northern wilderness. Construction crews could be supplied only by building 500 miles of highway and trails, which were buried at times by blizzards and sandstorms. Finally, on November 5, 1913, some 40,000 Angelenos turned out to watch the Owens River water cascade into a San Fernando Valley reservoir. Many of those who came out had brought along tin cups to take their first drink. "There it is," said Mulholland, "take it" (Weaver 1973, 43, 46).

Irrigation, however, was a reorganization of nature, and all such reorderings have their risks. In October 1904, the California Development Company cut a second canal to augment one that had been completed in 1901 by George Chafee, who upon opening the canal, christened the former desert the "Imperial Valley." This second canal began on the western bank of the Colorado River and cut across northern Mexico into the Imperial Valley. Done illegally and on the cheap, the cut was a disaster waiting to happen, which did in the spring of 1905 when the Colorado River wrenched westward, as if seeking its ancient destination. Gorged by spring rains, the Colorado River over-

Train of the Southern Pacific Railway Company, c. 1900. Library of Congress.

whelmed the second canal and ran at levels of 25 to 200 feet above the rim of the Imperial Valley. As the unbridled Colorado flooded the entire valley, it looked as if southern California would be drowned beneath a vast inland sea. Finally, the Southern Pacific Railroad (SP), the only civil engineering entity capable of dealing with a catastrophe of this proportion, stopped the flooding by pouring some 2,500 carloads of rock, gravel, and clay into the break. This provided a temporary respite that gave engineers time to design and build an eight-foot-high levee that stretched for 15 miles on both sides of the original rupture. During the construction that took almost two years, 1,500 men had been pressed into service. President Theodore Roosevelt promised Southern Pacific president E. H. Harriman that the federal government would compensate the railroad for, in effect, preventing much of southern California from being permanently submerged. But Congress declined to go along with the president, and all that SP got for its efforts was gratitude of southern Californians and ownership of the bankrupt California Development Company.

In San Francisco another talented engineer brought water and waterpower to that city. Michael O'Shaughnessy of San Francisco pushed a major water project to a successful conclusion also by tapping a river, the Tuolumne, and bringing its water to the city through a system of dams, reservoirs, and aqueducts that took years to construct. As with Los Angeles, the San Francisco project involved its own long and intricate political and financial history, from first filing of water claims to finished construction.

On July 7, 1923, San Francisco mayor James "Sunny Jim" Rolph dedicated the O'Shaughnessy Dam, named in honor of the city engineer. But not until 1934, after 90 lives were lost, 4 more dams and 5 more reservoirs were built, and miles of tunnels constructed and pipelines put in place, would San Francisco benefit from water brought in from the Tuolumne.

The man-made water systems developed in Los Angeles and San Francisco enabled a population growth that would have been unsupportable otherwise. But these advancements came at a tremendous cost to the natural environment. San Francisco lost the magnificent Hetch-Hetchy Valley near Yosemite when the Tuolumne River was dammed and the valley filled to create a reservoir, and the Los Angeles canals devastated the once-fertile Owens Valley when the Owens River was siphoned off to Los Angeles. Each project, moreover, was plagued by claims of deception, double-dealing, and conflicts of interest that became the subject of many histories, novels, and films—including the Oscar-winning *Chinatown* (1974)—in the decades to come (Starr 2005, 172).

NAVIGATION

San Francisco, with its port facilities, railway terminals, banks, and factories, seemed obviously destined to be the commercial, financial, and industrial capital of the American West, but the powerful downtown Angelenos set out to dredge a deep-water harbor and build an aqueduct. The harbor project pitted Harrison Otis, editor of the *Los Angeles Times*, against Collis P. Huntington, president of the Southern Pacific, in a battle for federal funds. The money should go into harbor improvements at San Pedro, the *Times* insisted. The Southern Pacific, eager to control the city's waterfront traffic (and the city as well, of course), fought for a port at Santa Monica. The San Pedro forces organized what they called the Free Harbor League and, with the help of Stephen M. White in the U.S. Senate, managed to derail the Southern Pacific.

Work on the San Pedro breakwater began April 26, 1899, accompanied by suitable oratory, band music, and a barbecue. It was finished in 1910. The task of dredging the inner harbor was well along by the time the Panama Canal opened four years later. San Diego and San Francisco, with their splendid natural harbors, found themselves sharing the world's maritime commerce with an inland city. In the meantime, the Los Angeles city fathers had resorted to some artful gerrymandering. First, in 1906, they had annexed a "shoestring strip," which gave the city a corridor from its southern limits to the San Pedro-Wilmington area. Under state law, however, one incorporated city could not annex another, so Angelenos got the law changed to permit "consolidation." In August 1909, San Pedro and Wilmington agreed to be consolidated, and together the two small towns became a seaport city (Weaver 1973, 42).

Although a reciprocity treaty with Hawaii in 1874 had given the United States rights to lease navigation facilities at Pearl Harbor, the navy did not undertake serious construction of a base there until after the Spanish American War in 1898. In 1908, the navy dredged the harbor and over the next two decades, American workers turned Pearl Harbor into the finest naval facility in the Pacific. In 1935, the U.S. Navy staged a mock attack on Pearl Harbor, and the exercise exposed the weakness of the defense capabilities of the naval base. The significance of this liability of course became apparent to all Americans on December 7, 1941, when the successful attack on Pearl Harbor by the Japanese drew the United States into World War II.

TRANSPORTATION

Henry E. Huntington left San Francisco in 1902 and moved to Los Angeles, determined to "join this whole region in one big family." A generation of Angelenos rode his red (interurban) and yellow (local) trolley cars to the office, the theater, the beach, and the mountains. Racing along at speeds of 40 and 50 miles an hour (the horsecar had moved at the rate of seven and one-half miles an hour), the Pacific Electric cars enabled southern Californians to live among orange trees and work in downtown buildings.

"Los Angeles is a busy center for short trips, chiefly made now by electric cars," *Baedeker's United States* informed travelers in 1909. The local fare was 5 cents. It cost 15 cents to make the half-hour trip to Pasadena ("a thriving business city and health resort"). The hour-long, 50-cent journey to Santa Monica took tourists through Hollywood ("a suburb of charming homes"), and could be extended to Venice ("with canals, etc., in imitation of its European namesake"). For a dollar, the big spenders could travel a hundred miles along the Pacific Electric's "Great Surf Route," which included not only Long Beach ("a frequented summer resort, with 2,250 inhabitants") and San Pedro ("the National Government is now constructing a huge breakwater here"), but also Compton ("the center of the dairy district").

In the first decade of the new century, as Pacific Electric tracks snaked across the countryside, the population of Los Angeles tripled (from 102,479 to 319,198). Long Beach shot up from 2,252 to 17,809, Santa Monica from 3,057 to 7,847, Redondo Beach from 855 to 2,935, and Burbank from 3,048 to 12,255. "City making now is different from that of previous times," the editor of the *Express* pointed out on a fall day in 1905, shortly after Angelenos had agreed to go along with the acquisition of Owens Valley water rights. "Modern transportation methods make it possible to weave into a harmonious unit a larger section than was possible until late years."

Even if Greater Los Angeles stretched out 25 miles to both the northwest and the southeast, as seemed probable, a commuter would still be able to pick a fresh boutonniere from his garden, catch an interurban electric car, and reach his downtown office within an hour. Warming to the message of his tea leaves, the editor went on to describe a future city that would serve as "the world's symbol of all that is beautiful and healthful and inspiring." "It will retain the flowers and orchards and lawns, the invigorating free air from the ocean, the bright sunshine and the elbow room, which have marked it as peculiar in the past and which now are secured for all time by the abundance of the water supply. It will not become congested like the older cities, for the transportation lines, built in advance of the demands, have made it possible to get far out in the midst of the orchards and fields for home making."

The pattern for the city's sprawling development had been established by the world's finest mass rapid transit system. No one foresaw its doom when, at two o'clock on a May morning in 1897, a pair of tinkerers rolled a four-cylinder horseless carriage out of a West Fifth Street shop and took a few friends on a trial spin through the business district. "One fear which had been felt beforehand was that the machine would scare horses, because of its unique appearance and because of the noise of the gasoline motors and the gasoline explosions," the *Times* reported. "A number of teams were passed during the trial trip, but they showed not the slightest fear of the novel spectacle. The traffic question has become a problem," the *Times* observed on December 18, 1910, and called on the city council to do something "to keep the automobiles moving." Ten years later, when Rob Wagner was predicting that undertakers would soon be setting up branch mortuaries at all crossings and wags were referring to Los Angeles as "the city of the quick and the dead," the city fathers came up with a plan to protect pedestrians by outlawing parking in the downtown area. "The problem before the City Council of making the downtown streets safe for democracy has stirred up a war that makes the Battle of Gettysburg seem like a checker game by comparison," the *Times* observed on January 3, 1920, when the ordinance was being debated.

It took effect the following April, and Angelenos awakened to the realization that, like it or not, they had become dependent on automobiles. A *Times* headline trumpeted the discovery: "Business Can't Do without Them." Hollywood came to the rescue of downtown businessmen in the shapely form of Clara Kimball Young, who led a protest parade of cars through the business district. The no-parking ordinance was lifted, except for two evening rush hours. The city had capitulated to the automobile.

"Too bad we cannot make Broadway a three-deck affair," the *Times* sighed, momentarily struck by a fantasy that turned the streets over to automobiles, put public transportation underground, and had pedestrians walking "on a viaduct level with the second floor of the shops." City planners dreamed of the central city of 1990, proposing what they called "pedways" to accomplish the same visionary objective. So, too, would state and county roadways be necessary for a population increasingly wedded to the private automobile. By the end of 1924, approximately 310,000 automobiles—more than the total number of automobiles registered in the state

---

Snapshot

San Francisco Cable Cars

Andrew Smith Hallidie tested the first cable car at 4 o'clock in the morning, August 2nd, 1873, on Clay Street, in San Francisco. His idea for a steam engine powered—cable driven—rail system was conceived in 1869, after witnessing horses being whipped while they struggled on the wet cobblestones to pull a horsecar up Jackson Street. Clay Street Hill Railroad began public service on September 1st, 1873, and was a tremendous success.

By the beginning of 1906, many of San Francisco's remaining cable cars were under the control of the United Railroads company (URR), although Cal Cable and the Geary Street company remained independent. URR was pressing to convert many of its cable lines to overhead electric traction, but this was being resisted by opponents who objected to what they saw as ugly overhead lines on the major thoroughfares of the city center.

But at 5:12 A.M. on April 18, 1906, those objections were swept away as the great San Francisco earthquake struck. The quake and resulting fire destroyed the power houses and car barns of both the Cal Cable and the URR's Powell Street lines, together with the 117 cable cars stored within them. The subsequent race to rebuild the city allowed the URR to replace most of its cable car lines with electric streetcar lines. At the same time the independent Geary Street line was replaced by a municipally owned electric streetcar line, the first line of the San Francisco Municipal Railway.

By 1912, only eight cable car lines remained, all with steep gradients impassable to electric streetcars. In the 1920s and 1930s these lines came under pressure from the much improved buses of the era, which could now climb steeper hills than the electric streetcar. By 1944, the only cable cars remaining were the two Powell Street lines, by then in municipal ownership, and the three lines owned by the still independent Cal Cable. (www.cablecarmuseum.org/heritage.html)

of New York—were daily entering Los Angeles, where the corner of Adams and Figueroa, passed by 69,797 cars a day, was the busiest intersection in the United States. By 1933, streetcar usage in Los Angeles was half that of its peak year of 1924. By 1935, it had halved once again. Metropolitan Los Angeles was an integrated plain, hence amenable to automobile traffic via the great boulevards—Figueroa, Pico, Western, Olympic, Wilshire, Sunset—that were either inaugurated or expanded in the 1920s. In March 1938, construction began on the Arroyo Seco Parkway

A cable car on Sutter Street in San Francisco in the late nineteenth century. The Granger Collection, New York.

linking Pasadena and downtown Los Angeles on a continuously moving basis, with no intersections. Dedicated on December 30, 1940, just two days before the annual Tournament of Roses, the parkway anticipated the freeway system of post–World War II California (Weaver 1973, 48–52).

In northern California, the Caldecott Tunnel, which was dug through the Contra Costa Range in 1937, linked the automotive traffic of the Bay Area with the spacious plain of Contra Costa. The Bay Area presented a different transportation problem. Comprised of a series of populated land masses that were separated by water, the area had 50,000 commuters who depended on ferries to bring them into and out of San Francisco daily. With the popularity and ownership of automobiles growing exponentially, pressure steadily increased for the construction of bridges to connect the water-trapped population centers. San Franciscans had been talking about the possibility of a bridge linking their city to Oakland on the East Bay shore since the middle of the nineteenth century. In 1869 the completion of a railroad intensified such talk, because the city of San Francisco could be approached by rail only from San Jose via the San Francisco peninsula. Finally in 1906, the Southern Pacific spanned the southern portion of San Francisco Bay with a low-level trestle across the shoals and mudflats between Dumbarton Point and Palo Alto. A parallel span for automobiles was not added until 1927.

By 1929 President Herbert Hoover, a Stanford-trained engineer, was spearheading discussions regarding a great bridge linking Oakland and San Francisco. Hoover directed the Reconstruction Finance Corporation—which had been created to bring relief to Depression-wracked businesses—to purchase $62 million in state bonds from the California Toll Bridge Authority toward the construc-

The Golden Gate Bridge under construction, San Francisco, 1934. Photo by Charles M. Hiller. Library of Congress.

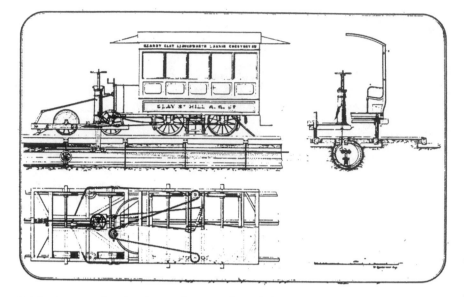

Original patent drawing for Andrew Smith Hallidie's cable car system, the world's first, introduced in San Francisco in 1873. The Granger Collection, New York.

tion of such a bridge. Later the New Deal's Public Works Authority authorized another $15.2 million in loans and grants, bringing the total budget for the bridge to $77.2 million, which made the San Francisco–Oakland Bay Bridge, dedicated in November 1936, one of the most expensive public works projects in American history.

While plans were being made for the Oakland bridge, the counties surrounding San Francisco Bay, joined by Del Norte County on the Oregon border (eager to bring automotive tourists into the Redwood Empire), organized the Golden Gate Bridge and Highway District in order to build a bridge across the Golden Gate Strait between San Francisco and Marin County, thereby linking the Bay Area directly to the North Coast. In November 1930, voters in the district authorized the issuance of $35 million in bonds to construct a bridge across the Golden Gate. The bridge, designed by Charles Alton Ellis, combined the architectural stylizations of San Francisco architect Irving Morrow and a color scheme based on international orange. His design resulted in a bridge built between January 1933 and April 1937 that not only linked the San Francisco peninsula to the North Coast but created a masterpiece of art and engineering that ranks, so its historian John van der Zee has justifiably claimed, with the Parthenon as a harmonization of site and structure, nature and public work. Soon the Golden Gate Bridge, like the Brooklyn Bridge, asserted itself as an icon of American civilization (Starr 2005, 186–87).

The Wright brothers flew their powered heavier-than-air craft on December 17, 1903, near Kitty Hawk, North Carolina. But neither North Carolina nor the Wrights' home state of Ohio was destined to capitalize upon the new invention. That role belonged to California. Over the next 10 years, the names associated with aviation in California—Glenn Curtiss, Allan and Malcolm Loughead (later changed to Lockheed), John Northrop, Glenn Martin, Donald Douglas, T. Claude Ryan—would become names that Americans associated with flight.

In 1910, the Lockheed brothers were busy with the design and production of a passenger-carrying seaplane, first flown in 1911. Glenn Curtiss and Glenn Martin were also designing and building pioneering aircraft. Graduating from MIT in 1914 with the first degree in aeronautical engineering granted by that institution, Donald Douglas joined Glenn Martin the next year at an assembly building near the present-day Los Angeles International Airport. In 1920, after a brief sojourn in Cleveland, Douglas opened his own aviation company in the back room of a barbershop on Pico Boulevard. By the fall of 1922, Douglas was manufacturing an airplane a week out of a former movie studio on Wilshire Boulevard in Santa Monica. T. Claude Ryan, meanwhile, had established Ryan Airlines of San Diego, a mail and passenger carrier. This got Ryan interested in the problem of long-distance flight. The result was the M-1, soon refined into the M-2 monoplane. Further modified as the N-X-22 Ryan NYP, Ryan's monoplane, christened the *Spirit of St. Louis,* was flown across the Atlantic in May 1927 by one of Ryan's young pilots, Charles Lindbergh.

So, too, did California pioneer passenger flight. By the mid-1920s, fully a third of the aviation traffic in the United States was operating from 50 private landing fields in greater Los Angeles, where there were some 3,000 licensed pilots (a group that included a notable number of women and minorities, especially African Americans). Four passenger lines—Western Air Express, Maddux Air Lines, Pacific Air Transport, and Standard Airlines—were offering regularly scheduled service to Salt Lake City, San Francisco, Seattle, and the Southwest. In 1929, Western announced plans for service to Kansas City, connecting to New York, in Fokker DP-32 passenger planes. Maddux Airlines, in which film director Cecil B. DeMille was an early investor, flew Ford Tri-Motors. On August 26, 1929, the gigantic (776 feet in length) German passenger dirigible *Graf Zeppelin* arrived in Los Angeles at Mines Field, site of the present-day Los Angeles International Airport, on a round-the-world cruise. An estimated 150,000 visitors flocked to the airport by automobile and streetcar to catch a glimpse of the tethered behemoth whose very arrival signaled an impending era of international flight.

The following decade, thanks in part to pioneering aeronautical research at Caltech, Donald Douglas took a two-engine passenger/freight carrier through the evolutions of DC-1 and DC-2 to the DC-3, arguably the most serviceable aircraft in the history of aviation. Announcing the DC-3 in 1935, Douglas sold 803 of these aircraft in the next two years. By 1937, DC-3s were carrying 95 percent of the civilian traffic in the United States. During World War II, more than 10,000 DC-3s (redesignated the C-47 Sky Train or the C-54 by the Americans, the Dakota by the British) ferried hundreds of thousands of troops and an uncountable amount of freight.

To the north in Seattle, Washington, William E. Boeing was also making aviation history. In 1916 Boeing began building seaplanes. A year later he incorporated his operations as the Boeing Airplane Company. Over the next decade Boeing joined with Pacific Airplane Company to launch United Airlines, and in the 1930s Boeing developed an aircraft capable of transatlantic passenger travel. Pan American used these Boeing seaplanes to begin passenger travel to England in 1939.

Political Life

In the first half of the twentieth century a strong contrast can be seen between the states of the Pacific West that were dominated by special interests and those where a strong pioneer spirit of rugged individualism put more democratic forces in play.

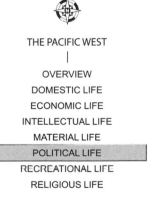

California and Hawaii fit into the former group and Washington, Nevada, Oregon, and Alaska into the latter. For example, when Washingtonians entered the Union in 1889, they created a constitution that divided the executive branch among nine elected offices to restrict the concentration of power in too few hands. This section will explore the governments these political forces created and how these political bodies responded to societal challenges such as crime and war.

GOVERNMENT

California, despite its self-propagated and self-authenticated image of itself as a free and easy society, had at the center of its complexity a tendency toward hard conservatism, which was evident from its earliest days of statehood with political gangs such as the San Francisco vigilance committees of 1851, 1856, and 1876.

And into the early twentieth century the state allowed a hard-nosed corporation, the Southern Pacific, to exercise significant political and economic control over its citizens. California was also an agricultural state in which farming was conducted on a quasi-industrial basis, and most big farmers who were living close to the edge supported a political system that opposed the organization of agricultural labor. California was also, outside San Francisco and Los Angeles, a suburban and small-town state, characterized by conservative political values.

On the other hand, with a militant labor union tradition that emerged in reaction to the unbridled supremacy of economic powers such as the Southern Pacific, the state also cultivated a leftist tradition, and in the early twentieth century the IWW had found a receptive environment in California, and so in the 1930s would the Communist Party (Starr 2005, 202–3).

As with the rest of the nation, complacency settled on California and the rest of the Pacific West during the prosperous decade following World War I. The entire West voted solidly Republican in those years, and in the national arena, Herbert Hoover, who had become an adopted son of California, served as U.S. secretary of commerce under President Calvin Coolidge and won the presidency in 1928. California entered the Great Depression with a pervasively moderate Republican orientation, tinged by reformist Progressivism. To the right were hard-nosed corporate oligarchs, busy perfecting a number of merchants' and manufacturers' associations, and a cadre of ultraconservative ranchers, many of them of southern ancestry. To the left were old-fashioned socialists (especially in Oakland, Berkeley, and Los Angeles), remnants of the IWW, utopian radicals of various persuasions, disciplined and dedicated Communists, and various other ideologues.

Because certain booming industries, such as the construction trades and tourism, were keenly sensitive to national trends and fell into a slump immediately, the Great Depression hit Californians hard. Adding to the economic stress were the "Okies," the refugees from the Dust Bowl, who swarmed into California and congregated in makeshift camps, where they suffered from hunger and disappointment until organized relief was forthcoming. In the mid-1930s, at the height of the Depression, more than 100,000 migrants, with no more possessions than they could carry on their backs or in their beat-up old jalopies, wandered into the Central Valley looking for work, shelter, and opportunities that, for the moment, did not exist.

California had also begun to attract retired farmers and businesspeople from throughout the Midwest. Although industrious and intelligent, in this pre–Social Security era, their resources were rather limited, so that they often had to engage in part-time employment, which put them into direct competition with native Californians in the already scarce job market. With time on their hands, these "senior citizens" became receptive to the myriad politicians preaching utopian solutions to the nation's economic woes. Perhaps, as journalist John Gunther suggested, it was the bright sunshine that caused previously conservative midwesterners to "go crazy" in California.

The first panacea that attracted support was "technocracy," a proposal advanced by Howard Scott of Columbia University. He contended that if the national economy were regimented by scientific planning to utilize all available technical improvements, then everyone would need to work only two or three hours daily and laborers could be retired with pensions at age 45. While this scheme was gathering some support, two others advanced in 1934 soon overshadowed it. One was the End Poverty in California (EPIC) crusade of Upton Sinclair, a Socialist and the author of many plays and novels. He advocated the elimination of the sales tax, the enactment of heavy income and corporation taxes, and the issuance of state "scrip" as a substitute for the money then so scarce. His proposal included the founding of state land colonies for the unemployed and the payment of pensions of 50 dollars a month to retired persons. His plan won him the Democratic nomination for governor in 1934, but he lost in the general election to businessman Frank Merriam.

The other panacea that blossomed in the year 1934 in the West was the Townsend Plan, which promised a simple solution for all economic ills. The originator, Dr. Francis E. Townsend, a retired physician, proposed that the state levy a tax of 2.5 percent on all business transactions and use the revenue for the payment of pensions of $200 a month to all persons over 60, who would spend the money and thus stimulate the economy. For several years afterward this plan continued to have a devoted band of followers, and hundreds of Townsend Clubs across the nation beat the drum for "old age survivors' pensions." Although unsuccessful, the enthusiasm demonstrated by the Townshendites certainly influenced New Dealers in the development of their own Social Security plan.

Meanwhile, many Californians became devotees of another scheme, which was dubbed "Ham and Eggs." A radio commentator, Robert Noble, proposed that all persons over 50 be paid a pension of $25 every Tuesday, and an advertising agent, Willis Allen, lent promotion, but with a change to $30 every Thursday. The labor unions and the Communist Party endorsed this proposal, and thousands turned out and even paid for admission to the spectacular mass meetings staged by the promoters. When the plan was made an issue in the election of 1938, over a million people voted for it, but soon the enthusiasm waned. When the proposal was submitted again in a special election the next year, it was soundly defeated.

Indirectly, these plans were a boon to Democratic leaders in Washington who were trying to push their own economic reforms. Obviously, a California that could be carried off by such radical panaceas would accept the relatively mild measures of the New Deal with little opposition. California, as well as the entire West, voted Democratic in the national elections through the 1930s and into the 1940s, thereby contributing a large bloc of electoral votes to Roosevelt and Truman (Starr 2005, 210–13).

In Hawaii, politics in the first decades on the twentieth century was controlled by the "Big Five" holding companies that began as shipping companies in the mid-nineteenth century, started by the sons of the missionaries who had come to the islands in the early nineteenth century. By the twentieth century these companies held controlling interest in most of the sugar plantations and processing and canning plants, as well as the shipping facilities (Barnes 2007, 38–39). This powerful group guided Hawaii to annexation to the United States in 1898 despite the wishes of a majority of native Hawaiians to return to monarchy and self-rule. During most of the territorial period, which lasted until 1959, the Big Five controlled the legislature, which was the most powerful political force on the island. They maintained power despite the fact that during the early territorial period two-thirds of the voters were native Hawaiians, most of whom advocated the home-rule policies of the pro-monarchists. Until the end of World War II the government was controlled from the lounge of the exclusive Pacific Club in Honolulu, where wealthy sugar planters met to plan strategies for the future over snifters of brandy and Cuban cigars (Barnes 2007, 57).

Without strong special interest groups, Alaska came under the control of the federal government to a greater degree than its sister territory Hawaii. The best example of this influence occurred during the Great Depression, when power in Washington, D.C., expanded as more and more people looked to their federal government for help to combat the economic catastrophe that had fallen on them. The Great Depression had hit Alaska hard, but times had been rough for so long in so many places that some folks did not seem to notice. In the summer of 1934, with no upturn in sight, President Franklin D. Roosevelt told Ernest Gruening, head of the newly created Division of Territories and Island Possessions, "Alaska needs more people and we ought to do something to promote agriculture. Next Spring I would like you to move a thousand or fifteen hundred people from the drought stricken states of the Midwest and give them a chance to start a new life in Alaska."

Alaska was not the only place where the New Deal tried to resettle the destitute from poverty-stricken rural areas, but thanks in part to Alaska's special mystique, the proposed project "up north" got considerable press and took center stage. In Alaska even those traditionally opposed to the federal government involvement in territorial affairs were guardedly optimistic. The area selected was the Matanuska Valley, 40 miles north of Anchorage. The area had soil that in some areas was rich and fertile and a growing season of 110 days. In 1935, the federal government restricted homesteading in the area and designated it as an area reserved for those families the government would send in to colonize it. In all some 200 families traveled north to the new colony in the spring of 1935. Despite the promise of sunny skies, the colonists were welcomed by torrential rain. Furthermore, promised homes had not been built, wells had not been dug, there were no schools, and there were perennial complaints about the high prices at the government commissary. Rather than complain, 106 of the families simply gave up and went home, but for those that remained progress eventually came. Within the year 140 houses of the 200 promised were built, and a school building was opened. By 1940, 150 of the 200 tracts were occupied, despite the fact that many of the original families had abandoned the project. In the end, the federal government had saved the colony and eased its transition into a regular settlement.

But it was not New Deal domestic policy but rather military policy that stimulated growth. In 1940 the military constructed Fort Richardson and Elmendorf Air Base nearby, which provided a job market as well as a farm market for the colonists of Matanuska Valley. Some critics called the Matanuska colony a social experiment gone awry—just another socialist New Deal scheme by that Democrat Franklin Delano Roosevelt (FDR). Others sang FDR's praises and called Matanuska the best thing that could have happened to them. Regardless, the fact remains that the town survived and prospered through federal government intervention (Borneman 2004, 311–16).

At the turn of the century Nevada was a subject for discussion in periodicals as the rotten borough of the nation, which should never have been admitted to the Union. There was even discussion as to whether a state, once in the Union, could constitutionally be put out of it when it became depopulated. The effect of this discussion upon native Nevadans can readily be imagined. They became fiercely assertive concerning their state sovereignty, the more so because the paucity of their population gave them a personal experience of sovereignty that was lacking in the populous states.

Nevada politics in the twentieth century until World War II had a town-meeting air about it. Had not the expanse of the state prohibited it, all of the voters could have assembled conveniently on the beautiful lawn of the state university campus at Reno and there argued out their affairs and selected their public officers. Once the Southern Pacific Political Bureau dismantled itself, Nevada politics became small townish and gossipy. Nevada Senator Key Pittman boasted that he knew almost every one of his constituents personally, and he could not have doubted that his constituents in turn knew all about him.

Nevadans were attracted to politics by the unusual opportunities for political participation. There were the same county and state central committees for the political parties that existed in other states and the same public offices, but the number of political participants was few. Nevadans, consequently, lived their political lives in a way that was not to be conceived of in the large states. This helped give them a sense of citizenship that was unexcelled in the nation.

The hero and the spokesman and, for many Nevadans, the apotheosis of this twentieth-century Nevada spirit was Senator Pat McCarran, standing forth in the name of Americanism against Communist subversion from within and invasion by aliens from without. In Nevada's roster of heroes, McCarran stands with John W. Mackay and no one else, for he personified citizenship as the concept that had been enlarged by Nevada's peculiar circumstances.

Gold and silver strikes in the early part of the century did much to emancipate Nevada politically as well as economically. Withdrawal of the Southern Pacific from Nevada politics, taking place at the time of the new discoveries, created a vacuum into which anything might have rushed. Aside from the railroad, the only economic interest in the state of any considerable importance was the livestock industry, which was largely absentee-owned. The best guess is that, except for the new bonanzas, Nevada's political destinies would have been determined by Nevada cattle corporations, united by common interests, whether they were in San Francisco or New York. This possibility was obviated by Jim Butler's discovery of gold and silver in west-central Nevada. A rich home-owned industry, Tonopah mining, came into being and provided an economic basis for home rule. During the next half century, nearly every nationally important political figure in the state was a man from Tonopah (Ostrander 1966, 133–34).

In the twentieth century the people of Oregon demonstrated in their creation of government the same innovative spirit of their pioneer predecessors. In the early decades of the century, for example, they implemented reforms that collectively became known as the "Oregon Plan." These innovations included initiative and referendum established in 1902, which allows citizens to create and remove laws through the ballot. In 1908, they were the first state to establish the right of recall, and in 1923 they were the first state to institute an income tax.

LAW, CRIME, AND PUNISHMENT

Throughout the latter part of the nineteenth century, romanticized accounts of the exploits of criminals from the West like Jesse James, Cole Younger, Butch Cassidy, and Billy the Kid had fascinated Americans. But by the beginning of the new century the old West had become much tamer and the more colorful criminals had moved on to the new frontier of Alaska. One such character was Jefferson Randolph "Soapy" Smith of Skagway, Alaska, a turn-of-the-century gold boomtown. In 1898, already run out of other towns on the mining frontier, in the "lower forty-eight," Smith was destined to meet his end in Skagway. He received his nickname, "Soapy," from running a confidence game where 20—or even 100—dollar bills were wrapped around bars of soap. The "lucky" ones were then placed in a barrel with similarly wrapped, but valueless bars. Five dollars a shot was all it took to try to win, but of course the only winners of the big bucks were Smith's hired hands.

Like many crime bosses, he was revered by some and feared by most. While his gang of henchmen duped newcomers, fleeced returning prospectors, and even resorted to murder out on the trails, Smith stood innocently and supported everything from stray dogs to destitute stampeders, the latter frequently made so by the work of his gang. Finally Smith's gang pushed the locals too far. When a miner who had just returned from the Yukon was robbed, duped,

Snapshot

Soapy Smith: Crime Boss of Skagway, Alaska

Fact frequently blurs with fiction when recounting tales of Soapy's reign in Skagway, but one story is too good to pass up even if its sources are dubious. One of Smith's operations, it seems, was a telegraph station that purported to send messages to loved ones back home. No one seemed to notice that the telegraph lines ran a few miles out of town and then stopped. But that didn't stop Smith from receiving replies from the outside—always collect. (Borneman 2004, 190–92)

or otherwise conned—the versions of the story vary—out of some $3,000 in gold dust, a vigilante committee determined to confront Smith's iron rule, and on July 8, 1898, Smith was killed on Juneau wharf in a shoot-out with the town surveyor, Frank Reid. Smith died instantly. Reid lingered for days before being given a hero's burial that the *Skagway News* said was to Skagway and Alaska what General Grant's had been to New York's and the nation (Borneman 2004, 190–92).

REFORM

Much of the energy of reform movements of the early twentieth century came from newly organized women's movements. The new woman of the twentieth century was in most cases better educated, more likely to work outside the house, and more dedicated to public issues than her mother. In 1900 in the West, one-fourth of the nonfarm workforce was composed of women, and many went into nurturing professions of social welfare, teaching, and nursing. These professions brought women directly in contact with many of the social problems facing the nation. They recognized that poor schooling, poor housing, poor dietary habits, unsupervised canning of food, lack of access to open space, and exploitation of women and children in the workforce were problems for the entire community.

Unlike reform movements of the previous century, the twentieth-century reformers saw government as a vehicle for change, not an obstruction. Therefore, they struggled to take control of government. One political tactic in the reform movement was to unite with suffragists to get the vote for women, who, it was believed, would be more likely to vote in support of social reform. Western states took the lead in this battle. By 1913 every state in the West and the Alaska territory had granted women the right to vote. By contrast, east of the Mississippi no state granted suffrage until New York did so in 1917.

Armed with women's power of the vote, western states struggled to wrest control of government from special interests. Oregon led the way in reform in 1903 by being the first state to write the process of initiative and recall into its state constitution. Once in control of state legislatures, reformers passed myriad laws that would change the lives of their fellow westerners. As a result of reform movements, Americans throughout the West benefited from better schools, cleaner drinking water, and regulated public utilities. In many areas open space coveted by developers and manufacturers was safeguarded for all. In 1913, for example, reformers in Oregon persuaded Governor Oswald West to make the entire Oregon coastline available for public access, thus boosting coastal park development. Reform movements in the West also regulated the hours that children and women could work. Even in a state such as California, with powerful agricultural interests opposed to restricting the hours that women could work, reformers were able to get such a bill passed in 1911 (Mowry 1951, 144). As a result of the work of reformers in the early decades of the century, the life of Americans in the West changed. They were more likely to be protected by insurance on the job; had cleaner drinking water, better schools, and healthier food;

and enjoyed the benefits of the natural wonders that surrounded them in protected national and state parks.

WAR

In 1914, the U.S. navy established its Pacific Fleet, supported by a growing naval presence in San Diego. During World War I, California contributed its fair share of troops, including a number of locally raised regiments whose soldiers entered the trenches bonded to each other by local association and civic pride. Professor George Ellery Hale of the Mount Wilson Observatory in Pasadena also played a key role in organizing the national scientific establishment on behalf of the war effort. In the 1920s, the oligarchy of San Diego, operating through Congressman William Kettner, deliberately recruited a major naval and Marine Corps presence to that city, transforming San Diego into a kind of Gibraltar on the Pacific, complete with a Marine Corps training depot designed in Spanish Revival by Bertram Goodhue, architect of the California Building at the Panama California International Exposition. The U.S. army, meanwhile, was expanding its presence through a series of forts and installations in the San Francisco Bay Area, including Hamilton Field Air Station in Marin County. In 1931, the naval air service established Moffett Field, an important lighter-than-air facility, at the border between Sunnyvale and Mountain View on the San Francisco peninsula, centered on an airship hangar of such monumental proportions that it created its own weather system. Meanwhile Californians, such as Chester Nimitz, Henry "Hap" Arnold, Jimmy Doolittle, and George S. Patton, had earned, or were in the process of earning, distinguished military reputations that would propel them into leadership roles in the conflict to come. The San Francisco Bay Area and metropolitan Los Angeles had each finally developed important port and ship repair facilities, both military and civilian, and secured the sources of water and hydroelectricity necessary for an expanded defense industrial capacity (Starr 2005, 227–29).

Recreational Life

SPORTS

The outdoor life, which celebrated mountaineering, camping, fishing, sport boxing, swimming, and golf had characterized the California—and to some extent the Oregon—lifestyle since the late nineteenth century. California also has boasted an especially large proportion of athletic champions emanating from the state. Furthermore, because of generous public support of sports facilities, Californians promoted the democratization of sports such as swimming, tennis, and golf that were usually the domain of the elite. Most of the champions of the twentieth century who came from California first developed their skills in publicly subsidized circumstances: municipally supported swimming pools, golf courses, and tennis courts in particular.

The tennis courts of California, many of them municipally funded, tended to favor hard surfaces, which were more economical and could be used year-round, and encouraged a quicker and more competitive mode of play than the game played on the grass or clay surfaces of the East. Hence the early champions in this field—May Sutton (Wimbledon 1907), Maurice McLoughlin (Wimbledon 1913), Helen Wills (an eight-time Wimbledon winner in the 1920s and 1930s)—tended to come up through public courts rather than country clubs and to play a fast and edgy kind of game. The same is true for swimming champion Florence Chadwick, a policeman's daughter who set new English Channel records in August 1950. She had honed her skills as a youngster in the free public surf off San Diego. Rough-water swimming has also been a popular pursuit in California as attested by the many swimming and boating clubs fronting San Francisco Bay. One aspect of this rough-water-oriented culture, yachting, centered in the clubs and associations of San Francisco, Catalina, and San Diego, remained elite. Surfing, a rough-water sport brought to California in 1907 by Anglo-Hawaiian George Freeth, became yet another affordable, widespread pursuit. By the late twentieth century, in fact, the California surfer, male and female alike, had become an icon of the California lifestyle, celebrated in song, film, advertising, and other media. So, too, did another inexpensive shoreline pursuit, beach volleyball, gain comparable popularity during these years and become similarly representative of an endless summer on the shores of the sundown sea in a place called California, where youth ruled the popular imagination.

Golf also became a popular sport in the West in the early decades of the century, and California was home to one of the most popular links in the world, Pebble Beach. This beautiful course, which looks out over the Pacific Ocean, opened in 1919 on land located in a resort owned by the Pacific Improvement Company. Over the years Pebble Beach gained international fame among golf enthusiasts and in 2005 was named the best golf course in America by *Golf Digest*.

Although baseball was popular, California and the rest of the Pacific West remained minor league states until the arrival of the Giants and the Dodgers in California in 1958. Prior to the arrival of the "Big Leagues," the Pacific Coast League—organized in 1903 from the club-oriented California League that had emerged in the 1880s—was for more than half a century an extraordinarily popular and successful venture in terms of the number of cities represented, successful stadiums, and notable players, including two of baseball's greatest stars, Joe DiMaggio (San Francisco Seals) and Ted Williams (San Diego Padres). Another great California player, Jackie Robinson of Pasadena, became the first African American to integrate Major League Baseball via a team (the Dodgers) that subsequently came to Los Angeles.

Mountaineering, meanwhile, remained a largely elite endeavor, pursued by such upper-middle-class Sierra Club members as Walter A. Starr Jr., whose posthumously published *Starr's Guide to the John Muir Trail and the High Sierra Region* (1934) literally cost him his life to research. Skiing, an allied pursuit, was equally upper-middle-class in the pre–World War II era but, unlike mountaineering, expanded in the postwar era to a widespread resort-based culture. Rock climbing, however, an edge-sport affiliate of mountaineering, remained a sport of the few, given its great dangers (Starr 2005, 299–301).

Hawaiians traditionally had a fondness for sports. Many of these were water based, such as swimming, surfing, spear fishing, and canoeing. Many "sports" of the twentieth century were rooted in the economic life of an earlier era. For example, canoeing in heavy surf was an essential survival skill, but in the twentieth century it evolved into the official state sport of outrigger canoe racing. Hawaiian's two most important contributions to American sports have been surfing and catamaran sailing (Barnes 2007, 22).

MUSIC

In 1923, an opera company was established in San Francisco under the direction of emigre Gaetano Merola. Moved in 1932 to a magnificent new Beaux Arts opera house on Van Ness Avenue, the San Francisco Opera—along with its symphony orchestra established in 1911 and flourishing under the direction of Pierre Monteux—sustained for 50 years San Francisco's claim to be the performing arts capital of the Far West. Los Angeles, meanwhile, nurtured a burgeoning choral music community from the early 1900s, the legacy of its strong Anglo-Protestant population. In 1919 a philharmonic orchestra was established under the direction of Alfred Hertz with the financial support of mining heir William Andrews Clark, who sometimes sat in as second violin. In Daisy Dell, a canyon amphitheater in Hollywood, a tradition of religious services and choral music led to the establishment of the Hollywood Bowl in 1922, for which architect Lloyd Wright, son of Frank Lloyd Wright, designed a performance shell that soon emerged as one of the primary icons of southern California (Starr 2005, 296).

ENTERTAINMENT

Like the rest of the country, Westerners were entertained by movies, but unlike the rest of the nation, when they went to the movies they were enjoying a "home-grown" product. In the 1920s Los Angeles became the capital of the great film entertainment industry. Motion pictures did not initially establish themselves in California. The early studios were in New York, Philadelphia, New Jersey, and Chicago. But in the winter of 1907–1908 director Francis Boggs and cameraman Thomas Persons, working for Selig Films of Chicago, and needing good weather, left for Los Angeles, where they filmed the outdoor scenes for *The Count of Monte Cristo* (1908). Liking Los Angeles as a location, they established a Selig operation there, filming *In the*

Sultan's Power (1908), the first complete film to be made in Los Angeles, and then used a Classic Revival villa and gardens as background for *The Roman* (1908).

Those films were quickly followed by a production of *Carmen* (1908), which involved the building of an entire set. Not only did the Selig staff appreciate the reliably good weather of Los Angeles, they also relished the distance from the subpoena servers constantly being dispatched by the lawyers hired by Edison Laboratories to initiate suits against producers who were not always willing to pay what Edison considered their fair share of licensing and reel footage fees.

Between 1908 and 1909, a number of other filmmakers, equally reluctant to pay tribute to the so-called Edison Trust, arrived in Los Angeles. In the winter of 1910, director David Wark Griffith arrived, returning to southern California in the winters of 1911, 1912, and 1913 to film outdoor scenes. For his first all-California film, *The Thread of Destiny* (1910), a story of Old California starring Mary Pickford, Griffith moved his troupe out to Mission San Gabriel. Another all-California film, *In Old California* (1910), soon followed. Most of the movies Griffith made in these early years—including *The Converts* (1910), *The Way of the World* (1910), and *Over Silent Paths* (1910)—were set in Spanish or Mexican California and filmed in the missions of San Gabriel, San Fernando, or San Juan Capistrano. These settings gave Americans who saw these films a romanticized view of the West, and for many it became their fixed idea of the region. The mission settings depicted in these films celebrated the lost grandeur of an earlier way of life but were not representative of American life in the West as it really was in the early twentieth century.

Perhaps a more honest view of life in the West, at least in southern California, may have come from the creations of Mack Sennett, a disciple of Griffith, who came to Los Angeles in 1912. Within 30 minutes of his troupe's arrival at the train station, Sennett was busy filming the first of many Keystone comedies. A brash Irish Canadian given to liquor, cigars, and women (tradition assigns to him the invention of the casting couch), Sennett loved Los Angeles and featured it as the environment and background of countless Keystone comedies. Taking to the streets for innumerable chase scenes, Sennett caught Los Angeles in the process of becoming a major American city. Viewing these comedies across the country, Americans caught glimpses of inviting bungalows on broad avenues lined with palm, pepper, or eucalyptus trees. It was always sunny, and there was never any snow on the ground.

The New York director Cecil Blount DeMille arrived in Los Angeles in December 1913 to film a Western titled *The Squaw Man* (1914), which he was making in partnership with the San Jose–born New York vaudeville producer Jesse Lasky and Lasky's brother-in-law, Samuel Goldfish (later Goldwyn), who was in the wholesale glove business. "I'm in," said Goldfish the night the Jesse L. Lasky Feature Play Company was organized by Lasky, DeMille, and Goldfish over dinner at the Claridge Grill in New York. (As Samuel Goldwyn, Goldfish became famous for saying "Include me out" when he didn't like a deal.)

In Los Angeles, DeMille located an L-shaped barn abutting an orange grove on the corner of the dirt roads Selma and Vine, which he rented and transformed into a makeshift studio. Released in February 1914, *The Squaw Man* earned $244,700, which represented an enormous return on investment. Not only did DeMille decide to stay

Cecil B. DeMille, 1952. Library of Congress.

A scene with actor Lionel Atwill from *Doctor X,* 1932, directed by Michael Curtiz. © Warner Bros. Pictures. Photographer: Scotty Welbourne.

in Hollywood, he became, along with Griffith, the iconic Hollywood director, dressed in quasi-military style jodhpurs and riding boots, with epaulets on his shirt, directing large-scale films in the studio or outdoors like a general on campaign. Griffith's *The Birth of a Nation* (1915) and *Intolerance* (1916) set new standards for ambitious production, and in such films as *Carmen* (1915) and *The Ten Commandments* (1923), DeMille was not far behind. Each of them owed a debt (especially DeMille) to David Belasco, a San Francisco–born New York producer specializing in opulent presentations that Belasco helped transmute into the Hollywood approach, with its obsession with lavish production values, its taste for pageantry, and, above all, its belief that *story, story, story* must ever energize the film and move it forward. Perhaps it was DeMille's emphasis on the spectacular that gave Americans the impression that Hollywood was that, as the nation became captivated by these great extravaganzas.

What was amazing about Hollywood was that, decade after decade, it never fell into a slump. In the early 1900s, film was conceptualized as narrative and made a vital connection with the masses. In the 1910s, just about every genre—comedies, tragedies, biblical and historical epics, domestic dramas, westerns—was introduced in fully realized formats. In the domestic dramas of Cecil B. DeMille from this period—*The Cheat* (1915), *Old Wives for New* (1918), *Male and Female* (1919), *Don't Change Your Husband* (1919), *For Better or Worse* (1919), *Why Change Your Wife?* (1920)—a generation of recently derusticated Americans was exposed to the amenities, niceties, and dangers of urban life, including adultery and divorce. During the 1930s, Hollywood can be said to have helped stabilize the nation by offering intensities of psychological release for the stress everyone was experiencing: gangster films (*Little Caesar* [1930], *Public Enemy* [1931], *Scarface* [1932]) with which to question capitalism itself; horror films (*Dracula* [1931], *Frankenstein* [1931], *Freaks* [1932], *Doctor X* [1932]) to express the dread of sudden and catastrophic collapse; sexually charged films (*Dishonored* [1931], *Red Dust* [1932]) that expressed a sense of rebellion against the established order; and, toward the end of the decade, great costume dramas (*Anthony Adverse* [1936], *The Prisoner of Zenda* [1937]) that showed the triumph of individual courage over hostile historical forces; westerns (*Stage Coach* [1939], *Union Pacific* [1939]) renewing hope in the American experiment; and *Gone With the Wind* (1939), in a class by itself, recasting the American experience as an epic of defiance in the face of defeat. Never, as historian Arthur Schlesinger Jr., has pointed out, have so many great films been produced in such rapid succession, and never did Hollywood play such a powerful and direct role in the subliminal and public life of the nation. From its inception at the beginning of the century through World War II, Hollywood films not only entertained but educated, but they influenced American life more than any other single cultural force in the country (Starr 2005, 276–81).

The most important form of entertainment in the Hawaiian Islands was dance, which took many forms in Hawaii. Dance or hula was performed by both men and women. Some forms of hula were sacred while others were performed solely for entertainment for both the dancers and the audience. In addition to its entertainment value, hula played an important role in passing down the oral history from one generation to the next. All hula movements represented a particular action or event that together told a story in a most beautiful fashion (Barnes 2007, 21).

HOLIDAYS, CELEBRATIONS, AND FESTIVALS

Those who lived on the West Coast celebrated Christmas much as the rest of the United States with Christmas trees, lights, Santa Claus, family dinners, and presents, but the unique weather of southern California provided opportunities to add special distinctions to the universal celebration. In Newport Beach, for example, the town celebrated a Christmas Boat Parade, which started in the early 1900s when Venetian gondolier John Scarpa put lights on eight canoes and his gondola and floated them around the bay.

Since the end of the nineteenth century the people of Los Angeles have been celebrating the Tournament of Roses, which began in 1890 when members of the Pasadena Valley Hunt Club, former residents of the East and Midwest, wanted to showcase their new home's mild winter weather. "In New York, people are buried in snow," announced Professor Charles F. Holder at a Club meeting. "Here our flowers are blooming and our oranges are about to bear. Let's hold a festival to tell the world about our paradise." During the next few years, the festival expanded to include marching bands, games, and motorized floats. The games on the town lot (which was renamed Tournament Park in 1900) included ostrich races, bronco busting demonstrations, and a race between a camel and an elephant (the elephant won). Reviewing stands were built along the parade route, and eastern newspapers began to take notice of the event. In 1895, the Tournament of Roses Association was formed to take charge of the festival, which had grown too large for the Valley Hunt Club to handle. In 1902 the Tournament of Roses Association decided to enhance the day's festivities by adding a football game. Stanford University accepted the invitation to take on the powerhouse University of Michigan, but the West Coast team was flattened 49–0 and gave up in the third quarter. The lopsided score prompted the tournament to give up football in favor of a polo match. When that event drew only 2,000 people, they opted for a Roman-style chariot race. The races lasted until 1915. But by then college football was well on its way to becoming the premier sporting attraction in the country and the tournament committee brought the sport back in 1916.

Religious Life

RELIGION, SPIRITUALITY, AND RITES OF PASSAGE

In Los Angeles in 1906, on Azusa Street, a religious movement began, which some historians call the birth of the modern Pentecostalism. To read the newspapers in 1906, one might have wondered about all the excitement in an old building on Azusa Street in the industrial part of the city. According to the *Los Angeles Times*, a bizarre new religious sect had started with people "breathing strange utterances and mouthing a creed which it would seem no sane mortal could understand." Furthermore, "Devotees of the weird doctrine practice the most fanatical rites, preach the wildest theories, and work themselves into a state of mad excitement." The article continued by saying that "Colored people and a sprinkling of whites compose the congregation, and night is made hideous in the neighborhood by the howlings of the worshippers who spend hours swaying forth and back in a nerve-racking attitude of prayer and supplication." To top it all off, they claimed to have received the "gift of tongues," and what's more, "comprehend the babel."

Nonetheless, for the spiritually hungry who came from far and wide to receive their Pentecost, "the very atmosphere of heaven" had descended, according to one. A visiting Baptist pastor said, "The Holy Spirit fell upon me and filled me literally, as it seemed to lift me up, for indeed, I was in the air in an instant, shouting, 'Praise God,' and instantly I began to speak in another language. I could not have been more surprised if at the same moment someone had handed me a million dollars" (http://www.ag.org/enrichmentjournal/199904/026_azusa.cfm).

Little could the subscribers of the *Times* have guessed that in years to come, historians would say that the Azusa Street revival played a major role in the development of modern Pentecostalism—a movement that changed the religious landscape and became the most vibrant force for world evangelization in the twentieth century. Azusa Street became the most significant revival of the century in terms of global perspective.

The movement had been started by William Seymour, a black preacher from Topeka, Kansas, who had been moved by Charles Parham, who preached that the end of times was near and the signs could be seen through those who, filled with the Holy

Spirit, began to speak in tongues. The first woman to speak in tongues supposedly began speaking Chinese for hours after receiving the Holy Spirit but could not speak in her own language. Moved by the Spirit himself, Seymour came to Los Angeles. He preached that glossolalia, or "speaking in tongues," was evidence of Holy Spirit baptism; his first Los Angeles parish expelled him, but Seymour continued preaching until he and a small group experienced glossolalia. Crowds began to gather, and a mission space was found on Azusa Street, in a run-down building in downtown Los Angeles. Worship there was frequent, spontaneous, and ecstatic, drawing people from around the world to a revival that lasted about three years. The Azusa revival was multiracial. It welcomed poor people and encouraged the leadership of women. Azusa's "five-fold doctrine" was: (1) salvation; (2) sanctification or holiness; (3) tongues as evidence of Spirit baptism; (4) divine healing; and (5) the "very soon" return of Christ. The movement continues throughout the world to the present, and, although Pentecostalism has earlier roots, the Azusa Street revival launched it as a worldwide movement (http://enrichmentjournal.ag.org/199904/026_azusa.cfm).

In the 1920s, California produced what would become the prototypes for radio evangelism throughout the country, Bob Schuler and Aimee Semple McPherson. It began with fierce and patriarchal Bob Schuler, who personified the Bible Belt and all its relish for hellfire and damnation. Of poor white stock, raised in a log cabin in the hardscrabble hills of Tennessee, Schuler first rose to prominence as a Methodist preacher in Texas. Soon his style of denunciation from the pulpit brought him trouble and he left Texas in 1920 (under the shadow of a number of libel suits) for Los Angeles, where he became pastor of the Trinity Methodist Church, an embattled downtown church with dwindling membership and growing debt. In 1922, he began publishing *Bob Schulers Magazine*, which he wrote mostly himself. In his magazine he praised the Bible and William Jennings Bryan while railing against Jews, Catholics, movies, evolution, jazz, and dancing. Within the decade he had expanded his congregation from 940 to over 42,000 and had paid off most of the church's debt.

Schuler (and his avid followers) considered himself the savior of Los Angeles, which he described as the last Anglo-Saxon city of more than a million people left in America. During the Christmas season of 1926, Elizabeth Glide, a devout Methodist follower and oil heiress, bought Schuler a radio station, KGEF. Now, with a radio audience of over 200,000, Schuler exhorted, scolded, named names, and soon became a political power in his own right. His power reached a peak in 1928 when his candidate for mayor of Los Angeles, John Porter, a church-going used auto parts salesman and former Klan member, won the contest. When Porter's incompetence and inability to run the city became obvious, Schuler's credibility plummeted.

Schuler's despised counterpart, Aimee Semple McPherson, made her Los Angeles shrine the epicenter of religiosity for the common folk of California and eventually the entire United States. She presided over the new (as of January 1923) $1.5 million Angelus Temple on the northwest edge of Echo Park in Los Angeles. There, on a Sunday morning, evangelist McPherson, a charismatic preacher given to flamboyant theatricality, preached to congregations of 4,000 and more people her "Foursquare Gospel" of evangelical healing and hope. Weekly sermons were announced from an electric marquee over the temple entrance, as in a motion picture palace. For McPherson, the message was in the medium. Entering the temple on a motorcycle in a policeman's uniform, McPherson placed sin under arrest and urged her audience not to speed to ruin. Prodding him with a pitchfork, she chased the devil from the stage. Dressed as a University of Southern California football player, she urged her congregation to carry the ball for Christ. Dressed as a nurse, she prayed over the sick. McPherson's healing ministry in fact was at the core of her success, because so many of the people had come to southern California in late middle or old age in the hope of regaining lost health. By the late 1920s, a special display area at the temple featured the canes, crutches, and braces that so many of the people, now healed, no longer found necessary. Her message went out to the nation on radio station KFSG (Kall Four Square Gospel).

In May 1926, McPherson mysteriously disappeared, in a swimming area near the small town of Venice, California. After a month of mournful searching for her remains, McPherson resurfaced with a kidnapping story that was seriously doubted. When it was discovered that her presumed lover had also been unaccounted for during the same period, her story became less credible, as did her influence as a preacher. She continued to minister to smaller congregations until her death from a drug overdose in 1944 (Starr 1991, 136, 139, 142–43).

The adobe walls and Spanish mission red tile roofs of Los Angeles churches stake their claim as the seedbed of North American Catholicism. Franciscan padres followed the Spanish conquistadores into California more than a century before Anglo-Catholics landed in the East Coast colonies of England. But after the mass immigrations from Europe of the mid-nineteenth century, the center of gravity of the American Church became solidly grounded at a point somewhere between the East Coast and the Great Lakes. The sole western outpost of American-style institutional Catholicism in the first decades of the twentieth century was San Francisco, dominated by highly successful Irish and Italian transplants from the East. Mexican Catholic southern California was regarded as mission territory well into the twentieth century. Not until the post–World War II era would mass migration to southern California transform the former mission of Los Angeles into one of the largest archdioceses in the country (Morris 1997, 257–58).

Despite the diligent work of nineteenth-century American missionaries, many native Hawaiian religious traditions lasted well into the twentieth century, and the major gods played an important role in the rich and diverse mythology of Hawaii. The Hawaiians worshipped four major gods: Kane, the creator; Lono, the god of fertile soil and a rich harvest; Ku, the god of war; and Kanaloa, the god of the sea. There are also a large number of lesser gods, the most famous of which is Pele, the goddess of volcanoes. Natives and visitors alike continue to visit her home in Halema'uma in Hawaii Volcanoes National Park. Along with these universal gods, native Hawaiian families have their own ancestral gods, called *aumakua*. They were often represented by a fish or a bird or other animal that has had significance for the family (Barnes 2007, 18).

Although in the Northwest no social stigma attached itself to the nonchurchgoer, the influence of the church in the Northwest remained evident. For example, in Oregon, well into the twentieth century stores were closed on Sundays, and in Washington no liquor was sold by the bottle or the drink from midnight on Saturday until 6:00 A.M. Monday. Although attacked by the Washington convention and tourist industry, the strict regulations prevailed against all opposition until the late twentieth century.

WORLDVIEW

The Pacific Coast West encompassed the last frontier of America and likewise the last of the pioneers. The last two states to enter the Union are included in this region. Frontiers attract those who are open to change and new ideas. It creates an environment that encourages experimentation. In this environment new industries of the twentieth century, such as the cinema and aviation, prospered. As in all areas deemed frontiers by the newly arriving majority, the old and established often becomes displaced. Mexicans in southern California with cultural roots centuries deep saw themselves displaced, as did the Native Americans of Alaska, Oregon, and Washington.

Experimentation in the Pacific West was a virtue that manifested itself in forms as varied as innovative government in Oregon and Pentecostal religion in California. Wherever one lived in the Pacific West one could find a spirit of openness to change and acceptance of individual differences, to a degree not as common in the other regions of the country.

FOR MORE INFORMATION

Books

Barnes, Phil. *A Concise History of the Hawaiian Islands*. Hilo, HI: Petroglyph Press, 2007.

Black, Brian. *Nature and the Environment in Twentieth-Century American Life*. Westport, CT: Greenwood Press, 2006.

Borneman, Walter. *Alaska: Saga of a Bold Land*. New York: Perennial, 2004.

Carpenter, Frank G. *Alaska: Our Northern Wonderland*. New York: Doubleday, Doran and Company, 1972.

Daniels, Roger, and Spencer Olin. *Racism in California: A Reader in the History of Oppression*. New York: Macmillan and Company, 1972.

Fenton, Frank. *A Place in the Sun*. New York: Random House, 1942.

Green, Harvey. *The Uncertainty of Everyday Life, 1915–1945*. Fayetteville: University of Arkansas Press, 2000.

Grier, Katherine C. *Pets in America*. Chapel Hill: University of North Carolina Press, 2006.

Hill, Daniel Delis. *As Seen in Vogue*. Lubbock: Texas Tech University Press, 2004.

Ingham, John N., and Lynne B. Feldman. *African-American Business Leaders: A Biographical Dictionary*. Westport, CT: Greenwood Press, 1994.

Jones, Kirkland C. *Renaissance Man from Louisiana: A Biography of Arna Wendell Bontemps*. Westport, CT: Greenwood Press, 1992.

Kyvig, David E. *Daily Life in the United States 1920–1940: How Americans Lived through the Roaring Twenties and the Great Depression.* Chicago: Ivan R. Dee, 2002.

Lindenmeyer, Kristine. *The Greatest Generation Grows Up.* Chicago: Ivan R. Dee, 2005.

London, Jack. *John Barleycorn.* New York: Oxford University Press, 1989.

MacDonald, Betty. *The Egg and I.* Philadelphia: J. B. Lippincott, 1945.

Morris, Charles. *American Catholic: The Saints and Sinners Who Built America's Most Powerful Church.* New York: Random House, 1997.

Mowry, George. *The California Progressives.* Chicago: Quadrangle Paperbacks, 1951.

Ostrander, Gilman. *Nevada: The Great Rotten Borough 1859–1964.* New York: Knopf, 1966.

Reich, Steven, ed. *Encyclopedia of the Great Black Migration.* Westport, CT: Greenwood Press, 2006.

Starr, Kevin. *California: A History.* New York: Modern Library, 2005.

_____. *Endangered Dreams: The Great Depression in California.* New York: Oxford Press, 1997.

_____. *Inventing the Dream: California in the Progressive Era.* New York: Oxford, 1986.

_____. *Material Dreams: Southern California through the 1920s.* New York: Oxford Press, 1991.

Thompson, Nile, and Carolyn Marr. *Building for Learning: Seattle Public Schools 1862–2000.* Seattle, WA: Seattle Public Schools, 2001.

Weaver, John. *El Pueblo Grande: A Non Fiction Book about Los Angeles.* Los Angeles: Ward Ritchie Press, 1973.

Zinn, Howard. *A People's History of the United States 1492–Present.* New York: Harper Perennial, 2003.

Articles

Cook, Katherine. "Education among Native and Minority Groups in Alaska, Puerto Rico, Virgin Islands and Hawaii." *Journal of Negro Education* 3, no. 1 (January 1934): 20–41.

Hayner, Norman. "Regional Family Patterns: The Western Family." *American Journal of Sociology* 53, no. 6 (May 1948): 432–34.

Lange, Emil. "Character Education in Long Beach Schools." *Journal of Educational Sociology* 4, no.7 (March 1931): 426–29.

Web Sites

Enrichment Journal. http://enrichmentjournal.ag.org/199904/026_azusa.cfm.

Ingham, John N., and Feldman, Lynne B. "Nickerson, William, Jr." African-American Business Leaders: Biographical Dictionary. Westport CT: Greenwood Press, 1994. The African American Experience. Greenwood Group March 24, 2008. http://aae.greenwood.com/doc.aspx?fileID=IBL&chapterID=IBL-2239&path=/encyclopedias/greenwood//.

McGee, Gary. "William J Seymour and the Azusa Street Revival." *Journal for Pentecostal Ministry.* http://www.ag.org/enrichmentjournal/199904/026_azusa.cfm.

"OREGON." http://ca.encarta.msn.com/encyclopedia_761558216_9/oregon.html.

San Francisco Cablecar Museum. http://www.cablecarmuseum.org/heritage.html.

Yosemite National Park, California. http://www.nps.gov/yose/historyculture/index.htm.

PRIMARY DOCUMENTS

1. PRESIDENT THEODORE ROOSEVELT'S COROLLARY TO THE MONROE DOCTRINE (DECEMBER 6, 1904)

Although Theodore Roosevelt liked to invoke the African proverb, "Walk softly and carry a big stick," he hardly walked softly in the Caribbean and Latin America. Roosevelt epitomized the moralistic tone of Progressive diplomacy, which saw the American system of democracy as superior and inevitable for the rest of the world. Roosevelt understood that the final collapse of Spain in the Caribbean after 1898 had left a power vacuum, which he was eager to see the Unites States fill. The first step in this direction took place with the Platt Amendment of 1902, which gave the United States the right to intervene in Cuba if the independence or the internal order of the country was threatened. Using that power, the United States sent troops to Cuba in 1906 and 1923, and in 1933 orchestrated the departure of President Gerardo Machado.

In his annual message to Congress in December 1904, Roosevelt, fearing that corrupt governments in South America and rising debt in the region would give Europeans reason to reintervene in the hemisphere, added a corollary to the Monroe Doctrine of 1823, which had warned Europe against further military intervention in Latin America. Roosevelt's corollary established the right of the United States to intervene directly in any Latin American country that failed to keep its financial and political households in order. Under this self-proclaimed power, the United States, in the first four decades of the twentieth century, sent American soldiers into Haiti, the Dominican Republic, Cuba, Nicaragua, Panama, and Mexico.

In treating of our foreign policy and of the attitude that this great Nation should assume in the world at large, it is absolutely necessary to consider the Army and the Navy, and the Congress, through which the thought of the Nation finds its expression, should keep ever vividly in mind the fundamental fact that it is impossible to treat our foreign policy, whether this policy takes shape in the effort to secure justice for others or justice for ourselves, save as conditioned upon the attitude we are willing to take toward our Army, and especially toward our Navy. It is not merely unwise, it is contemptible, for a nation, as for an individual, to use high-sounding language to proclaim its purposes, or to take positions which are ridiculous if unsupported by potential force, and then to refuse to provide this force. If there is no intention of providing and keeping the force necessary to back up a strong attitude, then it is far better not to assume such an attitude.

The steady aim of this Nation, as of all enlightened nations, should be to strive to bring ever nearer the day when there shall prevail throughout the world the peace of justice. There are kinds of peace which are highly undesirable, which are in the long run as destructive as any war. Tyrants and oppressors have many times made a wilderness and called it peace. Many times peoples who were slothful or timid or short-sighted, who had been enervated by ease or by luxury, or misled by false teachings, have shrunk in unmanly fashion from doing duty that was stern and that needed self-sacrifice, and have sought to hide from their own minds their shortcomings, their ignoble motives, by calling them love of peace. The peace of tyrannous terror, the peace of craven weakness, the peace of injustice, all these should be shunned as we shun unrighteous war. The goal to set before us as a nation, the goal which should be set before all mankind, is the attainment of the peace of justice, of the peace which comes when each nation is not merely safe-guarded in its own rights, but scrupulously recognizes and performs its duty toward others. Generally peace tells for righteousness; but if there is conflict between the two, then our fealty is due first to the cause of righteousness. Unrighteous wars are common, and unrighteous peace is rare; but both should be shunned. The right of freedom and the responsibility for the exercise of that right can not be divorced. One of our great poets has well and finely said that freedom is not a gift that tarries long in the hands of cowards. Neither does it tarry long in the hands of those too slothful, too dishonest, or too unintelligent to exercise it. The eternal vigilance which is the price of liberty must be exercised, sometimes to guard against outside foes; although of course far more often to guard against our own selfish or thoughtless shortcomings.

If these self-evident truths are kept before us, and only if they are so kept before us, we shall have a clear idea of what our foreign policy in its larger aspects should be. It is our duty to remember that a nation has no more right to do injustice to another nation, strong or weak, than an individual has to do injustice to another individual; that the same moral law applies in one case as in the other. But we must also remember that it is as much the duty of the Nation to guard its own rights and its own interests as it is the duty of the individual so to do. Within the Nation the individual has now delegated this right to the State, that is, to the representative of all the individuals, and it is a maxim of the law that for every wrong there is a remedy. But in international law we have not advanced by any means as far as we have advanced in municipal law. There is as yet no judicial way of enforcing a right in international law. When one nation wrongs another or wrongs many others, there is no tribunal before which the wrongdoer can be brought. Either it is necessary supinely to acquiesce in the wrong, and thus put a premium upon brutality and aggression, or else it is necessary for the aggrieved nation valiantly to stand up for its rights. Until some method is devised by which there shall be a degree of international control over offending nations, it would be a wicked thing for the most civilized powers, for those with most sense of international obligations and with keenest and most generous appreciation of the difference between right and wrong, to disarm. If the great civilized nations of the present day should completely disarm, the result would mean an immediate recrudescence of barbarism in one form or another. Under any circumstances a sufficient armament would have to be kept up to serve the purposes of international police; and until international cohesion and the sense of international duties and rights are far more advanced than at present, a nation desirous both of securing respect for itself and of doing good to others must have a force adequate for the work which it feels is allotted to it as its part of the general world duty. Therefore it follows that a self-respecting, just, and far-seeing nation should on the one hand endeavor by every means to aid in the development of the various movements which tend to provide substitutes for war, which tend to render nations in their actions toward one another, and indeed toward their own peoples, more responsive to the general sentiment of humane and civilized mankind; and on the other hand that it should keep prepared, while scrupulously avoiding wrongdoing itself, to repel any wrong, and in exceptional cases to take action which in a more advanced stage of international relations would come under the head of the exercise of the international police. A great free people owes it to itself and to all mankind not to sink into helplessness before the powers of evil.

We are in every way endeavoring to help on, with cordial good will, every movement which will tend to bring us into more friendly relations with the rest of mankind. In pursuance of this policy I shall shortly lay before the Senate treaties of arbitration with all powers which are willing to enter into these treaties with us. It is not possible at this period of the worlds development to agree to arbitrate all matters, but there are many matters of possible difference between us and other nations which can be thus arbitrated. Furthermore, at the request of the Interparliamentary Union, an eminent body composed of practical statesmen from all countries, I have asked the Powers to join with this Government in a second Hague conference, at which it is hoped that the work already so happily begun at The Hague may be carried some steps further toward completion. This carries out the desire expressed by the first Hague conference itself.

It is not true that the United States feels any land hunger or entertains any projects as regards the other nations of the Western Hemisphere save such as are for their welfare. All that this country desires is to see the neighboring countries stable, orderly, and prosperous. Any country whose people conduct themselves well can count upon our hearty friendship. If a nation shows that it knows how to act with reasonable efficiency and decency in social and political matters, if it keeps order and pays its obligations, it need fear no interference from the United States. Chronic wrongdoing, or an impotence which results in a general loosening of the ties of civilized society, may in America, as elsewhere, ultimately require intervention by some civilized nation, and in the Western Hemisphere the adherence of the United States to the Monroe Doctrine may force the United States, however reluctantly, in flagrant cases of such wrongdoing or impotence, to the exercise of an international police power. If every country washed by the Caribbean Sea would show the progress in stable and just civilization which with the aid of the Platt Amendment Cuba has shown since our troops left the island, and which so many of the republics in both Americas are constantly and brilliantly showing, all question of interference by this Nation with their affairs would be at an end. Our interests and those of our southern neighbors are in reality identical. They have great natural riches, and if within their borders the reign of law and justice obtains, prosperity is sure to come to them. While they thus obey the primary laws of civilized society they may rest assured that they will be treated by us in a spirit of cordial and helpful sympathy. We would interfere with them only in the last resort, and then only if it became evident that their inability or unwillingness to do justice at home and abroad had violated the rights of the United States or had invited foreign aggression to the detriment of the entire body of American nations. It is a mere truism to say that every nation, whether in America or anywhere else, which desires to maintain its freedom, its independence, must ultimately realize that the right of such independence can not be separated from the responsibility of making good use of it.

In asserting the Monroe Doctrine, in taking such steps as we have taken in regard to Cuba, Venezuela, and Panama, and in endeavoring to circumscribe the theater of war in the Far East, and to secure the open door in China, we have acted in our own interest as well as in the interest of humanity at large. There are, however, cases in which, while our own interests are not greatly involved, strong appeal is made to our sympathies. Ordinarily it is very much wiser and more useful for us to concern ourselves with striving for our own moral and material betterment here at home than to concern ourselves with trying to better the condition of things in other nations. We have plenty of sins of our own to war against, and under ordinary circumstances we can do more for the general uplifting of humanity by striving with heart and soul to put a stop to civic corruption, to brutal lawlessness and violent race prejudices here at home than by passing resolutions and wrongdoing elsewhere. Nevertheless there are occasional crimes committed on so vast a scale and of such peculiar horror as to make us doubt whether it is not our manifest duty to endeavor at least to show our disapproval of the deed and our sympathy with those who have suffered by it. The cases must be extreme in which such a course is justifiable. There must be no effort made to remove the mote from our brothers eye if we refuse to remove the beam from our own. But in extreme cases action may be justifiable and proper. What form the action shall take must depend upon the circumstances of the case; that is, upon the degree of the atrocity and upon our power to remedy it. The cases in which we could interfere by force of arms as we interfered to put a stop to intolerable conditions in Cuba are necessarily very few. Yet it is not to be expected that a people like ours, which in spite of certain very obvious shortcomings, nevertheless as a whole shows by its consistent practice its belief in the principles of civil and religious liberty and of orderly freedom, a people among whom even the worst crime, like the crime of lynching, is never more than sporadic, so that individuals and not classes are molested in their fundamental rights—it is inevitable that such a nation should desire eagerly to give expression to its horror on an occasion like that of the massacre of the Jews in Kishenef, or when it witnesses such systematic and long-extended cruelty and oppression as the cruelty and oppression of which the Armenians have been the victims, and which have won for them the indignant pity of the civilized world.

Source: http://www.ourdocuments.gov/doc.php?doc=56; excerpted from President Theodore Roosevelt's annual message to Congress, December 6, 1904.

2. PRESIDENT THEODORE ROOSEVELT'S MUCKRAKER SPEECH—"THE MAN WITH THE MUCK RAKE" (APRIL 15, 1906)

With his muckraker speech, President Theodore Roosevelt brought new meaning and use to a seventeenth-century phrase. Although he attacked over-enthusiastic journalists eager to rake up the muck of American society, he at the same time promised to bring the power of the American government against the "men of wealth who . . . are trying to prevent the regulation and control of their business in the interest of the public by the proper government authorities," and to put government on the side of "The wage worker, [and] the tiller of the soil, [on whom we all] depend [for] the welfare of the entire country."

Over a century ago Washington laid the corner stone of the Capitol in what was then little more than a tract of wooded wilderness here beside the Potomac. We now find it necessary to provide by great additional buildings for the business of the government.

This growth in the need for the housing of the government is but a proof and example of the way in which the nation has grown and the sphere of action of the national government has grown. We now administer the affairs of a nation in which the extraordinary growth of population has been outstripped by the growth of wealth in complex interests. The material problems that face us today are not such as they were in Washington's time, but the underlying facts of human nature are the same now as they were then. Under altered external form we war with the same tendencies toward evil that were evident in Washington's time, and are helped by the same tendencies for good. It is about some of these that I wish to say a word today.

In Bunyan's "Pilgrim's Progress" you may recall the description of the Man with the Muck Rake, the man who could look no way but downward, with the muck rake in his hand; who was offered a celestial crown for his muck rake, but who would neither look up nor regard the crown he was offered, but continued to rake to himself the filth of the floor.

In "Pilgrim's Progress" the Man with the Muck Rake is set forth as the example of him whose vision is fixed on carnal instead of spiritual things. Yet he also typifies the man who in this life consistently refuses to see aught that is lofty, and fixes his eyes with solemn intentness only on that which is vile and debasing.

Now, it is very necessary that we should not flinch from seeing what is vile and debasing. There is filth on the floor, and it must be scraped up with the muck rake; and there are times and places where this service is the most needed of all the services that can be performed. But the man who never does anything else, who never thinks or speaks or writes, save of his feats with the muck rake, speedily becomes, not a help but one of the most potent forces for evil.

There are in the body politic, economic and social, many and grave evils, and there is urgent necessity for the sternest war upon them. There should be relentless exposure of and attack upon every evil man, whether politician or business man, every evil practice, whether in politics, business, or social life. I hail as a benefactor every writer or speaker, every man who, on the platform or in a book, magazine, or newspaper, with merciless severity makes such attack, provided always that he in his turn remembers that the attack is of use only if it is absolutely truthful.

The liar is no whit better than the thief, and if his mendacity takes the form of slander he may be worse than most thieves. It puts a premium upon knavery untruthfully to attack an honest man, or even with hysterical exaggeration to assail a bad man with untruth.

An epidemic of indiscriminate assault upon character does no good, but very great harm. The soul of every scoundrel is gladdened whenever an honest man is assailed, or even when a scoundrel is untruthfully assailed.

Now, it is easy to twist out of shape what I have just said, easy to affect to misunderstand it, and if it is slurred over in repetition not difficult really to misunderstand it. Some persons are sincerely incapable of understanding that to denounce mud slinging does not mean the endorsement of whitewashing; and both the interested individuals who need whitewashing and those others who practice mud slinging like to encourage such confusion of ideas.

One of the chief counts against those who make indiscriminate assault upon men in business or men in public life is that they invite a reaction which is sure to tell powerfully in favor of the unscrupulous scoundrel who really ought to be attacked, who ought to be exposed, who ought, if possible, to be put in the penitentiary. If Aristides is praised overmuch as just, people get tired of hearing it; and overcensure of the unjust finally and from similar reasons results in their favor.

Any excess is almost sure to invite a reaction; and, unfortunately, the reactions instead of taking the form of punishment of those guilty of the excess, is apt to take the form either of punishment of the unoffending or of giving immunity, and even strength, to offenders. The effort to make financial or political profit out of the destruction of character can only result in public calamity. Gross and reckless assaults on character, whether on the stump or in newspaper, magazine, or book, create a morbid and vicious public sentiment, and at the same time act as a profound deterrent to able men of normal sensitiveness and tend to prevent them from entering the public service at any price.

As an instance in point, I may mention that one serious difficulty encountered in getting the right type of men to dig the Panama canal is the certainty that they will be exposed, both without, and, I am sorry to say, sometimes within, Congress, to utterly reckless assaults on their character and capacity.

At the risk of repetition let me say again that my plea is not for immunity to, but for the most unsparing exposure of, the politician who betrays his trust, of the big business man who makes or spends his fortune in illegitimate or corrupt ways. There should be a resolute effort to hunt every such man out of the position he has disgraced. Expose the crime, and hunt down the criminal; but remember that even in the case of crime, if it is attacked in sensational, lurid, and untruthful fashion, the attack may do more damage to the public mind than the crime itself.

It is because I feel that there should be no rest in the endless war against the forces of evil that I ask the war be conducted with sanity as well as with resolution. The men with the muck rakes are often indispensable to the well being of society; but only if they know when to stop raking the muck, and to look upward to the celestial crown above them, to the crown of worthy endeavor. There are beautiful things above and round about them; and if they gradually grow to feel that the whole world is nothing but muck, their power of usefulness is gone.

If the whole picture is painted black there remains no hue whereby to single out the rascals for distinction from their fellows. Such painting finally induces a kind of moral color blindness; and people affected by it come to the conclusion that no man is really black, and no man really white, but they are all gray.

In other words, they neither believe in the truth of the attack, nor in the honesty of the man who is attacked; they grow as suspicious of the accusation as of the offense; it becomes well nigh hopeless to stir them either to wrath against wrongdoing or to enthusiasm for what is right; and such a mental attitude in the public gives hope to every knave, and is the despair of honest men. To assail the great and admitted evils of our political and industrial life with such crude and sweeping generalizations as to include decent men in the general condemnation means the searing of the public conscience. There results a general attitude either of cynical belief in and indifference to public corruption or else of a distrustful inability to discriminate between the good and the bad. Either attitude is fraught with untold damage to the country as a whole.

The fool who has not sense to discriminate between what is good and what is bad is well nigh as dangerous as the man who does discriminate and yet chooses the bad. There is nothing more distressing to every good patriot, to every good American, than the hard, scoffing spirit which treats the allegation of dishonesty in a public man as a cause for laughter. Such laughter is worse than the crackling of thorns under a pot, for it denotes not merely the vacant mind, but the heart in which high emotions have been choked before they could grow to fruition. There is any amount of good in the world, and there never was a time when loftier and more disinterested work for the betterment of mankind was being done than now. The forces that tend for evil are great and terrible, but the forces of truth and love and courage and honesty and generosity and sympathy are also stronger than ever before. It is a foolish and timid, no less than a wicked thing, to blink the fact that the forces of evil are strong, but it is even worse to fail to take into account the strength of the forces that tell for good.

Hysterical sensationalism is the poorest weapon wherewith to fight for lasting righteousness. The men who with stern sobriety and truth assail the many evils of our time, whether in the public press, or in magazines, or in books, are the leaders and allies of all engaged in the work for social and political betterment. But if they give good reason for distrust of what they say, if they chill the ardor of those who demand truth as a primary virtue, they thereby betray the good cause and play into the hands of the very men against whom they are nominally at war.

In his Ecclesiastical Polity that fine old Elizabethan divine, Bishop Hooker, wrote:

He that goeth about to persuade a multitude that they are not so well governed as they ought to be shall never want attentive and favorable hearers, because they know the manifold defects whereunto every kind of regimen is subject, but the secret lets and difficulties, which in public proceedings are innumerable and inevitable, they have not ordinarily the judgment to consider. This truth should be kept constantly in mind by every free people desiring to preserve the sanity and poise indispensable to the permanent success of self-government. Yet, on the other hand, it is vital not to permit this spirit of sanity and self-command to degenerate into mere mental stagnation. Bad though a state of hysterical excitement is, and evil though the results are which come from the violent oscillations such excitement invariably produces, yet a sodden acquiescence in evil is even worse.

At this moment we are passing through a period of great unrest—social, political, and industrial unrest. It is of the utmost importance for our future that this should prove to be not the unrest of mere rebelliousness against life, of mere dissatisfaction with the inevitable inequality of conditions, but the unrest of a resolute and eager ambition to secure the betterment of the individual and the nation.

So far as this movement of agitation throughout the country takes the form of a fierce discontent with evil, of a determination to punish the authors of evil, whether in industry or politics, the feeling is to be heartily welcomed as a sign of healthy life.

If, on the other hand, it turns into a mere crusade of appetite against appetite, of a contest between the brutal greed of the "have nots" and the brutal greed of the "haves," then it has no significance for good, but only for evil. If it seeks to establish a line of cleavage, not along the line which divides good men from bad, but along that other line, running at right angles thereto, which divides those who are well off from those who are less well off, then it will be fraught with immeasurable harm to the body politic.

We can no more and no less afford to condone evil in the man of capital than evil in the man of no capital. The wealthy man who exults because there is a failure of justice in the effort to bring some trust magnate to account for his misdeeds is as bad as, and no worse than, the so-called labor leader who clamorously strives to excite a foul class feeling on behalf of some other labor leader who is implicated in murder. One attitude is as bad as the other, and no worse; in each case the accused is entitled to exact justice; and in neither case is there need of action by others which can be construed into an expression of sympathy for crime.

It is a prime necessity that if the present unrest is to result in permanent good the emotion shall be translated into action, and that the action shall be marked by honesty, sanity, and self-restraint. There is mighty little good in a mere spasm of reform. The reform that counts is that which comes through steady, continuous growth; violent emotionalism leads to exhaustion.

It is important to this people to grapple with the problems connected with the amassing of enormous fortunes, and the use of those fortunes, both corporate and individual, in business. We should discriminate in the sharpest way between fortunes well won and fortunes ill won; between those gained as an incident to performing great services to the community as a whole and those gained in evil fashion by keeping just within the limits of mere law honesty. Of course, no amount of charity in spending such fortunes in any way compensates for misconduct in making them.

As a matter of personal conviction, and without pretending to discuss the details or formulate the system, I feel that we shall ultimately have to consider the adoption of some such scheme as that of a progressive tax on all fortunes, beyond a certain amount, either given in life or devised or bequeathed upon death to any individual—a tax so framed as to put it out of the power of the owner of one of these enormous fortunes to hand on more than a certain amount to any one individual; the tax of course, to be imposed by the national and not the state government. Such taxation should, of course, be aimed merely at the inheritance or transmission in their entirety of those fortunes swollen beyond all healthy limits. Again, the national government must in some form exercise supervision over corporations engaged in interstate business—and all large corporations engaged in interstate business—whether by license or otherwise, so as to permit us to deal with the far reaching evils of overcapitalization.

This year we are making a beginning in the direction of serious effort to settle some of these economic problems by the railway rate legislation. Such legislation, if so framed, as I am sure it will be, as to secure definite and tangible results, will amount to something of itself; and it will amount to a great deal more in so far as it is taken as a first step in the direction of a policy of superintendence and control over corporate wealth engaged in interstate commerce; this superintendence and control not to be exercised in a spirit of malevolence toward the men who have created the wealth, but with the firm purpose both to do justice to them and to see that they in their turn do justice to the public at large.

The first requisite in the public servants who are to deal in this shape with corporations, whether as legislators or as executives, is honesty. This honesty can be no respecter of persons. There can be no such thing as unilateral honesty. The danger is not really from corrupt corporations; it springs from the corruption itself, whether exercised for or against corporations.

The eighth commandment reads, "Thou shalt not steal." It does not read, "Thou shalt not steal from the rich man." It does not read, "Thou shalt not steal from the poor man." It reads simply and plainly, "Thou shalt not steal."

No good whatever will come from that warped and mock morality which denounces the misdeeds of men of wealth and forgets the misdeeds practiced at their expense; which denounces bribery, but blinds itself to blackmail; which foams with rage if a corporation secures favors by improper methods, and merely leers with hideous mirth if the corporation is itself wronged.

The only public servant who can be trusted honestly to protect the rights of the public against the misdeeds of a corporation is that public man who will just as surely protect the corporation itself from wrongful aggression.

If a public man is willing to yield to popular clamor and do wrong to the men of wealth or to rich corporations, it may be set down as certain that if the opportunity comes he will secretly and furtively do wrong to the public in the interest of a corporation.

But in addition to honesty, we need sanity. No honesty will make a public man useful if that man is timid or foolish, if he is a hot-headed zealot or an impracticable visionary. As we strive for reform we find that it is not at all merely the case of a long uphill pull. On the contrary, there is almost as much of breeching work as of collar work. To depend only on traces means that there will soon be a runaway and an upset.

The men of wealth who today are trying to prevent the regulation and control of their business in the interest of the public by the proper government authorities will not succeed, in my judgment, in checking the progress of the movement. But if they did succeed they would find that they had sown the wind and would surely reap the whirlwind, for they would ultimately provoke the violent excesses which accompany a reform coming by convulsion instead of by steady and natural growth.

On the other hand, the wild preachers of unrest and discontent, the wild agitators against the entire existing order, the men who act crookedly, whether because of sinister design or from mere puzzle headedness, the men who preach destruction without proposing any substitute for what they intend to destroy, or who propose a substitute which would be far worse than the existing evils—all these men are the most dangerous opponents of real reform. If they get their way they will lead the people into a deeper pit than any into which they could fall under the present system. If they fail to get their way they will still do incalculable harm by provoking the kind of reaction which in its revolt against the senseless evil of their teaching would enthrone more securely than ever the evils which their misguided followers believe they are attacking.

More important than aught else is the development of the broadest sympathy of man for man. The welfare of the wage worker, the welfare of the tiller of the soil, upon these depend the welfare of the entire country; their good is not to be sought in pulling down others; but their good must be the prime object of all our statesmanship.

Materially we must strive to secure a broader economic opportunity for all men, so that each shall have a better chance to show the stuff of which he is made. Spiritually and ethically we must strive to bring about clean living and right thinking. We appreciate that the things of the body are important; but we appreciate also that the things of the soul are immeasurably more important.

The foundation stone of national life is, and ever must be, the high individual character of the average citizen.

Source: http://www.usconstitution.com/documents.htm.

3. THE *NEW YORK SUN* DESCRIBES THE 1906 SAN FRANCISCO EARTHQUAKE (APRIL 19, 1906)

The San Francisco earthquake of April 18, 1906, was followed by a fire lasting four days and destroying 497 city blocks covering five square miles. The earthquake resulted in the demolition of 28,188 buildings, causing approximately a billion dollars in damage and costing 500 lives. Just three years later, 20,000 new fireproof buildings had been erected.

The greatest earthquake disaster in the history of the United States visited San Francisco early yesterday morning. A great part of the business and tenement district was shaken down, and this was followed by a fire which is still burning and which has covered most of the affected area. . . .

. . . Happening at 5 o'clock in the morning, the earthquake caused practically no loss of life among the business houses, but the tenement houses, especially the cheap lodging houses, suffered severely in this respect. Directly afterward a fire started in seven or eight places, helped out by broken gas mains. The water system failed, and all through the morning the fire was fought with dynamite. . . .

. . . Almost all the greater buildings of San Francisco are lost. These include the City Hall, the new Post Office, the "Call" Building, twenty stories high; the Parrott Building, housing the largest department store in the West; the "Chronicle" and "Examiner" buildings, Stanford University at Palo Alto, the Grand Opera House and St. Ignatius's Church.

Oakland, Cal., April 18.—The great shock which did the damage happened at 5:15 o'clock this morning, just about daybreak. Beginning with a slight tremor, it increased in violence every moment. Before it was over, the smaller and older buildings in the business districts had fallen like houses of cards, the great steel buildings were mainly skinned of walls, and the tenement district, south of Market, was in ruins. . . .

Hardly were the people of the hill district out of their houses when the dawn of the east was lit up in a dozen places by fires which had started in the business district below. The first of these came with a sheet of flame which burst out somewhere in the warehouse district near the waterfront. Men from all over the upper part of town streamed down the hills to help. No cars could run, for the cable car slots and the very tracks were bent and tossed with the upheavals of the ground.

The fire department responded. . . . The firemen, making for the nearest points, got their hose out. There was one rush of water; then the flow stopped. The great water main, which carries the chief water supply of San Francisco, ran through the ruined district. It had been broken and the useless water was spurting up through the ruins in scores of places.

The firemen stood helpless, while fire after fire started in the ruined houses. Most of these seem to have been caused by the ignition of gas from the gas mains, which were also broken. The fires would rush up with astonishing suddenness, and then smoulder in the slowly burning redwood, of which three-quarters of San Francisco is built. When day came the smoke hung over all the business part of the city. Farther out fires were going in the Hayes Valley, a middle class residence district, and in the old Mission part of the city. Dynamite was the only thing. . . .

. . . Chief of Police Dinan got out the whole police force, and General Funston, acting on his own initiative, ordered out all the available troops in the Presidio military reservation. After a short conference the town was placed under martial law, a guard was thrown about the fire, and all the dynamite in the city was commandeered.

The day broke beautifully clear. The wind, which usually blows steadily from the west at this time of year, took a sudden veer and came steadily from the east, sending the fire, which lay in the wholesale district along the waterfront, toward the heart of the city, where stood the modern steel structure buildings, mainly stripped of their cement shells. . . .

Meantime there had been a second and lighter shock at 8 o'clock which had shaken down some walls already tottering and taken the heart out of many of the people who had hoped that the one shock would end it. . . .

There was an overpowering smell of gas everywhere from the broken mains. Now and again these would catch fire, making a great spurt of fire, which would catch in the debris. The first concern of the firemen was to stop these leakages. They piled on them bags of sand, dirt clods, even bales of cloth torn from the wreckage of burning stores. In the middle of the morning, however, there came a report from the south louder and duller than the reports of the dynamite explosions. There followed a burst of flame against the dull smoke. The gas works had blown up and the tanks were burning. After that the gas leaks stopped. . . .

It seemed to be two or three minutes after the great shock was over before people found their voices. There followed the screaming of women, beside themselves with terror, and the cries of men. With one impulse people made for the parks, as far as possible from the falling walls. These speedily became packed with people in their nightclothes, who screamed and moaned at the little shocks which followed every few minutes. The dawn was just breaking. The gas and electric mains were gone and the street lamps were all out. But before the dawn was white there came a light from the east—the burning warehouse district. . . .

On Portsmouth Square the panic was beyond description. This, the old Plaza about which the early city was built, is bordered now by Chinatown, by the Italian district, and by the "Barbary Coast," a lower tenderloin. A spur of the quake ran up the hill upon which Chinatown is situated and shook down part of the crazy little buildings on the southern edge. . . . The rush to Portsmouth Square went on almost unchecked by the police, who were more in demand elsewhere.

The denizens came out of their underground burrows like rats and tumbled into the square, beating such gongs and playing such noise instruments as they had snatched up. . . . They were met on the other side by the refugees of the Italian quarter. The panic became a madness. At least two Chinamen were taken to the morgue dead of knife wounds, given for no other reason, it seems, than the madness of panic. There are 10,000 Chinese in the quarter and there are thousands of Italians, Spaniards and Mexicans on the other side. It seemed as though every one of these, with the riffraff of "Barbary Coast," made for that one block of open land. The two uncontrolled streams met in the center of the square and piled up on the edges. There they fought all the morning, until the Regulars restored order with their bayonets. . . .

Source: The New York Sun, April 19, 1906.

4. PURE FOOD AND DRUG ACT (JUNE 30, 1906)

Thanks to exposés such as Upton Sinclair's *The Jungle*, Americans in the early decades of the twentieth century discovered that not everything that was packaged for consumption was healthy. In fact, it could be dangerous. In one section of Sinclair's book, people learned of tubercular cows being butchered for sale, rat dung mixed into meat, body parts included in ground meat, and whole human bodies that had fallen into boiling vats being sold as lard. The public demanded action from Congress, and what they got was the Pure Food and Drug Act of 1906, which continues to regulate what Americans eat and drink.

Be it enacted by the Senate and House of Representatives of the United States of America in Congress assembled, That it shall be unlawful for any person to manufacture within any territory or the District of Columbia any article of food or drug which is adulterated or misbranded, within the meaning of this Act; and any person who shall violate any of the provisions of this section shall be guilty of a misdemeanor, and for each offense shall, upon conviction thereof, be fined not to exceed five hundred dollars or shall be sentenced to one year's imprisonment, or both such fine and imprisonment, in the discretion of the court, and for each subsequent offense and conviction thereof shall be fined not less than one thousand dollars or sentenced to one year's imprisonment, or both such fine and imprisonment, in the discretion of the court.

Section 2. That the introduction into any State or Territory or the District of Columbia from any other State or Territory or the District of Columbia, or from any foreign country, or shipment to any foreign country of any article of food or drugs which is adulterated or misbranded, within the meaning of this Act, is hereby prohibited; and any person who shall ship or deliver for shipment from any State or Territory or the District of Columbia to any other State or Territory or the District of Columbia, or to a foreign country, or who shall receive in any State or Territory or the District of Columbia from any other State or Territory or the District of Columbia, or foreign country, and having so received, shall deliver, in original unbroken packages, for pay or otherwise, or offer to deliver to any other person, any such article so adulterated or misbranded within the meaning of this Act, or any person who shall sell or offer for sale in the District of Columbia or the Territories of the United States any such adulterated or misbranded foods or drugs, or export or offer to export the same to any foreign country, shall be guilty of a misdemeanor, and for such offense be fined not exceeding two hundred dollars for the first offense, and upon conviction for each subsequent offense not exceeding three hundred dollars or be imprisoned not exceeding one year, or both, in the discretion of the court: Provided, That no article shall be deemed misbranded or adulterated within the provisions of this Act when intended for except to any foreign country and prepared or packed according to the specifications or directions of the foreign purchaser when no substance is used in the preparation or packing thereof in conflict with the laws of the foreign country to which said article is intended to be shipped; but if said article shall be in fact sold or offered for sale for domestic use or consumption, then this proviso shall not exempt said article from the operation of any of the other provisions of this Act.

Section 3. That the Secretary of the Treasury, the Secretary of Agriculture, and the Secretary of Commerce and Labor shall make uniform rules and regulations for carrying out the provisions of this Act, including the collection and examination of specimens of foods and drugs manufactured or offered for sale in the District of Columbia, or in any Territory of the United States, or which shall be offered for sale in unbroken packages in any State other than that in which they shall have been respectively manufactured or produced, or which shall be received from any foreign country, or intended for shipment to any foreign country, or which may be submitted for examination by the chief health, food, or drug officer of any State, Territory, or the District of Columbia, or at any domestic or foreign port through which such product is offered for interstate commerce, or for export or import between the United States and any foreign port or country.

Section 4. That the examinations of specimens of foods and drugs shall be made in the Bureau of Chemistry of the Department of Agriculture, or under the direction and supervision of such Bureau, for the purpose of determining from such examinations whether such articles are adulterated or misbranded within the meaning of this Act; and if it shall appear from any such examination that any of such specimens is adulterated or misbranded within the meaning of this Act, the Secretary of Agriculture shall cause notice thereof to be given to the party from whom such sample was obtained. Any party so notified shall be given an opportunity to be heard, under such rules and regulations as may be prescribed as aforesaid, and if it appears that any of the provisions of this Act have been violated by such party, then the Secretary of Agriculture shall at once certify the facts to the proper United States district attorney, with a copy of the results of the analysis or the examination of such article duly authenticated by the analyst or officer making such examination, under the oath of such officer. After judgment of the court, notice shall be given by publication in such manner as may be prescribed by the rules and regulations aforesaid.

Section 5. That is shall be the duty of each district attorney to whom the Secretary of Agriculture shall report any violation of this Act, or to whom any health or food or drug officer or agent of any State, Territory, or the District of Columbia shall present satisfactory evidence of any such violation, to cause appropriate proceedings to be commenced and prosecuted in the proper courts of the United States, without delay, for the enforcement of the penalties as in such case herein provided.

Section 6. That the term "drug," as used in this Act, shall include all medicines and preparations recognized in the United States Pharmacopoeia or National Formulary for internal or external use, and any substance or mixture of substances intended to be used for the cure, mitigation, or prevention of disease of either man or other animals. The term "food," as used herein, shall include all articles used for food, drink, confectionery, or condiment by man or other animals, whether simple, mixed, or compound.

Section 7. That for the purposes of this Act an article shall be deemed to be adulterated:

In case of drugs:

First. If, when a drug is sold under or by a name recognized in the United States Pharmacopoeia or National Formulary, it differs from the standard of strength, quality, or purity, as determined by the test laid down in the United States Pharmacopoeia or National Formulary official at the time of investigation: Provided, That no drug defined in the United States Pharmacopoeia or National Formulary shall be deemed to be adulterated under this provision if the standard of strength, quality, or purity be plainly stated upon the bottle, box, or other container thereof although the standard may differ from that determined by the test laid down in the United States Pharmacopoeia or National Formulary.

Second. If its strength or purity fall below the professed standard or quality under which it is sold.

In the case of confectionery:

If it contain terra alba, barytes, talc, chrome yellow, or other mineral substance or poisonous color or flavor, or other ingredient deleterious or detrimental to health, or any vinous, malt or spirituous liquor or compound or narcotic drug.

In the case of food:

First. If any substance has been mixed and packed with it so as to reduce or lower or injuriously affect its quality or strength.

Second. If any substance has been substituted wholly or in part for the article.

Third. If any valuable constituent of the article has been wholly or in part abstracted.

Fourth. If it be mixed, colored, powdered, coated, or stained in a manner whereby damage or inferiority is concealed.

Fifth. If it contain any added poisonous or other added deleterious ingredient which may render such article injurious to health: Provided, That when in the preparation of food products for shipment they are preserved by any external application applied in such manner that the preservative is necessarily removed mechanically, or by maceration in water, or otherwise, and directions for the removal of said preservative shall be printed on the covering or the package, the provisions of this Act shall be construed as applying only when said products are ready for consumption.

Sixth. If it consists in whole or in part of a filthy, decomposed, or putrid animal or vegetable substance, or any portion of an animal unfit for food, whether manufactured or not, or if it is the product of a diseased animal, or one that has died otherwise than by slaughter.

Section 8. That the term, "misbranded," as used herein, shall apply to all drugs, or articles of food, or articles which enter into the composition of food, the package or label of which shall bear any statement, design, or device regarding such article, or the ingredients or substances contained therein which shall be false or misleading in any particular, and to any food or drug product which is falsely branded as to the State, Territory, or country in which it is manufactured or produced.

That for the purposes of this Act an article shall also be deemed to be misbranded:

In case of drugs:

First. If it be an imitation of or offered for sale under the name of another article.

Second. If the contents of the package as originally put up shall have been removed, in whole or in part, and other contents shall have been placed in such package, or if the package fail to bear a statement on the label of the quantity or proportion of any alcohol, morphine, opium, cocaine, heroin, alpha or beta eucaine, chloroform, cannabis indica, chloral hydrate, or acetanilide, or any derivative or preparation of any such substances contained therein.

In the case of food:

First. If it be an imitation of or offered for sale under the distinctive name of another article.

Second. If it be labeled or branded so as to deceive or mislead the purchaser, or purport to be a foreign product when not so, or if the contents of the package as originally put up shall have been removed in whole or in part and other contents shall have been placed in such package, or if it fail to bear a statement on the label of the quantity or proportion of any morphine, opium, cocaine, heroin, alpha or beta eucaine, chloroform, cannabis indica, chloral hydrate, or acetanilide, or any derivative or preparation of any such substances contained therein.

Third. If in package form, and the contents are stated in terms of weight or measure, they are not plainly and correctly stated on the outside of the package.

Fourth. If the package containing it or its label shall bear any statement, design, or device regarding the ingredients or the substances contained therein, which statement, design, or device shall be false or misleading in any particular: Provided, That an article of food which does not contain any added poisonous or deleterious ingredients shall not be deemed to be adulterated or misbranded in the following cases:

First. In the case of mixtures or compounds which may be now or from time to time hereafter known as articles of food, under their own distinctive names, and not an imitation of or offered for sale under the distinctive name of another article, if the name be accompanied on the same label or brand with a statement of the place where said article has been manufactured or produced.

Second. In the case of articles labeled, branded, or tagged so as to plainly indicate that they are compounds, imitations, or blends, and the word "compound," "imitation," or "blend," as the case may be, is plainly stated on the package in which it is offered for sale: Provided, That the term blend as used herein shall be construed to mean a mixture of like substances, not excluding harmless coloring or flavoring ingredients used for the purpose of coloring and flavoring only: And provided further, That nothing in this Act shall be construed as requiring or compelling proprietors or manufacturers of proprietary foods which contain no unwholesome added ingredient to disclose their trade formulas, except in so far as the provisions of this Act may require to secure freedom from adulteration or misbranding.

Section 9. That no dealer shall be prosecuted under the provisions of this Act when he can establish a guaranty signed by the wholesaler, jobber, manufacturer, or other party residing in the United States, from whom he purchases such articles, to the effect that the same is not adulterated or misbranded within the meaning of this Act, designating it. Said guaranty, to afford protection, shall contain the name and address of the party or parties making the sale of such articles to such dealer, and in such case said party or parties shall be amenable to the prosecutions, fines, and other penalties which would attach, in due course, to the dealer under the provisions of this Act.

Section 10. That any article of food, drug, or liquor that is adulterated or misbranded within the meaning of this Act, and is being transported from one State,

Territory, District, or insular possession to another for sale, or, having been transported, remains unloaded, unsold, or in original unbroken packages, or if it be sold or offered for sale in the District of Columbia or the Territories, or insular possessions of the United States, or if it be imported from a foreign country for sale, or if it is intended for export to a foreign country, shall be liable to be proceeded against in any district court of the United States within the district where the same is found, and seized for confiscation by a process of libel for condemnation. And if such article is condemned as being adulterated or misbranded, or of a poisonous or deleterious character, within the meaning of this Act, the same shall be disposed of by destruction or sale, as the said court may direct, and the proceeds thereof, if sold, less the legal costs and charges, shall be paid into the Treasury of the United States, but such goods shall not be sold in any jurisdiction contrary to the provisions of this Act or the laws of that jurisdiction: Provided, however, That upon the payment of the costs of such libel proceedings and the execution and delivery of a good and sufficient bond to the effect that such articles shall not be sold or otherwise disposed of contrary to the provisions of this Act, or the laws of any State, Territory, District, or insular possession, the court may by order direct that such articles be delivered to the owner thereof. The proceedings of such libel cases shall conform, as near as may be, to the proceedings in admiralty, except that either party may demand trial by jury of any issue of fact joined in any such case, and all such proceedings shall be at the suit of and in the name of the United States.

Section 11. The Secretary of the Treasury shall deliver to the Secretary of Agriculture, upon his request from time to time, samples of foods and drugs which are being imported into the United States or offered for import, giving notice thereof to the owner or consignee, who may appear before the Secretary of Agriculture, and have the right to introduce testimony, and if it appear from the examination of such samples that any article of food or drug offered to be imported into the United States is adulterated or misbranded within the meaning of this Act, or is otherwise dangerous to the health of the people of the United States, or is of a kind forbidden entry into, or forbidden to be sold or restricted in sale in the country in which it is made or from which it is exported, or is otherwise falsely labeled in any respect, the said article shall be refused admission, and the Secretary of the Treasury shall refuse delivery to the consignee and shall cause the destruction of any goods refused delivery which shall not be exported by the consignee within three months from the date of notice of such refusal under such regulations as the Secretary of the Treasury may prescribe: Provided, That the Secretary of the Treasury may deliver to the consignee such goods pending examination and decision in the matter on execution of a penal bond for the amount of the full invoice value of such goods, together with the duty thereon, and on refusal to return such goods for any cause to the custody of the Secretary of the Treasury, when demanded, for the purpose of excluding them from the country, or for any other purpose, said consignee shall forfeit the full amount of the bond: And provided further, That all charges for storage, cartage, and labor on goods which are refused admission or delivery shall be paid by the owner or consignee, and in default of such payment shall constitute a lien against any future importation made by such owner or consignee.

Section 12. That the term "Territory" as used in this Act shall include the insular possessions of the United States. The word "person" as used in this Act shall be construed to import both the plural and the singular, as the case demands, and shall include corporations, companies, societies and associations. When construing and enforcing the provisions of this Act, the act, omission, or failure of any officer, agent, or other person acting for or employed by any corporation, company, society, or association, within the scope of his employment or office, shall in every case be also deemed to be the act, omission, or failure of such corporation, company, society, or association as well as that of the person.

Section 13. That this Act shall be in force and effect from and after the first day of January, nineteen hundred and seven.

Approved, June 30, 1906.

Source: http://faculty.washington.edu/qtaylor/documents_us/pure_fda.htm.

5. SIXTEENTH AMENDMENT TO THE U.S. CONSTITUTION— "THE INCOME TAX AMENDMENT" (RATIFIED FEBRUARY 3, 1913)

Throughout the second half of the nineteenth century, the idea of an income tax had lingered on the fringes of American politics. During the Civil War, Congress had enacted a flat tax of 3 percent on all income over $800, but the tax was repealed soon after the end of the war. During the last decades of the nineteenth century, however, as manufacturers were reaping windfall profits and farmers and workers felt unfairly beleaguered by high tariffs, which remained the country's principal source of income, populist groups began calling again for a graduated income tax. Eventually an income tax was attached to the tariff of 1894, but it was struck down by a 5–4 Supreme Court decision.

At the turn of the century, Progressives picked up the banner and began to call for a graduated income tax. Hoping to end the discussion once and for all, conservative congressmen in 1909 called for a constitutional amendment on the issue. They believed that such a measure would never pass through the required number of states, and the issue could be put to rest forever. But, much to their surprise, one state after another approved the constitutional amendment and, in February 1913, with the certification of Secretary of State Philander C. Knox, the 16th Amendment to the Constitution went into effect, and income tax became a fact of everyday American life.

Sixty-first Congress of the United States of America, At the First Session,

Begun and held at the City of Washington on Monday, the fifteenth day of March, one thousand nine hundred and nine.

Joint Resolution

Proposing an Amendment to the Constitution of the United States.

Resolved by the Senate and House of Representatives of the United States of America in Congress assembled (two-thirds of each House concurring therein), That the following article is proposed as an amendment to the Constitution of the United States, which, when ratified by the legislature of three-fourths of the several States, shall be valid to all intents and purposes as a part of the Constitution:

"**ARTICLE XVI.** The Congress shall have power to lay and collect taxes on incomes, from whatever source derived, without apportionment among the several States, and without regard to any census or enumeration."

[Endorsements]

Source: http://www.ourdocuments.gov/doc.php?doc=57.

6. PRESIDENT WOODROW WILSON'S FIRST INAUGURATION ADDRESS (MARCH 4, 1913)

On March 4, 1913, Woodrow Wilson was inaugurated as the nation's 28th president. He was the first Democrat elected to the office since 1892. In his inaugural speech, Wilson noted this change in the political landscape and promised the American people a government that would be put to the service of humanity.

There has been a change of government. It began two years ago, when the House of Representatives became Democratic by a decisive majority. It has now been completed. The Senate about to assemble will also be Democratic.

The offices of President and Vice-President have been put into the hands of Democrats. What does the change mean? That is the question that is uppermost in our minds to-day. That is the question I am going to try to answer, in order, if I may, to interpret the occasion.

It means much more than the mere success of a party. The success of a party means little except when the Nation is using that party for a large and definite purpose. No one can mistake the purpose for which the Nation now seeks to use the Democratic Party. It seeks to use it to interpret a change in its own plans and point of view.

Some old things with which we had grown familiar, and which had begun to creep into the very habit of our thought and of our lives, have altered their aspect as we have latterly looked critically upon them, with fresh, awakened eyes; have dropped their disguises and shown themselves alien and sinister.

Some new things, as we look frankly upon them, willing to comprehend their real character, have come to assume the aspect of things long believed in and familiar, stuff of our own convictions. We have been refreshed by a new insight into our own life.

We see that in many things that life is very great. It is incomparably great in its material aspects, in its body of wealth, in the diversity and sweep of its energy, in the industries which have been conceived and built up by the genius of individual men and the limitless enterprise of groups of men.

It is great, also, very great, in its moral force. Nowhere else in the world have noble men and women exhibited in more striking forms the beauty and the energy of sympathy and helpfulness and counsel in their efforts to rectify wrong, alleviate suffering, and set the weak in the way of strength and hope.

We have built up, moreover, a great system of government, which has stood through a long age as in many respects a model for those who seek to set liberty upon foundations that will endure against fortuitous change, against storm and accident. Our life contains every great thing, and contains it in rich abundance.

But the evil has come with the good, and much fine gold has been corroded. With riches has come inexcusable waste. We have squandered a great part of what we might have used, and have not stopped to conserve the exceeding bounty of nature, without which our genius for enterprise would have been worthless and impotent, scorning to be careful, shamefully prodigal as well as admirably efficient.

We have been proud of our industrial achievements, but we have not hitherto stopped thoughtfully enough to count the human cost, the cost of lives snuffed out, of energies overtaxed and broken, the fearful physical and spiritual cost to the men and women and children upon whom the dead weight and burden of it all has fallen pitilessly the years through.

The groans and agony of it all had not yet reached our ears, the solemn, moving undertone of our life, coming up out of the mines and factories, and out of every home where the struggle had its intimate and familiar seat. With the great Government went many deep secret things which we too long delayed to look into and scrutinize with candid, fearless eyes.

The great Government we loved has too often been made use of for private and selfish purposes, and those who used it had forgotten the people.

At last a vision has been vouchsafed us of our life as a whole. We see the bad with the good, the debased and decadent with the sound and vital. With this vision we approach new affairs. Our duty is to cleanse, to reconsider, to restore, to correct the evil without impairing the good, to purify and humanize every process of our common life without weakening or sentimentalizing it.

There has been something crude and heartless and unfeeling in our haste to succeed and be great. Our thought has been "Let every man look out for himself, let every generation look out for itself," while we reared giant machinery which made it impossible that any but those who stood at the levers of control should have a chance to look out for themselves.

We had not forgotten our morals. We remembered well enough that we had set up a policy which was meant to serve the humblest as well as the most powerful, with an eye single to the standards of justice and fair play, and remembered it with pride. But we were very heedless and in a hurry to be great.

We have come now to the sober second thought. The scales of heedlessness have fallen from our eyes. We have made up our minds to square every process of our national life again with the standards we so proudly set up at the beginning and have always carried at our hearts. Our work is a work of restoration.

We have itemized with some degree of particularity the things that ought to be altered and here are some of the chief items: A tariff which cuts us off from our proper part in the commerce of the world, violates the just principles of taxation, and makes the Government a facile instrument in the hand of private interests; a banking and currency system based upon the necessity of the Government to sell its bonds fifty years ago and perfectly adapted to concentrating cash and restricting credits; an industrial system which, take it on all its sides, financial as well as administrative, holds capital in leading strings, restricts the liberties and limits the opportunities of labour, and exploits without renewing or conserving the natural resources of the country; a body of agricultural activities never yet given the efficiency of great business undertakings or served as it should be through the instrumentality of science taken directly to the farm, or afforded the facilities of credit best suited to its practical needs; watercourses undeveloped, waste places unreclaimed, forests untended, fast disappearing without plan or prospect of renewal, unregarded waste heaps at every mine.

We have studied as perhaps no other nation has the most effective means of production, but we have not studied cost or economy as we should either as organizers of industry, as statesmen, or as individuals.

Nor have we studied and perfected the means by which government may be put at the service of humanity, in safeguarding the health of the Nation, the health of its men and its women and its children, as well as their rights in the struggle for existence.

This is no sentimental duty. The firm basis of government is justice, not pity. These are matters of justice. There can be no equality or opportunity, the first essential of justice in the body politic, if men and women and children be not shielded in their lives, their very vitality, from the consequences of great industrial and social processes which they can not alter, control, or singly cope with.

Society must see to it that it does not itself crush or weaken or damage its own constituent parts. The first duty of law is to keep sound the society it serves. Sanitary laws, pure food laws, and laws determining conditions of labour which individuals are powerless to determine for themselves are intimate parts of the very business of justice and legal efficiency.

These are some of the things we ought to do, and not leave the others undone, the old-fashioned, never-to-be-neglected, fundamental safeguarding of property and of individual right. This is the high enterprise of the new day: To lift everything that concerns our life as a Nation to the light that shines from the hearthfire of every man's conscience and vision of the right.

It is inconceivable that we should do this as partisans; it is inconceivable we should do it in ignorance of the facts as they are or in blind haste. We shall restore, not destroy. We shall deal with our economic system as it is and as it may be modified, not as it might be if we had a clean sheet of paper to write upon; and step by step we shall make it what it should be, in the spirit of those who question their own wisdom and seek counsel and knowledge, not shallow self-satisfaction or the excitement of excursions whither they can not tell. Justice, and only justice, shall always be our motto.

And yet it will be no cool process of mere science. The Nation has been deeply stirred, stirred by a solemn passion, stirred by the knowledge of wrong, of ideals lost, of government too often debauched and made an instrument of evil.

The feelings with which we face this new age of right and opportunity sweep across our heartstrings like some air out of God's own presence, where justice and mercy are reconciled and the judge and the brother are one. We know our task to be no mere task of politics but a task which shall search us through and through, whether we be able to understand our time and the need of our people, whether we be indeed their spokesmen and interpreters, whether we have the pure heart to comprehend and the rectified will to choose our high course of action.

This is not a day of triumph; it is a day of dedication. Here muster, not the forces of party, but the forces of humanity. Men's hearts wait upon us; men's lives hang in the balance; men's hopes call upon us to say what we will do.

Who shall live up to the great trust? Who dares fail to try? I summon all honest men, all patriotic, all forward-looking men, to my side. God helping me, I will not fail them, if they will but counsel and sustain me!

Source: http://www.firstworldwar.com/source/wilson1913inauguration.htm.

7. PRESIDENT WOODROW WILSON'S DECLARATION OF NEUTRALITY (AUGUST 19, 1914)

As Europe went to war in 1914, Woodrow Wilson feared that the immigrant population in the United States would create factions that reflected the divisions in Europe. He believed the best policy for America was strict neutrality, and, in the following speech delivered to the Senate on August 19, 1914, just weeks after the start of World War I, Wilson urged Americans to be neutral in thought as well as deed. Although Wilson insisted on neutrality, events were already in motion that would eventually draw America into the conflict.

The effect of the war upon the United States will depend upon what American citizens say and do. Every man who really loves America will act and speak in the true spirit of neutrality, which is the spirit of impartiality and fairness and friendliness to all concerned. The spirit of the nation in this critical matter will be determined largely by what individuals and society and those gathered in public meetings do and say, upon what newspapers and magazines contain, upon what ministers utter in their pulpits, and men proclaim as their opinions upon the street.

The people of the United States are drawn from many nations, and chiefly from the nations now at war. It is natural and inevitable that there should be the utmost variety of sympathy and desire among them with regard to the issues and circumstances of the conflict. Some will wish one nation, others another, to succeed in the momentous struggle. It will be easy to excite passion and difficult to allay it. Those responsible for exciting it will assume a heavy responsibility, responsibility for no less a thing than that the people of the United States, whose love of their country and whose loyalty to its government should unite them as Americans all, bound in honor and affection to think first of her and her interests, may be divided in camps of hostile opinion, hot against each other, involved in the war itself in impulse and opinion if not in action.

Such divisions amongst us would be fatal to our peace of mind and might seriously stand in the way of the proper performance of our duty as the one great nation at peace, the one people holding itself ready to play a part of impartial mediation and speak the counsels of peace and accommodation, not as a partisan, but as a friend.

I venture, therefore, my fellow countrymen, to speak a solemn word of warning to you against that deepest, most subtle, most essential breach of neutrality which may spring out of partisanship, out of passionately taking sides. The United States must be neutral in fact, as well as in name, during these days that are to try men's souls. We must be impartial in thought, as well as action, must put a curb upon our sentiments, as well as upon every transaction that might be construed as a preference of one party to the struggle before another.

Source: Woodrow Wilson, *Message to Congress*, 63rd Cong., 2d Sess., Senate Doc. No. 566 (Washington, 1914), pp. 3–4.

8. GERMAN WARNING OF SUBMARINE ATTACKS ON BRITISH SHIPS (MAY 2, 1915)

On May 1, 1915, the day before the British luxury ocean liner *Lusitania* was set to sail from New York to Liverpool, the German Embassy took out an ad in the travel section of the *New York Times*, which reminded readers of the state of war that existed between Great Britain and Germany and warned readers that all British ships, including passenger ships, were subject to attack. The following day, the *New York Times* reported the departure of the *Lusitania* without incident and with her passenger list undiminished by the German threat. The *New York Times* also reported that when Captain W. T. Turner of the *Lusitania* was advised of the warning, he laughed and told the *Times* reporter, "I wonder what the Germans will do next." The *Lusitania* was torpedoed by a German submarine on May 7 and sank quickly, causing the deaths of almost 1,200 people.

Notice
Travellers intending to embark on the Atlantic voyage are reminded that a state of war exists between Germany and her allies and Great Britain and her allies; that the zone of war includes the waters adjacent to the British Isles; that, in accordance with formal notice given by the Imperial German Government, vessels flying the flag of Great Britain, or any of her allies, are liable to destruction in those waters and that travelers sailing in the war zone on ships of Great Britain or her allies do so at their own risk
IMPERIAL GERMAN EMBASSY
Washington D.C.
April 22, 1915

Source: New York Times, May 2, 1915.

9. ZIMMERMAN NOTE (JANUARY 16, 1917)

In January 1917, although their country seemed to be drifting toward war, most Americans remained opposed to intervention, believing that the war was too far away to threaten them. That attitude changed radically when English intelligence decoded a German message to the Mexican government promising not only aid and assistance, but the return of territory lost to the United States in the war of 1846–1848 if they would ally themselves with Germany in an attack on the United States. The Zimmerman Note, as it came to be known, changed the opinion of the American people and opened the door to American entry into the war, which assured an eventual Allied victory over Germany. Never before had a decoded message had such an impact on world events.

Decoded message text of the Zimmerman Telegram
From 2nd from London
We intend to begin on the first of February unrestricted submarine warfare. We shall endeavor in spite of this to keep the United States of America neutral. In the event of this not succeeding, we make Mexico a proposal or alliance on the following basis: make war together, make peace together, generous financial support and an understanding on our part that Mexico is to reconquer the lost territory in Texas, New Mexico, and Arizona. The settlement in detail is left to you. You will inform the President of the above most secretly as soon as the outbreak of war with the United States of America is certain and add the suggestion that he should, on his own initiative, invite Japan to immediate adherence and at the same time mediate between Japan and ourselves. Please call the President's attention to the fact that the ruthless employment of our submarines now offers the prospect of compelling England in a few months to make peace.
Signed, Zimmerman

Source: http://wwi.lib.byu.edu/index.php/The_Zimmerman_

10. PRESIDENT WOODROW WILSON'S WAR MESSAGE TO CONGRESS (APRIL 2, 1917)

On February 3, 1917, President Wilson addressed Congress to announce that diplomatic relations with Germany were severed. In a Special Session of Congress held on April 2, 1917, President Wilson delivered this "War Message." Four days later, Congress overwhelmingly passed the War Resolution that brought the United States into the Great War.

Gentlemen of the Congress:
I have called the Congress into extraordinary session because there are serious, very serious, choices of policy to be made, and made immediately, which it was nei-

ther right nor constitutionally permissible that I should assume the responsibility of making.

On the 3d of February last I officially laid before you the extraordinary announcement of the Imperial German Government that on and after the 1st day of February it was its purpose to put aside all restraints of law or of humanity and use its submarines to sink every vessel that sought to approach either the ports of Great Britain and Ireland or the western coasts of Europe or any of the ports controlled by the enemies of Germany within the Mediterranean. That had seemed to be the object of the German submarine warfare earlier in the war, but since April of last year the Imperial Government had somewhat restrained the commanders of its undersea craft in conformity with its promise then given to us that passenger boats should not be sunk and that due warning would be given to all other vessels which its submarines might seek to destroy, when no resistance was offered or escape attempted, and care taken that their crews were given at least a fair chance to save their lives in their open boats. The precautions taken were meagre and haphazard enough, as was proved in distressing instance after instance in the progress of the cruel and unmanly business, but a certain degree of restraint was observed. The new policy has swept every restriction aside. Vessels of every kind, whatever their flag, their character, their cargo, their destination, their errand, have been ruthlessly sent to the bottom without warning and without thought of help or mercy for those on board, the vessels of friendly neutrals along with those of belligerents. Even hospital ships and ships carrying relief to the sorely bereaved and stricken people of Belgium, though the latter were provided with safe-conduct through the proscribed areas by the German Government itself and were distinguished by unmistakable marks of identity, have been sunk with the same reckless lack of compassion or of principle.

I was for a little while unable to believe that such things would in fact be done by any government that had hitherto subscribed to the humane practices of civilized nations. International law had its origin in the attempt to set up some law which would be respected and observed upon the seas, where no nation had right of dominion and where lay the free highways of the world. By painful stage after stage has that law been built up, with meagre enough results, indeed, after all was accomplished that could be accomplished, but always with a clear view, at least, of what the heart and conscience of mankind demanded. This minimum of right the German Government has swept aside under the plea of retaliation and necessity and because it had no weapons which it could use at sea except these which it is impossible to employ as it is employing them without throwing to the winds all scruples of humanity or of respect for the understandings that were supposed to underlie the intercourse of the world. I am not now thinking of the loss of property involved, immense and serious as that is, but only of the wanton and wholesale destruction of the lives of noncombatants, men, women, and children, engaged in pursuits which have always, even in the darkest periods of modern history, been deemed innocent and legitimate. Property can be paid for; the lives of peaceful and innocent people can not be. The present German submarine warfare against commerce is a warfare against mankind.

It is a war against all nations. American ships have been sunk, American lives taken, in ways which it has stirred us very deeply to learn of, but the ships and people of other neutral and friendly nations have been sunk and overwhelmed in the waters in the same way. There has been no discrimination. The challenge is to all mankind. Each nation must decide for itself how it will meet it. The choice we make for ourselves must be made with a moderation of counsel and a temperateness of judgment befitting our character and our motives as a nation. We must put excited feeling away. Our motive will not be revenge or the victorious assertion of the physical might of the nation, but only the vindication of right, of human right, of which we are only a single champion.

When I addressed the Congress on the 26th of February last, I thought that it would suffice to assert our neutral rights with arms, our right to use the seas against unlawful interference, our right to keep our people safe against unlawful violence. But armed neutrality, it now appears, is impracticable. Because submarines are in effect outlaws when used as the German submarines have been used against merchant shipping, it is impossible to defend ships against their attacks as the law of nations has assumed that merchantmen would defend themselves against privateers or cruisers, visible craft giving chase upon the open sea. It is common prudence in such circumstances, grim necessity indeed, to endeavour to destroy them before they have shown their own intention. They must be dealt with upon sight, if dealt with at all. The German Government denies the right of neutrals to use arms at all within the areas of the sea which it has proscribed, even in the defense of rights which no modern publicist has ever before questioned their right to defend. The intimation is conveyed that the armed guards which we have placed on our merchant ships will be treated as beyond the pale of law and subject to be dealt with as pirates would be. Armed neutrality is ineffectual enough at best; in such circumstances and in the face of such pretensions it is worse than ineffectual; it is likely only to produce what it was meant to prevent; it is practically certain to draw us into the war without either the rights or the effectiveness of belligerents. There is one choice we can not make, we are incapable of making: we will not choose the path of submission and suffer the most sacred rights of our nation and our people to be ignored or violated. The wrongs against which we now array ourselves are no common wrongs; they cut to the very roots of human life.

With a profound sense of the solemn and even tragical character of the step I am taking and of the grave responsibilities which it involves, but in unhesitating obedience to what I deem my constitutional duty, I advise that the Congress declare the recent course of the Imperial German Government to be in fact nothing less than war against the Government and people of the United States; that it formally accept the status of belligerent which has thus been thrust upon it, and that it take immediate steps not only to put the country in a more thorough state of defense but also to exert all its power and employ all its resources to bring the Government of the German Empire to terms and end the war.

What this will involve is clear. It will involve the utmost practicable cooperation in counsel and action with the governments now at war with Germany, and, as incident to that, the extension to those governments of the most liberal financial credits, in order that our resources may so far as possible be added to theirs. It will involve the organization and mobilization of all the material resources of the country to supply the materials of war and serve the incidental needs of the nation in the most abundant and yet the most economical and efficient way possible. It will involve the immediate full equipment of the Navy in all respects but particularly in supplying it with the best means of dealing with the enemy's submarines. It will involve the immediate addition to the armed forces of the United States already provided for by law in case of war at least 500,000 men, who should, in my opinion, be chosen upon the principle of universal liability to service, and also the authorization of subsequent additional increments of equal force so soon as they may be needed and can be handled in training. It will involve also, of course, the granting of adequate credits to the Government, sustained, I hope, so far as they can equitably be sustained by the present generation, by well conceived taxation. . . .

While we do these things, these deeply momentous things, let us be very clear, and make very clear to all the world what our motives and our objects are. My own thought has not been driven from its habitual and normal course by the unhappy events of the last two months, and I do not believe that the thought of the nation has been altered or clouded by them. I have exactly the same things in mind now that I had in mind when I addressed the Senate on the 22d of January last; the same that I had in mind when I addressed the Congress on the 3d of February and on the 26th of February. Our object now, as then, is to vindicate the principles of peace and justice in the life of the world as against selfish and autocratic power and to set up amongst the really free and self-governed peoples of the world such a concert of purpose and of action as will henceforth ensure the observance of those principles. Neutrality is no longer feasible or desirable where the peace of the world is involved and the freedom of its peoples, and the menace to that peace and freedom lies in the existence of autocratic governments backed by organized force which is controlled wholly by their will, not by the will of their people. We have seen the last of neutrality in such circumstances. We are at the beginning of an age in which it will be insisted that the same standards of conduct and of responsibility for wrong done shall be observed among nations and their governments that are observed among individual citizens of civilized states.

We have no quarrel with the German people. We have no feeling towards them but one of sympathy and friendship. It was not upon their impulse that their Government acted in entering this war. It was not with their previous knowledge or approval. It was a war determined upon as wars used to be determined upon in the old, unhappy days when peoples were nowhere consulted by their rulers and wars were provoked and waged in the interest of dynasties or of little groups of ambitious men who were accustomed to use their fellow men as pawns and tools. Self-governed nations do not fill their neighbour states with spies or set the course of intrigue to bring about some critical posture of affairs which will give them an opportunity to strike and make conquest. Such designs can be successfully worked out only under cover and where no one has the right to ask questions. Cunningly contrived plans of deception or aggression, carried, it may be, from generation to generation, can be worked out and kept from the light only within the privacy of courts or behind the carefully guarded confidences of a narrow and privileged class. They are happily impossible where public opinion commands and insists upon full information concerning all the nation's affairs.

A steadfast concert for peace can never be maintained except by a partnership of democratic nations. No autocratic government could be trusted to keep faith within it or observe its covenants. It must be a league of honour, a partnership of opinion. Intrigue would eat its vitals away; the plottings of inner circles who could plan what they would and render account to no one would be a corruption seated at its very heart. Only free peoples can hold their purpose and their honour steady to a common end and prefer the interests of mankind to any narrow interest of their own.

Does not every American feel that assurance has been added to our hope for the future peace of the world by the wonderful and heartening things that have been happening within the last few weeks in Russia? Russia was known by those who knew it best to have been always in fact democratic at heart, in all the vital habits of her thought, in all the intimate relationships of her people that spoke their natural instinct, their habitual attitude towards life. The autocracy that crowned the summit of her political structure, long as it had stood and terrible as was the reality of its power, was not in fact Russian in origin, character, or purpose; and now it has been shaken off and the great, generous Russian people have been added in all their naive majesty and might to the forces that are fighting for freedom in the world, for justice, and for peace. Here is a fit partner for a league of honour.

One of the things that has served to convince us that the Prussian autocracy was not and could never be our friend is that from the very outset of the present war it has filled our unsuspecting communities and even our offices of government with spies and set criminal intrigues everywhere afoot against our national unity of counsel, our peace within and without our industries and our commerce. Indeed it is now evident that its spies were here even before the war began; and it is unhappily not a matter of conjecture but a fact proved in our courts of justice that the intrigues which have more than once come perilously near to disturbing the peace and dislocating the industries of the country have been carried on at the instigation, with the support, and even under the personal direction of official agents of the Imperial Government accredited to the Government of the United States. Even in checking these things and trying to extirpate them we have sought to put the most generous interpretation possible upon them because we knew that their source lay, not in any hostile feeling or purpose of the German people towards us (who were, no doubt, as ignorant of them as we ourselves were), but only in the selfish designs of a Government that did what it pleased and told its people nothing. But they have played their part in serving to convince us at last that that Government entertains no real friendship for us and means to act against our peace and security at its convenience. That it means to stir up enemies against us at our very doors the intercepted note to the German Minister at Mexico City is eloquent evidence.

We are accepting this challenge of hostile purpose because we know that in such a government, following such methods, we can never have a friend; and that in the presence of its organized power, always lying in wait to accomplish we know not what purpose, there can be no assured security for the democratic governments of the world. We are now about to accept gage of battle with this natural foe to liberty and shall, if necessary, spend the whole force of the nation to check and nullify its pretensions and its power. We are glad, now that we see the facts with no veil of false pretence about them, to fight thus for the ultimate peace of the world and for the liberation of its peoples, the German peoples included: for the rights of nations great and small and the privilege of men everywhere to choose their way of life and of obedience. The world must be made safe for democracy. Its peace must be planted upon the tested foundations of political liberty. We have no selfish ends to serve. We desire no conquest, no dominion. We seek no indemnities for ourselves, no material compensation for the sacrifices we shall freely make. We are but one of the champions of the rights of mankind. We shall be satisfied when those rights have been made as secure as the faith and the freedom of nations can make them.

Just because we fight without rancour and without selfish object, seeking nothing for ourselves but what we shall wish to share with all free peoples, we shall, I feel confident, conduct our operations as belligerents without passion and ourselves observe with proud punctilio the principles of right and of fair play we profess to be fighting for.

I have said nothing of the governments allied with the Imperial Government of Germany because they have not made war upon us or challenged us to defend our right and our honour. The Austro-Hungarian Government has, indeed, avowed its unqualified endorsement and acceptance of the reckless and lawless submarine warfare adopted now without disguise by the Imperial German Government, and it has therefore not been possible for this Government to receive Count Tarnowski, the Ambassador recently accredited to this Government by the Imperial and Royal Government of Austria-Hungary; but that Government has not actually engaged in warfare against citizens of the United States on the seas, and I take the liberty, for the present at least, of postponing a discussion of our relations with the authorities at Vienna. We enter this war only where we are clearly forced into it because there are no other means of defending our rights.

It will be all the easier for us to conduct ourselves as belligerents in a high spirit of right and fairness because we act without animus, not in enmity towards a people or with the desire to bring any injury or disadvantage upon them, but only in armed opposition to an irresponsible government which has thrown aside all considerations of humanity and of right and is running amuck. We are, let me say again, the sincere friends of the German people, and shall desire nothing so much as the early reestablishment of intimate relations of mutual advantage between us—however hard it may be for them, for the time being, to believe that this is spoken from our hearts. We have borne with their present government through all these bitter months because of that friendship—exercising a patience and forbearance which would otherwise have been impossible. We shall, happily, still have an opportunity to prove that friendship in our daily attitude and actions towards the millions of men and women of German birth and native sympathy, who live amongst us and share our life, and we shall be proud to prove it towards all who are in fact loyal to their neighbours and to the Government in the hour of test. They are, most of them, as true and loyal Americans as if they had never known any other fealty or allegiance. They will be prompt to stand with us in rebuking and restraining the few who may be of a different mind and purpose. If there should be disloyalty, it will be dealt with with a firm hand of stern repression; but, if it lifts its head at all, it will lift it only here and there and without countenance except from a lawless and malignant few.

It is a distressing and oppressive duty, gentlemen of the Congress, which I have performed in thus addressing you. There are, it may be, many months of fiery trial and sacrifice ahead of us. It is a fearful thing to lead this great peaceful people into war, into the most terrible and disastrous of all wars, civilization itself seeming to be in the balance. But the right is more precious than peace, and we shall fight for the things which we have always carried nearest our hearts—for democracy, for the right of those who submit to authority to have a voice in their own governments, for the rights and liberties of small nations, for a universal dominion of right by such a concert of free peoples as shall bring peace and safety to all nations and make the world itself at last free. To such a task we can dedicate our lives and our fortunes, everything that we are and everything that we have, with the pride of those who know that the day has come when America is privileged to spend her blood and her might for the principles that gave her birth and happiness and the peace which she has treasured. God helping her, she can do no other.

Source: http://wwi.lib.byu.edu/index.php/Wilson's_War_Message_to_Congress.

11. CIVIL LIBERTIES DURING WORLD WAR I—THE ESPIONAGE ACT (JUNE 15, 1917)

Not every American embraced the declaration of war against Germany enthusiastically. To ensure public support, President Woodrow Wilson created a Committee on Public Information (CPI) under publicist George M. Creel to rally support for the war. Creel commissioned an army of "Four Minute Men" who entered movie theaters, churches, sporting events, wherever the public gathered, to give short speeches designed to raise enthusiasm for the war and to sell war bonds. In addition, Wilson urged the passing of a sedition act that made it a crime to speak out against the war, or even against the government. Under this Espionage Act, over 1,500 citizens were arrested for offenses such as criticizing the Red Cross, or speaking out against wartime taxes. One film producer was even arrested and convicted for producing a film about the American Revolution that cast an ally, Great Britain, in an unfavorable light. The Espionage Act was subsequently repealed in 1921.

Espionage Act
United States, *Statutes at Large*, Washington, D.C., 1918, Vol. XL, pp 553 ff.
A portion of the amendment to Section 3 of the Espionage Act of June 15, 1917. The act was subsequently repealed in 1921.
SECTION 3. Whoever, when the United States is at war, shall willfully make or convey false reports or false statements with intent to interfere with the operation or success of the military or naval forces of the United States, or to promote the success of its enemies, or shall willfully make or convey false reports, or false statements, . . . or incite insubordination, disloyalty, mutiny, or refusal of duty, in the military or naval forces of the United States, or shall willfully obstruct . . . the recruiting

or enlistment service of the United States, or . . . shall willfully utter, print, write, or publish any disloyal, profane, scurrilous, or abusive language about the form of government of the United States, or the Constitution of the United States, or the military or naval forces of the United States . . . or shall willfully display the flag of any foreign enemy, or shall willfully . . . urge, incite, or advocate any curtailment of production . . . or advocate, teach, defend, or suggest the doing of any of the acts or things in this section enumerated and whoever shall by word or act support or favor the cause of any country with which the United States is at war or by word or act oppose the cause of the United States therein, shall be punished by a fine of not more than $10,000 or imprisonment for not more than twenty years, or both.

Source: http://wwi.lib.byu.edu/index.php/The_U.S._Sedition_Act.

12. CONSCIENTIOUS OBJECTION—ONE OBJECTOR'S STORY

Not everyone marched to the rhythm of the war drums. Local draft boards granted conscientious objector status to 57,000 men. About 21,000 of these accepted induction into noncombat duty, but the rest refused induction and many went to prison, while others suffered other indignities. Below is the story of one of these objectors.

Reminiscences of a Rebel Conscientious Objector

My informant was a conscientious objector during the period of the War and declined to give me his name. "It's hard enough to hunt a job, as it is," he explained, "without making it still more difficult by naming myself as one who opposed the war. Nearly everyone now agrees with what we C.O.'s said at the time; nearly every sane person now admits that the war was everything we predicted it would be; nearly everybody laments the loss of life and ruination the war left in its wake, they all now know that it was one hell of a big blunder, but they all still denounce and ridicule us for not going crazy too when they did. We still are an unhonored lot. Unlike those who marched uncritically and abjectly into the slaughter, our stand, as C.O.'s, was such that we as yet cannot also strut, brag and swagger as heroes. Of course, as things turned out, a long depression, with the 'heroes' favored on jobs and civil service, we may have been foolish not to have gone crazy along with all the rest. But we, despite what they say, were certainly no cowards. The joy-ride over to France, with the cheers of the business elements and the flattering attention from the ladies, even though after a training spell we were thrown into the trenches, was more alluring than the abuse and misunderstanding, the starvation and rotting away in solitary cells, that many of us knew awaited us as objectors. Don't kid yourself, nor let anyone else kid you, about the C.O.'s being afraid of fighting; it took a damned sight more guts to resist the national hysteria than to fall in line with it. And at that, there were times when we had no more assurance of emerging alive from the jails and penitentiaries than were the more glorified and subservient guys in the trenches. After all, our refusing to be fed as fodder to the bloody war, was a financial saving to Uncle Sam. When, with his pants down, and dizzy with the clamorous demands upon him in the heart of the depression, we, at least, didn't bother him for a bonus!"

"In Chicago, during the excitement attending the daily expectation of the United States entering the war, I was arrested on suspicion of being instrumental in opposing the preparations. The jailor, pausing before my cell, rather politely asked 'What are you in for?' I answered that I really didn't know, but that it was probably because they feared I would prevent the war. 'You mean to say that you're agin it?' he queried. 'I'm not particularly hankering for it,' I replied. 'Why in the hell ain't you' he asked, 'don't you know that the Kaiser, or Germany anyhow, has been tryin' to get a hold of this country for over 400 years?'"

"Another time, two city and one government detectives raided my room. Having made a thorough search of my belongings, and apparently ready to leave, satisfied that nothing then warranted my arrest, one of the bulls spied the title of the book I was reading. It was Dostoievsky's *Crime and Punishment*. 'UH huh! Crime and punishment, huh? Makin' a real study of it, huh? Readin' up all about it, huh? Come on!' I was turned loose the following day. Possibly someone more learned, informed them that the book was not a treatise on how to commit crime and escape punishment."

"A friend of mine, a Scotchman by the name of Mackay, was standing before a store window, trying to decide what shirt to buy. A buxom woman approached him and said: 'Young man, you look physically fit. Why aren't you in the trenches?' 'Madame' he returned, 'did you ever see me walk? 'No!' somewhat pityingly, thinking perhaps he was already a cripple, 'No I haven't seen you walk.' 'Then just watch me madame,' said Mac, as he walked swiftly away from her."

"Some of the fellows, on visiting us in the can, tried to bring us in some literature. Some of it was Wobbly papers and similar matter, but most was as innocent of subversive ideas as the Literary Digest. The jailor, however, confiscated the entire bundle. Looking it over, and seeing Emma Goldman's "Mother Earth" most radical of them all he said, "Here, you can take in this farm book."

Source: Library of Congress, American Life Histories: Manuscripts from the Federal Writers' Project, 1936–1940 http://lcweb2.loc.gov/cgi-bin/query/D?wpa:1:./temp/~ammem_2MTL::

13. PRESIDENT WOODROW WILSON'S FOURTEEN POINTS (JANUARY 8, 1918)

In addition to providing a vast arsenal of war supplies and food, the American entry into the war also provided the Allies with Wilson's idealism, which gave them a propaganda edge. Wilson's dream of a postwar world was not embraced by the Allies, who rejected his ideas at the Versailles peace talks in 1919. But, in 1918, Wilson's idealism gave the Allies an added advantage over the Central Powers, whose people could see no further reason for fighting if Wilson's Fourteen Points were to be the basis of a just peace. German liberals, encouraged by the Fourteen Points, contacted Wilson by telegram in October 1918, and a month later Kaiser Wilhelm II was overthrown and a truce was declared.

Delivered in Joint Session, January 8, 1918

Gentlemen of the Congress:

Once more, as repeatedly before, the spokesmen of the Central Empires have indicated their desire to discuss the objects of the war and the possible basis of a general peace. Parleys have been in progress at Brest-Litovsk between Russian representatives and representatives of the Central Powers to which the attention of all the belligerents have been invited for the purpose of ascertaining whether it may be possible to extend these parleys into a general conference with regard to terms of peace and settlement.

The Russian representatives presented not only a perfectly definite statement of the principles upon which they would be willing to conclude peace but also an equally definite program of the concrete application of those principles. The representatives of the Central Powers, on their part, presented an outline of settlement which, if much less definite, seemed susceptible of liberal interpretation until their specific program of practical terms was added. That program proposed no concessions at all either to the sovereignty of Russia or to the preferences of the populations with whose fortunes it dealt, but meant, in a word, that the Central Empires were to keep every foot of territory their armed forces had occupied—every province, every city, every point of vantage—as a permanent addition to their territories and their power.

It is a reasonable conjecture that the general principles of settlement which they at first suggested originated with the more liberal statesmen of Germany and Austria, the men who have begun to feel the force of their own people's thought and purpose, while the concrete terms of actual settlement came from the military leaders who have no thought but to keep what they have got. The negotiations have been broken off. The Russian representatives were sincere and in earnest. They cannot entertain such proposals of conquest and domination.

The whole incident is full of significances. It is also full of perplexity. With whom are the Russian representatives dealing? For whom are the representatives of the Central Empires speaking? Are they speaking for the majorities of their respective parliaments or for the minority parties, that military and imperialistic minority which has so far dominated their whole policy and controlled the affairs of Turkey and of the Balkan states which have felt obliged to become their associates in this war?

The Russian representatives have insisted, very justly, very wisely, and in the true spirit of modern democracy, that the conferences they have been holding with the Teutonic and Turkish statesmen should be held within open, not closed, doors, and all the world has been audience, as was desired. To whom have we been listening, then? To those who speak the spirit and intention of the resolutions of the German Reichstag of the 9th of July last, the spirit and intention of the Liberal leaders and parties of Germany, or to those who resist and defy that spirit and intention and insist upon conquest and subjugation? Or are we listening, in fact, to both, unreconciled and in open and hopeless contradiction? These are very serious and pregnant questions. Upon the answer to them depends the peace of the world.

But, whatever the results of the parleys at Brest-Litovsk, whatever the confusions of counsel and of purpose in the utterances of the spokesmen of the Central Empires, they have again attempted to acquaint the world with their objects in the war and have again challenged their adversaries to say what their objects are and what sort of settlement they would deem just and satisfactory. There is no good reason why that challenge should not be responded to, and responded to with the utmost candor. We did not wait for it. Not once, but again and again, we have laid our whole thought and purpose before the world, not in general terms only, but each time with sufficient definition to make it clear what sort of definite terms of settlement must necessarily spring out of them. Within the last week Mr. Lloyd George has spoken with admirable candor and in admirable spirit for the people and Government of Great Britain.

There is no confusion of counsel among the adversaries of the Central Powers, no uncertainty of principle, no vagueness of detail. The only secrecy of counsel, the only lack of fearless frankness, the only failure to make definite statement of the objects of the war, lies with Germany and her allies. The issues of life and death hang upon these definitions. No statesman who has the least conception of his responsibility ought for a moment to permit himself to continue this tragical and appalling outpouring of blood and treasure unless he is sure beyond a peradventure that the objects of the vital sacrifice are part and parcel of the very life of Society and that the people for whom he speaks think them right and imperative as he does.

There is, moreover, a voice calling for these definitions of principle and of purpose which is, it seems to me, more thrilling and more compelling than any of the many moving voices with which the troubled air of the world is filled. It is the voice of the Russian people. They are prostrate and all but hopeless, it would seem, before the grim power of Germany, which has hitherto known no relenting and no pity. Their power, apparently, is shattered. And yet their soul is not subservient. They will not yield either in principle or in action. Their conception of what is right, of what is humane and honorable for them to accept, has been stated with a frankness, a largeness of view, a generosity of spirit, and a universal human sympathy which must challenge the admiration of every friend of mankind; and they have refused to compound their ideals or desert others that they themselves may be safe.

They call to us to say what it is that we desire, in what, if in anything, our purpose and our spirit differ from theirs; and I believe that the people of the United States would wish me to respond, with utter simplicity and frankness. Whether their present leaders believe it or not, it is our heartfelt desire and hope that some way may be opened whereby we may be privileged to assist the people of Russia to attain their utmost hope of liberty and ordered peace.

It will be our wish and purpose that the processes of peace, when they are begun, shall be absolutely open and that they shall involve and permit henceforth no secret understandings of any kind. The day of conquest and aggrandizement is gone by; so is also the day of secret covenants entered into in the interest of particular governments and likely at some unlooked-for moment to upset the peace of the world. It is this happy fact, now clear to the view of every public man whose thoughts do not still linger in an age that is dead and gone, which makes it possible for every nation whose purposes are consistent with justice and the peace of the world to avow now or at any other time the objects it has in view.

We entered this war because violations of right had occurred which touched us to the quick and made the life of our own people impossible unless they were corrected and the world secure once for all against their recurrence. What we demand in this war, therefore, is nothing peculiar to ourselves. It is that the world be made fit and safe to live in; and particularly that it be made safe for every peace-loving nation which, like our own, wishes to live its own life, determine its own institutions, be assured of justice and fair dealing by the other peoples of the world as against force and selfish aggression. All the peoples of the world are in effect partners in this interest, and for our own part we see very clearly that unless justice be done to others it will not be done to us. The program of the world's peace, therefore, is our program; and that program, the only possible program, as we see it, is this:

I. Open covenants of peace, openly arrived at, after which there shall be no private international understandings of any kind but diplomacy shall proceed always frankly and in the public view.

II. Absolute freedom of navigation upon the seas, outside territorial waters, alike in peace and in war, except as the seas may be closed in whole or in part by international action for the enforcement of international covenants.

III. The removal, so far as possible, of all economic barriers and the establishment of an equality of trade conditions among all the nations consenting to the peace and associating themselves for its maintenance.

IV. Adequate guarantees given and taken that national armaments will be reduced to the lowest point consistent with domestic safety.

V. A free, open-minded, and absolutely impartial adjustment of all colonial claims, based upon a strict observance of the principle that in determining all such questions of sovereignty the interests of the populations concerned must have equal weight with the equitable claims of the government whose title is to be determined.

VI. The evacuation of all Russian territory and such a settlement of all questions affecting Russia as will secure the best and freest cooperation of the other nations of the world in obtaining for her an unhampered and unembarrassed opportunity for the independent determination of her own political development and national policy and assure her of a sincere welcome into the society of free nations under institutions of her own choosing; and, more than a welcome, assistance also of every kind that she may need and may herself desire. The treatment accorded Russia by her sister nations in the months to come will be the acid test of their good will, of their comprehension of her needs as distinguished from their own interests, and of their intelligent and unselfish sympathy.

VII. Belgium, the whole world will agree, must be evacuated and restored, without any attempt to limit the sovereignty which she enjoys in common with all other free nations. No other single act will serve as this will serve to restore confidence among the nations in the laws which they have themselves set and determined for the government of their relations with one another. Without this healing act the whole structure and validity of international law is forever impaired.

VIII. All French territory should be freed and the invaded portions restored, and the wrong done to France by Prussia in 1871 in the matter of Alsace-Lorraine, which has unsettled the peace of the world for nearly fifty years, should be righted, in order that peace may once more be made secure in the interest of all.

IX. A readjustment of the frontiers of Italy should be effected along clearly recognizable lines of nationality.

X. The peoples of Austria-Hungary, whose place among the nations we wish to see safeguarded and assured, should be accorded the freest opportunity to autonomous development.

XI. Rumania, Serbia, and Montenegro should be evacuated; occupied territories restored; Serbia accorded free and secure access to the sea; and the relations of the several Balkan states to one another determined by friendly counsel along historically established lines of allegiance and nationality; and international guarantees of the political and economic independence and territorial integrity of the several Balkan states should be entered into.

XII. The Turkish portion of the present Ottoman Empire should be assured a secure sovereignty, but the other nationalities which are now under Turkish rule should be assured an undoubted security of life and an absolutely unmolested opportunity of autonomous development, and the Dardanelles should be permanently opened as a free passage to the ships and commerce of all nations under international guarantees.

XIII. An independent Polish state should be erected which should include the territories inhabited by indisputably Polish populations, which should be assured a free and secure access to the sea, and whose political and economic independence and territorial integrity should be guaranteed by international covenant.

XIV. A general association of nations must be formed under specific covenants for the purpose of affording mutual guarantees of political independence and territorial integrity to great and small states alike.

In regard to these essential rectifications of wrong and assertions of right we feel ourselves to be intimate partners of all the governments and peoples associated together against the Imperialists. We cannot be separated in interest or divided in purpose. We stand together until the end. For such arrangements and covenants we are willing to fight and to continue to fight until they are achieved; but only because we wish the right to prevail and desire a just and stable peace such as can be secured only by removing the chief provocations to war, which this program does remove. We have no jealousy of German greatness, and there is nothing in this program that impairs it. We grudge her no achievement or distinction of learning or of pacific enterprise such as have made her record very bright and very enviable. We do not wish to injure her or to block in any way her legitimate influence or power. We do not wish to fight her either with arms or with hostile arrangements of trade if she is willing to associate herself with us and the other peace-loving nations of the world in covenants of justice and law and fair dealing. We wish her only to accept a place of equality among the peoples of the world,—the new world in which we now live,—instead of a place of mastery.

Neither do we presume to suggest to her any alteration or modification of her institutions. But it is necessary, we must frankly say, and necessary as a preliminary to any intelligent dealings with her on our part, that we should know whom her spokesmen speak for when they speak to us, whether for the Reichstag majority or for the military party and the men whose creed is imperial domination.

We have spoken now, surely, in terms too concrete to admit of any further doubt or question. An evident principle runs through the whole program I have outlined. It is the principle of justice to all peoples and nationalities, and their right to live on equal terms of liberty and safety with one another, whether they be strong or weak.

Unless this principle be made its foundation no part of the structure of international justice can stand. The people of the United States could act upon no other principle; and to the vindication of this principle they are ready to devote their lives, their honor, and everything they possess. The moral climax of this the culminating and final war for human liberty has come, and they are ready to put their own strength, their own highest purpose, their own integrity and devotion to the test.

Source: http://wwi.lib.byu.edu/index.php/President_Wilson%27s_Fourteen_Points.

14. WOMEN'S RIGHT TO VOTE—THE NINETEENTH AMENDMENT TO THE U.S. CONSTITUTION (RATIFIED AUGUST 18, 1920)

In 1920, after more than a half century of struggle and in the wake of World War I, women in the United States received the right to vote with the passage of the 19th Amendment to the U.S. Constitution.

Sixty-sixth Congress of the United States of America; At the First Session,
Begun and held at the City of Washington on Monday, the nineteenth day of May, one thousand nine hundred and nineteen.
JOINT RESOLUTION
Proposing an amendment to the Constitution extending the right of suffrage to women.
Resolved by the Senate and House of Representatives of the United States of America in Congress assembled (two-thirds of each House concurring therein), That the following article is proposed as an amendment to the Constitution, which shall be valid to all intents and purposes as part of the Constitution when ratified by the legislature of three-fourths of the several States.

"ARTICLE————.

"The right of citizens of the United States to vote shall not be denied or abridged by the United States or by any State on account of sex.

Congress shall have power to enforce this article by appropriate legislation."

[endorsements]

Source: http://www.ourdocuments.gov/doc.php?flash=true&doc=63.

15. PROHIBITION ENFORCEMENT (JANUARY 26, 1922)

The Prohibition Era, which lasted from 1920 to 1933, produced its share of stories and characters. None were more colorful than Izzy Einstein and his partner Moe Smith. These well-publicized federal agents devised numerous schemes to trap bootleggers and reported their exploits to reporters eager for a story. The *New York Times* story reprinted here is typical of the exploits of the famed federal agents who simply became known as "Izzy and Moe."

Izzy and Moe

Rum Stills Found Near Graveyard
Izzy Einstein Posing As a Farmer Seizes Two Plants in Barns Upstate
Federal Judge Howe promises Jail Sentences for Violators of Volstead Act

Even upstate farmers located on the edge of graveyards and removed by many miles from a railroad station are not safe from detection by Izzy Einstein, the widely known "hootch hound," and his fellow agent Moe Smith. Returning to headquarters in West 27th Street yesterday morning from a hurried trip, Einstein reported to John S. Parsons, head of the field agents of the state, the seizure of two stills found in barns, destruction of 1,000 gallons of mash, confiscation of a quantity of alcohol in milk and oil cans, and the arrest of three persons, one a woman.

To reach one place the agents had to go by sleigh for thirty miles from the nearest railroad station Einstein said. The agents first stopped at Monticello where they were joined by agents Fanell and Stafford. They drove out some distance from the town and came upon the farmhouse of Harris Gordon. Einstein posing as a prosperous farmer seeking another farm engaged Gordon's attention while Smith and the other two agents took a stroll around the premises, winding up at the barn only a short distance from the graveyard. They found, according to the report to Chief Parsons, a still having a capacity of thirty gallons and a quantity of alcohol put up in milk and oil cans, and destroyed five hundred gallons of mash. The alcohol was shipped to New York.

Einstein said that he understood that the use of milk cans for the transportation of moonshine from upstate towns to New York City and from one point in the city to another had become quite general.

Source: New York Times, January 26, 1922.

16. IMMIGRATION ACT OF 1924 (MAY 26, 1924)

The Immigration Act of 1924 created a permanent quota system (that of 1921 was only temporary), reducing the 1921 annual quota from 358,000 to 164,000.

In addition, the act reduced the immigration limit from 3 percent to 2 percent of each foreign-born group living in the United States in 1890. Using 1890 rather than 1910 or 1920 excluded the new wave of foreign-born from southern and eastern Europe from quotas truly proportionate to their new numbers in the population. Finally, the act provided for a future reduction of the quota to 154,000.

The quota system did not apply to countries in the Western Hemisphere. The United States did not want to alienate its neighbors, and it needed workers, especially those from Mexico. During World Wars I and II, the United States recruited thousands of temporary workers from Mexico to harvest crops in its labor-short farmland.

From 1924 to 1947, only 2,718,006 immigrants came to the United States, a total equal to the number entering during any two-year period before World War I. In the 1930s, for the first time in U.S. history, those leaving the United States outnumbered those entering.

Immigration Bill of 1924

An act to limit the migration of aliens into the United States. . . . " (approved May 26, 1924). The Statutes at Large of the United States of America, from December 1923 to March 1925. Vol. XLII, Part 1, pp. 153–169 (Washington, D.C.: Government Printing Office, 1925.)

SIXTY EIGHTH CONGRESS. SESS.I. Ch. 185, 190. 1924.

Be it enacted by the Senate and House of Representatives of the United States of America in Congress assembled, That this Act may be cited as the "Immigration Act of 1924."

Sec. 2. (a) A consular officer upon the application of any immigrant (as defined in section 3) may (under the conditions hereinafter prescribed and subject to the limitations prescribed in this Act or regulations made thereunder as to the number of immigration visas which may be issued by such officer) issue to such immigrant an immigration visa which shall consist of one copy of the application provided for in section 7, visaed by such consular officer. Such visa shall specify (1) the nationality of the immigrant; (2) whether he is a quota immigrant (as defined in section 5) or a non-quota immigrant (as defined in section 4); (3) the date on which the validity of the immigration visa shall expire; and such additional information necessary to the proper enforcement of the immigration laws and the naturalization laws as may be by regulations prescribed.

b. The immigrant shall furnish two copies of his photograph to the consular officer. One copy shall be permanently attached by the consular officer to the immigration visa and the other copy shall be disposed of as may be by regulations prescribed.

c. The validity of an immigration visa shall expire at the end of such period, specified in the immigration visa, not exceeding four months, as shall be by regulations prescribed. In the case of an immigrant arriving in the United States by water, or arriving by water in foreign contiguous territory on a continuous voyage to the United States, if the vessel, before the expiration of the validity of his immigration visa, departed from the last port outside the United States and outside foreign contiguous territory at which the immigrant embarked, and if the immigrant proceeds on a continuous voyage to the United States, then, regardless of the time of his arrival in the United States, the validity of his immigration visa shall not be considered to have expired.

(d) If an immigrant is required by any law, or regulations or orders made pursuant to law, to secure the visa of his passport by a consular officer before being permitted to enter the United States, such immigrant shall not be required to secure any other visa of his passport than the immigration visa issued under this Act, but a record of the number and date of his immigration visa shall be noted on his passport without charge therefor. This subdivision shall not apply to an immigrant who is relieved, under subdivision (b) of section 13, from obtaining an immigration visa.

(e) The manifest or list of passengers required by the immigration laws shall contain a place for entering thereon the date, place of issuance, and number of the immigration visa of each immigrant. The immigrant shall surrender his immigration visa to the immigration officer at the port of inspection, who shall at the time of inspection indorse on the immigration visa the date, the port of entry, and the name of the vessel, if any, on which the immigrant arrived. The immigration visa shall be transmitted forthwith by the immigration officer in charge at the port of inspection to the Department of Labor under regulations prescribed by the Secretary of Labor.

(f) No immigration visa shall be issued to an immigrant if it appears to the consular officer, from statements in the application, or in the papers submitted therewith, that the immigrant is inadmissible to the United States under the immigration laws, nor shall such immigration visa be issued if the application fails to comply with the provisions of this Act, nor shall such immigration visa be issued if the consular officer knows or has reason to believe that the immigrant is inadmissible to the United States under the immigration laws.

(g) Nothing in this Act shall be construed to entitle an immigrant, to whom an immigration visa has been issued, to enter the United States, if, upon arrival in the United States, he is found to be inadmissible to the United States under the immigration laws. The substance of this subdivision shall be printed conspicuously upon every immigration visa.

(h) A fee of $9 shall be charged for the issuance of each immigration visa, which shall be covered into the Treasury as miscellaneous receipts.

DEFINITION OF IMMIGRANT

SEC. 3. When used in this Act the term "immigrant" means an alien departing from any place outside the United States destined for the United States, except (1) a government official, his family, attendants, servants, and employees, (2) an alien visiting the United States temporarily as a tourist or temporarily for business or pleasure, (3) an alien in continuous transit through the United States, (4) an alien lawfully admitted to the United States who later goes in transit from one part of the United States to another through foreign contiguous territory, (5) a bona fide alien seaman serving as such on a vessel arriving at a port of the United States and seeking to enter temporarily the United States solely in the pursuit of his calling as a seaman, and (6) an alien entitled to enter the United States solely to carry on trade under and in pursuance of the provisions of a present existing treaty of commerce and navigation.

NON-QUOTA IMMIGRANTS

SEC. 4. When used in this Act the term "non-quota immigrant" means—

(a) An immigrant who is the unmarried child under 18 years of age, or the wife, of a citizen of the United States who resides therein at the time of the filing of a petition under section 9;

(b) An immigrant previously lawfully admitted to the United States, who is returning from a temporary visit abroad;

(c) An immigrant who was born in the Dominion of Canada, Newfoundland, the Republic of Mexico, the Republic of Cuba, the Republic of Haiti, the Dominican Republic, the Canal Zone, or an independent country of Central or South America, and his wife, and his unmarried children under 18 years of age, if accompanying or following to join him;

(d) An immigrant who continuously for at least two years immediately preceding the time of his application for admission to the United States has been, and who seeks to enter the United States solely for the purpose of, carrying on the vocation of minister of any religious denomination, or professor of a college, academy, seminary, or university; and his wife, and his unmarried children under 18 years of age, if accompanying or following to join him; or

(e) An immigrant who is a bona fide student at least 15 years of age and who seeks to enter the United States solely for the purpose of study at an accredited school, college, academy, seminary, or university, particularly designated by him and approved by, the Secretary of labor, which shall have agreed to report to the Secretary of Labor the termination of attendance of each immigrant student, and if any such institution of learning fails to make such reports promptly the approval shall be withdrawn.

EXCLUSION FROM UNITED STATES

SEC. 13. (a) No immigrant shall be admitted to the United States unless he (1) has an unexpired immigration visa or was born subsequent to the issuance of the immigration visa of the accompanying parent, (2) is of the nationality specified in the visa in the immigration visa, (3) is a non-quota immigrant if specified in the visa in the immigration visa as such, and (4) is otherwise admissible under the immigration laws.

(b) In such classes of cases and under such conditions as may be by regulations prescribed immigrants who have been legally admitted to the United States and who depart therefrom temporarily may be admitted to the United States without being required to obtain an immigration visa.

(c) No alien ineligible to citizenship shall be admitted to the United States unless such alien (1) is admissible as a non-quota immigrant under the provisions of subdivision (b), (d), or (e) of section 4, or (2) is the wife, or the unmarried child under 18 years of age, of an immigrant admissible under such subdivision (d), and is accompanying or following to join him, or (3) is not an immigrant as defined in section 3.

(d) The Secretary of Labor may admit to the United States any otherwise admissible immigrant not admissible under clause (2) or (3) of subdivision (a) of this section, if satisfied that such inadmissibility was not known to, and could not have been ascertained by the exercise of reasonable diligence by, such immigrant prior to the departure of the vessel from the last port outside the United States and outside foreign contiguous territory or, in the case of an immigrant coming from foreign contiguous territory, prior to the application of the immigrant for admission.

(e) No quota immigrant shall be admitted under subdivision (d) if the entire number of immigration visas which may be issued to quota immigrants of the same nationality for the fiscal year already has been issued. If such entire number of immigration visas has not been issued, then the Secretary of State, upon the admission of a quota immigrant under subdivision (d), shall reduce by one the number of immigration visas which may be issued to quota immigrants of the same nationality during the fiscal year in which such immigrant is admitted; but if the Secretary of State finds that it will not be practicable to make such reduction before the end of such fiscal year, then such immigrant shall not be admitted.

(f) Nothing in this section shall authorize the remission or refunding of a fine, liability to which has accrued under section 16.

DEPORTATION

SEC. 14. Any alien who at any time after entering the United States is found to have been at the time of entry not entitled under this Act to enter the United States, or to have remained therein for a longer time than permitted under this Act or regulations made thereunder, shall be taken into custody and deported in the same manner as provided for in sections 19 and 20 of the Immigration Act of 1917: Provided, That the Secretary of Labor may, under such conditions and restrictions as to support and care as he may deem necessary, permit permanently to remain in the United States, any alien child who, when under sixteen years of age was heretofore temporarily admitted to the United States and who is now within the United States and either of whose parents is a citizen of the United States.

MAINTENANCE OF EXEMPT STATUS

SEC. 15. The admission to the United States of an alien excepted from the class of immigrants by clause (2), (3), (4), (5), or (6) of section 3, or declared to be a non-quota immigrant by subdivision (e) of section 4, shall be for such time as may be by regulations prescribed, and under such conditions as may be by regulations prescribed (including, when deemed necessary for the classes mentioned in clauses (2), (3), (4), or (6) of section 3, the giving of bond with sufficient surety, in such sum and containing such conditions as may be by regulations prescribed) to insure that, at the expiration of such time or upon failure to maintain the status under which he was admitted, he will depart from the United States.

SEC 28. As used in this Act—

(a) The term "United States," when used in a geographical sense, means the States, the Territories of Alaska and Hawaii, the District of Columbia, Porto Rico, and the Virgin Islands; and the term "continental United States " means the States and the District of Columbia;

(b) The term "alien" includes any individual not a native-born or naturalized citizen of the United States, but this definition shall not be held to include Indians of the United States not taxed, nor citizens of the islands under the jurisdiction of the United States; (c) The term "ineligible to citizenship," when used in reference to any individual, includes an individual who is debarred from becoming a citizen of the United States under section 2169 of the Revised Statutes, or under section 14 of the Act entitled "An Act to execute certain treaty stipulations relating to Chinese," approved May 6, 1882, or under section 1996, 1997, or 1998 of the Revised Statutes, as amended, or under section 2 of the Act entitled "An Act to authorize the President to increase temporarily the Military Establishment of the United States," approved May 18, 1917, as amended, or under law amendatory of, supplementary to, or in substitution for, any of such sections;

(d) The term "immigration visa" means an immigration visa issued by a consular officer under the provisions of this Act;

(e) The term "consular officer" means any consular or diplomatic officer of the United States designated, under regulations prescribed under this Act, for the purpose of issuing immigration visas under this Act. In case of the Canal Zone and the insular possessions of the United States the term "consular officer" (except as used in section 24) means an officer designated by the President, or by his authority, for the purpose of issuing immigration visas under this Act; (f) The term "Immigration Act of 1917" means the Act of February 5, 1917, entitled "An Act to regulate the immigration of aliens to, and the residence of aliens in, the United States";

(g) The term "immigration laws" includes such Act, this Act, and all laws, conventions, and treaties of the United States relating to the immigration, exclusion, or expulsion of aliens;

(h) The term "person" includes individuals, partnerships, corporations, and associations;

(i) The term "Commissioner General" means the Commissioner General of Immigration;

(j)The term "application for admission" has reference to the application for admission to the United States and not to the application for the issuance of the immigration visa;

(k) The term "permit" means a permit issued under section 10;

(l) The term "unmarried," when used in reference to any as of any time, means an individual who at such time is not married, whether or not previously married;

(m) The terms "child," "father," and "mother," do not include child or parent by adoption unless the adoption took place before January 1, 1924;

(n) The terms "wife" and "husband" do not include a wife or husband by reason of a proxy or picture marriage.

Source: http://www.usconstitution.com/immigrationactof1924.htm.

17. FLORIDA HURRICANE OF 1926 (SEPTEMBER 19, 1926)

On September 17, 1926, a hurricane crashed into the rapidly growing and romanticized city of Miami. The hurricane killed 113 persons, injured another 854, and effectively ended the Florida land boom of the early 1920s. Printed here is the first account of the storm as it was reported under large two-column headlines on the front page of the *New York Times*.

75 Reported Dead in Miami;
Hurricane Sweeps Coast;
2000 Buildings in Ruins

$100,000,000 Damage in City
Meager Facts of Disaster
Reach Mobile by Wireless Message

Docks Gone;
Boats Sunk
100 Mile Gale Drove Sea into the Streets,
Covering Them to Depth of Six Feet

Palm Beach Is Also Hit
Only Scant Details from the Devastated Area
Storm Is Called Worst in History
Mobile Ala., Sept. 18 (A.P.)

Seventy-Five known dead, property loss of $100,000,000 in the city, and every boat in the harbor sunk, was the toll of the hurricane that struck Miami, according to fragmentary messages picked up by the Tropical Radio Telegraph Company station here today. The station is working the American steamship Siboney, which has established communication with a makeshift transmitting plant in Hialeah. Every vestige of the city dock system was swept away, and 2,000 buildings were ruined said the message, which added that troops, food, and medical supplies are needed urgently.

Source: New York Times, September 19, 1926.

18. POVERTY IN THE PROSPEROUS 1920s—CASE STUDIES OF UNEMPLOYED WORKERS I

Case studies of unemployment, like the one reproduced below, were compiled in the mid-1920s by the Unemployment Committee of the National Federation of Settlements. The committee conducted a national survey of unemployed workers from various backgrounds. These case studies provide a window into life among the forgotten poor in what is often remembered as the "prosperous twenties."

CASE 1 Union Settlement CARDANI* New York City, N.Y.
* The names in all the cases are fictitious in order not to reveal the identity of the persons included in the study.

Ital. (*M. 37; W. 28*)

Chn: *11, 10, 8*

Laborer (*bricklayer's helper*)

Unemployment Reported Due to:

seasonal slackness; oversupply of labor

The Cardani family of mother and father, 11-year-old daughter and two sons, aged 10 and 8 have lived in neighborhoods close to the settlement for ten years. Mrs. Cardani has been a star member of the nutrition class for mothers, a proficient pupil in English, and a real asset to the settlement because of her cooperativeness,—always ready to break the ice at a party by singing an Italian song, or to coach her children and help with their costumes when they have taken part in plays. All three children have entered with enthusiasm into any and every activity offered by the settlement for junior groups, and the excellence of their work has been noteworthy. Mr. Cardani has been shy to the point of aloofness; on the rare occasions when he has come to the settlement,—perhaps to a community gathering, or to see Bianca dance,—it has been impossible to engage him in conversation. For the last eight months, the family has been coming less and less frequently to the settlement, and this is the explanation given by Mrs. Cardani:

"Ever since last May I work so hard and so long at the factory that I cannot go to clubs and classes any more. My Bianca does some of the work home that I used to do, so she can't go either, with her lessons getting harder and everything."

Here Mrs. Cardani put aside her iron, wiped off a chair for her caller, and she sank into another, with a look of relief; 10-year-old Enrico took up the iron and slowly and painstakingly completed two boys' blouses and a pair of ruffled sash-curtains.

"I've always helped out some, sewing coats at home, or half-time in the factory. But this year my husband has been off since May. Only five days' work since May, right in the good season too, when we count on buying clothes and saving a little. So now I work all day long. I'm glad to do it. He has always brought home every dollar he's earned, and so good to the children, and just crazy when they're sick or when they don't seem to do well.

"Why couldn't he get a job last summer? Well, you see, he don't speak so good English and there aren't enough jobs to go round anyway, so he don't have much chance. Every morning he goes to see the bosses. They say, 'No, too many men come; not enough work; you got to wait.' Everywhere too many men, jobs for just a few.

"I could earn much more money if I went down town to work. But I don't want to let the children run wild, with nothing hot for lunch or anything. This boss, he knows we women don't want to leave our families and go way down there, so he says, 'Take what I pay or get out.'"

"But surely, Mrs. Cardani, you cannot earn enough to pay the rent, and buy coal and food, too?"

"No, I can't. For these four rooms we pay $20 a month. I make $12 a week. That's all we have. But you know what we do. If we pay the rent and there isn't enough left, you know what we do. If we're going to live honest, you know what we do."

Here Bianca, an interested listener, deciding that her mother was not making herself clear, explained, "We eat little—that's what we do."

"Yes," went on Mrs. Cardani, now that the truth was out, "that's the only place we can cut down. I buy a quart of loose milk every morning. The children have this with breakfast,—I usually cook cereal, too. Then what milk is left they can have at a noon, maybe mixed with cocoa and water, for something warm. Then at night we have something that fills our stomachs up. I can get four pounds of greens for fifteen cents, and that does fine for a meal. I haven't been buying eggs or meat this winter. From the time my babies were weaned they always had one egg a day. Now Bianca is getting so thin and white, my husband says we'll have to manage that egg again somehow. . . . No, I don't mind eating light—it just makes me kinda cold sometimes. But it's the children!

"I got some trouble too that pulls me down. The doctor said I should rest or have operation. But I haven't any time or any money. I stay up till one, two, three o'clock every night trying to keep the house clean and the children's clothes fit to wear to school. Maybe next summer if he gets a job, I'll get a chance to rest up."

Just then Mr. Cardani came in and when told what the talk was about, added in broken English, "I came to this country eighteen year ago. I live always with Italian people. All the men I know they do day labor same as me. I'm bricklayer's helper—$8 a day. We never make full week though—one day too cold, next day it rain, maybe the sand don't come, maybe the cement.

"What do I do when I got no job? Mornings I go out and look for job. Then I come home and sit. Nine months I sit around now. I can't read—just like a blind man! You see my father die when I was 5, and leave my mother with four little children. He was sick, my father, a long time. No money left. No free school in those days—my brother and my sisters and I, we never went to school.

"Why don't I go to English class? I go two year to the school in the next block. The teacher make the writing on the blackboard, so and so and so [scrolls]; I copy, so and so and so. But I don't know the letters. The other men, yes, they read Italian newspaper. But I don't know one letter. I don't tell the teacher—she have enough trouble. It's too late now."

At the door Mrs. Cardani remarked that it was getting colder out. "When it comes very cold," she said, "we have to spend the money for coal and then I just don't know what to do for food." There had been no fire in the stove that evening with the thermometer at 40° outdoors. The flat was cold and the floor draughty. The parents were wearing coats or sweaters turned up at the neck, and the children had only cotton stockings and thin shoes.

Source: Library of Congress: Case studies of unemployment, compiled by the Unemployment Committee of the National Federation of Settlements, with an intro. by Helen Hall and a foreword by Paul U. Kellogg. Edited by Marion Elderton.

National Federation of Settlements and Neighborhood Centers. Unemployment Committee http://lcweb2.loc.gov/cgi-bin.

19. POVERTY IN THE PROSPEROUS 1920s—CASE STUDIES OF UNEMPLOYED WORKERS II

This report by the Unemployment Committee National Federation of Settlements tells the story of a single father trying to keep his family together in New Orleans.

Case 16 Family Service Society MONTEREY New Orleans
Lat. Amer. (M. 52); Amer. (W. died 1927)
Chn: 18, 13, 9, 7
Painter and Carpenter, Later Boiler-Scaler
Eldest son also boiler-scaler
Unemployment Reported Due to:
depression and mechanization

Mr. Monterey is 52 years old and was born in Central America of Spanish parentage. Mrs. Monterey was born in one of the country districts of Louisiana. She died in the summer of 1927. There are three boys, aged 18, 9 and 7, and one girl, 13.

The family first came to our attention in August, 1927. At that time both Mr. Monterey and his son were working irregularly for a boiler concern.

The father had worked for several years as a boiler-scaler and prior to that had been a painter, carpenter's helper and sailor. Rudolpho, the eldest son, had completed the grammar grades and studied the trade of boiler-scaler under his father.

Before unemployment, the family lived in comfortable surroundings and although they were not able to afford luxuries, Mr. and Mrs. Monterey and the children were not deprived of any of the necessities. Because the parents did not approve of street play for the children and the seeking of amusements away from home, they endeavored to make the home as pleasant as possible and encouraged the children to invite their little friends to visit them. They often gave little parties at which the friends were present.

The father and Rudolpho became unemployed at the time of the general business depression. The firm for which they were working laid off over half of the workmen. This concern still gives day's work to the Montereys whenever possible, since the foreman considers them excellent workmen.

The installation of machinery in Mr. Monterey's line of work has also been a cause of his unemployment. He has been without steady work for almost two years. The day's work which he and his son secure now and then in one of the ship-building yards pays from $3.30 to $3.80 a day, but it is extremely irregular. The father and son applied from place to place for employment, always taking their working clothes with them in the event that they might secure work.

During the period when they were both regularly employed the family income was between $40 and $50 a week. They earn now as little as $3 or $4 a week and many weeks not even this much.

In telling his story, Mr. Monterey said: "In the past eight months I was only able to get two days' work a month. Then I got a job filling at the West End, at the rate of 40 cents an hour. I used to work twelve and thirteen hours a day. I worked forty days steady work and made $196, which was barely enough to cover my debts. From that date in August until the present date, I have not had a steady job."

This period of unemployment has had serious effects upon the family's financial arrangements. The family became burdened with rent and a grocery bill. In an effort to meet these debts, Mr. Monterey pawned articles of clothing, sold almost all of their furniture and moved from place to place in search of cheaper rent.

The family is now living in a somewhat undesirable neighborhood near the river. Mr. Monterey does not feel that the present location is a good one, but it is only $7 a month and within walking distance of several of the big ship yards and he hopes that his children, who have not presented problems in the past, will not be influenced by the many undesirable forces in their present environment.

The family has been forced to drop all insurance policies. About a month ago, the 13-year-old girl had to stop school, although she is making an effort to study at home as much as possible.

Mr. Monterey was given a small amount of relief at one period during his unemployment. He requested this money as a loan because he does not like to ask for charity.

The family has not been able to keep up their usual standards of health. The children's diets are not sufficiently varied to insure proper growth. Two of the children are undernourished and quite delicate. They also do not have adequate clothing. The children have had no winter coats or sweaters and in cold weather have gone to school without such clothing. The little girl, America, is obliged to wash several times a week in order to keep the family in clean clothing and underwear since their supply is so limited.

The rooms contain practically nothing but the necessary beds. A short time ago when neither father nor son had work for weeks, the two little boys went to the market where they picked up scraps of meat and cast-off vegetables for the family's food.

Mr. Monterey has faced the family's predicament with a great deal of courage. He has made valiant efforts to meet some of his debts and tries diligently to secure work. He seems to be reaching the breaking point, however, and has begun to feel that his situation is almost hopeless and eventually he will be forced to break up his home and place the children in an asylum. Such thoughts greatly upset him and he states that he is almost afraid to think of the future.

America, who has been forced to stop school, does not seem bitter or antagonistic. She is studying at home, so that she will be able to keep up with her class, as far as possible. It was one of her great ambitions, as well as that of her father, that she might at least complete the grade school.

Unemployment has practically curtailed the family's opportunities for securing relaxation and recreation. There is no money for books or shows. The victrola, which was one of the children's chief forms of recreation, has been sold. All of the children, especially the daughter, are fond of music. The little girl had hoped to be able to take violin lessons from one of her father's friends, and the lessons were to be free. America has, however, since abandoned the hope of this because she now knows that her father cannot afford to buy her the instrument.

Source: Library of Congress: Case studies of unemployment, compiled by the Unemployment Committee of the National Federation of Settlements, with an intro. by Helen Hall and a foreword by Paul U. Kellogg. Edited by Marion Elderton.

National Federation of Settlements and Neighborhood Centers. Unemployment Committee http:// lcweb2.loc.gov/cgi-bin.

20. BOULDER DAM PROJECT—TRANSCRIPT OF THE BOULDER CANYON PROJECT ACT (DECEMBER 21, 1928)

President Herbert Hoover called the building of Boulder Dam "the greatest engineering work of its character ever attempted by the hand of man." About 16,000 men and women worked on the project with approximately 3,500 people employed at any one time. It was dangerous work, and the official death toll was 96. Five thousand men and their families settled in the Nevada desert, most in Boulder City, an efficiently run, well-ordered company town built by the federal government. Others lived in dozens of tent cities and honky-tonk towns that sprang up on the road from the dam to the small town of Las Vegas. To a country struggling to come out of the Depression, the project was dramatic evidence of what American brains and manpower could accomplish, and it became a symbol of hope for the dispossessed. The dam was completed in 1935.

AN ACT To provide for the construction of works for the protection and development of the Colorado River Basin, for the approval of the Colorado River compact, and for other purposes.

Be it enacted by the Senate and House of Representatives of the United States of America in Congress assembled, That for the purpose of controlling the floods, improving navigation and regulating the flow of the Colorado River, providing for storage and for the delivery of the stored waters thereof for reclamation of public lands and other beneficial uses exclusively within the United States, and for the generation of electrical energy as a means of making the project herein authorized a self-supporting and financially solvent undertaking, the Secretary of the Interior, subject to the terms of the Colorado River compact hereinafter mentioned, is hereby authorized to construct, operate, and maintain a dam and incidental works in the main stream of the Colorado River at Black Canyon or Boulder Canyon adequate to create a storage reservoir of a capacity of not less than twenty million acre-feet of water and a main canal and appurtenant structures located entirely within the United States connecting the Laguna Dam, or other suitable diversion dam, which the Secretary of the Interior is hereby authorized to construct if deemed necessary or advisable by him upon engineering or economic considerations, with the Imperial and Coachella Valleys in California, the expenditures for said main canal and appurtenant structures to be reimbursable, as provided in the reclamation law, and shall not be paid out of revenues derived from the sale or disposal of water power or electric energy at the dam authorized to be constructed at said Black Canyon or Boulder Canyon, or for water for potable purposes outside of the Imperial and Coachella Valleys: Provided, however, That no charge shall be made for water or for the use, storage, or delivery of water for irrigation or water for potable purposes in the Imperial or Coachella Valleys; also to construct and equip, operate, and maintain at or near said dam, or cause to be constructed, a complete plant and incidental structures suitable for the fullest economic development of electrical energy from the water discharged from said reservoir; and to acquire by proceedings in eminent domain, or otherwise all lands, rights-of-way, and other property necessary for said purposes.

SEC. 2. (a) There is hereby established a special fund, to be known as the "Colorado River Dam fund" (hereinafter referred to as the "fund"), and to be available, as hereafter provided, only for carrying out the provisions of this Act. All revenues received in carrying out the provisions of this Act shall be paid into and expenditures shall be made out of the fund, under the direction of the Secretary of the Interior.

(b) The Secretary of the Treasury is authorized to advance to the fund, from time to time and within the appropriations therefor, such amounts as the Secretary of the Interior deems necessary for carrying out the provisions of this Act, except that the aggregate amount of such advances shall not exceed the sum of $165,000,000. Of this amount the sum of $25,000,000 shall be allocated to flood control and shall be repaid to the United States out of 62 1/2 per centum of revenues, if any, in excess of the amount necessary to meet periodical payments during the period of amortization, as provided in section 4 of this Act. If said sum of $25,000,000 is not repaid in full during the period of amortization, then 62 1/2 per centum of all net revenues shall be applied to payment of the remainder. Interest at the rate of 4 per centum per annum accruing during the year upon the amounts so advanced and remaining unpaid shall be paid annually out of the fund, except as herein otherwise provided.

(c) Moneys in the fund advanced under subdivision (b) shall be available only for expenditures for construction and the payment of interest, during construction, upon the amounts so advanced. No expenditures out of the fund shall be made for operation and maintenance except from appropriations therefor.

(d) The Secretary of the Treasury shall charge the fund as of June 30 in each year with such amount as may be necessary for the payment of interest on advances made under subdivision (b) at the rate of 4 per centum per annum accrued during the year upon the amounts so advanced and remaining unpaid, except that if the fund is insufficient to meet the payment of interest the Secretary of the Treasury may, in his discretion, defer any part of such payment, and the amount so deferred shall bear interest at the rate of 4 per centum per annum until paid.

(e) The Secretary of the Interior shall certify to the Secretary of the Treasury, at the close of each fiscal year, the amount of money in the fund in excess of the amount necessary for construction, operation, and maintenance, and payment of interest. Upon receipt of each such certificate the Secretary of the Treasury is authorized and directed to charge the fund with the amount so certified as repayment of the advances made under subdivision (b), which amount shall be covered into the Treasury to the credit of miscellaneous receipts.

SEC. 3. There is hereby authorized to be appropriated from time to time, out of any money in the Treasury not otherwise appropriated, such sums of money as may be necessary to carry out the purposes of this Act, not exceeding in the aggregate $165,000,000.

SEC. 4. (a) This Act shall not take effect and no authority shall be exercised hereunder and no work shall be begun and no moneys expended on or in connection with the works or structures provided for in this Act, and no water rights shall be claimed or initiated hereunder, and no steps shall be taken by the United States or by others to initiate or perfect any claims to the use of water pertinent to such works or structures unless and until (1) the States of Arizona, California, Colorado, Nevada, New Mexico, Utah, and Wyoming shall have ratified the Colorado River compact, mentioned in section 13 hereof, and the President by public proclamation shall have so declared, or (2) if said States fail to ratify the said compact within six months from the date of the passage of this Act then, until six of said States, including the State of California, shall ratify said compact and shall consent to waive the provisions of the first paragraph of Article XI of said compact, which makes the same binding and obligatory only when approved by each of the seven States signatory thereto, and shall have approved said compact without conditions, save that of such six-State approval, and the President by public proclamation shall have so declared, and, further, until the State of California, by act of its legislature, shall agree irrevocably and unconditionally with the United States and for the benefit of the States of Arizona, Colorado, Nevada, New Mexico, Utah, and Wyoming, as an express covenant and in consideration of the passage of this Act, that the aggregate annual consumptive use (diversions less returns to the river) of water of and from the Colorado River for use in the State of California, including all uses under contracts made under the provisions of this Act and all water necessary for the supply of any rights which may now exist, shall not exceed four million four hundred thousand acre-feet of the waters apportioned to the lower basin States by paragraph (a) of Article III of the Colorado River compact, plus not more than one-half of any excess or surplus waters unapportioned by said compact, such uses always to be subject to the terms of said compact. The States of Arizona, California, and Nevada are authorized to enter into an agreement which shall provide (1) that of the 7,500,000 acre-feet annually apportioned to the lower basin by paragraph (a) of Article III of the Colorado River compact, there shall be apportioned to the State of Nevada 300,000 acre-feet and to the State of Arizona 2,800,000 acre-feet for exclusive beneficial consumptive use in perpetuity, and (2) that the State of Arizona may annually use one-half of the excess or surplus waters unapportioned by the Colorado River compact, and (3) that the State of Arizona shall have the exclusive beneficial consumptive use of the Gila River and its tributaries within the boundaries of said State, and (4) that the waters of the Gila River and its tributaries, except return flow after the same enters the Colorado River, shall never be subject to any diminution whatever by any allowance of water which may be made by treaty or otherwise to the United States of Mexico but if, as provided in paragraph (c) of Article III of the Colorado River compact, it shall become necessary to supply water to the United States of Mexico from waters over and above the quantities which are surplus as defined by said compact, then the State of California shall and will mutually agree with the State of Arizona to supply, out of the main stream of the Colorado River, one-half of any deficiency which must be supplied to Mexico by the lower basin, and (5) that the State of California shall and will further mutually agree with the States of Arizona and Nevada that none of said three States shall withhold water and none shall require the delivery of water, which cannot reasonably be applied to domestic and agricultural uses, and (6) that all of the provisions of said tri-State agreement shall be subject in all particulars to the provisions of the Colorado River compact, and (7) said agreement to take effect upon the ratification of the Colorado River compact by Arizona, California, and Nevada. (b) Before any money is appropriated for the construction of said dam or power plant, or any construction work done or contracted for, the Secretary of the Interior shall make provision for revenues by contract, in accordance with the provisions of this Act, adequate in his judgment to insure payment of all expenses of operation and maintenance of said works incurred by the United States and the repayment, within fifty years from the date of the completion of said works, of all amounts advanced to the fund under subdivision (b) of section 2 for such works, together with interest thereon made reimbursable under this Act.

Before any money is appropriated for the construction of said main canal and appurtenant structures to connect the Laguna Dam with the Imperial and Coachella Valleys in California, or any construction work is done upon said canal or contracted for, the Secretary of the Interior shall make provision for revenues, by contract or otherwise, adequate in his judgment to insure payment of all expenses of construction, operation, and maintenance of said main canal and appurtenant structures in the manner provided in the reclamation law.

If during the period of amortization the Secretary of the Interior shall receive revenues in excess of the amount necessary to meet the periodical payments to the United States as provided in the contract, or contracts, executed under this Act, then, immediately after the settlement of such periodical payments, he shall pay to the State of Arizona 183/4 per centum of such excess revenues and to the State of Nevada 183/4 per centum of such excess revenues.

SEC. 5. That the Secretary of the Interior is hereby authorized, under such general regulations as he may prescribe, to contract for the storage of water in said reservoir and for the delivery thereof at such points on the river and on said canal as may be agreed upon, for irrigation and domestic uses, and generation of electrical energy and delivery at the switchboard to States, municipal corporations, political subdivisions, and private corporations of electrical energy generated at said dam, upon charges that will provide revenue which, in addition to other revenue accruing under the reclamation law and under this Act, will in his judgment cover all expenses of operation and maintenance incurred by the United States on account of works constructed under this Act and the payments to the United States under subdivision (b) of section 4. Contracts respecting water for irrigation and domestic uses shall be for permanent service and shall conform to paragraph (a) of section 4 of this Act. No person shall have or be entitled to have the use for any purpose of the water stored as aforesaid except by contract made as herein stated. After the repayments to the United States of all money advanced with interest, charges shall be on such basis and the revenues derived therefrom shall be kept in a separate fund to be expended within the Colorado River Basin as may hereafter be prescribed by the Congress. General and uniform regulations shall be prescribed by the said Secretary for the awarding of contracts for the sale and delivery of electrical energy, and for renewals under subdivision (b) of this section, and in making such contracts the following shall govern:

(a) No contract for electrical energy or for generation of electrical energy shall be of longer duration than fifty years from the date at which such energy is ready for delivery. Contracts made pursuant to subdivision (a) of this section shall be made with a view to obtaining reasonable returns and shall contain provisions whereby at the end of fifteen years from the date of their execution and every ten years thereafter, there shall be readjustment of the contract, upon the demand of either party thereto, either upward or downward as to price, as the Secretary of the Interior may find to be justified by competitive conditions at distributing points or competitive centers and with provisions under which disputes or disagreements as to interpretation or performance of such contract shall be determined either by arbitration or court proceedings, the Secretary of the Interior being authorized to act for the United States in such readjustments or proceedings.

(b) The holder of any contract for electrical energy not in default thereunder shall be entitled to a renewal thereof upon such terms and conditions as may be authorized or required under the then existing laws and regulations, unless the property of such holder dependent for its usefulness on a continuation of the contract be purchased or acquired and such holder be compensated for damages to its property, used and useful in the transmission and distribution of such electrical energy and not taken, resulting from the termination of the supply.

(c) Contracts for the use of water and necessary privileges for the generation and distribution of hydroelectric energy or for the sale and delivery of electrical energy shall be made with responsible applicants therefor who will pay the price fixed by the said Secretary with a view to meeting the revenue requirements herein provided for. In case of conflicting applications, if any, such conflicts shall be resolved by the said Secretary, after hearing, with due regard to the public interest, and in conformity with the policy expressed in the Federal Water Power Act as to conflicting applications for permits and licenses, except that preference to applicants for the use of water and appurtenant works and privileges necessary for the generation and distribution of hydroelectric energy, or for delivery at the switchboard of a hydroelectric plant, shall be given, first, to a State for the generation or purchase of electric energy for use in the State, and the States of Arizona, California, and Nevada shall be given equal opportunity as such applicants.

The rights covered by such preference shall be contracted for by such State within six months after notice by the Secretary of the Interior and to be paid for on the same terms and conditions as may be provided in other similar contracts made by said Secretary: Provided, however, That no application of a State or a political subdivision for an allocation of water for power purposes or of electrical energy shall be denied or another application in conflict therewith be granted on the ground that the bond issue of such State or political subdivision, necessary to enable the applicant to utilize such water and appurtenant works and privileges necessary for the generation and distribution of hydroelectric energy or the electrical energy applied for, has not been authorized or marketed, until after a reasonable time, to be determined by the said Secretary, has been given to such applicant to have such bond issue authorized and marketed.

(d) Any agency receiving a contract for electrical energy equivalent to one hundred thousand firm horsepower, or more, may, when deemed feasible by the said Secretary, from engineering and economic considerations and under general regulations prescribed by him, be required to permit any other agency having contracts hereunder for less than the equivalent of twenty-five thousand firm horsepower, upon application to the Secretary of the Interior made within sixty days from the execution of the contract of the agency the use of whose transmission line is applied for, to participate in the benefits and use of any main transmission line constructed or to be constructed by the former for carrying such energy (not exceeding, however, one-fourth the capacity of such line), upon payment by such other agencies of a reasonable share of the cost of construction, operation, and maintenance thereof. The use is hereby authorized of such public and reserved lands of the United States as may be necessary or convenient for the construction, operation, and maintenance of main transmission lines to transmit said electrical energy.

SEC. 6. That the dam and reservoir provided for by section 1 hereof shall be used: First, for river regulation, improvement of navigation, and flood control; second, for irrigation and domestic uses and satisfaction of present perfected rights in pursuance of Article VIII of said Colorado River compact; and third, for power. The title to said dam, reservoir, plant, and incidental works shall forever remain in the United States, and the United States shall, until otherwise provided by Congress, control, manage, and operate the same, except as herein otherwise provided: Provided, however, That the Secretary of the Interior may, in his discretion, enter into contracts of lease of a unit or units of any Government-built plant, with right to generate electrical energy, or, alternatively, to enter into contracts of lease for the use of water for the generation of electrical energy as herein provided, in either of which events the provisions of section 5 of this Act relating to revenue, term, renewals, determination of conflicting applications, and joint use of transmission lines under contracts for the sale of electrical energy, shall apply.

The Secretary of the Interior shall prescribe and enforce rules and regulations conforming with the requirements of the Federal Water Power Act, so far as applicable respecting maintenance of works in condition of repair adequate for their efficient operation, maintenance of a system of accounting, control of rates and service in the absence of State regulation or interstate agreement valuation for rate-making purposes, transfers of contracts, contracts extending beyond the lease period, expropriation of excessive profits, recapture and/or emergency use by the United States of property of lessees, and penalties for enforcing regulations made under this Act of penalizing failure to comply with such regulations or with the provisions of this

Act. He shall also conform with other provisions of the Federal Water Power Act and of the rules and regulations of the Federal Power Commission, which have been devised or which may be hereafter devised, for the protection of the investor and consumer. The Federal Power Commission is hereby directed not to issue or approve any permits or licenses under said Federal Water Power Act upon or affecting the Colorado River or any of its tributaries, except the Gila River, in the States of Colorado, Wyoming, Utah, New Mexico, Nevada, Arizona, and California until this Act shall become effective as provided in section 4 herein.

SEC. 7. That the Secretary of the Interior may, in his discretion, when repayments to the United States of all money advanced, with interest, reimbursable hereunder, shall have been made, transfer the title to said canal and appurtenant structures, except the Laguna Dam and the main canal and appurtenant structures down to and including Syphon Drop, to the districts or other agencies of the United States having a beneficial interest therein in proportion to their respective capital investments under such form of organization as may be acceptable to him. The said districts or other agencies shall have the privilege at any time of utilizing by contract or otherwise such power possibilities as may exist upon said canal, in proportion to their respective contributions or obligations toward the capital cost of said canal and appurtenant structures from and including the diversion works to the point where each respective power plant may be located. The net proceeds from any power development on said canal shall be paid into the fund and credited to said districts or other agencies on their said contracts, in proportion to their rights to develop power, until the districts or other agencies using said canal shall have paid thereby and under any contract or otherwise an amount of money equivalent to the operation and maintenance expense and cost of construction thereof.

SEC. 8. (a) The United States, its permittees, licensees, and contractees, and all users and appropriators of water stored, diverted, carried, and/or distributed by the reservoir, canals, and other works herein authorized, shall observe and be subject to and controlled by said Colorado River compact in the construction, management, and operation of said reservoir, canals, and other works and the storage, diversion, delivery, and use of water for the generation of power, irrigation, and other purposes, anything in this Act to the contrary notwithstanding, and all permits, licenses, and contracts shall so provide.

(b) Also the United States, in constructing, managing, and operating the dam, reservoir, canals, and other works herein authorized, including the appropriation, delivery, and use of water for the generation of power, irrigation, or other uses, and all users of water thus delivered and all users and appropriators of waters stored by said reservoir and/or carried by said canal, including all permittees and licensees of the United States or any of its agencies, shall observe and be subject to and controlled, anything to the contrary herein notwithstanding, by the terms of such compact, if any, between the States of Arizona, California, and Nevada, or any two thereof, for the equitable division of the benefits, including power, arising from the use of water accruing to said States, subsidiary to and consistent with said Colorado River compact, which may be negotiated and approved by said States and to which Congress shall give its consent and approval on or before January 1, 1929; and the terms of any such compact concluded between said States and approved and consented to by Congress after said date: Provided, That in the latter case such compact shall be subject to all contracts, if any, made by the Secretary of the Interior under section 5 hereof prior to the date of such approval and consent by Congress.

SEC. 9. All lands of the United States found by the Secretary of the Interior to be practicable of irrigation and reclamation by the irrigation works authorized herein shall be withdrawn from public entry. Thereafter, at the direction of the Secretary of the Interior, such lands shall be opened for entry, in tracts varying in size but not exceeding one hundred and sixty acres, as may be determined by the Secretary of the Interior, in accordance with the provisions of the reclamation law, and any such entryman shall pay an equitable share in accordance with the benefits received, as determined by the said Secretary, of the construction cost of said canal and appurtenant structures; said payments to be made in such installments and at such times as may be specified by the Secretary of the Interior, in accordance with the provisions of the said reclamation law, and shall constitute revenue from said project and be covered into the fund herein provided for: Provided, That all persons who served in the United States Army, Navy, Marine Corps, or Coast Guard during the War with Germany, the War with Spain, or in the suppression of the insurrection in the Philippines, and who have been honorably separated or discharged therefrom or placed in the Regular Army or Naval Reserve, shall have the exclusive preference right for a period of three months to enter said lands, subject, however, to the provisions of subsection (c) of section 4 of the Act of December 5, 1924 (43 Stat. 672, 702; 43 U.S.C., sec. 433); and also, so far as practicable, preference shall be given to said persons in all construction work authorized by this chapter: Provided further, That the above exclusive preference rights shall apply to veteran settlers on lands watered from the Gila canal in Arizona the same as to veteran settlers on lands watered from the All-American canal in California: Provided further, That in the event such entry shall be relinquished at any time prior to actual residence upon the land by the entryman for not less than one year, lands so relinquished shall not be subject to entry for a period of sixty days after the filing and notation of the relinquishment in the local land office, and after the expiration of said sixty-day period such lands shall be open to entry, subject to the preference in the section provided.

SEC. 10. That nothing in this Act shall be construed as modifying in any manner the existing contract, dated October 23, 1918, between the United States and the Imperial Irrigation District, providing for a connection with Laguna Dam; but the Secretary of the Interior is authorized to enter into contract or contracts with the said district or other districts, persons, or agencies for the construction, in accordance with this Act, of said canal and appurtenant structures, and also for the operation and maintenance thereof, with the consent of the other users.

SEC. 11. That the Secretary of the Interior is hereby authorized to make such studies, surveys, investigations, and do such engineering as may be necessary to determine the lands in the State of Arizona that should be embraced within the boundaries of a reclamation project, heretofore commonly known and hereafter to be known as the Parker-Gila Valley reclamation project, and to recommend the most practicable and feasible method of irrigating lands within said project, or units thereof, and the cost of the same; and the appropriation of such sums of money as may be necessary for the aforesaid purposes from time to time is hereby authorized. The Secretary shall report to Congress as soon as practicable, and not later than December 10, 1931, his findings, conclusions, and recommendations regarding such project.

SEC. 12. "Political subdivision" or "political subdivisions" as used in this Act shall be understood to include any State, irrigation or other district, municipality, or other governmental organization.

"Reclamation law" as used in this Act shall be understood to mean that certain Act of the Congress of the United States approved June 17, 1902, entitled "An Act appropriating the receipts from the sale and disposal of public land in certain States and Territories to the construction of irrigation works for the reclamation of arid lands," and the Acts amendatory thereof and supplemental thereto.

"Maintenance" as used herein shall be deemed to include in each instance provision for keeping the works in good operating condition.

"The Federal Water Power Act," as used in this Act, shall be understood to mean that certain Act of Congress of the United States approved June 10, 1920, entitled "An Act to create a Federal Power Commission; to provide for the improvement of navigation; the development of water power; the use of the public lands in relation thereto; and to repeal section 18 of the River and Harbor Appropriation Act, approved August 8, 1917, and for other purposes," and the Acts amendatory thereof and supplemental thereto.

"Domestic" whenever employed in this Act shall include water uses defined as "domestic" in said Colorado River compact.

SEC. 13. (a) The Colorado River compact signed at Santa Fe, New Mexico, November 24, 1922, pursuant to Act of Congress approved August 19, 1921, entitled "An Act to permit a compact or agreement between the States of Arizona, California, Colorado, Nevada, New Mexico, Utah, and Wyoming respecting the disposition and apportionment of the waters of the Colorado River, and for other purposes," is hereby approved by the Congress of the United States, and the provisions of the first paragraph of article II of the said Colorado River compact, making said compact binding and obligatory when it shall have been approved by the legislature of each of the signatory States, are hereby waived, and this approval shall become effective when the State of California and at least five of the other States mentioned, shall have approved or may hereafter approve said compact as aforesaid and shall consent to such waiver, as herein provided.

(b) The rights of the United States in or to waters of the Colorado River and its tributaries howsoever claimed or acquired, as well as the rights of those claiming under the United States, shall be subject to and controlled by said Colorado River compact.

(c) Also all patents, grants, contracts, concessions, leases, permits, licenses, rights-of-way, or other privileges from the United States or under its authority, necessary or convenient for the use of waters of the Colorado River or its tributaries, or for the generation or transmission of electrical energy generated by means of the waters of said river or its tributaries, whether under this Act, the Federal Water Power Act, or otherwise, shall be upon the express condition and with the express covenant that the rights of the recipients or holders thereof to waters of the river or its tributaries, for the use of which the same are necessary, convenient, or incidental, and the use of the same shall likewise be subject to and controlled by said Colorado River compact.

(d) The conditions and covenants referred to herein shall be deemed to run with the land and the right, interest, or privilege therein and water right, and shall attach as a matter of law, whether set out or referred to in the instrument evidencing any such patent, grant, contract, concession, lease, permit, license, right-of-way, or other privilege from the United States or under its authority, or not, and shall be deemed to be for the benefit of and be available to the States of Arizona, California, Colorado, Nevada, New Mexico, Utah, and Wyoming, and the users of water therein or thereunder, by way of suit, defense, or otherwise, in any litigation respecting the waters of the Colorado River or its tributaries.

SEC. 14. This Act shall be deemed a supplement to the reclamation law, which said reclamation law shall govern the construction, operation, and management of the works herein authorized, except as otherwise herein provided.

SEC. 15. The Secretary of the Interior is authorized and directed to make investigation and public reports of the feasibility of projects for irrigation, generation of electric power, and other purposes in the States of Arizona, Nevada, Colorado, New Mexico, Utah, and Wyoming for the purpose of making such information available to said States and to the Congress, and of formulating a comprehensive scheme of control and the improvement and utilization of the water of the Colorado River and its tributaries. The sum of $250,000 is hereby authorized to be appropriated from said Colorado River Dam fund, created by section 2 of this Act, for such purposes.

SEC. 16. In furtherance of any comprehensive plan formulated hereafter for the control, improvement, and utilization of the resources of the Colorado River system and to the end that the project authorized by this Act may constitute and be administered as a unit in such control, improvement, and utilization, any commission or commissioner duly authorized under the laws of any ratifying State in that behalf shall have the right to act in an advisory capacity to and in cooperation with the Secretary of the Interior in the exercise of any authority under the provisions of sections 4, 5, and 14 of this Act, and shall have at all times access to records of all Federal agencies empowered to act under said sections, and shall be entitled to have copies of said records on request.

SEC. 17. Claims of the United States arising out of any contract authorized by this Act shall have priority over all others, secured or unsecured.

SEC. 18. Nothing herein shall be construed as interfering with such rights as the States now have either to the waters within their borders or to adopt such policies and enact such laws as they may deem necessary with respect to the appropriation, control, and use of waters within their borders, except as modified by the Colorado River compact or other interstate agreement.

SEC. 19. That the consent of Congress is hereby given to the States of Arizona, California, Colorado, Nevada, New Mexico, Utah, and Wyoming to negotiate and enter into compacts or agreements, supplemental to and in conformity with the Colorado River compact and consistent with this Act for a comprehensive plan for the development of the Colorado River and providing for the storage, diversion, and use of the waters of said river. Any such compact or agreement may provide for the construction of dams, headworks, and other diversion works or structures for flood control, reclamation, improvement of navigation, division of water, or other purposes and/or the construction of power houses or other structures for the purpose of the development of water power and the financing of the same; and for such purposes may authorize the creation of interstate commissions and/or the creation of corporations, authorities, or other instrumentalities.

(a) Such consent is given upon condition that a representative of the United States, to be appointed by the President, shall participate in the negotiations and shall make report to Congress of the proceedings and of any compact or agreement entered into.

(b) No such compact or agreement shall be binding or obligatory upon any of such States unless and until it has been approved by the legislature of each of such States and by the Congress of the United States.

SEC. 20. Nothing in this Act shall be construed as a denial or recognition of any rights, if any, in Mexico to the use of the waters of the Colorado River system.

SEC. 21. That the short title of this Act shall be "Boulder Canyon Project Act."

Approved, December 21, 1928.

Source: Bureau of reclamation Web site, http://www.usbr.gov/lc/hooverdam/History/articles/chrono. html-US Bureau of Reclamation.

21. PRESIDENT FRANKLIN DELANO ROOSEVELT'S FIRST INAUGURAL ADDRESS (MARCH 4, 1933)

On March 4, 1933, an anxious nation awaited the words of their new president. In a time of uncertainty, Franklin Delano Roosevelt (known as FDR) exuded enthusiasm and gave people hope that help was on the way. After years of government paralysis, Roosevelt's policy of "try something try anything" to get the country going may or may not have been successful in the long run, but it did give the people confidence that the government was going to help lift them out of their personal economic morass.

First inaugural address, Saturday, March 4, 1933
I am certain that my fellow Americans expect that on my induction into the Presidency I will address them with a candor and a decision which the present

situation of our Nation impels. This is preeminently the time to speak the truth, the whole truth, frankly and boldly. Nor need we shrink from honestly facing conditions in our country today. This great Nation will endure as it has endured, will revive and will prosper. So, first of all, let me assert my firm belief **that the only thing we have to fear is fear itself**—nameless, unreasoning, unjustified terror which paralyzes needed efforts to convert retreat into advance. In every dark hour of our national life a leadership of frankness and vigor has met with that understanding and support of the people themselves which is essential to victory. I am convinced that you will again give that support to leadership in these critical days.

In such a spirit on my part and on yours we face our common difficulties. They concern, thank God, only material things. Values have shrunken to fantastic levels; taxes have risen; our ability to pay has fallen; government of all kinds is faced by serious curtailment of income; the means of exchange are frozen in the currents of trade; the withered leaves of industrial enterprise lie on every side; farmers find no markets for their produce; the savings of many years in thousands of families are gone.

More important, a host of unemployed citizens face the grim problem of existence, and an equally great number toil with little return. Only a foolish optimist can deny the dark realities of the moment.

Yet our distress comes from no failure of substance. We are stricken by no plague of locusts. Compared with the perils which our forefathers conquered because they believed and were not afraid, we have still much to be thankful for. Nature still offers her bounty and human efforts have multiplied it. Plenty is at our doorstep, but a generous use of it languishes in the very sight of the supply. Primarily this is because the rulers of the exchange of mankind's goods have failed, through their own stubbornness and their own incompetence, have admitted their failure, and abdicated. Practices of the unscrupulous money changers stand indicted in the court of public opinion, rejected by the hearts and minds of men.

True they have tried, but their efforts have been cast in the pattern of an outworn tradition. Faced by failure of credit they have proposed only the lending of more money. Stripped of the lure of profit by which to induce our people to follow their false leadership, they have resorted to exhortations, pleading tearfully for restored confidence. They know only the rules of a generation of self-seekers. They have no vision, and when there is no vision the people perish.

The money changers have fled from their high seats in the temple of our civilization. We may now restore that temple to the ancient truths. The measure of the restoration lies in the extent to which we apply social values more noble than mere monetary profit.

Happiness lies not in the mere possession of money; it lies in the joy of achievement, in the thrill of creative effort. The joy and moral stimulation of work no longer must be forgotten in the mad chase of evanescent profits. These dark days will be worth all they cost us if they teach us that our true destiny is not to be ministered unto but to minister to ourselves and to our fellow men.

Recognition of the falsity of material wealth as the standard of success goes hand in hand with the abandonment of the false belief that public office and high political position are to be valued only by the standards of pride of place and personal profit; and there must be an end to a conduct in banking and in business which too often has given to a sacred trust the likeness of callous and selfish wrongdoing. Small wonder that confidence languishes, for it thrives only on honesty, on honor, on the sacredness of obligations, on faithful protection, on unselfish performance; without them it cannot live.

Restoration calls, however, not for changes in ethics alone. This Nation asks for action, and action now.

Our greatest primary task is to put people to work. This is no unsolvable problem if we face it wisely and courageously. It can be accomplished in part by direct recruiting by the Government itself, treating the task as we would treat the emergency of a war, but at the same time, through this employment, accomplishing greatly needed projects to stimulate and reorganize the use of our natural resources.

Hand in hand with this we must frankly recognize the overbalance of population in our industrial centers and, by engaging on a national scale in a redistribution, endeavor to provide a better use of the land for those best fitted for the land. The task can be helped by definite efforts to raise the values of agricultural products and with this the power to purchase the output of our cities. It can be helped by preventing realistically the tragedy of the growing loss through foreclosure of our small homes and our farms. It can be helped by insistence that the Federal, State, and local governments act forthwith on the demand that their cost be drastically reduced. It can be helped by the unifying of relief activities which today are often scattered, uneconomical, and unequal. It can be helped by national planning for and supervision of all forms of transportation and of communications and other utilities which have a definitely public character. There are many ways in which it can be helped, but it can never be helped merely by talking about it. We must act and act quickly.

Finally, in our progress toward a resumption of work we require two safeguards against a return of the evils of the old order; there must be a strict supervision of all banking and credits and investments; there must be an end to speculation with other people's money, and there must be provision for an adequate but sound currency.

There are the lines of attack. I shall presently urge upon a new Congress in special session detailed measures for their fulfillment, and I shall seek the immediate assistance of the several States.

Through this program of action we address ourselves to putting our own national house in order and making income balance outgo. Our international trade relations, though vastly important, are in point of time and necessity secondary to the establishment of a sound national economy. I favor as a practical policy the putting of first things first. I shall spare no effort to restore world trade by international economic readjustment, but the emergency at home cannot wait on that accomplishment.

The basic thought that guides these specific means of national recovery is not narrowly nationalistic. It is the insistence, as a first consideration, upon the interdependence of the various elements in all parts of the United States—a recognition of the old and permanently important manifestation of the American spirit of the pioneer. It is the way to recovery. It is the immediate way. It is the strongest assurance that the recovery will endure.

In the field of world policy I would dedicate this Nation to the policy of the good neighbor—the neighbor who resolutely respects himself and, because he does so, respects the rights of others—the neighbor who respects his obligations and respects the sanctity of his agreements in and with a world of neighbors.

If I read the temper of our people correctly, we now realize as we have never realized before our interdependence on each other; that we can not merely take but we must give as well; that if we are to go forward, we must move as a trained and loyal army willing to sacrifice for the good of a common discipline, because without such discipline no progress is made, no leadership becomes effective. We are, I know, ready and willing to submit our lives and property to such discipline, because it makes possible a leadership which aims at a larger good. This I propose to offer, pledging that the larger purposes will bind upon us all as a sacred obligation with a unity of duty hitherto evoked only in time of armed strife.

With this pledge taken, I assume unhesitatingly the leadership of this great army of our people dedicated to a disciplined attack upon our common problems.

Action in this image and to this end is feasible under the form of government which we have inherited from our ancestors. Our Constitution is so simple and practical that it is possible always to meet extraordinary needs by changes in emphasis and arrangement without loss of essential form. That is why our constitutional system has proved itself the most superbly enduring political mechanism the modern world has produced. It has met every stress of vast expansion of territory, of foreign wars, of bitter internal strife, of world relations.

It is to be hoped that the normal balance of executive and legislative authority may be wholly adequate to meet the unprecedented task before us. But it may be that an unprecedented demand and need for undelayed action may call for temporary departure from that normal balance of public procedure.

I am prepared under my constitutional duty to recommend the measures that a stricken nation in the midst of a stricken world may require. These measures, or such other measures as the Congress may build out of its experience and wisdom, I shall seek, within my constitutional authority, to bring to speedy adoption.

But in the event that the Congress shall fail to take one of these two courses, and in the event that the national emergency is still critical, I shall not evade the clear course of duty that will then confront me. I shall ask the Congress for the one remaining instrument to meet the crisis—broad Executive power to wage a war against the emergency, as great as the power that would be given to me if we were in fact invaded by a foreign foe.

For the trust reposed in me I will return the courage and the devotion that befit the time. I can do no less.

We face the arduous days that lie before us in the warm courage of the national unity; with the clear consciousness of seeking old and precious moral values; with the clean satisfaction that comes from the stern performance of duty by old and young alike. We aim at the assurance of a rounded and permanent national life.

We do not distrust the future of essential democracy. The people of the United States have not failed. In their need they have registered a mandate that they want direct, vigorous action. They have asked for discipline and direction under leadership. They have made me the present instrument of their wishes. In the spirit of the gift I take it.

In this dedication of a Nation we humbly ask the blessing of God. May He protect each and every one of us. May He guide me in the days to come.

Source: Franklin and Eleanor Roosevelt Institute, http://www.feri.org/common/news/details.cfm?QID=2067&clientid=11005.

22. FRANKLIN D. ROOSEVELT'S FIRST FIRESIDE CHAT (MARCH 12, 1933)

When President Franklin Roosevelt took office on March 4, 1933, the country was in the worst financial crisis of its history—banks were closing, Americans were losing their homes and farms, unemployment was over 25 percent, and there seemed to be no relief in sight. One of Roosevelt's first acts in office was to declare a bank holiday to stop the run on the banks. Following this order, he went on the radio to explain his actions to the American people. This was the first of what would become known as his "fireside chats." Roosevelt, more than any of his predecessors, understood the power of the radio. And he knew how best to use that power to garner the support of the American people. Whereas other leaders in less democratic countries put radio loudspeakers on corners interrupting planned broadcasts with long speeches, Roosevelt personalized the radio, using it to come into American homes. Still unsophisticated audiences gave in to the emotion and feeling that the president was sitting in their living room talking to them personally. Roosevelt used this technique famously and frequently during his administration to explain his actions and policies to the public in plain language and simple metaphor.

On the Bank Crisis
Franklin D. Roosevelt
Sunday, March 12, 1933.
I want to talk for a few minutes with the people of the United States about banking—with the comparatively few who understand the mechanics of banking but more particularly with the overwhelming majority who use banks for the making of deposits and the drawing of checks. I want to tell you what has been done in the last few days, why it was done, and what the next steps are going to be. I recognize that

the many proclamations from State Capitols and from Washington, the legislation, the Treasury regulations, etc., couched for the most part in banking and legal terms should be explained for the benefit of the average citizen. I owe this in particular because of the fortitude and good temper with which everybody has accepted the inconvenience and hardships of the banking holiday. I know that when you understand what we in Washington have been about I shall continue to have your cooperation as fully as I have had your sympathy and help during the past week.

First of all let me state the simple fact that when you deposit money in a bank the bank does not put the money into a safe deposit vault. It invests your money in many different forms of credit-bonds, commercial paper, mortgages and many other kinds of loans. In other words, the bank puts your money to work to keep the wheels of industry and of agriculture turning around. A comparatively small part of the money you put into the bank is kept in currency—an amount which in normal times is wholly sufficient to cover the cash needs of the average citizen. In other words the total amount of all the currency in the country is only a comparatively small proportion of the total deposits in all the banks of the country.

What, then, happened during the last few days of February and the first few days of March? Because of undermined confidence on the part of the public, there was a general rush by a large portion of our population to turn bank deposits into currency or gold.—A rush so great that the soundest banks could not get enough currency to meet the demand. The reason for this was that on the spur of the moment it was, of course, impossible to sell perfectly sound assets of a bank and convert them into cash except at panic prices far below their real value.

By the afternoon of March 3 scarcely a bank in the country was open to do business. Proclamations temporarily closing them in whole or in part had been issued by the Governors in almost all the states.

It was then that I issued the proclamation providing for the nation-wide bank holiday, and this was the first step in the Government's reconstruction of our financial and economic fabric.

The second step was the legislation promptly and patriotically passed by the Congress confirming my proclamation and broadening my powers so that it became possible in view of the requirement of time to entend (sic) the holiday and lift the ban of that holiday gradually. This law also gave authority to develop a program of rehabilitation of our banking facilities. I want to tell our citizens in every part of the Nation that the national Congress—Republicans and Democrats alike—showed by this action a devotion to public welfare and a realization of the emergency and the necessity for speed that it is difficult to match in our history.

The third stage has been the series of regulations permitting the banks to continue their functions to take care of the distribution of food and household necessities and the payment of payrolls.

This bank holiday while resulting in many cases in great inconvenience is affording us the opportunity to supply the currency necessary to meet the situation. No sound bank is a dollar worse off than it was when it closed its doors last Monday. Neither is any bank which may turn out not to be in a position for immediate opening.

The new law allows the twelve Federal Reserve banks to issue additional currency on good assets and thus the banks which reopen will be able to meet every legitimate call. The new currency is being sent out by the Bureau of Engraving and Printing in large volume to every part of the country. It is sound currency because it is backed by actual, good assets.

Another question that you will ask is this: why are all the banks not to be reopened at the same time? The answer is simple, and I know that you will understand it. Your government does not intend that the history of the past few years shall be repeated. We do not want and will not have another epidemic of bank failures.

As a result we start tomorrow, Monday, with the opening of banks in the twelve Federal Reserve bank cities—those banks which on first examination by the Treasury have already been found to be all right. This will be followed on Tuesday by the resumption of all their functions by banks already found to be sound in cities where there are recognized clearing houses. That means about 250 cities of the United States.

On Wednesday and succeeding days banks in smaller places all through the country will resume business, subject, of course, to the Government's physical ability to complete its survey. It is necessary that the reopening of banks be extended over a period in order to permit the banks to make applications for necessary loans, to obtain currency needed to meet their requirements and to enable the Government to make common sense checkups.

Please let me make it clear to you that if your bank does not open the first day you are by no means justified in believing that it will not open. A bank that opens on one of the subsequent days is in exactly the same status as the bank that opens tomorrow.

I know that many people are worrying about State banks that are not members of the Federal Reserve System. These banks can and will receive assistance from members banks and from the Reconstruction Finance Corporation and of course they are under the immediate control of the state authorities. These state banks are following the same course as the national banks except that they get their licenses to resume business from the state authorities, and these authorities have been asked by the Secretary of the Treasury to permit their good banks to open up on the same schedule as the national banks. I am confident that the state banking departments will be as careful as the National Government in the policy relating to the opening of banks and will follow the same broad policy.

It is possible that when the banks resume a very few people who have not recovered from their fear may again begin withdrawals. Let me make it clear that the banks will take care of all needs—and it is my belief that hoarding during the past week has become an exceedingly unfashionable pastime. It needs no prophet to tell you that when the people find that they can get their money—that they can get it when they want it for all legitimate purposes—the phantom of fear will soon be laid aside. People will again be glad to have their money where it will be safely taken care of and where they can use it conveniently at any time. I can assure you that it is safer to keep your money in a reopened bank than under the mattress.

The success of our whole great national program depends, of course, upon the cooperation of the public—on its intelligent support and use of a reliable system.

Remember that the essential accomplishment of the new legislation is that it makes it possible for banks more readily to convert their assets into cash than was the case before. More liberal provision has been made for banks to borrow on these assets at the Reserve Banks and more liberal provision has also been made for issuing currency on the security of those good assets. This currency is not fiat currency. It is issued only on adequate security—and every good bank has an abundance of such security.

One more point before I close. There will be, of course, some banks unable to reopen without being reorganized. The new law allows the Government to assist in making these reorganizations quickly and effectively and even allows the Government to subscribe to at least a part of new capital which may be required.

I hope you can see from this elemental recital of what your government is doing that there is nothing complex, or radical in the process.

We had a bad banking situation. Some of our bankers had shown themselves either incompetent or dishonest in their handling of the people's funds. They had used the money entrusted to them in speculations and unwise loans. This was of course not true in the vast majority of our banks but it was true in enough of them to shock the people for a time into a sense of insecurity and to put them into a frame of mind where they did not differentiate, but seemed to assume that the acts of a comparative few had tainted them all. It was the Government's job to straighten out this situation and do it as quickly as possible—and the job is being performed.

I do not promise you that every bank will be reopened or that individual losses will not be suffered, but there will be no losses that possibly could be avoided; and there would have been more and greater losses had we continued to drift. I can even promise you salvation for some at least of the sorely pressed banks. We shall be engaged not merely in reopening sound banks but in the creation of sound banks through reorganization.

It has been wonderful to me to catch the note of confidence from all over the country. I can never be sufficiently grateful to the people for the loyal support they have given me in their acceptance of the judgment that has dictated our course, even though all of our processes may not have seemed clear to them.

After all there is an element in the readjustment of our financial system more important than currency, more important than gold, and that is the confidence of the people. Confidence and courage are the essentials of success in carrying out our plan. You people must have faith; you must not be stampeded by rumors or guesses. Let us unite in banishing fear. We have provided the machinery to restore our financial system; it is up to you to support and make it work.

It is your problem no less than it is mine. Together we cannot fail.

Source: Franklin and Eleanor Roosevelt Institute, http://www.feri.org/common/news/details.cfm?QID=2067&clientid=11005.

23. ANOTHER FIRESIDE CHAT—GOALS OF THE FIRST NEW DEAL (MAY 7, 1933)

Two months after his first fireside chat, President Franklin Roosevelt entered the living rooms of Americans once again to explain to them what was happening in the frenetic first hundred days of his administration. There had never been anything like it before, and Roosevelt believed he had to explain to the American people what their government was doing for them. In the process of reassuring the American people in this fireside chat, Roosevelt outlined the goals of the First New Deal.

May 7, 1933

On a Sunday night a week after my Inauguration I used the radio to tell you about the banking crisis and the measures we were taking to meet it. I think that in that way I made clear to the country various facts that might otherwise have been misunderstood and in general provided a means of understanding which did much to restore confidence.

Tonight, eight weeks later, I come for the second time to give you my report—in the same spirit and by the same means to tell you about what we have been doing and what we are planning to do.

Two months ago we were facing serious problems. The country was dying by inches. It was dying because trade and commerce had declined to dangerously low levels; prices for basic commodities were such as to destroy the value of the assets of national institutions such as banks, savings banks, insurance companies, and others. These institutions, because of their great needs, were foreclosing mortgages, calling loans, refusing credit. Thus there was actually in process of destruction the property of millions of people who had borrowed money on that property in terms of dollars which had had an entirely different value from the level of March, 1933. That situation in that crisis did not call for any complicated consideration of economic panaceas or fancy plans. We were faced by a condition and not a theory.

There were just two alternatives: The first was to allow the foreclosures to continue, credit to be withheld and money to go into hiding, and thus forcing liquidation and bankruptcy of banks, railroads and insurance companies and a re-capitalizing of all business and all property on a lower level. This alternative meant a continuation of what is loosely called "deflation," the net result of which would have been extraordinary hardship on all property owners and, incidentally, extraordinary hardships on all persons working for wages through an increase in unemployment and a further reduction of the wage scale.

It is easy to see that the result of this course would have had not only economic effects of a very serious nature but social results that might bring incalculable harm. Even before I was inaugurated I came to the conclusion that such a policy was too much to ask the American people to bear. It involved not only a further loss of homes, farms, savings and wages but also a loss of spiritual values—the loss of that sense of security for the present and the future so necessary to the peace and contentment of the individual and of his family. When you destroy these things you will find it difficult to establish confidence of any sort in the future. It was clear that mere appeals from Washington for confidence and the mere lending of more money to shaky institutions could not stop this downward course. A prompt program applied as quickly as possible seemed to me not only justified but imperative to our national security. The Congress, and when I say Congress I mean the members of both political parties, fully understood this and gave me generous and intelligent support. The members of Congress realized that the methods of normal times had to be replaced in the emergency by measures which were suited to the serious and pressing requirements of the moment. There was no actual surrender of power, Congress still retained its constitutional authority and no one has the slightest desire to change the balance of these powers. The function of Congress is to decide what has to be done and to select the appropriate agency to carry out its will. This policy it has strictly adhered to. The only thing that has been happening has been to designate the President as the agency to carry out certain of the purposes of the Congress. This was constitutional and in keeping with the past American tradition.

The legislation which has been passed or in the process of enactment can properly be considered as part of a well-grounded plan.

First, we are giving opportunity of employment to one-quarter of a million of the unemployed, especially the young men who have dependents, to go into the forestry and flood prevention work. This is a big task because it means feeding, clothing and caring for nearly twice as many men as we have in the regular army itself. In creating this civilian conservation corps we are killing two birds with one stone. We are clearly enhancing the value of our natural resources and second, we are relieving an appreciable amount of actual distress. This great group of men have entered upon their work on a purely voluntary basis, no military training is involved and we are conserving not only our natural resources but our human resources. One of the great values to this work is the fact that it is direct and requires the intervention of very little machinery.

Second, I have requested the Congress and have secured action upon a proposal to put the great properties owned by our Government at Muscle Shoals to work after long years of wasteful inaction, and with this a broad plan for the improvement of a vast area in the Tennessee Valley. It will add to the comfort and happiness of hundreds of thousands of people and the incident benefits will reach the entire nation.

Next, the Congress is about to pass legislation that will greatly ease the mortgage distress among the farmers and the home owners of the nation, by providing for the easing of the burden of debt now bearing so heavily upon millions of our people.

Our next step in seeking immediate relief is a grant of half a billion dollars to help the states, counties and municipalities in their duty to care for those who need direct and immediate relief.

In addition to all this, the Congress also passed legislation authorizing the sale of beer in such states as desired. This has already resulted in considerable reemployment and, incidentally, has provided much needed tax revenue.

Now as to the future:

We are planning to ask the Congress for legislation to enable the Government to undertake public works, thus stimulating directly and indirectly the employment of many others in well-considered projects.

Further legislation has been taken up which goes much more fundamentally into our economic problems. The Farm Relief Bill seeks by the use of several methods, alone or together, to bring about an increased return to farmers for their major farm products, seeking at the same time to prevent in the days to come disastrous over-production which so often in the past has kept farm commodity prices far below a reasonable return. This measure provides wide powers for emergencies. The extent of its use will depend entirely upon what the future has in store.

Well-considered and conservative measures will likewise be proposed which will attempt to give to the industrial workers of the country a more fair wage return, prevent cut-throat competition and unduly long hours for labor, and at the same time to encourage each industry to prevent over production t One of our bills falls into the same class, the Railroad Bill. It seeks to provide and make certain definite planning by the railroads themselves, with the assistance of the Government, to eliminate the duplication and waste that now results in railroad receiverships and in continuing operating deficits.

I feel very certain that the people of this country understand and approve the broad purposes behind these new governmental policies relating to agriculture and industry and transportation. We found ourselves faced with more agricultural products than we could possibly consume ourselves and surpluses which other nations did not have the cash to buy from us except at prices ruinously low. We found our factories able to turn out more goods than we could possibly consume, and at the same time we have been faced with a falling export demand. We have found ourselves with more facilities to transport goods and crops than there were goods and crops to be transported. All of this has been caused in large part by a complete failure to understand the danger signals that have been flying ever since the close of the World War. The people of this country have been erroneously encouraged to believe that they could keep on increasing the output of farm and factory indefinitely and that some magician would find ways and means for that increased output to be consumed with reasonable profit to the producer.

But today we have reason to believe that things are a little better than they were two months ago. Industry has picked up, railroads are carrying more freight, farm prices are better, but I am not going to indulge in issuing proclamations of over-enthusiastic assurance. We cannot ballyhoo ourselves back to prosperity. I am going to be honest at all times with the people of the country. I do not want the people of this country to take the foolish course of letting this improvement come back on another speculative wave. I do not want the people to believe that because of unjustified optimism we can resume the ruinous practice of increasing our crop output and our factory output in the hope that a kind providence will find buyers at high prices. Such a course may bring us immediate and false prosperity but it will be the kind of prosperity that will lead us into another tailspin.

It is wholly wrong to call the measure that we have taken Government control of farming, control of industry, and control of transportation. It is rather a partnership between Government and farming and industry and transportation, not partnership in profits, for the profits would still go to the citizens, but rather a partnership in planning and partnership to see that the plans are carried out.

Let me illustrate with an example. Take the cotton goods industry. It is probably true that ninety per cent of the cotton manufacturers would agree to eliminate starvation wages, would agree to stop long hours of employment, would agree to stop child labor, would agree to prevent an overproduction that would result in unsalable surpluses. But, what good is such an agreement if the other ten per cent of cotton manufacturers pay starvation wages, require long hours, employ children in their mills and turn out burdensome surpluses? The unfair ten per cent could produce goods so cheaply that the fair ninety per cent would be compelled to meet the unfair conditions. Here is where government comes in. Government ought to have the right and will have the right, after surveying and planning for an industry to prevent, with the assistance of the overwhelming majority of that industry, unfair practice and to enforce this agreement by the authority of government. The so-called anti-trust laws were intended to prevent the creation of monopolies and to forbid unreasonable profits to those monopolies. That purpose of the anti-trust laws must be continued, but these laws were never intended to encourage the kind of unfair competition that results in long hours, starvation wages and overproduction.

And my friends, the same principle that is illustrated by that example applies to farm products and to transportation and every other field of organized private industry.

We are working toward a definite goal, which is to prevent the return of conditions which came very close to destroying what we call modern civilization. The actual accomplishment of our purpose cannot be attained in a day. Our policies are wholly within purposes for which our American Constitutional Government was established 150 years ago.

I know that the people of this country will understand this and will also understand the spirit in which we are undertaking this policy. I do not deny that we may make mistakes of procedure as we carry out the policy. I have no expectation of making a hit every time I come to bat. What I seek is the highest possible batting average, not only for myself but for the team. Theodore Roosevelt once said to me: "If I can be right 75 per cent of the time I shall come up to the fullest measure of my hopes."

Much has been said of late about Federal finances and inflation, the gold standard, etc. Let me make the facts very simple and my policy very clear. In the first place, government credit and government currency are really one and the same thing. Behind government bonds there is only a promise to pay. Behind government currency we have, in addition to the promise to pay, a reserve of gold and a small reserve of silver. In this connection it is worth while remembering that in the past the government has agreed to redeem nearly thirty billions of its debts and its currency in gold, and private corporations in this country have agreed to redeem another sixty or seventy billions of securities and mortgages in gold. The government and private corporations were making these agreements when they knew full well that all of the gold in the United States amounted to only between three and four billion and that all of the gold in all of the world amounted to only about eleven billion.

If the holders of these promises to pay started in to demand gold the first comers would get gold for a few days and they would amount to about one twenty-fifth of the holders of the securities and the currency. The other twenty-four people out of twenty-five, who did not happen to be at the top of the line, would be told politely that there was no more gold left. We have decided to treat all twenty-five in the same way in the interest of justice and the exercise of the constitutional powers of this government. We have placed every one on the same basis in order that the general good may be preserved.

Nevertheless, gold, and to a partial extent silver, are perfectly good bases for currency and that is why I decided not to let any of the gold now in the country go out of it.

A series of conditions arose three weeks ago which very readily might have meant, first, a drain on our gold by foreign countries, and secondly, as a result of that, a flight of American capital, in the form of gold, out of our country. It is not exaggerating the possibility to tell you that such an occurrence might well have taken from us the major part of our gold reserve and resulted in such a further weakening of our government and private credit as to bring on actual panic conditions and the complete stoppage of the wheels of industry.

The Administration has the definite objective of raising commodity prices to such an extent that those who have borrowed money will, on the average, be able to repay that money in the same kind of dollar which they borrowed. We do not seek to let them get such a cheap dollar that they will be able to pay back a great deal less than they borrowed. In other words, we seek to correct a wrong and not to create another wrong in the opposite direction. That is why powers are being given to the Administration to provide, if necessary, for an enlargement of credit, in order to correct the existing wrong. These powers will be used when, as, and if it may be necessary to accomplish the purpose.

Hand in hand with the domestic situation which, of course, is our first concern, is the world situation, and I want to emphasize to you that the domestic situation is inevitably and deeply tied in with the conditions in all of the other nations of the world. In other words, we can get, in all probability, a fair measure of prosperity return in the United States, but it will not be permanent unless we get a return to prosperity all over the world.

In the conferences which we have held and are holding with the leaders of other nations, we are seeking four great objectives. First, a general reduction of armaments and through this the removal of the fear of invasion and armed attack, and, at the same time, a reduction in armament costs, in order to help in the balancing of government budgets and the reduction of taxation. Secondly, a cutting down of the trade barriers, in order to re-start the flow of exchange of crops and goods between nations. Third, the setting up of a stabilization of currencies, in order that trade can make contracts ahead. Fourth, the reestablishment of friendly relations and greater confidence between all nations.

Our foreign visitors these past three weeks have responded to these purposes in a very helpful way. All of the Nations have suffered alike in this great depression. They have all reached the conclusion that each can best be helped by the common action of all. It is in this spirit that our visitors have met with us and discussed our common problems. The international conference that lies before us must succeed. The future of the world demands it and we have each of us pledged ourselves to the best Joint efforts to that end.

To you, the people of this country, all of us, the Members of the Congress and the members of this Administration owe a profound debt of gratitude. Throughout the depression you have been patient. You have granted us wide powers, you have encouraged us with a wide-spread approval of our purposes. Every ounce of strength and every resource at our command we have devoted to the end of justifying your confidence. We are encouraged to believe that a wise and sensible beginning has been made. In the present spirit of mutual confidence and mutual encouragement we go forward.

And in conclusion, my friends, may I express to the National Broadcasting Company and to the Columbia Broadcasting System my thanks for the facilities which they have made available to me tonight.

Source: Franklin and Eleanor Roosevelt Institute, http://www.feri.org/common/news/details.cfm?QID=2068&clientid=11005.

24. REPEAL OF PROHIBITION—THE TWENTY-FIRST AMENDMENT TO THE U.S. CONSTITUTION (RATIFIED DECEMBER 5, 1933)

The "noble experiment" of Prohibition came to an end in 1933 with the ratification of the 21st Amendment, which repealed the 18th Amendment—the only time in the history of the U.S. Constitution that an amendment had been repealed.

Section 1. The eighteenth article of amendment to the Constitution of the United States is hereby repealed.

Section 2. The transportation or importation into any state, territory, or possession of the United States for delivery or use therein of intoxicating liquors, in violation of the laws thereof, is hereby prohibited.

Section 3. This article shall be inoperative unless it shall have been ratified as an amendment to the Constitution by conventions in the several states, as provided in the Constitution, within seven years from the date of the submission hereof to the states by the Congress.

Source: http://www.usconstitution.com/21stamendment.htm.

25. ENDING THE ALL-WHITE PRIMARY—*GROVEY V. TOWNSEND* (APRIL 1, 1935)

Ever since the end of Reconstruction, southern whites had been systematically disenfranchising blacks through devices such as intimidation, poll taxes, and literacy tests. As late as 1935, the U.S. Supreme Court upheld one of those barriers by declaring the all-white primary constitutional.

GROVEY v. TOWNSEND, 295 U.S. 45 No. 563.

Argued March 11, 1935.
Decided April 1, 1935.
[295 U.S. 45, 46] Mr. J. Alston Atkins, of Houston, Tex., for petitioner.
Mr. Justice ROBERTS delivered the opinion of the Court.

The petitioner, by complaint filed in the justice court of Harris county, Tex., alleged that although he is a citizen of the United States and of the state and county, and a member of and believer in the tenets of the Democratic Party, the respondent, the county clerk, a state officer, having as such only public functions to perform, refused him a ballot for a Democratic Party primary election, because he is of the negro race. He demanded ten dollars damages. The pleading quotes articles of the Revised Civil Statutes of Texas which require the nomination of candidates at primary elections by any organized political party whose nominees received 100,000 votes or more at the preceding general election, and recites that agreeably to these enactments a Democratic primary election was held on July 28, 1934, at which petitioner had the right to vote. Referring to statutes [295 U.S. 45, 47] which regulate absentee voting at primary elections, the complaint states the petitioner expected to be absent from the county on the date of the primary election, and demanded of the respondent an absentee ballot, which was refused him in virtue of a resolution of the state Democratic Convention of Texas, adopted May 24, 1932, which is:

'Be it resolved, that all white citizens of the State of Texas who are qualified to vote under the Constitution and laws of the state shall be eligible to membership in the Democratic party and as such entitled to participate in its deliberations.'

The complaint charges that the respondent acted without legal excuse and his wrongful and unlawful acts constituted a violation of the Fourteenth and Fifteenth Amendments of the Federal Constitution.

A demurrer, assigning as reasons that the complaint was insufficient in law and stated no cause of action, was sustained; and a motion for a new trial, reasserting violation of the federal rights mentioned in the complaint, was overruled. We granted certiorari, 1 because of the importance of the federal question presented, which has not been determined by this court. 2 Our jurisdiction is clear, as the justice court is the highest state court in which a decision may be had, 3 and the validity of the

Constitution and statutes of the state was drawn in question on the ground of their being repugnant to the Constitution of the United States. 4 [295 U.S. 45, 48] The charge is that respondent, a state officer, in refusing to furnish petitioner a ballot, obeyed the law of Texas, and the consequent denial of petitioner's right to vote in the primary election because of his race and color was state action forbidden by the Federal Constitution; and it is claimed that former decisions require us so to hold. The cited cases are, however, not in point. In Nixon v. Herndon, 273 U.S. 536, 47 S. Ct. 446, a statute which enacted that 'in no event shall a negro be eligible to participate in a Democratic party primary election held in the State of Texas,' was pronounced offensive to the Fourteenth Amendment. In Nixon v. Condon, 286 U.S. 73, 52 S.Ct. 484, 485, 88 A.L.R. 458, a statute was drawn in question which provided that 'every political party in this State through its State Executive Committee shall have the power to prescribe the qualifications of its own members and shall in its own way determine who shall be qualified to vote or otherwise participate in such political party.' We held this was a delegation of state power to the state executive committee and made its determination conclusive irrespective of any expression of the party's will by its convention, and therefore the committee's action barring negroes from the party primaries was state action prohibited by the Fourteenth Amendment. Here the qualifications of citizens to participate in party counsels and to vote at party primaries have been declared by the representatives of the party in convention assembled, and this action upon its face is not state action. The question whether under the Constitution and laws of Texas such a declaration as to party membership amounts to state action was expressly reserved in Nixon v. Condon, supra, pages 84, 85, of 286 U.S., 52 S.Ct. 484. Petitioner insists that for various reasons the resolution of the state convention limiting membership in the Democratic Party in Texas to white voters does not relieve the exclusion of negroes from participation in Democratic primary elections of its true nature as the act of the state. [295 U.S. 45, 49] First. An argument pressed upon us in Nixon v. Condon, supra, which we found it unnecessary to consider, is again presented. It is that the primary election was held under statutory compulsion; is wholly statutory in origin and incidents; those charged with its management have been deprived by statute and judicial decision of all power to establish qualifications for participation therein inconsistent with those laid down by the laws of the state, save only that the managers of such elections have been given the power to deny negroes the vote. It is further urged that while the election is designated that of the Democratic Party, the statutes not only require this method of selecting party nominees, but define the powers and duties of the party's representatives and of those who are to conduct the election so completely, and make them so thoroughly officers of the state, that any action taken by them in connection with the qualifications of members of the party is in fact state action and not party action.

In support of this view petitioner refers to title 50 of the Revised Civil Statutes of Texas of 1925, 5 which by article 3101 requires that any party whose members cast more than 100,000 ballots at the previous election shall nominate candidates through primaries, and fixes the date at which they are to be held; by article 2939 requires primary election officials to be qualified voters; by article 2955 declares the same qualifications for voting in such an election as in the general elections; by article 2956, as amended (Vernon's Ann. Civ. St. art. 2956), permits absentee voting as in a general election; by article 2978 requires that only an official ballot shall be used, as in a general election; by articles 2980, 2981 specifies the form of ballot and how it shall be marked, as other sections do for general elections; by article 2984 fixes the number of ballots to be provided, as another article does [295 U.S. 45, 50] for general elections; by articles 2986, 2987, and 2990 permits the use of voting booths, guard rails, and ballot boxes which by other statutes are provided for general elections; by articles 2998 and 3104 requires the officials of primary elections to take the same oath as officials at the general elections; by article 3002 defines the powers of judges at primary elections; by articles 3003–3025 provides elaborately for the purity of the ballot box; by article 3028 commands that the sealed ballot boxes be delivered to the county clerk after the election, as is provided by another article for the general election; and by article 3041 confers jurisdiction of election contests upon district courts, as is done by another article with respect to general elections. A perusal of these provisions so it is said will convince that the state has prescribed and regulated party primaries as fully as general elections, and has made those who manage the primaries state officers subject to state direction and control.

While it is true that Texas has by its laws elaborately provided for the expression of party preference as to nominees, has required that preference to be expressed in a certain form of voting, and has attempted in minute detail to protect the suffrage of the members of the organization against fraud, it is equally true that the primary is a party primary; the expenses of it are not borne by the state, but by members of the party seeking nomination (article 3108, as amended by Acts 1931, c. 105, 2 (Vernon's Ann. Civ. St. art. 3108)) and article 3116, as amended by Acts 1927, c. 54, 1 (Vernon's Ann. Civ. St. art. 3116); the ballots are furnished not by the state, but by the agencies of the party (Rev. St. arts. 3109, 3119); the votes are counted and the returns made by instrumentalities created by the party (articles 3123–3125, 3127, as amended (Vernon's Ann Civ. St. arts. 3123–3125, 3127)); and the state recognizes the state convention as the organ of the party for the declaration of principles and the formulation of policies (articles 3136, 3139, as amended (Vernon's Ann. Civ. St. arts. 3136, 3139)).

We are told that in Love v. Wilcox, 119 Tex. 256, 28 S.W.(2d) 515, 522, the Supreme Court of Texas held the state was within its province in prohibiting a party from [295 U.S. 45, 51] establishing past party affiliations or membership in nonpolitical organizations as qualifications or tests for participation in primary elections, and in consequence issued its writ of mandamus against the members of the state executive committee of the Democratic Party on the ground that they were public functionaries fulfilling duties imposed on them by law. But in that case it was said, page 272 of 119 Tex., 28 S.W.(2d) 515, 522:

'We are not called upon to determine whether a political party has power, beyond statutory control, to prescribe what persons shall participate as voters or candidates in its conventions or primaries. We have no such state of facts before us.'

After referring to article 3107, as amended by Acts 1927, 1st Called Sess. c. 67, 1 (Vernon's Ann. Civ. St. art. 3107), which limits the power of the state executive committee of a party to determine who shall be qualified to vote at primary elections, the court said:

'The committee's discretionary power is further restricted by the statute directing that a single, uniform pledge be required of the primary participants. The effect of the statutes is to decline to give recognition to the lodgment of power in a State Executive Committee, to be exercised at its discretion.'

Although it did not pass upon the constitutionality of section 3107, as we did in Nixon v. Condon, supra, the Court thus recognized the fact upon which our decision turned, that the effort was to vest in the state executive committee the power to bind the party by its decision as to who might be admitted to membership.

In Bell v. Hill, 74 S.W.(2d) 113, the same court, in a mandamus proceeding instituted after the adoption by the state convention of the resolution of May 24, 1932, restricting eligibility for membership in the Democratic Party to white persons, held the resolution valid and effective. After a full consideration of the nature of political parties in the United States, the court concluded that [295 U.S. 45, 52] such parties in the state of Texas arise from the exercise of the free will and liberty of the citizens composing them; that they are voluntary associations for political action, and are not the creatures of the state; and further decided that sections 2 and 27 of article 1 of the state Constitution guaranteed to citizens the liberty of forming political associations, and the only limitation upon this right to be found in that instrument is the clause which requires the maintenance of a republican form of government. The statutes regulating the nomination of candidates by primaries were related by the court to the police power, but were held not to extend to the denial of the right of citizens to form a political party and to determine who might associate with them as members thereof. The court declared that a proper view of the election laws of Texas, and their history, required the conclusion that the Democratic Party in that state is a voluntary political association and, by its representatives assembled in convention, has the power to determine who shall be eligible for membership and, as such, eligible to participate in the party's primaries.

We cannot, as petitioner urges, give weight to earlier expressions of the state courts said to be inconsistent with this declaration of the law. The Supreme Court of the state has decided, in a case definitely involving the point, that the Legislature of Texas has not essayed to interfere, and indeed may not interfere, with the constitutional liberty of citizens to organize a party and to determine the qualifications of its members. If in the past the Legislature has attempted to infringe that right and such infringement has not been gainsaid by the courts, the fact constitutes no reason for our disregarding the considered decision of the state's highest court. The legislative assembly of the state, so far as we are advised, has never attempted to prescribe or to limit the membership of a [295 U.S. 45, 53] political party, and it is now settled that it has no power so to do. The state, as its highest tribunal holds, though it has guaranteed the liberty to organize political parties, may legislate for their governance when formed, and for the method whereby they may nominate candidates, but must do so with full recognition of the right of the party to exist, to define its membership, and to adopt such policies as to it shall seem wise. In the light of the principles so announced, we are unable to characterize the managers of the primary election as state officers in such sense that any action taken by them in obedience to the mandate of the state convention respecting eligibility to participate in the organization's deliberations is state action.

Second. We are told that sections 2 and 27 of the Bill of Rights of the Constitution of Texas as construed in Bell v. Hill, supra, violate the Federal Constitution, for the reason that so construed they fail to forbid a classification based upon race and color, whereas in Love v. Wilcox, supra, they were not held to forbid classifications based upon party affiliations and membership or nonmembership in organizations other than political parties, which classifications were by article 3107 of Revised Civil Statutes, 1925, as amended, prohibited. But, as above said, in Love v. Wilcox the court did not construe or apply any constitutional provision and expressly reserved the question as to the power of a party in convention assembled to specify the qualifications for membership therein.

Third. An alternative contention of petitioner is that the state Democratic Convention which adopted the resolution here involved was a mere creature of the state and could not lawfully do what the Federal Constitution prohibits to its creator. The argument is based upon the fact that article 3167 of the Revised Civil Statutes of Texas, 1925, requires a political party desiring to elect [295 U.S. 45, 54] delegates to a national convention to hold a state convention on the fourth Tuesday of May, 1928, and every four years thereafter; and provides for the election of delegates to that convention at primary conventions, the procedure of which is regulated by law. In Bell v. Hill, supra, the Supreme Court of Texas held that article 3167 does not prohibit declarations of policy by a state Democratic Convention called for the purpose of electing delegates to a national convention. While it may be, as petitioner contends, that we are not bound by the state court's decision on the point, it is entitled to the highest respect, and petitioner points to nothing which in any wise impugns its accuracy. If, as seems to be conceded, the Democratic Party in Texas held conventions many years before the adoption of article 3167, nothing is shown to indicate that the regulation of the method of choosing delegates or fixing the times of their meetings was intended to take away the plenary power of conventions in respect of matters as to which they would normally announce the party's will. Compare Nixon v. Condon, supra, page 84 of 286 U.S., 52 S.Ct. 484. We are not prepared to hold that in Texas the state convention of a party has become a mere instrumentality or agency for expressing the voice or will of the state.

Fourth. The complaint states that candidates for the offices of Senator and Representative in Congress were to be nominated at the primary election of July 9, 1934, and that in Texas nomination by the Democratic Party is equivalent to election. These facts (the truth of which the demurrer assumes) the petitioner insists, without more, make out a forbidden discrimination. A similar situation may exist in other states where one or another party includes a great majority of the qualified electors. The argument is that as a negro may not be denied a [295 U.S. 45, 55] ballot at a general election on account of his race or color, if exclusion from the primary renders his vote at the general election insignificant and useless, the result is to deny him the suffrage altogether. So to say is to confuse the privilege of membership in a party with the right to vote for one who is to hold a public office. With the former the state need have no concern, with the latter it is bound to concern itself, for the general election is a function of the state government and discrimination by the state as respects participation by negroes on account of their race or color is prohibited by the Federal Constitution.

Fifth. The complaint charges that the Democratic Party has never declared a purpose to exclude negroes. The premise upon which this conclusion rests is that the party is not a state body but a national organization, whose representative is the national Democratic Convention. No such convention, so it is said, has resolved to exclude negroes from membership. We have no occasion to determine the correctness of the position, since even if true it does not tend to prove that the petitioner was discriminated against or denied any right to vote by the state of Texas. Indeed the contention contradicts any such conclusion, for it assumes merely that a state convention, the representative and agent of a state association, has usurped the rightful authority of a national convention which represents a larger and superior country-wide association.

We find no ground for holding that the respondent has in obedience to the mandate of the law of Texas discriminated against the petitioner or denied him any right guaranteed by the Fourteenth and Fifteenth Amendments.

Judgment affirmed.

Source: http://www.usconstitution.com/groveyvtownsend.htm.

26. INSURING THE FUTURE—THE SOCIAL SECURITY ACT (AUGUST 14, 1935)

In 1935, one of the centerpieces of Roosevelt's New Deal, the Social Security Act, passed Congress. The act guaranteed payments to workers who lost their employment through no fault of their own and set up a trust fund for old-age benefits. Below is Section 6 of the bill, which outlines the pension benefits plan.

The Social Security Act (Act of August 14, 1935) [H. R. 7260]

An act to provide for the general welfare by establishing a system of Federal old-age benefits, and by enabling the several States to make more adequate provision for aged persons, blind persons, dependent and crippled children, maternal and child welfare, public health, and the administration of their unemployment compensation laws; to establish a Social Security Board; to raise revenue; and for other purposes.

DEFINITION

SEC. 6. When used in this title the term old age assistance means money payments to aged individuals.

TITLE II-FEDERAL OLD-AGE BENEFITS OLD-AGE RESERVE ACCOUNT

Section 201. (a) There is hereby created an account in the Treasury of the United States to be known as the Old-Age Reserve Account hereinafter in this title called the Account. There is hereby authorized to be appropriated to the Account for each fiscal year, beginning with the fiscal year ending June 30, 1937, an amount sufficient as an annual premium to provide for the payments required under this title, such amount to be determined on a reserve basis in accordance with accepted actuarial principles, and based upon such tables of mortality as the Secretary of the Treasury shall from time to time adopt, and upon an interest rate of 3 per centum per annum compounded annually. The Secretary of the Treasury shall submit annually to the Bureau of the Budget an estimate of the appropriations to be made to the Account.

(b) It shall be the duty of the Secretary of the Treasury to invest such portion of the amounts credited to the Account as is not, in his judgment, required to meet current withdrawals. Such investment may be made only in interest-bearing obligations of the United States or in obligations guaranteed as to both principal and interest by the United States. For such purpose such obligations may be acquired (1) on original issue at par, or (2) by purchase of outstanding obligations at the market price. The purposes for which obligations of the United States may be issued under the Second Liberty Bond Act, as amended, are hereby extended to authorize the issuance at par of special obligations exclusively to the Account. Such special obligations shall bear interest at the rate of 3 per centum per annum. Obligations other than such special obligations may be acquired for the Account only on such terms as to provide an investment yield of not less than 3 per centum per annum.

(c) Any obligations acquired by the Account (except special obligations issued exclusively to the Account) may be sold at the market price, and such special obligations may be redeemed at par plus accrued interest.

(d) The interest on, and the proceeds from the sale or redemption of, any obligations held in the Account shall be credited to and form a part of the Account.

(e) All amounts credited to the Account shall be available for making payments required under this title.

(f) The Secretary of the Treasury shall include in his annual report the actuarial status of the Account.

OLD-AGE BENEFIT PAYMENTS

SEC. 202. (a) Every qualified individual (as defined in section 210) shall be entitled to receive, with respect to the period beginning on the date he attains the age of sixty-five, or on January 1, 1942, whichever is the later, and ending on the date of his death, an old-age benefit (payable as nearly as practicable in equal monthly installments) as follows: (1) If the total wages (as defined in section 210) determined by the Board to have been paid to him, with respect to employment (as defined in section 210) after December 31, 1936, and before he attained the age of sixty-five, were not more than $3,000, the old-age benefit shall be at a monthly rate of one-half of 1 per centum of such total wages; (2) If such total wages were more than $3,000, the old-age benefit shall be at a monthly rate equal to the sum of the following: (A) One-half of 1 per centum of $3,000; plus (B) One-twelfth of 1 per centum of the amount by which such total wages exceeded $3,000 and did not exceed $45,000;

plus (C) One-twenty-fourth of 1 per centum of the amount by which such total wages exceeded $45,000.

(b) In no case shall the monthly rate computed under subsection (a) exceed $85.

(c) If the Board finds at any time that more or less than the correct amount has theretofore been paid to any individual under this section, then, under regulations made by the Board, proper adjustments shall be made in connection with subsequent payments under this section to the same individual.

(d) Whenever the Board finds that any qualified individual has received wages with respect to regular employment after he attained the age of sixty-five, the old-age benefit payable to such individual shall be reduced, for each calendar month in any part of which such regular employment occurred, by an amount equal to one month's benefit. Such reduction shall be made, under regulations prescribed by the Board, by deductions from one or more payments of old-age benefit to such individual.

PAYMENTS UPON DEATH

SEC. 203. (a) If any individual dies before attaining the age of sixty-five, there shall be paid to his estate an amount equal to 3 per centum of the total wages determined by the Board to have been paid to him, with respect to employment after December 31, 1936.

(b) If the Board finds that the correct amount of the old-age benefit payable to a qualified individual during his life under section 202 was less than 3 per centum of the total wages by which such old-age benefit was measurable, then there shall be paid to his estate a sum equal to the amount, if any, by which such 3 per centum exceeds the amount (whether more or less than the correct amount) paid to him during his life as old-age benefit. (c) If the Board finds that the total amount paid to a qualified individual under an old-age benefit during his life was less than the correct amount to which he was entitled under section 202, and that the correct amount of such old-age benefit was 3 per centum or more of the total wages by which such old-age benefit was measurable, then there shall be paid to his estate a sum equal to the amount, if any, by which the correct amount of the old-age benefit exceeds the amount which was so paid to him during his life.

Source: http://www.ssa.gov/history/35actinx.html.

27. YOUNG AND OUT OF WORK DURING THE DEPRESSION— THE WPA WRITER'S PROJECT I

In 1935, New Deal legislation created the Works Progress Administration (WPA) to put Americans back to work. Among the many WPA projects was the Federal Writers' Project. Unemployed writers went to work for the federal government on various writing assignments, including writing local history, travel books, and biographies. One of the richest parts of the collection offers stories of the lives of ordinary people. These stories tell of their struggles, their joys, and their survival during a very difficult time.

These life histories were compiled and transcribed by the staff of the Folklore Project of the Federal Writers' Project for the U.S. Works Progress (later Work Projects) Administration (WPA) from 1936–1940. The Library of Congress collection includes 2,900 documents representing the work of over 300 writers from 24 states. Typically 2,000–15,000 words in length, the documents consist of drafts and revisions, varying in form from narrative, to dialogue, to report, to case history. The histories describe the informant's family education, income, occupation, political views, religion and mores, medical needs, diet, and miscellaneous observations. Collectively these interviews provide a rich picture of American life from 1936–1940. Reproduced below, Rodney's story captures some of the frustration of being young and unemployed.

DATE: SEP 21 1940

JUST HANGING AROUND

Rodney was a tall lanky youth of twenty-two, who walked with an eager loping stride and wore, in all weather, a brown felt hat pulled low over his spectacles. He looked immature and callow, but possessed to a high degree all the hardboiled [cynicism?] and [flippant?] bitterness of the youth of the Great Depression. He customarily associated with men older than himself, and it had left a mark on him.

"I've got to get out of this town. There's nothing here for me. I've been out of high school four years and what have I done[??] Nothing but write for some of these lousy newspapers. A newspaperman can't make a living in this state. Of course they're underpaid in other places, but it's worse around here. You wouldn't believe how little some of these guys get. Guys that have been working for these papers for years. They work like hell too, and they get chicken-feed. Maybe eighteen bucks a week. In five or ten years perhaps they work up to a little better than twenty. Isn't that swell pay? I've got to get out of here, I know that.

"The problem is how to get enough money to get out and look for a job. I owe plenty around town already. I don't know anybody who's very anxious to stake me. So I'm stranded, like so many other young fellows. We want to get out and work, find [ourselves?], do some living. But when you're busted flat it's not so easy to do. It's pretty tough, believe me. In the old days a young fellow could borrow money to get started with, but try and do it today. You've got to have security to get anything from the banks. And the finance companies soak you so much you can't afford to clip them. All you do is hang around and drink too much, and wise-crack and laugh at everything because you feel licked and empty inside.

"I hate to see winter coming again. When the leaves begin to fall I want to go, too. The winters here are pretty bad. I don't go in much for skiing or skating or any winter sports. I like basketball, but there's not much of that here for fellows after they're out of school. So there's nothing to do but hang around the poolroom, bowling alleys and beer gardens; go to a show or a basketball game; read, if you can get hold of a decent book; talk and bum cigarettes and go out with a girl once in awhile. I don't care about dancing—unless I'm drinking. I've got a girl, just a kid, still in high school. She bawls me out for drinking. But what else is there to do in a town like this? Especially in the winter. In the summer you can go swimming; I like to swim. And there are ball games to go to.

"I've covered the Northern League games for three summers now. It's good baseball and you get to know a lot of real baseball characters: Jeff [Tesreau?], Jack Barry, Doc Gautreau, Vim Clancy, [Will?] Barrett, Ray Fisher; men like that who've been up there in the Big Show and lived baseball all their lives. I get a kick out of that stuff.

"Now that my job is finished I don't know what to do. I could pick up a little money covering basketball games this winter, but not enough to get by on. I couldn't make a living at it. I've never really made a living, I guess. If I could get hold of some money I'd go to Connecticut or Ohio. I have relatives there, and I could stick around and look for work. But I can't very well go without a dime. I don't know. It makes a guy wonder.

"I do know one thing though. Somehow, some way, I've got to get away from here and get started in something. This is almost enough to make a guy join the army."

Source: Library of Congress, WPA Writers Project, http://memory.loc.gov/cgi-bin.

28. THE AMERICAN MIDDLE CLASS IN THE DEPRESSION— THE WPA WRITERS' PROJECT II

The story reproduced below was recorded by a WPA writer and provides interesting insight into middle-class values and hopes in the Depression years of the 1930s. A fact revealed in this story that was a common theme in the Depression was that often women had to go to work (or in this case become entrepreneurial) when their husbands found themselves unemployed.

SOUTH CAROLINA WRITERS' PROJECT
LIFE HISTORY
TITLE: THE HARDY FAMILY.
Date of First Writing March 7th, 1939
Name of Person Interviewed Mrs. Roe Remington (White)
Fictitious Name Mrs. Hardy
Street Address Windermere
Place Charleston, S. C.
Occupation Housewife
Name of Writer Muriel A. Mann
Name of Reviser State Office. {Begin handwritten}[???]{End handwritten}

Project #-1655
Muriel A. Mann
Charleston, S. C.
March 21, 1939 LIFE HISTORY. THE HARDY FAMILY.

Facing the highway, just outside an old southern city, stands an attractive modern ivy-colored brick house of English design, with an expanse of well cared for lawn in front and a lily pond and flower garden in the rear. An electrically lighted sign which reads "The Windermere Guests," stands prominently at the entrance to the driveway, advertising to passing motorists that they may find accommodations within. It is the home of Dr. and Mrs. Hardy, who, more by chance than any other reason, find themselves with a thriving tourist business.

Mrs. Hardy, a good-looking woman with a shock of dark bobbed hair, shot with gray, and snapping brown eyes, was seated in the comfortable living room telling how she happened to convert her home into a tourist's inn.

"About two years ago," she said, "the house began to feel lonely and altogether too large for two people. Our three boys, Jack, Dick, and Paul were in the north seeking their own careers, and Phyllis, our only daughter had just gotten married. We were hard pressed financially, and for the first time in my life I seemed to have time on my hands. I was seeking some new interest, something which would pay.

"One day, the thought occurred to me that a number of homes along the highway were displaying tourist signs, and perhaps I too, could rent my three bedrooms occasionally and pick up a few extra dollars. So I talked it over with my husband, and as the idea met with his approval, I prepared to carry out the plan.

"From the beginning the venture was a success, and scarcely a night passed that the three bedrooms were not occupied, and, although my rates were reasonable, my bank account grew steadily, and I was thoroughly enjoying my contacts with the traveling public. It was a pleasant surprise to me.

"Only one unpleasant incident occurred. That was when one of my neighbors resented the competition so much that she employed a little colored boy to stand out in front of our house and direct all inquirers to her home. But, when the matter was brought to the attention of the county sheriff, the boy was ordered away and we were declared to be within our rights. We have not been bothered with her since.

"It was about a year after I began to rent my rooms that I happened to hear that someone was thinking of buying the vacant lot next door for the purpose of building a tourist camp. This was not a particularly agreeable thought to us, so we decided to buy it ourselves and build another house—a house which could be used to accommodate tourists now and later turned into a home for one of the children should any of them want to return here to live. Anyway it seemed like a good investment, and if I could keep three bedrooms steadily occupied, why not more!"

Mrs. Hardy got up and let in Trixy, the family pet, a little brown terrier who had been standing patiently outside the screen door for some time. Then resuming her seat, went on with her story:

"We didn't lose any time in calling in an architect and before long the plans were drawn up, the contract signed and the building under way.

"It was completed a short time ago, giving me seven more rooms to rent. Last night every room was taken and there were twenty-two people in the ten rooms. But that is almost a nightly occurrence, and I am making so much money that before long it will be possible for my husband to give up his teaching and research work at the Medical College and retire."

The new house, which stands to the side and slightly to the rear of the brick house, is Colonial in style and painted gray with deep blue shutters. The lawn has been extended across the front, and at the foot of the iron-railed steps by which you enter, a semi-circle of spring flowers will soon be a riot of color in shades of yellow and blue.

Mrs. Hardy invited me to inspect the interior, and accompanied by Trixy, we strolled across the lawn.

"I paid cash for every piece of furniture here, and expect to have the house paid for within three years at the rate I am going," she informed me. "I have tried to think always of the comfort of my guests and have bought the best springs and mattresses obtainable because I know from experience how much a comfortable night means after a day on the road."

A servant was polishing the oak floors and putting everything in order. The rooms are attractively furnished, and well designed to please the comfort loving guest.

There is a roomy two-car garage provided for each house and ample parking space, nicely graveled, which will accommodate a number of extra cars.

Strains of a Bach Prelude were coming from the little apartment over the brick house garage which is now occupied by Phyllis and her husband, who have recently returned home to live. Phyllis is an accomplished musician.

No detail seems to have been overlooked. There is even a laundry room where all the linens are washed and ironed, and there is enough work to keep a laundress employed constantly as well as a man and two maids.

Seated again in the living room, Mrs. Hardy resumed her story.

"A short time ago a woman died here. She was on her way to Florida accompanied by a companion, and had just stopped for the night. I chatted with her for a few minutes before she retired, and she seemed to be in good health and the very best of spirits. Early in the morning I heard a commotion downstairs, but thought nothing of it until my husband came in and told me that she had died in her sleep.

"Happening in our home, there was no undue excitement, as the doctor is naturally familiar with the procedure in such matters. The coroner was called and the body removed early. There was nothing more that anyone could do. But you have to be prepared for anything which occurs in this business.

"Occasionally an old college classmate of ours stops by, giving us an opportunity to renew old friendships and memories, and we both like the tourist business so much that it looks now like a permanent thing.

"But times have not always been so easy or so prosperous for us," Mrs. Hardy went on. "Indeed there have been periods when the struggle for existence was far from an easy one. The doctor and I met when we were attending the University of Iowa from which we graduated, he in Chemistry and I in the arts' course. He obtained a position teaching chemistry at the University of North Dakota and I went to Boston to study at the Curry School of Expression. The course took three years, and after graduating I taught for three years at Smith College before we got married.

"We were married at my home in Minneapolis and moved to Fargo to live, and for twenty years it was a struggle to raise four children on a teacher's salary, even though I kept up my teaching and was a pioneer in the school of expression in that state.

"Our children were fairly well grown when my husband decided to go after his Ph.D. degree. He began by studying during the summer holidays towards that end. But it was very hard on him and the progress was slow in comparison, so I insisted that he resign his teaching position and devote an entire year to the work demanded for his degree, which he did, and during that time I supported the entire family with my teaching.

"It was a difficult year for the Hardy family, and it meant making many sacrifices, but we persevered, and in the end the reward was well worth the work and time it had taken, for my husband was offered a position here at the Medical College as head of the Department of Food Research, the field in which he had specialized, which meant making a new start in a new field. Not long ago he was awarded an honorary degree by one of the important colleges of the south for his discoveries in the field of research, and I feel justly proud of him.

"Ten years have passed since coming south, ten years of ups and downs, of toil and heartaches as well as success, for it was shortly after we moved here and had bought this home, that the great depression hit the country, and for eight months not a professor at the college received a cent of pay.

"So once again I took up teaching and was able to make enough to help us over this bad time. We joined the Rotary Club and other groups and made contacts in this way. It was very discouraging at times, but we kept right on, and everything had gradually worked out as it usually does.

"Jack attended the local college the first two years we lived here and then he decided that he wanted to study chemistry in the north and graduate from a northern university. But the outlook was not very bright for we were unable to help him.

"He was undaunted, however, and packed his things, including his drums, and hitch-hiked to Ohio. When he was unable to get a job in an orchestra he washed dishes in a restaurant or waited on tables. The only trouble about being a waiter was that he had so much difficulty in remembering the orders, that sometimes the results were disastrous."

There was a gleam of pride in Mrs. Hardy's eyes as she told of her son's achievement.

"When Jack graduated he was offered an assistantship which he accepted, and after four years of teaching he won the Baker Fellowship Award of $1000.00 over competitors from every university in the country which enabled him to give up teaching and devote his time entirely to research. Now he is earning a fine salary working for the Mellon Institute, has married the girl of his choice, and is living in Dayton, Ohio.

"About five summers ago we decided that we all needed a rest, and a summer in the mountains away from the heat, would be beneficial, especially for my husband. So we rented a cottage in the mountains for the summer. Dick was in college now and Phyllis was preparing to go, too.

"It was really a rest and complete change, even though it took an awful lot of cooking to keep up with the appetites. But it paid in the end, I'm sure. Anyway, when Jack joined us, hitch-hiking down from Ohio, he brought with him a classmate and chum, Jim Ross, a graduate of the Massachusetts Institute of Technology. Due to the depression and being unable to find work in his field, he had decided to return to the university to get a teacher's diploma, rather than wait for something to turn up. None of the boys had any money to spare, but in spite of this we had a jolly time fishing, swimming in the mountain streams, hiking and loafing, and it was soon apparent to everybody that Jim and Phyllis were very much in love.

"When our vacation was over Phyllis went off to College for three years, and Jim found a position teaching architecture in Ohio. After Phyllis graduated she and Jim married and went to live in Ohio. Phyllis kept up her music and taught, and at the end of the first year they had saved enough to take a two month trip to Europe. They had a glorious time, returning happy but broke, of course, and went to live in Alabama, Jim having accepted a position teaching there to get away from the cold northern winters. They were living there when my husband happened to hear that there was a vacancy in a local firm of architects, so he sent for Jim, and that is why they are living here now. It looks like it will be permanent, too, and Jim is happy to be working in his own field instead of teaching. They are going to have a baby next summer and are so happy about it.

"Our other boys, Dick and Paul, have done well too. Dick graduated with honors from the college here and won a scholarship to the University of New York. He is a biologist and has a good position in New York. Last summer he married Phyllis' college roommate, who is also a very fine musician, and she is continuing her studies at the Juilliard School of Music.

"Paul, our youngest, is at the Bryant College of Business in Providence, Rhode Island, and will finish in August. He is earning his own tuition by helping in the office and correcting English papers. For a time it was difficult for Paul to find himself. He was not happy at the college here, and after two years he decided to get a job. For eight months he worked at a wood preserving plant, and they liked him so well that he can have his job back any time he wants it. But a relative expects to find a place for him in New York when he graduates, so he will probably remain there."

Mrs. Hardy paused reflectively, and after a moment added: "Looking back over the busy years behind us, it is easy to understand why the house seemed lonely and why the demands upon our pocketbook have been so heavy, but little did we believe that we would end up in the tourist business and like it."

Source: Library of Congress, WPA Writers Project, http://memory.loc.gov/cgi-bin.

29. RECOVERY IN WASHINGTON, D.C.—THE WPA WRITER'S PROJECT III

In this WPA interview, the writer documents a familiar story of failed banks and lost savings.

January 5, 1940
Mr. W. W. Tarpley (White)
5001 Nebraska Ave., N. W.
Washington, D.C.
Finance Officer in U.S. Treasury
(Bank Conservator)
By Bradley

"Yes, I really went through the depression. My story may not be so interesting to anyone else, but I'll be glad for you to write it."

The consultant is Mr. Raymond Tarver and he is being interviewed at his home, in a fashionable section in Washington, D.C. In appearance he is tall and rather slender. Though only in his early forties his hair is showing a decided grey and his face has lines in it that are the result of much care and responsibility. He is not a handsome man but has an expression on his face and a personality that immediately inspires one with confidence. His genuineness and his affable disposition have won for him many friends. His home is modern, with every comfort and convenience. The furnishings are of the best and most luxurious with an absence of any display of wealth.

"I guess, in a way," he resumed, "the depression was a blessing in disguise for me. It's an ill wind that blows nobody any good, you know. Of course I felt like I was ruined at the time, but if the crash had not come, I might have still been down in that little South Georgia town working for a small salary.

"There were thousands who went down during the panic—lost fortunes, homes, business, and in fact everything. Some have survived, and many never will. A great many were too old to begin building up again. In the kind of work I'm in I have been in position to know some of the devastating effects of it, and it certainly gets on your sympathy.

"I guess you would say I am recovering from it. When I say that though, I'm not boasting, but I'm deeply grateful for the good fortunes that have came my way. Then, too, I feel under everlasting obligations to some of my friends who have helped me to get where I am.

"I had not accumulated a great deal at the time of the panic, but I did have some savings and a good job. That was the trouble, my savings and my job went at the same time. Now that was real trouble. Nobody but my wife and I knew just what we did go through.

"Not long after, my mother died. This was the first death in the family. It seemed so sad to think that of a family as large as ours, my sister, father, and I were the only ones left at home. The other children had all moved away to other states.

"I married the next year. For awhile we tried to live at home with my sister and father. Well, that didn't work so well. It seldom does, you know; no house was built big enough for two bosses.

"We moved out and began keeping house in two rooms and a bath. We didn't buy much furniture, just enough to get by with. We really began at the bottom. We were content to live that way until I saved enough to buy us a permanent home. We didn't stint ourselves by any means, but we didn't spend money extravagantly. Our first and only child, Gloria, was born while we were living in these two rooms. We needed more room, though, so we moved into a larger house and rented out half of it. We bought us a second-hand T-model Ford coupe. I don't suppose any couple ever started out life any happier then we. I was making a fine salary, had a growing savings account, and a host of friends, and no serious troubles to worry about. My wife is just the smartest thriftiest person you have ever seen. To her I owe a lot of my successes. She is fine with her needle and crocheting, and you never saw her idle. She made all her spending money that way. Even now since we have been in Washington she keeps it up. And her fruit cake! People here rave about it. She cooks an enormous amount of it every Christmas and sells it for a big profit. She can't fill all the orders she gets. She is very resourceful and right now, if I were to die and not leave her a thing, she would manage some way. One of my hobbies was gardening and it proved to be a profitable one too. This place we rented had a fine garden spot, the finest in Dublin, so every one said. I worked in it early every morning and in the afternoon after banking hours. I sold lots of vegetables, and realized a lot on them—especially the early variety that brought a good price.

"One morning we three were at the breakfast table when the phone rang. It was one of the fellows who worked at the bank.

"'Tarver, he said, 'have you heard the news?'

"'What news? No, I haven't heard any news,' said I. What's it all about?'

"'Well,' he said, 'hurry on down and see.'

"If you will excuse the expression, when he said that, the seat of my britches almost dropped out. I felt like it meant trouble of some kind. I had had a terrible feeling of uneasiness over the bank for some time. Banks had been closing all over the country. There had been a run on our bank some time previous to that, but we tided that over, and since then it had seemed stronger than ever.

"I hurried down and, sure enough, in front of the bank, there stood a crowd of employees, as blank expressions on their faces as I've ever seen. They were too dumbfounded to be excited even.

"The bank was closed and a notice to that effect on the door. We stood there just looking at each other until finally one said, 'Well, boys, guess we had better go on the inside and see if we can find out what it's all about. I guess there goes our jobs.'

"Not only my job was in the balance but my savings were gone, at least for the present.

"No one knows, unless they have experienced it, what it means to work in a place under such conditions. Of course, there were promises that the bank would soon open up and resume business and begin paying off. That gave the depositor something to hope for at least. The sad part was, this was the strongest bank in this town. In fact there had already been several failures, so this was almost the only bank open for business. It was a national bank too, so everybody thought their money was safe. We worked on awhile. To be frank, I didn't worry so much about my losses. I was so concerned about the other fellows. People were losing their homes and some their savings of a lifetime. The saddest part of it was to see widows who probably had been left a little insurance and had put it all in the bank. People have a feeling that all connected with a bank, from the directors, president, on down to the lowest employee, are responsible for a bank failure and that makes you feel bad.

"What do you think caused the depression?" he asked. "Well, almost everyone will tell you something different. Usually they will speak from a personal standpoint. Ask a farmer down in that section and they will say, 'the boll weevill.' The merchant will tell you, inflation in prices during the war and the slump following. The Florida boom eventually brought disaster in that state. I'll tell you more about that later. I haven't told you yet how the depression affected me personally. We worked on at the bank trying to get things in shape, with no hopes deep down in our hearts of ever opening up again. Of course, we couldn't tell people on the outside that. We tried to appear hopeful. One by one they began laying off employees and I knew, sooner or later, my time would come. I didn't worry very much right then because I was young and, with my experience and standing in the town, I just knew I would not have any trouble getting work. I soon found out, though, I was mistaken in that.

"Well, my turn came to be laid off. On my desk one morning I found a letter to that effect. Of course it read, 'With appreciation for my valuable service, deep regret, best wishes, etc.' But that didn't help my feelings much. My job was gone and my savings too. Except for the time I served during the war, that was the first day I was without a job since I was just a boy. I went on home to break the news to Louise. She was not surprised, for we had both been expecting it."

Source: Library of Congress, WPA Writers Project, http://memory.loc.gov/cgi-bin.

30. WOMEN IN THE DEPRESSION—THE WPA WRITER'S PROJECT IV

In this document, a Federal Writers Project writer tells her own story.

IN LIEU OF SOMETHING BETTER
Written by: Miss Minnie Stonestreet
Washington, Georgia

Edited by: Mrs. Leila H. Harris
Supervising Editor
Georgia Writer's Project
Area 7
Augusta, Georgia
January 9, 1940

About this time, came Washington's first bank failure. And of course it had to be the Exchange Bank, the one where our money was deposited.

After about ten years Mother got $12.00 from the over $300.00 she had there.

During all this time I was working at the Carrington Insurance Agency at a very nice salary. However, in 1928 things were very bad financially and my employer got behind with my salary. Times were so hard there was not another opening so I stayed on and kept up as best I could, ever hoping better times would come. "Prosperity was around the corner" in those days, so said everybody.

In 1929, the friend who owned the house we lived in had a splendid opportunity to sell it. He gave us the refusal but it was a larger house than we needed and much more expensive than we could afford after our big losses. We had always wanted a little home, so we bought the small lot next to where we lived and started a home on the unit plan—building only a small portion of what we hope to have some day.

Before starting on our house I had a talk with Mr. Carrington and he assured me that he would have money in hand to pay all he owed me and that my salary would go right on. He then told me glowing stories of his prospects, and I foolishly believed it all. We went ahead and built our house and then everything went to pieces. The bills were due and we paid out as far as we could. There was no money to go any farther, Mr. Carrington had failed in his contract and I could not collect anything. Creditors were urging payment and the plumbing man was most especially insistent and ugly. One material man was hard up himself, and through his attorney made things very difficult. He, however, owned an immense plantation down near ours, so as he thought well of my little place, he suggested taking a second mortgage on it. I gladly did this feeling very safe for then neither of them could foreclose without paying the other. With a note signed by both Mother and myself, we satisfied the other material man.

In the office things went from bad to worse. Mr. Carrington had failed completely. He suggested that I take over his recording fire business as part payment on what he owed me and that/ he would pay me $10.00 per week to stay on to do his life insurance office work.

This I agreed to do—having no other place to go.

His fire insurance business was scattered over several counties and most of it was very undesirable—but I was like a sinking person, I grabbed at anything. I thought I could weed out the bad risks and gradually build up a good business. This I started out to do, but I did not reckon on the town's keen fire insurance competition.

Before I could make any headway there were fires one after another bringing terrific losses to the companies I represented. Then to cap the climax, Mr. Carrington forged my name to some policies, collected the premiums and spent them. He collected some others and used the money, leaving me liable to the Company. I had to take legal steps to stop him, but is was too late to save me from financial embarrassment such as I had never thought possible.

About this time I was a physical and financial wreck I could neither eat nor sleep from worry and dread. I had an indebtedness of something like $1,700.00 or more with nothing to meet it and living expenses going on at home for my mother and me. Besides the $500.00 that Mr. Carrington had collected in premiums and used, and for which I was responsible to the fire insurance companies, he owed me over $700.00 in back salary. I appealed to his brother in Atlanta, a very prominent merchant there. He promised to aid me in every way saying that he would see that his brother paid me and that if he didn't that he would see that I did not lose a penny if I would just let him manage it. Since he was a big churchman, an official in the Presbyterian denomination and a great Billy Sunday Evangelistic Club member and worker, I believed him.

In fact the first time I ever saw him was some years before when he came here with some members of the Atlanta Billy Sunday Club to hold services in this little country town. He spoke in the morning at our Methodist Church and in the evening at the Baptist. I was not working for his brother at the time but I heard him and thought what a Christian gentleman he was. Little did I think that some day I would have a perfectly good opportunity to find out for myself. What a lot of difference there is between saying and doing.

Well one day a friend who had a dental office next to the Carrington set-up came in and offered me room in his office. I accepted, borrowed a desk, an old broken down typewriter and brought a chair from home. I had nothing to move across the hall but some insurance blanks and forms.

But that move proved to be the most fortunate one I ever made, and now that I look back on it, I feel sure that it was a kind Providence who directed it.

In 1933 I applied for work in the office of our Government County Administrator here. I was called in every few days for several hours work which helped immensely. Later as the work expanded I was given more work until a family connection of the Administrator was taken in, then I was transferred to the re-employment office for part time work. This I had for some time, owing the money to meet our obligations and only taking a little out for living expenses. Then came notice that this office would be closed so I registered for work the last thing I did before leaving. I registered for general office work, typist and historical research.

Right away I applied to the Administrator for work. She did not give me anything nor even encourage me, although my application showed how very much I was in need of work. In the meantime there was a shakeup in the administration here and a young man was sent to replace the county administrator. I went to see him and laid my case before him. My mother had never fully recovered from her lung illness and was unable to do anything so the entire financial burden was on me.

After waiting as patiently as prevailing conditions allowed for a reasonable length of time, I borrowed the money and went to Atlanta to put my case before someone in the State Office. Miss Shepperson was not in the city so I was interviewed by

Miss Jane Van de Vrede. When I finished my story, I asked: "Is there a place in the program for me?"

She replied kindly and emphatically, "There certainly is you will be put to work at once."

She wrote the local office to that effect and very soon I was indexing the oldest records in the Clerk's office. That project expired about the time Federal Writer's was started and greatly to my surprise and delight I was given a job on that project, which I have retained until the present time and I am still liking it more and more.

In 1935 my former employer passed away without paying me. His brother, when time came to make good his promises failed on some slight pretext. Which goes to show as the old Negro preacher said: "You sho' can't believe every thing folks promises you."

Being so deeply involved, I could not pay but in a very long time, if ever, and a dear friend stepped in and took charge of our affairs in 1935. He sold all of our land at $3.00 per acre, paid up as far as it would go and helped us get the tangled strands of our financial affairs in better order. We had been unable to pay State and County taxes for 5 years—they amounted to nearly $400.00.

All of this happened over a very short period of time but I feel like I lived a lifetime. My mother is frail and I could never let her know how bad our condition really was. She would ask me to bring groceries home when needed and many a time I would not have the money so would conveniently "forget" them. I remember once she told me among other things to bring some coffee that day. I hadn't the price so I "forgot" it thinking surely the next day I would got the money. I didn't get it, nor the next and so on for several days. We had to drink tea, it was in the winter time, and neither of us liked it. Finally Mother said: "I'll declare, your memory is getting as bad as mine and if you don't think of that coffee today, I'm going up town and get it myself." I laughed with her over the "joke" she thought it was, but my heart sank fearing she would find the real reason why I had kept "forgetting" the needed groceries.

Sometimes I was so panicky I almost collapsed when I heard the sheriff's voice in the building, I was so afraid some of my creditors were foreclosing and would put us out—every week I feared looking over the legal advertisements lest our land was listed among the tax sales.

My good friend, who took me in his office, and his wife have meant everything to me—he was always so jolly and helped me not to give up.

He gave me a desk and helped me buy a re-built typewriter. In exchange I helped him all I could. He was an elderly man partially retired, so that there was not much office work to do. He died last October but even in passing away he thought of me and provided an office for me for as long as I needed it.

Sometimes when I think of the hard time and terrific strain I have had, and still am having for that matter, I am reminded of the lines from an old hymn:

"Through many dangers, toils and snares,

I have already come."

But I do not like to think back too much, for I am so thankful that I did not go down completely; that there were kind friends who stood by me, and that I live in a land under the administration of such a great humanitarian as our noble President, who feels for those who were caught in the terrible depression and lost almost all they had. Who in his wonderful kindness of heart has made it possible for us to have the high and rightful privilege of working out our financial difficulties and winning back our rightful places in the world, and still keep our self respect and our faith in God and man. And I can say with all the earnestness of my soul:

Thank God for America!

Thank God for Franklin D. Roosevelt, the president with a heart!

Source: Library of Congress, WPA Writers Project, http://memory.loc.gov/cgi-bin.

31. PRESIDENT FRANKLIN ROOSEVELT'S "QUARANTINE THE ENEMY" SPEECH (OCTOBER 5, 1937)

As war clouds began to hover over Europe once again, President Franklin Roosevelt realized that Americans would almost certainly be drawn into the conflict. The Spanish Civil War and the looming larger war in Europe presented Roosevelt with three conflicting dilemmas. He had to convince aggressive European nations that the United States would not stand by passively if they attempted to overrun Europe, but at the same time he had to assure his own heavily isolationist constituents that they would not be embroiled again in Europe. He also had to gently bring the American public to the realization that the world was growing smaller every day, and that the isolationism they had collectively embraced was not a practical policy. He resolved these dilemmas with his famous "Quarantine the Enemy" speech, which was given a full two years before the outbreak of war in Europe.

I am glad to come once again to Chicago and especially to have the opportunity of taking part in the dedication of this important project of civic betterment.

On my trip across the continent and back I have been shown many evidences of the result of common sense cooperation between municipalities and the Federal government, and I have been greeted by tens of thousands of Americans who have told me in every look and word that their material and spiritual well-being has made great strides forward in the past few years.

And yet, as I have seen with my own eyes, the prosperous farms, the thriving factories and the busy railroads—as I have seen the happiness and security and peace which covers our wide land, almost inevitably I have been compelled to contrast our peace with very different scenes being enacted in other parts of the world.

It is because the people of the United States under modern conditions must, for the sake of their own future, give thought to the rest of the world, that I, as the responsible executive head of the nation, have chosen this great inland city and this gala occasion to speak to you on a subject of definite national importance.

The political situation in the world, which of late has been growing progressively worse, is such as to cause grave concern and anxiety to all the peoples and nations who wish to live in peace and amity with their neighbors.

Some 15 years ago the hopes of mankind for a continuing era of international peace were raised to great heights when more than 60 nations solemnly pledged themselves not to resort to arms in furtherance of their national aims and policies. The high aspirations expressed in the Briand-Kellogg Pact and the hopes for peace thus raised have of late given way to a haunting fear of calamity. The present reign of terror and international lawlessness began a few years ago.

It began through unjustified interference in the internal affairs of other nations or the invasion of alien territory in violation of treaties. It has now reached the stage where the very foundations of civilization are seriously threatened. The landmarks, the traditions which have marked the progress of civilization toward a condition of law and order and justice are being wiped away.

Without a declaration of war and without warning or justification of any kind, civilians, including vast numbers of women and children, are being ruthlessly murdered with bombs from the air. In times of so-called peace, ships are being attacked and sunk by submarines without cause or notice. Nations are fomenting and taking sides in civil warfare in nations that have never done them any harm. Nations claiming freedom for themselves deny it to others.

Innocent peoples, innocent nations are being cruelly sacrificed to a greed for power and supremacy which is devoid of all sense of justice and humane considerations.

To paraphrase a recent author, "perhaps we foresee a time when men, exultant in the technique of homicide, will rage so hotly over the world that every precious thing will be in danger, every book, every picture, every harmony, every treasure garnered through two millenniums, the small, the delicate, the defenseless—all will be lost or wrecked or utterly destroyed.".

If those things come to pass in other parts of the world, let no one imagine that America will escape, that America may expect mercy, that this Western hemisphere will not be attacked and that it will continue tranquilly and peacefully to carry on the ethics and the arts of civilization.

No, if those days come, "there will be no safety by arms, no help from authority, no answer in science. The storm will rage until every flower of culture is trampled and all human beings are leveled in a vast chaos."

If those days are not to come to pass—if we are to have a world in which we can breathe freely and live in amity without fear—then the peace-loving nations must make a concerted effort to uphold laws and principles on which alone peace can rest secure.

The peace-loving nations must make a concerted effort in opposition to those violations of treaties and those ignorings of human instincts which today are creating a state of international anarchy and instability from which there is no escape through mere isolation or neutrality.

Those who cherish their freedom and recognize and respect the equal right of their neighbors to be free and live in peace, must work together for the triumph of law and moral principles in order that peace, justice, and confidence may prevail throughout the world. There must be a return to a belief in the pledged word, in the value of a signed treaty. There must be recognition of the fact that national morality is as vital as private morality.

A bishop wrote me the other day: "It seems to me that something greatly needs to be said in behalf of ordinary humanity against the present practice of carrying the horrors of war to helpless civilians, especially women and children. It may be that such a protest might be regarded by many, who claim to be realists, as futile, but may it not be that the heart of mankind is so filled with horror at the present needless suffering that that force could be mobilized in sufficient volume to lessen such cruelty in the days ahead. Even though it may take 20 years, which God forbid, for civilization to make effective its corporate protest against this barbarism, surely strong voices may hasten the day."

There is a solidarity and interdependence about the modern world, both technically and morally, which makes it impossible for any nation completely to isolate itself from economic and political upheavals in the rest of the world, especially when such upheavals appear to be spreading and not declining. There can be no stability or peace either within nations or between nations except under laws and moral standards adhered to by all. International anarchy destroys every foundation for peace. It jeopardizes either the immediate or the future security of every nation, large or small. It is, therefore, a matter of vital interest and concern to the people of the United States that the sanctity of international treaties and the maintenance of international morality be restored.

The overwhelming majority of the peoples and nations of the world today want to live in peace. They seek the removal of barriers against trade. They want to exert themselves in industry, in agriculture and in business, that they may increase their wealth through the production of wealth-producing goods rather than striving to produce military planes and bombs and machine guns and cannon for the destruction of human lives and useful property.

In those nations of the world which seem to be piling armament on armament for purposes of aggression, and those other nations which fear acts of aggression against them and their security, a very high proportion of their national income is being spent directly for armaments. It runs from 30 to as high as 50 per cent. The proportion that we in the United States spend is far less—11 or 12 per cent.

How happy we are that the circumstances of the moment permit us to put our money into bridges and boulevards, dams and reforestation, the conservation of our soil, and many other kinds of useful works rather than into huge standing armies and vast supplies of implements of war.

Nevertheless, my friends, I am compelled, as you are compelled, to look ahead. The peace, the freedom, and the security of 90 per cent of the population of the world is being jeopardized by the remaining 10 per cent who are threatening a breakdown of all international order and law. Surely the 90 per cent who want to live in peace under law and in accordance with moral standards that have received almost universal acceptance through the centuries, can and must find some way to make their will prevail.

The situation is definitely of universal concern. The questions involved relate not merely to violations of specific provisions of particular treaties; they are questions of war and of peace, of international law and especially of principles of humanity. It is true that they involve definite violations of agreements, and especially of the Covenant of the League of Nations, the Briand-Kellogg Pact and the Nine Power Treaty. But they also involve problems of world economy, world security and world humanity.

It is true that the moral consciousness of the world must recognize the importance of removing injustices and well-founded grievances; but at the same time it must be aroused to the cardinal necessity of honoring sanctity of treaties, of respecting the rights and liberties of others and of putting an end to acts of international aggression.

It seems to be unfortunately true that the epidemic of world lawlessness is spreading.

AND MARK THIS WELL: When an epidemic of physical disease starts to spread, the community approves and joins in a quarantine of the patients in order to protect the health of the community against the spread of the disease.

It is my determination to pursue a policy of peace and to adopt every practicable measure to avoid involvement in war. It ought to be inconceivable that in this modern era, and in the face of experience, any nation could be so foolish and ruthless as to run the risk of plunging the whole world into war by invading and violating, in contravention of solemn treaties, the territory of other nations that have done them no real harm and are too weak to protect themselves adequately. Yet the peace of the world and the welfare and security of every nation are today being threatened by that very thing.

No nation which refuses to exercise forbearance and to respect the freedom and rights of others can long remain strong and retain the confidence and respect of other nations. No nation ever loses its dignity or its good standing by conciliating its differences, and by exercising great patience with, and consideration for, the rights of other nations.

War is a contagion, whether it be declared or undeclared. It can engulf states and peoples remote from the original scene of hostilities. We are determined to keep out of war, yet we cannot insure ourselves against the disastrous effects of war and the dangers of involvement. We are adopting such measures as will minimize our risk of involvement, but we cannot have complete protection in a world of disorder in which confidence and security have broken down.

If civilization is to survive, the principles of the Prince of Peace must be restored. Shattered trust between nations must be revived.

Most important of all, the will for peace on the part of peace-loving nations must express itself to the end that nations that may be tempted to violate their agreements and the rights of others will desist from such a course. There must be positive endeavors to preserve peace.

Source: http://www.usconstitution.com/franklinroosevelt'squarantinespeech.htm.

32. FRANKLIN ROOSEVELT'S FIRESIDE CHAT—"THE ARSENAL OF DEMOCRACY" (DECEMBER 29, 1940)

In December 1940, with the Nazis in control of Western Europe and preparing to attack the Soviet Union, England and the Soviet Union stood virtually alone and separated against the German juggernaut. Roosevelt realized that the United States represented the last hope of those who opposed fascism. In this fireside chat, he tells his still isolationist countrymen that Americans may remain out of the war but morally they could not remain neutral. The country had an obligation to materially help those still fighting against the fascist plan for world domination. The United States had to become, Roosevelt declared, "the arsenal of democracy."

My friends: This is not a fireside chat on war. It is a talk on national security; because the nub of the whole purpose of your President is to keep you now, and your children later, and your grandchildren much later, out of a last-ditch war for the preservation of American independence and all of the things that American independence means to you and to me and to ours.

Tonight, in the presence of a world crisis, my mind goes back eight years to a night in the midst of a domestic crisis. It was a time when the wheels of American industry were grinding to a full stop, when the whole banking system of our country had ceased to function.

I well remember that while I sat in my study in the White House, preparing to talk with the people of the United States, I had before my eyes the picture of all those Americans with whom I was talking. I saw the workmen in the mills, the mines, the factories; the girl behind the counter; the small shopkeeper; the farmer doing his Spring plowing; the widows and the old men wondering about their life's savings. I tried to convey to the great mass of American people what the banking crisis meant to them in their daily lives.

Tonight I want to do the same thing, with the same people, in this new crisis which faces America.

We met the issue of 1933 with courage and realism. We face this new crisis—this new threat to the security of our nation—with the same courage and realism. Never before since Jamestown and Plymouth Rock has our American civilization been in such danger as now.

For on September 27, 1940—this year—by an agreement signed in Berlin. Three powerful nations, two in Europe and one in Asia, joined themselves together in the threat that if the United States of America interfered with or blocked the expansion program of these three nations—a program aimed at world control—they would unite in ultimate action against the United States.

The Nazi masters of Germany have made it clear that they intend not only to dominate all life and thought in their own country, but also to enslave the whole of

Europe, and then to use the resources of Europe to dominate the rest of the world. It was only three weeks ago that their leader stated this: "There are two worlds that stand opposed to each other." And then in defiant reply to his opponents he said this: "Others are correct when they say: 'With this world we cannot ever reconcile ourselves.' . . . I can beat any other power in the world." So said the leader of the Nazis.

In other words, the Axis not merely admits but the Axis proclaims that there can be no ultimate peace between their philosophy—their philosophy of government—and our philosophy of government.

In view of the nature of this undeniable threat, it can be asserted, properly and categorically, that the United States has no right or reason to encourage talk of peace until the day shall come when there is a clear intention on the part of the aggressor nations to abandon all thought of dominating or conquering the world.

At this moment the forces of the States that are leagued against all peoples who live in freedom are being held away from our shores. The Germans and the Italians are being blocked on the other side of the Atlantic by the British and by the Greeks, and by thousands of soldiers and sailors who were able to escape from subjugated countries. In Asia the Japanese are being engaged by the Chinese nation in another great defense.

In the Pacific Ocean is our fleet.

Some of our people like to believe that wars in Europe and in Asia are of no concern to us. But it is a matter of most vital concern to us that European and Asiatic war-makers should not gain control of the oceans which lead to this hemisphere.

One hundred and seventeen years ago the Monroe Doctrine was conceived by our government as a measure of defense in the face of a threat against this hemisphere by an alliance in Continental Europe. Thereafter, we stood guard in the Atlantic, with the British as neighbors. There was no treaty. There was no "unwritten agreement."

And yet there was the feeling, proven correct by history, that we as neighbors could settle any disputes in peaceful fashion. And the fact is that during the whole of this time the Western Hemisphere has remained free from aggression from Europe or from Asia.

Does any one seriously believe that we need to fear attack anywhere in the Americas while a free Britain remains our most powerful naval neighbor in the Atlantic? And does any one seriously believe, on the other hand, that we could rest easy if the Axis powers were our neighbors there?

If Great Britain goes down, the Axis powers will control the Continents of Europe, Asia, Africa, Australia, and the high seas—and they will be in a position to bring enormous military and naval resources against this hemisphere. It is no exaggeration to say that all of us in all the Americas would be living at the point of a gun—a gun loaded with explosive bullets, economic as well as military.

We should enter upon a new and terrible era in which the whole world, our hemisphere included, would be run by threats of brute force. And to survive in such a world, we would have to convert ourselves permanently into a militaristic power on the basis of war economy.

Some of us like to believe that even if Britain falls, we are still safe, because of the broad expanse of the Atlantic and of the Pacific.

But the width of those oceans is not what it was in the days of clipper ships. At one point between Africa and Brazil the distance is less than it is from Washington to Denver, Colorado, five hours for the latest type of bomber. And at the north end of the Pacific Ocean, America and Asia almost touch each other. Why, even today we have planes that could fly from the British Isles to New England and back again without refueling. And remember that the range of the modern bomber is ever being increased.

During the past week many people in all parts of the nation have told me what they wanted me to say tonight. Almost all of them expressed a courageous desire to hear the plain truth about the gravity of the situation. One telegram, however, expressed the attitude of the small minority who want to see no evil and hear no evil, even though they know in their hearts that evil exists. That telegram begged me not to tell again of the ease with which our American cities could be bombed by any hostile power which had gained bases in this Western Hemisphere. The gist of that telegram was: "Please, Mr. President, don't frighten us by telling us the facts." Frankly and definitely there is danger ahead—danger against which we must prepare. But we well know that we cannot escape danger, or the fear of danger, by crawling into bed and pulling the covers over our heads.

Some nations of Europe were bound by solemn nonintervention pacts with Germany. Other nations were assured by Germany that they need never fear invasion. Nonintervention pact or not, the fact remains that they were attacked, overrun, thrown into modern slavery at an hour's notice or even without any notice at all.

As an exiled leader of one of these nations said to me the other day, "the notice was a minus quantity. It was given to my government two hours after German troops had poured into my country in a hundred places." The fate of these nations tells us what it means to live at the point of a Nazi gun.

The Nazis have justified such actions by various pious frauds. One of these frauds is the claim that they are occupying a nation for the purpose of "restoring order." Another is that they are occupying or controlling a nation on the excuse that they are "protecting it" against the aggression of somebody else.

For example, Germany has said that she was occupying Belgium to save the Belgians from the British. Would she then hesitate to say to any South American country: "We are occupying you to protect you from aggression by the United States"?

Belgium today is being used as an invasion base against Britain, now fighting for its life. And any South American country, in Nazi hands, would always constitute a jumping off place for German attack on any one of the other republics of this hemisphere.

Analyze for yourselves the future of two other places even nearer to Germany if the Nazis won. Could Ireland hold out? Would Irish freedom be permitted as an amazing pet exception in an unfree world? Or the islands of the Azores, which still fly the flag of Portugal after five centuries? You and I think of Hawaii as an outpost of defense in the Pacific. And yet the Azores are closer to our shores in the Atlantic than Hawaii is on the other side.

There are those who say that the Axis powers would never have any desire to attack the Western Hemisphere. That is the same dangerous form of wishful thinking which has destroyed the powers of resistance of so many conquered peoples. The plain facts are that the Nazis have proclaimed, time and again, that all other races are their inferiors and therefore subject to their orders. And most important of all, the vast resources and wealth of this American hemisphere constitute the most tempting loot in all of the round world.

Let us no longer blind ourselves to the undeniable fact that the evil forces which have crushed and undermined and corrupted so many others are already within our own gates. Your government knows much about them and every day is ferreting them out.

Their secret emissaries are active in our own and in neighboring countries. They seek to stir up suspicion and dissension, to cause internal strife. They try to turn capital against labor, and vice versa. They try to reawaken long slumbering racial and religious enmities which should have no place in this country. They are active in every group that promotes intolerance. They exploit for their own ends our own natural abhorrence of war.

These trouble-breeders have but one purpose. It is to divide our people, to divide them into hostile groups and to destroy our unity and shatter our will to defend ourselves.

There are also American citizens, many of them in high places, who, unwittingly in most cases, are aiding and abetting the work of these agents. I do not charge these American citizens with being foreign agents. But I do charge them with doing exactly the kind of work that the dictators want done in the United States. These people not only believe that we can save our own skins by shutting our eyes to the fate of other nations. Some of them go much further than that. They say that we can and should become the friends and even the partners of the Axis powers. Some of them even suggest that we should imitate the methods of the dictatorships. But Americans never can and never will do that.

The experience of the past two years has proven beyond doubt that no nation can appease the Nazis. No man can tame a tiger into a kitten by stroking it. There can be no appeasement with ruthlessness. There can be no reasoning with an incendiary bomb. We know now that a nation can have peace with the Nazis only at the price of total surrender.

Even the people of Italy have been forced to become accomplices of the Nazis; but at this moment they do not know how soon they will be embraced to death by their allies.

The American appeasers ignore the warning to be found in the fate of Austria, Czechoslovakia, Poland, Norway, Belgium, the Netherlands, Denmark and France. They tell you that the Axis powers are going to win anyway; that all of this bloodshed in the world could be saved, that the United States might just as well throw its influence into the scale of a dictated peace and get the best out of it that we can.

They call it a "negotiated peace." Nonsense! Is it a negotiated peace if a gang of outlaws surrounds your community and on threat of extermination makes you pay tribute to save your own skins?

Such a dictated peace would be no peace at all. It would be only another armistice, leading to the most gigantic armament race and the most devastating trade wars in all history. And in these contests the Americas would offer the only real resistance to the Axis powers. With all their vaunted efficiency, with all their parade of pious purpose in this war, there are still in their background the concentration camp and the servants of God in chains.

The history of recent years proves that the shootings and the chains and the concentration camps are not simply the transient tools but the very altars of modern dictatorships. They may talk of a "new order" in the world, but what they have in mind is only a revival of the oldest and worst tyranny. In that there is no liberty, no religion, no hope.

The proposed "new order" is the very opposite of a United States of Europe or a United States of Asia. It is not a government based upon the consent of the governed. It is not a union of ordinary, self-respecting men and women to protect themselves and their freedom and their dignity from oppression. It is an unholy alliance of power and pelf to dominate and to enslave the human race.

The British people and their allies today are conducting an active war against this unholy alliance. Our own future security is greatly dependent on the outcome of that fight. Our ability to "keep out of war" is going to be affected by that outcome.

Thinking in terms of today and tomorrow, I make the direct statement to the American people that there is far less chance of the United States getting into war if we do all we can now to support the nations defending themselves against attack by the Axis than if we acquiesce in their defeat, submit tamely to an Axis victory, and wait our turn to be the object of attack in another war later on.

If we are to be completely honest with ourselves, we must admit that there is risk in any course we may take. But I deeply believe that the great majority of our people agree that the course that I advocate involves the least risk now and the greatest hope for world peace in the future.

The people of Europe who are defending themselves do not ask where to do their fighting. They ask us for the implements of war, the planes, the tanks, the guns, the freighters which will enable them to fight for their liberty and for our security.

Emphatically we must get these weapons to them, get them to them in sufficient volume and quickly enough so that we and our children will be saved the agony and suffering of war which others have had to endure.

Let not the defeatists tell us that it is too late. It will never be earlier. Tomorrow will be later than today.

Certain facts are self-evident.

In a military sense Great Britain and the British Empire are today the spearhead of resistance to world conquest. And they are putting up a fight which will live forever in the story of human gallantry.

There is no demand for sending an American expeditionary force outside our own borders. There is no intention by any member of your government to send such a force. You can therefore, nail, nail any talk about sending armies to Europe as deliberate untruth.

Our national policy is not directed toward war. Its sole purpose is to keep war away from our country and away from our people.

Democracy's fight against world conquest is being greatly aided, and must be more greatly aided, by the rearmament of the United States and by sending every ounce and every ton of munitions and supplies that we can possibly spare to help the defenders who are in the front lines. And it is no more unneutral for us to do that than it is for Sweden, Russia and other nations near Germany to send steel and ore and oil and other war materials into Germany every day in the week.

We are planning our own defense with the utmost urgency, and in its vast scale we must integrate the war needs of Britain and the other free nations which are resisting aggression.

This is not a matter of sentiment or of controversial personal opinion. It is a matter of realistic, practical military policy, based on the advice of our military experts who are in close touch with existing warfare. These military and naval experts and the members of the Congress and the Administration have a single-minded purpose—he defense of the United States.

This nation is making a great effort to produce everything that is necessary in this emergency—and with all possible speed. And this great effort requires great sacrifice.

I would ask no one to defend a democracy which in turn would not defend every one in the nation against want and privation. The strength of this nation shall not be diluted by the failure of the government to protect the economic well-being of its citizens.

If our capacity to produce is limited by machines, it must ever be remembered that these machines are operated by the skill and the stamina of the workers. As the government is determined to protect the rights of the workers, so the nation has a right to expect that the men who man the machines will discharge their full responsibilities to the urgent needs of defense.

The worker possesses the same human dignity and is entitled to the same security of position as the engineer or the manager or the owner. For the workers provide the human power that turns out the destroyers, and the planes and the tanks.

The nation expects our defense industries to continue operation without interruption by strikes or lockouts. It expects and insists that management and workers will reconcile their differences by voluntary or legal means, to continue to produce the supplies that are so sorely needed.

And on the economic side of our great defense program, we are, as you know, bending every effort to maintain stability of prices and with that the stability of the cost of living.

Nine days ago I announced the setting up of a more effective organization to direct our gigantic efforts to increase the production of munitions. The appropriation of vast sums of money and a well-coordinated executive direction of our defense efforts are not in themselves enough. Guns, planes, ships and many other things have to be built in the factories and the arsenals of America. They have to be produced by workers and managers and engineers with the aid of machines which in turn have to be built by hundreds of thousands of workers throughout the land.

In this great work there has been splendid cooperation between the government and industry and labor. And I am very thankful.

American industrial genius, unmatched throughout all the world in the solution of production problems, has been called upon to bring its resources and its talents into action. Manufacturers of watches, of farm implements, of Linotypes and cash registers and automobiles, and sewing machines and lawn mowers and locomotives, are now making fuses and bomb packing crates and telescope mounts and shells and pistols and tanks.

But all of our present efforts are not enough. We must have more ships, more guns, more planes—more of everything. And this can be accomplished only if we discard the notion of "business as usual." This job cannot be done merely by superimposing on the existing productive facilities the added requirements of the nation for defense.

Our defense efforts must not be blocked by those who fear the future consequences of surplus plant capacity. The possible consequences of failure of our defense efforts now are much more to be feared.

And after the present needs of our defense are past, a proper handling of the country's peacetime needs will require all of the new productive capacity, if not still more.

No pessimistic policy about the future of America shall delay the immediate expansion of those industries essential to defense. We need them.

I want to make it clear that it is the purpose of the nation to build now with all possible speed every machine, every arsenal, every factory that we need to manufacture our defense material. We have the men—the skill—the wealth—and above all, the will.

I am confident that if and when production of consumer or luxury goods in certain industries requires the use of machines and raw materials that are essential for defense purposes, then such production must yield, and will gladly yield, to our primary and compelling purpose.

So I appeal to the owners of plants—to the managers—to the workers—to our own government employees—to put every ounce of effort into producing these munitions swiftly and without stint. With this appeal I give you the pledge that all of us who are officers of your government will devote ourselves to the same whole-hearted extent to the great task that lies ahead.

As planes and ships and guns and shells are produced, your government, with its defense experts, can then determine how best to use them to defend this hemisphere. The decision as to how much shall be sent abroad and how much shall remain at home must be made on the basis of our overall military necessities.

We must be the great arsenal of democracy. For us this is an emergency as serious as war itself. We must apply ourselves to our task with the same resolution, the same sense of urgency, the same spirit of patriotism and sacrifice as we would show were we at war.

We have furnished the British great material support and we will furnish far more in the future.

There will be no "bottlenecks" in our determination to aid Great Britain. No dictator, no combination of dictators, will weaken that determination by threats of how they will construe that determination.

The British have received invaluable military support from the heroic Greek Army and from the forces of all the governments in exile. Their strength is growing. It is the strength of men and women who value their freedom more highly than they value their lives.

I believe that the Axis powers are not going to win this war. I base that belief on the latest and the best of information.

We have no excuse for defeatism. We have every good reason for hope—hope for peace, yes, and hope for the defense of our civilization and for the building of a better civilization in the future.

I have the profound conviction that the American people are now determined to put forth a mightier effort than they have ever yet made to increase our production of all the implements of defense, to meet the threat to our democratic faith.

As President of the United States, I call for that national effort. I call for it in the name of this nation which we love and honor and which we are privileged and proud to serve. I call upon our people with absolute confidence that our common cause will greatly succeed.

Source: http://www.usconstitution.com/franklinrooseveltarsenalofdemocracy.htm.

33. PRESIDENT FRANKLIN ROOSEVELT'S FOUR FREEDOMS SPEECH (JANUARY 6, 1941)

In his annual message to Congress in 1941, President Franklin Roosevelt addressed the growing fears of Americans regarding the expanding World War II.

Mr. Speaker, members of the 77th Congress:

I address you, the members of this new Congress, at a moment unprecedented in the history of the union. I use the word "unprecedented" because at no previous time has American security been as seriously threatened from without as it is today.

Since the permanent formation of our government under the Constitution in 1789, most of the periods of crisis in our history have related to our domestic affairs. And, fortunately, only one of these—the four-year war between the States—ever threatened our national unity. Today, thank God, 130,000,000 Americans in forty-eight States have forgotten points of the compass in our national unity.

It is true that prior to 1914 the United States often has been disturbed by events in other continents. We have even engaged in two wars with European nations and in a number of undeclared wars in the West Indies, in the Mediterranean and in the Pacific, for the maintenance of American rights and for the Principles of peaceful commerce. But in no case has a serious threat been raised against our national safety or our continued independence.

What I seek to convey is the historic truth that the United States as a nation has at all times maintained opposition—clear, definite opposition—to any attempt to lock us in behind an ancient Chinese wall while the procession of civilization went past. Today, thinking of our children and of their children, we oppose enforced isolation for ourselves or for any other part of the Americas.

That determination of ours, extending over all these years, was proved, for example, in the early days during the quarter century of wars following the French Revolution. While the Napoleonic struggle did threaten interests of the United States because of the French foothold in the West Indies and in Louisiana, and while we engaged in the War of 1812 to vindicate our right to peaceful trade, it is nevertheless clear that neither France nor Great Britain nor any other nation was aiming at domination of the whole world.

And in like fashion, from 1815 to 1914—ninety-nine years—no single war in Europe or in Asia constituted a real threat against our future or against the future of any other American nation.

Except in the Maximilian interlude in Mexico, no foreign power sought to establish itself in this hemisphere. And the strength of the British fleet in the Atlantic has been a friendly strength; it is still a friendly strength. Even when the World War broke out in 1914 it seemed to contain only small threat of danger to our own American future. But as time went on, as we remember, the American people began to visualize what the downfall of democratic nations might mean to our own democracy.

We need not overemphasize imperfections in the peace of Versailles. We need not harp on failure of the democracies to deal with problems of world reconstruction. We should remember that the peace of 1919 was far less unjust than the kind of pacification which began even before Munich, and which is being carried on under the new order of tyranny that seeks to spread over every continent today. The American people have unalterably set their faces against that tyranny.

I suppose that every realist knows that the democratic way of life is at this moment being directly assailed in every part of the world—assailed either by arms or by secret spreading of poisonous propaganda by those who seek to destroy unity and promote discord in nations that are still at peace.

During sixteen long months this assault has blotted out the whole pattern of democratic life in an appalling number of independent nations, great and small. And the assailants are still on the march, threatening other nations, great and small.

Therefore, as your President, performing my constitutional duty to "give to the Congress information of the state of the union," I find it unhappily necessary to report that the future and the safety of our country and of our democracy are overwhelmingly involved in events far beyond our borders.

Armed defense of democratic existence is now being gallantly waged in four continents. If that defense fails, all the population and all the resources of Europe and Asia, Africa and Australia will be dominated by conquerors. And let us remember that the total of those populations in those four continents, the total of those populations and their resources greatly exceeds the sum total of the population and the resources of the whole of the Western Hemisphere—yes, many times over.

In times like these it is immature—and, incidentally, untrue—for anybody to brag that an unprepared America, single-handed and with one hand tied behind its back, can hold off the whole world.

No realistic American can expect from a dictator's peace international generosity, or return of true independence, or world disarmament, or freedom of expression, or freedom of religion—or even good business. Such a peace would bring no security for us or for our neighbors. Those who would give up essential liberty to purchase a little temporary safety deserve neither liberty nor safety.

As a nation we may take pride in the fact that we are soft-hearted; but we cannot afford to be soft-headed. We must always be wary of those who with sounding brass and a tinkling cymbal preach the ism of appeasement. We must especially beware of that small group of selfish men who would clip the wings of the American eagle in order to feather their own nests. I have recently pointed out how quickly the tempo of modern warfare could bring into our very midst the physical attack which we must eventually expect if the dictator nation win this war.

There is much loose talk of our immunity from immediate and direct invasion from across the seas. Obviously, as long as the British Navy retains its power, no such danger exists. Even if there were no British Navy, it is not probable that any enemy would be stupid enough to attack us by landing troops in the United States from across thousands of miles of ocean, until it had acquired strategic bases from which to operate.

But we learn much from the lessons of the past years in Europe—particularly the lesson of Norway, whose essential seaports were captured by treachery and surprise built up over a series of years.

The first phase of the invasion of this hemisphere would not be the landing of regular troops. The necessary strategic points would be occupied by secret agents and by their dupes—and great numbers of them are already here and in Latin America.

As long as the aggressor nations maintain the offensive they, not we, will choose the time and the place and the method of their attack.

And that is why the future of all the American Republics is today in serious danger. That is why this annual message to the Congress is unique in our history. That is why every member of the executive branch of the government and every member of the Congress face great responsibility—great accountability.

The need of the moment is that our actions and our policy should be devoted primarily—almost exclusively—to meeting this foreign peril. For all our domestic problems are now a part of the great emergency. Just as our national policy in internal affairs has been based upon a decent respect for the rights and the dignity of all of our fellow men within our gates, so our national policy in foreign affairs has been based on a decent respect for the rights and the dignity of all nations, large and small. And the justice of morality must and will win in the end.

Our national policy is this :

First, by an impressive expression of the public will and without regard to partisanship, we are committed to all-inclusive national defense.

Second, by an impressive expression of the public will and without regard to partisanship, we are committed to full support of all those resolute people everywhere who are resisting aggression and are thereby keeping war away from our hemisphere.

By this support we express our determination that the democratic cause shall prevail, and we strengthen the defense and the security of our own nation.

Third, by an impressive expression of the public will and without regard to partisanship, we are committed to the proposition that principle of morality and considerations for our own security will never permit us to acquiesce in a peace dictated by aggressors and sponsored by appeasers. We know that enduring peace cannot be bought at the cost of other people's freedom.

In the recent national election there was no substantial difference between the two great parties in respect to that national policy. No issue was fought out on the line before the American electorate. And today it is abundantly evident that American citizens everywhere are demanding and supporting speedy and complete action in recognition of obvious danger.

Therefore, the immediate need is a swift and driving increase in our armament production. Leaders of industry and labor have responded to our summons. Goals of speed have been set. In some cases these goals are being reached ahead of time. In some cases we are on schedule; in other cases there are slight but not serious delays. And in some cases—and, I am sorry to say, very important cases—we are all concerned by the slowness of the accomplishment of our plans.

The Army and Navy, however, have made substantial progress during the past year. Actual experience is improving and speeding up our methods of production with every passing day. And today's best is not good enough for tomorrow.

I am not satisfied with the progress thus far made. The men in charge of the program represent the best in training, in ability and in patriotism. They are not satisfied with the progress thus far made. None of us will be satisfied until the job is done.

No matter whether the original goal was set too high or too low, our objective is quicker and better results. To give you two illustrations: We are behind schedule in turning out finished airplanes. We are working day and night to solve the innumerable problems and to catch up.

We are ahead of schedule in building warships, but we are working to get even further ahead of that schedule. To change a whole nation from a basis of peacetime production of implements of peace to a basis of wartime production of implements of war is no small task. The greatest difficulty comes at the beginning of the program, when new tools, new plant facilities, new assembly lines, new shipways must first be constructed before the actual material begins to flow steadily and speedily from them.

The Congress of course, must rightly keep itself informed at all times of the progress of the program. However, there is certain information, as the Congress itself will readily recognize, which, in the interests of our own security and those of the nations that we are supporting, must of needs be kept in confidence. New circumstances are constantly begetting new needs for our safety. I shall ask this Congress for greatly increased new appropriations and authorizations to carry on what we have begun.

I also ask this Congress for authority and for funds sufficient to manufacture additional munitions and war supplies of many kinds, to be turned over to those nations which are now in actual war with aggressor nations. Our most useful and immediate role is to act as an arsenal for them as well as for ourselves. They do not need manpower, but they do need billions of dollars' worth of the weapons of defense.

The time is near when they will not be able to pay for them all in ready cash. We cannot, and we will not, tell them that they must surrender merely because of present inability to pay for the weapons which we know they must have.

I do not recommend that we make them a loan of dollars with which to pay for these weapons—a loan to be repaid in dollars. I recommend that we make it possible for those nations to continue to obtain war materials in the United States, fitting their orders into our own program. And nearly all of their material would, if the time ever came, be useful in our own defense.

Taking counsel of expert military and naval authorities, considering what is best for our own security, we are free to decide how much should be kept here and how much should be sent abroad to our friends who, by their determined and heroic resistance, are giving us time in which to make ready our own defense.

For what we send abroad we shall be repaid, repaid within a reasonable time following the close of hostilities, repaid in similar materials, or at our option in other goods of many kinds which they can produce and which we need. Let us say to the democracies : "We Americans are vitally concerned in your defense of freedom. We are putting forth our energies, our resources and our organizing powers to give you the strength to regain and maintain a free world. We shall send you in ever-increasing numbers, ships, planes, tanks, guns. That is our purpose and our pledge."

In fulfillment of this purpose we will not be intimidated by the threats of dictators that they will regard as a breach of international law or as an act of war our aid to the democracies which dare to resist their aggression. Such aid is not an act of war, even if a dictator should unilaterally proclaim it so to be.

And when the dictators—if the dictators—are ready to make war upon us, they will not wait for an act of war on our part.

They did not wait for Norway or Belgium or the Netherlands to commit an act of war. Their only interest is in a new one-way international law which lacks mutuality in its observance and therefore becomes an instrument of oppression. The happiness of future generations of Americans may well depend on how effective and how immediate we can make our aid felt. No one can tell the exact character of the emergency situations that we may be called upon to meet. The nation's hands must not be tied when the nation's life is in danger.

Yes, and we must prepare, all of us prepare, to make the sacrifices that the emergency—almost as serious as war itself—demands. Whatever stands in the way of speed and efficiency in defense, in defense preparations at any time, must give way to the national need.

A free nation has the right to expect full cooperation from all groups. A free nation has the right to look to the leaders of business, of labor and of agriculture to take the lead in stimulating effort, not among other groups but within their own groups.

The best way of dealing with the few slackers or trouble-makers in our midst is, first, to shame them by patriotic example, and if that fails, to use the sovereignty of government to save government.

As men do not live by bread alone, they do not fight by armaments alone. Those who man our defenses and those behind them who build our defenses must have the stamina and the courage which come from unshakeable belief in the manner of life which they are defending. The mighty action that we are calling for cannot be based on a disregard of all the things worth fighting for.

The nation takes great satisfaction and much strength from the things which have been done to make its people conscious of their individual stake in the preservation of democratic life in America. Those things have toughened the fiber of our people, have renewed their faith and strengthened their devotion to the institutions we make ready to protect. Certainly this is no time for any of us to stop thinking about the social and economic problems which are the root cause of the social revolution which is today a supreme factor in the world. For there is nothing mysterious about the foundations of a healthy and strong democracy.

The basic things expected by our people of their political and economic systems are simple. They are: Equality of opportunity for youth and for others. Jobs for those who can work. Security for those who need it. The ending of special privilege for the few. The preservation of civil liberties for all. The enjoyment of the fruits of scientific progress in a wider and constantly rising standard of living.

These are the simple, the basic things that must never be lost sight of in the turmoil and unbelievable complexity of our modern world. The inner and abiding strength of our economic and political systems is dependent upon the degree to which they fulfill these expectations.

Many subjects connected with our social economy call for immediate improvement. As examples:

We should bring more citizens under the coverage of old-age pensions and unemployment insurance.

We should widen the opportunities for adequate medical care.

We should plan a better system by which persons deserving or needing gainful employment may obtain it.

I have called for personal sacrifice, and I am assured of the willingness of almost all Americans to respond to that call. A part of the sacrifice means the payment of more money in taxes. In my budget message I will recommend that a greater portion of this great defense program be paid for from taxation than we are paying for today. No person should try, or be allowed to get rich out of the program, and the principle of tax payments in accordance with ability to pay should be constantly before our eyes to guide our legislation.

If the Congress maintains these principles the voters, putting patriotism ahead pocketbooks, will give you their applause.

In the future days which we seek to make secure, we look forward to a world founded upon four essential human freedoms.

The first is freedom of speech and expression—everywhere in the world.

The second is freedom of every person to worship God in his own way—everywhere in the world.

The third is freedom from want, which, translated into world terms, means economic understandings which will secure to every nation a healthy peacetime life for its inhabitants—everywhere in the world.

The fourth is freedom from fear, which, translated into world terms, means a world-wide reduction of armaments to such a point and in such a thorough fashion that no nation will be in a position to commit an act of physical aggression against any neighbor—anywhere in the world.

That is no vision of a distant millennium. It is a definite basis for a kind of world attainable in our own time and generation. That kind of world is the very antithesis of the so-called "new order" of tyranny which the dictators seek to create with the crash of a bomb.

To that new order we oppose the greater conception—the moral order. A good society is able to face schemes of world domination and foreign revolutions alike without fear. Since the beginning of our American history we have been engaged in change, in a perpetual, peaceful revolution, a revolution which goes on steadily, quietly, adjusting itself to changing conditions without the concentration camp or the quicklime in the ditch. The world order which we seek is the cooperation of free countries, working together in a friendly, civilized society.

This nation has placed its destiny in the hands, heads and hearts of its millions of free men and women, and its faith in freedom under the guidance of God. Freedom means the supremacy of human rights everywhere. Our support goes to those who struggle to gain those rights and keep them. Our strength is our unity of purpose.

To that high concept there can be no end save victory.

Source: http://www.usconstitution.com/franklinrooseveltfourfreedomsspeech.htm.

34. PRESIDENT FRANKLIN ROOSEVELT'S "DAY OF INFAMY" SPEECH (DECEMBER 8, 1941)

On December 7, 1941, the Japanese attacked the U.S. Naval Station at Pearl Harbor, Hawaii. The following day a shocked and bewildered country looked to the president for help in understanding what had occurred. Americans listened anxiously to President Franklin Roosevelt on the radio as he addressed the Congress. In his speech to Congress that day, the president put into words the grief that all Americans felt, as he memorialized December 7, 1941, as "a date which will live in infamy."

Yesterday, December 7, 1941—a date which will live in infamy—the United States of America was suddenly and deliberately attacked by naval and air forces of the Empire of Japan.

The United States was at peace with that nation and, at the solicitation of Japan, was still in conversation with its Government and its Emperor looking toward the maintenance of peace in the Pacific. Indeed, one hour after Japanese air squadrons had commenced bombing in Oahu, the Japanese Ambassador to the United States and his colleague delivered to the Secretary of State a formal reply to a recent American message. While this reply stated that it seemed useless to continue the existing diplomatic negotiations, it contained no threat or hint of war or armed attack.

It will be recorded that the distance of Hawaii from Japan makes it obvious that the attack was deliberately planned many days or even weeks ago. During the intervening time the Japanese Government has deliberately sought to deceive the United States by false statements and expressions of hope for continued peace.

The attack yesterday on the Hawaiian Islands has caused severe damage to American naval and military forces. Very many American lives have been lost. In addition American ships have been reported torpedoed on the high seas between San Francisco and Honolulu.

Yesterday the Japanese Government also launched an attack against Malaya. Last night Japanese forces attacked Hong Kong. Last night Japanese forces attacked Guam. Last night Japanese forces attacked the Philippine Islands. Last night the Japanese attacked Wake Island. This morning the Japanese attacked Midway Island.

Japan has, therefore, undertaken a surprise offensive extending throughout the Pacific area. The facts of yesterday speak for themselves. The people of the United States have already formed their opinions and well understand the implications to the very life and safety of our nation.

As Commander-in-Chief of the Army and Navy, I have directed that all measures be taken for our defense.

Always will we remember the character of the onslaught against us. No matter how long it may take us to overcome this premeditated invasion, the American people in their righteous might will win through to absolute victory.

I believe I interpret the will of the Congress and of the people when I assert that we will not only defend ourselves to the uttermost but will make very certain that this form of treachery shall never endanger us again.

Hostilities exist. There is no blinking at the fact that our people, our territory and our interests are in grave danger.

With confidence in our armed forces—with the unbounded determination of our people—we will gain the inevitable triumph—so help us God.

I ask that the Congress declare that since the unprovoked and dastardly attack by Japan on Sunday, December seventh, a state of war has existed between the United States and the Japanese Empire.

Source: Franklin and Eleanor Roosevelt Institute, http://www.feri.org/common/news/details. cfm?QID=2067&clientid=11005.

APPENDICES

APPENDIX 1: POPULATION OF THE UNITED STATES BY DECADE, 1900–1940

As the following Census figures show, the population of the United States grew by almost 56 million persons between 1900 and 1940, with particular spurts in growth during the first decade of the twentieth century, thanks to immigration, and during the 1920s, due to economic prosperity.

1900	76,212,168
1910	92,228,496
1920	106,021,537
1930	123,202,624
1940	132,164,569

Source: United States Bureau of Census

APPENDIX 2: PRESIDENTS OF THE UNITED STATES, 1900–1945

Listed below are the presidents of the United States who held office between 1900 and 1945, with their party affiliations and their terms of service.

William McKinley[1]	Republican	1897–1901
Theodore Roosevelt	Republican	1901–1909
William Howard Taft	Republican	1909–1913
Woodrow Wilson	Democrat	1913–1921
Warren G. Harding[2]	Republican	1921–1923
Calvin Coolidge	Republican	1923–1929

| Herbert Hoover | Republican | 1929–1933 |
| Franklin D. Roosevelt[3] | Democrat | 1933–1945 |

[1] Assassinated in office in September 1901
[2] Died in office on August 2, 1923
[3] Died in office on April 12, 1945
Source: www.whitehouse.gov/history/presidents

APPENDIX 3: VICE PRESIDENTS OF THE UNITED STATES, 1900–1940s

Listed below are the vice presidents of the United States who held office between 1900 and 1945, with the president under whom they served, their party affiliation, and their terms of service.

Theodore Roosevelt[1]	McKinley	Republican	1901
Office Vacant	T. Roosevelt		1901–1905
Charles W. Fairbanks	T. Roosevelt	Republican	1905–1909
James S. Sherman[2]	Taft	Republican	1909–1912
Office Vacant	Taft		1912–1913
Thomas R. Marshall	Wilson	Democrat	1913–1921
Calvin Coolidge[3]	Harding	Republican	1921–1923
Office Vacant	Coolidge		1923–1925
Charles G. Dawes	Coolidge	Republican	1925–1929
Charles Curtis	Hoover	Republican	1929–1933
John Nance Garner	F. D. Roosevelt	Democrat	1933–1941
Henry A. Wallace	F. D. Roosevelt	Democrat	1941–1945
Harry S Truman[4]	F. D. Roosevelt	Democrat	1945
Office Vacant	Truman		1945–1949

[1] Succeeded to the presidency upon the death of William McKinley on September 14, 1901
[2] Died in office on October 30, 1912
[3] Succeeded to the presidency upon the death of Warren G. Harding on August 2, 1923
[4] Succeeded to the presidency upon the death of Franklin D. Roosevelt on April 12, 1945
Source: http://americanhistory.about.com/library/charts/blchartpresidents.htm

APPENDIX 4: SECRETARIES OF STATE OF THE UNITED STATES, 1900–1940s

Listed below are the secretaries of state of the United States who held office between 1900 and 1945, with the president who appointed them, their party affiliations, and their terms of service.

John Hay	McKinley/T. Roosevelt	Republican	1898–1905
Elihu Root	T. Roosevelt	Republican	1905–1909
Robert Bacon	T. Roosevelt	Republican	1909
Philander C. Knox	Taft	Republican	1909–1913
William Jennings Bryan	Wilson	Democrat	1913–1915
Robert Lansing	Wilson	Democrat	1915–1920
Bainbridge Colby	Wilson	Democrat	1920–1921
Charles Evans Hughes	Harding/Coolidge	Republican	1921–1925
Frank B. Kellogg	Coolidge	Republican	1925–1929
Henry L. Stimson	Hoover	Republican	1929–1933
Cordell Hull	F. D. Roosevelt	Democrat	1933–1944
Edward R. Stettinis Jr.	F. D. Roosevelt/Truman	Democrat	1944–1945

Source: http://www.state.gov/r/pa/ho/po/1682.htm; Mihalkanin, Edward S. *American Statesmen: Secretaries of State from John Jay to Colin Powell.* Westport, CT: Greenwood Press, 2004.

APPENDIX 5: CHIEF JUSTICES OF THE U.S. SUPREME COURT, 1900–1940s

Listed below are the chief justices of the U.S. Supreme Court who served between 1900 and 1945, with the president who appointed them and their terms of service.

Melvin Weston Fuller	Cleveland	1888–1910
Edward Douglass White	Taft	1910–1921
William Howard Taft[1]	Harding	1910–1930
Charles Evans Hughes	Hoover	1930–1941
Harlan Fiske Stone	F. D. Roosevelt	1941–1946

[1] Taft, a Republican who served as 27th president of the United States from 1909 to 1913, succeeded White, the man he himself had appointed chief justice in 1910.
Source: Hall, Kermit L., ed. *The Oxford Companion to the Supreme Court of the United States.* 2nd ed. New York: Oxford University Press, 2005.

BIBLIOGRAPHY

BOOKS

Addams, Jane. *Twenty Years at Hull-House*. Urbana: University of Illinois Press, 1990.

Akin, Edward N. *Flagler: Rockefeller Partner and Florida Baron*. Gainesville: University of Florida Press, 1991.

Alexander, June Granatir. *Daily Life in Immigrant America, 1870–1920*. Westport, CT: Greenwood Press, 2007.

Alinsky, Saul. *Reveille for Radicals*. New York: Vintage Books, 1969.

Allen, Frederick Lewis. *Only Yesterday*. New York: Perennial Library, 1959.

Auchincloss, Louis. *Theodore Roosevelt*. New York: Henry Holt and Company, 2001.

Badger, Anthony. *New Deal: The Depression Years*. New York: MacMillan Publishing Company, 1989.

Bakken, Gordon Morris, and Brenda Farrington, eds. *Encyclopedia of Women in the American West*. London: Sage Publications, 2003.

Barnes, Phil. *A Concise History of the Hawaiian Islands*. Hilo, HI: Petroglyph Press, 2007.

Batchelor, Bob. *The 1900s*. Westport, CT: Greenwood Press, 2002.

Becker, Susan D. *The Origins of the Equal Rights Amendment: American Feminism between the Wars*. Westport, CT: Greenwood Press, 1981.

Berg, A. Scott. *Lindbergh*. New York: G. P. Putnam's Sons, 1998.

Black, Brian. *Nature and the Environment in 20th-Century American Life*. Westport, CT: Greenwood Press, 2006.

Blanke, David. *The 1910s*. Westport, CT: Greenwood Press, 2002.

Blum, John Morton. *The Progressive Presidents: Theodore Roosevelt, Woodrow Wilson, Franklin D. Roosevelt, Lyndon B. Johnson*. New York: W. W. Norton and Company, 1982.

———. *The Republican Roosevelt*. New York: Atheneum, 1962.

———. *Woodrow Wilson and the Politics of Morality*. Boston: Little, Brown and Company, 1956.

Bode, Carl. *Maryland: A History*. New York: W. W. Norton and Company, 1977.

Bodnar, John. *The Transplanted: A History of Immigrants in Urban America*. Bloomington: University of Indiana Press, 1985.

Borneman, Walter. *Alaska: Saga of a Bold Land*. New York: Perennial, 2004.

Brands, H. W. *Woodrow Wilson*. New York: Henry Holt and Company, 2003.

Burt, Elizabeth V. *The Progressive Era: Primary Documents on Events from 1890 to 1914*. Westport, CT: Greenwood Press, 2004.

Carpenter, Frank G. *Alaska: Our Northern Wonderland*. New York: Doubleday, Doran, and Company, 1972.

Carter, Paul. *The Twenties in America*. 2nd ed. Arlington Heights, IL: Harlan Davidson, 1975.

Chapelle, Suzanne. *Baltimore: An Illustrated History*. Sun Valley, CA: American Historical Press, 2000.

Clark, Norman H. *Deliver Us from Evil: An Interpretation of American Prohibition*. New York: W. W. Norton and Company, 1976.

Clymer, Jeffery A. *America's Culture of Terrorism: Violence, Capitalism, and the Written Word*. Chapel Hill: University of North Carolina Press, 2003.

Collier, Peter. *The Roosevelts: An American Saga*. New York: Simon and Schuster, 1994.

Couch, W. T., ed. *Culture in the South*. Chapel Hill: University of North Carolina Press, 1934.

Crouch, Tom. *The Bishop's Boys: A Life of Wilbur and Orville Wright*. New York: W. W. Norton and Company, 1990.

Cumo, Christopher. *Science and Technology in 20th-Century American Life*. Westport, CT: Greenwood Press, 2007.

Daniels, Roger, and Spencer Olin. *Racism in California: A Reader in the History of Oppression*. New York: Macmillan and Company, 1972.

Davidson, John West, William E. Gienapp, Christine Leigh Hyrman, Mark H. Lytle, and Michael B. Stoff. *Nation of Nations: A Narrative History of the American Republic*. 4th ed. New York: McGraw Hill, 2005.

Dean, John W. *Warren G. Harding*. New York: Henry Holt and Company, 2004.

Degler, Carl N. *At Odds: Women and the Family in America from the Revolution to the Present*. New York: Oxford University Press, 1980.

Drowne, Kathleen, and Patrick Huber. *The 1920s*. Westport, CT: Greenwood Press, 2004.

Fass, Paula S. *The Damned and the Beautiful: American Youth in the 1920's*. New York: Oxford University Press, 1977.

Fenton, Frank. *A Place in the Sun*. New York: Random House, 1942.

Fisher, James T. *Catholics in America*. New York: Oxford University Press, 2000.

Fleming, Thomas. *New Jersey: A History*. New York: W. W. Norton and Company, 1985.

Freidel, Frank. *FDR: Launching the New Deal*. Boston: Little, Brown and Company, 1973.

Galbraith, John Kenneth. *The Great Crash 1929*. Boston: Houghton Mifflin, 1988.

Giordano, Ralph G. *Fun and Games in Twentieth-Century America: A Historical Guide to Leisure*. Westport, CT: Greenwood Press, 2003.

Gossop, Michael. *Living with Drugs*. Burlington, VT: Ashgate Publishing Company, 2007.

Green, Harvey. *The Uncertainty of Everyday Life 1915–1945*. Fayetteville: University of Arkansas Press, 2000.

Greenberg, David. *Calvin Coolidge*. New York: Henry Holt and Company, 2006.

Grier, Katherine C. *Pets in America: A History*. Chapel Hill: University of North Carolina Press, 2006.

Grossman, James, Ann Duskin Keating, and Janice Reiff, eds. *The Encyclopedia of Chicago*. Chicago: University of Chicago Press, 2004.

Guthrie, Woody. *Bound for Glory*. New York: Penguin Books, 1983.

Hagood, Margaret Jarman. *Mothers of the South: A Portraiture of the White Tenant Farmer Woman*. Chapel Hill: University of North Carolina Press, 1939.

Hall, Jacquelyn Dowd. *Revolt against Chivalry: Jessie Daniel Ames and the Women's Campaign against Lynching*. New York: Columbia University Press, 1979.

Handlin, Oscar. *Al Smith and His America*. Boston: Little, Brown and Company, 1958.

Harrell, David Edwin, Edwin S. Gaustad, John B. Boles, Sally Foreman Griffith, and Randall Miller. *Unto a Good Land: A History of the American People*. Grand Rapids, MI: William B. Eerdmans Publishing Company, 2005.

Heckscher, August. *Woodrow Wilson: A Biography*. New York: Charles Scribner's Sons, 1991.

Heidler, David S., and Jeanne T. Heidler. *Daily Life of Civilians in Wartime Modern America: From the Indian Wars to the Vietnam War*. Westport, CT: Greenwood Press, 2007.

Heyman, Neil M. *Daily Life during World War I*. Westport, CT: Greenwood Press, 2002.

Hicks, John D. *Republican Ascendancy, 1921–1933*. New York: Harper and Row, 1963.

Hill, Daniel Delis. *As Seen in Vogue: A Century of Fashion in Advertising*. Lubbock: Texas Tech University Press, 2004.

Himmelberg, Robert F. *The Great Depression and the New Deal*. Westport, CT: Greenwood Press, 2000.

Hine, Robert V., and John Mack Faragher. *The American West: A New Interpretive History*. New Haven, CT: Yale University Press, 2000.

Hoffecker, Carol E. *Delaware: A Bicentennial History*. New York: W. W. Norton and Company, 1977.

Holli, Melvin. *Reform in Detroit: Hazen Pingree and Urban Politics*. New York: Oxford University Press, 1969.

Hughes, Thomas P. *American Genius: A Century of Invention and Technological Enthusiasm 1870–1970*. Chicago: University of Chicago Press, 2004.

Ingham, John N., and Lynne B. Feldman. *African-American Business Leaders: A Biographical Dictionary*. Westport, CT: Greenwood Press, 1994.

Jenkins, Roy. *Franklin D. Roosevelt*. New York: Henry Holt and Company, 2003.

Jenkins, Sally. *The Real All Americans: The Team That Changed a Game, a People, a Nation*. New York: Doubleday and Co., 2007.

Jones, Kirkland C. *Renaissance Man from Louisiana: A Biography of Arna Wendell Bontemps*. Westport, CT: Greenwood Press, 1992.

Josephy, Alvin M. *The Indian Heritage of America*. New York: Alfred A. Knopf, 1969.

Kazin, Michael. *A Godly Hero: The Life of William Jennings Bryan*. New York: Alfred A. Knopf, 2006.

Keene, Jennifer. *American Soldiers Lives: World War I*. Westport, CT: Greenwood Press, 2006.

Koenig, Louis W. Bryan. *A Political Biography of William Jennings Bryan*. New York: Capricorn Books, 1975.

Kyvig, David E. *Daily Life in the United States 1920–1940: How American Lived through the Roaring Twenties and the Great Depression*. Chicago: Ivan R. Dee, 2002.

Lacey, Robert. *Ford*. Boston: Little, Brown and Company, 1986.

LaFarge, Oliver. *A Pictorial History of the American Indian*. New York: Crown Publishers, 1956.

Leuchtenburg, William E. *Franklin D. Roosevelt and the New Deal 1932–1940*. New York: Harper and Row, 1963.

———. *The Perils of Prosperity, 1914–1932*. New York: Rand McNally, 1958.

Lewis, David L. *District of Columbia*. New York: Norton Publishing Company, 1976.

Lindenmeyer, Kristine. *The Greatest Generation Grows Up*. Chicago: Ivan R. Dee, 2005.

Link, Arthur S. *Wilson the Diplomatist: A Look at His Major Foreign Policies*. Chicago: Quadrangle, 1963.

————. *Wilson: The New Freedom*. Princeton, NJ: Princeton University Press, 1967.

————. *Woodrow Wilson and the Progressive Era*. New York: Harper and Row, 1963.

————. *Woodrow Wilson: Revolution, War, and Peace*. Arlington Heights, IL: AHM Publishing Corporation, 1979.

————, and Richard L. McCormick. *Progressivism*. Arlington Heights, IL: Harlan Davidson, 1983.

Lloyd, Norman. *The Golden Encyclopaedia of Music*. New York: Golden Press, 1968.

London, Jack. *John Barleycorn*. New York: Century, 1913.

Lynd, Robert S., and Helen Merrell Lynd. *Middletown: A Study in Modern American Culture*. New York: Harcourt Brace and World, 1929.

MacDonald, Betty. *The Egg and I*. Philadelphia: J. B. Lippincott, 1945.

Marsden, George. *Fundamentalism and American Culture*. 2nd ed. New York: Oxford University Press, 2006.

Mayer, Harold, and Richard Wade. *Chicago: Growth of a Metropolis*. Chicago: University of Chicago Press, 1969.

Mencken, H. L. *On Politics: A Carnival of Buncombe*. New York: Vintage Books, 1960.

Miller, Nathan. *Theodore Roosevelt: A Life*. New York: William Morrow and Company, 1992.

Miller, Randall, and George Pozetta, eds. *Shades of the Sunbelt: Essays on Ethnicity, Race, and the Urban South*. Boca Raton: Florida Atlantic University Press, 1989.

Millman, Chad. *The Detonators: The Secret Plot to Destroy America and an Epic Hunt for Justice*. New York: Little Brown and Company, 2006.

Milner, Clyde, Carol A. O'Connor, and Martha A. Sandweiss. *The Oxford History of the American West*. New York: Oxford University Press, 1994.

Mitchell, Broadus. *Depression Decade: From New Era through New Deal 1929–1941*. New York: Harper Torch Books, 1947.

Morgan, Ted. *FDR: A Biography*. New York: Simon and Schuster, 1986.

Morris, Charles. *American Catholic: The Saints and Sinners Who Built America's Most Powerful Church*. New York: Random House, 1997.

Morris, Edmund. *The Rise of Theodore Roosevelt*. New York: The Modern Library, 2001.

————. *Theodore Rex*. New York: Random House, 2001.

Mowry, George. *The California Progressives*. Chicago: Quadrangle Paperbacks, 1951.

————. *Theodore Roosevelt and the Progressive Movement*. New York: Hill and Wang, 1960.

Murray, Robert K. *The Politics of Normalcy: Governmental Theory and Practice in the Harding-Coolidge Era*. New York: W. W. Norton and Company, 1973.

Nugent, Walter. *Into the West: The Story of Its People*. New York: Alfred A. Knopf, 1999.

Ogren, Kathy J. *The Jazz Revolution: Twenties America and the Meaning of Jazz*. New York: Oxford University Press, 1992.

Olson, James S. *Historical Dictionary of the Great Depression, 1929–1940*. Westport, CT: Greenwood Press, 2001.

Opdyke, Sandra. *No One Was Turned Away: The Role of Public Hospitals in New York City Since 1900*. New York: Oxford University Press, 1999.

Ostrander, Gilman. *Nevada: The Great Rotten Borough 1859–1964*. New York: Knopf, 1966.

Parrish, Michael. *Anxious Decades: America in Prosperity and Depression 1920–1941*. New York: W. W. Norton and Company, 1994.

Percy, Will. *Lanterns on the Levy: Recollections of a Planter's Son*. Baton Rouge: Louisiana State University Press, 2006.

Perrigo, Lynn. *The American Southwest: Its Peoples and Cultures*. Albuquerque: University of New Mexico Press, 1971.

Peters, Thelma. *Biscayne Country, 1870–1926*. Miami, FL: Banyan Books, 1981.

Pringle, Henry F. *The Life and Times of William Howard Taft*. 2 vols. Hamden, CT: Archon Books, 1964.

———. *Theodore Roosevelt*. New York: Harcourt, Brace Jovanovich, 1956.

Reich, Steven A. *Encyclopedia of the Great Black Migration*. Westport, CT: Greenwood Press, 2006.

Riess, Steven A. *City Games: The Evolution of American Urban Society and the Rise of Sports*. Chicago: University of Chicago Press, 1991.

Riordan, William L. *Plunkitt of Tammany Hall*, ed. Terrence Mc Donald. New York: Bedford Books/St. Martins Press, 1994.

Roberts, Randy. *Jack Dempsey: The Manassa Mauler*. Baton Rouge: Louisiana State University Press, 1979.

Rucker, Walter, and James Nathaniel Upton, eds. *Encyclopedia of American Race Riots*. 2 vols. Westport, CT: Greenwood Press, 2006.

Russell, Francis. *The Shadow of Blooming Grove: Warren G. Harding and His Times*. New York: McGraw-Hill, 1968.

Shanabruch, Charles. *Chicago's Catholics: The Evolution of an American Identity*. Notre Dame, IN: University of Notre Dame Press, 1981.

Sinclair, Upton. *The Jungle*. New York: Doubleday, Page, and Company, 1906.

Sklar, Robert. *Movie-Made America: A Cultural History of American Movies*. New York: Vintage Books, 1994.

Smith, Gene. *The Shattered Dream: Herbert Hoover and the Great Depression*. New York: McGraw-Hill, 1984.

———. *When the Cheering Stopped: The Last Years of Woodrow Wilson*. New York: William Morrow and Company, 1964.

Soule, George. *Prosperity Decade: From War to Depression*. New York: Harper Torchbooks, 1968.

Spear, Allan. *Black Chicago: The Making of a Negro Ghetto 1890–1920*. Chicago: University of Chicago Press, 1967.

Starr, Kevin. *California: A History*. New York: Modern Library, 2005.

———. *Endangered Dreams: The Great Depression in California*. New York: Oxford University Press, 1997.

———. *Inventing the Dream: California in the Progressive Era*. New York: Oxford University Press, 1986.

———. *Material Dreams: Southern California through the 1920s*. New York: Oxford University Press, 1991.

Steffens, Lincoln. *Shame of the Cities*. New York: Hill and Wang, 1957.

Stevens, Sylvester. *Pennsylvania: Birthplace of a Nation*. New York: Random House, 1964.

Strickland, Laurie, and Elizabeth Dunn. *Old Time Southern Cooking*. Gretna, LA: Pelican Publishing Co., 2002.

Sullivan, Mark. *Our Times: The United States 1900–1925*. New York: Charles Scribner's Sons, 1933.

Terkel, Studs. *Hard Times: An Oral History of the Great Depression*. New York: Avon, 1971.

Thelen, David P. *Robert M. La Follette and the Insurgent Spirit*. Boston: Little, Brown and Company, 1976.

Thompson, Nile, and Carolyn Marr. *Building for Learning: Seattle Public Schools 1862–2000*. Seattle, WA: Seattle Public Schools, 2001.

Tischauser, Leslie V. *Race Relations in the United States, 1920–1940*. Westport, CT: Greenwood Press, 2008.

Tygiel, Jules. *Past Time: Baseball As History*. New York: Oxford University Press, 2000.

Urban, Wayne, and Jennings Wagoner. *American Education: A History*. New York: McGraw-Hill Companies, 2003.

VanTassel, David, and John J. Grabowski, eds. *Cleveland: A Tradition of Reform*. Kent, OH: Kent State University Press, 1986.

Ward, Geoffrey C. *A First-Class Temperament: The Emergence of Franklin Roosevelt*. New York: Harper and Row, 1989.

Watson, John B. *Behaviorism*. New York: W. W. Norton and Company, 1930.

Weaver, John. *El Pueblo Grande: A Non Fiction Book about Los Angeles*. Los Angeles, CA: Ward Ritchie Press, 1973.

Weigley, Russel F., ed. *Philadelphia: A Three-Hundred Year History*. New York: W. W. Norton and Company, 1982.

Wells, Robert V. *Facing the King of Terrors: Death and Society in an American Community 1750–1990*. New York: Cambridge University Press, 2000.

White, Richard. *A New History of the American West*. Norman: University of Oklahoma Press, 1991.

Williams, T. Harry. *Huey Long*. New York: Vintage Books, 1969.

Wilson, Charles Reagan, and William Ferris, eds. *Encyclopedia of Southern Culture*. Chapel Hill: University of North Carolina Press, 1989.

Wilson, Joan Hoff. *Herbert Hoover: Forgotten Progressive*. Boston: Little, Brown and Company, 1975.

Wiltz, John E. *From Isolation to War, 1931–1941*. New York: Thomas Y. Crowell Company, 1968.

Woodward, C. Vann. *Origins of the New South 1877–1913*. Baton Rouge: Louisiana State University Press, 1974.

Works Progress Administration, ed. *Arizona, A State Guide*. New York: Hastings House, 1940.

Young, William H., and Nancy K. Young. *The Great Depression in America: A Cultural Encyclopedia*. 2 vols. Westport, CT: Greenwood Press, 2007.

Young, William H., with Nancy K. Young. *The 1930s*. Westport, CT: Greenwood Press, 2002.

Youngs, J. William T. *Eleanor Roosevelt: A Personal and Public Life*. Boston: Little, Brown and Company, 1985.

Zinn, Howard. *A People's History of the United States: 1492–Present*. New York: Harper Perennial, 2003.

ARTICLES

Bailey, Kenneth. "Southern White Protestants at the Turn of the Century." *American Historical Review* 68, no. 3 (April 1963): 618–35.

Bateman, Fred. "Improvement in American Dairy Farming, 1850–1910: A Quantitative Analysis." *Journal of Economic History* 28, no. 2 (June 1968): 255–73.

Blackwelder, Julia Kirk. "Race, Ethnicity, and Women's Lives in the Urban South." In *Shades of the Sunbelt: Essays on Ethnicity, Race, and the Urban South*, ed. Randall Miller and George Pozetta. Boca Raton: Florida Atlantic University Press, 1989.

Bodnar, John, Michael Weber, and Roger Simon. "Migration, Kinship, and Urban Adjustment: Blacks and Poles in Pittsburgh, 1700–1730." *Journal of American History* 66, no. 3 (December 1979): 548–65.

Burma, John H. "Present Status of the Spanish-Americans in New Mexico." *Social Forces* 28, no. 2 (December 1949): 138.

Clinton, Catherine. "Stars and Bars Feminism." *Reviews in American History* 21, no. 4 (December 1993): 612–16.

Cook, Katherine. "Education among Native and Minority Groups in Alaska, Puerto Rico, Virgin Islands and Hawaii." *Journal of Negro Education* 3, no. 1 (January 1934): 20–41.

Daniel, Peter. Review of *Bad Blood: The Tuskegee Syphilis Experiment,* by James Jones. *Journal of Southern History* 48, no. 2 (May 1981): 303–4.

Dozier, Edward. "The Pueblos of Southwestern United States." *Journal of the Royal Anthropological Institute of Great Britain and Ireland* 90 (1960): 146–60.

Graham, Robert Charles. Review of *Taking the University to the People: Seventy-Five Years of Cooperative Extension,* by Wayne D. Rasmussen. *Journal of Economic History* 50, no. 1 (March 1990): 200–21.

Hackney, Sheldon. "Southern Violence." *American Historical Review* 74, no. 3 (February 1969): 906–25.

Hall, Jacquelyn Dowd, Robert Konstadt, and James Leloudi. "Cotton Mill People: Work, Community, and Protest in the Textile South." *American Historical Review* 91, no. 2 (April 1986): 245–86.

Hayner, Norman. "Regional Family Patterns: The Western Family." *American Journal of Sociology* 53, no. 6 (May 1948): 432–34.

Howe, Irving. "The Southern Myth and William Faulkner." *American Quarterly* 3, no. 4 (Winter 1951): 357–62.

Kingsdale, Jon M. "The 'Poor Man's Club': Social Functions of the Urban Working Class Saloon." *American Quarterly* 25, no. 4 (October 1973): 472–89.

Lange, Emil. "Character Education in Long Beach Schools." *Journal of Educational Sociology* 4, no. 7 (March 1931): 426–29.

Lears, Jackson. "The Way We Live, the American Way of Debt." *New York Times Sunday Magazine,* June 11, 2006, 13.

Link, William A. "Privies, Progressivism, and Public Schools: Health Reform and Education in the Rural South, 1909–1920." *Journal of Southern History* 54 (November 1988): 623–42.

Loftue, John J. "The Activity Program in New York Elementary Schools." *Journal of Educational Sociology* 17, no. 2 (October 1943): 71–72.

Marsh, Margaret. "Suburban Men and Masculine Domesticity, 1870–1915." *American Quarterly* 40, no. 2 (June 1988): 165–86.

Mohl, Raymond. Review of *Reform in Detroit: Hazen Pingree and Urban Politics* by Melvin G. Holli. *American Quarterly* 22, no. 2 (Summer 1970): 286–87.

Murphy, Mary. "Bootlegging Mothers and Drinking Daughters: Gender and Prohibition in Butte, Montana." *American Quarterly* 46, no. 2 (June 1994): 174–94.

Nash, Roderick. "The American Cult of the Primitive." *American Quarterly* 18, no. 3 (Autumn 1966): 517–37.

Norrell, Robert. "Caste in Steel: Jim Crow Careers in Birmingham Alabama." *Journal of American History* 73, no. 3 (December 1986): 669–94.

Orsi, Robert. "The Religious Boundaries of an In Between People: Street Fest and the Problem of the Dark-Skinned Other in Italian Harlem, 1920–1990." *American Quarterly* 44, no. 3 (September 1992): 313–47.

Patrick, Vincent. "Crime Story." *New York Times Review of Books*, September 9, 2007, 31.

Robinson, Reginald. "Leisure Time Activities of the Children of New York's Lower West Side." *Journal of Educational Sociology* 9, no. 8 (April 1936): 484–93.

Sicotte, Richard. "Economic Crisis and Political Response: The Political Economy of the Shipping Act of 1916." *Journal of Economic History* 59, no. 4 (December 1999): 103–10.

Smith, Nancy Midgette. "In Search of Professional Identity: Southern Scientists, 1883–1940." *Journal of Southern History* 54, no. 4 (November 2006): 597–622.

Stowe, Steven. Review of *The House of Percy: Honor, Melancholy, and Imagination in a Southern Family* by Bertram Wyatt-Brown. *Reviews in American History* 24 (March 1996): 138–43.

Strayer, George D., et al., eds. "General Report on School Buildings and Grounds of Delaware." *Bulletin of the Service Citizens of Delaware* 1, no. 3 (1919).

WEB SITES

Almind, Gert J. "Jukeboxes." http://www.jukeboxworks.com/historyTerm.html.

American Experience. http://pbs.org.

American Life Histories: Manuscripts from the Federal Writers' Project, 1936–1940. http://www.americanmemory.gov.

Association of Religious Data Archives (ARDA). http://www.thearda.com.

Crime Library. http://www.crimelibrary.com/gangsters_outlaws/outlaws/floyd/3.html.

"Dallas Fort Worth Radio History." http://www.knus99.com/amlist.html.

Diehl, Lorraine B., and Marianne Hardart. "The Automat: The History, Recipes, and Allure of Horn and Hardart's Masterpiece." http://www.theautomat.net/.

Duke University Libraries—Airlines History site. http://scriptorium.lib.duke.edu/adaccess/airline-history.html.

Enrichment Journal. http://enrichmentjournal.ag.org/199904/026_azusa.cfm.

Geostat Center: Historical Census Browser. http://fisher.lib.virginia.edu/collections/stats/histcensus/php/county.php.

German Immigration. http://rs6.loc.gov/learn/features/immig/german8.html.

History of Chicago. http://www.encyclopedia.chicagohistory.org/.

History of Crosley Field, 1912–1970. http://www.crosley-field.com/.

History of Merion Golf Club. http://sc.essortment.com/meriongolfclub_rlxs.htm.

History of the Blues. http://www.history-of-rock.com/blues.htm.

Journal Star Archives. http://www.journalstar.com/articles/2005/05/22/Sunday_am/doc428b981453c7e539709681.bat.

Legends of America. http//:www.legendsofamerica.com.

Library of Congress, Prints and Photographs Division, FSA-OWI Collection. http://www.americanmemory.org.

McGee, Gary. "William J Seymour and the Azusa Street Revival." *Journal for Pentecostal Ministry*. http://www.ag.org/enrichmentjournal/199904/026_azusa.cfm.

Middle States Association. http://www.msache.org.

Native American Peoples of Oregon. http://www.oregonmaiden.com/Native-Americans-of-Oregon.html.

San Francisco Cablecar Museum. http://www.cablecarmuseum.org/heritage.html.

Sears Archives. http://www.searsarchives.com/.

Steber, Bill. "Juke Joints." http://www.steberphoto.com/articles-1.htm.

United Airlines History. http://www.united.com/page/middlepage/0,6823,2286,00.html.

W.E.B. Du Bois Learning Center. http:www.duboislc.org/man.html.

Wickman, Patricia. "Seminoles." http://www.seminoletribe.com/tribune/40anniversary/history.shtml.

Yosemite National Park, California. http://www.nps.gov/yose/historyculture/index.htm.

CUMULATIVE INDEX

Boldface numbers refer to volume numbers. A key appears on all verso pages.

Columbia Broadcasting System (CBS)

Curran, Charles E., **4:**250–51
Currency Act, **1:**11
Curtis, Cyrus H. K., **3:**160
Curtiss, Glenn, **3:**454
Cushing, Caleb, **2:**246
Custer, George A., **2:**92, 222–23, 368, 433
Custer Myth, **2:**223
Custis, Eliza, **1:**42
Cutler, George, **2:**41
Cutty Sark, **2:**567
Cycling, **2:**567–69
Cyclotron, **3:**438
CYO. *See* Catholic Youth Organization
Czachowski, Ray, **3:**125

Dacre, Harry, **2:**594
Daggert, Ezra, **1:**503; **2:**272
Daily Tribune, **2:**197
Dainty Work for Pleasure and Profit, **2:**608
D'Alesandro, Thomas, **3:**140
Dana, Richard Henry, **2:**217, 477
Dance: balls, **1:**150; de Chastellus, Marquis, on, **1:**149; as entertainment, **3:**467; in military life, American Revolution homefront, **1:**149–50; in recreational life, **2:**447–48; **4:**230–39; in Western frontier, **1:**277
Danticat, Edwidge, **4:**296
"The Dark Ages of American Oceanic Enterprise," **2:**79
Darrow, Charles B., **3:**198–99
Darrow, Clarence, **3:**26, 65, 269, 335, 393, 417
Dartmouth, **1:**67, 430
Darwin, Charles, **3:**269; **4:**121
Darwinism, **2:**210, 326; **3:**2
Daughters of Liberty, **1:**155
Daughters of the Confederacy, **3:**210
David, Opad D., **4:**61
Davis, Alexander Jackson, **1:**468, 480; **2:**129
Davis, Gussie, **2:**594
Davis, Jacob, **2:**411
Davis, James, **3:**127
Davis, Jefferson, **1:**386; **2:**49, 260; administration, **2:**151–52; on Confederacy, **2:**148; as hero, **2:**149; inauguration, **2:**171; parodies, **2:**172; release of, **2:**203
Davis, Philip, **2:**531
Davis, Rebecca Harding, **2:**389
Davis, Samuel Cole, **1:**291
Davis, Theodore R., **1:**231, 466
Davy Crockett, **4:**37
Davy, Humphrey, **2:**263
Dawes, William, **1:**18
Dawson, Francis W., **3:**249
Day, Benjamin H., **1:**534
Day, Dorothy, **3:**445
Daylight saving time, **4:**24
"Day of Infamy," **3:**582–84
The Day Christ Died (Bishop, J.), **4:**123
Day, Thomas F., **3:**398
Dean, Clarence, **3:**219–20
Dean, James, **4:**27, 34, 81, 141
Death: of Adams, John, **1:**375; in American Republic (1789–1820), **1:**312–13; in childbirth, **1:**36–37; of Harrison, William Henry, **1:**383; of Jefferson, Thomas, **1:**375; of McPherson, Aimee Semple, **3:**470; penalty, **4:**323; of Presley, Elvis, **4:**234; of Reagan, Ronald, **4:**264; in religious life, **1:**312–13; of

Roosevelt, Franklin D., **4:**24; in U.S. Civil War, **2:**25, 31, 57; wakes/funerals, **1:**312–13; worship and, **1:**309
DeBow's Review, **1:**465
Debs, Eugene V., **2:**507–8; **3:**13–14
Debt: of American Republic (1789–1820), **1:**193; domestic life and, **4:**144–45, Hamilton, Alexander, and, **1:**250; taxes and, **4:**314–15
Decades of discord, 1960–1990, **4:**12, 141; domestic life, **4:**13; economic life, **4:**13; historical overview, **4:**12–17; intellectual life, **4:**13–14; material life, **4:**14–15; political life, **4:**15–16; recreational life, **4:**16; religious life, **4:**16–17
"Declaration of Causes for Taking Up Arms," **1:**19
Declaration of Conscience, **4:**98, 359–62
Declaration of Independence, **1:**20–21
"Declaration of Rights and Grievances," **1:**12
Declaratory Act (1776), **1:**13
Deep South, **1:**391; **2:**64, 74, 119, 139, 144
Deere, John, **1:**541; **2:**518
The Deerslayer (Cooper, J. F.), **1:**452
Defoe, Daniel, **1:**141
Defoe, Thomas, **2:**265
DeForest, John W., **1:**454; **2:**96, 192, 385
de Forest, Lee, **3:**70, 437
De Grasse, Francois Comte, **1:**26
Deidesheimer, Philip, **2:**355
Deism, **1:**291, 297, 305–6; Franklin, Benjamin, and, **1:**297; Paine and, **1:**297; Washington, George, and, **1:**297
de Kalb, Johann, **1:**24
Delacorte, George, **3:**159
Delaney, Martin R., **1:**580
De Leon, Edwin, **2:**156–57
De Lesseps, **2:**472
Delineator, **2:**610
Dell, Daisy, **3:**464
Delmonico's, **1:**514; **2:**553–54
DeMille, Cecil B., **3:**445, 455, 465–66
Democracy, **1:**545; **4:**11, 17. *See also* "Arsenal of Democracy"
Democracy (de Tocqueville), **4:**11
Democratic Party, **1:**378, 383, 555; **2:**148, 150, 152–53, 160, 570–71, 577–78; **3:**134, 255–56; **4:**11; African Americans in, **4:**93; conflicts in, **1:**379; labor unions and, **4:**47; during roaring twenties, **3:**27; Roosevelt, Franklin, as leader of, **4:**92
Democratic-Republicans, **1:**195, 330, 372, 374
Democratic Vistas (Whitman, W.), **2:**257
Dempsey, Jack, **3:**93, 196–98
Denison, Frederick, **2:**530
Denmark Vesey Conspiracy (1822), **2:**289
Department of Homeland Security, **4:**328
de Rochemont, Richard, **4:**192
Derrida, Jacques, **4:**300
Desegregation, **4:**28, 173–74
Deseret Costume, **2:**410
Despotism in America (Hildreth), **1:**461
Detroit, **2:**527
Detroit Free Press, **3:**314
"Devil's wagon," **3:**49
DeVoe, Thomas, **2:**267–69
Dewey, Chester, **1:**425
Dewey, John, **2:**530; **3:**308–10; **4:**57, 61, 96
Dewey, Thomas E., **4:**25
De Will, Robert, **2:**386
de Young, Michael H., **3:**428, 445
The Dial, **2:**197

Diaz, Junot, **4:**296
Diaz, Porfirio, **3:**9
Dichter, Ernest, **4:**82
Dickens, Charles, **1:**58, 447, 454–57, 526–27, 579; **2:**82–83, 92, 94, 102, 279, 313; **4:**17–18; on mill girls, **1:**601–2
Dickinson, Emily, **2:**538–39, **4:**70
Dickinson, John, **1:**19, 96, 141
Dickstein, Morris, **4:**70
Diedrich Knickerbocker's History of New York (Irving), **1:**449; **2:**185
Diet: of Mexican Americans, **3:**382–83; "summer," **3:**305. *See also* Food
Diet plans: food and, **4:**193–94; health and, **4:**178–79
Dietrich, Marlene, **3:**446
Dillinger, John, **3:**333
Dillingham Commission, **3:**59
Dilweg, Lavvie, **3:**342
DiMaggio, Joe, **4:**27
Dining out/cooking: fast-service restaurants, **3:**75, 318; food and, **1:**513–14; **2:**403–5, 552–53; **4:**195–99, 307–9; in material life, **4:**197–99; midday meal, **3:**74–75
Diphtheria, **1:**222; **3:**74
Diplomatic Correspondence of the American Revolution (Sparks), **1:**461
Directions for Cookery (Leslie, E.), **1:**512
Disciples of Christ, **1:**297–98, 307
Discretionary expenditures, **2:**371
Discrimination, **4:**9, 208; Chinese exclusion, **2:**581–83; in Indian reservations, **2:**430–33; in manufacturing, **3:**81; Native Americans and, **3:**303; Nativism, **2:**157–60; in political life, **2:**157–60, 294–95, 430–33, 581–83; in public buildings, **3:**431; White Supremacy Movement, **2:**294–95. *See also* Civil Rights Act (1964); Civil Rights Act (1968); Integration; Ku Klux Klan; Racialists; Racism
Disease, **3:**72–73; **4:**17, 135, 181–82; among African Americans, **3:**239; child, **3:**212–14; health and, **1:**226–28; Jefferson, Thomas, on, **1:**229; pellagra, **3:**241; "social," **3:**58. *See also* Health, Hospitals, Medicine; Nursing; *specific diseases*
Disneyland, **4:**27, 37
Divorce, **1:**212; **3:**44–45; **4:**142, 145–46; abandonment as "poor man's," **3:**47
Dix, Dorthea, **2:**110–11; **3:**49
"Dixie," **2:**171
Dixie Primer for Little Folks (Moore, M. B.), **2:**90
Dixon, Willie, **3:**344
Dock, Christopher, **1:**62
Doctorow, E. L., **4:**101
Documentary History of the American Revolution (Force), **1:**461
Dodd, Sam, **2:**106
Dodge City, Kansas, **2:**420
Dodge, Mary Abigail, **2:**389
Doheny, Edward, **2:**478
Dole, Robert, **4:**322
Dole, Sanford B., **2:**429
Domestic life, **2:**3–4; during American changes/conflict (1821–1861), **1:**391–406; during American Republic (1789–1820), **1:**210–23; children in, **1:**39–42; **2:**49–58, 217–21, 341–43, 485–94; **3:**52–54, 119–21, 212–14, 291–92, 406–13; **4:**35–38, 139–41, 268–69; cities and, **4:**142–44; during Colonial America (1763–1789), **1:**29–43; courtship

1: 1763–1861	3: 1900–1940
2: 1861–1900	4: 1940–Present

in, 1:211–16, 399–401; debt and, 4:144–45; in decades of discord, 1960–1990, 4:13; drugs in, 4:270; dueling in, 1:402–3; duty/honor in, 1:402; during Exploitation Period, 2:330–50; family in, 1:29–31, 216–23, 395–96; 2:35–40, 207, 331–34, 473–75; 3:43–47, 111–16, 208–9, 281–84, 353–57, 402–5; 4:32–35; freedmen in, 2:221–23; hospitality in, 1:401–2; during Industrial Age (1870–1900), 2:473–99; kinship in, 1:397–98; 2:33–35, 204–7, 330–31, 473; marriage in, 1:211–16, 399–401; men in, 2:207–10, 334–36, 475–79; 3:47–49, 209–10, 284–86, 405; 4:41–42, 141–42, 270–71; in Middle Atlantic U.S., 3:111–21; in Midwest U.S., 3:280–93; miscegenation in, 1:405–6; modern era, 1991–2005, 4:18; modernization in, 1:393–95; in Northeast U.S., 3:43–57; orphans in, 1:42–43; 2:343–44; "Other America," 4:137–40, 272–73; overview, 4:136–37, 267–68; in Pacific West U.S., 3:402–13; pets in, 2:59–62, 223–24, 347–48, 497–98; 3:54–57, 214, 292–93, 413; 4:271–72; planter aristocracy in, 1:396–97; postwar America, 1946–1959, 4:31–32; prostitution in, 1:404–5; during Reconstruction (1865–1877), 2:201–4; rural America and, 4:142–44; servants in, 2:58–59, 221–23, 344–47, 494–96; slaves in, 2:58–59, 344–47; in Southern U.S., 3:208–14; in Southwest/Rocky Mountain Western U.S., 3:353–57; suburban living, 4:142–44; technology and, 4:144–45; during U.S. Civil War, 2:32–63; during war years, 1940–1945, 4:30–31; women in, 2:40–49, 210–17, 336–41, 479–85; 3:49–52, 117–19, 210–12, 286–91, 356–57, 405–6; 4:38–41, 145–46, 273–75

Domestic Medicine (Gunn), 1:437
Domestic Medicine or the Family Physician (Whitfield), 1:142
Domestic sciences, 2:211
Dominican Republic, 2:472
Donnelley, Thorne, 3:314–15
Don't Change Your Husband, 3:466
Doolittle, Jimmy, 3:462
Dorchester, Daniel, 2:458
Dorsey, Jimmy, 3:94–95
Dorsey, Mollie, 2:332, 341
Dorsey, Tommy, 3:95
Dos Passos, John, 3:23, 68; 4:71
Doubleday, Abner, 2:165
Dougherty, Joseph, 3:133
Douglas, A. S., 4:312
Douglas, Donald, 3:454
Douglass, Frederick, 1:480–81, 565, 580–81, 602–4; 2:103–4, 173, 602
Douglass' Monthly Magazine, 1:580; 2:103
Douglas, Stephen A., 1:386; 2:148, 150, 153; Lincoln, Abraham, debates, 1:389–90
Douglas, William O., 3:366
Dow, Lorenzo, 1:561; 2:459
Downing, Andrew Jackson, 1:468, 480–81; 2:129
Dows, Gustavus, 2:272
Doyle, Arthur Conan, 2:533

Draft, 4:99–100, 142, 221, 226
Drake, Edwin, 2:15, 361–62, 364–65
Draper, Margaret, 1:145
Dr. Chase's Recipes, 2:271
Dr. Cladius (Crawford, F. M.), 2:254
Dred: A Tale of the Great Dismal Swamp (Stowe), 1:579
Dred Scott case, 1:388–89, 555; 2:418
Dreiser, Theodore, 2:470, 533; 3:52, 67–68, 79
Dresser, Paul, 2:594
Drew, Daniel, 2:509
Drinker, Elizabeth, 1:160–61
Driven to Distraction (Hallowell/Ratey), 4:181
Dr. Jekyll and Mr. Hyde (Stevenson), 2:533
"Dr. Morse's Root Pills," 2:448
Droughts, 2:239
Drugs: advertising, 4:297; cartels, 4:323–24; in domestic life, 4:270; miracle, 4:68; "narco-trafficking," 4:323; research, 4:297; during Vietnam War (1965–1975), 4:226. *See also* Medicine
Drury, Marion, 2:55
Dryden, John, 3:184
Drys, 3:19
Dr. Zhivago (Pasternak), 4:28
Du Bois, W. E. B., 3:3–4, 24, 67, 135, 236–37; 4:71
Dude ranches, 3:361
Dudley, Dorothy, 1:107, 114, 123, 156, 159, 168
Dueling, 1:274; 2:166–67; code, 1:403; in domestic life, 1:402–3; golden age, 1:402; weapons, 1:403
Duff, Mary Ann, 2:313
Dukakis, Michael, 4:313
Duke, James Buchanan, 3:247–48
Dulles, Foster Rhea, 4:97
Dulles, John Foster, 4:99
Dull Knife, 2:432
Duncan, Don, 3:439
Dunglison, Robley, 1:440
"Dunkers," 1:296
Dunlap, John, 1:21
Dunlap, William, 1:57
Dunlop, J. B., 2:568
Dunmore, John Murray, 1:105–6
Dunn, Red, 3:342
Dunston, M. R., 3:426
du Pont, Alfred, 3:183
du Pont, Pierre, 3:154, 183
Durand, Asher B., 1:450
Durand, Peter, 1:503
Durant, Will, 3:20, 58, 296, 327
Durst, Ralph, 3:417–18
Dust Bowl, 3:306
Dutch: as bricklayers, 1:46; education and, 1:61; settlement of, 1:6; smugglers, 1:16
Dutch ovens, 1:132; 2:402
The Duty of American Women to Their Country (Beecher, C.), 2:381
Dwight, John Sullivan, 2:302
Dwight, Timothy, 1:459
Dylan, Bob, 4:110, 231–32, 234

Eagle Brewery, 1:510
Eames, Charles, 4:79
Eames, Ray, 4:79
Early, Jubal A., 2:231, 260
Earned Income Tax Credit, 4:321
Earp, Jug, 3:342

Earp, Morgan, 2:422
Earp, Virgil, 2:422
Earp, Wyatt, 2:422
Earth Day, 4:129
East India Company, 1:16–17
Eastman, George, 2:250, 605; 3:162
Eating in America (Root/de Rochemont), 4:192
Eaton, Amos, 1:431, 434
Eaton, Fred, 3:448
E-commerce, 4:312
Economic life: during American changes/conflict (1821–1861), 1:515–54; during American Republic (1789–1820), 1:230–68; animal husbandry/hunting/fishing in, 3:62–63, 151–52, 227–28, 305–7, 376–79, 432–36; artisans in, 1:252–56; banking in, 1:264–68; benefits, growth, change, 4:49–52; builders in, 1:262–64; buying/selling in, 1:243–52; caste/class experience in, 3:59–60, 131–46, 222–25, 298–303, 369–74, 428–32; cattle market in, 2:241–44; during Colonial America (1763–1789), 1:68–90; commerce in, 1:84–86; communications in, 1:530–35; consumer protection, 4:154; cost of living in, 2:71–73, 231–34, 369–72, 513; credit cards, 4:281–82; crop harvesting in, 1:540–44; in decades of discord, 1960–1990, 4:13; dollar in, 2:63–64; employment in, 4:164; energy crisis, 4:154–55; environmental issues, 4:154; during Exploitation Period, 2:350–79; factories in, 1:256–62; farming in, 1:230–36, 545–48; 2:74–79, 235–41, 517–19; finance in, 2:69–70, 229–31, 367–69, 508–13; food preservation in, 1:544–45; globalization, 4:277; industrial accidents in, 2:505–6; during Industrial Age (1870–1900), 2:499–525; industrial competition in, 4:155–61; industrial production in, 4:280–81; industry in, 1:83–84; inventions in, 1:515–16; investing, 4:278–80; iron/steel in, 1:552; labor in, 1:516–17; 4:148–53; labor unions in, 2:365–67; 4:47–48; livestock in, 1:236–40; 2:76–79; malls/shopping centers, 4:153–54; mechanics in, 1:515; in Middle Atlantic U.S., 3:121–52; in Midwest U.S., 3:293–307; mining in, 1:553–54; modern era, 1991–2005, 4:18; in Northeast U.S., 3:57–63; nutrition and, 4:147; organized labor in, 2:506–8; "other America" in, 4:162–63; overview, 4:146–47, 275–76; in Pacific West U.S., 3:413–36; population in, 4:148; poverty in, 4:282–84; recharging, 4:284–85; during Reconstruction (1865–1877), 2:225–47; roads/rivers in, 1:259–60; rural America and, 4:163–64; slavery in, 1:75–80; in Southern U.S., 3:214–28; Southern U.S. agriculture, 1:240–48; in Southwest/Rocky Mountain Western U.S., 3:357–79; taxes in, 4:285–87; technology in, 1:535–40; 4:161–62, 288–90; textile mills in, 1:550–52; trade in, 2:79–81, 244–46, 376–78, 519–24; 3:58–59, 129–31, 220–22, 256–58, 425–28; transportation in, 1:517–30; urban/rural issues, 2:73–74, 234–38, 372–73, 514; 3:60–62, 146–51, 225–26, 303–5, 374–76; 4:163–64; urban street, 2:514–17; during U.S. Civil War, 2:63–82; wartime economy, 1940–1945, 4:44–45; women at work in, 4:48–49; work

4:106; kinetoscopes, 3:99; large-screen projection, 3:99; ratings, 4:167; in recreational life, 4:244–45; religious, 4:123; during roaring twenties, 3:22; ticket sales, 4:62; westerns, 3:467; wide-screen epics, 4:107; during World War II, 4:63–64. *See also* Entertainment; Films; Theater; *specific movies*

Moyer, Charles, 3:393
Moynihan, Daniel Patrick, 4:138
MPAA. *See* Motion Picture Association of America
Mravlag, Victor, 3:91
Mr. Isaac's (Crawford, F. M.), 2:254
Muck, Karl, 3:13
Muhammad, Elijah, 4:217
Muir, John, 3:434–35
Mulholland, William, 3:448
Mulock, Dinah, 2:22
Mulvagh, Jane, 3:445
Mumford, Lewis, 4:66–67
Mummers Parade, 2:612; 3:199–200
Munn vs. Illinois, 2:419, 434
Munro, George, 2:386–87
Munro, Norman, 2:386–87
Munsey's Magazine, 2:537; 3:70
Murgas, Joseph, 3:176
Murphy, Charles W., 3:339
Murray, John Courtney, 4:258
Murray's Rush, 2:308
Murray, Thomas E., 2:477
Murray, W. H. H., 2:308
Murrow, Edward R., 4:54
Music: African American, 4:107–8; in American Republic (1789–1820), 1:286–87; big band, 4:110; Black spirituals, 2:303–4, 599; blues, 2:599; 3:262–63, 343; boogie woogie, 3:344; brass-band, 2:169–70, 302–3, 597; bully songs, 2:595; classical, 2:168–69; classical, on radio, 3:71; of Confederacy, 2:170–71; contemporary, 4:236; coon songs, 2:595–96; cowboys, 2:441–42; Decca Record Company, 3:94–95; disco, 4:236; drinking songs, 1:287; folk, 4:110; *Grand Ole Opry*, 3:263–64; grunge movement, 4:298; in intellectual life, 4:298–99; jazz, 2:599; 3:95, 262–63; jukeboxes, 3:95; lamentations, 2:172; making of, 2:438–42; messages in, 4:299; military, 2:169–70; in military life, American Revolution homefront, 1:151; mining, 2:441; minstrelsy, 2:169, 304–5, 592; musicals, 3:98–99; Napster, 4:299; opera, 3:464; philharmonic orchestra, 3:464; player pianos, 2:591; ragtime, 2:596–97; rap, 4:238, 298–99; in recreational life, 2:167–74, 302–6, 438–42, 447–48, 591–99; 3:94–95, 262–64, 343–44, 464; 4:107–10, 230–39; religious melodies, 1:286; rock, 4:230–36; rock and roll, 4:26, 108–10; Second New England School, 2:598; sheet music, 2:592; of slaves, 1:320–21; 2:173–74; song, 2:167–68, 593–94; swing, 3:95, 411; symphonic orchestra, 2:598; Thomas Orchestra, 2:303; Tin Pan Alley, 2:593–94; Western, 2:447–48; of Western emigrants, 2:438; white gospel, 2:305–6. *See also specific musicians*

Muskets, 1:97, 117–18; 2:84–85
Mussolini, Benito, 3:36–37
My Ántonia (Cather), 2:227, 540
Myers, Myer, 1:86–87
Mystery Train (Marcus), 4:109

NAACP. *See* National Association for the Advancement of Colored People
Nabokov, Vladimir, 4:34, 70
NACW. *See* National Association of Colored Women
Nader, Ralph, 4:14, 149
NAFTA. *See* North American Free Trade Agreement
Naked Lunch (Burroughs), 4:72
The Naked and the Dead (Mailer), 4:69
The Name of the Rose (Eco), 4:185
Napoleon III, 2:157, 292
Narrative of the Life of Frederick Douglass (Douglass), 1:565, 602–4; 2:103
Narrative of William Wells Brown, Fugitive Slave Written by Himself (Brown, W. W.), 2:104
NASA. *See* National Aeronautics and Space Administration
NASCAR. *See* National Association of Stock Car Auto Racing
Nash, Tom, 3:342
The Nashville Banner, 1:464
Nason, Tama, 4:101
Nast, Thomas, 2:185, 283, 535
The Natchez Courier, 1:464
National Academy of Sciences, 2:106
National Aeronautics and Space Administration (NASA), 4:28, 186–87
National Association for the Advancement of Colored People (NAACP), 4:102; anti-lynching protests, 3:222; founding of, 3:24; support for, 3:430
National Association of Amateur Oarsmen, 2:298
National Association of Colored Women (NACW), 3:3, 431
National Association of Stock Car Auto Racing (NASCAR), 4:336–38
National Association of Women's Lawyers, 4:145
National Association of Working Women, 4:151
National Black Political Assembly, 4:208
National Board for the Promotion of Rifle Practice (NBPRP), 2:300
National Broadcasting Corporation (NBC), 4:110, 111
National Collegiate Athletic Association (NCAA), 2:167, 299, 300; 4:113, 118–19, 332–35
National Commission of Life Adjustment for Youth, 4:58
National Committee for a Sane Nuclear Policy (SANE), 4:100
National Consumers League, 2:491
National Defense Education Act (1958), 4:61
National Education Association, 2:507
National Football League (NFL), 4:113, 240, 242
National Grange, 2:17
National Housing Act (1949), 4:51
National Housing Agency, 4:86
National Industry Recovery Act (NIRA), 3:33
National Institute of Alcohol Abuse and Alcoholism (NIAAA), 4:191
National Institutes of Health (NIH), 4:68
Nationalism, 2:2, 150; in American Republic (1789–1820), 1:206–7; new, 3:6; of Southern U.S., 1:581–84

National Labor Relations Act (1935), 3:34, 424; 4:47
National Livestock Association, 2:423
National Organization for Women (NOW), 4:40, 275
National Park System, 3:6, 151, 434–35
National Party, 2:288
National Peace Jubilee (1869), 2:302
National Police Gazette, 2:22–23, 422
National Progressive Union of Miners and Mine Laborers, 2:508
National Recorder, 1:463, 481
National Rifle Association (NRA), 2:300; 4:323
National Road, 1:260, 518
The National Journal, 1:461
National Urban League, 3:430
A Nation at Risk, 4:210–11, 293
The Nation, 2:256
Native Americans, 1:88, 387, 558; 2:96, 361, 386, 395, 539, 607, 646–48; 3:223–25, 397; 4:273; animal husbandry/hunting/fishing of, 1:314–15; British alliances, 1:127–28, 196; clans, 1:315–16; confinement of, 2:330; customs of, 3:370; depiction of, 2:384; discrimination and, 3:303; education, 3:381; family life, 3:403; farming, 1:314–15; food, 1:128; 3:318–19; games, 1:315; during Great Depression of 1929, 3:306–7, 372; Indian Wars, 2:223; during Jacksonian Age, 1:377–78; literacy, 2:21; Long Walk, 2:431; as minority, 3:370; Native American Party, 1:382; in new hunting grounds, 1:6; orphans, 2:220; Plains Indian Wars, 2:433; poverty among, 3:432; religious beliefs, 3:395; reservations, 2:430–33, 471; 3:432; rituals/ceremonies, 1:316–17; in social life, 1:313–18; suppression, 1:317; towns, 1:316–17; "Trail of Tears," 1:378; U.S. Supreme Court and, 1:377; voting and, 1:373. *See also* Creek War; French and Indian War (1754–1763); *specific Native American peoples*; *specific Native Americans*
Nativism, 1:382; 2:1, 148, 152–53; discrimination, 2:157–60; evangelical movement and, 2:160
Nativist Party, 2:152–53
NATO. *See* North Atlantic Treaty Organization
Natural gas, 3:358–59
Naturalization Act, 1:200
Natural law, 1:9
Navajos, 3:354, 371, 372
Navigation, 3:82–83, 450–51; Navigation Acts, 2:566. *See also* Transportation
Nazism, 4:9, 63
NBC. *See* National Broadcasting Corporation
NBPRP. *See* National Board for the Promotion of Rifle Practice
NCAA. *See* National Collegiate Athletic Association
NCAS. *See* North Carolina Academy of Science
The Nebraska Farmer, 2:400
Necessary Rules For the Proper Behavior of Children (Dock), 1:62
Negro Leagues, 4:114–15
The Negro American Family (Moynihan), 4:138
Nelson, Baby Face, 3:333
Nelson, Ozzie, 3:95
Nelson, Ricky, 4:27
Nevin, J. W., 2:456
New Almanack & Ephemeris (Rivington), 1:146
Newbold, Charles, 1:232; 2:517
New Deal, 2:586; 3:43, 128, 283–84; 4:11, 15, 88; agencies of, 3:32–33; as "creeping socialism,"

EDITORS

General Editor

Randall M. Miller
St. Joseph's University
Philadelphia, Pennsylvania

Volume Editor

Francis J. Sicius
St. Thomas University
Miami Gardens, Florida